W9-CNM-413

Encyclopedia of

World
Environmental
History

Encyclopedia of

World Environmental History

Shepard Krech III
J. R. McNeill
Carolyn Merchant
Editors

Volume 3 O–Z
INDEX

A Berkshire Reference Work

Routledge
New York London

Published in 2004 by

Routledge
29 West 35th Street
New York, NY 10001
www.routledge-ny.com

Published in Great Britain by
Routledge
11 New Fetter Lane
London EC4P 4EE
www.routledge.co.uk

Routledge is an imprint of the Taylor and Francis Group.
A Berkshire Reference Work
314 Main Street, Suite 12
Great Barrington, MA 01230
berkshirepublishing.com

10 9 8 7 6 5 4 3 2 1

Library of Congress Cataloging-in-Publication Data

ISBN 0-415-93732-9 (set)
ISBN 0-415-93733-7 (vol. 1)
ISBN 0-415-93734-5 (vol. 2)
ISBN 0-415-93735-3 (vol. 3)

Encyclopedia of world environmental history / Shepard Krech III, J.R. McNeill,
Carolyn Merchant, editors.
        p. cm.
Includes bibliographical references and index.
    ISBN 0-415-93732-9 (set : acid-free paper) — ISBN 0-415-93733-7 (v. 1 :
acid-free paper) — ISBN 0-415-93734-5 (v. 2 : acid-free paper) — ISBN 0-415-
93735-3 (v. 3 : acid-free paper)
    1. Human ecology—Encyclopedias. 2. Human beings—Effect of environment
on—Encyclopedias. 3. Nature—Effect of human beings on—Encyclopedias.
I. Krech, Shepard, 1944– II. McNeill, John Robert. III. Merchant, Carolyn.
    GF10.E63 2003
    304.2'03—dc21
                                                                2003008288

Printed in the United States of America on acid-free paper.

CONTENTS

Oceania

A region of little land and much sea, Oceania covers 45 percent of the Earth's surface, but contains only 0.01 percent of its total land area and human population. Oceania's diverse environments range from Melanesia's large forested islands with a more continental geology, to small coral atolls of Micronesia and Polynesia, where fresh water and trees were scarce for their inhabitants. Within Micronesia and Polynesia too were high volcanic islands, such as tropical Tahiti and the Hawaiian Islands, which sustained significant indigenous populations as did New Zealand and Easter Island (Rapa Nui) on the cooler temperate fringes.

Resource Reconnaissance

Starting with Ferdinand Magellan of Spain in 1520 and ending with the last of three voyages of the Englishman, James Cook from 1776 to 1780, a convoy of European explorers criss-crossed the Pacific searching variously for gold, trade, the Great South Land, and new knowledge. Cook's discoveries resulted in the British settlement of Australia (1788) and New Zealand (1840), and a huge corpus of knowledge about the Pacific's resources. This attracted European and North American entrepreneurs to Oceania's potential.

Beginning the Exploitation

From the late eighteenth century, the newcomers' activities drew Oceania into the global economy. There were two trades that dominated Pacific Islands' resource extraction from the 1780s until the 1860s. The first linked Europe, North America, (and later Australia and New Zealand), and China. Beginning in 1785 seal, beaver, and otter on the northwest American coast attracted British, American, and Russian traders, seeking furs to trade with China for tea. The Hawaiian Islands became a refreshment center on the passage to China and for overwintering, involving its people in food production for the ships. The search for seal furs also reached the Pacific coast of Peru, the South Island of New Zealand, and its small offshore islands as well Tasmania. By 1830, seal numbers had fallen so much that the trade became unviable. Other China cargoes were sought from the Islands—bêche-de-mer (sea cucumbers) until about 1850 from tropic lagoons around Belau and Fiji, and sandalwood from Fiji, the Marquesas, and Hawaii until it was worked out by the 1820s, then the discovery of substantial stands in the New Hebrides and New Caledonia. By 1860 little sandalwood remained.

The second trade nexus had a similar outcome. The exhaustion of Atlantic stocks led whalers from England and the east coast of the United States into the Pacific from 1788 seeking whale oil for lubrication and lighting. First the sperm whale and then the right whale were hunted by 200 to 500 ships a year until the 1860s when catches had declined.

Ecological Shadowlands

The 1860s saw most islands drawn into the economic orbit of Europe, North America, and the British colonies of Australia and New Zealand. These linkages cast an ecological shadow over the islands. Whalers had found that Pacific Islanders produced coconut oil for

Attachment to the Land on Chuuk

In a region where land is scarce, it is not surprising that people are attached to the land and value land that is their own. This text extract from an ethnographic study of Chuuk (formerly called Truk), now a state in the Federated States of Micronesia, describes this strong feeling of attachment.

The Trukese have a very strong attachment to their land, which might best be described as a strong jealousy of it. The strength of their emotions concerning their land is hard for Americans to appreciate.

Children are taken around by their fathers and mother's brothers and are taught the names and boundaries of the family lands and something of the traditions associated with them although the most important traditions are liable to be withheld more or less until adulthood. Each small piece of land, on the hills as well as the shore, has a separate name. Many of the names are simply descriptive of the location but others are named to commemorate some important legendary event in the family history which occurred there.

In spite of the practically universal Christianization of Truk, strong supernatural ties to the land still exist. What is to us a rather ordinary spring or rock may be cherished as the place where the local Adam or Eve sprang from the earth. Other places are considered to be the homes of local gods and demons. Cemeteries are unpopular and little used as the people want to be buried on their own land "where others will not play on top of our grave."

Source: Fischer, John L. (1958) *Native Land Tenure in the Truk District.* Guam: Office of the High Commissioner, Trust Territory of the Pacific Islands, pp. 202–203.

cosmetic purposes and that this had a growing market in Europe. Traders collected the oil in the 1840s and 1850s, but depended on the inclinations of the islanders regarding the quantity and quality of the product. German traders discovered that pressing the dried coconut kernel under factory conditions produced a superior product. To ensure a regular supply, Europeans turned to plantation agriculture and thus needed land. At the same time, the American Civil War destroyed most of the increasingly redundant whaling fleet, and stimulated demand for cotton. Planters sought land for this in Fiji, Samoa, Tahiti, New Hebrides, and the British colony of Queensland, Australia. Although the Pacific cotton boom faded with the end of the American Civil War, plantation agriculture focused on sugar and copra was common on the larger islands by the 1890s and the first decade of the twentieth century. The Civil War also set the foundation for expansion of sugar growing in Hawaii. Planting everywhere resulted in increased forest clearance and swamp drainage, altering coastal and lowland ecology.

From the 1870s and 1890s, the need to regulate conflicts with the indigenous people over land and labor, guarantee European property, as well as prevent friction among themselves led European powers and the United States to annex the Pacific Islands. Colonial governments had few conservation regulations and often were more concerned with international politics than protection. With land access secured, Europeans now needed labor to clear the forest, plant, and harvest their crops. Islanders were now seen as a resource. About 250,000 Pacific Islanders (with 186,000 Asians) were taken to workplaces outside their home islands before World War I. These Pacific Islanders initially suffered high mortality in their first year from foreign microorganisms, but gradually populations became more resistant.

"Continental" diseases had entered the Pacific Islands on the first European ships and "virgin soil" island populations suffered dramatic declines of up to 80 percent or 90 percent from diseases such as measles, smallpox, and venereal afflictions. Though all declined to varying degrees, those most affected were on islands where large areas of land had been alienated, destroying their resource base and thus undermining their resistance to introduced illness. Population decline or forced removal by colonial governments led to the decay of indigenous horticultural and aquacultural systems, sometimes allowing the original fauna and flora to recover. More commonly they opened niches for introduced weed species, such as the guava, and introduced domesticated animals, such as cattle and goats, as well as the European rat and, in New Zealand, rabbits. These destroyed both habitat and the young of indigenous species, causing many extirpations. In temperate New Zealand, European settlers felled and fired forests for pastoral uses on a massive scale, changing the ecology of millions of acres. The way that remaining indigenous lands were managed altered too with the incoming technology. Machetes and steel axes meant land could be cleared more easily. Capitalism and colonial taxation systems led not only to commercial plantations, but also to small-scale crop production by Pacific Islanders. Incoming ideology also played a part as Christianity ousted many traditional methods of population limitation that, in some places, probably assisted the gradual recovery of numbers noted from 1880 to 1920. Christians contributed to church upkeep, reinforcing the need to produce cash crops.

Several tropical lagoons were home to pearlshell. European traders sought the shell and pearls, relying on local divers. Once the diving helmet became available in the 1870s, only Europeans had capital to invest, gaining access to shell at deeper levels along with considerable control of the industry. Local people resisted this, but colonial laws tended to favor open access. With the availability of inexpensive flippers, snorkels, and masks in the 1950s local people often depleted the resource themselves—a common pattern whenever new technology first enters islands' societies. To revive the industry in the twentieth century some governments encouraged farming the shell, with some success, though mollusk disease has occurred.

Although the advent of the steamship in the 1880s enhanced access for relatively small suppliers to large, distant consumers in the metropolises, economies of scale along with the vagaries of weather often meant that it was commercially marginal to use scattered islands as plantations. This was all the more so as the world market experienced periodic gluts of vegetable oils in the 1920s and collapsed in the Great Depression of the 1930s. On the larger archipelagos, sugar continued strong in Fiji and with it in Hawaii the pineapple, buoyed up by integrated companies that invested in improving varieties and equipment and maintaining the fertility of the soil, mainly by chemical fertilizers. The expansion of commercial agriculture here, but particularly pastoralism in Australia and New Zealand, saw the tiniest islands of the Pacific fall within the ecological shadows of these metropolitan areas. Micronesia had a similar experience when it became a Japanese

mandate after World War I. Australia and New Zealand from the mid to late nineteenth century had sent their wool to Britain. Following the introduction of refrigerated shipping in the 1880s, sheep and cattle meat boosted exports. But both countries had poor soils.

Uninhabited guano islands such as Laysan soon lost their guano to collectors to sell as fertilizers, but others proved a source for the raw material for superphosphate. Makatea in the Society Islands and Angaur in the Carolines were mined from the 1900s. Japan controlled Angaur after 1914 and used its phosphates at home and within Micronesia where 98,000 Japanese migrants grew mainly sugarcane, planting entire islands. Nauru became a British Empire mandate, and was mined; with nearby Ocean (Banaba) Island, part of the British Protectorate of the Gilbert and Ellice Islands. This Commission sold phosphate, mainly to Australia and New Zealand at cost, far below the price for Makatea phosphate for example. The British relocated the Banabans in 1947 to a Fiji island. By the 1960s, the Nauruan people were left with an island of coral pinnacles and little useful vegetation.

The War with Japan

Japan entered the war and the western Pacific as far as Guadalcanal during 1942 and 1943. The war ushered in Oceania's greatest human invasion relative to its brief span of four years. It also introduced the airplane as a means of rapid communication and the spread of potential pests and pathogens. Japanese and Allied forces bombarded islands and, despite later demolition operations, unexploded munitions remain a danger. In some areas, such as north of Guadalcanal, the sea floor is littered with wrecked battleships now leaking oil and there are fears that dumped chemicals, such as mustard gas, are deteriorating in Micronesian swamps. Throughout the Pacific thousands of tons of coral were crushed to make airfields, changing the lagoon environment. Construction often destroyed taro pits, the subsistence base of many atoll dwellers.

Alien biota followed the troops. To supplement their diet, the Japanese introduced the destructive Great African snail (*Achatina*) to north New Guinea and it spread rapidly. American equipment shipped from Manus after the war introduced to Guam the brown tree snake (*Boiga irregularis*), which has virtually wiped out bird and bat life and is a pest to human beings. The American army introduced the cattle tick (*Boophilus microplus*) to New Caledonia. Many weed

953

species radiated out from wartime airfields, island hopping in the cuffs of military trousers. Air transport and the rapid movement of warships meant insect transfer was more likely, so colonial health authorities were extra vigilant. The feared extension of the malarial mosquito, *Anopheles*, southeast and south of Buxton's line (170 degrees east longitude and 20 degrees south latitude) did not occur, though infected soldiers returning to north Queensland where the vector was endemic induced malaria epidemics in local military and civilian populations in 1942.

Rear areas became suppliers of fresh food. Islands such as Fiji, New Caledonia, and New Zealand found their herds and soils depleted by wartime demand. This also meant greater mechanization of the agricultural sector and more land under crops. In terms of the human population, in the battle areas of coastal New Guinea and western Solomons there was decline, mainly due to disturbed conditions, malnutrition, and dysentery. Behind the front, often the birth rate rose as American troops fathered hundreds of children by women in the Cooks, the Samoan Islands, Tahiti, and Tonga, though fewer, it seems, in Fiji.

Nuclear Shadows and Decolonization

Oceania's remoteness from the perspective of the United States, Britain, and France made it an ideal atomic testing ground. From the first U.S. atmospheric test on Bikini in 1946 to the last underground nuclear detonation by the French on Mururoa in 1996, the islands and the people have absorbed unmeasured quantities of radioactive elements. Some islands are uninhabitable. Long-term outcomes are unknown.

Elsewhere life generally returned to the old pattern, but the United Nations' emphasis on decolonization saw more systematic surveys of resources, such as minerals, forests, and soil throughout the colonial Pacific from the late 1940s through to the 1970s. Although some colonial governments attempted to set up sustainable regimes in forestry, it was this sector, along with mining, that has been associated with vast ecological changes in the Melanesian islands since the 1980s. These resources are exploited by transnational companies that contribute to the coffers of governments, but little to environmental management. In Papua New Guinea, for example, the tailings from copper mining at Ok Tedi have inundated the lowlands with heavy metals, killing the vegetation and thus the habitat of

30,000 human beings and other fauna. Forests in the Solomons have been logged unsustainably for almost twenty years and soon will be exhausted.

Oceania's resource base is under pressure. Population growth is 3.5 percent annually in some areas. Migration to metropolitan areas has helped. Natural forces beyond human control, however, have always shaped Oceania. The rising sea level due to global warming of today is one such example. This is an increasing concern in Oceania as low-lying islands and atolls are being drowned, gardens salinated, and coral reefs, a major food source for lagoon people, are dying. Populations of islands and, in Kiribati's case, entire countries will have to migrate or perish.

Since the 1980s agencies of the Pacific Forum, a regional organization of Pacific countries, have been working to ameliorate these environmental challenges. Some success with gaining financial returns for the region from the tuna fishery in 1987 has not been matched with conservation of the resource by foreign fishers. The Forum countries also negotiated a ban on drift net fishing in 1989. Within islands, consciousness of the need for more active conservation seems to be emerging. Donor countries now include environmental impact assessments in aid packages. However, agencies such as the World Bank in Papua New Guinea, in using fiscal incentives to control unsustainable logging for example, sometimes create social problems by decreasing employment opportunities.

Judith A. Bennett

Further Reading

Baker, J. V. T. (1965). *The New Zealand people at war: War economy*. Wellington, New Zealand: Department of Internal Affairs.

Beaglehole, J. C. (1934). *The exploration of the Pacific*. London: A. & C. Black.

Bennett, J. A. (2000). *Pacific forest: A history of resource control and conflict in Solomon Islands, c. 1800–1997*. Cambridge, UK: White Horse Press.

Bennett, J. A. (2001). War, emergency and environment: Fiji, 1939–1946. *Environment and History, 7*, 255–287.

Bennett, J. A. (forthcoming). *South Pacific: Environment and World War II*.

Campbell, I. C. (1989). *A history of the Pacific Islands*. Christchurch, New Zealand: University of Canterbury Press.

Daws, G. (1968). *Shoal of time: A history of the Hawaiian Islands*. New York: Macmillan.

Denoon, D., Firth, S., Lineekin, J., Meleisea, M., & Nero, K. (1997). *The Cambridge history of the Pacific Islanders*. Cambridge, UK & New York: Cambridge University Press.

Kunitz, S. (1994). *Disease and social diversity: The European impact on the health of non-Europeans*. Oxford: Oxford University Press.

MacNeill, J., Winsemius, P., & Taizo, Y. (1991). *Beyond Independence: The meshing of the world's economy and the Earth's ecology*. New York: Oxford University Press.

McNeill, J. R. (1994). Of rats and men: A synoptic environmental history of the island Pacific. *Journal of World History, 5*(2), 299–349.

Moore, C., Leckie, J., & Munro, D. (Eds.). (1990). *Labour in the South Pacific*. Townsville, Australia: James Cook University.

Nunn, Patrick D. (1999). *Environmental change in the Pacific Basin*. Chichester, UK: Wiley.

Rallu, J. L. (1991). Population of the French overseas territories in the Pacific: Past, present and projected. *Journal of Pacific History, 26*, 169–186.

Rapaport, M. (1995). Oysterlust: Islanders, entrepreneurs, and colonial policy over Tuamotu lagoons. *Journal of Pacific History, 30*(1), 39–52.

Spate, O. H. K. (1988). *The Pacific since Magellan: Volume 3, Paradise found and lost*. Sydney: Australian National University Press.

Spennemann, D. (1998). Japanese poaching and the enforcement of German colonial sovereignty in the Marshall Islands. *Journal of Pacific History, 33*(1), 51–67.

Oceania, Ancient

Oceania is the large region of islands and archipelagos stretching across the South Pacific Ocean. The region encompasses more than 88 million square kilometers, most of which is ocean. The total landmass in the region is 1.6 million square kilometers, made up of more than twenty-five thousand islands. Oceania is divided into three general areas: Melanesia, which includes New Guinea, the Solomon Islands, New Caledonia, Fiji, and other islands making up a belt roughly to the northeast of Australia; Micronesia, a collection of archipelagos including the Marshall Islands, the Palau Islands, Guam, and other smaller atolls (coral islands consisting of a reef surrounding a lagoon) lying to the east of the Philippines; and Polynesia, the scattered island groups including the Samoan Islands, the Cook Islands, and others lying in a large triangle running from New Zealand to Hawaii to Easter Island.

Although the history of human migration across ancient Oceania is still debated, most archaeological and linguistic evidence suggests that humans colonized the region in a succession of waves emanating from southeast Asia and moving eastward. The earliest known human settlements in New Guinea date from around 40,000 to 35,000 BCE, approximately the same time that humans first arrived in Australia, whereas parts of the Solomon Islands lying closest to New Guinea appear to have been colonized around 26,000 BCE. By 7000 to 5000 BCE much of western Melanesia was occupied by hunter-gatherer groups, although several sites in New Guinea show evidence of early patterns of crop cultivation, including irrigation systems for growing taro (a plant grown for its edible rootstock). However, the rest of Oceania remained uninhibited.

Between 2000 and 1000 BCE another wave of migration spread across Melanesia from southeast Asia, giving rise both to new language forms and new patterns of human settlement that had a significantly greater environmental impact than the first hunter-gatherers who occupied the region. The Lapita culture, named for the distinctive pottery found at archaeological sites in New Caledonia, was marked by larger settlements practicing a combination of marine and shell fishing along with an agricultural complex based on cultivation of yam, taro, and banana crops and the domestication of pigs, dogs, and chickens.

Rapid Colonization

However, the most important innovation of the Lapita culture was advanced maritime technologies that enabled the rapid colonization of eastern Melanesia and from there, for the first time, migration northward into Micronesia and eastward into Polynesia. Larger outrigger canoes of 15 to 20 meters, coupled with improved sail technologies and refined navigation techniques, permitted colonists to cross the large expanses of ocean, bringing with them the crops and animals needed to establish settlements. The first known settlements in Fiji, on the eastern edge of Melanesia, date from 1500 BCE, and by 1000 BCE voyagers had crossed the several hundred kilometers of open ocean separating Fiji from the Samoan and Tonga Islands in western Polynesia. At around the same time colonists pushed northward into Micronesia, settling the Caroline and Marshall Islands. Over the next fifteen hundred years the rest of Polynesia became inhabited, with humans arriving last in Hawaii around 650 CE and in New Zealand between 1000 and 1200 CE. However, internal settlement and migration continued after this period, the most notable being contacts between Polynesians and South America, which resulted in the introduction of sweet potatoes as a basic crop throughout eastern Polynesia.

The establishment of human settlements on the previously isolated islands of Oceania produced profound environmental changes. None of the islands had any mammal species, with the exception of bats, before humans introduced domesticated animals. The arrival of humans was marked by sharp depletions in the numbers of native fauna through overhunting and competition from domesticated animals, resulting in the extinction of many species. Likewise, the pioneering agriculture practiced by the colonists included extensive use of slash-and-burn techniques, which resulted in significant amounts of deforestation and corresponding erosion problems on many islands. This was especially true in parts of eastern and southern Polynesia, where a cooler and drier climate proved ill suited to the types of tropical agriculture that the arriving colonists attempted to introduce. In some extreme cases, such as Easter Island and on some of the Marquesas Islands in eastern Polynesia, the arrival of humans appears to have precipitated an environmental crisis resulting in a large-scale collapse of the ecosystem and a sharp population decline or abandonment of the settlement within a century or two after colonization. Also, a continuing pressure on natural resources was one of the major forces driving the rapid migration across Oceania as colonists sought to find new islands to exploit.

Sustenance Systems

However, by 1500, on the eve of European arrival in the region, most of the human settlements in Oceania had developed more or less stable sustenance systems that varied according to their local climate and ecological conditions. Fishing was the most important element, and the inhabitants of Oceania practiced a wide variety of techniques, including the use of elaborate nets and traps as well as lures and harpoons. The major agricultural staples were coconuts, breadfruit, yams, and taro roots, with domesticated pigs, dogs, and chickens providing additional protein. Although many islanders continued to practice swidden (slash-and-burn) agriculture in which fields were cleared, burned,

Types of Polynesian sail canoes and charts. SOURCE: ANDERSEN, JOHANNES C. (1995) *MYTHS AND LEGENDS OF THE POLYNESIANS.* NEW YORK: DOVER PUBLICATIONS. ORIGINALLY PUBLISHED IN 1928.

used for two to three years, and then allowed to lie fallow for up to two decades, some Oceania societies developed more extensive farming systems using terraced plots and elaborate irrigation systems. Also, the island inhabitants developed complex social structures designed to keep the population from rising beyond what could be sustained by local environmental limits.

For the European voyagers, who began visiting the South Pacific in larger numbers between 1600 and 1800, many of the Oceania islands assumed mythical status as tropical paradises. From a European perspective the relatively benign climate and apparent richness of natural resources disguised the fact that most Oceania societies rested on a fragile ecological balance that seldom lasted long after the initial contact with outsiders.

James Lide

Further Reading

Craig, R., & King, F. (1981). *Historical dictionary of Oceania*. Westport, CT: Greenwood Press.

Denoon, D., Malama, M., Firth, S., Linnekin, J., & Nero, K. (Eds.). (1997). *The Cambridge history of the Pacific islanders*. Cambridge, UK: Cambridge University Press.

Jennings, J. (Ed.). (1979). *The prehistory of Polynesia*. Cambridge, MA: Harvard University Press.

Scarr, D. (1990). *The history of the Pacific islands. Kingdoms of the reefs*. Melbourne: Macmillan Company of Australia.

Spate, O. (1988). *Paradise found and lost*. Minneapolis: University of Minnesota Press.

Oceans and Seas

The oceans of the Earth consist of four confluent (flowing together) bodies of saltwater that are contained in enormous basins on the Earth's surface. Seas are lesser bodies of saltwater. Oceans and seas cover 361 million square kilometers (70.8 percent of the Earth's surface) and 98 percent of the volume of the biosphere (the part of the world in which life can exist). Saltwater comprises about 97.2 percent of the water on the planet, the remainder being freshwater. By evaporation and precipitation water is circulated between the oceans and seas, the atmosphere, and the land. The hydrological cycle (the sequence of conditions through which water passes from vapor in the atmosphere through precipitation upon land or water surfaces and ultimately back into the atmosphere as a result of evaporation and transpiration) transports and stores chemicals and heat, determines the Earth's climate, and fertilizes and erodes the land. The average salinity of the oceans and seas is 3.5 percent, deviations being determined by evaporation and inflow of freshwater. Ocean surface temperatures around the equator may be 30° C or more, decreasing toward the poles, where seawater freezes at −2° C. Below-surface temperature is fairly constant, decreasing to around 0° C in the deep ocean.

The largest ocean is the Pacific, which has a surface area of 166 million square kilometers, almost the size of the three other oceans together: the Atlantic (84 million square kilometers), the Indian (73 million square kilometers), and the Arctic (12 million square kilometers).

The Antarctic, or Southern, Ocean is sometimes counted as the fifth ocean, consisting of the waters of the southern parts of the Pacific, Indian, and Atlantic. Sections of the oceans may be described as enclosed and marginal seas. Enclosed seas—such as the Mediterranean Sea, Hudson Bay, the White Sea, the Baltic, the Red Sea, and the Mexican Gulf—cut into continental landmasses. Marginal seas—such as the Caribbean and Bering Seas, the Sea of Okhotsk, the East China Sea, the Sea of Japan, and the North Sea—are separated from the oceans by archipelagos.

The depth of the oceans increases to about 200 meters on the continental shelves, increasing further to 3,000–4,000 meters on the ocean basin floor and to 6,000–11,000 meters in the deepest areas. The ocean bed is covered by sediments of dead marine organisms, eroded soil from the continents, and red clay.

The waters of the oceans are circulated by changing winds, air pressures, and tides. The gulf current brings warm water to the North Atlantic and thus makes it possible to sustain human life at more northerly degrees in Europe than anywhere else on the globe. The upwelling areas on the margins of the Pacific and Atlantic Oceans off the coasts of Chile and Peru, California, and Namibia in Africa bring cold, nutrient-rich waters to the surface of the sea, and the combination of sunlight and nutrient richness makes the relatively narrow continental shelves rich in marine life. However, El Niño (an irregularly occurring flow of unusually warm surface water along the western coast of South America) may reverse ocean currents in the Pacific and cause abnormal climate effects both on land and sea.

Life began in the oceans, but science has incomplete knowledge of marine life-forms. About fifteen thousand species of marine fish are known, but it is estimated that five thousand species remain to be identified. The estimate of 200,000 ocean floor species of the North Atlantic alone may be low by a factor of three or four. Whereas the open oceans are blue deserts due to the lack of nutrients, the continental shelves are home to abundant marine life, and tropical coral reefs are habitats of large biodiversity (biological diversity as indicated by numbers of species of animals and plants).

Marine Resources

Humans utilize the oceans as highways for transportation, exploit their marine life, and extract their resources on the ocean bottoms.

Ocean landscape at the Izembek National Wildlife Refuge at the tip of the Alaska Peninsula. COURTESY OF THE U.S. FISH AND WILDLIFE SERVICE.

Oceanic transportation is the cheapest and most important way to move goods between the continents, but it imposes severe environmental stress on marine habitats and biodiversity. Prior to the fifteenth century the oceans presented a formidable obstacle to contact between continents. Paleolithic (2 million–10,000 BCE)

migrants did spread from Africa and Eurasia to Australia and the Americas by crossing the Straits of Torres and Bering; the Polynesian migrations into the Pacific islands around 2000 BCE and the Viking migration across the North Atlantic also testify to early maritime skills. However, the first contact between a major civilization and another continent was aborted in 1435 when the Chinese emperor decided to discontinue the explorations of the Chinese fleet to Africa across the Indian Ocean. The subsequent voyages of Columbus across the Atlantic from Spain to the Caribbean Sea, however, opened the way for a sustained exchange—causing great environmental impact—with the New World. With the development of the three-masted sailing vessel and nautical instruments, global seafaring allowed an exchange of terrestrial plants and animals that had substantial consequences for the recipient countries. Marine habitat changes followed as ports and bunker areas for loading coal were extended along shorelines and estuaries and as mud-dredgers changed tidal currents and coastal erosion. In the twentieth century tanker ships impacted marine ecosystems substantially when they discharged ballast water transported over thousands of kilometers. Ballast water is one of the

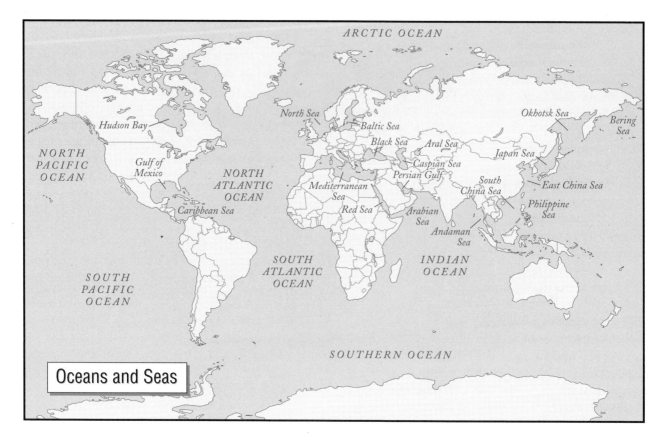

Oceans and Seas

most serious threats to marine biodiversity and has caused irreparable changes to ecosystems. Introduced species, which have no natural enemies in new environments, can multiply and eradicate original life-forms.

Humans have harvested inshore marine environments since earliest historical times. Whales, seals, fish, crustaceans, and algae have been fished for human consumption, and seaweeds, salt, sponges, corals, and pearls have been brought to consumers for diverse uses. Today important medicines, from anticoagulants to muscle relaxants, are derived from marine snails.

Beginning in the sixteenth century, thanks to the shipping revolution, whaling and fishing operations were taken to distant islands and continents. As marine life in these distant waters was depleted, the operations became oceanic, first in the Northern Hemisphere and later in the Southern Hemisphere. These operations extinguished some life-forms, such as the Stellar's sea cow in the Bering Sea, the gray whale in the European and later the American Atlantic, and the Caribbean monk seal. The early human impacts on pristine ecosystems are believed to have been important not only to a few signal species but also to the whole ecosystem, which may have experienced regime shifts when top predators that controlled ecosystem dynamics were fished out. Today most of the commercially important fish species are exploited to the full or beyond sustainable levels. Because of such heavy fishing pressure, many of the most valuable fish stocks of the world are in decline, and some have become locally extinct. The most dramatic case is the Newfoundland cod fishery, which collapsed in 1991, causing not only enormous and possibly irreparable harm to the ecosystem but also the disappearance of the very means of existence for many people in Atlantic Canada.

Commercial exploitation of minerals in the ocean bed is only beginning and is expected to increase dramatically in the twenty-first century. The ocean bed contains energy in the form of oil and natural gas, and minerals such as sodium chloride (salt), manganese, titanium, phosphate, and gold are found in the oceans. People also have begun to utilize tidal power from the oceans.

The development of industrialized societies has increased the discharge of sewage and other waste into the oceans and also has created the phenomenon of oil spills.

About two-thirds of the world's population live within 60 kilometers of a coast, and almost one-half of the world's cities with more than 1 million people are located near estuaries. This settlement pattern is a result of people choosing the oceans instead of agriculture as a source of food and employment; the oceans also have provided access to communication, transportation, and trade. However, people have had a prejudice against coastal settlement in some historical periods. The most marked instance of this prejudice occurred in many Neolithic (8000–5500 BCE) cultures with the introduction of agriculture, which increased the incentive to settle virgin inland territories. The nineteenth-century frontier movement of North America was also decidedly terrestrial, although migrants had to cross the Atlantic to pursue opportunities. In contrast, other colonizing experiences, such as the ancient Phoenician and Greek city-states, were decidedly maritime.

The French historian F. Braudel (1996) was the first to attempt a history of an enclosed sea—in this case, the Mediterranean—as a natural environment and a highroad for communication and cultural exchange. He argued that the common environmental conditions prevailing on the coasts of the Mediterranean provided the basis for a common culture. He showed how life in the mountains, plains, and coastal lowlands related with the sea across European and Arabic civilizations, and he stressed that the seaways were a key to the growth of the European economy. Braudel perceived of Europe as three regions: the Mediterranean, the Continent, and the Second Mediterranean of Europe, that is, the North Sea and the Baltic, or collectively the Northern Seas. Many other historians have since recognized that if the Mediterranean shores had a common culture, the same would hold true for other seas, with differences due to natural circumstances (such as enclosed or marginal character of the sea and accessibility of its shores) and historical experiences. The problem with the arguments of such historians is that they tend to list those aspects that the shores of a sea have in common but do not compare contacts inside and outside of the regional system.

Other approaches to the question of the role of oceans in human history have stressed the problems of overcoming distance. This is the dominant theme, of course, in the study of the Age of Exploration (c. 1491–1750), but it also resonates in the study of the more recent history of U.S. and European relations and most forcefully in the study of the history of Australia, which until the age of global airlines lived under the "tyranny of distance"—the fact that any visit abroad required weeks if not months of sea travel.

In the age before modern transport systems, sea transport was generally cheaper than land transport but not faster. Ship movements had many natural and unpredictable constraints. Delays of weeks occurred frequently because of unfavorable winds, and although some skippers would travel day and night because of a good knowledge of local waters, most dared sail only in daytime. Calculations of actual distances traveled by ships indicate that in spite of good winds sometimes bringing a ship's speed to 10 knots per hour (18 kilometers per hour), the distance covered during full trips, including the time spent waiting at anchor, seldom averaged more than 1 or 2 nautical miles (1.85–3.7 kilometers) per hour spent at sea. The distance covered per day thus works out to 45–90 kilometers. This calculation corresponds with actual travel distances on land. Whereas one cartload normally contained only twelve to eighteen barrels of grain or fish, even a small shipload might contain many times more. A typical ship of two hundred metric tons required a maximum crew of only ten men. The person-to-ton ratio would thus be 1:10 for the ship as against 1:1 for the cart, whereas distance traveled per day would be the same. Thus coastal urban markets received supplies by sea at a rate competitive with supplies from inland. A recent study of medieval England showed a ratio 1:4:8 for transport costs by sea, river, and road. Because the efficiency of land transport did not develop at the same pace that productivity increased in other trades such as agriculture, land transport costs grew relative to other costs until the eighteenth century.

The sea did not necessarily facilitate cultural impulses, such as aesthetic, dietary, or religious preferences, in the same way. The transportation of information and cultural impulses was not related to bulk freight rates but rather relied as much on individual travel patterns, most often by foot or horseback. Although enclosed and marginal seas may often have contained a well-developed trade and transport infrastructure, cultural relations do not necessarily mirror this and indeed may show quite different patterns of communication. Nevertheless, during the age of sail, roughly 1500 to 1850, maritime regions played a decisive role in many parts of the world. Coastal stretches of enclosed or marginal seas had an unusual concentration of maritime capital and labor that made possible the development of a distinctively maritime culture. This concentration was often based on the availability of timber for shipbuilding, although lack of forests did not preclude some regions rising to maritime preeminence.

The industrial transport revolution of the nineteenth century greatly enhanced long-distance and even global travel, but it lessened the importance of regional transport economics. Improved roads, railways, and steam shipping created a world market for many more goods than before, and regional markets gave way to the global market. Most small maritime communities were not able to raise the capital needed to participate in the global transport market, and as a result the coastal landscape changed from a string of human settlements to a few port towns with a concentration of maritime capital. In the industrial age, therefore, the age of regional seascapes came to an end.

Port towns are the nodes of the maritime transport system. The first port towns were well developed in the Mediterranean three thousand years ago. A port town may have its own home fleet, the crucial characteristic being that the town is a hub of inland and seaborne trade. Port towns tend therefore to utilize natural assets such as ease of multimodal transportation (land, river, and sea transport), access to a productive hinterland and a market, and strategic advantages such as control of waterways. Port towns provide access to the economic arteries of a country and therefore have historically been keenly regulated both for fiscal and military purposes. Occasionally they have gained full or partial sovereignty, as did the Italian city-states and the towns of the Hanseatic league, or have dominated a territorial state, such as the Netherlands in the sixteenth to eighteenth centuries, but most often they have been controlled by larger territorial powers. With the increase in shipping in the nineteenth century, port towns demanded more and more labor and sprawled along wharves and quays to become unwieldy entities, congested and heavily polluted. As a result of the spread of coal-fired steamer traffic in the second half of the nineteenth century, however, strict time schedules became possible and of utmost importance. To facilitate the steamers, a new infrastructure of bunker ports and dedicated quay facilities was built. To facilitate the steamers, a new infrastructure of bunker ports and dedicated quay facilities was built. Wind-powered ships continued to defeat the steam ships as long as a line of bunker ports did not dot the margins of the seas, but eventually the steam ships took possession of more and more sea routes so that by the early twentieth century the slow windjammers to Australia were the last to give in.

By that time diesel engines were being introduced, and by the 1950s coal was all but given up. At that point, passenger ships lost their edge in the oceanic transportation of people to the airlines, but a new era for the shipping of goods more than compensated for the loss to ship owners. In the first half of the twentieth century ships were designed to provide optimum cargo facilities and quicker turnaround times in ports. The Argentine meat industry and the Canary Island banana trade demanded refrigerated ships, and the oil industry gave rise to tanker ships. By the 1960s a design revolution took place, introducing the all-purpose shipping container, a metal box that could be refrigerated or otherwise modified and that conformed to standard measures and therefore allowed for convenient storage on board. The container ship became the vehicle for the globalization of trade, which severed the links between origin of resource, modification and packaging, and consumption.

To achieve optimum handling the once-prolific system of ocean ports has been minimized to a system of a few world ports that are the nodes of a few big container lines. Servicing the system are a number of feeder lines from lesser ports and a prolific number of trucking services that ensure that the individual container is brought to its final destination.

The environmental impact of the globalized container system is enormous. Although the system undoubtedly brings rationalization of the economic system, it is dependent on the availability of abundant and cheap energy, which will marginalize, for example, the costs of moving east Asian tiger prawns to Morocco to be peeled by cheap labor before they are moved to Germany to be packaged before they are eventually consumed in, for example, a restaurant in Paris.

Sea Law and Sea Powers

The oceans and seas have long been governed by law. The first principles for an international law of the seas were laid down by Hugo Grotius, a Dutch lawyer, historian, and theologian, in his work *Mare Liberum* (The Free Sea) (1609). He observed that the sea is an inexhaustible, common property and that all should have open access to it. These principles were adhered to in theory by all major European naval states and eventually were introduced as the guiding principles for access to all oceans and seas. Most states claimed dominion over territorial or coastal waters, but commercial ships were allowed free passage. The most important exception to this principle was the Danish Sound, providing access between the North Sea and the Baltic. The Danish government in 1857 lifted its toll on the sound and the right of inspection only after interna-

tional treaty and compensation. The shooting range of a cannon originally defined the width of territorial waters, but during the nineteenth century a 3-nautical-mile (5.5 kilometers) limit was increasingly accepted and laid down in international treaties. After World War II U.S. President Harry Truman claimed wider rights to economic interests on the North American continental shelf against Japan, and Chile and Peru claimed a 200-nautical-mile (370 kilometers) exclusive fishing zone off the coasts against U.S. tuna fishers. Iceland followed soon after with claims to exclude British fishers from Icelandic waters. Oil and fisheries were the main economic motives for these claims. In 1958 the United Nations called the first International Conference on the Law of the Sea to establish a new consensus on sea law. The conference extended territorial limits to 12 nautical miles (22 kilometers) but failed to settle the issue. A second conference in 1960 made little progress. During the 1960s and 1970s positions changed dramatically. It became much more evident that the supplies of fish stocks were limited and that depletion was becoming more prevalent. Attempts to manage resources through international bodies were proving to be largely ineffective. Many coastal states, both developed and developing, felt increasingly threatened by the large fleets of distant-water states off their coasts. Simultaneously, the issue of control over the mineral resources in the deep ocean beds raised the demands of developing states for a more equitable distribution of ocean wealth. The third international conference, which lasted from 1974 to 1982, resulted in a convention that is internationally recognized. The main innovation was the declaration of the right of coastal states to a 200-nautical mile "extended economic zone" (EEZ), which may be claimed by a coastal state for all mineral and living resources. The convention was signed by 157 states, while the United States, United Kingdom, and Germany took exception to the stipulations on seabed mineral resources. The EEZs represent the largest redistribution of territorial jurisdiction since nineteenth century colonialism.

The choice of 200 nautical miles as a limit for jurisdiction has no relevance to ecosystems or indeed to the distribution of mineral wealth but is simply a result of international negotiations. Whatever the imperfections of the convention, it has, however, provided coastal states with the authority to manage the resources within their zone. The short history of EEZs shows that they may be implemented to promote conservation interests in addition to the national economic interests for which they were designed.

Management and Protection

Whereas the law of the sea provides only a broad framework for international regulation of matters relating to oceans and seas, nation-states have developed intricate policies and institutions that impact the oceans. Two policies for the marine environment have been developed in recent years: integrated coastal zone management (ICZM) and marine protected areas (MPA). The specific policies that deal with issues such as watersheds and coastal development to seabed utilization by their very nature fail to grapple with the complete set of challenges that confronts people when they seek to manage, preserve, and develop the marine environment. This is the justification for the development of integrated coastal zone management. ICZM has developed as a cross-cutting policy for coastal and inshore management concerns since the 1980s, but it is implemented only to a limited degree in most countries. Marine protected areas have been designated throughout the world as areas where human access is restricted in order to conserve marine habitats. Coral reefs, fragile spawning areas, and hot spots of marine biodiversity have often been selected, but by 2000 only about 1 percent of the oceans were protected even by limited restrictions. The oceans and seas are still subject to open access and unrestricted human practices in most regions of the world, and the underwater world remains the last frontier, still to a large degree unexplored by humans.

Poul Holm

See also Aral Sea; Baltic Sea; Black Sea; Estuaries; Law of the Sea; Mediterranean Sea; Salton Sea; Yellow Sea

Further Reading

Anand, R. P. (1982). *Origin and development of the law of the sea: History of international law revisited.* The Hague, Netherlands: Nijhoff.

Borgese, E. M. (1998). *The oceanic circle: Governing the seas as a global resource.* New York: United Nations Publications.

Braudel, F. (1996). *The Mediterranean and the Mediterranean world in the age of Philip II.* Berkeley and Los Angeles: University of California Press.

Carlton, J. T., Geller, J. B., Reaka-Kudla, M. L., & Norse, E. (1999). Historical extinctions in the sea. *Annual Review of Ecology and Systematics, 30,* 515–538.

Chaudhuri, K. N. (1985). *Trade and civilisation in the Indian Ocean: An economic history from the rise of Islam to 1750.* Cambridge, UK: Cambridge University Press.

Chaudhuri, K. N. (1990). *Asia before Europe: Economy and civilisation of the Indian Ocean from the rise of Islam to 1750.* Cambridge, UK: Cambridge University Press.

Cicin-Sain, B., & Knecht, R. (1998). *Integrated coastal and ocean management: Concepts and practices.* Washington, DC: Island Press.

Day, T. (1999). *Oceans.* Chicago: Fitzroy Dearborn Publishers.

Garrison, T. (1995). *Oceanography: An invitation to marine science* (2nd ed.). Belmont, CA: Wadsworth Publishing.

Horden, P., & Purcell, N. (2000). *The corrupting sea: A study of Mediterranean history.* Oxford, UK: Oxford University Press.

Houde, E., & Brink, K. H. (2001). *Marine protected areas: Tools for sustaining ocean ecosystems.* Washington, DC: National Academy Press.

Masschaele, J. (1993). Transport costs in medieval England. *Economic History Review, 46,* 266–279.

McPherson, K. (1993). *The Indian Ocean: A history of people and the sea.* Bombay, India: Oxford University Press.

Mills, E. L. (1989). *Biological oceanography: An early history, 1870–1960.* Ithaca, NY: Cornell University Press.

Reid, A. (1993). *Southeast Asia in the age of commerce, 1450–1680.* New Haven, CT: Yale University Press.

Roding, J., & van Voss, L. H. (Eds.). (1996). *The North Sea and culture (1550–1800).* Hilversum: Verloren Press.

Thorne-Miller, B., & Earle, S. A. (1998). *The living ocean: Understanding and protecting marine biodiversity* (2nd ed.). Washington, DC: Island Press.

Oil

Oil has been the world's most important source of commercial energy since the late 1960s, and because of its high energy density and easy portability it will retain this primacy for decades to come. Natural seepages and pools of crude oil are common in the Middle East, and hence oil was known of since antiquity. However, its combustion was rare, and the heating of Constantinople's *thermae* (water baths) during the late Roman Empire is perhaps the best-known example of this infrequent use. Mass slaughter of whales during the first half of the nineteenth century spurred a search for a new source of lamp oil, and in 1853 Canadian physician and geologist Abraham Gessner performed the first distillation of kerosene from crude oil. A mere six years later, on 27 August 1859, at Oil Creek, Pennsylvania,

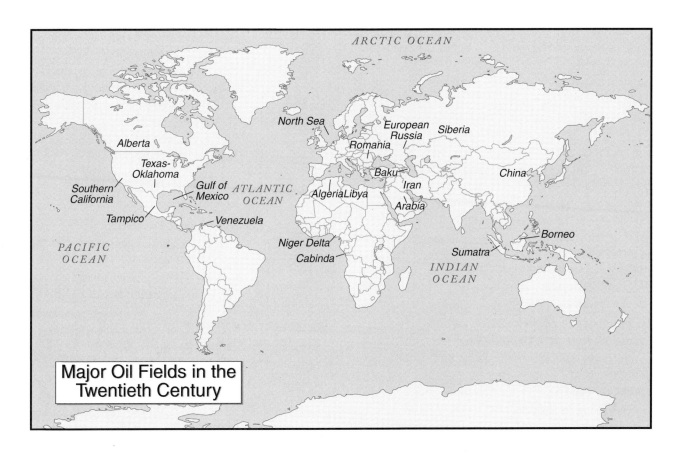

Major Oil Fields in the Twentieth Century

Colonel E. L. Drake's workers used the ancient Chinese percussion drilling technique (but powered by a steam engine) to complete the world's first oil well.

Gas lighting (especially after Austrian chemist Carl Welsbach's incandescent gas mantle in 1885) and U.S. inventor Thomas Edison's first electric power plants in 1882 obviated the need for petroleum as a new source of lighting, but this loss of a promising market was more than made up for by the introduction of internal combustion engines powered by gasoline. The first vehicle of this kind was patented by German inventor Gottlieb Daimler in 1885, and seven years later German mechanical engineer Rudolf Diesel introduced a different engine design that relied on high compression without sparking. Small-scale production of cars dominated the first two decades of the automotive era, but by 1913 the U.S. automaker Henry Ford introduced assembly lines in Detroit, where the Model T was built until 1927. Use of internal combustion engines for flight (for the first time in 1903) and introduction of heavy Diesel engines for rail and sea propulsion further increased the market for liquid fuels. Nonfuel products of crude oil refining—lubricating oils and as-

phalts used for hard-surface roads—also played an important role in the expanding demands for crude oil.

Rising Demands and Technical Innovation

All of these demands were in place before World War II, but, with the exception of U.S. car ownership, mass markets for private cars, worldwide deployment of heavy Diesels, long-distance trucking, and affordable intercontinental jet travel became the norm only after 1960. The oil industry has met these demands through continuous innovation that has gradually transformed exploration, drilling, extraction, refining, and distribution of liquid fuels. The industry's first four decades brought a rapid pioneering development not only in the United States (where California and Texas soon overshadowed Pennsylvania), but also in Romania (Ploesti fields), in Baku on the Caspian Sea, and in Sumatra. Countries that became major oil producers during the first half of the twentieth century included Mexico, Iran, Trinidad, and Venezuela before World War I and Iraq and Saudi Arabia before 1940. Most of the Middle East's oil fields were discovered between 1945 and 1965, and the Persian Gulf region now contains about 65 percent of the world's known oil reserves. Other major finds of the second half of the twentieth century included giant fields in both European and Siberian parts of Russia (before its collapse the USSR was the world's largest producer of crude oil), in China, Nigeria, Mexico, and the North Sea.

Key technical innovations in drilling were the introduction of the rolling cutter rock bit by U.S. industrialist Howard Hughes in 1909, development of anchored and semisubmersible offshore platforms after 1945, and a widespread adoption of directional and horizontal drilling after 1980. Long-distance transfers and exports of oil have been made possible by the introduction of large-diameter seamless-steel pipelines and by reliance on supertankers (carrying 250,000–500,000 metric tons) for overseas shipments. After 1936 crude oil refining was revolutionized by catalytic cracking, which makes it possible to produce lighter, high-octane distillates (above all, gasoline and jet fuel) from intermediate and heavy compounds.

Global oil production rose from only about 20 million metric tons in 1900 to nearly 500 million metric tons in 1950 and to about 3.5 billion metric tons by 2000, when the five largest crude producers were Saudi Arabia, United States, Russia, Iran, and Mexico. The United States, Japan, and Germany were the three largest importers. Until 1973 oil production increases were accompanied by declining or stable prices. This changed abruptly in 1973–1974, when the Organization of Petroleum Exporting Countries (OPEC) quintupled the price to more than $11 a barrel. This price was more than tripled in 1979–1980 amid the panic generated by the fall of the Iranian monarchy. Since this unsustainably high price collapsed in 1985 oil has been trading mostly at $15–$25 a barrel, but with unpredictable and often large (lows below $10, highs close to $40 a barrel) fluctuations. Although the affluent Western countries responded to higher prices by using less oil per unit of their gross domestic product, the overall global demand kept rising, aided particularly by huge import requirements of newly industrializing countries in Asia.

Resources and Environmental Impacts

This rising demand has led recently to renewed concerns about the ultimate magnitude of oil resources and about an early end of the oil era. But the best available estimates indicate that the ultimately recoverable resources of conventional oil are, at just over 3 trillion barrels, nearly four times as large as the total extracted

between 1860 and 2000 and that nonconventional sources (heavy oil sands and shales) may eventually supply a significant share of future demand. In any case, oil's high energy density (at 42 million Joules [a Joule is a unit of work or energy] per kilogram it is nearly twice as high as that of typical bituminous coal) and its easy portability and storage mean that it will remain a preferred (on land) or indispensable (in the air) source of transportation energy. Unfortunately, oil has done more than transform ways of travel, habitation, and leisure: Its extraction and marine transportation cause water pollution, and its combustion is one of the largest sources of air pollution. Crude oils are mixtures of complex hydrocarbons with mere traces of ash, but their heavy varieties contain as much sulfur or more (greater than 2 percent) than do bituminous coals. Combustion of high-sulfur fuel oils emits sulfur dioxide, a key precursor of acidifying deposition.

But the high-temperature combustion of liquid fuels in internal combustion engines and gas turbines is the main concern: It releases nitrogen oxides, carbon monoxide, and volatile organic compounds. Solar radiation energizes complex reactions of nitrogen oxides, carbon monoxide, and volatile organic compounds that produce photochemical smog. Its most aggressive component is highly reactive ozone, which impairs human health and damages plants and materials. Increasingly effective automotive controls have greatly reduced automotive emissions in the affluent countries, whereas the absence of such controls makes most Asian (outside Japan), African, and Latin American cities cloaked in seasonal or nearly permanent smog. Hybrid drive and fuel cells are the best choices for long-term management of this environmental problem. Future use of oil for fuel thus depends to a large extent on the success in controlling the resulting air pollution.

Vaclav Smil

Further Reading

Brantly, J. E. (1971). *History of oil well drilling.* Houston: Gulf Publishing.

British Petroleum. (2002). *Review of world energy.* London: British Petroleum.

Forbes, R. J. (1964). Bitumen and petroleum in antiquity. In *Studies in ancient technology: Vol. 1* (pp. 1–24). Leiden, Netherlands: E. J. Brill.

Hunt, J. M. (1979). *Petroleum geochemistry and geology.* San Francisco: W. H. Freeman.

Odell, P. R. (1999). *Fossil fuel resources in the 21st century.* London: Financial Times Energy.

Perrodon, A. (1985). *Histoire des Grandes Decouvertes Petrolieres* [History of great oil discoveries]. Paris: Elf Aquitaine.

Rogner, H.-H. (2000). Energy resources. In J. Goldemberg (Ed.), *World energy assessment* (pp. 135–171). New York: UNDP.

Smil, V. (1994). *Energy in world history.* Boulder, CO: Westview.

Smil, V. (2003). *Energy at the crossroads.* Cambridge, MA: MIT Press.

Womack, J. P., Jones, D. T., & Roos, D. (1991). *The machine that changed the world.* New York: Harper Perennial.

Oil Spills

Oil is a main source of energy. Because it is unevenly distributed in the world, it must be transported on the seas and in pipelines to distant lands. Although the major oil transport and transfer activities occur on the seas, ports, and rivers, they are not limited to these areas. Accidental spills can occur wherever oil is drilled, stored, handled, refined, transported, and transferred. These spills can be either massive and catastrophic or chronic. Few other environmental problems are as common or ubiquitous or have the potential for immediate environmental damage and long-range effects. Recent or dramatic oil spills have included those involving the ships *Amoco Cadiz, Exxon Valdez,* and *Sea Empress* and the massive oil spills during the Gulf War and in a northern Russian pipeline.

Crude petroleum or oil is a liquid or semiliquid mixture of hydrocarbon compounds that contains sulfur, oxygen, nitrogen, other elements, and metals. The hydrocarbons are the decayed remains of small marine animals and plants that flourished in the shallow inland seas that once covered large areas of the continents. Over hundreds of thousands of years, the dead remains of these tiny organisms drifted to the sea bottom. Covered by mud, this organic matter changed into the complicated hydrocarbons we call *petroleum.* For the past 600 million years, incompletely decayed plant and animal remains were buried under thick layers of rock, often accumulated one layer at a time. Because petroleum, natural gas, and coal formed from organisms that lived millions of years ago, they are called *fossil fuels.*

Since the Paleozoic era (from 570 to 245 million years ago), this organic matter has been slowly moving to more porous and permeable rocks, such as sandstone and siltstones, where it was trapped. The oil accumulates because of the presence of impermeable rock lying over these reservoirs. Some oil fields extend laterally in the rock over several kilometers and may be several hundred meters deep. Some oil enters the oceans through natural seeps, and these natural oil spills can have massive effects on the organisms living nearby.

Some of the hydrocarbon products of petroleum are dissolved natural gas, gasoline, benzene, naphtha, kerosene, diesel fuel and light heating oils, heavy heating oils, and tars of various weights. Petroleum yields these products through elaborate refining processes. They are then further refined and combined into other products such as solvents, paints, asphalt, plastics, synthetic rubber, fibers, soaps and cleansing agents, waxes and jellies, medicines, explosives, and fertilizers. Oil spills can occur during the refining process or during transport.

History of Small Oil Spills

For over six thousand years people have used asphalt, pitch (bitumen), and liquid oil. People living in river valleys of ancient Mesopotamia used local asphalt from hand-dug pits as building cement, jewelry, and caulking for boats. The legend of the flood described in the Book of Genesis records that the ark was well caulked. The Elamites, Chaldeans, Akkadians, and Sumerians mined shallow deposits of oil-derived pitch or asphalt to export to Egypt to preserve the mummies of great kings and queens and to make mosaics to adorn their coffins. The wrappings from Egyptian mummies were used for medicines. Nile River boats were caulked with asphalt, and the infant Moses was cradled in a raft of bulrushes "daubed with pitch" when he was set adrift. Liquid oil served as a purgative and wound dressing for the ancient Egyptians. It aided the healing process and kept wounds clean. Archaeological remains in Khuzestan, Iran, show that asphalt was commonly used for bonding and jewel-setting during the Sumerian epoch (4000 BCE). Asphalt served as cement in the Tower of Babel and in the walls and columns of early Babylonian temples. As early as 600 BCE the Babylonians set clay cones and tiny semiprecious stones in bitumen to form elaborate mosaics. According to the Greek biographer Plutarch, about 331 BCE Alexander the Great was impressed by the sight of a continuous flame issuing from the earth in Kirkuk, Iraq, probably a natural gas seep set ablaze. The Romans used oil lamps in the first century BCE. The Chinese first used oil as a fuel around 200 CE. They employed pulleys and hand labor to suction the oil from the ground through pipes. Oil spills from these uses were small and limited in scope.

Oil was quickly used for military purposes, which resulted in larger spills. Oil-filled trenches were set aflame to defend cities in ancient times. The Arabs developed the first distilling processes to obtain flammable products for military purposes, and they used arrows wrapped in oil-soaked cloths Greek fires during the siege of Athens in 480 BCE. The Byzantines used Greek fire against the Muslims in the seventh and eighth centuries. At close range, Greek fire was propelled through tubes onto Arab ships attacking Constantinople in 673 CE, and the fleet was nearly destroyed by the Greeks. The Saracens used Greek fire against St. Louis at the Crusades, and the Knights of St. John used it against the invading Turks at Malta. The Mongols also burned petroleum products in their siege of central Asia. Bukhara in western Asia fell in 1220 because Genghis Khan threw pots full of naphtha and fire at the gates of the castle, and it burst in flames. People poured from the city or died in the flames.

During the Renaissance, the transport of oil developed, leading to oil spills. In 1726 Peter the Great of Russia issued ordinances regulating the transport of oil from Baku on the Caspian Sea, by boat, up the Volga River. Oil became a valued commodity to barter, trade, or steal. In the New World, the natives of Venezuela caulked boats and hand-woven baskets with asphalt, and liquid oil was used for medicine and lighting. Native North Americans used oil in magic, medicines, and paints. The first barrel of Venezuelan oil was exported to Spain in 1539 to alleviate the gout of Emperor Charles V.

The modern era of oil transportation began in 1820 when a small-bore lead pipe was used to transport natural gas from a seep near Fredonia, New York, to nearby consumers, including the local hotel. From this time on, the possibility of oil spills due directly to transport and transfer increased with the decades.

The Modern Oil Spill Era

The majority of known oil reserves are in the Middle East, followed by North America. The Organization of Petroleum Exporting Countries has the greatest reserves, with Saudi Arabia leading the member nations. The global distribution of oil deposits influences production and transport patterns and thereby determines the potential distribution of oil spills. World oil production rose from 450 million metric tons in 1950 to 2.7 billion metric tons by 1996 and continues to rise slowly. Oil spills rise along with production.

The primary method of transportation of oil is by oil tanker, and traditional shipping lanes have developed between the oil-producing countries and the oil-importing countries. At present, major oil routes go from the Middle East to Japan, Europe, and the United States. Oil is also transported through pipes over vast distances to refineries. Oil spills occur mainly along these oceanic and land routes and along the shores where oil transfers take place. Small spills occur during the transfer of oil from tanker to tanker, from tanker to refinery, from damaged, underground pipes, and around oil refineries and storage facilities. About 7.56 billion liters of oil enter the oceans from spills and other accidents each year.

The large spills usually occur during tanker accidents. With the increase in the size of oil tankers, the potential for accidents has increased. The tankers of the 1880s had a capacity of 3,000 metric tons, compared to 16,500 in 1945, 115,000 in 1962, and 517,000 in 1977 (the modern era of tankers). The recent U.S. requirement that only double-hulled ships can enter U.S. waters should decrease the number of tanker spills.

Although the large oil spills receive media attention, only about 4 percent of oil entering the oceans comes from tanker accidents. Another 25 percent enters from tanker operations, 14 percent from other transport accidents, and 34 percent from rivers and estuaries. About 11 percent of the oil entering the oceans comes from natural seeps.

Major Spills

Since 1978 there has been a steady increase in the number of small spills, whereas the number of large spills has remained relatively constant. One to three spills of over 38 million liters happen each year. One or two catastrophic accidents in any given year can substantially increase the amount of oil spilled onto the land and into the oceans. The small spills of less than 378,000 liters apiece add up to about 38 million liters a year worldwide. Even without major spills, large quantities spill into marine and inland habitats; in 1999 alone approximately 120 million liters spilled.

The largest spill on record dumped 907 million liters into the Persian Gulf in 1991, but most spills are smaller. Since 1978 there have been thirty-five spills that involved more than 38 million liters per incident.

Other large spills have included the oil well Ixtoc–1 in Mexico (529 million liters, 1979), Norwruz Field in Arabia (302 million liters, 1980), Fergana Valley in Uzbekistan (302 million liters, 1992), Castillo de Bellver off South Africa (294 million liters, 1983), and the *Amoco Cadiz* off France (257 million liters, 1978). All other spills were less than 189 million liters each. The *Exxon Valdez* spill in Alaska was twenty-eighth on the list, with 41 million liters.

Effects of Oil Spills

Animals and plants and the nonliving parts of ecosystems are not equally vulnerable to oil spills. Some plants are fragile and have narrow habitat ranges, and they grow only in isolated sites. Some animals are very specialized, living in only a few places or eating only a few kinds of foods. Such species are particularly vulnerable to even small oil spills. Plants and animals in Arctic environments are fragile because of the limited growing season, limited diversity, and slow decay of the oil itself.

Other species are generalists, with wide tolerances for different environmental conditions, broad food requirements, and large geographical distributions. Such animals and plants are very adaptable and often can recover quickly from an oil spill, although the initial death toll may be high. Still other animals, such as some birds, fish, and mammals, can move away from a spill if its spread is slow.

Factors that determine whether an oil spill has devastating effects on plants and animals include size of the spill, type of oil, time of the spill (particularly in relation to the life cycle of the organisms), vulnerability of particular plants and animals, and the vulnerability of particular ecosystems. Location of a spill can determine effects. In spills in intertidal marshes or estuaries where there is little tidal flow, there is a reduced opportunity for the oil to be carried out to sea, where dilution can blunt the effects. Oil often concentrates at the edge of marshes where there is also a high concentration of invertebrates, young fish, and foraging birds. Many invertebrates do not have the ability to move or move only very short distances, making them particularly vulnerable to oil.

The timing of a spill is critical. A spill that occurs during the migratory season of birds, fish, or mammals may result in unusually high exposure of vast numbers of animals. A spill during the spawning season of invertebrates or fish can eliminate reproduction for a season, and a spill during the migration season of marine mammals can kill or weaken a significant portion of the local populations of seals, sea lions, sea otters, whales, and other mammals. Seabirds are particularly at risk because they spend most of their time in the oceans or in estuaries, where massive oil spills usually occur. Seabirds also nest in large colonies of hundreds or thousands, where an oil spill can "oil" or kill hundreds at a time. Oiled parents bring oil back to the nests, killing eggs or young chicks. Because they are so visible, birds often serve as bioindicators of the severity of oil spills, although only a fraction of the birds that die in oceanic or coastal oil spills are ever recovered.

People can be injured or become ill during oil spills or during the cleanup and can become ill by consuming oil-tainted fish or shellfish. Oil spill accidents can result in the death of workers on the tanker, refinery, or pipeline or the people employed in cleanup. Oil spills often occur during bad weather and stormy seas, making the hazards for the tanker crew more severe. During a recent fifteen-year period, an average of eighty-one mariner lives per year were lost due to oil spills, most because of fires or explosions.

The effect of oil spills on fishing communities can be devastating. Fishing communities are affected both in the short term and the long term. For many weeks or months the fish are tainted or contaminated, grounding the fisheries completely. The effects of oil on the fish may result in lower harvests for years after the oil has disappeared. Fishing losses were documented for at least six years after the *Exxon Valdez* spill. Fishers lost income because of the low yields and restricted fishing areas, and guides and hotels lost money because recreational fishers did not come back for many years. Fishers and guides lost their jobs and their lifestyle. Native American communities also lost their ability to harvest traditional resources, including fish and shellfish, resulting in a permanent change in their lives. The effects were cascading because much of the local economy depended upon fishing and tourism. The effects of oil spills on aesthetics and existence values, as well as on fishing and tourism, are massive and extensive.

Joanna Burger

Further Reading

Burger, J. (1997). *Oil spills.* New Brunswick, NJ: Rutgers University Press.

Cahill, R. A. (1990). *Disasters at sea: Titanic to Exxon Valdez.* San Antonio, TX: Nautical Books.

DeCola, E. (1999). *International oil spill statistics.* Arlington, MA: Cutter Information Corp.

Gin, K. Y. H., Huda, K., Lim, W. K., & Tkalich, P. (2001). An oil spill-food chain interaction model for coastal waters. *Marine Pollution Bulletin, 42*(7), 590–597.

Gottinger, H. W. (2001). Economic modeling, estimation and policy analysis of oil spill processes. *International Journal of Environment & Pollution, 15*(3), 333–363.

Griglunas, T. A., Oplauch, J. J., Diamatides, J., & Mazzotta, M. (1998). Liability for oil spill damages: Issues, methods, and examples. *Coastal Management 26* (2), 67–77.

Louma, J. R. (1999). Spilling the truth. Ten years after the worst oil spill in American history, Alaska is still feeling the effects of the Exxon Valdez disaster and cleanup. *Audubon 101* (2), 52–62.

Peterson, C. H. (2002). The "Exxon Valdez" oil spill in Alaska: Acute, indirect, and chronic effects on the ecosystem. *Advances in Marine Biology, 39*, 3–84.

Rice, S. D., et al. (2001). Impacts to pink salmon following Exxon Valdez oil spill: Persistence, toxicity, sensitivity, and controversy. *Reviews in Fisheries Science, 9*(3), 165–211.

U.S. Department of Energy. (1980–1998). *International energy annual reports.* Washington, DC: Author.

Orinoco River

The Orinoco forms the major river system in northern South America, with a watershed of 590,000 square kilometers. Its source is in the Guiana Highlands of southern Venezuela. The upper part of the river forms the border between Colombia and Venezuela. The river flows eastward in a gentle 2,700-kilometer-long arc, passing through a range of ecosystems, including the rain forests and plains of southern Venezuela, and through a large, swampy delta in eastern Venezuela. It drains into the Gulf of Paria in the Atlantic Ocean opposite the island of Trinidad. Although not one of the world's longest rivers, the Orinoco ranks third globally in terms of the volume of water discharged.

During the pre-Hispanic period, the river was densely settled by many different indigenous groups, including the Warao, Carib, Arawak, and Yanomamo. These groups used the riverine ecosystem in a variety of ways. Some groups fished from the river itself; others hunted game and gathered plants from the forests along the river's edge; still others farmed along the floodplain, cultivating cassava, corn, and other crops.

These groups organized large trading networks, some of which extended southward into the Amazon River basin and northward to the Caribbean Sea. This, for example, is most likely the route by which the cacao plant—a native of Amazonia—reached Mesoamerica. Tragically, the river also facilitated the movement of European conquerors—and European diseases—deep into the interior, leading to the demographic collapse of the indigenous populations. In the sixteenth century several European explorers, most famously Sir Walter Raleigh, explored the river and its tributaries in search of the fabled golden city of El Dorado. El Dorado remained elusive, however, and the region attracted few European settlers other than a handful of Jesuit missionaries. The only European settlement of any size was Angostura (now Ciudad Bolívar, Venezuela), founded in 1764. In the eighteenth century naturalists began to express interest in the region's abundant flora and fauna. In 1741 the Jesuit priest Jose Gumilla published the *Orinoco Ilustrado*, the first detailed study of the Orinoco River basin and its inhabitants. In the eighteenth and nineteenth centuries the basin was also explored and mapped by such well-known naturalists as Alexander von Humboldt.

The pace of human-caused environmental change accelerated rapidly during the twentieth century. The primary agent of environmental change has been the national government, which has sought to industrialize the region and to exploit its natural resources. In the early 1960s the government founded Ciudad Guayana, at the intersection of the Orinoco and Caroní Rivers, as an industrial center. It constructed the Guri dam, a hydroelectric project that created the second-largest lake in Venezuela. In the late 1990s large oil reserves were discovered in the Orinoco delta, which the government planned to exploit in collaboration with foreign oil companies. This pursuit of economic development has harmed many of the region's ecosystems and inhabitants.

Some of the region's most delicate species—including the West Indian manatee, the Orinoco crocodile, and the arrau river turtle—face extinction because of overhunting, pollution, and loss of habitat. Outbreaks of malaria have devastated the upriver communities of Yanomamo Indians. In response, many local, national, and international organizations—such as the Orinoco Oil Watch and the Amigos de la Gran Sabana—have begun to lobby for the establishment of nature preserves and more environmentally responsible programs of development. The largest of these is the

The Canoes of the Warao of the Orinoco Delta

The canoe plays an important role in the geographic environment in which the Warao play out their lives. The indigenes, without distinction by sex or age, are expert paddlers. Canoes transport the men to the areas in which they hunt and fish, to the rice fields (*Oryza* sp.) or the sawmills. Women use them to travel on a daily basis to the family plots under cultivation. The children bathe at the river's edge at the same time as they play with the boats tied up to the piles of their houses. The nuclear family, gathered together in the canoe, goes out in search of crabs (*Cardissoma* sp.) and iguanas (*Iguana iguana*), or paddles along the "*cañitos*" /creeks/ on its way to the moriche palm (*Mauritia flexuosa*) stands.

The manufacture of canoes is a strictly male task, which coincides with the summer or dry season. Usually this activity brings together, in a clearing in the forest, three or four individuals united by bonds of kinship, each of which, helped by the others, works on his own canoe. The Warao oldsters persist in applying themselves to this activity with the cooperation of their *aukatuma* (sons), *natoromo* (grandsons) or *dawatuma* (sons-in-law).

Source: Suárez, Maria Matilde. (1968). *The Warao: Natives of the Orinoco Delta*. Caracas, Venezuela: Deparemento de Antropología, Instituto Venezolano de Investigaciones Científicas, p. 35.

Upper Orinoco-Casiquare Biosphere Reserve, an area of almost 9 million hectares, established in 1993.

Stuart McCook

Further Reading

Coronil, F. (1997). *The magical state: Nature, money, and modernity in Venezuela.* Chicago: University of Chicago Press.

Gumilla, J. (1963). *El Orinoco ilustrado y defendido* [The Orinoco, illustrated and defended]. Caracas, Venezuela: Academia Nacional de la Historia. (Original work published 1741)

Humboldt, A. V. (1995) *Personal narrative of travels to the equinoctial regions of the new continent during the years 1799–1804.* London: Penguin Books. (Original work published 1818)

Lewis, W. M., Jr., Hamilton, S. K., Lasi, M. A., Rodriguez, M., & Saunders, J. F., III (2000). Ecological determinism on the Orinoco floodplain. *BioScience, 50*(8), 681–692.

O'Hanlon, R. (1998). *In trouble again: A journey between the Orinoco and the Amazon.* London: Hamish Hamilton.

Parisina, M. (1998). Current challenges on the Orinoco. *Americas, 50*(6), 6–14.

Ozone, Tropospheric

Ozone, a molecule made of three atoms of oxygen, is a trace constituent of the Earth's atmosphere. It was first identified in 1840 by the German chemist Christian Schoenbein (1799–1868). Elevated ozone concentrations in the stratosphere protect us from harmful ultraviolet radiation. This "good ozone" is seriously depleted by anthropogenic compounds such as chlorofluorocarbons. In the troposphere, the layer of air directly above ground, ozone is a major pollutant and one of the main compounds in photochemical or "Los Angeles type" smog, sometimes called "bad ozone." Nowadays, it is considered a major air pollution hazard worldwide.

A Tricky Kind of Air Pollution

Ozone is a secondary air pollutant: It is not emitted directly, but is formed in the atmosphere from so-called precursor substances. In a complex chain of reactions involving the presence of sunlight, nitrogen oxides (NO_x) react with volatile organic compounds (VOCs), a group of substances with varied individual properties such as ethylene, formaldehyde, or toluene, to form ozone. The formation process is influenced by meteorology (especially temperature and sunlight intensity) and by the concentrations of the individual precursors. Concentrations depend on emission density and atmospheric dilution, again a meteorological issue. Generally, the warmer, calmer, sunnier, and more industrialized an area is, the greater its ozone problem.

A number of further issues create obstacles for regulation. Both ozone and its precursor compounds can remain stable over several days, transporting pollution for more than 1,000 kilometers. At high concentrations, nitrogen oxides are able to destroy ozone. Ozone levels thus are lowest close to the nitrogen oxide emission sources. The same nitrogen oxide molecule that destroyed ozone can later act as a precursor compound tens or hundreds of kilometers downwind of the emission area. Due to such complex interactions, reduction of precursors does not have linear effects on the reduction of ozone levels. Furthermore, both ozone and its precursors occur naturally and thus anthropogenic production adds to a background.

There are many sources for the precursors, but automobile exhaust is one of the most important for both types of precursors. Nitrogen oxides derive from all combustion processes, especially from high-temperature combustion as in car engines, power plants, or lightning. VOCs are produced by incomplete combustion as in open fires, by gasoline evaporation, and solvent application. A considerable amount is also produced by plants as part of their natural metabolism. In remote areas of the world, biomass burning is an important source, leading to globally elevated levels of ozone in the troposphere.

Ozone is harmful for plants at levels that are close to background conditions. It is also seen as one of the main reasons for the new type of forest dieback encountered in many regions. In humans, it causes both short- and, more dangerously, long-term health effects, most important are damages to the respiratory system.

The History of an Unsolved Problem

Natural ozone-rich air, for example, that found after thunderstorms, was considered healthy in the nineteenth and beginning of the twentieth century; tourist resorts even used it in their marketing. Concern about ozone as a pollutant started with the first recognized episodes of smog in Los Angeles in 1943. Donora, Pennsylvania, experienced an air pollution episode in 1948 that killed 20 people and numerous animals and injured about 6,000 inhabitants. In 1950, the first scientific paper showing ozone damage to plants was published, and research on the problem became so abundant that a first summarizing monograph appeared in 1961.

In reaction to the great smog of 1943, the Los Angeles Air Control District was formed in 1947. Scientific evidence on pollution, including the causal links between precursors and ozone and on the adverse effects of ozone on plants, led to the Air Pollution Control Act, effective in 1955. This was the first nationwide regulation of air pollution. Extended in 1959, it was developed into the 1963 Clean Air Act, which was then updated with regular amendments, among which the 1970 amendment constituted a new phase in regulation. The Environmental Protection Agency (EPA) has since been the main agency responsible for monitoring and formulation of standards. The National Academy of Sciences (NAS) conducted several detailed assessments of the ozone problem. Due to the secondary nature of the pollutant, ozone pollution questions extended to the potential threat reformulated gasoline could pose, elaborated in an NAS study in 2000.

The EPA revised its ozone standard in 1979. A reassessment undertaken in 1993 proved the standard to be still adequate. Based on more than 3,000 studies published in the following years, EPA in 1997 again somewhat adapted the standard by using longer averaging times as basis for assessment.

Concern about emissions led to technical developments in combustion processes, especially in automobiles. Volvo led the way with the first three-way catalyst in its 1977 "smog free car" model. Only this type of catalytic device can effectively curb both precursors in car exhaust. But catalysts may degrade after some time. The "smog checks" done since 1984 in California show that this was, at least initially, a problem.

Developments in Europe were a bit different. Up until the late 1960s, the primary source of ozone over continental Europe was believed to be meteorological transport from the stratosphere. As was further believed, the cool climate, especially in northern Europe, would not constitute favorable meteorological conditions for photochemical formation of tropospheric ozone from anthropogenic emissions. In fact, peak concentrations are in general significantly lower. But after first experiments with indicator plants in the 1960s had shown considerable ozone concentrations, international monitoring and regulation started in the wake of acid rain research. From 1968 to the late 1970s, OECD (Organization for Economic Cooperation and Development) hosted a first working group addressing transboundary air pollution. Since then, the United Nations Economic Commission for Europe (UN-ECE) hosts the Convention on the Long-Range Transport for Air Pollution, which through its Co-operative Program for Monitoring and Evaluation of the Long-Range Transmission of Air Pollutants in Europe (EMEP) still is one of the main mechanisms for air pollution regulation throughout Europe. Damage to forests became a concern in Europe in the 1980s, leading to increased attention to ozone as a harmful pollutant. However, the first protocol specifically targeted at ozone was enforced as late as 1991, regulating VOCs. EUROTRAC, an initiative for research into long-range air pollution, started in 1988 and has produced a wealth of data and models since. Regulatory approaches switched from freezes or uniform decreases to country-specific targets (national emission ceilings), based on reduction effects as a more cost-effective solution.

How Far Have We Come?

In the U.S, the situation in the 1960s and 1970s was characterized by severe photochemical smog damage to public health and the environment. A similar situation developed in Mexico City in the 1980s. There, the successful reduction of particle pollution had enabled higher sunlight intensity than under polluted skies, facilitating ozone formation.

The situation has since improved in most urban areas, but sensitive parts of the population, in particular children, still suffer considerably during episodes. Ozone pollution is episodic, showing a buildup of pollution levels over days during longer periods of hot and sunny weather with slow exchange of air. Therefore, recent decreases in the number of episodes cannot safely be interpreted as a success of control, but may simply derive from different weather patterns in different years.

The most immediate health effects having been dealt with, the costs and benefits of further ozone regulation are a matter of ongoing discussion. The odd combination of natural emissions of forests and pollutants from city centers in forming ozone make effective measures extremely difficult. Not just human health, but crop productivity and aesthetic considerations such as the question of access to clean air offering high visibility, allow for seemingly endless argument, with ambient levels of ozone still high enough to merit serious concern.

Verena and Wilfried Winiwarter

Further Reading

Committee on Tropospheric Ozone, National Research Council (1992). *Rethinking the ozone problem in urban and regional pollution.* Washington, DC: National Academy Press.
Committee on Tropospheric Ozone, National Research Council (2000). *Ozone-forming potential of reformulated gasoline.* Washington, DC: National Academy Press.
Farrell, A. & Keating, T. J. (1998). Multi-jurisdictional air pollution assessment: A comparison of the eastern United States and Western Europe. ENRP Discussion Paper E–98–12, Kennedy School of Government, Harvard University. Retrieved June 4 2002, from http://environment.harvard.edu/gea/pubs
Keating, T. J., & Farrell, A. (1998). Problem framing and model formulation: The regionality of tropospheric ozone in the U.S. and Europe. ENRP Discussion Paper E–98–11, Kennedy School of Government, Harvard University. Retrieved June 4 2002, from http://environment.harvard.edu/gea/pubs
Leighton, P. A. (1961). *Photochemistry of air pollution.* New York: Academic Press.

Ozone Depletion

Ozone is a gas consisting of molecules of three atoms of oxygen (the oxygen gas we breathe has molecules of two such atoms). It is highly reactive and unstable, and formed by photochemical reactions in the atmosphere. In the lower atmosphere, this process requires additional trace compounds (from natural sources such as lightning and trees, but more pronounced from anthropogenic pollution). In the stratosphere, a layer of the atmosphere 10–50 kilometers above us, the intensity of ultraviolet (UV) light is sufficient to form ozone from oxygen. Ozone is able to absorb such UV radiation (in particular UV-B) and thus shields the lower atmosphere and the Earth's surface from this carcinogenic radiation. In addition, ozone plays an important role in stabilizing the temperature profile of the atmosphere. Stratospheric ozone is beneficial to humans and is sometimes called "good ozone."

Humans Influence the Stratosphere

The natural equilibrium of stratospheric ozone concentrations has been strongly affected by anthropogenic ozone depletion. The depletion is caused by a class of synthetic substances called CFCs (chlorofluorocarbons) and chemically related molecules, together called ODS or Ozone Depleting Substances. CFCs were invented in 1930 and produced in increasing quantities from the 1950s to the 1990s as propellants, coolants, and solvents. Halocarbons, the group of substances to which CFCs belong, are very stable, nonflammable, and nontoxic. Their stability enables them to eventually rise up into the stratosphere unchanged, a process that takes several years. Under certain conditions (extremely low temperatures in the presence of high-energy radiation) ODS are destroyed and chlorine or bromine is released from them. These halogens are able to destroy ozone without being used in the reaction themselves ("catalytically"). The low temperature and presence of sunlight required are most typical of the situation at the end of a polar winter; therefore ozone depletion is most notable above the Antarctic (and less pronounced above the Arctic) in spring, when the first sunlight reaches the polar region. Ozone concentration regenerates during the polar summer, but the hole reoccurs each late winter. With no ozone left, UV-B reaches the ground unabated. Health problems associated with increased UV B are skin cancer and cataracts. Photoaging and damages to the immune system are additional problem. UV-B seriously endangers phytoplankton, the basis of the aquatic food web in the seas; the decrease of phytoplankton will augment global warming due to decreased carbon fixation, and have adverse effects on the entire aquatic ecosystem. In general, polar aquatic ecosystems will suffer most. Physical and chemical properties of plastics will be adversely affected by UV-B, resulting in earlier wear and tear. In addition, CFCs and their substitutes are potent greenhouse gases.

Although the production and consumption of CFCs has been banned, effectively reducing the amount of CFCs released into the atmosphere, the ozone layer continues to be adversely affected by the CFC molecules already there and on their way into the stratosphere. A recovery is expected sometime in the mid-twenty-first century, unless new combined effects change chemical reactions in unexpected ways. There is no cure against the excess UV-B radiation.

Finding Depletion

Ozone depletion in the stratosphere was first discussed in considerations about supersonic air transport (SSTs or supersonic transports). In 1963, the U.S. launched a development program for SSTs. Sonic booms were considered the main adverse effect of such aircraft. Although SST development for commercial planes came to a halt soon after, the chemistry of the stratosphere became a matter of concern for the first time. Exhausts, in particular water vapor, were judged to have an ozone-depleting potential. A publication in the prestigious journal *Nature* in 1970 resulted. The stratosphere

and its ozone had become recognized as being prone to anthropogenic disturbance. In 1974, two separate groups of investigators arrived at alarming conclusions: Richard Stolarski and Ralph Cicerone concluded that chlorine in the stratosphere can break up ozone. F. Sherwood Rowland and Mario J. Molina showed that a man-made source of chlorine, CFCs, can catalytically destroy ozone. They immediately were aware of the size of the threat to the ozone layer and spoke along these lines at a press conference in December 1974. This marked the beginning of ozone as a public topic and concern.

A public interest law firm, the National Resource Defense Council, took the issue on its agenda and unsuccessfully sued the Consumer Product Safety Commission for a ban on aerosols, one of the main sources of CFCs at the time. The 1970s saw a "Ban the Can" media campaign, a 1975 decision of the State of Oregon to ban aerosol sprays, and voluntary action by manufacturers to seek substitutes for CFCs as propellants, altogether resulting in an October 1978 ban of CFCs in aerosols in the U.S. The substances continued to be used unabated as solvents in the microchip industry, in refrigerators, and in air-conditioning units. The National Academy of Sciences issued several reports on the problem. Whereas the first, 1976 report recommended no immediate governmental action, the second, November 1979 estimated ozone depletion to be as high as 16.5 percent and declared a wait-and-see approach to be impractical, revising its estimate again in March 1982, with a lower figure of 5–9 percent. Whereas the original Rowland-Molina hypothesis was never challenged as such, uncertainty was large enough to enable industry lobbyists to call for yet more research and postpone action. In April 1980, the Environmental Protection Agency had announced the intention of the U.S. to freeze all CFC production at 1979 levels. While government was proactive during the Carter administration (1977–1981), the antiregulatory policy of the Reagan administration (1981–1989) halted progress for several years.

A Hole That Could Be Spotted from Mars

But new scientific evidence, again produced by Rowland, surfaced in 1984. He showed that a different kind of chemical reaction in polar stratospheric clouds could speed up ozone destruction. Later that year a British group led by Joseph Farman published findings of an unexpected decline of ozone over Antarctica during the austral spring. In August 1985, the first visualization of the depletion became available, made from NASA's *Nimbus* satellite data that had been re-analyzed after the Farman publication. These were the first proofs of what later would be dubbed a "hole" in the ozone layer. In August 1986, with only a few months preparation time, the first Antarctic ozone expedition, led by Susan Solomon of the National Oceanic and Atmospheric Administration, attempted to assess the role of CFCs under the unique meteorological conditions of Antarctica. Polar stratospheric clouds magnify the ozone depletion rate by providing a reservoir for chlorine compounds during the austral winter, and thereby offsetting the counteracting nitrate chemistry at work at other latitudes. But at the time results of the first expedition became available in October 1986, stating—if cautiously—that chemicals were to blame, a dynamic theory of ozone depletion, arguing for natural weather phenomena, was still given credibility by respected researchers. A second, much larger expedition in 1987 used high-flying aircraft to measure the important chemical compounds, above all chlorine monoxide, directly in the stratosphere. This dangerous mission proved the chemical hypothesis beyond reasonable doubt, results being known by November 1987.

Ozone Diplomacy

Meanwhile, international negotiations had begun. The United Nations Environment Programme (UNEP), under the determined leadership of Mostafa Tolba, had formed a Coordinating Committee on the Ozone Layer in 1976, basically reviewing the new scientific results annually. Under the auspices of UNEP, an ad hoc working group of legal and technical experts for the preparation of a global framework had begun to work in January 1982. In 1983, the Toronto Group, named after the place of their first meeting, had formed. Canada, Finland, Norway, Sweden, and Switzerland brought the idea of reduction of CFC emissions into the negotiations. With the resignation of Anne Gorsuch as head of EPA the then anti-regulatory policy of the U.S. had suddenly changed and the U.S. joined the Toronto group in late 1983. In January 1985, ambassador Richard Benedick, over the next years one of the architects of international ozone agreements, led the U.S. delegation at a meeting in Geneva, which failed to come to any substantial agreement, but agreed on the need for an international treaty on information exchange, research, and monitoring. In the light of new scientific evidence and under more favorable political

conditions in the U.S., the Vienna Convention on Protection of the Ozone Layer, aimed at these rather informal goals, was signed by twenty-eight countries on 22 March 1985. On 16 September 1987, the Montreal Protocol on Substances that Deplete the Ozone Layer was signed by forty-six countries.

One of the main new features of the Protocol was its flexibility. Revisions of the original agreement have been undertaken in London (1990), Copenhagen (1992), Vienna (1995), Montreal (1997), and Beijing (1999). These were based on the assessments undertaken by the panels that were formed. A scientific, an environmental, and a technical and economic assessment panel were instrumental in revising the protocol. During the international negotiations, several companies changed their obstructive policies, making it easier for regulators to demand action from others, less active ones. In particular, DuPont, the largest manufacturer, and McDonalds, a key consumer of the substances, came to acknowledge their responsibility, at least partially driven by media pressure.

In 1995, Rowland and Molina, together with the Dutch chemist Paul Crutzen, whose work about the catalytic capability of nitrogen oxides was also of key importance in understanding ozone depletion, received the Nobel Prize in chemistry.

Action against Ozone Depletion: A Model Case?

International agreements attempted to halt ozone depletion. Their significance lies in their timing: They were both concluded prior to any directly attributable damaging effects (although such effects were reasonably predictable by that time). It was the global ozone depletion visualized in the ozone hole that made the world community adopt preventive and precautionary principles for the first time. Judgments were based on predicted dangers before scientists had closed the issue—in fact, while scientific consensus had not been reached. The role of scientists in the development of the issue is enormous, but tells a cautionary tale: Though a lot of researchers had long agreed upon the basic fact of ozone depletion as being beyond reasonable doubt, in congressional hearings and during negotiations, their differences often bore more weight than their basic agreement. Scientists were clearly unhappy with this process. For the purposes of public testimonial and quick media releases, their scientific integrity was being placed at risk. They were being asked to advocate measures prior to having had a chance to scrutinize their own findings on the ozone depletion issue. Ultimately, they felt their efforts at changing public opinion and policies were fruitless.

The ozone depletion issue was primarily a U.S. concern in the first place, the U.S. being both the largest producers and consumers of CFCs. Besides the EPA, who played a leading role in ozone politics, the Natural Resource Defense Council, a public interest law firm, was untiring in keeping the topic and the negotiations alive. The NRDC at a time of deadlock in negotiations sued the EPA for failure to comply with the Clean Air Act to create opportunities for action within the agency. In the international negotiations, relatively unaffected countries such as Norway and Canada played a leading role. Germany was the EEC country instrumental in changing the EEC policy, which had been against a ban for a long time. UNEP, based in Nairobi, was crucial for international implementation and still hosts the Ozone Secretariat (Secretariat for the Vienna Convention and its Montreal Protocol). In addition, through the Multilateral Ozone Layer Fund, the United Nations Development Programme (UNDP) provides third-world countries with monetary means to implement CFC reduction policies, a key to international success.

Learning from the Ozone Case

Several shifts of paradigm, both scientific and political, occurred in the ozone debate, which makes it a particularly noteworthy case. The stratospheric ozone case shows the long-term effects of accumulated pollution by substances that are harmless in direct use (as opposed to DDT for example, which was known as a poison) and in particular the problem of synthetic production of potentially catalytic substances. First, the stability of the compounds had to be recognized as a problem rather than an advantage. Second, the stratosphere, which was before ozone a most arcane object of study, had to be recognized as being connected to surface conditions. Teleconnections between the source of a pollutant and the area of its largest effect were unknown before the ozone problem. Likewise, it became the first pollutant to be regulated in international negotiations, and the only one so far for which a complete halt of production of the pollutant ever was discussed and implemented. The principle of ozone politics is anticipatory action: though the scientific results were not considered final or unambiguous, the size of the risk justified action. Certainly the success

only became possible because industry had replacement compounds at hand before they agreed on the ban. Most observers see the Montreal Protocol as a cornerstone also for further negotiations, as it was designed as a flexible instrument, rather than being concerned with the conservation of a status quo. Observers differ as to whether the ozone story is an example of success or a more cautionary tale of the difficulties arising from decision making under conditions of uncertainty. Being rewarded with the Nobel Prize certainly is a most welcome appreciation of scientific success. But the prizewinners Molina and Rowland, two main figures in the ozone debate, and many of their fellow scientists suffered during the decade following their seminal paper and their realization that the Earth was under a serious threat because they were unable to bring about the political measures they saw necessary.

Verena Winiwarter

Further Reading

Benedick, R. E. (1991). *Ozone diplomacy: New directions in safeguarding the planet.* Cambridge, MA, and London: Harvard University Press.

Cagin, S., & Dray, P. (1993). *Between earth and sky. How CFCs changed our world and endangered the ozone layer.* New York: Pantheon.

Canan, P., & Reichman, N. (2002). *Ozone connections: Expert networks in global environmental governance.* Sheffield: Greenleaf.

French, H. F. (1997). *Learning from the ozone experience. In: State of the World 1997.* A Worldwatch Institute Report, 151–218.

Nance, J. J. (1991). *What goes up: The global assault on our atmosphere.* New York: William Morrow and Company.

The ozone layer—the Achilles heel of the biosphere. (1995). Press release of the Nobel Committee: Retrieved May 29, 2002 from http://www.nobel.se/chemistry/laureates/1995/press.html

Ozone Secretariat, United Nations, Environment Programme (2000). *Action on ozone.* Kenya: UNEP.

Roan, S. (1989). *Ozone crisis.* New York: Wiley.

Rowland, S. F., & Molina, M. (1994). Ozone depletion: 20 years after the alarm. *Chemical and Engineering News,* 72, 8–13.

Rowland, S. F. & Molina, M. (2001). *The CFC-ozone puzzle: Environmental science in the global arena.* John H. Chafee Memorial Lecture on Science and the Environment,

December 7, 2000, Washington DC: National Council for Science and the Environment.

Rowlands, I. H. (1992). The international politics of global environmental change. In: I. H. Rowlands & M. Greene (Eds.), *Global environmental change and international relations* (pp. 19–37). London: Palgrave Macmillan.

Rowlands, I. H. (1995). *The politics of global atmospheric change.* Manchester, UK: Manchester University Press.

Sabogal, N. (2000). The depletion of the stratospheric ozone layer. *Meteorologica Colombiana, 2,* 73–79.

Solomon, S. (1999). Stratospheric ozone depletion: A review of concepts and history. *Reviews of Geophysics, 37*(3), 275–316.

Papua New Guinea

(2001 est. pop. 5 million)

Papua New Guinea (PNG) occupies the eastern half of New Guinea, the second-largest island in the world. The country of PNG also includes the smaller islands of New Britain, Manus, New Ireland, and Bougainville. Originally colonized by Germany and England in the nineteenth century, PNG was administered by Australia after World War I until becoming an independent nation in 1975.

Located in the South Pacific, just south of the equator, the island of New Guinea is entirely in the tropics. A chain of mountains stretches the length of the island. Earthquakes are frequent, and there are active volcanoes. New Guinea was still joined to Australia, forming a single continent called "Sahul," when it was settled by people at least forty thousand years ago.

Papua New Guinea's population is predominantly rural. The most densely settled rural areas are the broad valleys of the highlands. Archeologists have found evidence that these highland valleys have been farmed for at least nine thousand years. Several crops may have originally been domesticated in New Guinea, including sugarcane, some varieties of taro and bananas, and possibly the staple crop grown in swampy lowland areas, the sago palm. The dominant crop is sweet potato, introduced from South America only about three hundred years ago. The most important domestic animal is the pig, which was introduced at least ten thousand years ago.

The University of Papua New Guinea and the Wau Ecology Institute are among the institutions that have contributed to an understanding of PNG ecology, as have many visiting overseas scientists. These include anthropologists who studied traditional environmental knowledge and subsistence practices. Linguists grouped the hundreds of New Guinea languages into some 180 language families, each representing a distinctive way of viewing and categorizing the environment.

The Constitution of Papua New Guinea gives explicit protection to the environment. Supporting legislation is also protective of the environment, but its effectiveness in practice has been more controversial. Foreign logging companies (primarily Malaysian) have taken advantage of poor enforcement to harvest logs from the world's fourth-largest remaining tropical forest.

The largest share of PNG's export economy is based on mining gold, silver, and copper. Each of the three largest mines—Bougainville (closed by violence in 1989), Ok Tedi, and Porgera—disposed of mine wastes and tailings (residue) by dumping them into the river system. Riverine tailings disposal is severely criticized for causing overbank flooding that kills forests and water pollution that reduces fish populations. Two coastal mines—Lihir and Misima—pipe their tailings directly into the ocean, another controversial practice.

Most land is held communally by clan groups who are eager to receive the royalties paid for timber or mining because the landowners have few other prospects for earning income. Local environmental non-government organizations (NGOs) have begun to develop alternatives, such as small-scale sustainable forestry and ecotourism, with support from their coun-

Traditional Method of Growing the Sweet Potato

The sweet potato is the most important food crop on Papua New Guinea. The following account describes the traditional farming methods of the Kapauku people of western New Guinea.

After the planter has thrown her armful of sweet potato shoots on to the ground, she drives her planting stick into the earth by holding it in both hands and striking the same spot, usually, three times. Into the hole she has made she puts about five pieces of vine. These planted shoots are about 30 centimeters long and have generally been taken from a single vine. This was torn into the required lengths by pressing the stem between the thumb and index fingers of her right hand and sharply pulling the end with her left hand. The vines are usually planted 1 meter apart. After dropping the vines into the hole the planter fills it in with loose dirt, although she does not press it down. To utilize the ground to its limits the woman may decide to plant an intercrop of *idaja*, [spinach-like green] between the sweet potato shoots. Normally only part of the field would be thus exploited. The planting technique is the same as for the sweet potatoes except that, instead of segments of vines, seedlings are used. *Idaja* plants mature and are harvested after only two months, thus not interfering with the later growth of the tuberous plants. The native woman, if older, is often helped in her task by her young daughter, who thus learns early in life her future responsibilities.

Source: Pospisil, Leopold J. (1963). *Kapauku Papuan Economy*. New Haven, CT: Yale University Publications in Anthropology, pp. 67, 97.

---

terpart NGOs in nearby Australia and other wealthy, industrialized countries.

Although environmental destruction from industrial logging and large mining projects has received the most attention, smaller-scale damage has also resulted from the introduction of new technologies to indigenous people. Shotguns led to decimation of some species of birds. Fishing with dynamite destroyed sections of coral reefs near urban settlements. Papua New Guinea is an island nation that contains one of the richest, but most threatened, regions of biological diversity in the world.

Patricia K. Townsend

Further Reading

Hansen, L. W., Allen, B. J., Bourke, R. M., & McCarthy, T. J. (2001). *Papua New Guinea rural development handbook*. Canberra: Australian National University.

Morauta, L., Pernetta, J., & Heaney, W. (Eds.). (1982). *Traditional conservation in Papua New Guinea*. Boroko, Papua New Guinea: Institute of Applied Social and Economic Research.

Sekhran, N., & Miller, S. (1995). *Papua New Guinea country study on biological diversity*. Waigani, Papua New Guinea: Department of Environment and Conservation.

Sillitoe, P. (1998). *An introduction to the anthropology of Melanesia: Culture and tradition*. Cambridge, UK: Cambridge University Press.

White, J. P., and O'Connell, J. F. (1982). *A prehistory of Australia, New Guinea and Sahul*. New York: Academic Press.

Paraguay *See* Southern Cone

Parks and Recreation

Parks are designated public or shared open spaces provided for leisure and outdoor recreation. Parks range in scale from small, highly environmentally modified urban parks, including public gardens, to large national parks with wilderness characteristics. Parks are primarily a function of Western attitudes toward nature and urbanism, although they are now found throughout the world. However, although open space remains a key constituent, the concept of a park and its use for recreational and other purposes has changed substantially over time.

The parks around the imperial palaces of ancient Rome, although originally meant solely for private use, were among the earliest open urban spaces devoted to recreation. Julius Caesar's donation of his gardens to Rome was one of the first recorded examples of a private recreational privilege being passed on to the public. Early parklike open spaces, which were often similar to large private gardens, were the domain of the rich. Wealth and power were prerequisites to garden and park creation in Western society until the mid-nineteenth century as the establishment of gardens and parks reflected the financial or political ability to turn land from productive uses—for example, farming—to nonproductive uses related to leisure. Such a change in land use also required the development of attitudes to nature that regarded such land use as aesthetically desirable. The landscapes of power found in medieval parks are perhaps best illustrated by the creation of the New Forest in southern England in 1079 by King William I (William the Conqueror) as a royal hunting park with laws regarding forest management, grazing, and access by the common people. The special land-use status of the New Forest has continued, and now it has a role equivalent to that of a national park and receives millions of visitors per year.

In addition to the gradual closure and privatization of common land in Europe, the park idea has its origins in the protected gardens of the Middle East and Europe in the Middle Ages, such as those of monasteries, in which gardens were private, secluded, and often surrounded by a wall. Such private gardens exist today, including private parks such as Bedford Square in London. Together with royal gardens and hunting estates, initially accessible only by royalty and the aristocracy—for example, Regents Park in London—such gardens gradually became shared recreational spaces for the elite, then available to the general public over time.

From Common Land to Parkland

The greatest privatization of common land occurred in the United Kingdom in the eighteenth and nineteenth centuries and was known as the "enclosure of the commons." Between 1760 and 1820 approximately 20 percent of England's total acreage was enclosed. The enclosures led to a revolution not only in commercial agricultural production but also in the nature and aesthetics of the English landscape. The agricultural landscape was transformed into a commercial space of regular, hedge-rowed fields, and changes in the aesthetics of garden design moved away from tight, enclosed spaces to expansive landscapes of trees, lakes, and lawn, which are now represented as the ideal English or temperate countryside. These temperate English landscapes have influenced parks internationally in terms of both aesthetic conceptions and park design. Such landscapes are still referred to as parks or parkland scenery to the present day, even if they remain in private hands.

In the eighteenth century landscape designers such as Capability Brown and Humphry Repton transformed the gardens and grounds of the elite into such parklands, which still served to exclude the working classes and to provide seclusion for their owners from the industrial and rural poor. Such parklands became accessible for recreation by the wider public only in the late twentieth century as their owners sought to either avoid taxes by granting public access or sought additional funds to maintain heritage houses and landscapes through commercial recreation and leisure.

Medieval cities enjoyed substantial access to open space for private gardens and recreation, often on the fringe of the city or outside of the old city walls. The typical medieval city often had shooting and bowling grounds as well as areas for racing and archery. Many of these open spaces are similar to the village greens retained in some areas of Britain to the present. Most cities also had common areas immediately outside of the urban areas that were available not only for grazing but also for hunting and recreation. However, much of this urban open space was lost when the Industrial Revolution of the late eighteenth and early nineteenth centuries and the subsequent demand for labor led to the rapid growth of industrial cities.

British Public Parks

In Britain the first official government recognition of the need for urban public parks came in 1839 with a report to Parliament by the Select Committee on Public Walks. The case for urban public parks for recreation was taken up by the public health movement and by intellectuals who believed the new industrial areas to be evil as well as unhealthy places and who actively campaigned for the creation of parks as a source of healthy recreation and moral regeneration. In 1840 the first public park in Britain was given to the city of Derby by philanthropist Joseph Strutt. The first municipal park in Britain was established in Birkenhead in 1843. (The difference between a public and municipal park is that the latter is specifically established and managed by a municipal authority whereas the former may be established by private benefactors or organizations and may eventually be managed by a municipality.) In some cities, such as Leicester and London, the few commons that had survived the enclosures were gradually converted from grazing to public parks. Significantly, the history of grazing had actually contributed to the commons' parkland nature and provided an aesthetic for their retention as public open space. In his book *A History of British Gardening* Michael Hadfield commented, "many Victorian gardens, and . . . public parks, were within a permanent setting of a Brown or Repton landscape. The artistic merit of these were never questioned, and they were allowed to mature unharmed" (Hadfield 1985, 315).

In the latter half of the nineteenth century public open space was an important source of civic pride, with the Victorian public parks containing refreshment and tearooms, fountains, lakes, and ornamental trees and gardens that reflected the private parkscapes of the rural elite. The Victorian emphasis on the availability of public parks and gardens as a means of healthy recreation was exported throughout the British Empire and was incorporated in urban planning practice in the towns of Australia, Canada, India, New Zealand, and South Africa. Botanical and zoological gardens were also often integrated with park developments. Such gardens were usually associated with the formation of societies with scientific and economic interests, although they often received a degree of government support in recognition of their educational role. Throughout the British Empire such gardens served an important social function because they not only included plant and animal species that reminded the British settler of "home," but also served as a base for the spread of such species in the new country through the activities of acclimatization societies.

In the early twentieth century new urban open space tended to include recreation grounds, with far less emphasis given to aesthetic concerns. These new urban open spaces reflected the growth of organized sport, and, as professional sports emerged in towns, public parks were often transformed into sports stadiums occupied by professional sports teams. Examples include the Melbourne and Sydney Cricket Grounds in Australia and Eden Park in Auckland, New Zealand. This phenomenon appears almost universal in the industrialized world. The influence of the garden city movement at the turn of the twentieth century and the greenbelt movement in the early to mid-twentieth

century meant that the inclusion of public parks and open space in new town and suburban developments and at the urban edge is now widely accepted.

North American Public Parks

The Victorian urban park model, which emphasized the health benefits of outdoor recreation, was influential far beyond the British Empire. In the United States park advocates and designers such as landscape architect Frederick Law Olmsted argued for the development of public parks that would allow workers to improve their health and that might also provide a more moral alternative to other recreational pursuits such as drinking alcohol. In the mid-nineteenth century Olmsted proposed a park chain in San Francisco and a garden city in Berkeley, California. Perhaps more significantly, Olmsted designed Manhattan's Central Park, which became a model for many other urban parks in North American cities, including Mount Royal Park in Montreal, Canada. Olmsted's public parks in Boston and New York were intended to bring city dwellers some of the benefits of life in the country. They, too, were "modeled after English country estates and included grassy meadows, clumps or avenues of trees, and lakes" (Jenkins 1994, 25). The public park movement's vision of nature also contributed to the democratization of the English private park aesthetic in the front-lawn aesthetic of suburban middle-class America. In addition, Olmsted argued not only for the creation of urban parks and spaces but also for the creation of natural parklands in areas such as Niagara Falls, Yosemite, and the Adirondacks.

National Parks

As well as bringing an idealized European vision of nature, garden, and countryside to the American city, Olmsted and the public park movement's desire for open space coincided with the growing Romanticist and transcendentalist traditions in American intellectual life, which contributed to the development of the national park concept. Early national parks were primarily locations of aesthetic contemplation and recreational activity that were valued for their provision of nature's wonders to wealthy tourists rather than for their ecology. Many of the early national parks, such as Yosemite in California and Royal National Park in Sydney, had formal gardens, zoological gardens, sports grounds, and playgrounds at their core until well into the twentieth century. In the case of Australia, with the exception of Queensland, the first national parks were all established close to capital cities and were easily accessible by train, with many recreational activities being made available to daytrippers by park authorities. In such circumstances core areas of the parks were highly modified to provide playing areas, sports grounds, gardens, and tearooms. In many park jurisdictions, modification also included the introduction of species, particularly deer, foxes, and rabbits for hunting or trout for fishing. For example, in New Zealand's Tongariro National Park heather was planted in the 1920s in an attempt to introduce grouse from Scotland for hunting. In a number of national parks in Australia, New Zealand, and North America, ski runs were also developed as this form of winter recreation became popular. Although many of the recreational developments in national parks were initially for the benefit of the wealthier classes, access gradually became available to members of the increasingly mobile middle class who were able to purchase their own automobiles. Although this increased park accessibility, it also created tensions in national, state, and provincial park management that exist to the present day in terms of the potential conflicts between recreational and environmental conservation goals. Indeed, those people who set the legislative requirements for parks to provide recreational access and enjoyment as well as to conserve prized landscapes would never have anticipated the millions of people who now use the natural area park systems.

Parks and Social Control

The capacity of some of the early national parks to provide recreational opportunities to increasingly mobile urban dwellers helped generate support for the national park concept in metropolitan areas. As towns grew in size, a small but politically significant segment of the urban population argued for the setting aside of larger rural and natural areas as regional, state, provincial, and national parks offering more active outdoor recreational opportunities. Significantly, the development of such parks can be related not only to the development of commercial recreation activities but also to concerns about the physical and moral health of young boys and men in the cities. Such concerns reflected earlier Victorian attitudes toward the evils of urbanization and industrialization but also included concerns about the loss of contact with nature for national identity and culture as well as the potential fitness of young men for military service. Early users of some of the new

"natural" parks included groups such as the Boy Scouts and Boys Brigade, which were formed in reaction to the moral dangers of the cities and which provided outlets for Christian education and recreation.

The moral and social control dimensions of park creation and use continued through the twentieth century to today. Members of the garden city movement believed that their new cities with their parks and open spaces would provide a basis for the development of stronger community values. Despite a lack of empirical evidence, the belief that participation in sport helps reduce juvenile delinquency has also been a major impetus in the provision of parks and recreational facilities in post-World War II urban developments.

Since the 1960s urban parks have become recognized as significant environmental resources. Measures such as retaining dead plant matter, planting native species, and planting less lawn enhance habitat creation, although they are often at odds with traditional parkland aesthetics. However, the conservation of environmental values represents yet another function of public open spaces and reinforces the increasingly multiuse, multipurpose nature of public parks.

Future Directions

Parks are utilized by different, often conflicting, user groups for a range of active and passive activities. The use of parks by some minorities and socioeconomic groups remains limited. The multiplicity of users and functions means that park management and provision are harder than ever, although the cultural, environmental, and recreational significance of parks means that they will remain significant public property for the foreseeable future.

C. Michael Hall

Further Reading

Conway, H. (1991). *People's parks: The design and development of Victorian parks in Britain*. Cambridge, UK: Cambridge University Press.

Hadfield, M. (1985). *A history of British gardening*. Harmondsworth, UK: Penguin Books.

Hall, C. M., & Page, S. J. (2002). *The geography of tourism and recreation: Place, space and environment* (2nd ed.). New York: Routledge.

Jackson, K. T. (1985). *Crabgrass frontier: The suburbanization of the United States*. New York: Oxford University Press.

Jenkins, V. J. (1994). *The lawn: A history of an American obsession*. Washington, DC: Smithsonian Institution Press.

Short, J. R. (1991). *Imagined country: Society, culture and environment*. London: Routledge.

Solecki, W., & Welch, J. (1995). Urban parks: Green spaces or green walls? *Landscape and Urban Planning, 32*(1), 93–106.

Stevenson, E. (1977). *Park maker: A life of Frederick Law Olmsted*. New York: Macmillan.

Taylor, D. (1999). Central Park as a model for social control: Urban parks, social class and leisure behaviour in nineteenth century America. *Journal of Leisure Research, 31*(4), 426–477.

Wilson, W. H. (1989) *The City Beautiful movement*. Baltimore: John Hopkins University Press.

Passenger Pigeon

The passenger pigeon *(Ectopistes migratorius)* is legendary as a symbol of unbelievable abundance and of human-caused extinction. It was an essential living resource to eighteenth and nineteenth century America that was overexploited to extinction out of a combination of greed and ignorance.

The species occurred only in North America, primarily east of the Rocky Mountains, and bred almost exclusively in the eastern deciduous forest. There were some 3–5 billion passenger pigeons in America prior to the arrival of the Europeans; they composed perhaps a quarter of the continent's bird life. Yet, due entirely to human activities, the passenger pigeon was extinct in the wild by the end of the nineteenth century, and its last representative, the fabled Martha, died in the Cincinnati Zoo on 1 September 1914.

The Passenger Pigeon in Abundance

Reports of the huge numbers of passenger pigeons, in passing flocks so large that they obscured the sun, might appear to be beyond belief were they not so consistent among independent observers for three centuries. Flocks were described as "having neither beginning or end," and the birds themselves as being "in such prodigious numbers, as almost to surpass belief" and similar superlatives. These flocks had major impacts on the landscape, moving great quantities of nutrients, breaking tree limbs with the combined weight of roosting birds, consuming the food supply of some birds and mammals and becoming the food supply of others.

Fossil records extend back to 100,000 years before present and include western states not part of the recent range. There are many records from Native American sites during the Woodland period, early Holocene (ca. 500 BCE–1200 CE), particularly in what are now the Great Lake states. Bones were at settlement sites dating to about 1300 CE. but never in great quantities. Anthropologist Stephen Williams has speculated that pigeon populations rose beginning around 1450–1500 CE, coinciding with a major decline in human populations in the agricultural Mississippian culture that had occupied much of what is now the eastern United States since about 800 CE. The human decline occurred particularly in the lower Mississippi valley and partway up the Ohio River. The decline may have been caused by a cooling climate during the Little Ice Age (c. 1400–c. 1850 CE). Climate change and abandoned agricultural land may have created forested habitat for a rising population of passenger pigeons.

The sightings of French explorer Jacques Cartier are the first surviving record of passenger pigeon numbers; he recorded seeing "an infinite number" on 1 July 1534 at Prince Edward Island. From 1540 to 1580 Spanish conquistadors explored southern North America, but made no mention of skies filled by flocks of passenger pigeons. The explorer Samuel de Champlain recorded "countless numbers" on 12 July 1605 along the coast of southern Maine.

The enormous nomadic flocks roamed the continent, traveling hundreds of kilometers daily in search of food. In most seasons they fed primarily on acorns and beechnuts. In certain years, oaks and beech trees produce superabundant crops of nuts, known as mast. When the pigeons located a rich source of mast in the spring, they established a huge nesting colony (at least hundreds of thousands of pairs), known as a "city." Often there would be dozens of nests on a single tree. Each nest contained a single egg. Colonies ranged from 50 hectares to thousands of hectares. The largest nesting described (from 1871) covered much of the southern two-thirds of Wisconsin. The colonies had time only for a single nesting before the food supply was exhausted and the birds moved on. It is unlikely that the food was sufficient to allow for more than a single nesting in a year. During summer, the birds fed on abundant berries in the Great Lakes states and provinces.

Passenger Pigeons and Humans

Passenger pigeons were a source of fresh or preserved meat, feathers, and sport for native people and later for European settlers and their descendants. Essentially every flock that was encountered by humans at any time of year was subject to shooting, netting, and other means of killing.

Commercial trade in pigeon meat, fat, and feathers began in the eighteenth century. Tens of thousands of adults and young were killed at a colony. This extensive killing probably had little, if any, impact on pigeon populations until the infrastructure was available to transport pigeons and carcasses from nesting colonies to markets in urban areas, beginning around 1840. In 1851 nearly 2 million pigeons (dead and alive) were shipped from a single nesting. In the late nineteenth century from 600 to 1,200 men worked as professional pigeon trappers, using massive nets to capture live pigeons for shooting matches and using guns, poles, fire, and other means to kill birds for market.

Populations, although reduced, were still superabundant in the early 1870s. The nesting in Wisconsin in 1871 included nearly the entire population of the species, estimated to be more than 135 million adults (less than 10 percent of what had been estimated only decades earlier). The population declined drastically during the 1870s. The last huge nesting, "something like 100,000 acres" (Forbush 1927, 65), took place in 1878 in Michigan, near Petosky. There was a tremendous slaughter of perhaps 10 million birds, which were shipped out by the barrel. After that, no mass nestings were reported. Without the mass nestings, which had provided protection from predators, nestings of small groups and isolated pairs apparently produced insufficient numbers of offspring to maintain the species.

Although the population probably declined beyond point of recovery by late 1880s, as many as 2,000 pigeons were reportedly taken for market in the early 1890s. By the mid-1890s, flocks of hundreds were noteworthy. By 1895, a flock of just ten pigeons drew attention. The end of the century brought the end of the passenger pigeon. The last reliable specimen was taken in 1900 in Ohio.

The passenger pigeon was successful due to its nomadic behavior and its colonial habits, which allowed it to exploit superabundant food sources that were unpredictable in space and time. Additionally the numbers were so enormous that nonhuman predators could not reduce the population. Ironically, these same factors attracted the human predators from whose relentless persecution the passenger pigeon was unable to recover.

Major Factors in the Passenger Pigeon's Decline

Two factors predominated in causing the decline: habitat destruction and direct exploitation by humans for food. Other explanations have been proposed, including climate, disease, and weather-related catastrophe, but without evidence.

Every passenger pigeon colony that was accessible to humans was exploited. Ornithologists David Blockstein and Harrison. B. Tordoff have argued that the development of the transcontinental railroad and the telegraph in the nineteenth century were key factors leading to extinction. Railroads allowed access to nesting colonies, and the telegraph provided a way for scouts who located colonies to inform the professional pigeon trappers.

By the time the Civil War ended, the railroad covered most of the United States east of the Mississippi. Only a handful of nesting colonies were too far from rail or ship for market exploitation. Often hundreds of thousands of adults and squabs were shipped from a single nesting. Large numbers of birds were destroyed by locals or otherwise killed but not transported. A million birds could be lost at a single nesting. Yet, even the enormous numbers of birds killed were probably not sufficient to cause the precipitous decline in the population. Overhunting did not exterminate the passenger pigeon, as is commonly believed. Rather, the disturbance of the nesting colonies over a period of almost thirty years, well over twice the lifetime of the average bird, led the birds to abandon the colonies before they had raised young. This, coupled with slaughter of fat nestlings, these are squabs—more than 200 grams, full of fat and apparently very tasty—as well as adults largely eliminated replacement of the population.

Deforestation was also a major factor in the decline, because it reduced the area available to the pigeons and thus reduced the opportunities for nesting and roosting colonies. Being nomadic, passenger pigeons traveled enormous areas to find some conditions suitable for nesting colonies. Because nesting colonies formed only where there was sufficient mast, the reduction in the forest meant that in some years there was no nesting at all. Another nineteenth-century technology, the portable saw mill (introduced in 1870s), sped the destruction of what had once been a completely forested landscape. By 1880, about 80 percent of the original forest of New England had been cleared. Deforestation in the major nesting area of north central Pennsylvania began in 1872, but did not reach full speed until 1892. Michigan was still well wooded in 1883, and although it was being logged rapidly, the trees being harvested were largely pine, whose loss had less impact on the passenger pigeon than the loss of deciduous trees

The extinction of the passenger pigeon pre-dated any conservation movement in America. The extinction of the once "limitless" flocks of pigeons along with the near extermination of the American bison *(Bison bison)* introduced Americans to the concept of human-induced extinction. Some states approved laws requiring nets to be located away from nesting colonies, prohibiting disturbance at the nesting colony, but these laws were rarely enforced and were for the most part too late. The density and abundance of the pigeons were such that few people recognized that there were any risks to the species. Arguments that there was no need for protection generally doomed any proposed legal protection. In the words of Aldo Leopold:

> There will always be pigeons in books in museums, but these are effigies and images, dead to all hardships and to all delights. Book-pigeons can not dive out of a cloud to make the deer run for cover, or clap their wings in thunderous applause of mast-laden woods. Book-pigeons cannot breakfast on new-mown wheat in Minnesota, and dine on blueberries in Canada. They know no urge of seasons, no lash of wind and weather. They live forever by not living at all. (Leopold 1947, 3)

David E. Blockstein

Further Reading

Bendire, C. (1892). Passenger pigeon. In C. Bendire (Ed.), *Life histories of North American birds: With special reference to their breeding habits and eggs.* U.S. National Museum Special Bulletin No. 1. Washington DC: National Museum of Natural History.

Blockstein, D. E. (2002). Passenger pigeon (*Ectopistes migratorius*). In A. Poole & F. Gill (Eds.), *The birds of North America* (No. 611, 28). Philadelphia: The Birds of North America.

Blockstein, D. E., & Tordoff, H. B. (1985). A contemporary look at the extinction of the passenger pigeon. *American Birds, 39,* 845–852.

Forbush, E. H. (1913). The last passenger pigeon. *Bird Lore, 15,* 99–103.

Forbush, E. H. (1927). Passenger pigeon. In E. H. Forbush (Ed.), *Birds of Massachusetts and other New England states* (Vol. 2, pp. 54–82). Boston: Massachusetts Department of Agriculture.

Goodwin, D. (1983). *Pigeons and doves of the world.* (3rd ed.). London: British Museum of Natural History.

Leopold, A. 1947. On a monument to the pigeon. In W. E. Scott (Ed.), *Silent wings: A memorial to the passenger pigeon* (pp. 3–5). Madison: Wisconsin Society for Ornithology.

Mershon, W. B. (1907). *The passenger pigeon.* New York: Outing Publishing Co.

Mitchell, M. H. (1935). *The passenger pigeon in Ontario.* (Contribution No. 7 of the Royal Museum of Zoology.). Toronto, Canada: University of Toronto Press.

Schorger, A. W. (1955). *The passenger pigeon: Its natural history and extinction.* Madison: University of Wisconsin Press.

Wilson A. (1812). American Ornithology Volume 5, 102–112. Philadelphia: Bradford and Inskeep.

Pastoralism

The word *pastorale* evokes charming rurality; the word *pastoralism* evokes an arduous yet rewarding form of land use, a way of life in which people raise domestic livestock on natural pastures. Relying on grazing animals, pastoralists exploit dry rangelands, prairies, deserts, mountains, or tundra that are otherwise virtually uninhabitable. Pastoralist communities largely depend on their animals for subsistence, consuming meat and milk products or purchasing other foods and necessities from sale of livestock. Under highly variable and uncertain environmental conditions, pastoralists have devised strategies for sustaining herds and securing livelihoods. They usually raise numerous species, divide herds into smaller management units, and practice rapid and opportunistic herd mobility. By moving herds, they access better forage and water for their animals; by moving households with herds, they follow their own food and guarantee ready supplies of labor to defend and manage herds. Strategically, pastoralists aim for rapid herd growth but accept high losses if conditions worsen. Because keeping animals in remote, sparsely inhabited regions is demanding, pastoralists have gained a somewhat stereotypical reputation for hardy independence, skill in self-defense, and distinctiveness of culture.

Pastoralists are found on most continents and, according to environment, differ in the domestic animals they raise. Pastoralism is primarily practiced outside major cities and political centers, but many pastoralists historically have exercised significant military and political influence on the wider society and political states in their respective regions. On the high, dry, and cold plateau of Central Asia live the Mongols, who keep species of horses, two-humped Bactrian camels, cattle, sheep, and goats on the Himalayan Plateau, whereas Tibetan societies also keep yaks. The sheep is the preferred animal across southwestern Asia and in the Mediterranean basin, used both for meat and wool. Single-humped camels (dromedaries) prevail among Bedouins and other Arab-speaking communities who inhabit arid regions of the Arabian Peninsula, among Somalis of lowland Ethiopia and the Horn of Africa, and among Tuareg and Tubu of northern Africa and the Sahara Desert. Herded alongside sheep and goats in semiarid rangelands, the cow is the dominant animal raised by most African pastoralists: the Fulani of western Africa; Bagghara, Dinka, and Nuer of Sudan; Borana of Ethiopia; Turkana, Pokot, Samburu, and Masai of Kenya; Barabaig of Tanzania; Herero of Namibia; and Tswana of Botswana. In the New World, indigenous pastoralists herd camelid llama and alpaca across vertical zones of the high Andes. The Sami of Sweden and Norway herd reindeer across the northern latitudes. Domestic animals are also raised in nonpastoralist settings, where they are highly integrated into intensive farming or dairy systems in wetter areas of the Indian subcontinent, southeastern Asia, Melanesia, and Europe, or in extensive commercial ranching systems where hired herders and modern technology are used to raise animals strictly for sale. Pastoralism is invariably associated with indigenous societies, for whom it supports not only subsistence but also a culture and a way of life.

Pastoralism and Dryland Environments

As population pressure on pastoral lands has increased, debates have arisen regarding the impact pastoralism has on dryland environments. Did pastoralism arise as an adaptation to drylands, and do pastoralists represent distinctive socioeconomic systems there or are they part-societies (societies dependent on wider networks of trade and interaction)? Is pastoralism inherently destructive as a form of land use, or are pastoralists intrinsically conservationists? Is pastoralism compatible or in conflict with wildlife conservation? Is pastoral sedentarization a way of saving the environment, or does it cause increased degradation, and how should pastoralism best evolve today as a way of life and a strategy for using and conserving dryland environments?

The Origins of Pastoralism

Humans began domesticating wild grazing animals approximately nine thousand years ago, at the beginning of the Neolithic period. Domestication occurred as human communities intervened in biological selection of gregarious species of herbivores predisposed to engaging in herd behavior and to tolerating the proximity of humans. As more aggressive animals were killed and more docile animals preserved, the species evolved to accept management by humans. Just as plant domestication stabilized human communities in sites amenable to cultivation, so animal domestication allowed early pastoralists to make use of drier regions. Domestic grains offered early domestic animals incentives to approach human settlements, so plant and animal domestication may have arisen together. But herding specialists undoubtedly exploited more stringent grassy environments where crops could not be raised. The mountains and valleys of southwestern Asia, from today's Iran through Turkey, were likely sites for the first domestication of goats and sheep. It was long thought that the first domestic cattle evolved in Turkey or Greece, but recent evidence suggests that indigenous humpless African cattle were domesticated from wild oxen (Bos taurus) along the border between Egypt and the Sudan, lending support to an African origin of cattle.

Gregarious species highly adapted to specific environments were candidates for domestication, a process that arose independently in diverse areas of the world: Camels and dromedaries were adapted to high degrees of aridity in both cold and hot settings; llama, alpaca, and yak to high mountain ecologies; reindeer to tundra; buffalo to warm tropics; cattle, sheep, and goats to arid grasslands. Nomadic pastoralism, in which households shift with herds between sites of grazing, evolved in the broad, arid zone from Eurasia to Africa, where agricultural communities with traditional technologies were unable to take root but grasses could be seasonally exploited by domestic animals.

If, as was long thought, cattle migrated to Africa from southwestern Asia and were not well adapted to

African savanna, they might have been destructive of the dry grassland environment. That the first cattle were most likely domesticated from wild oxen indigenous to Africa helps explain the antiquity of pastoralism on the continent and the great physiological resistance of African cattle breeds to heat, sun, and a range of endemic parasitic diseases.

Rangeland Degradation and Desertification

In any locale, vegetation is highly correlated with rainfall, so arid and semiarid regions range from desert to open grasslands to open woodlands. Rainfall in arid lands is low and unpredictable, but occasional heavy downpours can result in erosion. Because domestic animals graze regions that are susceptible to erosion and localized degeneration and that undergo dramatic natural cycles of growth and desiccation each year, overstocking and overgrazing are often identified as major culprits in range degradation. Growing human populations who use wood for building and fuel are often deemed the cause of deforestation in the drylands.

After the nineteenth century, colonial foresters and agronomists began to draw the conclusion that denudation and desiccation of pastures in southern Africa were the result of the expansion of settler ranching and local pastoralism. "Veld (grassland) decline" was especially attributed to pastoral overstocking, heavy seasonal grazing, and prerain burning of pastures, which in light of the great Dust Bowl effect in North America supported government intervention to transform traditional systems. In the 1930s it was claimed that the Sahara Desert was progressively encroaching on grazing lands due to indigenous forms of land use and population growth. The great Sahelian (southern fringe of the Sahara) drought from 1968 to 1973 resulted in the loss of hundreds of thousands of livestock and 100,000 human deaths from starvation and disease, forcing herding families seeking famine relief to settle or flee to cities. This catastrophe was attributed by many to pastoralism itself as a prime source of desertification. At the 1977 U.N. Conference on Desertification it was claimed that one-third of the Earth is natural desert but that an additional one-tenth is human-made desert, with two-tenths under threat of desertification due to dryland farming and overgrazing. The Ethiopian famine of the 1980s was largely attributed to livestock-generated degradation of land. Also, based on extrapolation from the amount of wood needed to provide the fuel needs of households, rural dwellers, and especially pastoralists, were given much

of the blame for deforestation. It was said that as grasses and trees declined, rainfall itself would diminish. From being admired as the few who could inhabit drylands, pastoralists were redefined as authors not just of deserts but of aridity!

Reversal of Fortunes: Land and Pastoralists Rehabilitated

Retrospectively, ecologists have demonstrated that the African Sahel area is not experiencing progressive and incremental decline in biomass (living matter) and regenerativity that would define desertification, nor is the line between the desert and the savanna moving inexorably southward. Rather, the 1930s and 1970s represented periods of very low rainfall when as a matter of course dryland vegetation withered and retreated, only to regenerate when rainfall levels returned to normal. By moving out of grasslands at their driest, herders were able to return when conditions favorable to animal husbandry were restored. Human settlements, rather than being surrounded by widening circles of deforestation propagated by the desperate search for wood fuel, were in fact oases of green as dryland settlers planted and preserved trees for shade and cropping, gathering dead branches, or harvested trees planted for that purpose for wood fuel. Rather than an open-access resource, trees are often owned and subject to tenure rules.

Dry pastoral regions receive low rainfall, which varies widely and unpredictably, thus limiting and making uncertain the seasonal growth of grass; grasses grow, dry up, and disappear in relation to rainfall, whether grazed or not. In such contexts, the pastoral strategy is to make optimal use of scarce resources, encouraging high rates of herd growth in good seasons, practicing rapid and opportunistic herd mobility, and diversifying investments in herds. Maximal exploitation of pastures creates the appearance of degradation, and, given seasonal and annual rainfall variation, range areas will frequently be full of dry dust, and animals that depend on grass may die. But with rains, vegetation regenerates and herds increase, often without lasting damage to rangeland ecosystems.

With this reversal in environmental analysis, why was it for so long thought that pastoralist overgrazing caused desertification and deforestation? One reason is the observable association between heavy stocking and a denuded range during dry periods, another is the intuitive common-sense extrapolation of short-term desiccation to long-term degradation or desertification; and yet another is the tendency to grant authority to what appears to be scientific observation (casual though it might be) over indigenous knowledge.

The Effects of Pastoral Settlement

Land dedicated to pastoralism has diminished everywhere due to expansion of cultivation, commercial ranching, nature or wildlife parks and reserves, or appropriation by agencies of government. With less land available, population growth has resulted in pastoral diversification and sedentarization, some herders gathering in trading centers, settling in small towns, or migrating to larger cities. Speaking of the Pashtuns of the Middle East in a classic study, the Norwegian anthropologist Frederick Barth pointed out in 1961 that sedentarization was practiced by the very poor to survive and by the very rich to invest pastoral wealth in stable property and enhance their political position. Pastoralists have always considered themselves rich in livestock, an almost universal countercurrency, but due to environmental pressure, unpredictable losses of stock, and sedentarization, many now count themselves as impoverished. Pastoral poverty does often result from natural disasters, as in the Sahel and Ethiopia, but also from loss of resources to more influential competitors or officials of the state, political vulnerability due to low education, loss of markets to intensive husbandry or overseas competition, or misguided but ill-conceived development programs.

Pastoral sedentarization has been official policy of many countries with large pastoral populations on the grounds that settlement would halt environmentally destructive nomadism, enhance proper administration and political control of unruly populations, facilitate provision of social services and relief to pastoralists, and encourage development. But studies of pastoralists who settle or continue nomadic life have shown that settled populations have a higher incidence of malnutrition and suffer a wider range of serious health problems than do nomads with protein-rich diets based on animal products. Also, reduction of pastoral mobility actually increases rather than decreases range degradation, as animals concentrate around settlements. Yet, spontaneous settlement has long served as a safety valve, opening up opportunities for the poor and relieving pressure on those who continue pastoral life. But forced settlement of nomads—to assert centralized control by the Iranian state of Reza Shah Pahlavi, to achieve villagization in Tanzania and Ethiopia, to quell civil unrest in Niger and Mali, to create large-scale irrigated plantations in the Gezira Scheme in the Sudan, or to encourage dryland farming in Syria—has invariably increased poverty, reduced productivity of communities concerned, and increased degradation of lands formerly under pastoral management.

Disillusioning Changes: Conflict, Development

Borderlands between nations, being less inhabited, drier, and less fertile, are often ideal for pastoralism. Pastoralists in turn are often associated with cross-border conflicts, insurgencies, and strife with central governments to retain regional autonomy, maintain control of land, or resist attempts by central governments to control trade and contraband or to militarily subdue them. Multilateral strife in Afghanistan, the Tuareg revolt in Mali, the Somali civil war, the current resistance of the Oromo Liberation Front to the Tigrean-led government in Ethiopia, the perpetual movement for southern secession in the Sudan all reflect resistance of regional pastoral societies to the state. At the same time, local disorder and violence have increased among pastoralists with the weakening of civil security and the spread of cheap yet sophisticated weapons. Pastoral conflict has taken a toll not only in lost lives and foregone development but also in environmental conservation as herders increasingly concentrate animals and retreat from more vulnerable grazing areas.

Throughout the world, programs for pastoral development have followed a model for transforming largely subsistence-oriented, small-scale, family-based forms of husbandry into larger-scale commercial production. During the socialist period, in pastoral areas state-managed ranches were created that in their ideal blueprint resembled commercial ranches in capitalist areas. Scarce resources were in principle to be invested in creating modern ranches; paddocks were to be fenced, grazing rotations enforced, breeds upgraded, veterinary medicines provided, predetermined stocking rates established, and predetermined rates of offtake achieved, by removing animals from the herd for exchange, sale, or slaughter. The blueprints were rarely realized but also were rarely realizable, being based on inappropriately rigid models unsuited for pastoral areas with unpredictable rainfall and dramatically varying range conditions, for which highly flexible and responsive pastoralism was most adapted. Ranching associations were created to coordinate patterns of land use and encourage improved husbandry, but shrewd pastoralists persisted in managing herds as families, aimed at rapid herd growth, and sold animals cautiously to preserve their breeding stock. Among the Masai of Kenya, when group ranches were formed the land was privatized, leading the more influential to seek individualized land. The collapse of collective trust that followed the dubious allocation of individual parcels out of group lands finally led to comprehensive subdivision and massive loss of land to financial schemes, corruption, and pastoral land sales. Regarding environmental impacts, on lands taken for speculation, production decreased and grazing went unused; on individual ranchlands, the range tended to be degraded, given diminished herd movement; and, due to their diminished size, some group lands tended in dry periods toward greater degradation. Development initiatives encourage settlement and costly improvements that require marketing of livestock to justify, but they have largely failed to improve forms of husbandry or the quality of pastoralist lives. Pastoralists do engage in massive market production and feed vast populations across the world, but "development" has often made their lands and lives less rather than more secure.

Pastoralist Resilience in the Modern World

Pastoralism has historically made possible the occupation and productive use of vast dryland areas of the world unsuited for agriculture, whether rangelands, deserts, mountains, or tundra. It continues to do so today, even as new technologies and population pressures have resulted in the expansion of agriculture and as global interest in conservation has stimulated the excision of wildlife reserves from the herder's domain. The outcome has been reduction in the amount of pastoralist land and marginalization and frequent impoverishment of pastoralist communities. Changes have been justified by the claim that pastoralism degrades range environments through overgrazing pastures, a view that supports the transfer of land away from its indigenous trustees. However, recent findings in ecology demonstrate that many pastoralist regions are relatively impervious to grazing pressure and that pastoralists have many strategies—among them herd diversification, splitting, and mobility—for optimally utilizing pasture resources and preventing their overuse. Exploiting a niche in global environmental resources by using human labor, ingenuity, and modest technology, pastoralism will continue. But pastoralists will thrive most as citizens of a modern world when their land rights are secured and the aim of development is not to change them into cultivators, ranchers, or townspeople but rather to strengthen their capacity

to raise livestock in the world's most arduous areas for their own subsistence and the provision of the market. For this, the qualities of pride, autonomy, determination, and resilience will continue to prove well adapted.

John G. Galaty

Further Reading

Allan, T. (1996). *In search of cool ground: War, flight & homecoming in northeast Africa.* Trenton, NJ: Africa World Press.

Barth, F. (1961). *Nomads of south Persia.* Boston: Little, Brown.

Bonfiglioli, A. (1992). *Pastoralists at a crossroads: Survival and development in African pastoralism.* Nairobi, Kenya: UNICEF/UNSO Project for Nomadic Pastoralists in Africa (NOPA).

Bourgeot, A. (1999). *Horizons nomades en Afrique sahélienne: Sociétés, développement et démocratie* [Horizons for nomads in Sahelian Africa: Society, development, and democracy]. Paris: Karthala.

Clutton-Brock, J. (Ed.). (1989). *The walking larder: Patterns of domestication, pastoralism and predation.* London: Allen & Unwin.

Fratkin, E., Galvin, K., & Roth, E. (Eds.). (1994). *African pastoralist systems: An integrated approach.* Boulder, CO: Lynne Rienner Publishers.

Galaty, J., & Johnson, D. (Eds.). (1990). *The world of pastoralism: Herding systems in comparative perspective.* New York: Guilford Press.

Kurimoto, E., & Simonse, S. (1998). *Conflict, age & power in north east Africa: Age systems in transition.* Oxford, UK: James Currey.

Leach, M., & Mearns, R. (Eds.). (1996). *The lie of the land: Challenging received wisdom on the African environment.* Portsmouth, NH: Heinemann.

Scoones, I. (Ed.). (1996). *Living with uncertainty: New directions in rangeland management.* London: Intermediate Technology Publications.

Pathway Hypothesis

The Pathway Hypothesis was posited in 2002 by U.S. forester Dr. John Fedkiw to describe the evolution of forestry in the United States along a path of ever-increasing holism (relating to complete systems rather than parts) and consideration for the multiple values and services of forest ecosystems. The hypothesis suggests that the path began with concerns for the sustained yield of wood from managed forests in the early twentieth century and has now embraced the sustainability of forest ecosystems for multiple benefits. This evolution, Fedkiw says, occurred one step at a time as science and society's values changed.

The pathway is a metaphor; it has a starting point, it leads somewhere, and one must travel the early parts to reach the later parts. Prior to the late 1800s there was no forestry in America, no pathway, so to speak. Forests were cleared for farms and towns or cut for timber or wood fuels and left behind as loggers moved to the next natural stands. This stage has been replicated in every nation with forests throughout human history. During the late nineteenth century concern over the effects of these "cut and run" practices led visionaries such as the U.S. forester Bernhard Fernow and the U.S. conservationist Gifford Pinchot to suggest the adoption of scientific forestry to perpetuate forests and sustainable yields of timber. The sustained yield stage of managed forests in America began as the twentieth century began. But it was not universally applied. Logging natural forests without attention to renewing or regenerating a new stand of trees was practiced well into the twentieth century while sustained yield forestry continued to take shape. Dr. Fedkiw would say that forestry started on the pathway to sustainability with Fernow's and Pinchot's ideas.

Sustained Yield

The Pathway Hypothesis suggests that from this initial stage, forestry has broadened from a focus on sustained yield of wood in response to scientific advances and stimuli from a growing conservation ethic. The current stage goes by names such as "ecosystem management" and "sustainable forest management." If all forestry at any point in time used similar methods to strive for similar goals, one could say that the pathway is narrow, that everyone on it progresses in lock-step stages, and that it includes only minor side paths. On the other hand, if methods and goals diverge at some point, then the pathway must be more like a deciduous (leaf-dropping) tree with its familiar dendritic (branching) pattern. Furthermore, forest managers can be at many different places along the pathway at any point in time depending on their goals and methods.

A good hypothesis must be capable of being proven wrong, and it must be amenable to alternative views. What evidence would show the pathway to be false or what might that evidence say about the kind of pathway that forestry's evolution reflects? One line of evidence that would nullify the Pathway Hypothesis would be if forestry unfolded in such a way that each "new" version appeared without linkage to prior versions. There is no evidence for this; each new variant of American forestry has built upon prior approaches, and the linkages and legacies are still apparent.

Dr. Fedkiw suggests that the pathway has a goal: sustainability, which itself continually evolves as people learn more about forests and as societal values and expectations change. This postulation of an ever-changing goal is also supported by evidence. Historic changes in state and federal legislation and in practices on the land show that the evolution of forestry has been greatly influenced by new scientific knowledge and by changing societal values.

A New Path

So, the Pathway Hypothesis is plausible as an explanation for forestry's evolution. Each new stage is founded on prior stages, some of which are still in practice as the new stages emerge. However, U.S. forestry is not on a narrow pathway with only limited courses to follow and a singular goal. The latter half of the twentieth century was marked by a dramatic divergence in goals and methods for how forests are managed in the United States. Beginning around the mid-twentieth century, foresters and landowners started planting trees after harvests. They started managing those planted trees to increase the yields of wood from their lands. This initiated a major new path in forestry: managed planted forests to complement managed natural forests. At first these planted forests were diverse in species composition, and they grew into forests that resembled natural forests. Over time the intensity of tree culture increased, and many planted forests began to look more like what many people called them: tree farms. Meanwhile, yet another path was emerging in park and wilderness forests—management of people and their activities to reduce human impact but no harvest of trees except for safety reasons.

These divergent branches along the pathway became dramatically clear during the latter twentieth century and are now well established as different approaches to sustaining forest values: high yields of wood on the one hand and high yields of naturalness on the other. The original path of multivalue forestry or multiple-use forestry still exists and is practiced by many forest owners, including many forests managed by state and federal agencies. So, the evolutionary pathway now has several main branches, and all branches make major although different contributions to sustaining the full benefits of forests: healthy environments and ecosystem services, raw materials and jobs to meet people's needs, and diverse cultural values.

At the start of the twenty-first century the pathway of American forestry has many branches, each reflecting variations in goals and methods. Each branch is connected to its historical antecedents. Each changes over time in response to new understandings, new technologies, and new societal goals. Although the original notion of forestry to sustain wood yield has evolved into ecosystem management and sustainable forest management, it is unlikely that the final pathway or branch has emerged. Forestry is only a little over one hundred years old in the United States. A long pathway remains, with a lot more branching.

Hal Salwasser

Further Reading

Fedkiw, J. (2002). *Sustainability and the Pathway Hypothesis.* Durham, NC: Forest History Society.

MacCleery, D. W. (1996). *American forests: A history of resiliency.* Durham, NC: Forest History Society.

Perlin, J. (1989). *A forest journey: The role of wood in the development of civilization.* New York: W. W. Norton.

Williams, M. (1989). *Americans and their forests: An historical geography.* New York: Cambridge University Press.

Peat

Peat is the product formed by the partial decomposition of various plants in ancient bogs (called peat bogs) that formed wherever stagnant water prevailed in the moderate climate zones. Thin layers of peat cover large areas of Canada, Scandinavia, and Russia. Historically of most interest is the large belt of raised peat bogs (2–8 meters thick and 300 kilometers wide) that covered the coastal plains of northern Europe, stretching from northern France, along Belgium, the Netherlands, Germany, Poland, Russia, Lithuania, Latvia, and Estonia. Human exploitation of peat lands have often come in several historical stages, often tied to whether the peat lands were being exploited for agriculture or as a source of fuel.

Peat Bogs as Agricultural Land

Living peat bogs take the shape of a round pillow with a diameter of a couple of kilometers. The high centers are bare plains of peat-forming vegetation, primarily mosses. Toward the more mineral-rich edges water-loving trees and shrubs such as willow, alders, and hazel grow. The first phase of humanization of the peat bogs was using them as a natural resource: for grazing sheep, providing fuel and construction wood, and as a source for fruits and herbs. The second phase of humanization was turning them into arable lands. A vast labor of drainage and canal building had to be carried out before the surface was dry enough to carry grain crops. However, the more intensive use of the peat lands had some unintended consequences. The surface level sunk at the surprisingly high rate of about 1 meter per century. Peat is like a sponge. It is 90 percent water, so when it is drained, little is left. Also the dried peat soil oxidized in reaction with air, a sort of flameless fire. Over time the subsidence of the raised peat bogs led to perpetual adaptation of the drainage system, replacing and enlarging the capacity of ditches, canals, embankments, and sluices. When the (average) peat surface level, mostly in the fifteenth century, reached the mean water level of the North Sea, mechanical pumping was introduced to prevent the land from flooding. The windmill, equipped with wooden scoops and fitted with sails, like a gristmill, was the response to this human-induced ecological challenge. Invented in Holland in 1408, it spread quickly and reached England and Germany in the seventeenth century.

Peat Bogs as a Source of Fuel

As a fuel peat comes between wood and coal. It has the same low energetic value as wood, 8–16 joules per kilogram, but geologically it is a carbon layer on its way to becoming lignite and coal. Like coal it is a grayish-brown-black substance. Its energy content depends on its purity: The less sand and clay particles it contains, the more heat it gives. Peat is very easy to process. It suffices to cut a layer 30–60 centimeters thick into small blocks in the spring, pile them up to dry over the summer, and take them away for use in the autumn. Peat used as a fuel is first described in reports of Arab travelers in Roman times, but archaeological evidence of peat burning goes back far into the Iron Age. Commercial peat digging, financed and organized by urban capitalists, first developed in twelfth-century Flanders, then the industrial center of northern

Europe. When resources there were depleted, the center of peat extraction moved to the western Netherlands (fourteenth century), then on to the eastern Netherlands (sixteenth century). In coastal Germany peat mining was commercial from the seventeenth century onwards; in Estonia it is still an active industry. In Great Britain it never became commercial on a large scale, because of low population pressure, large wood reserves, and the competition of coal.

Due to scarcity of peat and low labor costs, a particular peat-extraction technology developed in the Netherlands in the fifteenth century. Dredging peat from below the groundwater level became widespread, destroying the arable surface, displacing villages, and creating enormous lakes. From the seventeenth century onwards land was reclaimed from these lakes using windmills.

Nowadays very little remains of Europe's peat bogs. Some stretches are still intact along the German and Baltic coast and in Ireland. Apart from their value as wetland habitats for rare species, their capacity to absorb carbon dioxide from the air makes them valuable. Worldwide they absorb more than the rain forests. For the historian and archeologist they are valuable because they preserve ancient deposits of organic materials such as cloth, skins, pollen, and bones. The remaining peat bogs are under high pressure from the market for fertilizer and soil. Private gardening and the intensive vegetable and flower industry, in particular the greenhouse sector, consume 6 million cubic meters of peat per year. Since the 1990s national laws protect wetlands and subsidize regeneration.

Petra J. E. M. van Dam

Further Reading

Heathwaite, A. L. (Ed.). (1990). *Mires: Process, exploitation and conservation.* Chichester, UK: Hohn Wiley & Sons.

van Dam, P. J. E. M. (2000). Sinking peat bogs: Environmental change in Holland, 1350–1550. *Environmental History, 5*(4), 32–45.

Peru

(2000 est. pop. 27 million)

The varied Peruvian environment and its rich history are the product of the dynamic interaction of its multi-faceted biophysical conditions and its complex human cultural process. Peru is the third-largest country in South America (1.2 million square kilometers), with an additional jurisdiction over 370 square kilometers of ocean. Contemporary Peru is the result of an anthropogenic (resulting from the influence of humans) environmental history. Native Americans, who arrived as hunter-gatherers approximately 25,000 BCE and slowly evolved into complex civilizations, gradually mixed with the descendants of the Spanish conquistadores, reformulating their subsistence systems and their patterns of natural resources utilization. Peru's population stands today at 27 million with an annual growth rate of 1.6 percent.

Stretching along western South America between the equator and 18° S latitude, Peru comprises three distinctive regions. A narrow Pacific coast covers approximately 10 percent of its territory, framing the Andean highlands. The Andes are characterized by massive ranges, deep, narrow, and wide mountain valleys, and high plateaus. This abrupt sierra makes up another 30 percent of Peru's landmass. To the east the Andes gradually drop into lowland plains, holding the major portion of the upper watershed of the Amazon River basin. Sixty percent of Peru is covered by the Amazonian rain forest.

The Andes

The Andean ranges run in a north-south direction and imprint the geological character of the country. These ranges are the result of the convergence of the South American and the South Pacific tectonic plates, where the latter is subducted (the edge of one plate descending below the edge of another) into the former. The Andean geosyncline (a large linear trough along the margin of the continent) uplift started in the Late Paleozoic era and continued during the Mesozoic and Cenozoic, reaching its peak during the Upper Tertiary period in a dynamic process that continues to date. This uplift resulted in intense folding and faults, prompting seismic and volcanic activity. Magmatism partly explains the intensive mineralization of the Andes and the current diversity and wealth of mineral ores in the country. The Pleistocene epoch also brought extensive glaciation and further transformed the Andean landscape.

Peru exhibits one of the most diversified distributions of animals and plants on Earth. Based on Holdridge's (1947) life zone (a region characterized by specific animals and plants) system constructed on bioclimatic criteria, Tosi (1960) and Oficina Nacional de Evaluacion de Recursos Naturales (ONERN [National Office of Evaluation of Natural Resources] 1976) classified the country into 101 life zones, of which 17 are transitional (out of a total world system of 114 life zones). Ceballos's biogeographical criteria (1984) classifies Peru into two subregions, four areas, six subareas, and seventeen zones. A more recent and comprehensive classification of the country (Braack 1984) divides Peru into eleven eco-regions. The national weather service identifies twenty-eight microclimates.

Environmental Threats

The main environmental threats to coastal Peru are unplanned urban growth and associated industrial pollution of rivers and the coastline and overfishing. The rich and ancient agro-pastoral traditions in the high Andes, cradle of a record number of domesticated plants, are nowadays affected by genetic erosion. The area also suffers from mining-related pollution. The upper watershed of the Amazon basin is severely affected by deforestation and oil exploitation.

Lima, the capital city (2000 est. pop. 7.5 million), is particularly severely affected by particles in suspension, lead poisoning, carbon monoxide, and sulfuric gases. Other urban centers with over 1 million inhabitants (Arequipa and Trujillo) experience increased environmental problems due to motorized traffic, industrial pollution, waste disposal, improper sewage treatment, and lack of green areas. Expanding cities are covering the limited arable land of the country (3.5

percent), and the demand of coastal cities for water is pressing for engineering works to divert water from the Amazon watershed into the Pacific.

Peru is considered one of the world's most biodiverse countries, ranking second in birds (1,701 species), sixth in mammals (361 species), seventh in amphibians (251 species), and eighth in reptiles (297 species) and flowering plants (20,000 species). Since the 1970s fifty-one protected areas have been established to protect endangered species. The areas represent most of the 101 classified life zones. In total they cover 15.31 percent of the national territory. Conservation of biodiversity is under the Ministry of Agriculture's National Institute of Natural Resources (INRENA). Peru is a signatory of the World Convention on Biological Diversity. A special law on conservation and sustainable use of the country's biological diversity was enacted in 1997.

Academics and activists have expressed Peru's environmental concerns since the 1920s. A structured environmental movement started in the mid-1970s, mostly represented by nongovernmental organizations. Only during the last decade have universities increased their advocacy of the environment. Environmental issues were brought to public attention in political campaigns only during the 1990s. More recently the financial sector has started to express its environmental concerns as part of its lending operations, particularly with the mining sector.

In 1997 the government established the National Environmental Council (CONAM). CONAM is a public council, with private sector representation in its board, in charge of drafting environmental policy and coordinating the different environmental divisions in most ministries. The Ministry of Foreign Affairs has a most dynamic environmental division that participates in most U.N. forums on the environment. Peru has signed the Antarctic treaties and keeps a research station in the South Pole. During the year 2002 Peru played a leading role in the U.N.'s International Year of the Mountains.

Peru's National Environmental Code was enacted in 1998 and is currently under revision. Since 1980 local governments have started advocating for conservation and pollution control and have active programs aimed at environmental management.

Alejandro Camino

Llama herders in the Peruvian Andes Mountains stand near a pile of rocks, created both to clear the land of obstructions and to mark a path through the mountains. COURTESY OF NICOLE LALIBERTE.

Further Reading

Braack, E. A. (1984). Ecologia de un pais complejo [Ecology of a complex country]. In *Gran geografia del Peru*

[Large geography of Peru] (pp. 177–319). Barcelona, Spain: Grafos S. A.

Camino Diez Canseco, A., & Recharte, J. (1991). Analisis de la situacion del medio ambiente en el Peru [Analysis of the environmental situation in Peru]. In *La situacion ambiental en America Latina* [The environmental situation in Latin America]. Buenos Aires, Argentina: CIEDLA.

Ceballos, B. I. (1984). Nuevo esquema biogeografico del Peru [New biogeographical plan of Peru]. *Revista Universitaria, 63*(130), 1–26.

Holdridge, L. R. (1947). Determination of world plant formations from simple climatic data. *Science, 105* (2727), 367–368.

Oficina Nacional de Evaluacion de Recursos Naturales (ONERN [National Office of Evaluation of Natural Resources]). (1976). *Mapa ecologico del Peru: Guia* explicativ [Ecological map of Peru: Explanatory guide]. Lima, Peru: ONERN.

Tosi, J. (1960). *Zonas de vida natural en el Peru* [Natural life zones in Peru]. Turrialba, Costa Rica: IICA-OEA.

Zimmerer, K. S. (1997). *Changing fortunes: Biodiversity and peasant livelihood in the Peruvian Andes.* Berkeley: University of California Press.

Peru, Coastal

Despite Peru's location in the tropics of western South America (3°25′ to 18°20′ S latitude), coastal Peru is a stark desert. Nevertheless, it is home to millions of people and has supported large populations for millennia. The secret to prosperity in this extreme environment is twofold: Upwelled nutrients from the Antarctic Humboldt (Peru) current make the Pacific Ocean in this region one of the world's most productive fisheries, and irrigation canal water drawn from rivers fed by snowmelt and rainfall in the adjacent highlands permits intensive agriculture in the coastal valleys. However, the oceanic phenomenon El Niño (an irregularly occurring appearance of unusually warm surface water along the western coast of South America) impacts the region periodically, bringing warmer, less-nutrient-rich water and destructive rainfall to parts of the coast; impacts diminish to the south, and events are variable in intensity.

In such a setting, climate and environment play a major role in human adaptations, and both have changed over the span of human occupation. The first people arrived about thirteen thousand years ago; they were fishers, hunters, and gatherers who exploited the rich ocean, the river valleys, and the *lomas* (fog-based plant communities on the coastal foothills between 200 and 1,000 meters above sea level). At that time, sea level was about 60 meters below the present level (it reached the present level about six thousand years ago), and the climate in northern coastal Peru was probably somewhat warmer and wetter than it is today. Central and southern coastal Peru, however, has remained hyperarid for millions of years and has not changed substantially during the span of human occupation. From eighty-nine hundred to fifty-eight hundred years ago, northern Peru was definitely warmer and wetter than it is at present, and El Niño was absent or extremely rare. People continued hunting, fishing, and gathering, but by the end of that period sedentary life had begun, and some domesticated plants such as gourd and squash were in use.

Fifty-eight hundred years ago the coast of northern Peru cooled, and El Niño began, although with low frequency. At the same time people began to live in larger settlements, to build irrigation canals and cultivate a variety of crops, and to build monumental temple architecture. Fishing remained important in the economy, providing virtually all animal protein. Indeed, the northward emplacement of the Humboldt current at that time implies increased biomass (the amount of living matter) available to fishers. The monumental temple-building tradition continued until about three thousand years ago, when El Niño's frequency increased, and the last temples were abandoned. Changing climate undoubtedly played a role in these transitions, although many other cultural factors must also have been critical. Populations continued to grow, and after a hiatus of several centuries, monumental structures of even greater scale were built. Most food now came from agriculture, although intensive fishing continued (domestic animals—llamas, alpacas, and guinea pigs—were present, but only guinea pigs were common on the coast).

The rise and fall of subsequent civilizations in coastal Peru, such as the Moche and the Sicán, have been linked in part to El Niño occurrences or to frequency changes, along with other factors. After the Spanish conquest in 1532, the first really strong El Niño occurred in 1578. The Spanish administration had recently consolidated the much-reduced native population into centralized settlements placed squarely in the floodpaths, and damage was severe.

Daniel H. Sandweiss

Further Reading

Copson, W., & Sandweiss, D. H. (1999). Native and Spanish perspectives on the 1578 El Niño. In M. Boyd, J. C. Erwin, & M. Hendrickson (Eds.), *The entangled past: Integrating history and archaeology* (pp. 208–220). Calgary, Canada: University of Calgary.

Fagan, B. M. (1999). *Floods, famines, and emperors: El Niño and the fate of civilizations.* New York: Basic Books.

Sandweiss, D. H., Maasch, K. A., Burger, R. L., Richardson J. B., III, Rollins, H. B., & Clement, A. (2001). Variation in Holocene El Niño frequencies: Climate records and cultural consequences in ancient Peru. *Geology, 29*(7), 603–606.

Pesticides

Pesticides are agents that reduce or eradicate plants, animals, fungi, and microorganism populations that compete with organisms of specific interest to humans, such as crops and farmed animals, or that represent hazards to human health. (See table 1.)

Uses

Some pesticides have no counterparts in nature and are thus truly synthetic chemicals, others are modeled on naturally occurring pesticides but are produced synthetically, and yet others are organisms such as bacteria, fungi, and viruses; which are pathogenic to specific pests; the latter pesticides are biopesticides.

Pesticides are widely used in agriculture (including crop storage), horticulture, and forestry; other relatively minor uses include the protection of wood (e.g., in buildings to prevent rot and insect attack) and fiber (e.g., wool). Many regulatory authorities, such as the U.S. Environmental Protection Agency, also classify as pesticides other categories of crop- and animal-protection compounds, notably defoliants and desiccants, which facilitate crop harvesting, and plant and insect growth regulators, which affect plant architecture and growth rates to improve crop output and disrupt insect pest growth stages, respectively. Because most pesticides are produced from fossil fuels, they constitute a significant input of fossil-fuel energy into agricultural systems. Thus one form of carbon is employed to enhance the capture of light energy to produce another form of carbon as food or fiber.

Pesticides enhance agricultural production by eliminating competitors for resources such as sunlight energy, nutrients, space, food energy, and water or by preventing disease. They have been used since prehistoric times, but the modern pesticide industry began in the mid-nineteenth century when two natural insecticides were discovered. Rotenone, from the root of the derris plant, and pyrethrum, from the flowers of a species of chrysanthemum, were employed as insecticides. Further developments occurred as a result of chemical research before and during World War II, notably the invention of DDT (dichlorodiphenyltrichloroethene) and organochlorine compounds (compounds containing carbon, oxygen, hydrogen, and chlorine), as well as various phosphorus-containing chemicals that impair nervous systems. The large-scale production of these substances underpinned the post-1940 pesticide industry and is associated with the industrialization of agriculture throughout the developed world. However, the adverse impact of many of these substances, recognized since the 1960s as reflected in the publication of Rachel Carson's book *Silent Spring* (1962), has prompted the establishment of registration procedures that require stringent laboratory and field testing to ensure nil or minimum risks to flora, fauna, the environment, and human health. Regulatory authority approval is essential before such substances can be marketed.

Moreover, emphasis has shifted from the production of synthetic chemicals to the identification and mimicking of naturally occurring pesticides and to the genetic modification of crops so that they exhibit insecticidal properties or tolerance to herbicides. In 2002 the value of the world pesticide industry was $30 billion.

Herbicides

Herbicides are used against undesirable plants, so-called weeds. The biggest targets of herbicides are those plants in agricultural systems that compete with crops for nutrients, water, and so forth and thus cause economic losses. Traditionally the control of weeds has been achieved by manual or mechanical weeding, but herbicides eliminate these labor-intensive activities. Herbicides thus contribute to increased agricultural productivity, reduce labor costs, and provide a degree of environmental protection because less disturbance reduces soil and water losses. Although some inorganic chemicals (e.g., sodium arsenite and sodium chloride mixed with ashes) have been used as herbicides historically, the modern herbicide industry began in the 1930s when the first synthetic organic com-

TABLE 1.
CATEGORIES OF PESTICIDES

Herbicides	Fungicides	Insecticides	Acaricides	Nematicides	Molluscicides	Rodenticides	Plant growth regulators
Weeds	Fungi	Insects	Mites	Nematode Worms	Snails, slugs	Rodents	Crops Ornamentals
Phenoxyacetic acids 2,4-D, MCPA	*Pyrimidines* Ethirmol, Fenarimol	*Organochlorines* DDT, Dieldrin	*Organochlorines* Dicofol	*Fumigants* Methylbromide, Dibromo-Chloropropane	*Aldehydes* Metaldehyde	*Coumarins* Warfarin, Coumatetryl, Brodifacoum	*Hormones* Gibberellins, Ethylene, Auxins, Cytokinin, Abscisic acid
Biprilliums Paraquat, Diquat	*Alarines* Furalaxyl, Ofurace	*Organo phosphates* Terbuphos, Dimethoate	*Organotins* Cyhexatin	*Carbamates* Aldicarb, Oxamyl	*Carbamates* Methiocarb, Thiocarboxime, Mexacarbamate	*Inorganic* Zinc phosphide, Yellow phosphorus, Thallium sulfate	*Triazoles* Paclobutrazol
Phosphonates Glyphosate	*Triazoles* Triadimefon, Flutriafol	*Carbamates* Aldicarb, Carbofuran	*Tetrazines* Clofentezine	*Organo phosphates* Fenamiphos, Fosthiazate	*Inorganic* Calcium arsenate, Copper sulfate	*Convulsants* Crimidine, Sodium Fluoroacetate, Fluoroacetamide, Strychnine	*Dikegulac*
Pyrazoliums Difenzoquat	*Strobilurins* Azoxystrobin, Picoxystrobin, Trifloxystrobin, Pyraclostrobin	*Pyrethroids* Permethrin, Cypermethrin, Fenvalerate, Tefluthrin, Cyhalothrin	*Avermectins* Abmectin, Emamectin *Nicotinoids* Imidacloprid, Nicotine				
Aryloxy-Phenoxyacetic acid Diclofop-Methyl, Fluazifop-butyl *Nitro-Diphenylethers* Fomesafen *Sulphonylureas* Chlorosulfuron, Metasulfuron-methyl							

pounds for weed control were developed. Currently herbicides dominate the world pesticide market by value. Only six multinational companies are involved, which is a cause for concern in light of recent developments involving herbicide-resistant, genetically modified crops. Herbicides are used mainly in the developed world, especially in North America and Europe, which account for about 60 percent of their use. The major crops treated are maize, soybeans, wheat, and rice. Together with artificial fertilizers, which have been used more since World War II, and the breeding of high-yield crop varieties, herbicides have made a major contribution to increased crop yields. There are also many nonagricultural applications for herbicides where a weed-free condition is desirable, for example, roadsides, railroad tracks and embankments, recreation areas, and irrigation channels.

Herbicides are generally divided into two categories: selective and nonselective. Selective herbicides eliminate weeds but do not damage the crop; nonselective herbicides eliminate all plants. Herbicides are applied to either the foliage or the soil, depending on how the chemical operates; many herbicides are applied as sprays, whereas others are applied when seed is planted by direct drilling. Some herbicides can be applied broadly, but if used at recommended doses they will effectively be selective because they act against some plants but not others. Alternative classifications of herbicides relate to their mode of action, timing of application, and the part of the plant in which the pesticide is effective. For example, if the chemical enters the plant via its roots, it is systemic, in contrast with chemicals that cause plant death when contact is made with the foliage. In terms of timing, herbicides may be used in preplanting, preemergent, or postemergent stages. The area covered may be a band, the entire field, small areas, or selected weeds or areas.

The majority of herbicides are organic chemicals, that is, they are based on carbon compounds. Organic compounds can be classified into groups according to their chemical structure, and many groups contain one or more chemicals with herbicidal properties. (See table 1.) Included in the bipyridliums are paraquat and diquat, which are contact broad-spectrum herbicides. They inhibit photosynthesis and cause plant cells to fracture, which manifests as wilting and desiccation. Consequently, they are widely used to clear arable fields prior to seeding and immediately before harvest to facilitate the collection of seed crops, for example, sunflower, cotton, and soybean. They are suited to direct drilling, or minimum tillage, which involves the mechanized placement of seed, herbicide, and fertilizer without plowing. Although they are toxic to mammals, these herbicides have few adverse environmental impacts; they are immobilized when they reach the soil and so do not easily contaminate the wider environment. Glyphosate is another widely used, broad-spectrum herbicide with uses similar to those of the bipyridliums; it works physiologically by inhibiting the production of essential amino acids. It is inactivated in soils, but if it enters aquatic ecosystems it causes fish mortality. Herbicides that act as defoliants include the phenoxyacetic acids 2,4-D (2.4-dichlorophenoxy), 2,4,5T (2,4,5-trichlorophenoxy), and MCPA (4-chloro–2-methylphenoxy). The former two were the components of Agent Orange, which was used during the Vietnam War (1965–1971) by the U.S. military as a jungle defoliant. Unfortunately some batches of Agent Orange were contaminated with dioxins that caused human health problems such as fetal deformity. The phenoxyacetic acids, or hormone herbicides, were developed in the late 1940s and are used for weed management in cereal crops and pastures. In their targets they mimic the plant hormone auxin, which controls cell division, to cause excessive growth and eventual death. Nonagricultural uses include weed control on roads, railroads, and lawns. These herbicides cause few environmental problems and exhibit only low toxicity to humans and other mammals. However, indirect effects include a decline in broad-leaved plant species in field margins due to imprecise spraying; this, in turn, causes reduced insect populations, which are a likely reason for high mortality rates of partridge chicks and the overall decline of partridge populations throughout Europe.

Examples of selective herbicides include the diphenyl ethers, which act on contact to cause chlorosis (the destruction of chlorophyll) in weeds in the preemergent or early postemergent stages of various crops. Fomesafen and bifenox are members of this group and are used to combat grass and broad-leaved weeds in preemergent legume crops such as soybean and peanut and weeds in postemergent wheat, barley, and sugar beet. The sulphonylureas are another large group of herbicides that is widely used. Causing death by preventing cell division at root tips, these herbicides are particularly effective against broad-leaved species and are used to control such weeds in cereal crops.

New approaches to weed control involve biotechnology and the engineering of crop plants with genes to promote herbicide resistance. Engineered maize and wheat are already available; fields of such crops can be treated with broad-spectrum herbicides to eliminate weeds without impairment of the crop.

Insecticides

A major cause of crop loss is damage by insects, some types of which also damage animal products such as fiber and reduce overall productivity. The first modern chemical insecticides produced in the period from 1930 to 1945 were broad-spectrum rather than target-specific, the disadvantage of which is that they kill beneficial as well as harmful insects. They included the thiocyanates, which work by disrupting insect enzyme systems, and the organochlorines, which work by interfering with the transmission of nerve impulses. The use of both groups is prohibited in many countries because of their adverse ecological effects. However, the development of the organochlorine insecticides in the late 1930s represented a major advance for the embryonic pesticide industry, notably the synthesis of the diphenyl aliphatics, which include DDT. Now notorious, DDT nonetheless saved many human lives between 1940 and 1973 when it was used for public health purposes worldwide, including the control of louse-borne typhus and malaria. It is still used in insect control programs in some developing countries because it is inexpensive to manufacture, stable chemically, easy to apply, nontoxic to humans, and immediately effective. These properties were precisely what encouraged DDT's use as a crop protection chemical, although initial success gave way to concerns about the loss of beneficial insects in cropping systems and the later discovery, in the 1960s, that DDT has long-term adverse environmental impacts. It is persistent in soils onto which it is washed by rain, so crop foliage soon loses its protection while soil insects are considerably reduced. DDT residues and their breakdown products undergo biological magnification as they pass through food chains and food webs (the totality of interacting food chains in an ecological community); eventually concentrations become sufficiently high to cause damage to organisms at the tops of food chains, notably through the impairment of their reproductive capacities. These organisms include many birds of prey whose populations have declined substantially, even in areas to which DDT and related compounds—for example, aldrin, dieldrin, and endrin—were not directly applied because the compounds have been disseminated by air, water, and organisms in terrestrial and aquatic environments. Among the organochlorine insecticides used today are lindane and endosulfan, which are biodegradable, and the recently synthesized fipronil, which is selectively toxic. Problems have also been caused by the use of organophosphate compounds, which were developed from World War II research on nerve gases; these inhibit the enzyme cholinesterase in insect nervous systems and, like DDT, are broad-spectrum insecticides. So are the carbamates, which also work by inhibiting cholinesterase and which were developed in the mid-1950s. The carbamates—for example, carbofuran—are toxic to mammals and honeybees.

Having noted the many problems generated by these early synthetic pesticides, crop protection and animal health industries turned their attention from broad-spectrum products to target-specific products that have minimal environmental impact. Among the first such insecticides to be developed were the pyrethroids. Although established as having insecticidal properties, the flowers of *Chrysanthemum cinerariaefolium* were too expensive to cultivate on a large scale, and the active ingredient, pyrethrum, proved to be unstable in sunlight. Nevertheless, the potential began to be realized in the late 1940s when the first artificial pyrethroid, allethrin, was produced synthetically. Three further generations of pyrethroids have since been produced, and they are now highly significant in the arsenal of crop-protection chemicals available to farmers worldwide. Interestingly, the pyrethroid mode of action is similar to that of DDT; it focuses on sodium channels in nerve membranes, which causes paralysis. Unlike DDT, the pyrethroids are not environmentally persistent because they break down rapidly in soils, and as hydrophobic compounds their spread beyond the point of application by dissolving in or combining with water is limited. Another advantage is that they are effective at low dose rates, for example, 10 to 100 grams per hectare; thus they are economical for farmers, and the prospect of environmental impairment is limited. However, most pyrethroids are toxic to fish, so care is required to prevent contamination of watercourses.

The avermectins are another group of organic chemicals that derives from natural compounds. Developed in the late 1980s, avermectins are antibiotics that control mites and helminth and nematode worms as well as ticks and lice. They derive from lactones (chemicals comprising a ring of carbon atoms and oxygen) produced by the actinomycete fungus *Streptomyces avermitilis* and cause death in target species by blocking specific neurotransmitters. Because these compounds are unstable in sunlight they do not persist in the environment, but they can be toxic to mammals.

They also have applications in animal health care for controlling parasites.

Among the most recent insecticides to be developed are the nicotinoids, which are based on nicotine, an alkaloid found in tobacco. Several nicotinoids have been developed, of which the most widely used is imidacloprid. This was introduced to Europe in 1990. It can be applied to soil, seed, or foliage and controls a range of insects—for example, Colorado potato beetle, termites, whiteflies, and aphids—by blocking the nervous system.

The fact that target insects can develop resistance to insecticides means that there is an ongoing need to produce new insecticides, to adopt integrated pest management (IPM) strategies that combine rotation, chemicals, sowing, and harvesting techniques and to innovate with new technologies. Currently biotechnology is being used to exploit the insecticidal properties of the bacterium *Bacillus thuringiensis* (Bt). As a commercial preparation, populations of this bacterium have been in use as a biocide for the last thirty years because it produces chemicals that are pathogenic to insects, especially lepidopteran (butterflies and moths) pests. Bt preparations have been widely used to control cotton bollworm in cotton crops, but now transgenic (genes that have been altered artificially, i.e., by human intervention in the laboratory) cotton is available, which has been genetically modified by introducing the genetic code for Bt toxin. This provides the cotton with a built-in insecticide. Transgenic cotton is widely grown in the United States, China, and South Africa, and productivity has generally increased as costs have declined; the reduced need for chemical pesticides should also be an environmental benefit. However, there are concerns, so far unproven, that beneficial insect populations may be harmed. The possibility of insect resistance to the Bt toxin is also of concern; there is evidence for the development of resistance in areas where conventional Bt has been used. Consequently, transgenic cotton may have limited use, and strategies to curtail resistance must be an integral component of the agricultural system. This may involve the maintenance of so-called refugia comprising patches of non-transgenic cotton to support populations of insects that have not developed a genetic predisposition for resistance and that can interbreed with insects exposed to Bt cotton that may have begun to develop resistance.

Fungicides

Fungi can cause economic losses in agriculture in several ways. They can infect leaves or roots, impairing crop plants' optimal utilization of resources, and they can infect harvested crops so that there is less product to use or sell. Fungicides were developed to reduce such losses. Prior to the 1940s most chemicals used as fungicides were inorganic. Examples include sulfur, lime-sulfur, and compounds of copper and mercury. However, these chemicals contaminate the wider environment, and many are toxic to humans and other mammals. Modern fungicides are complex organic compounds; because most are aimed at preventing fungal diseases they are applied as protectant fungicides by either coating seeds before planting or spraying fields before seedling emergence. These are mostly broad-spectrum fungicides. Alternatively, curative fungicides, which are usually disease-specific, are applied in the early stages of the disease and operate systemically by being absorbed by the plant. Limitation and possibly cure of fungal disease may be achieved by systemic eradicant fungicides The main crops requiring fungicides are vegetables, fruits, cereals, and rice.

The organochlorides were among the first synthetic fungicides to be developed, but mercury-containing substances are dangerous to handle and not environmentally friendly. The triazoles, introduced in the 1960s, control fungal pests by interfering with their metabolism and are considered to be environmentally benign because no persistent residues are produced. Their long-term use, however, has caused the development of resistance in some fungi. (See table 1.) Recently developed fungicides include the methoxy acrylates, which are synthetic variations on strobilurin, a natural product found in the fungus *Strobilurin tenacellus*. They were registered for use in 1996 and are effective against mildews, late blight, rynchosporium, net blotch, and eyespot. Their mode of operation involves the inhibition of respiration. The strobilurins are protectant and mostly systemic fungicides and have additional benefits, which include improving nitrogen uptake and delaying senescence (aging). Environmentally, the strobilurins are harmless to most insects and humans, although they are toxic to algae and so can harm fish populations. They are used in cereal, rice, grapevine, vegetables, and pome (apple-like) fruits. There are already concerns about resistance, and best practice requires the use of more than one type of fungicide.

Acaricides

The grazing of crops by mites causes serious economic losses in many agricultural systems, and ticks and mites cause health problems for cattle and pigs. Consequently chemical compounds have been developed to combat these pests. Such compounds are known as "acaricides" after Acarida, the taxonomic order to which mites and ticks belong. (See table 1.) Dicofol is an organochlorine and is used to treat mite infestations in fruits, vegetables, ornamental plants, and cotton. It is often included in sprays for insect and disease control. It is toxic to fish, nontoxic to honeybees, and can be harmful to humans. Cyhexatin is used to control mites in nut crops, such as almonds and walnuts, hops, ornamental plants, and some fruits, especially where resistance to other acaricides has developed. Although it is nontoxic to bees, cyhexatin is harmful to fish and humans. Because use of chemicals that contain heavy metals such as tin is not environmentally friendly, cyhexatin is no longer widely used and is banned in many countries. Many compounds that are used as insecticides—for example, the pyrethroids and avermectins—are also effective acaricides. For example, since 1985 abamectin has been used to control two-spotted and rust mites and leafminers and psylia in citrus and pome fruits as well as cotton and vegetables. Several acaricides are available for outdoor and indoor use on ornamentals; they disrupt growth patterns to prevent maturity and cause paralysis through interference with the nervous system.

Nematicides

Nematodes (also known as "eelworms," "roundworms," "pinworms," or "threadworms") are microscopic, usually circular organisms that live in the soil. Whereas many species are free-living and feed on bacteria, fungi, and other soil microorganisms, other species, notably eelworms, are parasitic, entering plants via the root systems. This parasitism is manifested as root knots and cysts (hence the terms *root-knot* and *cyst nematodes*) in crop plants; nematodes can cause substantial losses by absorbing carbohydrates produced by the plant. As a nematode swells and produces eggs the root enlarges until it fractures, expelling the eggs into the soil so that infestation can occur again. Acknowledged as a major crop pest, especially in root crops, nematodes are difficult to combat because they live below ground; early nematicides comprised fumigants but had limited success. (See table 1.) Other compounds that were developed as insecticides—for example, the carbamates and organophosphates—have also been developed as nematicides. Fosthiazate is a contact organophosphate nematicide that causes death by inhibiting cholinesterase and is widely used to treat potatoes, vegetables, citrus fruits, and bananas. Its en-

vironmental effects are limited because it does not accumulate in or leach out of soils, and it is not toxic to beneficial organisms.

Recent approaches to nematode control involve genetic modification of crops to generate plants that have improved resistance. The first stage is to identify crop plants and then the specific genetic code that confers enhanced resistance and then to amplify the effect of this code. Thereafter clones can be produced for planting. Currently research is under way on potatoes, pineapples, and bananas. In the case of the latter, genetic modification for nematode resistance (and for other advantageous attributes) is particularly important because conventional breeding is slow in tree crops.

Molluscicides

Mollusk pests of crops include snails and slugs. These pests cause substantial crop losses in agricultural and horticultural enterprises and are major garden pests. Snails and slugs are herbivorous, that is, they feed on living and dead plant material, and are thus consumers of crops and ornamentals. They cause plant death by grazing the emergent seedlings and crop losses by grazing the foliage of mature crops. Economically, they can also reduce the value of products by disfiguration. Inorganic compounds, such as calcium arsenate and copper sulfate, have been used with some success, but the control of such organisms is difficult. Several compounds that were developed as insecticides—for example, the carbamates—are also effective against slugs and snails. (See table 1.) Mexacarbamate, for example, is particularly effective against slugs but is toxic to mammals. The most widely used molluscicide is metaldehyde. It is applied to the soil around plants as pellets, flakes, or a liquid. Snail and slug death is caused by excessive loss of water, although when conditions are wet the animals may recover. Metaldehyde is relatively harmless to humans, but beneficial organisms, such as hedgehogs, as well as pets may be poisoned.

Rodenticides

Increasing rodent populations, especially of rats, are a problem worldwide. Not only are such animals a significant cause of crop losses, notably in storage as well as in the field, but also they are a threat to animals in some environments and a serious problem for human health. Rats and their pests carry a range of diseases that are potentially fatal to humans. For example, bubonic plague is caused by a bacterium that is carried by rat fleas that transmit the disease to humans.

Inorganic compounds that have been used as rodenticides include thallium sulfate, yellow phosphorus, and zinc phosphide. (See table 1.) All are harmful to humans and other mammals. Indeed, the similarity of rodent physiology to that of humans and other mammals means that developing a truly safe pesticide is impossible. As a means of safeguarding human health rodenticides are required by regulatory authorities to have a proven antidote.

The best-known and most widely used rodenticide is warfarin. (See table 1.) This and related coumarins and indiandiones are crystalline compounds comprising carbon, hydrogen, and oxygen and are toxic to humans; they are absorbed into the bloodstream via the stomach and intestines and cause death, as they do in rats, by reducing the synthesis of blood-clotting factors based on vitamin K, for example, prothrombin. The antidote is vitamin K_1. The emergence of resistance to the first generation of warfarins has resulted in new rodenticides, which are superwarfarins, for example, brodifacoum. Brodifacoum is also an anticoagulant, but it kills more rapidly than its predecessors, which may require several ingestions of bait rather than a single ingestion; it is also effective against rats and mice, which are resistant to warfarin. The antidote remains vitamin K_1.

Chemicals that cause convulsions and death have also been developed as rodenticides. (See table 1.) They are organic—for example, crimidine, which is a synthetic chlorinated pyrimidine, and strychnine, which is a natural toxin present in seeds of *nux vomica* (from the east Indian tree *Strychnos nux-vomica*)—as well as inorganic chemicals. (See table 1.) All are harmful to humans and other mammals. Treatment for crimidine and strychnine poisoning in humans involves the administration of charcoal, which will absorb the chemicals.

Plant Growth Regulators

The capacity to control the growth of plants and their architecture has many applications in agriculture, horticulture, and recreational facilities that depend on turf, for example, sports stadiums, golf courses, and playgrounds. The crop protection industry has harnessed the inherent capacity of plants to control rooting, fruiting, flowering, branching, and coloring. The identification of hormones that are responsible for these processes and the determination of their chemical structure have facilitated the production of hormone sprays that control plant growth. These sprays include gibberellic acid, which stimulates growth through cell elongation, promotes fruit and seed production, and arrests leaf aging. (See table 1.) Applications of gibberellins can thus control plant height to maintain it at a convenient level for harvest as well as control the timing of flowering and fruiting in relation to weather conditions and pest life cycles. Applications are mainly in fruit crops. Ethylene is a gaseous hormone and is associated with fruit ripening. Its production can be genetically manipulated to delay ripening so that fruits such as tomatoes can develop flavor while still on the vine but retain firmness for marketing. Indeed, the so-called flavorsaver tomato is one of the first genetically modified crops to reach the marketplace. Several synthetic compounds have also been developed to regulate plant growth. They include dikegulac, which is absorbed by leaves; it encourages flower bud formation and the side branching of many ornamental plants—for example, fuchsia and azalea—rather than apical (at the apex or top) growth. Paclobutrazol, a triazole (a compound with a ring structure comprising two carbon atoms and three nitrogen atoms), causes stunting, mainly in fruit trees, without damaging fruit production. (See table 1.) This makes harvesting easier than in nontreated orchards. It is also used to encourage tillering in rice (tillers are intertwining roots that give a plant a firm anchor in the soil) and to retard growth in turf. The latter use reduces the need for frequent cutting and is thus a cost saver. No plant growth regulators are known to cause environmental damage.

A. M. Mannion

See also Agribusiness; Agriculture

Further Reading

Alford, D. V. (Ed.). (2000). *Pest and disease management handbook*. Oxford, UK: Blackwell Science.

Basra, A. S. (Ed.). (2000). *Plant growth regulators in agriculture and horticulture: Their role and commercial uses*. New York: Food Products Press.

CABI (CAB International). (2001). *Crop protection compendium*. Wallingford, UK: CAB International.

Cobb, A. H., & Kirkwood, R. C. (Eds.). (2000). *Herbicides and their mechanisms of action*. Boca Raton, FL: CRC Press.

Copping, L. G. (Ed.). (2001). *The biopesticide manual* (2nd ed.). Farnham, UK: British Crop Protection Council.

Monaco, T. J., Weller, S. C., & Ashton, F. M. (Eds.). (2002). *Weed science: Principles and practices.* New York: John Wiley and Sons.

Phelps, W., Winton, K., & Effland, W. R. (Eds.). (2002). *Pesticide environmental fate: Bridging the gap between laboratory and field studies.* Washington, DC: American Chemical Society.

Tomlin, C. D. S. (Ed.). (2000). *The pesticide manual: A world compendium* (12th ed.). Farnham, UK: British Crop Protection Council.

Whitford, F. (Ed.). (2002). *The complete book of pesticide management: Science, regulation, stewardship, and communication.* New York: Wiley-Interscience.

Philippines

(2000 est. pop. 81 million)

The Philippines is an archipelago of 7,107 tropical islands scattered across 1.3 million square kilometers between the South China Sea and the Philippine Sea. Only about 1,000 of the islands are populated; 462 islands are 2.6 square kilometers or larger; and 11 islands contain 94 percent of the country's total landmass. The islands are exposed to more than twenty typhoons per season and even a tidal wave or two per year. The terrain of most of the islands is for the most part steep, and the monsoon rains make them naturally prone to soil erosion. Even the most environmentally sound techniques, appropriate know-how, and technology rarely prevent substantial soil erosion.

After the United States seized the islands from Spain in 1898, Americans encouraged the rapid development of sugarcane and other cash crops. To meet demand for sugar as well as for tobacco, pineapples, hemp, and copra and other coconut products, peasants on the larger islands such as Cebu moved into the hills and cleared the forests, triggering massive soil erosion. By 1950 the pace of soil erosion had begun to slow on the island of Cebu in part because little soil was left. In the 1970s the introduction of contour plowing on the slopes and agroforestry (land management for the simultaneous production of food, crops, and trees) helped to slow, but not curtail, erosion.

The International Rice Research Institute (IRRI) was established in 1960 to develop varieties of high-yield rice. The IRRI promoted monoculture, or the produc-

tion of a single crop, and turned the Philippines into a rice-exporting nation. The capital generated from exports, in turn, was used for industrialization. But the pest-resistant crops that the IRRI introduced eventually proved vulnerable to infestation. This forced farmers to use heavier and heavier doses of pesticides. Often the pesticides would end up in the water supplies and make their way into the human food chain. Yet, with all of this technological innovation, the Philippines still has among the lowest crop yields in Asia and produces only about 25 percent of the rice achieved per unit of land in Japan.

The Japanese demand for timber in the 1950s and 1960s accelerated exports of hardwoods from the Philippines. In 1960, 60 percent of the country was forested. By the late 1970s the Philippines had nearly exhausted its supply of marketable timber and even developed an acute shortage of timber for domestic use. Attempts at reforestation in the 1980s failed largely due to a corrupt bureaucracy. In 2000 only 10 percent of the land remained covered by forests.

Between 1918 and 2000 the Philippines eliminated 71 percent of its mangroves, which are coastal trees valued for their tannic acid and wood and vital to marine and terrestrial wildlife. After 1980 high global demand for shrimp prompted the further removal of mangrove forests for shrimp farms, which harmed the ecosystem and disrupted the local communities dependent upon mangroves. Mismanagement and disease led to a drop in the number of farms in the late 1990s. With a greater understanding of the ecological importance of mangrove forests, the government and some international organizations have begun rehabilitation efforts but with limited success because of the amount of corruption and indifference they face. Much of that can be said about the government's overall handling of the environment as well.

James G. Lewis

Further Reading

Dolan, R. E. (1993). *Philippines: A country study.* Washington, DC: Federal Research Division, Library of Congress.

McNeill, J. R. (2000). *Something new under the sun: An environmental history of the twentieth-century world.* New York: W. W. Norton.

Steinberg, D. J. (2000). *The Philippines: A singular and a plural place* (4th ed.). Boulder, CO: Westview Press.

Philosophy *See* Environmental Philosophy

Photography *See* Nature Photography

Phylloxera

The phylloxera *(Viteus vitifolii, Phylloxera vastatrix)* is an insect that in its adult stage measures around 1 millimeter in length and has a whitish or yellowish color. It has a complicated life cycle, with at least nineteen stages below ground and above ground. It infests the roots and leaves of grape plants, as in vineyards, causing the vine stock to die. Phylloxera was discovered by the American entomologist Asa Fitch in 1856, and it became clear that phylloxera originated on wild species of grapevine in North America.

Wine growing has been threatened since its beginning by crises caused by diseases and pests. The worst crisis was experienced by European wine growers as they battled mildew beginning in the 1850s. Mildew was carried over from America on ornamental vines and then appeared in many European countries. It was discovered that a few American vines were resistant to mildew. The result was the importation of such American vines, but these vines were infected with phylloxera. The first indications of phylloxera infestations in Europe were observed in southern France in 1864. Only twenty years later all wine-growing regions of France were infested. The importation of infected American vines caused devastations in nearly all wine-growing countries of the world. Phylloxera was first observed, for example, in Portugal in 1871, Austria in 1872, Switzerland in 1874, Germany in 1874, Spain in 1877, Italy in 1879, South Africa in 1886, Peru in 1888, New Zealand in 1890, and Lebanon in 1910. In the United States, California was affected around 1873. Many experiments were conducted to find a defense against phylloxera, such as the application of sterile sand or the flooding of vineyards by water. Another method tried was treatment with chemicals such as petroleum or carbon disulphide (CS_2). But only a few remaining insects are sufficient to establish a new and fast-growing colony of phylloxera, so these treatments were useless. Other steps taken included the intensive monitoring of vineyards, the control of the trade of

vines, and the exchange of information, which was regulated by an international phylloxera convention in 1878 and in 1881. In the early 1880s experts argued that the best solution was the grafting of vines onto American rootstocks, which are resistant to phylloxera. Subsequently, vineyards all over the world were replanted with grafter vines. In major wine-growing countries like France, this process came to an end in the 1920s. Some vineyards, especially in marginal locations and at the northern frontier of viticulture in Europe, were abandoned and replaced by orchards or woodland. Because the replanting required a lot of capital, a socioeconomic concentration took place: Many wine growers had to look for a new workplace. Especially in France this caused social tensions between the larger and smaller wine-growing estates. Thus the phylloxera crisis can be seen as one of the earliest global environmental crises, having enormous economic and social consequences in wine-growing countries.

Andreas Dix

Further Reading

Garrier, G. (1989). *Le Phylloxéra. Une guerre de trente ans 1870–1900* [The phylloxera : A thirty years' war 1870–1900]. Paris: Albin Michel.

Ordish, G. (1987). *The great wine blight* (2nd ed.). London: Sidwick & Jackson.

Pouget, R. (1990). *Histoire de la lutte contre le Phylloxéra de la vigne en France (1868–1895)* [History of the fight against phylloxera of the grapevine in France]. Paris: Institut National de la Recherche Agronomique.

Unwin, T. (1996). *Wine and the vine: An historical geography of viticulture and the wine trade* (2nd ed.). New York: Routledge.

Pig

Pigs, which are also called swine or hogs, were probably the earliest domesticated animals, following the dogs. Bones from domesticated pigs have been found in a 10,000-year-old archaeological site in southeastern Turkey, from a settlement of people who were otherwise still depending on gathering clams and wild plants and hunting wild sheep and deer. Pigs seem to have been domesticated from the wild boar, *Sus scrofa*, in more than one location from Europe to Southeast

Asia. Domesticated pigs may be identified by differences in the skull and teeth from those of wild boars. Escaped domesticated pigs readily become feral and the feral populations may again interbreed with domesticated animals, resulting in hybrids. In some areas, such as eastern Europe and New Guinea, people have long hunted wild boars as well as kept domesticated pigs.

Pigs are omnivorous. In the wild, they root in moist soil, foraging for fungi, leaves, roots, acorns, fruits, earthworms, insect larvae, frogs, mice, and other small animals. Domesticated and living in traditional villages or impoverished urban neighborhoods, they became excellent scavengers, feeding on vegetable peels, garbage, and human feces. By doing this they contributed to controlling hookworm and other diseases, producing manure that could be used in agriculture without the danger of spreading disease by fertilizing crops directly with human wastes. In the highlands of Papua New Guinea, pigs were fed on the surplus and wastes of sweet potato gardens, converting this into fat and protein that were otherwise scarce in the human diet. New Guinea pigs were consumed in ritual sacrifices that may have served to regulate environmental relationships among pigs, people, and crops, according to the anthropologist Roy Rappaport.

Pigs prefer moist conditions like the natural habitat of their wild ancestors—the oak forests of Europe and the tropical forests and mangroves of Asia. They have little body hair to protect them from sun and they cannot sweat to cool off. They wallow in water or mud to keep cool. For these reasons, and also because of their temperament and diet, they are not suited to herding with sheep, goats, and cattle.

Although they were first domesticated in the Middle East and were once important throughout the area, pigs fell out of favor and came to be taboo as a source of food in the region, especially among Jews and Muslims. Anthropologists and others seeking to understand the reasons for the emergence of these prohibitions have frequently used ecological explanations. As agriculture developed and people drained swampy areas such as the Nile Delta and cleared the forests, there was less habitat for pigs to forage for their own food. If they had to be hand fed, they would be competing with people for food, as their digestive systems are similar to those of humans. They are not cud-chewing animals, and cannot digest cellulose in grasses or shrubs, so they were not readily incorporated into nomadic pastoralism.

High-density industrial hog farming has almost entirely replaced the hand rearing of a few pigs as a sideline on family farms in the United States. These huge operations cause significant environmental problems. Lagoons containing hog wastes sometimes leak, contaminating water sources. Volatilized ammonia, hydrogen sulfide, and other gases pollute the air, causing health problems for neighbors. Antibiotics fed to the pigs may also lead to the evolution and spread of antibiotic resistance in other populations of bacteria. These environmental problems are in addition to those caused by the large-scale industrial agriculture that produces animal feed.

Pigs produce large litters at short intervals and grow rapidly, making them extraordinarily effective in providing a high return of meat for the investment in feeding them, compared to other animals raised for meat. Pork provides about one quarter of the meat eaten in the United States and a much larger proportion in China and northern and eastern Europe. Therefore domesticated pigs are an important part of the ecology of these regions.

Patricia K. Townsend

Further Reading

Harris, M. (1985). *Good to eat: Riddles of food and culture*. New York: Simon and Schuster.

Nelson, S. M. (Ed.). (1998). *Ancestors for the pigs: Pigs in prehistory*. MASCA Research Papers in Science and Archaeology, Vol. 15. Philadelphia: University of Pennsylvania Museum of Archaeology and Anthropology.

Rappaport, R. A. (1968). *Pigs for the ancestors: Ritual in the ecology of a New Guinea people*. New Haven: Yale University Press.

Thu, K. M., & Durrenberger, E. P. (Eds.). (1998). *Pigs, profits, and rural communities*. Albany: State University of New York Press.

Pinchot, Gifford
(1865–1946)
First professional U.S. forester

Gifford Pinchot was born in Simsbury, Connecticut, and graduated from Yale University in 1889, intent on becoming a forester at a time when there were no American forests under management and no forestry

> **Worldwide practice of Conservation and the fair and continued access by all nations to the resources they need are the two indispensable foundations of continuous plenty and of permanent peace.**
>
> **Gifford Pinchot**

schools in North America. After training in France and Germany for a year, he returned home hoping to introduce forestry methods and influence federal forestry policies. With his first job as private forester for George Vanderbilt's Biltmore Estate in North Carolina, he initiated the first systematic forest management in America in 1892. His book, *Biltmore Forest* (1893), was the first of many publications on forestry and conservation. In 1896, Pinchot served on the National Forestry Commission and the following year as a special agent for the Department of the Interior, both positions that allowed him to help shape a national forest policy. Pinchot then accepted appointment as chief of the U.S. Agriculture's Division of Forestry in 1898, even though the Department of the Interior had control of the national forests. Pinchot held that post until 1910.

As chief forester, Pinchot immediately launched a government cooperative program to assist private forest owners, and began his efforts to transfer control of the forests over to his bureau. With President Theodore Roosevelt's support, this effort led to the creation of the U.S. Forest Service in 1905, and made Pinchot the most influential bureau chief before or since. He used his position and access to Roosevelt to lead a national conservation crusade. To help staff the Forest Service, the Pinchot family founded the Yale Forest School in 1900 by donating $150,000.

Pinchot was at the pinnacle of his power during the final two years of Roosevelt's administration. Pinchot organized the Governor's Conference on Conservation (1908), and served on the Commission on Country Life (1908) and the National Conservation Commission (1909). He founded the National Conservation Association (NCA) in 1909 to advance his national conservation agenda. He was dismissed as chief of the Forest Service in 1910 for a disagreement over conservation policy with Secretary of the Interior Richard A. Ballinger. The NCA then gave Pinchot a platform from which to continue his crusade after his dismissal.

After 1910, Pinchot remained active in forestry matters. He lobbied for federal regulation of private forestry in 1919, served two years as Pennsylvania's Com-

mission of Forestry (1920–1922), and worked to prevent transfer of the Forest Service from the Department of Agriculture to the Department of the Interior in the 1930s. After retirement from public office, he and his wife, Cornelia, worked toward making conservation the foundation of world peace.

James G. Lewis

Further Reading

McGeary, M. N. (1960). *Gifford Pinchot: Forester-politician.* Princeton, NJ: Princeton University Press.

Miller, C. (2001). *Gifford Pinchot and the making of modern environmentalism.* Washington, DC: Island Press.

Pinchot, G. (1947). *Breaking new ground.* New York: Harcourt, Brace, and Co.

Pinchot, G. (2001). *The conservation diaries of Gifford Pinchot* (H. K. Steen, Ed.). Durham, NC: Forest History Society.

Pinkett, H. T. (1970). *Gifford Pinchot: Private and public forester.* Chicago: University of Illinois Press.

Steen, H. K. (1976). *The U.S. Forest Service: A history.* Seattle: University of Washington Press.

Taylor, B. P. (1992). *Our limits transgressed: Environmental political thought in America.* Lawrence: University Press of Kansas.

Plato

(c. 428–348 BCE)
Greek philosopher

Opinion about the Greek philosopher Plato's role in the development of Western environmental thought is strongly divided. For some critics his work offers an organic view of nature that respects and celebrates the Earth as a divine, ensouled being (a deity with a soul). For other critics Plato leads development in the dominant tradition of a concept of human identity that is alienated from the body, the animal, and the feminine, identifying the human essence as "a celestial and not a terrestrial plant" (*Timaeus* 48, 90). The implications of this divided opinion are extensive. If, as the latter critics urge, "the essential ingredients of an alienated [human] identity are already present in a major way and as major themes in pre-Enlightenment thought" (Plumwood 1993, 77), the main problem of the origins of the dominant culture's ecological insensitivity and neglect of nature cannot be located in the transition to science and modernity, as so many claim.

Indisputably, Platonic philosophy affirms an extreme hierarchical dualism (an order strongly marked by ranking in terms of perceived superiority) and separation between a higher, imperishable sphere of reason or logos (designated as Being) and a lower, perishable sphere of alterity (designated as Becoming). The hyperseparation (an extreme form of division or separation) of these two orders of being corresponds to strong class and gender divisions between their respective representatives in Greek society: the lower sphere of matter, the body, the "world of changes" (the world of coming into being and passing away of the temporal and biological world) being associated with the woman, the slave, and the animal, the higher sphere being associated with the ideal realm of reason and of elite males. In every sphere of life there is a corresponding division, the higher form always governing the lower. The timeless, abstract, and male-associated world of the Forms (the sphere of reason or logos) must rule irrational and corrupting female matter. The same applies to the higher and lower aspects of love, beauty, knowledge, art, education, ontology (the theory of what is or what exists), causation, human selfhood, art, and music that the Platonic dialogues discuss. Born in 427 BCE to an upper class Athenian family, the Greek philosopher Plato is famous for his philosophical dialogues, including the *Phaedo*, the *Republic*, the *Symposium*, and the *Timaeus*. The dialogues take the dramatic form of conversation on philosophical themes between Plato's philosophical master Socrates and various other dramatic characters representing unreflective or opposing views.

There are two main issues regarding the significance of this schism for environmental thought. The first issue is whether Plato's later philosophy reconciles the two orders of being making a "return journey" in which the lower sphere is ultimately rehabilitated by its relationship to the higher. For Plato's critics this relationship remains basically limited and instrumental and cannot rescue Plato's consistent denigration of

the condition of particularized embodiment in the terrestrial order. The mathematical and other abstract qualities of the sensible world partake of divinity, and ephemeral natural items themselves do so only in a secondary, indirect, and inferior way, or are conceived as downright corrupting.

The second issue is that much turns on the meaning of the term *nature*. The concept of nature is complex and does not correspond in any simple way to the categories of Plato's thought. "Nature" in one or other of its many senses can be found on both sides of this dualism. Plato's work reveals as many as nine senses of "nature," treated as "Other" or lower in all but one of these senses, that of intelligible celestial and lawlike nature. Plato systematically devalues matter and most other candidates for a concept of nature: the sensible world, the "world of changes," physical embodiment, nonhuman biological nature, and the sphere of necessity. Female-coded chaos, the unordered matter that Plato describes in the *Timaeus* (one of Plato's last and most influential dialogues, and perhaps the most relevant to his ecological philosophy, discusses Plato's conception of human identity) as "the mother and receptacle of visible and sensible things" (Plato, *Timaeu 18*, 51), is an inferior element, contaminating its contrast of cosmos, form, or rational order.

Supporters of Plato emphasize his affirmation of nature in the sense of cosmos, the universe of rational laws. But this must be asked: Which concept of nature matches contemporary environmental concern? The perfectly ordered and mathematically expressible realm of eternal laws and celestial revolutions is not the kind of "nature" able to suffer environmental degradation. Plato's reverence for cosmos does not mean that his philosophy was respectful of nature in senses relevant to contemporary environmental problems. It is primarily material and biological nature, the realm of "coming to be and passing away" (a phrase used often in the dialogues) that is subject to contemporary environmental degradation and contest. Plato's persistent and emphatic devaluation of material and sensible nature, nonhuman animals, and human embodiment must weigh heavily in any assessment of the significance of his philosophy for Western environmental thought.

Val Plumwood

Further Reading

Adam, J. (1911). *The vitality of Platonism*. Cambridge, UK: Cambridge University Press.

Collingwood, R. G. (1945). *The idea of nature*. Oxford, UK: Clarendon Press.

Hughes, J. D. (1982). Gaia: An ancient view of our planet. *Environmental Review, 6*(2).

Lee, D. (Ed.). (1965). *Plato: Timaeus and Critias*. New York: Penguin Books.

Mahoney, T. (1997). Platonic ecology: Response to Plumwood's critique of Plato. *Ethics and the Environment, 2*(1), 25–42.

Plumwood, V. (1993). *Feminism and the mastery of nature*. London: Routledge.

Plumwood, V. (1997). Prospecting for ecological gold among the Platonic forms. *Ethics and the Environment, 2*(2), 149–168.

Vlastos, G. (1973). *Platonic studies*. Princeton, NJ: Princeton University Press.

Pleistocene Overkill

Animal life during the Pleistocene epoch or Ice Age (1.9 million to 8000 BCE) was rich beyond measure, but massive mammalian extinctions at its close changed this forever. Mammoths, mastodons (an extinct genus of elephant), horses, camelops (an extinct genus of large camels), ground sloths, various bison species, saber-tooth cats, and seventy other genera disappeared from North and South America. In Eurasia woolly mammoths, woolly rhinoceros, and Irish elk became extinct. Africa lost 15 to 20 percent of its large mammals.

Species extinctions have occurred throughout geological history, but Pleistocene extinctions are unusual: (1) They occurred worldwide in a brief period between 10,000 and 6000 BCE, (2) the ecological niches of most extinct species remained unclaimed by new forms of animals, (3) more large species (megafauna) than smaller ones became extinct, and (4) they coincided with the dispersal of anatomically modern humans over the Earth.

Debate persists between scientists who say that these extinctions were due to climatic and environmental change and those who say that such extinctions were due to the interaction of humans and environment. Terminal Pleistocene climate change was rapid. Glacial expansion terminated abruptly about 10,000 BCE, and one thousand years of warmer, moister climate followed. About 9000 BCE glacial conditions abruptly returned for another thousand years. These rapid climate shifts must have had a severe impact on plant and animal life. However, ice remissions and climatic changes occurred many times during the Pleistocene without triggering waves of extinctions. Further, some animals such as the horse became extinct in North America only to be reintroduced in historic times. If the post-Pleistocene environment of North America was fatal to the horse, why do wild descendants of Spanish mustangs roam the western United States today? Climatic explanations are not altogether satisfactory.

Hunting by humans on a grand scale ("anthropogenic overkill") is an alternative explanation, at least in North America. There, archaeologists have found bones of extinct megafauna associated with unique stone projectile points of the Paleo-Indian tradition. Paleo-Indians appeared abruptly in North America between 9500 and 9000 BCE; megafauna disappeared there between 10,000 and 6000 BCE. The correlation is striking. If Paleo-Indians were the first people to arrive in the New World, they found a hunter's paradise. Never hunted by humans, animals there lacked behavioral means of dealing with two-legged predators. As growing Paleo-Indian populations expanded across the continent, their profligate hunting extinguished megafauna along an ever-widening front. Computer models suggest that descendants of a mere one hundred people entering Alaska at 9500 BCE could have destroyed 3.3 million New World mammoths in five hundred years!

Computer simulation aside, archaeological evidence of overkill by Paleo-Indians is strong. For example, at the Olson-Chubbuck Paleo-Indian bison kill site in Colorado, a buried arroyo contains the bones of two hundred extinct bison. Paleo-Indians apparently stampeded them into the arroyo and butchered animals only near the top of the pile. Animals out of reach at the bottom of the arroyo were left to rot. This population contained adult, immature, and juvenile animals of both sexes. Wasteful hunting, practiced in a time of changing climate, may have proven fatal to other species as well. By the time Paleo-Indian peoples reached the tip of South America around 7000 BCE, the megafauna were gone.

D. Bruce Dickson

Further Reading

Alroy, J. (2001). A multispecies overkill simulation of the end-Pleistocene megafaunal mass extinction. *Science, 292,* 1893–1896.

Grayson, D. K. (1984). Explaining Pleistocene extinctions: Thoughts on the structure of a debate. In P. S. Martin & R. G. Klein (Eds.), *Quaternary extinctions* (pp. 807–823). Tucson: University of Arizona Press.

Grayson, D. K. (1987). An analysis of the chronology of late Pleistocene mammalian extinctions in North America. *Quaternary Research, 28*(2), 281–289.

Klein, R. G. (1984). Mammalian extinctions and Stone Age people in Africa. In P. S. Martin & R. G. Klein (Eds.), *Quaternary extinctions* (pp. 553–573). Tucson: University of Arizona Press.

Martin, P. S. (1984). Prehistoric overkill: The global model. In P. S. Martin & R. G. Klein (Eds.), *Quaternary extinctions* (pp. 354–403). Tucson: University of Arizona Press.

Martin, P. S., Thompson, R. S., & Long, A. (1985). Shasta ground sloth extinctions: A test of the Blitzkrieg model. In J. I. Mead & D. J. Meltzer (Eds.), *Environments and extinctions: Man in late glacial North America* (pp. 5–14). Orono: Center for the Study of Early Man, University of Maine at Orono.

Martin, P. S., & Wright, H. E. (Eds.). (1967). *Pleistocene extinctions: The search for a cause.* New Haven, CT: Yale University Press.

Meltzer, D. J., & Mead, J. I. (1985). Dating late Pleistocene extinctions: Theoretical issues, analytical bias, and substantive results. In J. I. Mead & D. J. Meltzer (Eds.). *Environments and extinctions: Man in late glacial North America* (pp. 145–173). Orono: Center for the Study of Early Man, University of Maine at Orono.

Mosimann, J. E., & Martin, P. S. (1975). Simulating overkill by Paleo-Indians. *American Scientist, 63*(3), 304–313.

Wheat, J. B. (1972). *The Olsen-Chubbuck site: A Paleo-Indian bison kill* (Society for American Archaeology Memoir No. 26). Washington, DC: Society for American Archaeology.

Whittington, S. I., & Dyke, B. (1989). Simulating overkill: Experiments with the Mosimann and Martin model. In P. S. Martin & R. G. Klein (Eds.), *Quaternary extinctions* (pp. 451–465). Tucson: University of Arizona Press.

Poland

(2000 est. pop. 39 million)

When Communism fell, Poland was among Europe's most environmentally damaged countries. In 1985, sulfur dioxide emissions totaled 116 kg per capita (compared to 301 in East Germany—GDR, but only 33 in France), while dust emissions totaled 48.0 kg per capita (compared to 140.7 in GDR, but only 3.5 in France). Poland was the third worst in Europe in sulfur deposition behind GDR and Czechoslovakia, with annual deposition of 4.55 metric tons per square km.

Poland does better in vehicular emissions and agriculture-related environmental problems. A high percentage of small farms remained private under Communism—76 percent of cultivated land as of 1985. These farms maintained mixed land use without the monocultures, intensive mechanization, or intensive chemical fertilizer and pesticide use that degraded the soil and groundwater in other Communist countries. Soil erosion due to a high proportion of cultivated land and under 29 percent forest cover was, however, a problem.

Distribution and Hot Spots

Much of Poland's pollution stems from the early development of mining and heavy industry. Industry was initially concentrated in Silesia and Upper Silesia, regions of Poland in Prussia up to 1871 and later part of Germany. In Katowice, Gliwice, and Ruda Śląska in Upper Silesia, the mining of bituminous coal, iron ore, and zinc starting in the mid eighteenth century, led to the development of iron and steel milling a century later. By World War II, while still under German sovereignty, Upper Silesian industry had diversified, and industry had spread between Wrocław and the Sudeten Mountains. Besides these, only Łódź and Warsaw (Russian possessions until the end of World War I) had become minor centers of environmentally harmful industry.

World War II did not particularly damage Silesian industry. The old industries of Upper and Central Silesia developed further, spreading to new locations elsewhere in Poland. These include the large Nowa Huta iron and steel mill near Kraków, iron works and chemical production in Stalowa Wola and Tarnobrzeg along the upper Vistula River, and copper mining and processing in Lower Silesia.

In Poland and other Communist countries industrialization meant heavy industry, with an emphasis on increasing output. Under central planning inefficiency was rife, especially in terms of energy use: in 1987–1988 primary energy consumption was 0.73 kg per dollar of GDP in Poland compared to 0.35 kg for the European Community (EC). Coal supplied 79 percent of Poland's energy needs at the time, compared to 28 percent in Hungary and 25 percent in the EC; high coal consumption also worsened air pollution.

Concentration of heavy industry and thermoelectric power production meant ecological hazards were concentrated in southern Poland. Together with southern GDR and northern Czechoslovakia, this formed a zone of severe environmental degradation. Southern Poland included several pollution "hot spots." Lower Silesia was affected by copper mining and processing, and the Sudeten Mountain forelands by chemical production, thermoelectric power production, and windborn pollution from GDR and Czechoslovakia. The Upper Silesian and Kraców regions were affected by bituminous coal, zinc, and tin mining, iron and steel milling, and chemical production, and the upper Vistula Valley by sulfur production and steel milling. These locations suffered from severe air pollution, pollution-damaged forests, and surface and groundwater contamination. The coal-mining region of Upper Silesia covered 6,650 square km and produced all Poland's bituminous coal, half its steel, and one-third of its coke. Industrial and mining waste and large-scale land subsidence (by as much as 35 m) are severe problems here.

The chemical industry was responsible for most pollution in other areas, including the lower Vistula Valley, the Gdansk and Szczecin regions, and Warsaw. Coal-fired thermoelectric power production around Belchatów and in the upper Warta Valley was another major polluter.

The regions of Podlasia, much of Mazovia, the Masurian Lakeland, and Pomerania were unspoiled compared to elsewhere in the Communist bloc and even to western Europe. In all, about 9 percent of Poland was relatively unspoiled, while another 19 percent was less polluted.

Poland's major rivers originate in the south. They were heavily polluted, and were responsible for the poor water quality along Poland's 528-km Baltic coastline. The Oder River entered Poland from Czechoslovakia already heavily polluted, to be further contaminated in Poland's Upper Silesia. The Vistula River drains part of Upper Silesia, but received additional pollution from Kraców, the Tarnobrzeg-Stalowa Wola Industrial Region, and Warsaw and Plock. The Warta, the Oder's largest tributary, was heavily polluted from its source in Upper Silesia; the Bug, the Vistula's largest tributary, entered Poland from Ukraine already heavily polluted.

Changes in the 1990s

Since Communism fell in 1989, abandoning central planning has resulted in "passive sanitation": closing, scaling-back, and converting heavily polluting industries has reduced energy consumption. There have been active measures too, and new environmental policy (1991) meant that 1.0–1.6 percent of GDP was invested in environmental remediation from 1993 to 1997. These measures together cut sulfur dioxide emissions by 51 percent (1989 to 1998), atmospheric emissions of lead, cadmium, and mercury by 46, 40, and 11 percent, respectively (1990 to 1998), and carbon dioxide emissions by 31 percent (1989 to 1998). The proportion of forest that is damaged declined from 55 percent in 1994 to 37 percent in 1997. Though conditions also improved in former hot spots in southern Poland, these are still among the most polluted places in central Europe. This is largely because heavily polluting bituminous coal still supplies 66.6 percent of primary energy needs (1998), and problems from underground mining still persist in Upper Silesia. Additional problems the industrial south shares with urban areas elsewhere in Poland include sewage treatment, solid waste disposal, and air pollution from transport.

As of 1999, sewage treatment facilities served only 47 percent of the population, compared to 73 percent in the EU. Two-thirds of all major enterprises and 150 urban areas had no sewage treatment plants, although some 300 were being constructed annually. Consequently, only 4.8 percent of rivers were in Class I condition (Polish standard) and a third were excessively polluted. Three-fifths of Poland's approximately 500 lakes are still seriously contaminated with sewage and industrial effluent.

A Polish farmer riding his horse-drawn cart near Kraców in 1985. COURTESY KAREN CHRISTENSEN.

Waste disposal is a growing problem: municipal waste increased from 368 kg per capita in 1992 to 776 kg in 1997, and is mostly deposited, unseparated, in landfills. Landfills have tripled in area since 1975, and their technical standards are generally unsatisfactory. Industrial and mining waste (3.5 percent of which is hazardous) amounted to 94 tons per million dollars of GDP, compared to 52 tons in the EU. The Waste Act of 1997 provides a regulatory framework to improve this situation.

Private car ownership has risen from 14 per 100 inhabitants in 1990 to 26 in 2000, and transport now contributes one-third of carbon dioxide, carbon monoxide, hydrocarbon, and lead emissions. Erosion is still serious in rural areas, and most likely exacerbated the 1997 floods that affected over 4,000 square km in the Oder and Vistula watersheds.

Current Environmental Policy

A 1991 act set policy concerning the establishment of a system of national parks, nature reserves, and protected areas linked by biological corridors. In addition to the seventeen existing ones, in 1995 and 1996 five new national parks were established; national parks now total 3,054 square km, or 0.97 percent of Poland. During territorial restructuring in 1999, several environmental responsibilities were devolved to the regional and local levels; further decentralization is expected.

Environmental policy is being integrated with that of the OECD and EU countries; however, application of EU environment standards was limited as of 2003. Enforcement is weak with regard to air pollution, waste treatment, and water purification due to a lack of monitoring. Poland has asked the EU for partial transitional status up to 2015 in the areas of sewage, waste, and hazardous waste.

Poor implementation of environmental policy partly stems from the weakness of the environmental movement. Major political parties pay scant attention to the environment, since economic issues are still the focus. It falls to external pressure, mainly from the EU, and to international financial aid to move things forward (4 percent of Polish investment in environmental protection in the 1990s came from EU funds). In January 2000, the ISPA (Infrastructure Strategy for the Preparation of Accession) Management Committee estimated that adopting EU environmental standards would cost Poland EUR 22,100–42,800 million. This far exceeds recent spending: In 1996 and 1997 Poland's investment in environmental measures amounted to just EUR 2,266.4 and 2,059.2 million, respectively.

Peter Jordan

Further Reading

Austrian Institute of East and Southeast European Studies (Ed.). (1996). *Atlas of Eastern and Southeastern Europe.* Vienna, Austria: Gebr. Borntraeger.

Breu, J. (Ed.). (1970–1989). *Atlas of the Danubian countries.* Vienna, Austria: Deuticke.

Carter, F. W., & Kantowicz, E. (2002). Poland. In F. W. Carter & D. Turnock (Eds.), *Environmental problems of East Central Europe* (2nd ed.). New York: Routledge.

Clarke, J., & Cole, D. H. (1998). *Environmental protection in transition: Economic, legal and socio-political perspectives on Poland.* Aldershot, UK: Ashgate.

European Parliament, General Directorate of Research. (1991). *Selected examples from the area of energy and research.* Brussels, Strasbourg: General Directorate for Research.

Ministry of Environmental Protection, Natural Resources and Forestry. (1991). *National environmental policy of Poland.* Warsaw, Poland: Author.

OECD. (1994). *Environmental performance review of Poland.* Paris: Author.

Trafas, K. (1991). Air Pollution in Southern Poland. In Austrian Institute of East and Southeast European Studies (Ed.), *Atlas of Eastern and Southeastern Europe* (No. 1.1-PL1). Vienna, Austria: Gebr. Borntraeger.

United Nations (Ed.). (1987). *Environment statistics in Europe and North America: An experimental compendium.* New York: United Nations.

Warner, J. (1999). Poland: The environment in transition. *Geographical Journal, 165*(2), 209–221.

Welfens, P. (Ed.). (1991). *Economic aspects of German unification.* New York: Springer.

Politics *See* Environmental Politics

Pollution *See* Air Pollution

Population, Human

The relationship between human population and environment, contrary to popular belief, is anything but simple. In the past half-century, as concern over environmental degradation mounted, popular discussion more often than not emphasized the simple, appealing equation: More population equals more environmental degradation. Although this is true in many circumstances, it is by no means invariably so. Scholars have expended great energy trying to tease out the relationship, but with limited success. The question, in both popular and scholarly debate, has been for fifty years and remains to this day a highly political one, with deeply felt principles involved.

History of Human Population

Efforts to count the number of people in a given territory began in ancient times. The first effort to take a census for an entire polity (Tuscany) was made in 1427. Reasonably reliable censuses date from about 1800 and for most of the world from about 1950. So, reconstructing the history of the entire human population inevitably involves a hefty amount of inference and educated guesswork. Opinions vary, although there is remarkable consensus on the general trajectory. (See table 1.)

Although it is unclear exactly when humans became humans, when they did there were few of them. Living as hunter-gatherers they were constantly on the move. Carrying multiple small children was a great burden, so early humans checked their fertility by prolonged breast-feeding (which reduces a woman's fertility) and probably checked population growth via infanticide and abandonment. In any case, population growth was extremely slow by today's standards, although it should be understood that today's standards are a bizarre anomaly: For most of human history pop-

The world population is increasingly urbanizing. This photo of the city of Maleka, Malaysia, in 2001 shows the mix of old and new buildings typical of many cities in the developing world. COURTESY MARY CORINNE LOWENSTEIN.

ulation growth in net terms was close to zero, and population declined almost as often as it grew.

With the shift to food production and more sedentary ways of life, the chief constraint on population growth, the difficulty of carrying around small children, eased. The origins of agriculture date to about ten thousand years ago, at which time there were 4 million (more cautiously, 2 to 20 million) people on the Earth. Where agriculture first took root, in southwestern Asia and the tropical lowlands of the Americas, population growth accelerated somewhat. Birthrates climbed, and although death rates eventually did as well, they did not keep pace. Death rates eventually climbed because agricultural societies acquired new diseases, most of them transfers from herd animals such as pigs, cattle, and camels, that quickly killed people, especially young children. Crowding helped spread such diseases rapidly and promoted others that flourished where human beings lived amid their own wastes.

Gradually agriculture spread throughout much of the suitable terrain on Earth, and most of the human population lived in agrarian societies in which villages formed the social nucleus. Irrigation, especially in Egypt, southern Asia, and East Asia, allowed more productive farming and still denser populations. By 3500 BCE cities began to emerge, first in Mesopotamia. The efficiency of agriculture is extremely variable, depending on soils, crops, tools, and other factors, but as a general rule it can support ten times the population density that hunting and gathering can. For this and other reasons agricultural societies spread fairly rap-

TABLE 1.
ESTIMATED GLOBAL
POPULATIONS (IN MILLIONS)

Date	Population
300,000 BCE	1
10,000 BCE	4
1000 BCE	50
1 CE	200
500 CE	200
1000 CE	270
1200 CE	380
1400 CE	370
1600 CE	550
1800 CE	920
1900 CE	1,625
2000 CE	6,000

Source: (Cohen 1995, appendix 2)

idly at the expense of the less populous communities of hunter-gatherers.

In agrarian societies, children from the age of about five could perform useful labor, such as tending chickens or weeding gardens. Without the requirement of constant migration, children were more an economic asset than a liability, and so, except in conditions of land scarcity (and even sometimes in such conditions), people tended to marry young and reproduce prolifically. Fertility (here presented in the form of the crude birthrate) reached levels of perhaps 50 per 1,000 per year (about four times as high as the current birthrate in the United States), although rates of 35–40 per 1,000 were probably more typical. Even so, reproductive exuberance barely kept up with the toll from disease and famine, which every now and then reached catastrophic levels, pruning back the population growth of happier years. This, in broad strokes, was the demographic regime of agrarian society, the majority experience of humankind from at least 3000 BCE until 1800 CE.

During that time population grew much faster than it had during preagricultural times, although still slowly in comparison to today's growth rates. And there were times when population declined. On local and regional scales, epidemics and famines produced such catastrophes fairly regularly, normally at least once or twice within every generation. On the global scale there were at least two great catastrophes, each of which probably brought global population decline (although the figures are not reliable enough to say with assurance). The first of these was the great pandemic of the fourteenth century known as the Black Death, probably a result of the spread of bubonic plague throughout most of Asia, Europe, northern Africa, and perhaps parts of sub-Saharan Africa. It reduced the population of Europe, Egypt, and southwestern Asia by perhaps one-quarter or one-third and on a global level by perhaps one-seventh or one-tenth. In Europe the population took 150 years to recover from the plague's ravages. The second great catastrophe came when the population of the Americas was exposed to Eurasian and African diseases in the wake of Christopher Columbus's voyages. Estimates of the population loss for the period from 1500 to 1650 range from 50 to 90 percent. Because there are no good data on the size of the pre-Columbian population in the Americas, it is impossible to know how large the global effect of this disaster may have been. It might have lowered total global population, although more likely, because there were far more people in Eurasia and Africa than in the Americas, the total effect repressed world population growth without forcing it below zero.

Accelerating Growth

During the eighteenth century human population embarked on its current spectacular expansion. In several parts of the world epidemics and famines started to recede, and death rates fell. The reasons behind this remain uncertain, although ecological adjustment among pathogens (agents of disease) and their human hosts was surely part of it, as were improvements in food supply and famine management. In some places birthrates also rose slightly. During the nineteenth century world population almost doubled, and then in the twentieth century it almost quadrupled as death rates tumbled. Better sanitation, vaccines, and antibiotics lowered the toll from disease, and much more productive agriculture increased the food supply sharply. In Europe by the 1890s families responded by consciously limiting the number of births, a reaction that occurred later but more quickly in most other parts of the world. When and where birthrates shrank, population growth slowed; when and where birthrates remained robust, as in much of Africa, Central America, and parts of southern and southwestern Asia, population growth spurted after 1950. Globally, the growth rate peaked around 1970 at perhaps 2.1 percent per year. In 2001 it had declined to 1.3 percent per year, or about 79 million additional people per year. Demographers now expect the world's population to reach 9 or 10 billion around 2050.

For most of history roughly three-fourths of humanity lived in Eurasia. That remains the case today, but the proportion who lived in the Americas grew sharply after 1750, and the proportion living in Africa leapt upward after 1950. (See table 2.)

Population Policy

People have voiced concern that humanity is too thick on the ground since at least 1600 BCE. Such concern, however, has been rare until recently. Political authorities, when they gave any consideration at all to population, generally took the view that the more people there were within their borders, the better. All the major religions favored population growth, too. This is not surprising: Until the last 250 years survival was so precarious that maximizing births was usually a sensible insurance policy against disaster. But in the mid- and late twentieth century a few governments began to see

TABLE 2.
REGIONAL POPULATIONS FROM 1750 TO 2000 (IN MILLIONS)

	1750	1800	1850	1900	1950	2000
Asia	480	602	749	937	1,386	3,766
Europe	140	187	266	401	576	728
Africa	95	90	95	120	206	840
N. America	1	6	26	81	167	319
South and Central America	11	19	33	63	162	531
Australia and Oceania	2	2	2	6	13	32

Source: McNeill (2000, 271).

matters differently. India and China, by far the two most populous countries, committed themselves to birth control, and in China's case to stern restrictions that between 1978 and 2000 kept the population 250 million lower than it would otherwise have been (it was 1.2 billion in 2000). Other countries in the twentieth century, especially in Europe, sought to increase their birthrates but to very little effect.

Population and Environment

At all times and places the relationship between population and environment is one of mutual interaction. Environmental conditions affect population's trajectory and population growth (or decline) affects the environment.

Historically, the environmental conditions that influenced population were climate, disease, and agriculture. Major climate shifts, such as the waxing and waning of ice ages, strongly affected human population by changing the proportion of the Earth that was habitable and by changing the biological productivity of the parts not covered with ice. The onset of the last Ice Age presumably reduced human population, and its end encouraged population growth. Since the end of the last Ice Age ten thousand years ago, climate change has played only a small role in determining human population size on the global level.

As noted, the human burden of disease became markedly heavier when and where people took up cultivation, especially settled cultivation, especially when domesticated animals were involved. In tropical lands, except at high altitudes, sustaining dense settled populations was difficult because so many more disease organisms flourished in the warmth. The emergence of cities also created lethal disease environments, mainly because people lived cheek by jowl, communicating infections daily, and because few cities adequately disposed of wastes. So, cities generally, perhaps invaria-

bly, were black holes for humanity, sustained only by recurrent migration from healthier, rural landscapes. This situation remained in force until the end of the nineteenth century and in many countries until the middle of the twentieth century. Eventually, mainly through scientific sanitation after 1880, cities became even healthier than rural areas, and one of the great historic constraints on population growth, the lethality of city life, was lifted.

Changes in agricultural conditions also helped to regulate human population by affecting the food supply. Irrigation agriculture, as noted, could support more people than could rainfall agriculture. But irrigation often generated salinization (the accumulation of salts, harmful to plant growth), which over centuries could spoil farmland, as in Mesopotamia, where environmental degradation probably played a role in episodes of depopulation around 1900 BCE, around 1375 BCE, and before 1250 CE. Over centuries, even over decades, soil erosion could also significantly lower the productivity of agricultural land, which, if not otherwise compensated for, could reduce population. Salinization and erosion could easily affect local and regional populations severely, although at the global level their impacts have always been negligible.

A more recent change in agricultural conditions, the Green Revolution, has had impacts at every scale. Since the 1950s agronomists (agricultural scientists dealing with field-crop production and soil management) have bred new strains of most of the major food crops of the world, making them responsive to heavy doses of fertilizer and timely doses of irrigation water, more resistant to crop diseases and pests, and more suited to machine harvesting. As a result, modern chemicalized agriculture doubled and quadrupled crop yields. The global effect as of 2000 was to increase the world's food supply by about one-third, an essential component of the contemporary surge in world population.

Population growth, or decline, also affects the environment. Just how much it does depends on many factors, including rates of growth, existing densities of population, resilience and stability of ecosystems, the technologies available, and just which aspect of the catch-all phrase *the environment* one chooses to measure. The amount of nuclear wastes around the world, for example, has had little to do with population levels or growth rates but everything to do with technology and politics. Conversely, urban sprawl has resulted directly from population growth (although other factors have been involved).

The circumstances under which population growth proved maximally disruptive to environments were probably those in which initial levels of population were either zero or very low, the growth rate vigorous, and the transformative technologies at hand powerful. The history of New Zealand provides an apt illustration. New Zealand was long isolated from outside influence and had no human population for millions of years—a sanctuary for species from the Cretaceous era. People first arrived around 1300 CE (perhaps as early as 1000), at first probably only a few. But the Maori—New Zealand's original settlers—found ample resources in seals, mollusks, and large flightless birds (moas), which they hunted. They burned the forest to make better forage for creatures they hunted and to make room for crops. In the course of a few centuries, they drove the moa and a few other species to extinction and reduced the forest cover of New Zealand by about one-third or one-half. Similar dramatic changes followed upon initial human settlement of other isolated islands such as Madagascar (c. 400 CE) and Iceland (c. 870 CE). Presumably the impacts of initial human settlement in the preagricultural past were less pronounced, although the occupation of Australia (about sixty thousand years ago) and the Americas (about fifteen thousand years ago) may have brought on—this is the majority view but by no means a consensus view—numerous extinctions of large and midsized mammals. Even without much technology beyond spears and fire, humans, when entering landscapes in which species had no prior experience of human ways, proved highly disruptive.

With more powerful technologies at hand, population growth could be even more disruptive. After 1769, and especially after 1840, New Zealand acquired another settler population, primarily from Great Britain. These settlers had metal tools, which the Maori had not had, grazing animals, and eventually steam engines and the entire panoply of industrial machines.

In the span of two centuries, New Zealand's population went from less than 100,000 to about 3 million, almost all of whom used modern technologies. New Zealand lost most of the rest of its forest cover and many more of its indigenous species (mostly birds), and most of the landscape (discounting inhospitable extremes) became pastureland. Population growth alone, of course, was not responsible for this transformation of New Zealand, although it was crucial. Also crucial was the existence of overseas markets for wool, mutton, and butter, on which New Zealand's pastoral economy rested.

Population growth has been least disruptive where heavy labor has been required to stabilize an environment. The best examples of this concern soil erosion. Farmers, when working on slopes, inevitably risk rapid soil erosion unless they can construct and maintain terraces. But that is extremely labor intensive. In the Machakos Hills district of Kenya, for example, early in the twentieth century farmers caused high erosion rates by tilling the soil. They did not have enough people to undertake the backbreaking labor of terrace construction. But by the 1960s population growth had changed that. Farmers built and maintained terraces, stabilizing their soils. A reduction in population density in terraced mountain environments can bring accelerated soil erosion because too few people remain to keep the terracing in place. This happened in the twentieth century in the mountain regions of southern Europe when birthrates fell and young people emigrated. The endless terraces of Java or southern China would be difficult to maintain without dense population.

Population decline destabilized other landscapes as well. In eastern Africa, for example, by the nineteenth century people had learned that to keep sleeping sickness at bay they had to burn off the bush (which reduced the habitat for the tsetse fly that carries sleeping sickness). Sleeping sickness killed cattle more easily than people; it was an economic as well as a health problem. But bush control required labor, and when lethal epidemics broke out at the end of the nineteenth century and the beginning of the twentieth, one result was to make it difficult for people to control the vegetation surrounding their villages. Thus a costly ecological change proceeded: more bush, more tsetse fly, more sleeping sickness. This example, like the terraces of southern Europe, is a case in which an environment, already modified by human action and in a more or less stable state, was disrupted by population decline.

These examples show that a simple formula (more people equals more environmental disruption) does not necessarily apply. Nonetheless, in most circumstances, population growth has brought accelerated environmental change and continues to do so. In the context of the last half-century, when human population growth reached its maximum rate, the role of population has probably been greater than in previous times (with the exception of local- and regional-scale examples such as New Zealand's initial settlement). Cropland has increased by one-third since 1950, a process mainly driven by population growth. The proportion of land occupied by roads and buildings has grown roughly in step with population and chiefly because of population. The transformation of habitats, including deforestation, the extension of cropland, pastureland, and developed land has put heightened pressure on many species lately, especially in tropical forests. This pressure, one of the signal environmental changes of modern history, has been driven in part by population growth, although it is difficult to specify how large that part might be.

Population growth also has been a factor in the increased pollution loads of modern history. In cases such as water pollution derived from human wastes, it has been a large factor indeed. But in other cases, such as the pollution of the stratospheric ozone layer by chlorofluorocarbons, population growth played only a little role, and technological change (the invention of chlorofluorocarbons) a much larger one. Thus, among types of pollution, as among environmental changes in general, the degree to which population growth can logically be held responsible varies tremendously from case to case.

In the future it is likely that population will decline in importance as a variable in shaping environmental change. This is partly because the extraordinary pulse of population growth of the past century, and especially the past half-century, will sooner or later come to an end. But this is also because technology looms ever larger as a mediator between people and their environments, and the pace of technological change seems unlikely to slow any time soon. If global population stabilizes after 2050, as many demographers suppose it will, population shifts locally and regionally will still exert pressures of one sort or another. And it remains possible that because there are already so many people on Earth the addition of another 2 or 3 billion will have a much stronger impact than the addition of the last 2 or 3 billion. That is, there may be

nonlinear effects with respect to the consequences of population growth, thresholds that, if surpassed, bring major changes. Observers have predicted catastrophic consequences from population growth for millennia but most consistently (and most plausibly) in the last forty years. It has not happened yet. If it does, it will happen within the next fifty years.

J. R. McNeill

See also Disease, Human

Further Reading

Bogin, B. (2001). *The growth of humanity*. New York: Wiley-Liss.

Caldwell, J., & Schindlmayer, T. (2002). Historical population estimates: Unraveling the consensus. *Population and Development Review, 28*(2), 183–204.

Cipolla, C. (1962). *The economic history of world population*. Harmondsworth, UK: Penguin.

Cohen, J. (1995). *How many people can the Earth support?* New York: Norton.

Demeny, P. (1990). Population. In B. L. Turner II, W. C. Clark, R. W. Kates. J. F. Richards, J. T. Matthews, & W. B. Meyer (Eds.), *The Earth as transformed by human action* (pp. 41–54). New York: Cambridge University Press.

Erickson, J. (1995). *The human volcano: Population growth as geologic force*. New York: Facts on File.

Lourdes Arizpe, M., Stone, P., & Major, D. C. (Eds.). (1994). *Population and environment: Rethinking the debate*. Boulder, CO: Westview.

Lutz, W., Prskawetz, A., & Sanderson, W. C. (Eds.). (2002). Population and environment: Methods of analysis. *Population and Development Review, 28*, 1–250.

Massim, L. B. (2001). *A concise history of world population*. Malden, MA: Blackwell.

Mazur, L. A. (Ed.). (1994). *Beyond the numbers: A reader on population, consumption, and the environment*. Washington, DC: Island Press.

Ts'ui-jung, L., Lee, J., Reher, D. S., Saito, O., & Feng, W. (Eds.). (2001). *Asian population history*. Oxford, UK: Oxford University Press.

Whitmore, T. M., Turner, B. L., Johnson, D. L., Kates, R. W., & Gottschang, T. R. (1990). Long-term population change. In B. L. Turner, W. C. Clark, R. W. Kates. J. F. Richards, J. T. Matthews, & W. B. Meyer (Eds.), *The Earth as transformed by human action* (pp. 25–40). New York: Cambridge University Press.

Potato

The potato *(Solanun tuberosum)* first figured in human history as the principal crop of people living in the cool, high plains of the Andes Mountains of South America. No exact date can be assigned to the domestication of the potato, but long before frozen, air-dried potatoes—which could be stored underground for years—fed the laborers who built the fortresses and roads of the Inca Empire, potatoes were a staple food from Ecuador in the North to coastal Chile in the South. As such, potatoes sustained one of the two major civilizations of the New World.

The Spanish conquest of the area (in 1532) meant that Spanish administrators of the viceroyalty (the office of the ruling representative of a sovereign) of Peru continued to rely on frozen, air-dried potatoes to feed the thousands of Indians they conscripted to work for them. Those assigned to work in the silver mines of Potosi (modern Bolivia) produced so much silver between 1545 and 1650, when the richest lodes began to run out, that they inflated prices and upset monetary regimes throughout the world—in China as well as in Europe, and everywhere in-between. Across the whole of Eurasia religious and political upheavals were exacerbated by the rapid inflation of traditional prices. Everywhere people were sure that wicked greed was responsible. Consequently, the price revolution provoked by the flood of Peruvian silver embittered Protestant-Catholic conflicts in Christian Europe, Sunni-Shi'a struggles among Muslims, and sectarian Buddhist uprisings in China. Without potatoes to feed the native miners, such unprecedented amounts of silver could not have been put on the market and thus raise prices so rapidly. This was the first time that potatoes played a hidden, world-transforming role in history.

However, it would not be the last time they did so. For when potatoes reached Europe and other parts of the Old World, they fit the older styles of agriculture in diverse and sometimes revolutionary ways. Best known is what happened in Ireland, but the greatest impact on world affairs occurred on the continent of Europe. Potatoes reached Europe initially when anonymous Spanish sailors, returning from the Pacific Coast of North America, carried a few potatoes ashore and planted them in local gardens in Spain. Most of Spain is too hot and dry for potatoes to flourish. Only in Basque country along the northern coast does enough rain fall in summer to assure a good crop. But potatoes were a cheap and nutritious food, and within a generation or so Basque fishermen, sailing to the Grand Banks near Newfoundland in North America, routinely fed themselves on the new food.

"Potatoes of Virginia"

From northern Spain potatoes spread to the Po River plain in Italy, where they were still a novelty in 1588 when botanists first took notice. In that year an Italian priest forwarded samples to French botanist Carolus Clusius in the Low Countries (Netherlands, Belgium, Luxembourg). However, before Clusius published information about the new plant in his *Rariorum plantarum historia* [History of rare plants] (Antwerp, 1601), an English botanist, John Gerard, printed a handsome woodcut in his *Herball: Or General Historie of Plantes* (London 1597), erroneously calling the new plant "potatoes of Virginia." Nonetheless, Gerard's misinformation points to a second introduction of the potato to Europe by an English navigator—perhaps Francis Drake, who, during his round-the-world voyage, went ashore at Valparaiso, Chile, in 1597 to reprovision his ship. Potatoes were undoubtedly the only food readily available there, but Drake's subsequent stop in Virginia resulted in the mistaken notion that the potato was picked up in the colony. In any case, Gerard's potato blossoms were purple; Clusius's were white, so they were genetically different.

The white-blossoming potatoes were the kind that spread initially within continental Europe and to the west coast of Ireland, where Basque fishermen were accustomed to coming ashore for rest and refreshment en route to and from the Grand Banks.

The new crop first became important in Ireland at the time of the conquest by English soldier and statesman Oliver Cromwell (1649–1652), when the Catholic Irish were banished to Connaught and the Protestant English took possession of the rest of the island. In crowded Connaught, the fact that an acre of potatoes could feed a family for a year if supplemented by the milk of a single cow made survival possible for the banished Irish. But because English laborers refused to accept a potato diet, the new landlords in the rest of Ireland found it less expensive to employ Irish on their estates than to find the bread needed to feed the English. Consequently, within less than a century in most of the country rural laborers came to be Irish Catholic and deeply alienated from their Protestant landlords. They subsisted by renting potato land annually and growing enough grass for a cow. Yet, because potatoes and milk constituted an adequate diet, the Catholic population grew so rapidly that work became hard to find after 1815, and wages remained barely enough to pay rising rents. Not surprisingly, hostility between the Catholic Irish and their Protestant oppressors mounted.

Potatoes played a quite different role on the continent. Starting in northern Italy, peasant farmers living along the so-called Spanish Road took to potatoes spontaneously. When in 1588 the Spanish Armada failed to drive Dutch and English sailors from the seas, Spanish soldiers had to sail to Italy and march overland to the main theater of war in the Low Countries. But marching soldiers had to eat along the way and could do so only by seizing grain from peasants' barns, leaving little or nothing behind. Peasants along the Spanish Road from northern Italy to the Low Countries quickly learned that planting potatoes in their gardens produced food that was safe from military marauders because potatoes, left hidden in the ground, can be dug as needed throughout the winter, permitting survival even after soldiers had taken all the grain.

For a long time landowners and urban dwellers paid little attention to the spread of potato gardens along the Spanish Road. They ate bread, and grain fields supplied the towns as before. Yet, even after the Dutch wars ended (1648), potatoes continued to spread among peasants in the Rhinelands and southern Germany—wherever the armies of French King Louis XIV (1643–1715) operated. Then, during the War of the Austrian Succession (1740–1748), Prussian King Frederick the Great noticed that even prolonged campaigning did not reduce Rhineland peasants to starvation, and he quickly discovered why. He decided that peasants in Prussia needed the same cushion against military requisitioning and ordered local Prussian administrators to find seed potatoes and show peasants how to grow them.

They obeyed with such effect that when the Seven Years' War (1756–1763) broke out and Prussia was invaded year after year by French, Austrian, and Russian armies, Frederick's peasant subjects had enough potatoes in their gardens to survive. That, in turn, allowed the Prussian state and army to survive, with fateful consequences for subsequent German history. Moreover, each of the invading armies became aware of how potatoes sustained Prussia's strength. Accordingly, when peace returned, agents of the French, Austrian, and Russian governments set out to propagate potatoes among their own peasants. Suddenly official policy accelerated the spread of potato cultivation

throughout the north European plain and simultaneously translated potatoes from a garden crop into a field crop.

Food Resources Multiply

This cultivation vastly multiplied the food resources of northern Europe. The calorie yield from an acre of potatoes was up to four times as great as that from rye, the only grain that did well east of the Elbe River. Moreover, by planting potatoes in fields that had to be fallowed to keep weeds from overwhelming the grain, and then hoeing the potatoes during the growing season to check the weeds, farmers made potatoes a field crop without reducing the output of grain at all. This required extra labor in summer, but potatoes could feed a larger rural labor force with plenty to spare. Population spurted upward, and when employment in mines and factories started to spread from Great Britain after 1815, surplus rural labor was available to sustain the Industrial Revolution. Without all the extra food, Europe's meteoric increase in wealth and power between 1815 and 1914 could not have occurred. This, then, was the second time that potatoes affected history worldwide, making western Europe exceptionally, if only temporarily, superior to the rest of the world.

A short but severe setback to potato cultivation took place between 1845 and 1847 when blight blasted potato fields throughout Europe, provoking hunger and even starvation among rural populations who had become dependent on them. The blight was caused by a fungus, probably imported inadvertently from South America. Cool, damp weather promoted its spread, and the resultant catastrophe in Ireland was especially severe. On the continent the "hungry forties" were long remembered, but because potatoes had not displaced grain, their failure did not provoke outright starvation. In Ireland, however, the climate was too wet for grain to grow well, and landlords, responding to market prices, largely gave up grain farming after 1815. Instead they raised beef cattle while allowing the poverty-stricken Irish to subsist on plots devoted to the production of potatoes and milk as before, imposing rents that underemployed laborers often could not pay.

Failure of the Irish potato crop therefore meant famine. Belated efforts by the British government to import and distribute corn meal from the United States did not prevent more than 1 million persons from dying. In the next few years population was further reduced by a wave of emigration from Ireland—sometimes financed by landlords desiring to clear their land of surplus laborers. The resulting Irish diaspora (scattering of people) in Britain, the United States, Canada, and Australia altered local society and politics throughout the English-speaking world. Parallel but smaller emigration from Germany, provoked by political disappointment as well as by economic distress, also affected the ethnic patterns of the United States.

After 1847 the crisis subsided when sunnier weather made the potato blight recede. Within less than a generation, rapid industrialization absorbed surplus German labor, and Germany even began to import Poles to work in Silesian coal mines and on east German estates. In Ireland memories of the famine bit far deeper. In particular, rigorous efforts to avoid poverty by postponing marriage until land was available to support a new family slowed population growth. Emigration also continued to relieve local crowding; political movements aimed at ousting the Protestant establishment gathered momentum and became irresistible after 1919. Mixed farming superseded dependence on potatoes alone. Never again would the Irish expose themselves to the disaster of the famine years.

Elsewhere in Europe potato cultivation continued to expand and was increasingly mechanized. Before the end of the nineteenth century chemical sprays checked blight as well as potato bugs; with every war, including World War II, potato acreage increased because calorie yields were so much superior to those from grain.

Potato cultivation also became important in northern China, in North America, and wherever else a cool, moist climate favored the crop. Only rice and wheat exceed potatoes as a source of calories for the world's peoples today.

William H. McNeill

Further Reading

Langer, W. L. (1963). Europe's initial population explosion. *American Historical Review, 69*(1), 1–17.

Langer, W. L. (1975, Winter). American foods and Europe's population growth, 1750–1850. *Journal of Social History, 8*, 51–66.

McNeill, W. H. (1947). *The influence of the potato on Irish history.* Unpublished doctoral dissertation, Cornell University, Ithaca, NY.

McNeill, W. H. (1999, Spring). How the potato changed the world's history. *Social Research, 66*, 67–83.

Powell, John Wesley
(1834–1902)
U.S. explorer

John Wesley Powell was born in upstate New York to evangelical Protestant immigrants from Great Britain and grew up in Ohio, Wisconsin, and Illinois. Although college educated, he was largely self-taught in the natural sciences, including his specialty of geology. Science became for him a substitute for religion; throughout his life, he believed in the promise of science to create progress and the good life, dismissing most religious ideas as superstitions. What he took from his parents was a belief in the common origins of all people and an opposition to slavery and racial bigotry. He fought on the Union side in the Civil War, losing part of his right arm in the battle at Shiloh in 1862. Five years later he led a group of college students on a field expedition to the Rocky Mountains, and there was born his ambition to penetrate the hidden mysteries of the Southwest.

Powell led the first scientific expeditions down the Colorado River in 1869 and 1871–1872. After mapping that river system and its Grand Canyon, he organized a federally funded topographic survey of the entire Colorado Plateau. On the basis of his reputation as explorer and scientist, Powell was named Director of the U.S. Geological Survey in 1881, a position he held until 1894. He also became director of the Bureau of Ethnology, which did much to promote the study of Native Americans. During Powell's tenure the Geological Survey became the government's most important scientific research agency. He organized the first government program to investigate irrigation possibilities in the West, and from that effort came the U.S. Bureau of Reclamation, founded the year Powell died.

Powell's most important writings include two government reports, *Exploration of the Colorado River of the West* (1875) and *Report on the Arid Lands of the United States* (1878). The latter opened a fierce debate over the agricultural possibilities of the drier side of the continent. Powell argued that, west of the hundredth meridian, rainfall was generally inadequate for traditional farming, a condition that would put severe limits on westward expansion. Irrigation would be essential, but because of the limited water supply most of the land must forever remain beyond the reach of farming. Powell presented a set of reforms in the public land laws that would encourage grazing and irrigation and would secure the water in the hands of small farmers organized into colonies. He was profoundly worried that the scarcity of natural resources would lead to monopoly and injustice unless the nation took careful steps to design a new dryland commonwealth.

Powell lost his battle to bring realism to federal land policy and to secure agrarian principles for the West. He has stood nonetheless as one of the founders of the conservation movement, and he has inspired millions with his love of the American landscape and particularly of the stark beauty of the Colorado River and its canyons.

Donald Worster

Further Reading

DeBuys, W. (Ed.). (2001). *Seeing things whole: The essential John Wesley Powell*. Washington, DC: Island Press.

Stegner, W. (1954). *Beyond the hundredth meridian: John Wesley Powell and the second opening of the American West*. Boston: Houghton Mifflin.

Worster, D. (2001). *A river running west: The life of John Wesley Powell*. New York: Oxford University Press.

Preservationism

Preservationism is the desire to protect parts of the natural world from human change and development. A modern term for a general movement that arose in industrialized countries after 1860, it often is opposed to conservation—the concept of scientific, sustainable resource use.

Accelerating expansion, economic development, and urbanization in the nineteenth century created awareness of the human impact on the natural world. George Perkins Marsh's influential *Man and Nature* (1864) documented how human action could turn a forest to a desert. Observers worried that American reliance on wood for building and fuel would cause national deforestation. Hunting, particularly professional market hunting, threatened bird and animal populations. The sudden disappearance of once-numerous bison ("buffalo") and the passenger pigeon shocked Americans. Egg collecting, a popular pastime, threatened rare species, while in Europe gathering eggs for food reduced bird populations. Fashion was another factor. In the early nineteenth century trappers eliminated beaver from most of their original range; a decline in the popularity of beaver-felt hats saved

remnant populations in remote areas. By century's end a craze for women's feathered hats threatened many bird species, most of which were only saved when such hats went out of style in the 1920s.

Governments had long regulated useful or harmful wild animals and certain valuable trees; preservationists sought to protect often economically useless animals, plants, and places. Mainly private citizens such as scientists and urban middle- or upper-class amateurs, preservationists worked to protect vulnerable nature through moral suasion, private action, and government regulation. Charles Sprague Sargent of Boston's Arnold Arboretum led a movement to save American trees, resulting in the establishment of government forest reserves in 1891 (later reorganized as National Forests). Bird protection societies such as the Audubon Society appeared across the industrialized world. Sport hunters and fishermen in such societies as the Boone and Crockett Club and the Izaak Walton League pressed for hunting and fishing regulation and for wildlife sanctuaries. North American and European nations instituted hunting seasons and licenses, adopted laws and treaties protecting migratory birds, and established wildlife sanctuaries. Continued threats by development, pesticides, and hunting led by the 1970s to laws and treaties to protect endangered species.

Threats to scenic natural wonders in the American West inspired a new preservation tool, the national park. In 1864, the Lincoln administration gave Yosemite to California as a state park (after 1890 expanded as a national park). In 1872 Congress created the world's first national park, Yellowstone National Park, to protect its unique features. Nature writer John Muir crusaded for protection of wild beauty and founded the Sierra Club in 1892 to defend the new parks. The Wilderness Society, founded in 1935, won passage of the 1964 Wilderness Act preserving undeveloped areas. Groups like Sierra Club, along with radicals like Earth First!, have fought to limit or even roll back development within parks and to expand park and wilderness lands. The European national park movement generally followed German biologist Hugo Conwentz's concept of "nature monuments," preservation of landscapes of both natural and cultural significance.

In the twentieth century European nations created national parks, wildlife refuges, and hunting regulations both in their homelands and throughout their empires in Africa and Asia. In the 1980s and 1990s, the movement to preserve global biodiversity and the world's rain forests gained prominence. Although preservationism has left an important legacy of protected biota and natural areas around the world, local people were often removed or prevented from traditional subsistence uses of parkland.

Mark Stoll

See also Audubon Society; Biodiversity; Izaak Walton League; National Park Service; Wilderness; Wilderness Society

Further Reading

Dominick, R. H., III. (1992). *The environmental movement in Germany: Prophets and pioneers, 1871–1971.* Bloomington: Indiana University Press.
Nash, R. (2001). *Wilderness and the American Mind* (4th ed.). New Haven, CT: Yale University Press.
Reiger, J. F. (2001). *American sportsmen and the origins of conservation* (3rd ed.). Corvallis: Oregon State University Press.
Runte, A. (1997). *National parks: The American experience* (3rd ed.). Lincoln: University of Nebraska Press.
Schama, S. (1995). *Landscape and memory.* New York: Knopf.

Prickly Pear

The prickly pear (genus *Opuntia*) includes over two hundred species of cactus native to North, Central, and South America. In the Americas prickly pears are valued as sources of food, medicine, and animal fodder. In Mexico *tunas*—the berries—are eaten fresh or prepared as syrup, juice, or marmalade; the flat stems (cladophylls) are eaten fresh, cooked, or pickled. Prickly pears have been cultivated for centuries to produce cochineal—a traditional Mexican red dye—made from a scale insect *(Dactylopius coccus)* that feeds on cladophyll fluids. Cochineal production, once a Spanish monopoly, spread to Haiti when cactus and cochineal were smuggled there in 1777 and later to South America, India, the Canary Islands, and Portugal.

Introduced to many arid regions, prickly pears have sometimes naturalized and become pests, dominating pasturelands and outcompeting desirable plant species. A spectacular biological invasion occurred when prickly pears were introduced to Australia. In 1839 *Opuntia stricta* was brought to Australia from the

A prickly pear cactus in Spain. COURTESY SARAH CONRICK.

United States as an ornamental and flourished. Between 1840 and 1850 New South Wales and Queensland landowners planted prickly pear cuttings as pastureland hedges. Hedges quickly became overgrown and encroached pastures. In response, landowners leveled invasive hedges and scattered cladophylls, which rooted and formed new plants, unwittingly multiplying the cactus. During the great drought of the early 1900s, prickly pear was fed to starving sheep and cattle, spreading cladophylls and berries widely. Human actions and an opportunistic, competitive life history strategy allowed *O. stricta* to infest over 4 million hectares of Queensland and New South Wales by 1900 and over 24 million hectares by 1925. Dense stands of prickly pear, 1–2 meters tall, choked pastures and forced abandonment of farms and grazing operations. In heavily infested areas, tunnels were cut through stands to allow movement of people and animals.

In 1886 New South Wales passed the Prickly Pear Destruction Act, but the low value of grazing lands and the high cost of chemical control hampered prickly pear eradication. Interest in biological control of prickly pear began in 1899, and by 1912 Queensland appointed the Prickly Pear Traveling Commission, charged with identifying natural enemies in countries where prickly pears were native or naturalized. An early success was control of *Opuntia monacantha* by the cochineal insect *Dactylopius ceylonicus* by 1915. In 1920 the Commonwealth Prickly Pear Board was formed to hasten development of biological controls. One hundred and fifty species of cactus-feeding arthropods were evaluated for control potential; twelve species were selected for rearing and release. *Cactoblastis cactorum*, a South American moth whose larvae feed only on prickly pear cladophylls, was effective in controlling *O. stricta* and *O. inermis*. First released in 1926, *Cactoblastis* achieved complete control of these species by 1940. Prickly pears persist in Australia as scattered, low-density populations regulated by *Cactoblastis*. Ironically, *Cactoblastis*, a recent immigrant to Central and North America, is now a threat to desirable prickly pear species.

Today production of prickly pears for food, animal feed, and phytochemicals (plant chemicals) is increasing in the United States and Mexico, providing a potential basis for sustainable arid land agriculture.

Charles E. Williams

Further Reading

Chisholm, A. E. (Ed.). (1958). *The Australian encyclopedia*. East Lansing: Michigan State University Press.

Krebs, C. J. (2001). *Ecology: The experimental analysis of distribution and abundance* (5th ed.). San Francisco: Benjamin/Cummings.

Mabberley, D. J. (1997). *The plant-book: A portable dictionary of the vascular plants* (2nd ed.). Cambridge, UK: Cambridge University Press.

Queensland Department of Natural Resources and Mines. (2001). *Prickly pear identification and their control* (NRM Facts No. QNRM01246). Queensland, Australia: Queensland Department of Natural Resources and Mines.

Stiling, P. (2000, June). A worm that turned. *Natural History, 109*(5), 40–43.

Primates

Humans belong to the order of mammals called Primates. We share enormous biological similarity with our fellow primates: the apes, monkeys, and prosimians. However, our culture, language, and technology make the humans of today qualitatively different from the nonhuman primates. For over two million years human and nonhuman primates have coexisted in areas of Africa and Asia. For over fifteen thousand years monkeys and humans have coexisted in the Americas. Throughout that time humans have seen the nonhuman primates as food, pets, pests, jokesters, mythical beings, companions, demons, and even sometimes as people. Today humans and our nonhuman relatives share a diverse set of interconnections spanning geography, culture, and context.

The Branches and Distribution of the Primates

The various types of primates can be divided into three main groups, the prosimians, the New World monkeys, and the Old World monkeys and apes. The prosimians are the lemurs and lorises, an ancient group of primates inhabiting the island of Madagascar and much of Africa and South and Southeast Asia. New World monkeys are found in Central and South America and have been evolving separately from the other monkeys for nearly 35 million years. The monkeys and apes of Africa and Asia and humans share a close evolutionary history. Humans belong to the super-family Hominoidea along with four ape groups: the gibbons, the orangutans, the chimpanzees, and the gorillas.

All primates are highly social mammals, and they are found in a diverse array of grouping patterns. The majority of monkeys and apes live in complex social groups consisting of multiple adult females, males, and young. These groups can range from under ten to over three hundred individuals. Some monkeys and apes are found in communities, where members live in the same general area but are not always in the same precise place together (much like humans). Many prosimians live in small groups and some even spend a good deal of their time by themselves. Humans share much of their basic social patterns with the other primates: group living, complex social relationships, and very strong bonds between mothers and their offspring.

While humans can be found all across the globe, most nonhuman primates can be found between the Tropic of Cancer and the Tropic of Capricorn. This distribution is related to the prevalence of forested areas and tropical environments in these regions. Currently it is in these areas that humans and nonhuman primates exhibit the highest degree of overlap and therefore interact most frequently.

Nonhuman Primates in Human Religion and Folklore

Because of our physical similarities and the geographical overlap of human and nonhuman primates in much of the world, the apes, monkeys and prosimians have become included in many aspects of human culture.

Many of the world's religions have special roles for nonhuman primates. In Hinduism, monkeys play a primary role in the *Ramayana*, an epic story that dates from approximately 300 BCE. In the tale, Sita, the wife of the hero Rama, is abducted by a demon king. The monkey general (often called the monkey king) Hanuman uses his magic powers and army of monkeys to help defeat the evil demon and reunite Rama and Sita. Because of the popularity of the *Ramayana* in Hindu art, dance, and theater, the macaque (genus *Macaca*) and langur (genus *Semnopithecus*) monkeys of India receive favorable treatment in much of that country. This treatment takes the form of food provisions, offerings, and relative protection, even when the monkeys are living within cities and causing serious damage to property. In fact, the common langur monkey in India is referred to as the "Hanuman langur" because of its supposed direct relationship to Hanuman.

In Buddhist traditions, especially in China, monkeys and gibbons are seen as both tricksters and wise men because of the role of the monkey king in folklore. The monkey king, Sun Wugong, makes a prominent appearance in the ancient novel *Xiyou ji* (The Journey to the West). This novel recounts the journey of the monk Xuanzang (602–664 CE) from China to India to retrieve important texts of Mahayana Buddhism. Sun Wugong is one of the monk's traveling companions and is a central figure in the adventure and misadventures of the traveling party. He is a metaphor for much of humanity, part of nature, yet divine, filled with strength and honor and at the same time devious and disobedient. The monkey also plays a prominent role on the Chinese zodiac and is well represented as an icon in modern Chinese popular culture.

Unlike the central and benevolent, yet guileful, role that nonhuman primates have in Asia, in European history they take on a more sinister guise. By 800 CE or earlier, devils and demons were frequently depicted as having monkey or apelike traits. Because of the similarities between human and nonhuman primates, monkeys and apes were seen as degenerate humans, perversions and demons. This may have been due to the lack of wild European populations of monkeys and consequent lack of exposure to any nonhuman primates.

In Africa nonhuman primates also play central roles in religion and myth. In ancient Egypt baboons (genus *Papio*) played prominent religious roles as much as three thousand years ago. The monkey god, Thoth, was tied to the lunar cycle and timekeeping and a similar deity, Hapi, the monkey-headed god, was thought to watch over the spirits of the dead as they went before the central deity, Osiris. Baboons are found as mummies throughout portions of ancient Egypt, and a monkey cemetery has been excavated in the ancient city of Thebes. Among Bantu-speaking peoples of southern Africa, baboons frequently appear in folklore as vicious tricksters who occasionally steal human babies. Alternatively, in these same groups other types of monkeys are sometimes reflected as carefree and foolish, teasing other animals and generally engaging in tomfoolery.

Nonhuman Primates as Family or Food

In South and Central America, particularly the Amazonian basin, monkeys can be treated both as prey items and as cultural cousins. In an extreme case, among the Guaja, a Tupi-Guarani-speaking group in Brazil, young monkeys whose mothers have been killed in hunts are brought into the villages and raised by human females. For the Guaja, monkeys are both food and relatives, with pet monkeys becoming part of an extended kin network and wild monkeys part of the regular diet.

Throughout the tropical areas of Africa, Asia, and the Americas many traditional foraging societies rely on monkeys for food but also recognize a kinship between human and nonhuman primates. This kinship is usually played out in myths about the co-origins of human and nonhuman primates from a common ancestral form or family.

As a food source, it is not uncommon for nonhuman primates to make up 25 percent or more of the bushmeat (meat of wild animals) for sale at markets in Africa. In Asia and South America, nonhuman primate meat is less likely to be sold in markets, but is very likely to be a part of forest dwelling peoples' diets.

Nonhuman primates are also captured and processed for organs and body parts. In many areas of Asia, certain parts of monkeys and apes are held to have medicinal value and bring high prices in both formal and informal markets.

Nonhuman Primates as Sources of Entertainment

In many cultures nonhuman primates play significant roles in entertainment. In Japan, the monkey is seen as reflecting aspects of humanity and as an animal jokester, and images of monkeys are heavily used in advertising and cartoons. In general, in countries where nonhuman primates exist in the wild (such as Japan) there appears to be more use of the images of monkeys and apes in advertising, whereas in countries with no wild populations (such as the United States), nonhuman primates are more prominent in motion pictures, television, and occasionally books. In the United States, nonhuman primates have been the focus of numerous movies and television shows, whether it be the giant gorilla in *King Kong* or the genial orangutan in *Every Which Way But Loose*. H. A. Ray's *Curious George* book series (popular since 1941) is particularly interesting because the main character is a generalized nonhuman primate, with a mix of monkey and ape characteristics. For most citizens of Europe and North America the only exposure to nonhuman primates is in zoos or though moving or still images. This may accentuate the role of nonhuman primates as entertainment oddities rather than regular features of everyday life.

Nonhuman Primates and Human Economics

As mentioned earlier, nonhuman primates are eaten as food in Africa and South and Central America, and for this reason they can be said to figure as a food commodity in those areas. In the United States and Europe medical research relies heavily on the use of nonhuman primates as test subjects. In Asia and the United States breeding colonies of laboratory subjects are managed and maintained as revenue-generating units.

Nonhuman primates are integrated into human economies in other ways, as well. In Thailand, male macaque monkeys are used as expert coconut pickers. Humans raise a male macaque from infancy and train it to climb the coconut trees and retrieve the fruits. In many cases a single macaque can produce a higher daily income from coconuts than a human doing the same job. In circuses and zoos throughout the world, shows by nonhuman primates are main attractions. Whether it is having breakfast with an orangutan at the Singapore Zoo or watching chimpanzees perform at a wild-animal park in California, people are willing to pay to interact with nonhuman primates. Recently, primate ecotourism, or tours to see nonhuman primates in their natural habitat, has grown substantially as an industry. Currently, tour agencies operate primate ecotours in Africa, Asia, and Central and South America. In Europe and the United States there are wild-animal parks that mimic natural environments as well.

Conflicts between Human and Nonhuman Primates

From the human perspective, a primary conflict with nonhuman primates arises from agriculture. In many parts of the tropical world humans rely on garden plots to satisfy their nutritional needs. When these gardens border forests or other nonhuman primate habitats, they can become an easy and favored food source for the monkeys and apes. In Asia, both macaque monkeys and leaf monkeys raid human gardens. These monkeys range in size from 5 to over 15 kilograms and a troop of over 20 can do significant damage. In Africa the main crop raiders are baboons (12–25 kilograms) and vervets (3–6 kilograms). However, in some areas of central and western Africa chimpanzees and gorillas have begun using human crops as food sources. These much larger apes can substantially impact a garden's yield. In South and Central America crop raiding is less common, as the monkeys there are generally smaller than those in Africa and Asia and spend much more time in trees (they are mostly arboreal).

While it is easy to see the damage of crop raiding as a problem caused by nonhuman primates, it is important to realize that this type of interaction is increasing due to the conversion of forestland to cropland. As more and more habitat is lost, nonhuman primates are faced with diminishing feeding opportunities in their natural habitat and turn to human agriculture as a food source. However, even when forest foods are available, the types of fruits and vegetables that humans grow are easier to obtain and more nutritionally rewarding than their wild counterparts.

When humans and nonhuman primates compete it is not always in forests or gardens. Today, especially in India and a few parts of Southeast Asia, monkeys and humans are sharing village and city environments. In India, because of the extensive human population and the tolerance of nonhuman primates that Hinduism promotes, as monkeys are running out of wild habitat they are joining the humans in cities and towns. In fact, some researchers estimate that a majority of rhesus monkeys in India today live in village or city environments. This demographic shift results in daily encounters between urban monkeys and humans.

Disease Transmission

Changing human social, economic, and political conditions and associated deforestation result in nonhuman primates coming into increasingly regular contact with humans. Hunting, logging, farming, the pet trade, ecotourism, and research all provide contact opportunities in which diseases can jump the species barrier.

While research has demonstrated the devastating effect that human diseases (such as tuberculosis, polio, and respiratory viruses) can have on nonhuman primates in captivity, relatively little research has focused on the effects of these diseases on populations of wild nonhuman primates. It is quite likely that one result of increased interactions with humans is that many wild nonhuman primate populations will be negatively impacted by human disease. This can be especially dangerous for those populations or species that are currently endangered or threatened with extinction.

In the other direction, it has become apparent that many human diseases may have origins in nonhuman primates. For example, recent research suggests that the chimpanzee virus SIVcpz made the jump to humans and mutated into the human HIV 1 virus at some point in the last century.

Looking to the Future of Nonhuman Primates

Human and nonhuman primates share intertwined destinies. Nonhuman primates are our closest evolutionary relatives and integrated into our mythologies, diets, and economies. There is no longer the possibility of studying a group, or population, of nonhuman primates without coming into contact with some element of human interaction. Ninety percent of the world's primates are found in tropical forests, and these forests are being converted to human use faster and more dramatically than any other habitats on earth. Fifty percent of all primate species are a conservation concern to the Species Survival Commission (SSC) and the World Conservation Union (IUCN), and 20 percent are considered endangered or critically endangered. Human and nonhuman primates have been interacting for millions of years. It is now up to humans to decide how much longer the other primates will be around to continue this pattern.

Agustin Fuentes

Further Reading

Carter, A., & Carter, C. (1999). Cultural representation of nonhuman primates. In P. Dolhinow & A. Fuentes (Eds.), *The nonhuman primates.* (pp. 270–276). Mountain View, CA: Mayfield Publishing Co.

Corbey, R., & Theunissen, B. (1995). *Ape, man, apeman: Changing views since 1600.* Leiden, Netherlands: Department of Prehistory Publication.

Fuentes, A., & Wolfe, L. (2002). *Primates face to face: The conservation implications of human-nonhuman primate interconnections.* Cambridge, UK: Cambridge University Press.

Ohnuki-Tierney, E. (1987). *Monkey as mirror: Symbolic transformations in Japanese history and ritual.* Princeton, NJ: Princeton University Press.

Rowe, N. (1996). *The pictorial guide to the living primates.* East Hampton, NY: Pogonias Press.

Pristine Myth

The pristine myth is the widely held belief that until 1492 most of North America and Amazonian South America was a wild, sparsely populated, wilderness, pure and unspoiled, full of virgin forests, and teeming with wild animals. The few "primitive" Indians lived so in tune with nature that they barely disturbed their environments.

While various versions of the pristine myth have been popular in America and Western Europe for a few hundred years, the term itself was created and popularized by U.S. geographer William M. Denevan (b. 1931) in his important 1992 article "The Pristine Myth." The myth continues to be perpetuated by Hollywood, the general media, in schoolbooks, and in some anthropology texts. Denevan's essay, followed the same year by articles by Martin Bowden and Arturo Gomez-Pompa and Andrea Kaus, soon precipitated *The Great New Wilderness Debate* (Callicott and Nelson 1998).

Perceptions of the Forest

Denevan (1992, 369) states, "The pristine view is to a large extent an invention of nineteenth-century romanticist and primitivist writers such as W. H. Hudson, Cooper, Thoreau, [and] Longfellow. . . . The wilderness image has since become part of the American heritage, associated with a heroic pioneer past in need of preservation." The myth is closely connected to other romantic notions, of a golden age, for instance, or of the noble savage, the virgin wilderness, and the "ecological Indian" (which represents indigenous peoples as natural conservationists).

In the mid-1900s, geographers, historians, and anthropologists began questioning the idea that the American environment was pristine in 1492. By the end of the 1980s, the myth was being discredited by new studies in historical ecology. In the 1990s writers presented revisionist arguments that forests in the Americas, and tropical forests in Asia and Africa, were not virgin, but anthropogenic (human-modified). Earth was a humanized landscape everywhere that people were present. In America, geographers found that what had appeared to be empty lands actually contained remains of earthworks, roads, fields, settlements, deforested areas, severe erosion, and wildlife extinction. At the same time, other studies were concluding that contrary to the assumption that there had always been only small isolated groups of indigenes in the Americas, there had been a severe Indian depopulation in America, from at least 50 million in 1492 to 6 million in 1650, further supporting the revisionist view. By the end of the twentieth century, it was generally accepted that this drastic population decline was caused by deadly epidemics of European diseases introduced into the New World in the 1500s, to which the indigenous populations had no immunity.

The Debate over Rain Forest Foraging

As applied to Asia, Africa, and the Amazon, the pristine myth envisioned tropical rain forests filled with a cornucopia of wild foods, so much so that prehistoric foraging peoples must have found plenty of nutritious wild foods to eat with almost no labor. By the late 1980s, however, anthropologists presented evidence that such forests are actually so food-poor that humans could never have lived there without agriculture. In the 1990s others disputed that claim, presenting archaeological evidence that prehistoric peoples lived in some rain forests before agriculture. Summary arguments from both sides may be found in Headland and Bailey (1991), McKey (1996), and Roosevelt et al. (1996).

Since the mid 1990s, most geographers and anthropologists have come to agree that the pristine myth is false. But students should be careful not to discard too quickly every argument in support of it. While there are many documented examples today that indicate most forests are anthropogenic and not pristine, and that most indigenous tribal peoples are not the ecological conservationists they were thought to be, there are a few known cases where Indian groups did practice

a traditional conservation ethic. (Two examples of such are the Uwa Tunebo Indians and the Tucano Indians, both in Colombia.) Likewise, students should keep in mind that the dispute is soaked in strong ideological biases. Extremists on one side argue that Primitive Man was just as much a destroyer of his environment as is Industrial Man. Those on the other side defend the opposite view, that all tribal indigenes practiced a perfect conservationist ethic, one that would save our planet if everyone followed it. The truth is somewhere in between.

Thomas N. Headland

Further Reading

Balee, W. (Ed.). (1998). *Advances in historical ecology*. New York: Columbia University Press.

Bowden, M. J. (1992). The invention of American tradition. *Journal of Historical Geography, 18*(1), 3–26.

Callicott, J. B., & Nelson, M. P. (1998). *The great new wilderness debate*. Athens: University of Georgia.

Crumley, C. L. (Ed.). (1994). *Historical ecology*. Santa Fe, NM: School of American Research Press.

Denevan, W. (1992). The pristine myth: The landscape of the Americas in 1492. *Annals of the Association of American Geographers, 82*(3), 369–385.

Gomez-Pompa, A., & Kaus, A. (1992). Taming the wilderness myth. *BioScience, 42*(4), 271–279.

Headland, T. N. (1997). Revisionism in ecological anthropology. *Current Anthropology, 38*, 605–630.

Headland, T. N., & Bailey, R. C. (Eds.). (1991) *Human foragers in tropical rain forests*. New York: Plenum. [A special issue of the journal *Human Ecology, 19*(2).]

Kirch, P. V., & Hunt, T. L. (Eds.). (1997) *Historical ecology in the Pacific Islands: Prehistoric environmental and landscape change*. New Haven, CT: Yale University Press.

McKey, D. B. (1996). Wild yam question. In D. Levinson & M. Embers (Eds.), *Encyclopedia of cultural anthropology, Vol. 4*. (pp. 1363–1366). New York: Henry Holt.

Roosevelt, A. C., et al. (1996). 1996 Paleoindian cave dwellers in the Amazon: The Peopling of the Americas. *Science, 19*, 373–384.

Protestantism

Christianity's rich mixture of Jewish and classical Greek and Roman thought contains many, sometimes contradictory, ideas about nature. Various strands of

Protestantism have accentuated and expanded elements of Christianity that emphasize the significance of nature in knowing God, giving rise to a strong emphasis on nature that shapes culture and environmentalism. Other strands have minimized nature's role and have produced some of the most vocal opponents of the environmental movement.

Christianity is a creation religion: The first chapter of the Bible focuses on the creation of the world, barely mentioning humans, and the Bible frequently refers to God as creator (Job 38–41, Psalms 104) whom creation praises (Psalms 148). God works miracles through nature (such as manna in Exodus) and shows his wrath or providence through natural events like droughts or bountiful harvests. Wilderness was both a place of testing, such as during the Exodus or the temptations of Jesus, and a place where Moses and the prophets heard God. God created the world and its plants and animals for humans to conquer (Genesis 1:28), but the world was God's, and humans were merely managers (Genesis 2:15). God saw creation was good (Genesis 1) but cursed it after the Fall (Genesis 3:17); and it would groan in travail until Jesus returned (Romans 8:22), a new heaven and Earth appeared, and Eden was restored (Isaiah, Revelation). Nevertheless, creation exhibited the goodness and wisdom of God and thus was proof against disbelief (Psalms 19, Romans 1:20).

Church Fathers like St. Augustine wedded Greek philosophy and science to biblical theology, particularly the ideas that nature had a purpose, was made for humans, and showed evidence of design. Platonic philosophy was particularly agreeable to theology, especially the third-century neo-Platonism of the Roman philosopher Plotinus. Neo-Platonism taught that the world is an organically interrelated whole that emanates from the Divine Spirit and reflects patterns or ideas in the Divine Mind; through meditation on the beauty of creation, mystics could achieve union with God via the idea of beauty in the Divine Mind. Another Church Father, St. John Chrysostom, preached that God would not lock up all knowledge of himself in a revealed book where only a few people literate in Greek and Hebrew could find it; everyone, however, could learn of God through the so-called "Book of Nature," which like the Bible came directly from his hand and told of his attributes.

In the century after the Reformation, Protestant theologians began to lay great emphasis on nature. In contrast to the Catholic Church, to which the influence of the Holy Spirit on the body of the faithful was theologically far more significant than the action of the

Spirit in nature, Protestants saw in the "Book of Nature" an aid to faith and support for the truth of Protestantism. Calvinists in particular supported this view; the first words of the Calvinist 1648 Westminster Confession of Faith of the Puritans and Presbyterians restate Romans 1:20, giving pride of place to the concept of the presence of God in nature. Emphasizing predestination and the need for God's grace, Calvinists contrasted fallen and sinful humans with pure nature, the ongoing creation of God. Puritan John Milton's *Paradise Lost*, with its theme of sinful man banned from Paradise, is the most famous expression of this view. Calvin also formulated the influential concept of stewardship: God gave humans control of the Earth, and like good stewards humans must leave it in better condition than they received it.

Natural Theology

Hence Protestants equated study of the "Book of Nature" with study of the Bible and, like Sir Isaac Newton and John Ray, considered science a religious activity. Natural theology (theology based on the evidences of God in nature) enjoyed a tremendous vogue throughout the Enlightenment. Major works included Ray's *The Wisdom of God Manifested in the Works of the Creation* (1691), William Derham's *Physico-Theology* (1713), William Paley's *Natural Theology* (1803), and the *Bridgewater Treatises* of 1833–1840. Many clerics, including Cotton Mather, Gilbert White, and Joseph Priestley, were amateur natural scientists. During the Enlightenment, at both the popular and elite levels people thought that species are fixed as God created them and that nature is little changed in the few thousand years since Adam and Eve left Eden. Works like Thomas Burnet's *Telluris Theoria Sacra* (1691) and William Buckland's *Reliquiae Diluvianae* (1823) explained how current landforms appeared after the cataclysms of the Noachic Flood. By the turn of the nineteenth century, geologists like Thomas Hutton and Charles Lyell theorized how the Earth could have arisen from entirely natural processes, preparing the way for Charles Darwin's *Origin of Species* (1859), which theorized how species could arise without supernatural aid. Thereafter the popular appeal of natural theology declined.

In its place, a more mystical attitude toward nature developed. In the late 1600s Leibniz in Germany and Cambridge Platonists Henry More and Ralph Cudworth in England revived Christian neo-Platonism, which grew in influence until the early nineteenth cen-

---

God, The Creator

Psalm 104:24

O LORD, how manifold are thy works! In wisdom hast thou made them all: the earth is full of thy riches.

Romans 1:20

For the invisible things of him from the creation of the world are clearly seen, being understood by the things that are made, even his eternal power and Godhead.

---

tury. By then German theologians like Schelling and American Transcendentalists like Emerson in *Nature* (1836) expounded almost pure neo-Platonism. Philosopher Alfred North Whitehead's process theology of "pantheism," the idea of an organic universe, the source of whose evolution was God, revised neo-Platonism for the twentieth century, and in recent works John B. Cobb has interpreted Whitehead in terms of environmental concerns. Norwegian philosopher Arne Naess in 1973 coined the term *deep ecology*, a vaguely mystical philosophy whose principles are based on the intrinsic value of all life and a spiritual change in each person to have a "deep" understanding of humans' holistic interrelationship with nature.

Infused with God and untouched by the corrupting hand of humans, primeval nature as moral influence was a central concept to Protestant Romanticism. This theme informs the literature of Goethe, Wordsworth, Coleridge, John Clare, William Cullen Bryant, and Henry David Thoreau and the art of Kaspar David Friedrich, John Ruskin, and Hudson River School painters such as Thomas Cole. In England and America, Frederick Law Olmsted and other landscape architects designed such grand city parks as Central Park in New York City, where nature would morally influence the citizenry. The American Transcendentalist principle that nature is a spiritual and moral resource heavily influenced a wide range of people, including nature writers John Burroughs and Scots-American John Muir, advocate of Yosemite National Park and founder of the Sierra Club; nature photographer Ansel Adams; architect Frank Lloyd Wright, whose early work blended with the landscape; and the directors and landscape architects who created the American national park system. Founded on the ideal of a holy landscape uninhabited by corrupt humans, American national parks became the model for national parks worldwide.

Influence on Natural Sciences

Protestant neo-Platonism influenced the development of the natural sciences. The ideas of the interconnectedness of life in an organic unity influenced biology, particularly the creation of ecology, a nearly exclusively Protestant science. Heavily influenced by German Romanticism, Ernst Haeckel coined the word *ecology* in 1866. Early developments by the German K. A. Möbius (1877), the American Stephen Forbes (1887), and the Dane Eugenius Warming (1895) emphasized the microcosmic aspects of an ecosystem. The American Frederic Clements saw the plant community as a living organism. James Lovelock's Gaia hypothesis gives new scientific basis for the view of life as an interrelated organic unity. Ecological theory from plant succession to ecosystem has an implicit moralism in that it views humans as disturbers of nature's harmonies or processes—intruders in Paradise.

Protestant nations acted early and forcefully to establish conservation and environmental agencies or ministries. After 1880 strong bird, animal, and nature protection societies appeared. The German Hugo Conwentz's idea of the "nature monument" shaped European national park ideas. Scandinavian nature groups like the Danish Naturfredningsforening have been popular and politically influential. The Swiss Green movement began in the Protestant North. German Greens are most numerous and radical in Protestant areas. The Danish Environmental Protection Board (1967) and Environmental Protection Law (1968) were the world's first and strongest, followed in 1970 by the American Environmental Protection Agency and National Environmental Policy Act. Sweden organized and hosted the 1972 United Nations Conference on the Human Environment.

Nature's moral and spiritual aspects play a significant role in American, Swiss, German, Dutch, Scandinavian, and British environmentalism, along with a

Protestant-style idea that individual conversion to right belief is key to solving the environmental crisis. For example, Dutch organization Kleine Aarde (Small Earth, 1971) stressed individual lifestyle changes. Dutchman E. de Vries's 1948 *De Aarde Betaalt* ("The Earth Pays") and American Aldo Leopold's 1948 *Sand County Almanac* proclaimed individuals' moral responsibility to respect life and restrain greed. Danish environmentalism emphasizes the ecological responsibility of each individual. Britain's 1945 Dower Report, which led to the establishment of British national parks in 1949, identified their purposes as the preservation and enjoyment of the beauty of landscapes (as opposed to social, economic, or patriotic purposes). Puritanism colored American environmentalism with mistrust of resource exploitation for profit, fear of waste, and emphasis on efficiency. Strong moralistic rhetoric accompanied establishment of national parks under the influence of John Muir and national forests under the aegis of President Theodore Roosevelt and Chief Forester Gifford Pinchot. In addition, evangelicalism influenced the styles and rhetoric of environmental figures including Muir, the Sierra Club president David Brower, and the Earth First! founder Dave Foreman. Restorationism—the Protestant principle that Christianity was corrupt and that its early form must be restored—re-emerges in notions that modern people have fallen away from an ideal past and must return to a paleolithic relationship with nature.

Liberal Activism

Liberal, historically Lutheran and Calvinist denominations (like Presbyterianism and Congregationalism) have been environmentally active for decades. Ministers of the West German Lutheran (or "Evangelical") Church participated in environmental battles in the 1950s and sponsored a series of air pollution conference after 1957. In communist East Germany the Lutheran churches became a haven for critics of government industrial and pollution policies. The American Lutheran theologian Joseph Sittler wrote "A Theology for Earth" in 1954 and "Ecological Commitment as Theological Responsibility" in 1970. The Danish religious society Forsoningsforbundet participated in the fight against nuclear power in the 1970s. The American National Council of Churches assisted the Faith-Man-Nature Group as it met from the 1960s until 1974.

Yet, in the 1960s leading academics, including Lynn White Jr., Ian McHarg, and Roderick Nash, blamed Christianity for the environmental crisis. Many moderate and liberal denominations were stung into action by this accusation. Led by the American Lutheran and Presbyterian (U.S.A.) churches in 1970, national church organizations actively supported environmentalism in the 1970s and again, after a lull in the 1980s, quite conspicuously in the 1990s. Liturgies began to include "Earth Sundays." Churches of all denominations began to discuss the idea of stewardship. The North American Conference on Christianity and Ecology began meeting in 1987. Presbyterians established the Task Force on Eco-Justice in the 1990s, followed by the National Council of Churches Eco-Justice Working Group. British churches launched the interdenominational Eco-Congregation Programme in 2001. Protestant ecumenical groups like the National Council of Churches, the World Council of Churches, and the Conference of European Churches have given increasing attention to creation and social justice issues since the 1970s. The European Christian Environmental Network dates from 1999. In the 1990s, inspired by new environmental, theological, and feminist movements, a number of theologians, including H. Paul Santmire, John B. Cobb Jr., and Sallie McFague, produced works highlighting the significance of nature.

The Arminian Tradition

The Arminian tradition denies Calvinist predestination and emphasizes the ability of believers to attain salvation through their own efforts. The tradition includes the Anglican, Methodist, Holiness, and Pentecostal churches. Like Catholics, Anglicans and Methodists emphasize the corporate nature of worship. Black Protestants of all denominations have also focused on the social aspects of Christianity. For all these groups, believers' Christian duty to help other believers or improve society outweighs the search for God in the "Book of Nature"; their environmental thinking considers nature through its social utility and the environment through principles of social justice. The Methodist theologian Cobb examined process theology's implications for furthering the common good. Beginning in the late 1980s, the growing association of environmental issues (especially urban pollution and job health issues) with the goal of social justice inspired Catholics and black Protestants alike to become environmentally active. Benjamin Chavez, a black minister then in the United Church of Christ (i.e., Congregational), popularized the term *environmental racism*.

Some Protestant denominations have laid little stress on the spiritual aspects of nature and have contributed few major leaders of environmental art, literature, or activism. Eighteenth- and nineteenth-century British and American revival movements created churches that valued experiential over intellectual religion. Appealing to less-educated farmers and workers, these churches favored a more literal Biblicism (adherence to the letter of the Bible) in which nature played a minor role. For example, American Protestantism in the South and parts of the West—particularly in the Southern Baptist denomination, the largest American Protestant denomination—focused on evangelization and strict Biblicism, mistrusted mysticism, and rejected environmentalism as a potentially pagan distraction to believers. Consequently environmental sentiment there is exceptionally weak. Other denominations founded on evangelism and an emotional experience of conversion or of the Holy Spirit include Methodism, Holiness, and Pentecostalism.

When President Ronald Reagan appointed conservative Pentecostal James G. Watt as secretary of the Interior Department in 1981, many saw his policies of retreat on all environmental issues as proof of Lynn White's criticism. Some evangelicals, led by Calvin De-Witt of the Au Sable Institute, became environmentally active, but most fundamentalists and evangelicals reject the idea of environmental crisis and see environmentalism as a liberal, pagan, or secular-humanist movement. Evangelical Protestants organized the Evangelical Environmental Network, but it has had little impact.

Mark Stoll

Further Reading

Abrams, M. H. (1971). *Natural supernaturalism: Tradition and revolution in romantic literature.* New York: Norton.

Bramwell, A. (1989). *Ecology in the twentieth century: A history.* New Haven, CT: Yale University Press.

Fowler, R. B. (1995). *The greening of Protestant thought.* Chapel Hill: University of North Carolina Press.

Glacken, C. J. (1967). *Traces on the Rhodian shore: Nature and culture in Western thought from ancient times to the end of the eighteenth century.* Berkeley & Los Angeles: University of California Press.

Lovejoy, A. O. (1960). *The great chain of being: A study of the history of an idea.* New York: Harper & Row. (Original work published 1936)

Nash, R. (1989). *The rights of nature: A history of environmental ethics.* Madison: University of Wisconsin Press.

Nicolson, M. H. (1959). *Mountain gloom and mountain glory: The development of the aesthetics of the infinite.* Ithaca, NY: Cornell University Press.

Oelschlaeger, M. (1994). *Caring for creation: An ecumenical approach to the environmental crisis.* New Haven, CT: Yale University Press.

Santmire, H. P. (1985). *The travail of nature: The ambiguous ecological promise of Christian theology.* Philadelphia: Fortress Press.

Stoll, M. (1997). *Protestantism, capitalism, and nature in America.* Albuquerque: University of New Mexico Press.

Thomas, K. (1983). *Man and the natural world: A history of the modern sensibility.* New York: Pantheon Books.

White, L., Jr. (1967). The historical roots of our ecologic crisis. *Science, 155,* 1203–1207.

Public Health *See* Industrial Health and Safety; Toxicity

Public Interest Research Groups

The Public Interest Research Groups (PIRGs) are an alliance of organizations that advocate for social and environmental justice. Located in cities throughout the United States and Canada, PIRGs research threats to public health and fight these threats through media exposés, grassroots organizing, advocacy, and litigation. PIRGs concentrate on activism for the environment, consumer protection, and democratic government. The PIRG movement was founded and stimulated by Ralph Nader (b. 1934), a spokesperson for environmental, social, and political causes.

Each Public Interest Research Group in the United States is independent and state-based. Most PIRGs have main offices in the state capital, which allows them to lobby politicians, intervene in administrative hearings, and take court action. The state PIRGs work together nationally to share ideas and resources and cooperate on regional and national issues. All PIRGs, for example, are opposed to oil drilling in the Arctic National Wildlife Refuge and support labels on genetically engineered food. Public Interest Research Groups are supported by member donations, and each is governed by a board of trustees. PIRGs have been lobbying for progressive legislation change in the United States since 1971.

Each year, state PIRGs issue scorecards that rank members of Congress according to whether they voted for the public interests or for special interests. PIRGs attempt to build awareness about key campaigns and influence public policy. PIRG staff members include attorneys, scientists, and other professionals who monitor government and corporate decisions, research and craft policy solutions, and advocate on the public's behalf. PIRGs frequently urge the public to take action on pertinent issues, such as government energy proposals, food safety, tobacco legislation, and environmental conservation. State PIRGs often issue groundbreaking reports that influence legislation to protect citizens. Grassroots action campaigns are designed to increase government response to average citizen concerns.

PIRG Priorities

Some of the larger and more influential PIRG chapters are located in Massachusetts, California, and Alaska. Priorities for the Massachusetts Public Interest Research Group (MASSPIRG) in 2002 included unfair credit card interest rates, clean elections laws, and power plant emissions. Priorities for the California group (CALPIRG) in 2002 included clean energy solutions, elimination of toxic pesticides near schools, and accounting reforms for investors and taxpayers. CALPIRG has helped write and pass laws for clean energy, clean water, healthy schools, car safety, and increased federal financial aid. The Alaska Public Interest Research Group (AkPIRG) publishes reports used for public education and policy analysis or in support of specific issues, such as campaign financing, workers compensation, and playground safety. Contributions to most PIRGs, unlike nonprofit and nonpartisan AkPIRG, are not deductible as charitable contributions because the groups engage in political action.

PIRGs are active in at least twenty-six states; the United States Public Interest Group (U.S. PIRG) serves as a watchdog in Washington, D.C. State PIRGs founded the National Lobbying Office as an independent voice that attempts to counter the powerful special interests in the nation's capital.

Many PIRGs have student chapters that encourage activism on American college campuses and teach students to become effective citizens. Student PIRGs, located in twelve states, are independent organizations that work on public problems of interest to college stu-

dents. Recent work by student PIRGs included fighting global warming, cleaning up polluted rivers and streams, and protecting the remaining roadless areas in the national forest system. PIRG chapters frequently send members door to door to raise awareness about pertinent issues. Some PIRGs organize public demonstrations on crucial legislation.

Canadian PIRGs are set up differently from those in the United States due to Canada's parliamentary party system and less-accessible court system. The eighteen Canadian PIRGs are primarily grassroots student efforts. They do not have strong provincial or national offices to organize larger-scale campaigns.

Canadian PIRGs

In Canada PIRGs owe their birth to a 1972 speech at the University of Waterloo by Ralph Nader, who condemned pollution and corporate irresponsibility to an audience of students. Nader described his vision of a system of independent consumer groups across the continent, linked by a central research body. Four days later, the first PIRG was established in Canada. In the 1970s PIRGs organized chapter by chapter and expanded rapidly at several universities, including those at Waterloo, Ottawa, McMaster, Guelph, and Trent. Canadian PIRGs are locally based and depend on participatory democracy.

The Canadian PIRG model for student involvement includes working groups who identify programs and projects for the organization. PIRGs are supported by student fees and run by a volunteer board of student directors. Canadian PIRGs have adopted a consensus decision-making process, drawn from the success of the antinuclear movement and women's movement. Students learn to balance process and goals, training, and activism. Year-around PIRG staff members help implement the students' policies. The separate groups meet periodically to conduct networking sessions, combine their resources, write grant applications, and hire joint staff for campaigns on the provincial level.

In the 1970s Canadian PIRGs addressed the antinuclear debate and published groundbreaking research on other controversial issues, including mercury poisoning, asbestos, forestry, and agriculture. In the 1980s student PIRGs established recycling programs in Canada and raised awareness about the effects of acid rain. Concordia PIRG students run a natural food store. Simon Fraser PIRG organized an Earth Fair and protested the threat of clear-cutting to the Stoltmann Wilderness. Quebec PIRG published a book about socially responsible food choices. Dalhousie PIRG ran a successful campaign to stop an incinerator in the Halifax area.

Public Interest Research Groups in both the United States and Canada publish consumer guides for the general public, and each individual PIRG issues a newsletter for its members and supporters.

Robin O'Sullivan

Further Reading

Farbridge, K., & Cameron, P. (1998, summer). PIRG power: Public interest research groups in Canada celebrate 25 years of student activism. *Alternatives, 24*(3), 22–27.

Lehn, A. (1983). *In the public interest: Ten years of PIRG at Waterloo.* Waterloo, Canada: WPIRG.

Robertson, D., & Moore, T. (1976). *Public interest research: An historical and organizational perspective, OPIRG 1st annual retreat.* Waterloo, Canada: OPIRG.

R

Rabbits

Rabbits belong to the order Lagomorpha and their ancestors were present in Asia 45 million years ago. All modern rabbits, wild and domestic, are descended from the European rabbit, *Oryctolagus cuniculus*, which managed to survive in Spain during the Ice Age ten thousand years ago. Few other animals have profited from humans as much as the rabbit has or had their status changed so often and so profoundly.

It is important to understand the distinction between rabbits and hares (Lepus). Apart from small differences in appearance—the back legs of hares are much longer—there are two very clear differences. First, whereas rabbits dig rather deep and complex burrows, hares live on flat beds aboveground. Second, hares have adapted to immediate exposure to the elements so their young are born with fur and able to see, like lambs, calves, or guinea pigs. Rabbits, on the other hand, are born blind and naked, like mice. The young rabbits need the protection of the burrow.

The ancient Romans encountered the rabbit in Spain and introduced it to Italy and many isles in the Mediterranean Sea. They kept rabbits for consumption in small enclosures called *leporaria*. During the Middle Ages the rabbit became a common wild animal in southern Europe. Its fur was listed in wills as a valued lining of winter clothes, and its meat was a valued dish for well-to-do town dwellers. In northern Europe, however, rabbits did not occur in the wild because of the climate. Rabbits do not cope well with snow and ice-covered plants and starve in harsh winters. They remained a prestigious animal seen only at the courts of the nobility, where they were kept in small enclosures.

A new phase in the dispersion of the rabbit began when many common fur-bearing animals such as bear, beaver, and squirrel became extinct because of habitat destruction by deforestation and reclamation for agriculture and by overhunting. In order to create a new fur supply, medieval landowners established rabbit warrens. Sovereigns set aside large areas of otherwise unproductive soil under a special statute in Great Britain and France from 1100 on and in the Germanic countries in the fourteenth century. In East Anglia, England, more than fifty warrens operated between 1270 and 1460, producing up to three thousand rabbits annually. The total production of the twenty-plus warrens of the count of Holland in the coastal sand dunes of the Netherlands is estimated to have been at least forty thousand annually. The warren rabbit was well cared for. Hunting and agricultural treatises and administrative sources reveal how warren keepers systematically eradicated predators such as fox, wildcat, weasel, polecat, and birds of prey. Warren keepers drilled holes to facilitate burrow building and provided fodder in winter. Selection of rabbits for size took place during the commercial hunting campaigns, carried out with nets and ferrets to start the rabbits out of their burrows. Big does (females) were marked with a cut in the ear and put back, whereas small does and old males were removed. The rabbit increased in size substantially, as bones from excavations show.

The northern European "coney culture" (or warren practice) explains why the feral descendants of warren rabbits in the North of Europe are bigger than those in the South today. Coney culture involves a historic form of interaction between humans and animals that does not exist any more in modern Western industrialized society. It designates a very extensive regime of husbandry practices intended to promote the number of rabbits by maintaining a favorable environment, but with very little protection and feeding. Although not necessarily intended to create different breeds, it allowed for the possibility of manipulating procreation. It includes a specialized form of commercial hunting that included selection of animals, thus influencing the gene reserves of the population. Selection for size meant that humans manipulated the gene pool of the rabbit population to the advantage of bigger rabbits. As a result of this practice, the modern rabbit populations in northern Europe that are descended from those earlier rabbits continue to be characteristically larger than those in the South.

Rabbit Dispersal

By 1500 the rabbit had developed into a pest in certain areas of the North. Complaints and court cases of the time show that rabbits escaped from warrens and feasted on fields of corn and vegetables. However, until the eighteenth century populations of feral rabbits remained small and scattered. They survived only near warrens, where they could supplement their populations after severe winters. With the Agricultural Revolution a new phase of rabbit dispersion began. Farmers introduced new crops and drained wet areas that had formerly served as barriers. Governments laid out sand bodies to build railways, roads, and dikes, providing new burrowing opportunities for rabbits.

The worldwide spread of the European rabbit began in the nineteenth century, although, prior to

White-tailed Jackrabbit. COURTESY DEAN BIGGINS/U. S. FISH AND WILDLIFE SERVICE.

that, on occasion seafarers had set out rabbits on islands to provide for their future needs for food (often to the detriment of the local vegetation). The introduction of the rabbit to Australia is famous because of its devastating effect. There, in the state of Victoria in 1859, the human agent went further than just setting out rabbits. Ranchers unwittingly built a rabbit paradise, sowing grass, making ponds (for livestock), and killing off competitors (kangaroos) and predators (dingo, birds of prey). This interference with the natural ecosystem also led to the extinction of the rat kangaroo, which left behind a network of tunnels perfect for rabbit burrows. By 1950 there were an estimated 500,000 rabbits, which ate as much grass as 50,000 sheep. Officials in Australia and elsewhere introduced rabbit diseases—in the 1980s myxomatosis and in the 1990s viral hemorrhagus syndrome—both killing up to 99 percent of rabbit populations. But in most places this was only a temporary relief.

The Hutched Rabbit

The history of the hutched rabbit began in the courtyards of medieval castles and abbeys. By 1600 breeding techniques had developed to such an extent that four colors were available (gray, silver-gray, black, and white). Commercial rabbit keeping in cages, to supply the felt industry, expanded. Black rabbit fur was used to make the cheaper varieties of the so-called beaver hat in Paris in the eighteenth century. In the nineteenth century the development of new dyes turned rabbit fur into simulated-leopard and other highly desired furs.

Keeping rabbits as pets has been practiced since at least the seventeenth century. Breeding show rabbits for competition has developed into a widespread sport. One hundred breeds exist, with dozens of coat types, colors, and sizes ranging from dwarf (1 kilogram) to giant (10 kilograms). The general public has changed its opinion about wild rabbits, once regarded as pests, under the influence of their experience with the sweet, hutched, pet rabbits. This change in opinion is also facilitated in Europe because the number of rabbits has decreased so substantially due to disease and the introduction of predators such as foxes, that the wild rabbits are no longer pests. Yet, nature reserve managers have discovered that rabbits play an essential role in preserving biodiversity, in particular maintaining wild meadow vegetation communities and their associated animals and insects. The new interest in the rabbit is fed by a growing positive feeling of people who identify wild rabbits with their pet rabbits. So, in its long history with humans, the rabbit is assuming a new meaning again: Having been a prestigious animal for the nobility, a valued dish for town dwellers, and a pest for the farmer, it now becomes a highly appreciated aid of the nature manager.

Petra J. E. M. van Dam

Further Reading

Sheail, J. (1991). The management of an animal population: Changing the attitude towards the wild rabbit in Britain. *Journal of Environmental Management, 33,* 189–203.

Thompson, H. V., & King, C. M. (1994). *The European rabbit: The history and biology of a successful colonizer.* Oxford, UK: Oxford University Press.

Van Dam, P. J. E. M. (2001). Status loss due to ecological success. Landscape change and the spread of the rabbit. *Innovation: The European Journal of Social Science Research, 14*(2), 157–170.

Ranching

Ranching is an animal production system that uses livestock or other herbivores to harvest forage from extensive pastures or rangelands. Rangelands are grasslands, shrublands, and woodlands that although unsuitable for cultivation or forestry, produce plants edible by herbivores. A ranch usually includes significant amounts of individually held or used land and produces commercial products, while traditional pastoral systems are characteristically subsistence oriented and use some common grazing lands. Ranching is unlike farming and feedlot livestock production because most grazing is of naturally growing vegetation.

The term ranch is derived from the Spanish term *rancho*, as modified in the New World to describe a livestock-producing property. In the Iberian Peninsula ranching might be considered to have evolved from pastoral forms with the development of markets and changes in land tenure, but in much of the world ranching is historically linked to nineteenth- and twentieth-century colonial expansion. Labor and infrastructure needs are not great, so extensive acreages can be occupied and claimed by few people. Hides, tallow, and other preserved livestock products were traded across the seas. European colonists brought ranching to many

areas where it remains an important part of the economy, including North and South America, Australia, New Zealand, and Africa.

Cattle and sheep have always been the most commonly ranched livestock, with some ranching of other livestock such as buffalo, goats, llamas, yaks, and camels. Standardization and single-species production are hallmarks of the modern industry. The implantation of closed pastures, private holdings, and commercial livestock production into traditional pastoral systems in the twentieth century as a means of fostering "third world development" has had multiple social, economic, and environmental consequences, few of them believed to be beneficial.

Game ranching, the rangeland-based production of native and non-native wildlife species, may use deer, reindeer, moose, bison, emus, and ostriches. Commercial products may include "hunting" opportunities, meat, feathers, antlers, or specialty leather. In recent decades, ranching of red deer in New Zealand for antler velvet has become an important commercial enterprise.

Because forage quality and amount varies spatially and temporally, it is not uncommon for a ranch cycle of production to include annual herding to seasonal grazing areas, termed "transhumance." Ranching is often associated with mixed tenure arrangements. For example, a rancher in the Intermountain West of the United States may use Forest Service, Bureau of Land Management, and private lands in order to complete an annual herding cycle. The Homestead Act of 1862 and other nineteenth-century land distribution schemes of the U.S. government were for crop cultivation, and made the acquisition of extensive rangelands by private owners difficult. Ranchers claimed watered lands for cultivation and habitation, grazing their stock on the surrounding arid public domain. Starting in 1891, Forest Reserves were removed from the public domain and grazing was to varying degrees controlled on them, but the remaining public domain was kept in open access tenure, with no formal control of use, until the 1934 Taylor Grazing Act established Grazing Districts and a formal process for controlling grazing was initiated. In the meantime, competition among ranchers and transient herders for forage, speculative overstocking by investors, and droughts and unusually harsh winters led to overgrazing and sporadic livestock die-offs. In the Intermountain West and Rockies, unusually harsh winters killed millions of animals in the 1890s. Eventually, the Forest Reserves came to be administered by the Forest Service and much of the arid public domain by the Bureau of Land Management.

Almost all ecologists agree that the impacts of historic overgrazing damaged watercourses, changed plant communities, and caused soil erosion that is still a factor today. At this point the agreement ends, however, with some scientists arguing that rangeland conditions in general continue to decline under the influence of livestock grazing, and others arguing that rangeland conditions have steadily but slowly improved with the twentieth-century introduction of control of the timing and numbers of livestock on the public range. All do agree that introduced species, wildlife management, wild horses, climate change, water diversion, and changes in fire regimes have had major effects, but the relationship between these factors and ranching activity remains a debate and a subject of research.

Most modern North American ranches market calves weaned annually from a beef-cow herd. Sheep production has declined since its peak in the early twentieth century, although in New Mexican and Arizonan Native American and Hispanic communities ranching sheep for wool and meat remains of great economic and cultural significance. Ranch practices in the United States retain Spanish, Mexican, and Southern characteristics, just as in other countries they include northern and southern European, as well as local, influences. Because ranch production relies on the characteristics and natural capacity of local environments, each ranch and herd is unique. On the other hand, many of values and beliefs of ranchers, as well as practices and management goals, are widely shared.

Overproduction of grains in the United States, most notably corn, stimulated the development of a grain-fed livestock industry as a way of adding value to the crop beginning in the 1930s and expanding after World War II. Calves are purchased, usually from ranches, and put in feedlots to fatten them for market for five months to a year, resulting in low-priced, mass-produced beef. American ranchers today are subject to the vicissitudes of this industry, composed largely of speculative corporate investment, while the American consumer has learned to expect the flavor and look of grain-fed meat.

Recent research showing the superior health benefits of "grass-fattened" beef, interest in ranching for environmental goals including the conversion of cropland to grassland, concerns about the feeding of hormones and sub-therapeutic doses of antibiotics to feedlot animals, and interest in animal welfare,

have generated a small countertrend toward range-produced meats. The American model for grain-fed livestock production has been followed in a limited sense in other parts of the world, but grass-fattened lamb and beef is still marketed on a large scale in South America, New Zealand, Australia, and some other countries.

Conservationists have viewed ranching as a continuing cause of environmental destruction, and alternatively, as a means of conserving vast acreages of private lands as open space and wildlife habitat. In addition to the ecological impacts of grazing animals, ranchers throughout the world have altered water sources and vegetation to suit ranch production. This can include fencing, digging wells, diverting and consuming water, road construction, removal of trees and shrubs by burning, herbicides, and other means. Impacts are usually not as severe as those of cultivation, and ranches may continue to provide habitat for numerous wildlife species, as well as watershed, under the right conditions. In some areas, wildlife species have come to depend on the vegetation management practices and stockponds of ranchers. Various non-governmental conservation groups and land trusts have acquired ranches or conservation easements on ranches to prevent subdivision and development. On the other hand, the ranch environment cannot be termed environmentally pristine.

Environmental historians have looked at North American ranches as examples of colonial exploitation and destruction of North American natural resources, or, as a uniquely American lifeway expressive of the spirit of independence and self-sufficiency that defines "American culture." Perhaps because ranching is so closely intertwined with the settlement history of several nations, its local forms are often widely considered to be part of cultural heritage. The Australian and New Zealand "sheep station," the "finca" of the pampas in Argentina, and the American ranch, have become symbolic of human efforts to subdue a vast "wilderness," and are either championed or vilified accordingly.

Lynn Huntsinger and James Bartolome

Further Reading

Austin, M. D. (1904). *The land of little rain*. Boston: Houghton, Mifflin and Co.

Bell, S. (1989). *Campanha Gaúcha: A Brazilian ranching system, 1850–1920*. Stanford, CA: Stanford University Press.

Evans, S. M., Carter, S., & Yeo, B. (Eds.). (2000). *Cowboys, ranchers, and the cattle business: Cross-border perspectives on ranching history.* Boulder: University Press of Colorado.

Gressley, G. M. (1971). *Bankers and cattlemen.* Lincoln: University of Nebraska Press.

Heathcote, R. L. (1983). *The arid lands: Their use and abuse.* New York: Longman.

Jordan-Byychkov, T. G. (1993). *North American cattle ranching frontiers: Origins, diffusion, and differentiation.* Albuquerque: University of New Mexico Press.

Knight, R. L., Gilgert, W. C., & Marston, E. (2002). *Ranching west of the 100th meridian: Culture, ecology, and economics.* Washington, DC: Island Press.

Marshall, H. W., & Ahlborn, R. E. (1980). *Buckaroos in paradise: Cowboy life in northern Nevada.* Washington, DC: Library of Congress, Publications of the American Folklife Center, Number 6.

Sandford, S. (1983). *Management of pastoral development in the Third World.* New York: Wiley & Sons.

Sandoz, M. (1935). *Old Jules.* Boston: Little, Brown, and Co.

Slatta, R. W. (1990). *Cowboys of the Americas.* New Haven, CT: Yale University Press, Yale Western Americana series.

Starrs, P. F. (1998). *Let the cowboy ride: Cattle ranching in the American West.* Baltimore: Johns Hopkins University Press.

Stegner, W. E. (1954). *Beyond the hundredth meridian: John Wesley Powell and the second opening of the West.* Boston: Houghton, Mifflin.

United States Dept. of Agriculture. Office of the Secretary. (1936) *The western range; letter from the Secretary of Agriculture transmitting in response to Senate Resolution no.289. A report on the western range, a great but neglected natural resource.* Washington, DC: U.S. Govt. Printing Office.

Recreation *See* Parks and Recreation; Sports; Summer Camps

Redwoods

Forests of redwood *(Sequoia sempervirens)* covered approximately 800,000 hectares of the Pacific Coast region of North America at the time of European contact in the eighteenth century. Early in the twentieth century almost all of the covered area—extending from Monterey County, California, north to the border of California and Oregon—was claimed out of the public domain by timber companies and other private parties, forcing those interested in saving old-growth redwood to purchase the trees from private landowners. But old-growth redwoods provide lumber of such high quality that purchasing them was costly. Nevertheless, many people were distressed by the logging of redwoods, which are among the tallest living things in the world and as much as two thousand years old. Largely due to pressure from the Sempervirens Club (now known as the Sempervirens Fund), the California state legislature appropriated funds in 1902 to purchase the Big Basin redwoods in the Santa Cruz Mountains. Later, the Save-the-Redwoods League, founded in 1918, played the pivotal role in the creation of the California state park system in the 1930s and in following decades in the establishment of Prairie Creek, Jedediah Smith Redwoods, Humboldt Redwoods, and Del Norte Redwoods State Parks. The league raises private funding (often matched by state funds), largely through the establishment of memorial groves, many lining the Redwood Highway, which runs north-south through California's Humboldt and Del Norte Counties. In the mid-1950s floodwaters sweeping through fresh logging sites tore at the soils of the magnificent Founders Grove in Humboldt Redwoods State Park, necessitating stream restoration and erosion control and efforts to acquire the park's entire Bull Creek watershed.

In 1960 the Sierra Club launched a campaign to convince Congress to appropriate federal funds to save "the last redwoods" outside of the state parks. Redwood National Park, established in 1968, was, however, a political compromise, protecting only 12,342 hectares in two units (at an initial appropriation of $92 million). The southern unit was situated on Redwood Creek; logging on the still privately held slopes above Redwood Creek caused erosion that threatened the "Tall Trees" of the national park. Led by the Sierra Club, environmentalists convinced Congress to acquire 19,424 hectares in the Redwood Creek watershed in 1978 (at an initial cost of $379 million). Because 15,786 of these hectares had already been logged, the act provided $33 million for reforestation and rehabilitation of the watershed. The act also included substantial sums to compensate loggers and mill workers. The state and national parks are now under the combined management of the California State Division of Parks and Recreation and the National Park Service in the U.S. Department of the Interior.

The logging of privately held old-growth trees, especially in Humboldt County, continued to spark dissent. In 1990 members of Earth First! organized the Redwood Summer campaign, calling on college students across the nation to gather in northern California for a protest. Through the 1990s the issue of old-growth forest threatened by logging radicalized some grass-roots environmentalist, resulting in tree sittings and other forms of civil disobedience. The Save-the-Redwoods League continues to purchase lands for the state and national parks, including its acquisition in 2002 of 10,117 hectares along Mill Creek in Del Norte County that will protect the watershed of Jedediah Smith Redwoods State Park. Despite such efforts, less than 10 percent of the original acreage of old-growth redwoods is located in public parks.

Susan Schrepfer

Further Reading

Hyde, P., & Leydet, F. (1964). *The last redwoods: Photographs and story of a vanishing scenic resource*. San Francisco: Sierra Club Books.

Schrepfer, S. R. (1983). *The fight to save the redwoods: A history of environmental reform, 1917–1978*. Madison: University of Wisconsin Press.

Reforestation

Reforestation is the process of planting and growing trees in areas that historically have supported forests. Reforestation may be accomplished by deliberate planting or by "natural" means, under which trees regenerate on lands that have been cut over or abandoned. A related term, afforestation, usually refers to the planting of trees on lands that have not supported forests in the past.

Recent decades have seen considerable debate over the terms of global reforestation—what type of trees shall be grown, under what conditions, and for whose benefit. Besides providing raw material for the lumber and paper industries, forests during the twentieth century came to be valued for less-tangible benefits such as flood control and recreational opportunities. Especially since 1980, forests have been recognized for their role in mitigating global climate change ("global

warming"). Forests—particularly tropical forests—are now viewed as crucial reservoirs of biodiversity, being home to thousands of as-yet-uncounted species. More nations are committing themselves to "sustainable" forest management, under which forests can provide annual increments of goods and services in perpetuity. And foresters are being urged to manage their lands as part of larger "ecosystems," acknowledging the delicate web of connections between forests and water, air, plant, and animal resources. The heightened importance attached to forests at the beginning of the twenty-first century portends a growing battle over the conditions under which reforestation will occur. Key actors include governments, scientists, forest-products companies, transnational groups such as the United Nations, and a growing flock of non-government organizations interested in environmental and development issues.

A History of Depletion

From the beginnings of civilization, human beings cut trees for use as fuel and shelter, and cleared forests for agriculture and grazing, often by burning them. But the global impact was relatively slight until the beginning of the Industrial Revolution. A burgeoning, increasingly affluent population cut more trees after 1800, particularly in North America and Europe. Industrialized countries such as the United States experienced rapid forest depletion until about 1920. Public concern over a potential "timber famine" helped build support for government planting of forests on lands that were considered poor for agriculture. At the same time, much land in developed nations reverted to forest naturally as farms failed. As the amount of forested area in industrialized countries leveled off, however, cutting accelerated in developing nations. Brazil, for example, experienced relentless depletion of its tropical rain forest for mining and ranching. At the end of the twentieth century the Earth was still experiencing a net loss of forests each year. According to the Union of Concerned Scientists, forests in 1999 covered 27 percent of the Earth's land surface—about 35 million square kilometers. About half the planet's forests had disappeared since the end of the last Ice Age.

Concern over forest depletion dates to ancient times. The Romans codified provisions against forest cutting as early as 450 BCE. Forest guardians of the Middle Ages were more concerned with private rights than with any public utility attached to forests. Particularly in central Europe, they spelled out harsh penalties for timber destruction on crown lands, which were used by nobles for hunting. The Swiss recognized the usefulness of forests in preventing floods and avalanches as early as the fourteenth century. Their local, site-specific ordinances against forest cutting were replicated elsewhere in Europe.

"Inventing" Reforestation

Jean-Baptiste Colbert (1619–1683), named by Louis XIV as administrator of French forests in the 1660s, might fairly be described as the "father" of reforestation. His "Ordonnance des Eaux et Forets," promulgated in 1669, brought about the widespread planting of oak forests with one long-term aim: the provision of wood for building warships. Others had called for forest planting earlier—England, for example, had launched a short-lived program to stock its woodlands in the late sixteenth century. But Colbert's work was more far-reaching and systematic. A pioneer in forest data collection, he sent teams of workers into the woods to measure and otherwise assess standing timber. The forerunners of today's "timber cruisers," these workers provided hard evidence of forest depletion, enough so that the monarchy continued to bankroll Colbert's fledgling bureaucracy until the French Revolution more than a hundred years later. Scattered specimens of Colbert's magnificent oaks, including some in what are now the exurbs of Paris, survived into the twentieth century.

Efforts in forest science and management were undergirded by the appearance of numerous polemical works arguing for reforestation. John Evelyn (1620–1706) published an early forest text, *Silva, or a Discourse of Forest Trees and the Propagation of Timber in His Majesty's Dominion*, in 1664. Evelyn, like many of his contemporaries, viewed forests chiefly as a source of oak for warships. Hans Carl von Carlowitz (1645–1714), a civil servant in Saxony, first articulated the concept of "sustainable" forestry in his *Sylvicultura Oeconomica* in 1713. He wrote in response to the timber depletion that threatened the economic health of Saxony's mining and smelting industries.

Influenced by the economic theories of Adam Smith, many European nations repealed their forest laws after 1790. State-owned timberlands also were sold off; France alone had transferred a million hectares into private hands by 1823. But the resulting devastation inspired new forest laws after about 1850. In Europe and elsewhere, ordinances often were drafted in response to specific environmental calamities brought about by deforestation. Crews planted tens of thousands of trees, for example, in the denuded Tijuca Forest in the heart of Rio de Janeiro, Brazil, after 1860. The tropical forest had been stripped to make way for coffee plantations; the resulting runoff had contaminated streams that supplied city residents with water.

Forging a Discipline

Laws alone, many foresters realized, were not always sufficient to bring about forest protection and replanting. Forestry had to be established as an academic and managerial discipline. France and Prussia offered classroom study in forestry by the 1870s. Incorporating pursuits from silviculture to soil science and economics, the Prussian foresters would have wide influence. Several founders of American forestry, such as Bernhard E. Fernow (1851–1923), were Prussian immigrants. Other Americans, most notably Gifford Pinchot, the first chief of what would become the U.S. Forest Service, learned their craft in Europe. Pinchot (1865–1946) studied forestry in France and Germany. In 1892 he began managing the forests of the sprawling Biltmore estate in North Carolina, a demonstration project in sustained-yield forestry.

A few ardent foresters could not halt the reckless depletion of American timber in the decades after the Civil War. Westward expansion created an almost insatiable demand for sawlogs, which were milled into lumber and shipped to the prairies to build homes, churches, and schools. The virgin softwood of the Great Lakes states was nearly depleted by 1910. Lumbermen themselves then moved west, leaving behind a scarred landscape of stumps and brush.

Fearing a "timber famine," foresters worked tirelessly to rejuvenate this devastated land, but the terms of the battle soon changed in ways they did not expect. Agricultural interests had hoped to fill the cutover lands with farms, but poor soils caused many farmers to fail. The agricultural sector, made more productive by fertilizer and mechanization, was growing more food than the nation could consume, and the amount of land under tillage actually decreased in the early 1920s, a phenomenon unprecedented in American history. Under these harsh conditions, cutover farming was all but doomed. In a pattern that would be repeated in many developed nations, the cutover regions lost population, and much of the land reverted to government ownership for non-payment of taxes. At the onset of the Great Depression in the 1930s, foresters suddenly found themselves in possession of a vast swath of the public domain. Increasingly efficient agriculture had left a smaller and smaller footprint, and more land was left open for growing trees.

What to Plant?

Confronted with barren land, foresters often responded by filling it with a monoculture of trees to provide timber and a modicum of scenery and other amenities. Germany stocked much of its cutover land with Scotch pine and Norway spruce, shifting the composition of that country's forests from mostly hardwoods to mostly conifers. Most timber crops were planted plantation-style, in neat rows of trees of uniform age. Plantings that veered too far from "natural" sometimes angered people who attached sentimental or historical value to forests. England encountered much public resistance in the 1930s over the large-scale planting of conifers, hitherto a rare sight in that land of oak and beech.

Before World War II, Germany briefly embraced the "Dauerwald" model of forest management, which called for mixed-species, uneven-aged plantings to imitate the complexity of an indigenous forest. The American forester and game manager Aldo Leopold (1886–1948), an inventor of the science of restoration ecology, applauded the Dauerwald concept as an appealing alternative to the plodding uniformity of most replanted forests. After failing to take hold in Leopold's time, the Dauerwald ideal would be resurrected many years later as a model for instilling biodiversity and sustainability in replanted forests.

Especially in places with huge swaths of cutover land, much forest regeneration in the twentieth century simply happened on its own. Self-generating lands often were brush-filled and prone to fire, and unproductive in terms of timber growth. But the sheer volume of these lands was so great as to be beyond the reach of the state forestry apparatus. In parts of the northeastern United States, for example, the exodus of farmers cleared the way for the widespread, largely spontaneous return of forests. New York was 20 percent forested in 1890; a century later trees covered more than 60 percent of the state. Finnish scientists in the 1980s reported that forests in the world's mid- and high latitudes were increasing, not just in area covered but in the volume of wood and other living matter per hectare of land.

The Plantation Era

With the advent of the modern environmental movement about 1970, the politics of forestry grew increasingly fractious and complicated. Foresters who had once counted on the public to accede to their "expertise" now found themselves being questioned on many fronts. Cutting of old-growth forests, for example, came under sharp attack from environmental interest groups. Falling trade barriers and the ascendance of global capitalism raised new concerns about the impact of industrial forests on the people and environments of developing nations. Beginning about 1980, scientific research began to attach new and vital importance to forests. These findings were enunciated politically at the 1992 Rio "Earth Summit," which called for sustainable forest management, and by the 1997 Kyoto Protocol, which specified the role of forests in sequestering carbon to mitigate global warming. Striving for biodiversity, some scientific and political groups called for rejection of clear-cutting and age-class silviculture in favor of Dauerwald principles of planting and harvest. Foresters who had managed woodlands primarily for timber a generation before now were beset with multiple, sometimes conflicting goals for their work.

Forest plantations would evoke many of these conflicts. Systematic planting of trees dated to Colbert's France, but late-twentieth-century plantations were unique in their size and scope. Usually monocultures of fast-growing trees such as eucalyptus, pine, or poplar, the plantations were intensively managed to provide reliable outputs of pulpwood or lumber. By 2000, pine plantations accounted for almost a third of all the forests in the southeastern United States. Growing at twice the rate of natural stands, these forests helped the region supply 15 percent of the world's industrial timber. A major impetus for this planting was the clampdown on logging in the U.S. Pacific Northwest and Canada's British Columbia, where environmental concerns had reduced the felling of old-growth forests. Similar scenarios unfolded elsewhere. China, Malaysia, Thailand, and Indonesia, among others, restricted the cutting of old-growth forests in the 1990s. Such measures often were undone by illegal logging, but their net effect was to increase the uncertainty of supply. Worldwide, this uncertainty boosted the cost of old-growth timber. Plantation logs were cheap by comparison, so forest planting accelerated. As of 2000, about three-fifths of plantation forestland was located in Asia. Chile, Brazil, South Africa, and New Zealand also were among the pioneers in this new, and largely untested, forest discipline.

Forests for Tomorrow

At the start of the twenty-first century, visions of the world's future forest are divided into two camps. The polarization of the debate is exceeded perhaps only by its contentiousness.

One side predicts a "Great Restoration" of the world's forests by 2050, powered by increasingly efficient agriculture and a global network of high-output forest plantations. Developing nations, under this scenario, will pass through a "forest transition" much like that encountered by industrialized countries early in the twentieth century. Forest depletion will slow, agriculture will be mechanized, and plantation forests will supply industrial wood reliably and economically. Genetically altered trees will grow faster and resist pests and disease. Such intensive inputs will allow plantations to produce outsize yields of wood in relatively small spaces. The larger "natural" forests, meanwhile, will be left unmolested, free to provide recreation, scenery, wildlife habitat, biodiversity, and other amenities.

The opposing camp argues that plantations are not really "forests" at all, but utterly artificial monocultures that require constant intervention to keep them functioning. Because they deplete the soil, upset ecosystems, and perpetuate poverty in developing countries, they ultimately will prove unsustainable. The idea that plantations will spare the rest of the world's forests from abuse is only diverting attention from larger issues, such as loss of biodiversity, which may gravely affect the planet's ecological health. As an alternative vision, this group envisions true sustainability through ecosystem management, conservation, and local citizen involvement in forestry, especially in developing nations.

James Kates

Further Reading

Carley, M., & Christie, I. (2000). *Managing sustainable development* (2nd ed.). London: Earthscan Publications Ltd.

Drummond, J. (1996). The garden in the machine: An environmental history of Brazil's Tijuca Forest. *Environmental History, 1*(1), 83–104.

Hays, S. P. (1959). *Conservation and the gospel of efficiency: The progressive conservation movement, 1890–1920.* Cambridge, MA: Harvard University Press.

Higman, S., Bass, S., Judd, N., Mayers, J., & Nussbaum, R. (2000). *The sustainable forestry handbook.* London: Earthscan Publications Ltd.

Kennedy, J. J., Dombeck, M. P., & Koch, N. E. (1998). Values, beliefs and management of public forests in the Western world at the close of the twentieth century. *Unasylva, 49*(1), 16–26.

Mann, C. C., & Plummer, M. L. (2002). Forest biotech edges out of the lab. *Science,* 295 (1 March), 1626–1629.

Mather, A. (1992). The forest transition. *Area, 24*(4), 367–379.

Miller, C. (2000). The pivotal decade: American forestry in the 1870s. *Journal of Forestry, 98*(11), 6–10.

Morris, J. (Ed.). (2002). *Sustainable development: Promoting progress or perpetuating poverty?* London: Profile Books.

Schabel, H. G., & Palmer, S. L. (1999). The Dauerwald: Its role in the restoration of natural forests. *Journal of Forestry, 97*(11), 20–25.

Steen, H. K. (1976). *The U.S. Forest Service: A history.* Seattle: University of Washington Press.

United Nations Food and Agriculture Organization. (2001). *State of the world's forests 2001.* Rome: U.N. FAO.

Victor, D. G., & Ausabel, J. H. (2000). Restoring the forests. *Foreign Affairs, 79*(6), 127–144.

Williams, M. (1989). *Americans and their forests: A historical geography.* Cambridge, UK: Cambridge University Press.

Regulation *See* Environmental Regulation; International Law; Law—Biological Conservation; Law—Land Use and Property Rights; Law—Toxic Waste; Law—Water Pollution and Air Pollution; Law of the Sea

Religion *See* Catholicism; Confucianism; Cosmology; Ecology, Christian; Ecology, Spiritual; Eden; Hinduism; Islam; Jainism; Judaism; Millennialism; Protestantism; Religion, American Indian; Sacred Places; Shamanism; Shinto; Taoism

Religion, American Indian

The basis for religion in the cultures of American Indians is their relationship with the land. As members of subsistence-based societies that derived their living from hunting, gathering, fishing, and agriculture, American Indians lived intimately with the cycles of nature. They guided their collective lives in ceremonies timed by the cycles of the sun, moon, and stars. They adapted to an incredibly diverse range of environments, from the high deserts of the Southwest to the densely forested and humid regions of the Southeast. These environments influenced such diverse cultures as the highly individualistic societies of the Navajo and Apache and the hierarchical Natchez society of the Mississippi River valley.

Environment is not, however, the deterministic element in American Indian cultures. Although cultures adapt, quite different cultures may share the same environment. The highly communal Pueblos arose in the Southwest long before the arrival and emergence of the Navajos and Apaches. A number of tribes, including the Kiowa, Cheyenne, Lakota, Oto, Ponca, and Pawnee, migrated to the Great Plains. The Kiowa were hunters, and the Cheyenne were agriculturalists, and both adapted aspects of their social organization to the highly mobile lifestyle of the Great Plains. The Cheyenne, for example, retained in oral traditions the story of their origins in the region of the Great Lakes, but they also had memories of how new ceremonies were given to them by White Buffalo Calf Woman on the Great Plains.

Any discussion of American Indian religions should acknowledge that an essential aspect of their power lies in secrecy. Esoteric knowledge is at the heart of religious experiences. The power of a vision is in the personal and emotional experience of the individual, something impossible to convey in purely intellectual terms. The power of an initiation ritual is in the knowledge that an individual gains as a result of the experience, something that sets him or her apart from the uninitiated. Although the written word privileges the notion of an absolute truth, the power of American Indian religious beliefs comes from their very personal nature.

American Indian communities are also highly dynamic and have adopted new ideas and new ceremonies through both intertribal contacts and historical contacts with European religions. Pueblo peoples in the Southwest have assimilated the practices of Catholicism into traditional religious cycles. The very names of Pueblo communities—Santa Clara, San Ildefonso, San Juan—are evidence of this adaptation.

A Sense of Place

Despite centuries of European colonization and attempts to destroy the religious beliefs of Native American peoples in the name of civilization, the very source of American Indian identity, association with a land base, has remained the basic source of the political and cultural persistence of tribes, and it remains a source of cultural identity. Place names are a source of cultural values for the Apache, for instance. By reference to events that occurred long ago in certain places, people are reminded of the consequences of inappropriate behavior. The Black Hills in South Dakota are an important source of Lakota identity. It was there that the great race between the two-leggeds (birds, bears, and humans) and the four-leggeds took place. It went on so long that the racetrack was worn down, pushing up the land in the center and forming the Black Hills. Buffalo was ahead in the race, but Magpie had perched on his back and flew across the finish line first, thus establishing the hierarchy that humans would hunt animals. The contemporary cultural and political struggle of the Oglala Lakota to preserve their rights to the Black Hills in South Dakota is still important to contemporary Lakota identity.

The source of spirituality in American Indian religions is the sense of immanent power in the physical environment. Trees, rivers, animals, plants, rocks—physical phenomena—are alive in that they exhibit the ability to move and to change. Their actions are not under human control. The movement of storms is unpredictable. This sense of spiritual power in the world is expressed in the terms *wakan* (sacred) and *wakonda* (Lakota and other Siouian languages), *Manitou* (Chippewa and other Algonquian languages), and *orenda* (Iroquois). *Wakan* is manifest in the blue of the sky, the sun and moon, the winds, the earth, buffalo, the rocks, which exhibit the power of endurance, and White Buffalo Calf Woman, the spiritual being who taught the Lakota their sacred rituals. *Orenda* is found in the sounds of nature, and the term in Iroquoian languages refers both to spiritual power and the human act of praying. *Manitou* shows itself in the behavior of animals and storms and even rocks. A Chippewa man, asked by an anthropologist, "Are all the stones we see around us alive?" responded, "No, but some are." The "some" demonstrates the essence of American Indian religions. American Indians live in and utilize the resources of their environments on a daily basis, but they are always aware that things can act in unexpected ways. "Some" stones fall through the smoke holes of lodges or speak or move on their own and thus exhibit spiritual characteristics.

The environment is the source of religious experience, but that experience comes in two ways. For many societies, it must take place outside the confines of village life, where kinship and common knowledge structure behavior. Men must go to places where spirits dwell. Cheyenne vision quests often took place at Bear Lodge, called "Devil's Tower" by contemporary Americans. Bear Lodge is a spectacular volcanic plug in Wyoming now maintained by the National Park Service and is a major tourist site. For other societies, it must take place in a communal setting but in ceremonies that suspend regular social activity and create sacred time and space. In both ways, however, the experience is intensely personal and emotional.

The Black Hills are a source of that power for the Lakota. Young men go there to fast and pray for the appearance of a spirit to give them knowledge. By depriving themselves of food, water, and sleep, they offer their human suffering to the spirits and seek their pity. Menominee children were sent out into the forests from an early age to spend the day without food. This early preparation culminated in an extended period of fasting and praying to establish a relationship with a spirit. In northern California, men dived into deep pools of water in rivers to seek spiritual power, or they went to areas in the forests where they could fast and pray to seek power. The essence of these rituals was and is to establish an ongoing personal relationship between an individual and the spiritual world. The vision quest is an acknowledgment of the dependence of human beings on the forces of nature, an offering of the suffering associated with human deprivation to seek pity and power from the spiritual world.

The Power of Dreams

If visions are consciously sought, dreams are also a source of personal knowledge and power. Where the environment is viewed as highly uncertain and threatening, dreams offer access to personal power. The Seneca in upstate New York saw dreams as harbingers of illness, which could be avoided by acting out their dreams. The Mohave in southern California believed that dreams of infants in the womb gave the special talents and inclinations that shaped their lives as adults. Navajo saw their world as essentially dangerous. Winds, lightning, and sudden floods threatened human life. The Navajo relied on dreams to sustain their relationships with the spiritual world.

Other societies in similar environments established their relationships in much more structured ways. In Pueblo societies, which are sedentary and highly dependent on agriculture, many ceremonies involve all members, but initiation into secret societies is the key to individual knowledge. In kivas, underground rooms devoted to ceremonial activity, children encounter the kachinas, spirits who live in the mountains or lakes and who spend part of the year living in the villages with the people. The kachinas dance in the plazas of the villages, and they threaten unruly children. In the initiation rites, they whip children with yucca leaves, but they also take off their masks to reveal that they are the male relatives of the children. This shock of revelation leads ultimately to the realization that the men dress as the kachinas and dance to embody their spirits.

Through humans' knowledge of the spiritual world, whether gained in dreams, visions, or initiation, humans enter into relationships with the spirits that allow them to influence their manifestations in the forces of the natural world. Humans are not subject to impersonal forces of nature but play causal roles. Their prayers and actions evoke the response of the spirits. The Pueblo sustain their relationship with the environment through a cycle of ceremonies throughout the year. When bean seedlings are planted during a ceremony in February, they presage the growth of beans planted in the fields for food. Human prayer is the incentive for the crops to grow in the fields. Individuals may use the power they derive from spiritual relationships to influence the environment. Some people have the ability to cure illness, others to influence the movement of storms. Religion in American Indian societies is a matter of ongoing relationships with spiritual beings, maintained by ritual activity carried out in specific physical environments.

Ceremonies maintain the world, but they can also re-create it. They create a sense of space and time that transcends the ordinary and becomes sacred, that is, the realm in which humans have immediate access to the spiritual world. They are the ways in which humans renew their worlds. The White Deer Dance of the Hupa of northern California and the Green Corn Ceremony of the Cherokee in the Southeast share this characteristic of renewing the world with a specific ceremony at a particular time of year. The form of the Green Corn Ceremony has changed in more recent times, but in early historical accounts, women swept their homes and cleaned the village. Quarrels were settled. Household fires were put out and then relit from a central fire. This ceremony thus restored social relationships to an appropriate state and marked a new beginning for the Cherokee world.

Traditional Navajo chants, which are curing ceremonies, derive from the origin tradition that tells of the emergence of the people from worlds below. Bless-ingway, the basic ceremony, is the story of emergence, and each of the twenty-three recorded chants is then derived from traditions of events thereafter. The retelling of these traditions becomes a way of renewing the world and restoring it to a state of perfect balance and harmony known as *hozho*. This sense of renewal demonstrates the power of humans in their ongoing relationship with the spiritual world.

Spiritual Power

The spiritual power in the world is ambivalent, neither totally good nor totally evil. The forces of nature have their own will and volition, and human beings are not their primary concern. Origin traditions in some tribes describe a dichotomy between creative and destructive forces. Seneca traditions tell of the woman who fell from the sky to become the progenitor of life on Earth. She produced two children. One was born in the human way, and the other burst out through her side, killing her. The first twin went on to create the good things of the world—domesticated crops—and the other created the unpleasant things—thistles, weeds, annoying insects, poisonous snakes.

The ethical implications of spiritual power in the human community come from the ambiguity of power. Humans who have access to power can choose to use it for positive ends such as foretelling the future, controlling the weather, or curing illnesses. Good and evil in the human world are defined by the expectations of the community rather than by dogma. Good for the individual is generally expressed as health, long life, and happiness. The Chippewa term *pimidaziwin* has this meaning. For the society, it is the sense of balance and harmony that means that all beings, spiritual and human, stand in respectful and appropriate relationship with each other.

These social norms are enforced in human society by community opinion. In the setting of the village, people are aware of their relationships to community members. Kin relations are defined in terms of social obligations and privileges. In matrilineal societies such as the Hopi in the Southwest, male relatives in the mother's line have paternal obligations to their sister's children. On the Great Plains, where extended families constituted the basic unit of social organization, the family as a whole assumed responsibility for children.

In the human world, people can use the powers that they derive from spiritual relationships to influence not only natural phenomena but also, in a nega-

tive sense, the behavior or circumstances of other individuals. The term *witchcraft* is generally used for this use of spiritual power. In American Indian societies, which value the integrity of the individual above all else, the power of a witch to cause someone to become sick or to fall in love, to impose his or her will upon another, is the ultimate wrong. Charms, sometimes certain plants, and spells control spiritual power and turn it against other human beings. The result may be sickness, loss of property, or unexplained death.

This notion of the ambiguity of power is manifest most dramatically in the figure of the trickster—Wene-bojo, Nanbojo, or Nanabusho in Algonquian societies, Iktome the spider for the Lakota, the Kiowa Saynday figure, or the widely known Coyote. Coyote is constantly on the move, never becoming fully integrated into any social group, and he thus remains the outsider whose power is not fully explained through kin relations. The trickster embodies uncontrolled appetites for food, sex, revenge, and control over other beings. His powers encompass both creative and destructive elements. His actions, intentionally or unintentionally, account for certain aspects of the physical environment, but he is often made the fool by other animals and suffers physical mutilation or death as a result of his actions. Depending on the culture, he is viewed as more creative (Wenebojo kills the Snake King, causing a flood, into which he sends various animals to dive to the bottom to bring up mud, which he then causes to expand into this Earth), or more foolish, where Coyote is constantly trying to trick other animals but ends up the fool. Essentially, the trickster figure embodies the best and worst of human nature. He also represents the consequences of uncontrolled behavior.

Sacred Clowns

In Pueblo societies, sacred clowns play an essential role within their highly structured ceremonial life. Clowns reverse ordinary human behavior, representing disorder and chaos. They may mimic unrestrained sexual behavior or use ashes for logs in building simulated houses. They turn meaning on its head and by negative example reinforce notions of proper social order. Although such behavior would endanger the social standing and possibly the physical health of a human, the spiritual nature of the clowns is that they can behave this way without fear of punishment. Indeed, it is their role to embody such behaviors. They also define social boundaries by making fun of foreigners (other tribes and sometimes disrespectful tourists). In this regard their role in society is similar to that of tricksters. This reversal of meaning occurs in many other cultures—Heyokas in Lakota ceremonies, the Bluejay figure among tribes in Washington and Oregon. Human social behavior is disciplined not by dogma but by the personal experience of observing inappropriate action.

The sacred clowns demonstrate that there is a close connection between the realm of humor and the idea of the sacred. The clowns behave in ways that evoke laughter. Shame and ridicule are powerful tools in American Indian societies, but ultimately their power is that they arise from something contrary to ordinary and expected human behavior. The realm of the spiritual is that realm where something in the environment—a rock, a plant, a storm—exhibits behavior that is unpredictable. Suddenly a rock is alive, a plant has special powers to cure a particular physical condition, or an old woman walking down a path suddenly disappears, to be replaced by a bear.

If ordinary social behavior is governed by laws of kinship or community expectations, human beings who have special spiritual powers stand both inside and outside of the social realm. The man who goes through initiation rites into the Midewiwin, or Medicine Society of the Chippewa, begins by seeking to be cured of an illness but also has access to greater spiritual powers in successive initiations into higher levels of the society. Those who reach the fourth level can cure illness, but they can also exercise that ultimate power of controlling the behavior of others. Again, human behavior is not ultimately good nor ultimately evil. It depends on the expectations of society and upon the relationship of the individual with spiritual forces in the environment. Native American religions derive ultimately from the intimate relationships that Native American people had and in many ways still have with the physical environment around them. Attuned to the rhythms of that environment, keenly aware of its vicissitudes, and dependent upon their relationships with the animals and plants that provided sustenance, Native American societies understood the basic spirituality of the world, and their religions came from that understanding.

Clara Sue Kidwell

Further Reading

Beck, P. V., & Walters, A. L. (1977). *The sacred: Ways of knowledge sources of life*. Tsaile, AZ: Navajo Community College.

Devereux, G. (1961). *Mohave ethnopsychiatry: The psychic disturbances of an Indian tribe*. Washington, DC: Smithsonian Institution Press.

Goodman, R. (1992). *Lakota star knowledge: Studies in Lakota stellar theology*. Rosebud, SD: Sinte Gleska University.

Hallowell, A. I. (1955). *Culture and experience*. Philadelphia: University of Pennsylvania Press.

Ortiz, A. (Ed.). (1972). *New perspectives on the Pueblos*. Albuquerque: University of New Mexico Press.

Reichard, G. (1983). *Navaho religion: A study of symbolism*. Tucson: University of Arizona Press.

Simmons, L. W. (Ed.). (1963). *Sun Chief: The autobiography of a Hopi Indian*. New Haven, CT: Yale University Press.

Stands in Timber, J., & Liberty, M. (1967). *Cheyenne memories* (2nd ed.). New Haven, CT: Yale University Press.

Tooker, E. (Ed.). (1979). *Native North American spirituality of the eastern woodlands*. New York: Paulist Press.

Wallace, A. F. C. (1969). *The death and rebirth of the Seneca*. New York: Random House.

Reptiles

Living reptiles are the turtles, crocodilians, birds, tuataras, lizards, and snakes. In our everyday language, birds are separated from the other reptiles, yet in a phylogenetic (evolutionary history) sense, birds are reptiles because they are most likely members of the dinosaur lineage and are definitely members of the Archosauria group. Archosaurs include the crocodilians and dinosaurs and their relatives, such as pterosaurs and birds. Among living reptiles, tuataras, lizards, and snakes comprise the Lepidosauria group. The turtles are commonly postulated to have arisen from an early or basal branch of the reptilian stock, although a few scientists recently have proposed a closer relationship to the lepidosaurs and archosaurs (i.e., diapsid [having two pairs of temporal openings in the skull] reptiles). No matter what their relationships, turtles (order Testudines) are an ancient group, with the earliest known turtle *(Proganochelys)* from the Upper Triassic period, about 220 million years ago. *Proganochelys* was unquestionably a turtle with a well-developed shell and many other features present in living turtle species. The first crocodilians (order Crocodilia) appeared in the Late Cretaceous period, approximately eighty million years ago; they were less like modern crocodilians than early turtles were to modern ones. Lepidosaurs appeared in the Middle Jurassic period with the tuatara ancestors (order Sphenodontia). The earliest lizards (order Squamata) are from the Middle Triassic period, but squamates (having scales) show little diversity until the Middle Cretaceous. Sphendontians remained a low-diversity group, with only a few species available at any particular geologic moment. Snakes arose from lizards, with the first fossil from the Middle Cretaceous.

All reptiles (class Reptilia) have epidermal scales of one sort or another, although scales may not cover the entire body. These scales range in size from tiny tubercle-scales of geckos to the large scutes or shields on the bony shells of turtles or tail feathers (modified scales) of a peacock. Reptilian scales are keratinous structures formed by the surface cells of the epidermal portion of the skin dying and flattening to form the dry, scaly surface. All vertebrates produce alpha keratin, but only reptiles also produce beta-keratin in the development of their scales. All reptiles also develop within a set of extraembryonic membranes (the amniotic sac), a trait shared with their sister group, the class Synapsida, today represented by mammals.

A Wide Diversity

Among living reptiles, the tuataras are represented by only two living species, *Sphenodon punctatus* and *S. guentheri*, living on some offshore islets of New Zealand. There are twenty-two or twenty-three crocodilians, depending upon the authority followed. Although not speciose (having a large number of species), crocodilians are a successful group and the top predator in many habitats. They can also be quite abundant in some areas. Turtles are the next most speciose group, with approximately 280 species, ranging from strictly terrestrial species to nearly fully marine species (only female sea turtles return to land to lay eggs), and from dwarf species with shell lengths of 8 centimeters to giants with shell lengths of over 1.5 meters. The squamates are very speciose, with at least 4,600 species of lizards and more than 2,600 species of snakes. The diversity of squamates ranges from tiny Caribbean geckos *(Sphaerodactylus)* with head-body lengths of 11–12 millimeters to giants like the anaconda *(Eunectes murinus)* and reticulated python *(Python reticulatus)*, both with confirmed lengths exceeding 8 meters. Squamates occur on all continents except Antarctica and most oceanic islands. Some species are burrowers, seldom emerging on the surface, others are totally marine, giving birth at sea and totally helpless if washed ashore (e.g., hydrophiid sea snakes).

Among living reptiles, in the common parlance excluding birds, tuataras have the least economical and environmental importance. Their importance lies in what scientists can learn about their biology because they represent the sole survivors of an ancient reptilian lineage and one that has remained largely unchanged for millions of years. The tuataras occurred on the main New Zealand islands prior to the arrival of humans (Polynesians), but owing to their moderate size (19–28 centimeters in head-body length), they were harvested for food. The Polynesians also introduced the Pacific rat *(Rattus exulans)*, which preys on young tuataras and eggs. The problem of rat predation increased with the arrival of Europeans and the black rat *(Rattus rattus)*, and tuataras have been extinct on the main islands for more than a century. Their current survival on offshore islands requires the proactive support of humans through the elimination of rats. Adult tuataras are long-lived (more than thirty-five years) and can survive on islands with rats, but all eggs and juveniles are killed by rats.

Reptiles, however, can be alien or invasive species as well and endanger the local (native) fauna. The red-eared slider, a river turtle from the lower Mississippi River, now occurs in South America, Asia, and Europe. It may be out-competing the local turtle species for space and food. However, the brown treesnake is most notorious of the alien reptiles. This snake was transported from its home in New Guinea to Guam with war materials in the late 1940s. It remained largely invisible in its new home, owing to small population size, but then its population exploded in the late 1980s. Guam residents begin to see fewer and fewer birds and eventually none as the treesnake ate them all.

The economical value of many lizards and snakes is greatly underestimated because people fail to value their role in rodent control. Rodent-eating snakes occur worldwide and consist of many species and genera. For example, two groups *(Elaphe* and allies and *Ptyas)* have the vernacular name "ratsnake" because of the high proportion of rodents in their diets. Rodent-eating snakes include nonvenomous and venomous species. Many pythons and boas eat mainly rodents and birds. These snakes and some of the colubrid (a family of chiefly nonvenomous snakes) snakes are constrictors. That is, they strike their prey, bite and hold the prey in their jaws, then throw a coil or two of their body around the prey. Until recently, it was assumed that constriction killed by suffocation; however, elaborate biomechanical experiments demonstrate that constriction suppresses the prey's normal heartbeat. Lack of blood flow and oxygen supply to the brain anesthetizes and kills the prey more rapidly than would suffocation.

The Value of Venom

Venom is usually proposed to have evolved as an evolutionary adaptation to minimize injury to a snake during prey capture. Venom can be highly specific for prey so that it quickly kills a fish, frog, or slug and yet has only a slight effect on a bird or mammal. For centuries, venoms have played an important role in various folk medicines, some physiologically effective, others psychologically effective. Modern science developed one of the first major heart attack medicines from snake venom in the 1950s. Research on biomedical application of venoms now is aimed mainly at pain reduction or elimination and control of blood clotting. With about seven hundred snake species with some type of venom, the search for biomedical uses has barely begun, and the possibilities are even broader because some species have different components in different geographic areas, usually depending upon the major prey eaten. Even though about one-quarter of the living snake species are venomous, only two lizards (Mexican beaded lizard and the Gila monster, family Helodermatidae) are venomous. These two lizards are desert denizens of the southwestern United States and north-central Mexico. These lizards create no health hazard to humans because of their secretive habits and remote habitats. Such is not the case for snakes in some areas; in the United States, venomous snake populations can be quite dense and occur in close association with humans. In South Asia, cobras, kraits, and Russell's vipers are common in rice-growing areas. The venom of these snakes is very toxic and a real threat to farmers. Over one hundred deaths occur each year in Myanmar from viper bites, particularly during harvest time when mice and rats attracted by the ripe grain attract the vipers.

Other dangerous reptiles are the saltwater crocodile and the Nile crocodile, the only two crocodilians that are confirmed to kill and eat people. The crocodilians, however, have more to fear from people than people from the crocodilians. Leather from crocodilian skin remains a specialty wildlife product. During the 1950s and 1960s, crocodilians were hunted heavily worldwide and in some areas to extinction. The decimation of crocodilian populations resulted in worldwide conservation and management efforts. The protection afforded the American alligator is a notable success. Alligators are again abundant in most rivers and swamps of the Southeast. Regulated hunting is now permitted to provide skins for the leather trade and meat for the gourmet market and to regulate alligator populations to maintain an ecological balance.

Presently turtles suffer the greatest human predation for the food trade, pet trade, and traditional Asian medicines. Land and freshwater turtle populations and species are extinct or nearly so in many areas of Asia, and the market has spread widely throughout the world, threatening turtles everywhere. Turtles are generally long-lived; most species mature slowly, commonly requiring ten to twenty years to reach sexual maturity. Thus, removal of adults quickly threatens the survival of a local population by removing the reproducing females, which are only slowly replaced. The problem is even greater for sea turtles, most of which require over twenty years to mature and which travel widely as they mature and as adults migrating between feeding grounds and nesting beaches. Slow maturation and wide travel expose them to many natural hazards as well as an increasing number of human hazards. Their conservation requires and is receiving a worldwide effort. It remains uncertain whether this effort will protect them through the twenty-first century.

George Zug

Further Reading

Benton, M. J. (1997). *Vertebrate paleontology* (2nd ed.). London: Chapman & Hall.

Cogger, H. G., & Zweifel, R. G. (Eds.). (1998). *Encyclopaedia of amphibians and reptiles* (2nd ed.). San Diego, CA: Academic Press.

Ernst, C. H., & Barbour, R. W. (1989). *Turtles of the world*. Washington, DC: Smithsonian Institution Press.

Ernst, C. H., & Zug, G. R. (1996). *Snakes in question*. Washington, DC: Smithsonian Institution Press.

Farlow, J. O., & Brett-Surman, M. K. (Eds.) (1997). *The complete dinosaur*. Bloomington: Indiana University Press.

Greene, H. W. (1997). *Snakes: The evolution of mystery in nature*. Berkeley & Los Angeles: University of California Press.

Halliday, T., & Adler, K. (Eds.). (2002). *The new encyclopedia of reptiles and amphibians*. Oxford, UK: Oxford University Press.

Orenstein, R. (2001). *Survivors in armor: Turtles, tortoises and terrapins*. Toronto: Key Porter Press.

Pough, F. H., Andrews, R. M., Cadle, J. E., Crump, M. L., Savitzky, A. H., & Wells, K. D. (2000). *Herpetology* (2nd ed.). Upper Saddle River, NJ: Prentice Hall.

Ross, C. A. (Ed.). (1989). *Crocodiles and alligators*. Silverwater, Australia: Golden Press.

Shine, R. (1991). *Australian snakes: A natural history*. Ithaca, NY: Cornell University Press.

Zug, G. R., Vitt, L. J., & Caldwell, J. P. (2001). *Herpetology: An introductory biology of amphibians and reptiles* (2nd ed.). San Diego, CA: Academic Press.

Reservoirs *See* Dams, Reservoirs, and Artificial Lakes

Resettlement

Substantial changes in the environment often transform the patterns of human settlement and may result in population resettlement. Resettlement is the process through which populations displaced from their habitat and/or economic activities relocate to another site and reestablish their productive activities, services, and community life. In sociology and anthropology, as well as in the environmental literature, the term *resettlement* is used most frequently in the context of policies, planning activities, and social research dealing with displacements caused by development. The term appears in such expressions as "involuntary resettlement," "involuntary displacement and resettlement," "forced resettlement," and "resettlement and rehabilitation" (called "R & R," particularly in Asia). Environmental changes that cause resettlement fall into two categories: natural and human-made. The first category includes environmental disasters such as floods, droughts and famines, desertification, volcanic eruptions, and so forth. The second category includes environmental interventions such as the construction of highways, the building of hydropower dams and reservoirs, the expansion of strip mining, the conversion of forested areas into cultivated agricultural lands, and the construction of airports, railways, or ports.

Causes

Natural environmental changes that may cause forced population resettlement are either sudden events (such as floods or volcanic eruptions) or the result of human practices that damaged the environment. An example is the overexploitation and gradual shrinkage of the Aral Sea in Asia, causing salinization and desertification of vast areas around the sea and forcing the surrounding population to abandon the area and resettle elsewhere. Conversely, environmental interventions for development (dams, highways, open-pit mining, etc.), which also result in involuntary population resettlement, are planned and are meant to be implemented with resettlement measures and social safeguards. In such interventions governments expropriate lands for development and compel the land users to allow right-of-way by moving out. However, even though announced in advance, these resettlements are defined as "involuntary" because the inhabitants are not given the choice to remain in their present location. Consequently, involuntary resettlers face more risks than opportunities.

Magnitude and Content

The frequency of such environmental interventions results in high numbers of people being displaced and resettled. During the last two decades of the twentieth century 180–200 million people worldwide were subjected to development-caused involuntary displacement. Such displacement is expected to continue at a rate of 8 to 10 million people annually as a companion of development programs. The resistance of population groups affected by such displacements is also increasing worldwide and embraces multiple forms—from negotiating compensation rates to engaging in active political opposition.

Each development-caused involuntary resettlement consists of three phases: the displacement of a population, the population's physical transfer to a different site or site(s), and reconstruction of the resettled population's livelihood, often termed "rehabilitation" (particularly in Asia). Displacement is the legal expropriation of land, trees, and other assets to allow the right-of-way for development. Transfer is the actual moving and assistance of the displaced people during their physical move. Reconstruction is reestablishing livelihoods of those displaced at the site of their relocation. Each phase has its own demands, risks, costs, logistics, and sociocultural and economic effects, but reconstruction is by far the most complex and difficult process. In theory the three phases are segments of one continuum; in practice, however, displacement and transfer do not necessarily bring about reconstruction.

Expropriation, displacement, and physical relocation of displaced people may occur without full and immediate reconstruction as an integral part of the process. In India, for instance, researchers have calculated that some 33 to 40 million people were displaced and relocated by dam construction projects between 1950 and 2000; it is estimated that only 25 percent of those displaced by dams were "rehabilitated." Consequently, some 75 percent—that is, tens of millions of people, have ended up worse off than before their relocation. Likewise, in Africa the resettlement caused by the establishment of national parks, particularly in the central Congo River basin, has not included any systematic reconstruction, leaving the relocated populations to struggle with impoverishment.

Social and Environmental Risks in Resettlement

Given their complexity, the processes of displacement, transfer, and resettlement involve substantial socioeconomic risks for the affected populations, particularly impoverishment risks, as well as secondary risks to the environment and the natural resources at resettlement sites.

The "impoverishment risks and reconstruction" (IRR) model for resettling displaced populations, formulated by Michael M. Cernea, identifies the impoverishment risks embedded in displacement and shows that several of these basic risks also have an environmental dimension. These risks are: (1) landlessness, which occurs when expropriation of land removes the foundation upon which people's productive systems and livelihoods are constructed; (2) joblessness, which occurs when resettlers lose access to their employment and remain unemployed or underemployed; (3) homelessness, which occurs when the displaced people lose shelter and cultural spaces; (4) marginalization, which occurs when families lose economic power and other assets and spiral on a downward mobility path; (5) food insecurity, which occurs when resettlers fall into temporary or extended undernourishment; (6) increased morbidity and mortality as a result of the outbreak of relocation-related illnesses, transmitted diseases, social stress, and psychological trauma; (7) education loss, particularly by children who because of displacement interrupt school or do not return to school; (8) loss of access to the previous common property natural resources (pastures, forests, rivers quarries, etc.), which causes drops in incomes and livelihood levels and increases pressures on natural resources at the resettlement sites; and (9) social disarticulation, which tears apart the social fabric and dismantles mutual help networks and patterns of community organization.

Depending on circumstances at the old and the new sites, the intensity of these resettlement risks may vary, and some risks may not be experienced in a favorable environment. However, other risks, which are site specific and are not reflected in the IRR model, may also emerge. Indigenous groups, children, women, and the elderly are particularly vulnerable. In addition, host populations are affected when resettlers increase population densities suddenly and the carrying capacity (the population that an area will support without deterioration) of the local environment is exceeded.

The IRR model for resettlement also outlines a set of strategies necessary to achieve socially responsible resettlement, that is, resettlement apt to restore or improve resettlers' livelihoods. The main strategies are: (1) systematic economic reconstruction, helping resettlers to move from induced landlessness to land-based resettlement, from joblessness to employment, providing them with access to common property natural resources—all in order to ensure food security and improved incomes; (2) house reconstruction and public services to restore access to education and basic health care; and (3) community reconstruction at the new site, integration within host populations, and rebuilding of social cohesion through empowerment and participation of resettlers. In short, involuntary resettlement does not end with the act of physical transfer, but rather must continue through a lengthy process of socioeconomic reconstruction.

Mitigation Policies and Social Research

Given its magnitude and frequency, as well as its socioeconomic and environmental effects, involuntary resettlement caused by development programs gained a prominent place on the international development agenda during the last two decades of the twentieth century. Internationally financed projects that cause involuntary resettlement mandate special social-impact assessments (SIAs) and environmental-impact assessments (EIAs) as part of the project feasibility studies as well as a detailed resettlement action plan (RAP). Until the late 1970s involuntary resettlement implications of development projects were addressed usually under environmental-impact assessments. Yet, as knowledge has developed, it is now increasingly recognized that their social nature and complexity require distinct social analyses and planning to complement the EIAs with SIAs and RAPs. In developing countries, in particular, the use of such instruments is still uneven and evolving. Making more efforts to mitigate the effects of involuntary resettlement can reduce their scope and raise their standards but are not likely to eliminate them completely. Therefore, a consensus is emerging that the standards for involuntary resettlements must be raised by adopting responsible national policies and legal frameworks on resettlement. These policies and frameworks will improve the design and the financial foundations of resettlement programs, thus enabling the resettled populations to share in the benefits of development and achieve sustainable resettlement.

The increased prominence of resettlement issues on the international development agenda has led to increased research in sociology, anthropology, geography, and environmental sciences. During the last twenty years scientific studies on resettlement have grown exponentially; conceptualizations, models, and analytical tools have been refined; and resettlement research has become a recognized subfield in social research. In addition, social theory and research findings on resettlement have powerfully influenced the formulation of the policies of some governments and of development aid agencies in conceiving, planning, and carrying out involuntary resettlement operations. To contain the impoverishment risks of displacement, major agencies (e.g., the World Bank, Asian Development Bank, aid agencies of the Organization for Economic Co-Operation and Development countries, and others) have adopted as their basic policy objective in resettlement the improvement or at least the restoration of the livelihood levels of those displaced. Research has found, however, that the funds allocated to this objective (essentially compensation for lost assets) are not adequate and that, therefore, investments beyond compensation are necessary. Development social research has also distilled and codified "best practice" aids apt to enhance the quality of resettlement planning and implementation, such as the *Handbook for Preparing a Resettlement Action Plan* issued by the International Finance Corporation (IFC) and the IRR model.

Other Uses of the Resettlement Concept

The concept of resettlement is used also to describe certain development programs that encourage and finance "voluntary" resettlement. Voluntary resettlement has taken place under some government-sponsored programs that made available large areas of uncultivated and uninhabited lands to farming families who reside elsewhere and who possess little or no land. These programs have facilitated also the transfer and reestablishment of families who registered voluntarily to move to the newly settled lands. Such programs for encouraging voluntary resettlement were organized in the 1960s and 1970s in Africa, in the 1980s in Indonesia, in Latin America, and so forth. Yet, some of these resettlement programs, as in Indonesia, were predicated on systematic deforestation at the new settlement sites and had disastrous environmental effects, which eventually were recognized and led to closure of the programs. One successful voluntary resettlement program was implemented in the onchocerciasis (river blindness) areas of western Africa after the disease was eradicated through an effective environmental and health-care program. During the 1990s large-scale voluntary resettlement programs became relatively rare.

The concept of resettlement is also used sometimes in the context of assisting cross-border refugees from wars and civil strife when these refugees, rather than repatriating to their country of origin, are formally accepted for permanent resettlement in the country of asylum. Usually, only a small fraction of refugee populations receive permission to resettle permanently in the asylum country.

Michael M. Cernea

See also Migration

Further Reading

Aronson, I. (2002). *Negotiating involuntary resettlement: A study of local bargaining during the construction of the Zimapan Dam—Mexico.* Uppsala, Sweden: Uppsala Universitet.

Cernea, M. M. (1991). Involuntary resettlement: Social research, policy and planning. In M. M. Cernea (Ed.), *Putting people first: Sociological variables in development projects* (2nd ed., pp. 188–215). New York: Oxford University Press.

Cernea, M. M. (1997). The risks and reconstruction model for resettling displaced populations. *World Development, 25*(10), 1569–1588.

Cernea, M. M. (Ed.). (1999). *The economics of involuntary resettlement: Questions and challenges.* Washington, DC: World Bank.

Cernea, M. M. (2000). Risks, safeguards and reconstruction: A model for population displacement and resettlement. In M. M. Cernea & C. McDowell (Eds.), *Risks and reconstruction: Experiences of resettlers and refugees.* Washington, DC: World Bank.

Cernea, M. M. (2003). For a new economics of resettlement: The sociological critique of the compensation principle. *International Social Science Journal, 175*(1), 41–50.

Downing, T. E. (1996). Mitigating social impoverishment when people are involuntarily resettled. In C. McDowell (Ed.), *Understanding impoverishment: The consequences of development-induced resettlement* (pp. 33–48). Oxford, UK: Berghahn Books.

Guggenheim, S. E. (1993). Peasants, planners, and participation: Resettlement in Mexico. In M. M. Cernea & S. E. Guggenheim (Eds.), *Anthropological approaches to resettlement: Policy, practice, theory* (pp. 201–228). Boulder, CO: Westview Press.

International Finance Corporation. (2002). *Handbook for preparing a resettlement action plan.* Washington, DC: International Finance Corporation.

Koenig, D. (2002). Towards local development and mitigating impoverishment in development-induced displacement and resettlement (RSC Working Paper Series). Oxford, UK: University of Oxford Press.

Mahapatra, L. K. (1999). *Resettlement, impoverishment and reconstruction in India: Development for the deprived.* New Delhi, India: Vikas Publishing House.

Mathur, H. M. (1998). The impoverishment risk model and its use as a planning tool. In H. M. Mathur & D. Marsden (Eds.), *Development projects and impoverishment risks: Resettling project-affected people in India* (pp. 67–78). New Delhi, India: Oxford University Press.

McMillan, D. (1995). *Sahel visions: Planned settlement and river blindness control in Burkina Faso.* Tucson: University of Arizona Press.

Ota, A. B. (1998). Countering impoverishment risks: The case of Rengali dam projects. In H. M. Mathur & D. Marsden (Eds.), *Development projects and impoverishment risks: Resettling project-affected people* (pp. 125–133). New Delhi, India: Oxford University Press.

Pandey, Balaji and Associates. (1998). *Depriving the underprivileged by development.* Bhubaneshwar, India: Institute for Socioeconomic Development.

Pearce, D. W. (1999). Methodological issues in the economic analysis for involuntary resettlement operations. In M. M. Cernea (Ed.), *The economics of involuntary resettlement: Questions and challenges* (pp. 50–82). Washington, DC: World Bank.

Scudder, T. (1993). Development-induced relocation and refugee studies: 37 years of change and continuity among Zambia's Grebe Tonga. *Journal of Refugee Studies, 6*(3), 123–152.

Sorensen, B. (1996). *Relocated lives, displacement and resettlement within the Mahaweli project, Sri Lanka.* Amsterdam, Netherlands: VU University Press.

World Bank. (1994). *Resettlement and development: Report of the task force on resettlement, 1987–1994.* Washington, DC: World Bank.

Rhine River

The Rhine originates in the Swiss Alps and flows in a northwestward direction to the North Sea via Switzerland, Liechtenstein, Austria, Germany, France, and the Netherlands. It is 1,250 kilometers long and has a discharge of 2,200 cubic meters per second at its delta. Its watershed is 185,000 square kilometers, over half of which lies in Germany. The Aare, Neckar, Main, Mosel, and Ruhr are its principal tributaries.

The ancient Celts named the river "Renos," from which "Rhenus" (Latin), "Rhein" (German), "Rhin" (French), "Rijn" (Dutch), and "Rhine" (English) are all derived. It has been a trade route since Roman times, though the reefs and cliffs of the Rhenish Slate Mountains (between Mainz and Bonn) acted as a navigational hindrance, as did the proliferation of German principalities and toll booths during the medieval era. Dutch and British immortalized the river in poems and paintings in the seventeenth century, giving birth to Rhine Romanticism and a still-thriving tourist industry.

In 1815, the Congress of Vienna established the International Commission for Rhine Navigation to promote flood control projects as well as the removal of in-channel hazards such as islands, reefs, and curves. The river has been under a free-trade regime since ratification of the Mannheim Acts in 1868. The coal-rich Ruhr region jump-started industrial growth on the Rhine after 1850, especially in the iron, steel, and chemical sectors. Hydroelectric dams allowed industrialization to spread upstream to the Swiss-German and French-German borders at the beginning of the twentieth century. After 1945, oil from the Middle East turned the Rotterdam harbor at the Rhine mouth into a major refining and petrochemical site. Today, the Rhine transports over 200 million metric tons of coal, steel, chemicals, and other freight annually, making it the second-busiest river (behind the Mississippi) in the world.

Economic progress came at a high environmental price, and by the 1970s the Rhine channel was so polluted with chemicals and salts that it was commonly referred to as "Europe's most romantic sewer." The number and variety of plant and animal life living in or near the river had plummeted. Especially hard hit were migratory fish, notably salmon. In 1986, a fire at a Sandoz chemical facility in Basel resulted in the accidental release of agricultural chemicals into the river, killing flora and fauna for hundreds of kilometers downstream. Equally troublesome were four "hundred-year" floods (so-called because floods of that magnitude are supposed to happen only once every hundred years) of 1983, 1988, 1993, 1994, caused as much by ill-conceived land-reclamation and channel-straightening projects as by unseasonable weather.

In 1963, the riparian states established the International Commission for the Protection of the Rhine to address the river's many environmental problems. Water quality has vastly improved since then, and the channel is once again capable of supporting most life forms, a remarkable turnabout given the river's heavy usage. Efforts to restore the Rhine's former floodplains and migratory routes, however, have been hampered by the large number of dams, factories, cities, and other human-built fixtures along its channel and banks. As long as the river remains Europe's premier navigational route, only a partial restoration will be feasible.

Mark Cioc

Further Reading

Cioc, M. (2002). *The Rhine: An eco-biography, 1815–2000.* Seattle: University of Washington Press.

Clapp, E. J. (1911). *The navigable Rhine.* Boston: Houghton Mifflin.

Heinberg, N. L., & Mayr, A. (Eds.). (1996). *The Rhine Valley: Urban, harbour and industrial development and environmental problems.* Leipzig, Germany: Institut für Länderkunde.

Rees, G. (1967). *The Rhine.* New York: Putnam.

Rhone River

The Rhone is France's most powerful river. Its volume is the country's largest. The source of the Rhone is the Furka glacier, located at 8,700 kilometers in the Swiss Alps. The river flows west into Lake Geneva, crosses the border into France, and then turns south at Lyon until it reaches the Mediterranean Sea. It is 813 kilometers long.

The Rhone's basin includes mountains that receive ample snowfall and important tributaries. As the river approaches the Mediterranean, its flow increases from less than 500 cubic meters per second north of Lyon to more than 1,500 cubic meters per second by Avignon. Extreme floods can reach ten times these levels. In addition to its large volume, the Rhone's course is steep and its flow rapid.

The Rhone has been one of Europe's most important rivers for over two millennia. Lugdunum, modern-day Lyon, served as the capital of Roman Gaul. Until the mid-nineteenth century, most projects to use the Rhone for energy, irrigation, or transportation were local, small scale, and subject to the river's unpredictability. In the 1870s conflicts between hydroelectric, navigation, and agricultural interests emerged. After five decades of debate, the French state authorized the multipurpose development of the river and the creation of the Compagnie Nationale du Rhone (Rhone River Authority, or CNR) on 21 May 1921. Between 1934 and 1986, the CNR built nineteen projects, eighteen of which followed the "Rhone formula." A canal diverted most of the river's waters through a hydroelectric plant and locks. This canal rejoined the riverbed downstream. The CNR's projects were part of state efforts to industrialize and modernize France after World War II. Since the 1950s nuclear power and agricultural reorganization have also significantly transformed the river valley.

The French state proposed a Rhone-Rhine liaison in order to link the North Sea and the Mediterranean Sea by building a lengthy canal that would have connected two major continental rivers, thereby bypassing ocean-going transportation routes around Spain and through the Atlantic Ocean. The first proposals for the liaison date back to the Roman era and were periodically reconsidered. The state revived the Rhone-Rhine liaison beginning in the 1970s within the context of European integration. However, after several decades of preliminary studies, technical designs, and some legal action, the new Minister of Territorial Development and Environment cancelled the liaison in 1997.

Sara B. Pritchard

Further Reading

Bethemont, J. (1972). *Le Thème de l'Eau Dans la Vallée du Rhone: Essai sur la genèse d'un espace hydralique* [The theme of water in the Rhone Valley]. Saint-Etienne, France: Imprimerie "Le Feuillet Blanc."

Bravard, J.-P. (1988). *The French upper Rhone: Historical geography and management of a river*. Denver, CO: Bureau of Reclamation.

Giandou, A. (1999). *La Compagnie Nationale du Rhone (1933–1998): Histoire d'un partenaire régional de l'Etat* [The Rhone River Authority (1933–1998): History of a regional partner of the state]. Grenoble, France: Presses Universitaires de Grenoble.

Pritchard, S. (2001). *Recreating the Rhone: Nature and technology in France since World War II* (Doctoral dissertation, Stanford University, 2001). *Dissertation Abstracts International, 1*, 369.

Rice

Rice is the world's most important food grain, providing just over one-fourth of total world cereal production. According to data of the United Nation's Food and Agriculture Organization, between 1961 and 2000 world rice production increased from 215 million to 600 million metric tons and yields from 1.87 metric tons per hectare to almost 3.9 metric tons. These and corresponding increases in production and yield of wheat were the main reasons why the world famine widely feared in the 1960s never materialized. About 91 percent of the world's rice is produced in Asia. The five most important rice-producing countries, in order, are China, India, Indonesia, Bangladesh, and Thailand. Together they account for two-thirds of all rice grown.

Origins and Ecology

Rice is the only major cereal crop that can grow in standing water, although it does not require it. It is therefore uniquely adapted to the periodic heavy flooding that often accompanies the Asian monsoons. Worldwide, there are two domestic species and about twenty-six wild species. The domestic species are *Oryza sativa* and *O. glabberima. O. sativa* evolved in Asia and is divided into two subspecies: *indica* and *japonica*. The *indica* varieties are dominant in southern Asia, *japonica* in eastern Asia. Both are now distributed worldwide. *O. glabberima* is indigenous to western Africa and is still localized there. Both domestic species appear to have the same wild ancestor: *O. rufipogon*, an inhabitant of ponds and flooded ditches. The native wild rice of North America is a separate genus, *Ziziana*.

O. sativa was most probably domesticated from its wild ancestor at several places and times beginning about seven thousand years ago in a zone that extends from the upper Ganges River valley in northern India through Bangladesh, Myanmar (Burma), and Thailand and across southern China. It seems probable that *indica-japonica* differentiation occurred in different niches toward southeastern Asia, with the *japonica* varieties emerging in lowlands and *indica* in the higher areas. Such differentiation is found in those areas today. The indigenous *aus* and *aman* varieties of Bangladesh appear in many characteristics to be midway between the two subspecies. Rice has spread through the wetter areas of monsoon Asia, mainly replacing systems of cultivation based on taro, like that which survives today in Papua New Guinea.

The main differences between the *indica* and *japonica* subspecies are that the former have a taller growth habit and long, thin grains that are separate when cooked. The *japonica* grains are shorter and wider and stickier when cooked, and the plants are shorter stemmed, but there are variations in both subspecies. These variations involve taste, texture, yield, whether the rice is floating or not, whether it can survive submergence or not, the length of time it takes to mature, and whether its growth cycle is photo-period sensitive or not. "Floating" means that the stems can elongate rapidly as water depth increases, thus preventing the plant from being drowned in deep water. Some floating rices can extend 20 centimeters in a day, to total heights of several meters. "Photo-period sensitive" means that there is a tendency for the onset of grain production to be controlled by length of daylight. Although all rice can withstand submergence for one to three days, some can withstand it for up to twelve days but do not elongate like the floating rices. These are called "deepwater rices." Little research to improve productivity has focused on deepwater or floating rices.

Cultivation

Systems of rice cultivation differ according to whether the fields are permanent or shifting; bunded (with raised borders to contain water) or not bunded; irrigated, rainfed, or subject to flooding; the tools used; and the varieties of rice. The most general way to describe systems of rice cultivation is in terms of increasing labor and capital intensification.

The least intensive system is slash-and-burn, or swidden. This system is found worldwide in associa-

A family threshing rice in a village on a "char" – a transitory island – in the Jamuna River in central Bangladesh. COURTESY MURRAY LEAF.

tion with many crops and usually requires no tools besides an ax, a pointed stick (dibble stick), and fire. Swidden systems for rice still occur in remote mountainous areas from the Himalayas to Oceania (lands of the Pacific Ocean). In swidden rice cultivation, a patch of forest or bamboo brush is cut and allowed to dry in the dry season and ignited just before the rains. Seeds are then dibbled into the ashes or ground. The landholders may return to protect and harvest the crops for two or three years thereafter, and then the field is abandoned for between ten and fifty years. For swidden systems in general, yields are high in relation to labor input and to the actual cropped surface but very low in relation to total land required. When the land available comes to be restricted by the encroachment of more settled systems or other types of land use, regrowth is incomplete, fertility is depleted, and soil erosion is widespread.

A second system is upland cultivation. It is more intensive than swidden and involves direct seeding in permanent fields, usually on sloping ground. Tools are the hoe and perhaps the plow. Fields are not bunded to retain water. Yields are low, and soil erosion is endemic.

A third system is rainfed agriculture that utilizes fields that are leveled, bunded, and puddled. (Puddling is the process of agitating soil when the field is wet in order to build up a relatively impermeable layer of fine soil at the base of the agitated layer, which would hold water.) Although sometimes called "lowland cultivation," this system occurs at a wide range of elevations from mountain slopes to river deltas. The rice varieties are "upland" types, however, with good drought resistance but low tolerance for flooding. Transplanting requires more water and gives lower yields but reduces time to harvest. This type of cultivation can maintain high levels of productivity indefinitely. Almost all research for improving yield has been on rices of this type.

A fourth system is rainfed agriculture that occurs in floodplains where rising water may submerge the fields for many weeks. Land preparation is the same as for rainfed lowland cultivation, but the crops differ, with floating or deepwater rices predominating in the period of rising water, usually followed by another crop of upland rice or deepwater rice sown by seed or transplanted as the waters begin to recede.

A fifth system is irrigated lowland cultivation, which involves the same land preparation as rainfed lowland cultivation but adds the construction and operation of a water distribution system. This system accounts for most of the world's total production as well as for most of the recent expansion associated with the Green Revolution (the adoption and spread of agricultural technologies that allow farmers to substantially increase food production per unit of land and per unit of labor).

Prospects

The recent increases in rice production have depended on greatly increased use of fertilizers and a wide range of related agrochemicals and machinery, along with a substantial spread of irrigation. There is now little area to which to expand irrigation, and the agrochemicals and machinery are causing serious and increasing environmental damage. For the future, increasing yields alone will not be enough. The aim now is to produce increasing yields and sustainability. It is not clear how this will be done, but there is no doubt that it must be done.

Murray J. Leaf

Further Reading

Barker, R., Herdt, R. W., & Rose, B. (1985). *The rice economy of Asia*. Washington, DC: Resources for the Future.

Randhawa, M. S. (1980–1986). *A history of agriculture in India*. New Delhi, India: Indian Council of Agricultural Research.

U.N. Food and Agriculture Organization (FAO). (2000). FAO stat database gateway. Retrieved June 27, 2002, from http://apps.fao.org/lim500/nph-wrap.pl? Production.Crops.Primary& Domain = SUA& servlet = 1

Richards, Ellen Swallow

(1842–1911)

U.S. chemist and educator

A native of Massachusetts, Ellen Swallow Richards was a chemist and educator who conceptualized ecology as the study of the human home, or community. She entered Vassar College at the age of twenty-six, after only four years of education, and received her bachelor's degree in 1870, completing the four-year curriculum in two years. She was then admitted to the Massachusetts Institute of Technology, where she became the first woman in the United States to earn a bachelor's degree in chemistry, but she was denied admission to the doctoral program after MIT voted not to admit women.

She nevertheless remained a special student in chemistry at MIT, where she instructed students in the fields of sanitary chemistry and nutrition. In 1875 she married Robert Richards, an Earth science professor at MIT with whom she collaborated. In their home she set up a small chemistry laboratory in the kitchen, where she tested food, water, and other items. In addition to concepts about the Earth derived from research with her husband, Richards incorporated into her framework the ideas of Frank Storer, a professor studying the atmosphere.

Richards was not only a researcher and theorist, but also an educator. In 1876 she obtained funding from the Women's Education Association to establish the Woman's Laboratory at MIT, where she and other women scientists did experiments on food and water contamination. In 1881 she opened a summer laboratory in Annisquam, Massachusetts (also funded by the Women's Education Association), which eventually moved to Woods Hole, Massachusetts, and became the Marine Biological Laboratory. In 1884 she was appointed an instructor in the new field of sanitary chemistry at MIT, teaching sanitary engineers the analysis of food, water, sewage, and air. She collaborated with Thomas M. Drown to analyze 100,000 samples of water and sewage for the Massachusetts State Board of Health to produce water purity tables that established the first water quality standards in the United States.

In 1892 Richards introduced to America the term *oekology*, derived from "oekologie" (a term created by German biologist Ernst Haeckel in 1866), as the science of the environment. She refined the concept as *human ecology* in her 1907 book, *Sanitation in Daily Life*, as "the study of the surroundings of human beings in the effects they produce on the lives of men" (Richards 1907, v). The features of the environment, according to her theory, come both from the climate, which is natural, and from human activity, which is artificial, or superimposed on it. "Human ecology" intersected with the sanitation and home economics movements and raised public consciousness about problems, such as smoke, sewage, and contaminated food products, caused by humans living in industrializing cities.

Richards's other publications included *The Chemistry of Cooking and Cleaning* (1882), *Home Sanitation* (1887), *Air, Water, and Food* (1890), and *Euthenics, the Science of Controllable Environment* (1910). She argued that fresh air and clean water that are free of pollutants from factories are as necessary to human health as is good nutrition. Her approach to ecology, which included humans as an integral part of nature, differed from that of the developing field of scientific ecology, which focused primarily on the environment as it existed prior to and uninfluenced by humans. In 1910, just a few months before she died, Richards received an honorary doctorate from Smith College.

Carolyn Merchant

Further Reading

Clarke, R. (1973). *Ellen Swallow, the woman who founded ecology*. Chicago: Follette.

Hunt, C. L. (1910, December 31). Woman of the hour—Ellen H. Richards. *Follette's Weekly Magazine, 2*(51).

Hunt, C. L. (1912). *The life of Ellen H. Richards*. Boston: Whitcomb & Barrows.

McIntosh, R. P. (1985). *The background of ecology*. New York: Cambridge University Press.

Merchant, C. (2002). *The Columbia guide to American environmental history*. New York: Columbia University Press.

New science . . . Mrs. Richards names it oekology. (1892, December 1). *Boston Daily Globe*, (pp. 1).

Richards, E. S. (1907). *Sanitation in Daily Life*. Boston: Whitcomb & Barrows.

Río de la Plata River

The Río de la Plata, one of the largest tidal rivers (rivers whose regimes are marked by the water movements derived from the rise and fall of the sea tides) in the world, is a shallow estuary covering 38,800 square kilometers on South America's southeastern coast. The river is about 270 kilometers long and has a funnel shape with a width of about 40 kilometers at its head widening to a maximum breadth of about 200 kilometers at its mouth, where it meets the Atlantic Ocean. It was discovered by the Spanish explorer Juan Díaz de Solís in 1516, and the first settlement on its banks, Buenos Aires, Argentina, was established in 1536.

The Río de la Plata basin is composed of the Paraná, Tietê, Paraguay, Pilcomayo, Bermejo, Iguazú, Uruguay, and Río de la Plata river systems. The basin is the second largest in the continent, the fifth largest in the world, and drains an area of 3.1 million square kilometers in Brazil, Bolivia, Paraguay, Argentina, and Uruguay. The basin includes the most densely populated areas of the subcontinent, including large urban centers such as São Paulo, Brazil, and Buenos Aires, and accounts for about 70 percent of the five countries' gross domestic product, being rich in the production of grains (rice, corn, wheat, and soybean), beef and dairy products, timber, minerals, and hydroenergy. A number of large hydroelectric dams have been built in the basin since the 1970s, notably Itaipú (between Brazil and Paraguay) and Yaciretá (between Argentina and Paraguay), both on the Paraná River.

Dam building and deforestation to expand the croplands in the region have been blamed for irreversible damage to the region's fragile ecosystems, altering river flows and rainfall regimes, and the flooding of extensive areas required by the dams has displaced human settlements. Because of the flat terrain of the Río de la Plata estuary, particularly on the Argentinean side, large areas are exposed to flooding throughout the year. The threat of flooding is especially acute during winter, when strong Atlantic winds cause the meteorological phenomenon called *sudestada*, which raises the river level by pushing water against the coast. Recent climatic changes caused by global warming, the recurrent phenomenon El Niño, and anthropogenic (human-caused) transformations have exacerbated the impact of these events.

The Río de la Plata basin's river system has been historically the main access into central South America. It supports a number of important activities, including shipping, fishing, and tourism, and also serves both as the main freshwater resource and sink (receptacle of filth) for the untreated wastewaters of a large number of urban and industrial centers. This situation has been accentuated since the 1990s as a result of the increased integration between the basin's countries after creation of the Southern Common Market (MERCOSUR). This integration has fostered a number of projects with potentially far-reaching environmental impacts, including a bridge over the Río de la Plata between the cities of Buenos Aires and Colonia and the Paraná-Paraguay Hidrovía (a large-scale project to improve navigation in the Paraguay and Paraná Rivers in order to allow fluvial transportation of goods between the Brazilian Matto Grosso and the maritime ports in the Río de la Plata estuary) to connect upstream production centers with the large maritime ports of Buenos Aires and Montevideo, Uruguay. These processes, together with the continued urban development in surrounding areas and the increasing flows of river traffic and tourism, are placing further pressure on the local environment and its rich biodiversity (biological diversity as indicated by numbers of species of animals and plants).

José Esteban Castro

Further Reading

Instituto, H. L. (1997). *MERCOSUR: Un atlas social, cultural y económico* (MERCOSUR: A social, cultural, and economic atlas). Buenos Aires, Argentina: Manrique Zago Ediciones.

United Nations Environment Programme. (2000). *GEO Latin America and the Caribbean: Environment outlook 2000*. San José, Costa Rica: United Nations Environment Programme.

United Nations Environment Programme. (2001). *GEO environmental data and statistics for Latin America and the Caribbean*. San José, Costa Rica: United Nations Environment Programme–World Bank.

Rivers

By common definition, a river refers to water flowing within the confines of a channel (as suggested by its Latin root, *ripa*, meaning "bank"). More precisely, a river forms the stem of a drainage system that transports water, soil, rocks, minerals, and nutrient-rich debris from higher to lower elevations. In a broader sense, rivers are part of the global water cycle: They collect precipitation (snow, sleet, hail, rain) and transport it back to lakes and oceans, where evaporation and cloud formation begin anew. Energized by gravity and sunlight, rivers sculpt the land around them, wearing down mountains, grinding rocks, and carving floodplains through the earth's crust. As carriers of water and nutrients, rivers also provide complex biological niches for fish, sponges, insects, birds, trees, and many other organisms.

Rivers are compared by measuring basin size, discharge rate, and channel length, though there are no universally recognized statistics for any of these dimensions. The Amazon forms the world's largest drainage basin at approximately 7 million square kilometers, followed distantly by the Congo (3.7 million square kilometers) and the Mississippi-Missouri (3.2 million square kilometers). As regards discharge rate, the Amazon once again stands supreme at around 180,000 cubic meters per second, followed by the Congo (41,000 cubic meters per second), the Ganges-Brahmaputra (38,000 cubic meters per second), and the Chang, or Yangtze (35,000 cubic meters per second). At around 6,650 kilometers, the Nile is the world's longest river, followed closely by the Amazon (6,300 kilometers) and the Mississippi-Missouri (6,100 kilometers). Other rivers with large area-discharge-length combinations include the Ob'-Irtysh, Paraná, Yenisey, Lena, Niger, Amur, Mackenzie, Volga, Zambezi, Indus,

Tigris-Euphrates, Nelson, Huang He (Yellow River), Murray-Darling, and the Mekong. Two rivers—the Huang He and Ganges-Brahmaputra—also stand out for their huge annual sediment load, which makes them especially prone to severe flooding. There is no agreed-upon minimum size, length, or volume for a river, but small rivers are usually called streams, brooks, creeks, or rivulets. Great or small, rivers that form part of a larger drainage system are known as tributaries, branches, or feeder streams.

Although rivers vary greatly in size, shape, and volume, most rivers share certain characteristics. A typical river has its headwaters in a mountainous or hilly region, where it is nurtured by glaciers, melting snow, lakes, springs, or rain. Near the headwaters, swift currents prevail and waterfalls are common, owing to the rapid drop in elevation or the narrowness of the valley though which the river flows. As a river leaves the high region, its velocity typically slackens and its channel begins to meander, bifurcate, or braid. Often its floodplain broadens as it picks up tributary waters. As the river reaches its mouth, it usually loses most of its gradient. It becomes sluggish, allowing some of its sediment load to settle to the bottom, clogging the channel. The river responds by fanning around the sediment deposits, classically forming the shape of a delta (the fourth letter in the Greek alphabet, δ), before emptying in a lake, sea, or ocean.

Unique climatic and geographic conditions determine a river's annual discharge regime (its seasonal variations in water quantity), but as a rule rain-fed tropical rivers flow more steadily year-round than do snow-fed temperate rivers. A river is called perennial if it carries water all or almost all of the time, and intermittent or ephemeral if it does not. A water-carved channel in an arid region is often called an arroyo or dry gulch if it carries water only on rare occasions. For hydrologists, the term *flood* refers to a river's annual peak discharge period, whether it inundates the surrounding landscape or not. In common parlance, a flood is synonymous with the act of a river overflowing its banks. In 1887, a massive flood on the Huang He caused the death of nearly a million Chinese people. In 1988, flooding on the Ganges-Brahmaputra temporarily displaced over 20 million in Bangladesh.

Human Manipulation of Rivers

Rivers contain only a minuscule portion of the total water on Earth at any given time, but along with lakes, aquifers, and springs they are the principal sources of fresh water for humans as well as for many plants and animals. Rivers are therefore closely associated with the emergence of settled agriculture, irrigated crops, and early urban life. The great civilizations of Mesopotamia (literally "the land between the rivers") from Sumer to Babylonia emerged beginning around 4500 BCE along the Tigris and Euphrates floodplains of modern-day Iraq. Egypt, as the Greek historian Herodotus once famously noted, was "the gift of the Nile." The Huang He spawned early Chinese civilization, just as the Indus produced the first cultures of southwest Asia, and the river valleys of coastal Peru shaped urban life in the Andes. "All the great historic cultures," the social philosopher Lewis Mumford noted with only slight exaggeration, "have thriven through the movement of men and institutions and inventions and goods along the natural highway of a great river" (McCully 1996, 9).

For most of human history, river manipulation was slight, consisting mostly of diverting or impounding a portion of a river's water for the purpose of irrigating crops. Even modest modifications of this type, however, can have severe environmental consequences. In arid regions, salinization is a common problem. Unless properly drained, irrigated fields slowly accumulate the minuscule amounts of dissolved salts naturally found in soil and water. Over time this salt buildup will eventually render the fields incapable of growing most crop species. Siltation is a common problem caused when farmers and pastoralists deforest or overgraze river valleys, inadvertently setting in motion excessive erosion downstream. As the silt settles to the channel bottom, it elevates the river above the landscape, making it more prone to flooding.

Ancient Roman, Muslim, and Chinese engineers possessed a sophisticated understanding of the art of hydraulics, as the still-extant aqueducts, canals, and waterworks of Rome, Baghdad, Beijing, and other Eurasian cities amply demonstrate. But river engineering as a mathematical science first emerged in Europe between 1500 and 1800 CE. The crucial breakthrough came when Italian engineers calculated the formula for

The River Alto rushes through the forest in Teno, Ecuador, February 2000. COURTESY NICOLE LALIBERTE.

determining the amount of water flowing in a river at any given time by measuring width, depth, and flow rate. Thereafter, water experts knew how to "tame" a river—that is, manipulate its banks, bed, and velocity in order to contain floods, reclaim land, and promote navigation—with a greater degree of precision, and therefore a higher chance of success, than had previously been feasible.

Today's methods for controlling rivers are remarkably similar to those employed in the past—chiefly the construction of dams and weirs, the reinforcement of banks, and the straightening (and often widening) of channels—but materials and techniques have improved greatly over the past two centuries. Modern dams are designed to store water, regulate minimum channel depth (usually in connection with a lock), generate electricity, or perform all three tasks. Reinforced banks help keep the water in a designated channel, thereby reducing the frequency of flooding and opening up former floodplain for agricultural, urban, industrial, and other human uses. Channel straightening gives a river a steeper gradient and thus a faster discharge rate; by reducing the total length of a river, it also facilitates the transportation of goods between ports. Collectively, these engineering methods transform a mercurial and free-flowing stream (a "floodplain river") into a predictable deliverer of energy, goods, and water (a "reservoir river"). Nowadays, the Nile and Chang produce kilowatts for industries and cities, just as the Mississippi and Rhine transport freight for companies and consumers, and the Colorado and Rio Grande deliver water for farmers and homeowners.

The Environmental Consequences of Hydraulic Engineering

River engineering fosters bank-side economic growth by opening up arable land, reducing floods, promoting trade, and generating electricity, but it also has a disruptive impact on riverine environments. The problems can be divided into two interrelated types: Those that compromise the purity of the water in the channel (water pollution) and those that reduce the amount of living space in its channel and floodplain (habitat loss). Both typically result in a reduction in a river's biodiversity.

River Pollution

Water pollutants can be divided into three broad categories: nutrient-based, chemical, and thermal. The most common nutrient-based pollutants are fecal matter from untreated human sewage and agricultural runoff from phosphorus and nitrogen fertilizers. When introduced into a lake or river, these organic substances serve as food for phytoplankton (free-floating algae), which are huge consumers of the water's dissolved oxygen. If the river moves slowly, and if the "algal blooms" are large or frequent enough, the river will gradually become eutrophied (oxygen-depleted), with negative consequences for other organisms that require dissolved oxygen for respiration. The Po and Ganges are examples of sewage-fertilizer rivers.

The most pernicious chemical pollutants include heavy metals (zinc, copper, chromium, lead, cadmium, mercury, and arsenic), and chlorinated hydrocarbonssuch as polychlorinated biphenyls (PCBs) and dichlorodiphenyltrichloroethane (DDT). These substances bioaccumulate; that is, they pass unmetabolized from simple organisms to more complex organisms, magnifying in concentration as they move up the food chain. The Mersey, Rhine, Hudson, Ohio, and Donets are all examples of industrial-chemical rivers.

Thermal pollution is a problem on rivers that have numerous nuclear, coal, or oil-based power plants on their banks. The heated wastewater from the plant-cooling facilities artificially raises the water temperature, and the higher temperature in turn affects the type of species capable of living in the streambed. The Rhône and Rhine are examples of thermal rivers.

Most of the world's manipulated rivers can loosely be labeled "agricultural" since the majority of engineering projects are geared toward land reclamation (flood control) and the lion's share of dam water is still utilized for the purpose of irrigating crops. As industrialization spreads globally, however, chemical pollutants are increasingly becoming the single greatest threat to river systems; indeed, few rivers remain completely free of any trace of industrial contaminants. Today, the cleanliness or filth of a river is often more determined by the average income of the humans who live on its banks than by the number of farms and factories in its watershed. Wealthy nations have invested in urban and industrial sanitation plants over the past fifty years, and water quality has correspondingly improved. Poorer countries, unable to afford these techno-fixes, have seen their rivers continue to deteriorate.

Habitat Loss

Water pollution compromises a river's biological robustness by killing off organisms and by creating an unfavorable environment for nourishment and reproduction. But it is the engineering projects themselves that account for most of the habitat loss on rivers and are thus primarily responsible for the drop in biodiversity. Natural ("untamed") rivers contain an abundance of diverse biological niches: headwaters and tributaries, main and secondary channels, deep pools and islands, banks and bed, and marshes and backwaters. Channels provide longitudinal passageways along which organisms travel, while river edges provide access routes to the adjacent marshes and floodplains where many organisms find their nourishment and reproduction sites. Floodplains nurture trees, shrubs, and reeds, which help stabilize the channel bank while providing shade and protection to other organisms. A river basin hosts a complex web of life, ranging from simple organisms such as fungi, bacteria, algae, and protozoa, to more complex organisms such as flatworms, roundworms, and wheel animals, and on up to mollusks, sponges, insects, fish, birds, and mammals.

Engineering alters a basin's natural structure in ways that are detrimental to many species. Dams and weirs block a river's longitudinal passageways, making it difficult for organisms to take full advantage of the channel's living space. Migratory fish are particularly hard hit because their life cycles require them to move from headwaters to delta and back again. Most famously, salmon disappeared from the Columbia, Rhine, and many other rivers when dams were built on their banks. Reinforced banks have a similar impact: They sever the links between a river's channel and its floodplain, depriving many organisms of their feeding and breeding sites. As a river loses all or part of its natural channel, bed, banks, islands, backwaters, marshes, and floodplain, it is transformed into a narrow and uniform rather than a broad and diverse biological site. Typically this results in a precipitous drop in both the number and type of species that it supports.

Aside from reducing the total amount of living space on a river, engineering can also trigger dramatic population upsurges in certain species, creating an ecological imbalance. The zebra mussel—a hearty algae eater and rapid reproducer—has migrated from its home in the Caspian Sea to the industrial rivers of America and Europe, displacing local mollusk species along the way. Similarly, after the completion of the Aswan Dam in the mid-1930s, snails infected with deadly schistosomes (parasitic worms) began to colonize the Nile's new irrigation canals, debilitating and killing Egyptian farmers and fishermen.

Responding to environmentalists and to reformers from within their own ranks (such as Gilbert F. White), engineers have developed new and more sophisticated methods of river manipulation since the 1970s. More attention is now paid to preserving the original river corridor as channel beds and banks are fortified and dredged. Dams and weirs are fitted (or retrofitted) with fish ladders to aid fish migration. More floodplain is left intact. In some cases, rivers have even been re-meandered and rebraided so that they better replicate the natural conditions that once prevailed on their banks. Nevertheless, the Three Gorges Dam project under way on the Chang—the largest dam-building project of all time—serves as a reminder that the environmentally unfriendly practices of the past are still in widespread use today.

Mark Cioc

See also Amazon River; Chang River; Colorado River; Columbia River; Congo (Zaire) River; Danube River; Ganges River; Great Lakes and St. Lawrence River; Huang River; Hudson River; Indus River; Mackenzie River; Mekong River; Mississippi and Missouri Rivers; Murray River; Nile Valley; Niger Delta; Orinoco River; Río de la Plata; Rhine River; Rhone River; Volga River

Further Reading

Cowx, I. G., &. Welcomme, R. L. (Eds.). (1998). *Rehabilitation of rivers for fish: A study undertaken by the European Inland Fisheries Advisory Commission of FAO.* Oxford, UK: Fishing News Books.

Czaya, E. (1983). *Rivers of the world.* Cambridge, UK: Cambridge University Press.

Giller, P. S., & Malmqvist, B. (1998). *The biology of streams and rivers.* Oxford, UK: Oxford University Press.

Goubert, J.-P. (1986). *The conquest of water: The advent of health in the industrial age.* Princeton, NJ: Princeton University Press.

Harper, D. M., & Ferguson, A. J. D. (Eds.). (1995). *The ecological basis for river management.* Chichester, UK: John Wiley & Sons.

Hillel, D. (1994). *Rivers of Eden.* New York: Oxford University Press.

McCully, P. (1996). *Silenced rivers: The ecology and politics of large dams.* London: Zed Books.

Moss, B. (1988). *Ecology of freshwaters: Man and medium.* Oxford, UK: Blackwell Scientific Publications.

Nienhuis, P. H., Leuven, S. S. E. W., & Ragas, A. M. J. (Eds.). (1998). *New concepts for sustainable management of river basins.* Leiden, Netherlands: Backhuys.

Przedwojski, B., Blazejewski, R., & Pilarczyk, K. W. (1995). *River training techniques: Fundamentals, design and applications*. Rotterdam, Netherlands: A. A. Balkema.

Rand McNally and Company (1980). *Rand McNally encyclopedia of world rivers*. Chicago: Rand McNally.

Rocky Mountains

The Rocky Mountains, commonly known as the Rockies, are the longest mountain system in North America and the second longest in the world. Only South America's Andes Mountains are longer. The Rockies are composed of more than one hundred individually named ranges that form a vast mountain chain extending slightly more than 5,000 kilometers or 30 degrees of latitude from northern Alaska through Canada and much of the American West to northern New Mexico. The Rockies vary in width from about 100 to 600 kilometers, and summits vary in elevation from about 1,800 to 4,399 meters at Mount Elbert, Colorado. They are bordered by the Great Plains on the east and by a series of high plateaus and extensive basins on the west. The crestline of the Rockies forms the Continental Divide, which acts as a watershed boundary separating the flow of rivers east to the Atlantic Ocean from those west to the Pacific Ocean and north to the Arctic Ocean. Many of North America's largest western rivers, including the Yukon, Fraser, Columbia, Missouri, Colorado, Arkansas, and Rio Grande, have their headwaters in the Rockies.

The Rockies were formed during a succession of mountain-building episodes that lasted nearly 100 million years. The episodes are known collectively as the Laramide Orogeny and the post-Laramide Exhumation of the Rockies. Most of the relief seen today is the product of post-Laramide uplift, faulting, and volcanism that occurred during the late Tertiary period (5–24 million years ago). Although tectonically related, the Rockies are marked by significant differences in geology, climate, vegetation, and wildlife from one end of the chain to the other and from piedmont to summit. At the northern end of the chain, the remote Brooks Range is largely treeless, and alpine tundra extends from the foothills to the edge of ice-clad summits. At the southern end of the Rockies, the Sangre de Cristo Mountains rise from semiarid grasslands through approximately 2,000 meters of pine-spruce-fir forests before giving way to alpine tundra. Caribou and musk oxen are found only in the Arctic, whereas black bear, grizzly bear, elk, deer, moose, bighorn sheep, mountain lions, beaver, and numerous bird and reptile species are found in many areas.

At the time of European contact, the Rockies were inhabited by a number of Native American peoples, including Kutenai, Nez Perce, Blackfoot, Crow, and Ute. The first European to reach the Rockies was Francisco Vasquez de Coronado (1510–1544), who skirted the Rockies' southern edge in 1540. Sir Alexander Mackenzie (1764–1820) became the first person of European descent to cross the Canadian Rockies in 1793, and Meriwether Lewis (1774–1809) and William Clark (1770–1838) became the first to cross the American Rockies in 1805. Fur trappers and traders scoured the Rockies from about 1800 to 1840, but large-scale settlement did not occur until the gold rushes to Colorado, Idaho, Montana, and British Columbia, which occurred between 1858 and 1864. Mining established numerous settlements in the Rockies and had (and continues to have) a significant impact on the environment—destruction of vegetation and wildlife, alteration of land and drainage basins, and pollution of air and water. Today, the Rockies' major industries are mining, lumbering, ranching, farming, and tourism. The Rockies contain numerous ski resorts, national forests, and the largest percentage of national park land of any geographic region in North America. Notable parks include Jasper, Banff, and Waterton Lakes in Canada and Glacier, Yellowstone, and Rocky Mountain in the United States. Current issues include wildlife conservation, population growth, forest fire suppression policies, reintroduction of wolves, and lumbering and grazing on national forest lands.

George Vrtis

Further Reading

Lavender, D. (1981). *The Rockies*. Lincoln: University of Nebraska Press. (Original work published 1968)

Madole, R. F., Bradley, W. C., Loewenherz, D. S., Ritter, D. F., Rutter, N. W., & Thorn, C. E. (1987). Rocky Mountains. In W. L. Graf (Ed.), *Geomorphic systems of North America* (pp. 211–257). Boulder, CO: Geological Society of America.

McPhee, J. (1986). *Rising from the Plains*. New York: Farrar, Straus & Giroux.

Thybony, S. (1996). *The Rockies: Pillars of a continent*. Washington, DC: National Geographic Society.

Wyckoff, W., & Dilsaver, L. M. (1995). *The mountainous West: Explorations in historical geography*. Lincoln: University of Nebraska Press.

Rodale, J. I.
(1898–1971)
Organic farming advocate

J. I. (Jerome Irving) Rodale was one the earliest and loudest advocates of organic farming and sustainable agriculture in the United States. He pioneered methods of farming without chemical fertilizers and pesticides, promoting these methods through magazines and books published by his printing company, Rodale Press. Rodale popularized the term *organic* to describe methods of farming that do not rely on chemicals.

Rodale took a circuitous route to his career as the guru of organic agriculture. He was born in a tenement in the Lower East Side of New York City, far from farms of any kind but linked to food through his father's job as a grocer. After working as a tax auditor for the federal government for several years, Rodale, with his brother, opened a small manufacturing company. Rodale used profits from this venture to pursue his hobby of publishing, creating several short-lived humor magazines. He became interested in organic farming in 1941 when he encountered the ideas of the British agronomist Sir Albert Howard, who maintained that fertilizing agricultural produce with plant and animal waste—rather than chemical fertilizers—produces healthier soil, healthier plants, and healthier humans. Shortly thereafter, Rodale purchased a run-down farm in Erasmus, Pennsylvania, and began to test these principles. In 1942 he published the first issue of *Organic Gardening and Farming* to promote these principles. The focus of the magazine gradually expanded to include opposing chemical pesticides and food processing in addition to advocating organic fertilizers.

Initially few people embraced Rodale's ideas. He mailed ten thousand copies of his magazine's initial issue to farmers—but not one responded with a subscription request. In the 1960s, however, Rodale's promotion of organic farming found a more receptive ear. His antiinstitutional, antitechnological, and antichemical stances earned him thousands of admirers. Rodale's theories about the dangers of chemicals reflected national concerns about pollution in general and pesticides (such as DDT) in particular. By 1970 Rodale's magazine claimed a circulation of over seven hundred thousand. Rodale even became something of a prophet to those experimenting with back-to-the-land movements and simple living; the *New York Times Magazine* labeled him "the guru of the organic food cult." On the other hand, mainstream agronomists rejected many of Rodale's ideas. The scientific merits of organic farming remained unclear, and, more importantly, chemical fertilizers and pesticides were essential to the highly productive industrial farming that had developed in the mid-twentieth century. The bulkier organic substitutes were hard to transport and apply. By the early 1970s Rodale enjoyed a reputation as both a genius and a crackpot.

Organic farming moved closer to the mainstream of American agriculture in the late twentieth century, and the Rodale name has remained closely associated with the organic movement. The Rodale Institute has continued to promote organic methods and sustainability, working in partnerships with the U.S. Department of Agriculture and other organizations. Rodale Press publishes a wide variety of books and magazines on topics such as organic agriculture and healthy living, and *Organic Gardening* remains one of the most widely read gardening publications in the world.

James W. Feldman

Further Reading

Greene, W. (1971, June 6). Guru of the organic food cult. *New York Times Magazine*. J. I. Rodale biography and history. (n.d.). Retrieved October 5, 2002, from http://www.rodale.com

J. I. Rodale and the Rodale family: Celebrating 50 years as advocates of sustainable agriculture. (n.d.). Retrieved October 5, 2002, from http://www.dep.state.pa.us/dep/PA_Env-Her/rodale_bi o.htm

Shi, D. E. (1985). *The simple life: Plain living and high thinking in American culture*. New York: Oxford University Press.

Romanticism

At the end of the eighteenth and beginning of the nineteenth centuries a transformation in consciousness swept Europe and the Americas; this transformation of philosophy, music, art, and literature is known generally as "Romanticism," a heading under which people may include the U.S. variety of idealist poetics and philosophy known as "Transcendentalism." In concert with the political revolutions throughout Europe and the Americas that sought to liberate peoples from the unjust hold of colonial powers or absolute monarchies,

---

To sit in the shade on a fine day and look upon verdure is the most perfect refreshment.

—Jane Austen

Romanticism inaugurated a correspondent revolution in philosophy and the arts that sought to liberate thinkers and artists from the Lockean empiricism and the Neoclassical (relating to a revival or adaptation of the classical) conventions of the eighteenth century. Whereas the English philosopher John Locke (1632–1704) had discounted the presence of innate ideas, holding instead that the mind is a blank slate dependent upon sense impressions to form ideas, the Romantics emphasized the importance of innate ideas, feeling, and imagination, which they described as modes of truth that could free the mind from the imperial hold of the external world. And whereas Neoclassical artists, such as the French dramatist Jean Racine (1639–1699) and the English poet Alexander Pope (1688–1744), emphasized the importance of strictly following rules derived from the poetics of the Greek philosopher Aristotle and the Roman poet Horace and sought in their works to hold a mirror up to nature, the Romantics sought to illuminate nature with the light of the mind.

As empiricism gave way to idealism, so, too, did mechanism (the belief that the natural world and its processes are a machine governed by fixed and ultimately knowable laws) give way to organicism (the belief that nature is alive, even, in some formulations, sentient). In the seventeenth and eighteenth centuries Europeans increasingly thought of the natural world and its processes as a machine. As Carolyn Merchant and others have shown, nature was objectified as a lifeless machine over which humans could exercise dominion. As Merchant puts it, viewing nature "as a system of dead, inert particles moved by external, rather than inherent forces, the mechanical framework itself could legitimate the manipulation of nature" (Merchant 1989, 193). In the name of "improvement" humans tampered with the machine of nature, taming the wild and imposing the human imprint on nature, as evidenced by formal gardens and parks laid out according to mathematical principles and decorated with manicured topiary conforming to geometric designs.

By the end of the eighteenth century mechanism was challenged by the Romantic rediscovery of organi-

cism. Preferring the raw and unadorned to the cooked and clothed, the Romantics for the most part rejected the artificial environments of the city and the formal garden, favoring instead the picturesque beauty of the countryside and the sublimity of wild places. The American naturalist and writer Henry David Thoreau captures this sense best in his *Atlantic Monthly* essay "Walking" (1862) where he exclaims, "Give me a wildness whose glance no civilization can endure. . . ." (Thoreau 2000, 644). The country, as opposed to the city, was a repository for values uncorrupted by the artificial demands of civil society. Rural retreats, woodlands, and river valleys mirrored and promoted imaginative reverie and subjective feeling; mountains, lakes, and the wilderness, especially in the United States, became sites of spiritual transformation and psychic restoration, as well as symbols of individual freedom and the power of the imagination.

The Variety of Romanticisms

The Romantic movement was a complex set of unevenly developing ideas and cultural practices that took many forms in different countries at different times throughout the early nineteenth century. Appearing in Germany and England by the 1790s, not until the 1820s and after did Romanticism take firm hold in France, Italy, Spain, Russia, Poland, and Latin America. The Swiss writer and critic Madame de Staël (Germaine Necker, 1766–1877) was one of the first to recognize this new movement afoot in her *On Germany* (1810, 1813), which described the new literature of Germany as "romantic," a term by which she meant an aesthetic free from rules, focused upon indigenous cultural traditions, drawing upon folklore and the literature of the Middle Ages, and exhibiting the force and amplitude of nature itself. Given the distinctive religious and national character of each of these countries, Romanticism found adherents among Protestants, Catholics, and secular humanists; in the wake of new translations of the Chinese philosophers Confucius and Mencius and Sanskrit texts such as the Bhagavad Gita and the Vedas, some Romantic writers, particularly among the Transcendentalists in the United States, fused some tenets of Confucianism and Hinduism with Western beliefs. From this ferment of political, aesthetic, religious, and philosophical ideas, the Romantic movement saw the rise of some of the world's greatest writers, composers, and artists, most of whom had a strong sense of kinship with nature. Among the writers whose work reflects a strong interest in nature are Johann Wolfgang von Goethe (Germany, 1749–1832), Alphonse Lamartine (France, 1790–1869), Alexander Pushkin (Russia, 1799–1837), Domingo Faustino Sarmiento (Argentina, 1811–1888), Victor Hugo (France, 1828–1873), Emily Dickinson (United States, 1830–1886), and Gustavo Adolfo Bécquer (Spain, 1836–1870); among the painters, Francisco de Goya (Spain, 1746–1828), Eugène Delacroix (France, 1798–1863), J. M. W. Turner (England, 1775–1851), and Thomas Cole (United States, 1801–1848); and among the musicians, Ludwig von Beethoven (Germany, 1770–1827), Franz Schubert (Austria, 1797–1828) and Richard Wagner (Germany, 1813–1883). Although no list can do justice to the many talented artists of the Romantic period, the brief sample here should give some idea of the diversity and breadth of the movement.

This article focuses on a few key writers from France, Germany, England, and the United States whose ideas have influenced contemporary attitudes about the human place in nature. Although any brief characterization of Romanticism, nature, and ecology must be somewhat reductive, the fundamental ideas found within French, German, English, and U.S. Romanticism were shared by many of the major writers in the various national traditions. Despite all the differences among the various versions of Romanticism, one key commonality is the quest for transcendence, a quest, ironically, that is rooted in a deep appreciation for nature. Thus the Romantic striving for transcendence, to attain by means of an imaginative transformation of the mundane world a vision and feeling akin to spiritual bliss, leads to important contradictions and tensions that animate and complicate the Romantics' relation to the life world and that also vex Romanticism's relation to ecology.

Influence of Rousseau

Among the most influential of the early Romantic writers was the French philosopher and writer Jean Jacques Rousseau (1712–1778). As Jonathan Bate points out in *Romantic Ecology*, "If the French Revolution was one great root of Romanticism, then what used to be called 'the return to nature,' associated above all with the Rousseau of the second *Discourse* and the *Nouvelle Héloïse*, was surely the other" (Bate 1991, 7). Rousseau represents the transformation from Neoclassicism to Romanticism in its broadest sense because his philosophical and literary works, such as the *Discourse on Inequality* (1754), *The New Heloise* (1761), and *Confessions* (1781, 1788), provided a conceptual framework for the increased interest in individualism and political equality and spurred the turn away from the city to the country, from reason to feeling. Rousseau believed that every advance in civilization further separates human beings from nature. Guided by custom, education, and ambition, men and women in civil society exchange their true nature for an artificial, alienated self. One way to recuperate the natural man or woman and to reinstate a sense of unity with the life world is to relinquish society and to seek the restorative powers of simplicity and solitude in a quiet retreat. Another way is to experience or witness the grandeur and might of nature by seeking encounters with sublime scenes: steep cliffs, high mountains, treacherous ravines, and deep wilderness. In book 1 of *The Prelude* (1805) the English poet William Wordsworth describes his boyhood experience of nature precisely in these terms: "Fair seed-time had my soul, and I grew up / Fostered alike by beauty and by fear" (Wordsworth 1979, 44)—or, in the language of the time, fostered alike by the beautiful and the sublime.

The Sublime, the Beautiful, and the Picturesque

These two poles of experience—the beautiful and the sublime—were codified in English statesman Edmund Burke's *A Philosophical Enquiry into Our Ideas of the Sublime and Beautiful* (1757). Theorizing the effects of objects upon human passions, Burke (1729–1797) identifies the beautiful with objects eliciting love; the sublime, with those eliciting astonishment and fear. Smallness, smoothness, gradual variation, clarity, and delicacy Burke associates with the beautiful; greatness, ruggedness, vastness, privation, obscurity, infinity, and power, with the sublime. The sublime object, when not posing an immediate threat, arouses a state of astonishment, which Burke describes as "that state of the soul, in which all its motions are suspended, with some degree of horror" (Burke 1990, 53). Readers of Burke readily associated the sublime with mountains, deserts, wastelands, and wilderness; the beautiful with gardens, parks, woodlands, and rural scenes.

Providing not only a theory but also a vocabulary by which to measure and articulate the experience of nature and landscape, Burke's treatise profoundly influenced the increasing numbers of painters, poets, landscape architects, estate owners, and tourists who ventured into the countryside or who redesigned their properties in accordance with the new principles of taste. Among those readers were the English writers Richard Payne Knight (1750–1824), Uvedale Price (1747–1829), and William Gilpin (1724–1804), the authors of several popular treatises on the "picturesque," a new term added to the vocabulary of landscape description. The picturesque sought a middle ground between the sublime and the beautiful, locating picturesque beauty in scenes characterized by roughness, chiaroscuro (pictorial representation in terms of light and shade without regard to color), variety, and the play of line and surfaces. Gilpin's works especially, many of them written in the form of guidebooks to scenic places in England such as the Wye River valley, the Lake District, and the Scottish Highlands, promoted such a wide and enthusiastic following that the picturesque tourist, Claude glass and sketchbook in hand, became an object for parody in the 1790s. A Claude glass is a compact camera-like device with a mirror used by tourists for framing scenic views. So named after the French painter Claude Lorraine, whose landscape paintings helped to shape the taste for picturesque landscape viewing in the eighteenth century.

Meanwhile, in Germany the philosopher Immanuel Kant (1724–1804) married the concepts of the sublime and the beautiful to his idealist philosophy. In his *Critique of Judgment* (1790), Kant elevated the aesthetic interest in landscape to a high level of sophistication and complexity. Whereas Burke, following Locke's empiricism, believed that qualities of the sublime and beautiful reside in the objects that produce certain effects upon their beholders, Kant located the source of aesthetic experience in the mind of the beholder. For Kant, grand objects, such as mountain peaks or high waterfalls, initially overwhelm the beholder, making him or her feel subordinate to the power and magnitude of nature; but in a reflexive act of recovery, the beholder imagines a quantity or dimension that exceeds the physical limits of the object in view, thereby reasserting the superiority of the mind to nature. Thus the experience of the sublime allows the mind to realize its limitless power and its autonomy from the phenomenal

world. This dynamic and idealistic theory of the sublime points to one of the key contradictions in Romantic nature philosophy: Although praising nature as a source of moral guidance and beneficial impressions, the Romantics also sought to transcend the limits of nature and the world of objects in order to realize the fullest potentials of human freedom.

Romantic Idealism

Critics have long recognized that despite Romanticism's acknowledgment of kinship with nature, the Romantic spirit is driven by a transcendental humanism that ultimately celebrates the mind's triumph over the material conditions that threaten to limit its horizon. In Geoffrey Hartman's view, for example, "Nature, for Wordsworth, is not an 'object' but a presence and a power; a motion and a spirit; not something to be worshiped and consumed, but always a guide leading beyond itself" (Hartman 1970, 290). Other Romantics, like Wordsworth, believe that the separation from nature leads to a philosophic and artistic quest for unity that takes them beyond nature—not back to some lost unity, but forward to an unfolding—an infinite unfolding—of human potential. The German philosopher and poet Friedrich Schiller (1759–1805) expresses this distinction as the difference between the naive and the sentimental, by which he means the modern, or Romantic, self-conscious poet. In *On Naive and Sentimental Poetry* (1795–1796), Schiller writes "the poet . . . *is* nature or he will *seek* it. The former makes for the naive poet, the latter for the sentimental poet" (Schiller 1993, 200). The gap between the self-conscious mind and the nature it has lost leads not to desire for a simple return to nature; rather, it leads the mind to recognize its essential human nature, which is different from and superior to phenomenal nature. Following Schiller, later Romantic writers sought to find value and a sense of power in the creative attempt to achieve some compensatory state of mind or being—what Wordsworth calls "abundant recompense" in "Lines Composed a Few Miles above Tintern Abbey" (Wordsworth 1988, 134).

In this move to find not only compensation but also power in the fall from nature, Romanticism complicates the human relation to other living things and risks reinforcing an anthropocentric (human-centered), if not androcentric (male-centered), relation to nature. Ralph Waldo Emerson, one of the United States' most important Transcendentalist writers, proclaimed in his foundational essay "Nature" (1836) that "philosophically considered, the universe is composed of Nature and the Soul. Strictly speaking, therefore, all that is separate from us, all which Philosophy distinguishes as the NOT ME, that is, both nature and art, all other men and my own body, must be ranked under this name, NATURE" (Emerson 1985, 36).

Many Romantic writers such as Emerson engage in what Lawrence Buell in *The Environmental Imagination* calls a "metaphysics of correspondence" (Buell 1995, 129) whereby the spiritual world inhabited by the mind finds in nature simply a reflection and affirmation of its own powers. Given the drive for transcendence paradoxically grounded in a receptivity to nature, the Romantic relation to the natural world involves a double movement: on the one hand, a move toward identity and the recovery of the bond between human and the life world; on the other hand, a move toward difference and the celebration of the distance between human and nonhuman. This dialectic of identity and difference goes far to explain the often contested and contradictory relationship toward Romanticism found in environmental and ecological literature that often tends to oversimplify Romanticism as a naive and nostalgic return to nature or to see it as an anthropocentric celebration of the self. The dilemma for ecologically minded readers of Romantic texts is to reconcile the Romantics' love for nature with their sense of their autonomy from it and to sort out the Romantic acknowledgment of nature for its own sake from its treatment of nature as a means to aggrandize the human.

Romantic Ecology

One way to begin to resolve the paradox is to focus on the way the desire for transcendence is rooted in an effort to reconcile human nature with a principle of unity that drives all living things. As James McKusick writes in his introduction to a special issue of *The Wordsworth Circle* on Romanticism and ecology, although "much Romantic writing emerges from a desperate sense of alienation from the natural world," it also "expresses an anxious endeavor to re-establish a vital, sustainable relationship between [hu]mankind and the fragile planet on which [we] dwell" (McKusick 1997, 123). Many Romantic writers and artists identified a spirit of harmony and love operating throughout the natural world, a force that could serve as an anchor and model for humanity. For such writers and artists nature does not serve merely as a backdrop or soothing setting for their meditations; rather nature is a kindred spirit, a correspondent power, in whose dynamic processes and creativity the poet shares. In book 1 of *The Prelude* (1805, 1850), Wordsworth expresses this affinity between mind and nature as a correspondent breeze:

> For I, methought, while the sweet breath of
>   Heaven
> Was blowing on my body, felt within
> A corresponding mild creative breeze,
> A vital breeze which travell'd gently on . . .
>   (Wordsworth 1979, 30)

Here nature serves not as a palette for the poet's paintbrush, but rather as a companion spirit that guides the poet's mind in the act of creation. Moreover, for Wordsworth, nature is a benevolent force, a presence that provides moral guidance for those who are open to what he calls its "ministrations." Similarly, Emerson finds in nature a source for spiritual renewal and philosophical inspiration; in "Nature" he writes, "In the woods, we return to reason and faith" (Emerson 1985, 39).

This sense of community with nature provides one of the key affinities between ecology and Romanticism. In *Nature's Economy*, Donald Worster articulates that connection this way: "in its campaign to restore man to nature, Romanticism was fundamentally biocentric. This doctrine proposes that all nature is alive, and that whatever is alive has a claim on man's moral affections. With the Romantics, a sense of antagonistic dualism gave way to a movement toward fusion, and anthropocentric indifference toward nature yielded to a love for the whole order of being and an acknowledgment of natural kinship" (Worster 1994, 85). Similarly, Karl Kroeber argues in *Ecological Literary Criticism* that the Romantics "believed that humankind *belonged* in, could and should be at home within, the world of natural processes" (Kroeber 1994, 5). For Kroeber, this sense of belonging is the ground of what he calls the "proto-ecological views" of English Romanticism (Kroeber 1994, 5).

The ideal Romantic relationship between human beings and nature is reflexive and mutually interdependent—a meeting halfway or more. The Romantics' encounter with nature was not that of the spectator to a well-wrought canvas of beautiful scenery—a *natura naturata*, or world of mere phenomena, but rather that of a participant in a dynamic theater of creation and transformation—a *natura naturans*, a vital, active force. They attempted to move beyond reverence or admiration before the creative power of nature and to discern a sense of kinship with such powers and to recognize the mutual interdependence between nature and human beings.

Romanticism and the Environment

Although Romanticism presents a paradoxical relation to nature, many recent critics would agree with Donald Worster's characterization that "at the very core of [the] Romantic view of nature was what later generations would come to call an ecological perspective: that is, a search for holistic or integrated perception, an emphasis on interdependence and relatedness in nature, and an intense desire to restore man to a place of intimate intercourse with the vast organism that constitutes the earth" (Worster 1994, 82). Jonathan Bate echoes Worster's view, stating that "The 'Romantic ecology' reverences the green earth because it recognizes that neither physically nor psychologically can we live without green things; it proclaims that there is 'one life' within us and abroad, that the earth is a single vast ecosystem which we destabilize at our peril" (Bate 1991, 40). If, as Bate says, Romanticism strives to "enable mankind the better to live in the material world by entering into harmony with the environment" (Bate 1991, 40), then it also thematizes the problem of doing so by showing how far human consciousness is given to separate itself from nature and to celebrate its apparent superiority to other living things. Thus, as people attempt to recuperate and realize within their contemporary ecological discourse the constructive, ecocentric ideals of Romanticism, they must keep sight of those anthropocentric tendencies inherent in Romantic nature philosophy that would simply reaffirm human claims to superiority over nature. By sorting out the complexities of Romanticism's position on the environment, people may make better use of its insights and recognize that the quest for understanding their place in the life world, a quest first explored self-consciously by Romantic writers, is an ongoing, dialectical process. As Ralph Pite succinctly puts it in "How Green Were the Romantics?" "For the romantics to be green, we will need to read them in a green way" (Pite 1996, 359).

Gary Harrison

Further Reading

Abrams, M. H. (1971). *Natural supernaturalism: Tradition and revolution in Romantic literature*. New York: W. W. Norton.

Bate, J. (1991). *Romantic ecology: Wordsworth and the environmental tradition*. London: Routledge.

Bate, J. (2000). *The song of the earth*. Cambridge, MA: Harvard University Press.

Buell, L. (1995). *The environmental imagination: Thoreau, nature writing, and the formation of American culture*. Cambridge, MA: Belknap Press of Harvard University Press.

Burke, E. (1990). *A philosophical enquiry into the origins of our ideas of the sublime and beautiful*. Oxford and New York: Oxford University Press. (Original work published 1757)

Clark, K. (1973). *The Romantic rebellion: Romantic versus classic art*. New York: Harper & Row.

Cranston, M. (1994). *The Romantic movement*. Cambridge, MA: Blackwell.

Curran, S. (Ed.). (1993). *The Cambridge companion to British Romanticism*. Cambridge, UK: Cambridge University Press.

Day, A. (1996). *Romanticism*. New York: Routledge.

Emerson, R. W. (1985). Nature. In L. Ziff (Ed.), *Ralph Waldo Emerson: Selected essays*. (pp. 35–82). New York: Penguin. (Original work published 1836)

Evernden, N. (1985). *The natural alien: Humankind and environment*. Toronto, Canada: University of Toronto Press.

Hartman, G. (1970). The romance of nature and the negative way. In H. Bloom (Ed.), *Romanticism and consciousness: Essays in criticism*. (pp. 287–305). New York: W. W. Norton.

Herndl, C. G., & Brown, S. C. (Eds.). (1996). *Green culture: Environmental rhetoric in contemporary America*. Madison: University of Wisconsin Press.

Hinderer, W., & Dahlstrom, D. O. (Eds.). *The German library: Vol. 17. Friedrich Schiller: Essays*. New York: Continuum.

Kroeber, K. (1994). *Ecological literary criticism: Romantic imagining and the biology of mind*. New York: Columbia University Press.

Lovejoy, A. O. (1924). On the discrimination of Romanticisms. *Publications of the Modern Language Association of America (PMLA), 39*(2), 229–253.

McKusick, J. C. (1997, Summer). Introduction: Romanticism and ecology. *The Wordsworth Circle, 28*(3), 123–124.

McKusick, J. C. (2000). *Green writing: Romanticism and ecology*. New York: St. Martin's Press.

Merchant, C. (1989). *The death of nature: Women, ecology and the scientific revolution*. San Francisco: Harper.

Peckham, M. (1995). *The Romantic virtuoso*. Hanover, NH: Wesleyan University Press.

Phillips, A. (Ed.). *World's classics*. New York: Oxford University Press.

Pite, R. (1996, Fall). How green were the Romantics? *Studies in Romanticism, 35*(3), 357–374.

Porter, R., & Teich, M. (Eds.). (1988). *Romanticism in national context.* London: Macmillan Education.

Rousseau, J. J. (1977). *The confessions of Jean Jacques Rousseau* (J. M. Cohen, Trans.). Harmondsworth, UK: Penguin. (Original work published 1781–1788)

Rousseau, J. J. (1994). *Discourse on inequality* (F. Philip, Trans.; Patrick Coleman, Ed.). Oxford, UK: Oxford University Press. (Original work published 1755)

Schiller, F. (1993). On naive and sentimental poetry. In F. Schiller, *Aesthetic writings* (W. Hinderer & D. O. Dahlstrom, Eds.). New York: Continuum. (Original work published 1795–1796)

Thoreau, H. D. (2000). Walking. In B. Atkinson (Ed.), *Walden and other writings* (pp. 627–663). New York: Modern Library. (Original work published 1862)

Wordsworth, W. (1979). In J. Wordsworth, M. H. Abrams, & S. Gill (Eds.), *The prelude: 1799, 1805, 1850: William Wordsworth.* (pp. 28–482). New York: W. W. Norton. (Original work published 1805)

Wordsworth, W. (1988). Lines composed a few miles above Tintern Abbey. In S. Gill (Ed.), *William Wordsworth* (pp. 66–70). Oxford, UK: Oxford University Press.

Worster, D. (1994). *Nature's economy* (2nd ed.). Cambridge, UK: Cambridge University Press.

Roosevelt, Franklin Delano
(1882–1945)
U.S. president

Twice elected governor of New York, Franklin Delano Roosevelt was the only man elected four times to the presidency of the United States. The first eight years of Roosevelt's presidency saw the most concerted effort made by any American chief executive before or since to emphasize the wise use of natural resources to benefit the greatest number of citizens.

Born in Hyde Park, New York, he was the only son of James and Sara Delano Roosevelt. Educated privately until age fourteen, he then attended Groton School (graduated 1900), Harvard College (B.A., 1904), and Columbia University Law School (1904–1907), though he did not take a degree there. Roosevelt was a practicing attorney from 1907 to 1910, served in the New York State Senate from 1910 to 1913, and was Assistant Secretary of the Navy, 1913–1920. A Democrat, he was the party's nominee for vice-president of the United States in 1920. He was elected governor of New York State in 1928 and 1930. Four times elected president of the United States, in 1932, 1936, 1940, and 1944, he served as the nation's thirty-second chief executive from 1933 until 1945.

Roosevelt was chair of the New York State Senate Committee on Forests, Fish and Game, and attempted unsuccessfully to secure passage of a bill that would have restricted tree cutting on private property. As governor during the early stages of the Great Depression, he directed that jobless men be hired to plant trees through the Temporary State Emergency Relief Administration, and initiated studies of the conservation and use of state water resources. During his first two terms as president, Roosevelt's administration initiated the so-called New Deal, which involved a pragmatic approach to the nation's economic and social problems through a number of relief, recovery, and reform initiatives. More than any other president before or since, Roosevelt's programs emphasized the wise use of the nation's natural resources to benefit the greatest number of its citizens. Many of these conservation measures achieved considerable success, despite the fact that disputes between competing New Deal agencies sometimes prevented a coordination of efforts. They included the Civilian Conservation Corps (CCC), which placed several million young men to work in national parks, national forests, and wildlife refuges. The Tennessee Valley Authority (TVA) harnessed water resources through a series of dams built in impoverished regions of the south-central United States. The U.S. Bureau of Reclamation and the U.S. Army Corps of Engineers undertook a number of projects, including dam construction and other flood control initiatives. These helped to limit potential flood damage, provided cheap public electric power, and in some instances, made new recreational opportunities available to the public. Unfortunately, however, some unanticipated long-run environmental damage resulted from these efforts.

The administration embarked on a number of soil conservation enterprises, both before and during the Dust Bowl crisis of the mid and late 1930s. Much of the nation's exhausted farmland was reclaimed through reforms in farming methods. Examples include the Taylor Grazing act of 1934, which regulated the grazing of domestic animals on public lands, and the creation of a Soil Conservation in the Department of Agriculture (1935), which instructed farmers in better methods of planting and harvesting and the control of soil erosion. The planting of shelterbelts of trees in the northern plains states (an idea proposed by Roosevelt) met with some success. Secretary of the Interior Harold Ickes loyally served his chief throughout Roosevelt's twelve years in office, but Roosevelt rejected Ickes's proposal that Interior be reconstituted a Department of Conservation with expanded responsibilities. Overall, however, through Roosevelt's appointment and strong support of the many dedicated conservationists in his administration, a number of valuable programs were vigorously initiated and maintained during his presidency.

Keir B. Sterling

Further Reading

Nixon, E. B. (Ed.) (1957). *Franklin D. Roosevelt and conservation* (Vols. 2). Hyde Park, NY: FDR Library.

Riesch-Owen, A. L. (1983). *Conservation under FDR*. New York: Praeger.

Salmond, J. (1967). *The civilian conservation corps, 1933–1942: A new deal case study*. Durham, NC: Duke University Press.

Watkins, T. H. (1990). *Righteous pilgrim: The life and times of Harold L. Ickes (1874–1952)*. New York: Henry Holt.

Worster, D. L. (1979). *Dust bowl: The southern plains in the 1930s*. New York: Oxford University Press.

Roosevelt, Theodore

(1858–1919)

U.S. president, naturalist, cofounder of Boone and Crockett Club

Born in New York City, Theodore Roosevelt developed an early interest in natural history and ornithology. Roosevelt hoped to become a zoologist and even published two ornithology books while in college. But by his senior year, he had decided on a career in politics. He graduated from Harvard and enrolled at Columbia Law School but never finished. He was elected to the New York State Assembly in 1882 and served with distinction for three years. He also launched a career as a historian in 1882 with *The Naval Warfare of the War of 1812*, one of some three dozen books he wrote on a variety of topics. In 1883, he purchased a cattle ranch in what is now North Dakota and worked it on and off for the next five years. His cowboy days gave him a firsthand education about the environment.

In 1887, Roosevelt cofounded the Boone and Crockett Club, a gentlemen hunters club with a strong interest in the preservation of large game animals of the Western Plains. The club quickly became involved in the conservation movement, too. It fought for the preservation of Yellowstone Park, contributed to the passage of the Forest Reserve Act in 1891, and helped found the Bronx Zoo in 1895.

From 1889 to 1895, Roosevelt served on the U.S. Civil Service Commission, then for two years as a commissioner of the New York City Police Board. He then was appointed assistant secretary of the U.S. Navy and prepared the service for war with Spain. When war came in April 1898, he resigned to form the first U.S. Volunteer Cavalry regiment, better known as the Rough Riders. He returned from Cuba a war hero and was elected governor of New York in 1898. In 1900, he was elected vice president of the United States and became president in September 1901 upon the assassination of President William McKinley.

Besides his reputation as a trustbuster, Roosevelt is noted for his accomplishments in the conservation of natural resources. Roosevelt's administration brought nearly 1.2 million hectares of arid land in a dozen states under irrigation. He withdrew a total of 93.6 million hectares of public domain to prevent entry by or sale to the public and created the U.S. Forest Service in 1905 to manage much of that land. He established several national monuments and national parks. He also established the first federal wildlife refuges to protect wildlife and their habitats. The White House Conference of Governors, held in 1908, helped publicize conservation and make it a national goal.

After leaving the presidency in 1909, Roosevelt embarked on an African expedition to collect specimens for the Smithsonian Institution. After his defeat in 1912 as a third-party candidate for president, he then explored a newly discovered river in Brazil. The trip nearly killed him, but his party mapped the river and collected specimens. In Roosevelt's honor, Brazil renamed the river for him. His last years were spent writing articles and reviews for various publications. Of his many accomplishments, Roosevelt's conservation work remains arguably his greatest legacy.

James G. Lewis

To waste, to destroy our natural resources, to skin and exhaust the land instead of using it so as to increase its usefulness, will result in undermining in the days of our children the very prosperity which we ought by right to hand down to them amplified and developed.

Source: Roosevelt, Theodore, *Seventh Annual Message to Congress*, December 3, 1907.

Further Reading

Collins, M. L. (1989). *That damned cowboy: Theodore Roosevelt and the American West, 1883–1898*. New York: P. Lang.

Cutright, P. (1985). *Theodore Roosevelt: The making of a conservationist*. Chicago: University of Illinois Press.

Dalton, K. (2002). *Theodore Roosevelt: A strenuous life*. New York: Alfred A. Knopf.

Gould, L. L. (1991). *The presidency of Theodore Roosevelt*. Lawrence: University Press of Kansas.

Harbaugh, W. (1961). *Power and responsibility: The life and times of Theodore Roosevelt*. New York: Farrar, Straus, and Cudahy.

Miller, N. (1992). *Theodore Roosevelt: A life*. New York: Morrow.

Morris, E. (1979). *The rise of Theodore Roosevelt*. New York: Coward, McCann, and Geoghegan.

Morris, E. (2001). *Theodore rex*. New York: Random House.

Roosevelt, T. (1913). *An autobiography*. New York: Macmillan.

Root Crops

Root crops are an important component of the human diet as they provide about 80 percent of human energy consumption. Root crops are grown worldwide on about 53 million hectares. Root crops may include all plant species whose underground organs are grown for human consumption. A narrower definition would limit such crops to those that are roots or tubers, botanically speaking, rather than bulbs or corms. Originating in different regions, there are more than thirty root/tuber crops grown worldwide; some for human consumption directly or in processed form, some for animal feed, and others for starch or sugar extraction that are the basis of specific industries, including alcoholic beverages. Roots/tubers are especially important in developing countries. Approximately 70 percent of the roots/tubers harvested for human use (mainly potatoes) were consumed in developing countries while the remaining 30 percent were consumed in developed countries.

Most species have been selected because they contain large amounts of carbohydrates in enlarged underground organs, though they have high water content when compared with cereal (seed) crops and little protein. All roots/tubers are bulky and are usually propagated vegetatively but collectively they provide some 8–10 percent of the total energy source for humans. Potatoes, manioc or cassava, sweet potatoes, yams, beets, and carrots are among the most important in terms of area planted and productivity (see table 1), while species such as taro, yautia, arrowroot, ullucu, oca, mashua, kohlrabi, radish, ginger, and numerous others are significant in specific localities.

Potato

As table 1 shows, the potato is one of the most important root/tuber crops along with manioc. In terms of edible energy produced per unit area, the potato is one of the highest achievers, exceeding that of yam and sweet potato as well as the seed crops of maize, wheat, and rice. Today, it is a major world crop along with wheat, maize, and rice and is grown in agricultural systems ranging from subsistent to commercial. It also has a high vitamin C content and some protein, characteristics that have contributed to its importance and its cultivation has intensified in many countries where agricultural systems have been pressed to maintain food supplies for an increasing population and which are also required to generate agricultural products for export. It is a seasonal crop widely cultivated in the temperate zone, especially in the Northern Hemisphere; some 64 percent of world production is in developed countries. A crop may be achieved in only sixty days given good growing conditions of nutrient-

TABLE 1.
PRODUCTION AND AREA PLANTED OF THE WORLD'S MAIN ROOT/TUBER CROPS IN 2000

	Production (tonnes) in 2000	Area planted (ha) in 2000
Potato	328,050,784	19,940,259
Sweet potato	138,848,631	9,111,979
Yam	38,304,339	4,040,247
Sugar beet	245,419,567	5,968,770
Carrot	19,791,176	917,630
Manioc	176,784,378	17,032,269

Source: Food and Agriculture Organisation. (2002). FAOSTAT. Retrieved July 20, 2002, from www.fao.org.

rich soil, abundant water, and the absence of pests to which potato is particularly susceptible.

The cultivated potato is *Solanum tuberosum* subspecies *tuberosum* (also known as the Irish potato), a member of the family Solanaceae to which the tomato, aubergine (eggplant), and various peppers also belong. It is consumed directly in the many forms that cooked potatoes take, but flour and starch are also produced. The latter may be used in nonfood industries such as adhesive production. Its current distribution pattern belies its origins in the Peruvian Andes where it is most likely that domestication originally occurred, probably from *S. tuberosum* subspecies *andigena* and probably between 3,000 and 5,000 years ago. Sources of evidence for early use are mainly depictions on pottery from archeological sites; the artifacts indicate that the potato was used in fertility rites and divination. Today this mountain region (up to 4,000 meters above sea level) is home to some 5,000 varieties of various colors, shapes, sizes, and flavors with local farmers growing as many as seventy varieties on individual holdings to take advantage of the microhabitats that exist with rapidly changing altitude, soils, aspect, and length of growing season. It is this biodiversity that scientists are examining to reveal the potato's genetic characteristics for developing disease and pest resistance. The potato has thus returned to its roots!

Europeans encountered the potato when South America was annexed in the early 1500s. The first contact may have been in the Magdalena Valley in the Colombian Andes in 1537 while the first recorded use in Europe was in the Sangre Hospital in Seville, Spain, in 1573. It was present in Britain by 1586, though who effected the introduction is disputed; Sir Walter Raleigh and Sir John Hawkins have both been implicated but another possibility is Thomas Heriot, a botanist on Drake's expedition. The potato returned to the Americas from Europe in the 1700s, but to North America, and then spread throughout Europe where it became the crop of the poor, not only in Ireland but also in Eastern Europe and Russia. Here the genetic pool was depleted in comparison with that in the potato's homeland and so susceptibility to disease was high, especially to the fungal infection of late blight (*Phytophthora infestans*). A combination of accidental introduction of this disease to Ireland and potato monoculture enforced by colonial rule resulted in crop failure. This induced famine causing the deaths of 2.5 million people and the emigration of a further 1 million people to North America.

Today the potato is a popular food worldwide. Boiled, mashed, roasted, and as the ubiquitous French fry (chip) and crisp, the potato is a staple food that has undergone globalization. Production is likely to increase in the future as it is adopted as a major crop in many developing countries where it will supplement traditional crops such as rice and contribute to food-processing industries. The value of the potato is also reflected in research activities and policy options. Conventional plant breeding and biotechnology involving genetic modification are being used to produce varieties with enhanced resistance to late blight and other viral diseases while productivity will be increased with improved integrated crop management strategies. Local and rapid production of disease-free plants through tissue culture would reduce costs to farmers, as importation of plants would become unnecessary. The resulting increased food supply may help to alleviate poverty and lead to improved human health, especially in rural communities.

Sweet Potato

The sweet potato (*Ipomoea batatas* (L) Lam.) is a member of the Convolvulaceae family and is a tropical climbing plant with an underground storage root comprising pink sweetish flesh. Although it has 30 percent less energy content than the potato, to which it is not related, the sweet potato is richer in vitamins A, B, and C, and calcium. It is most widely grown in the tropics and subtropics, the major producers being China, which produces 85 percent of the world crop (see table 1), India, Indonesia, Nigeria, and Uganda. In many African countries sweet potato is considered a lifesaver as it provides food security for many rural poor, especially when other crops fail. Consumed mainly as fresh or dried tubers, it is also made into flour for bread and porridge, and pellets for animal feed.

A harvest of sugar beets on a farm near Calais, France, in 1994. COURTESY KAREN CHRISTENSEN.

The actual place of domestication is unknown but research at the International Potato Center, Peru, indicates that the greatest genetic diversity occurs in Central America. This is therefore considered as the most likely center of origin, with Peru-Ecuador as a secondary center. Sweet potato spread through Asia, Africa, and Latin America during the seventeenth and eighteenth centuries, but it had arrived in many Pacific islands, where there is higher per capita consumption than elsewhere, prior to European influence.

Sweet potato grows well in low-rainfall areas with poor soils up to altitudes of 3,000 meters. Its major pests are virus diseases and the sweet-potato weevil. Current research is focusing on the improvement of starch quality, pre-beta carotene content, and yield, while small- and medium-scale farmers in many developing countries are being encouraged to grow the crop. Increased production is likely to be important in China, where yields will rise as the area planted contracts, and in Vietnam, especially for feed for pigs and starch production.

Yam

Domesticated yams are climbing vines and are grown mostly in tropical and subtropical regions. All are members of the family Dioscoreaceae, a name derived from that of Pedanius Dioscorides, a physician in the Roman army in the first century CE who wrote a book entitled *De materia medica* that contained over 400 plant descriptions. The major yam species cultivated include *Dioscorea rotundata* (white or white Guinea yam) and *D. cayenensis* (yellow or yellow Guinea yam) which were domesticated in West Africa, *D. alata* (greater, water, or winged yam), *D. esculenta* (lesser yam), and *D. bulbifera* (aerial or potato yam) whose origins lie in New Guinea. *D. trifida* (Cush-cush or yampi yam) is an American species but it, along with several other species from Africa and Southeast Asia, is not widely grown for food. The food source is in an underground stem tuber rich in starch and, in comparison with other root crops, rich in protein.

Table 1 shows that 38 million tonnes of yams were produced in 2000 from about 4 million hectares. Between 90 and 95 percent of both the land and the production lies in tropical Africa, in a so-called yam belt or yam zone in the sub-Saharan countries of Cameroon, Nigeria, Benin, Togo, Ghana, and Côte d'Ivoire. Here *D. rotundata* is the species cultivated in labor-intensive agricultural systems; planting takes place prior to the rainy season using either saved seed or new material, staking is required to support the plant, and frequent weeding is necessary to reduce the competition for light, water, and nutrients which can be acute. Most of the produce is consumed as food for humans; boiled, grilled, fried, or roasted, the yam is a staple food that has a longer storage life than manioc or sweet potato. Yams are also dried as chips, which are sold for making flour. This is used to produce a dough known as *amala* or *telibowo*. Yam cultivation is set to increase in the future as population continues to increase rapidly in the yam zone; efforts to improve resistance to pests such as nematodes through plant breeding and biotechnology could improve productivity and commercial use could be developed.

Sugar Beet

Sugar beet *(Beta vulgaris* variety *altissima)* contrasts with the root/tuber crops detailed above as it is almost entirely confined to regions with a temperate to Mediterranean-type climate. Moreover, most of the crop is used in the production of sugar rather than consumed directly and is thus highly commercialized; beet pulp is used as animal feed. Several beets are used for fodder and as vegetables (collectively known as chards); all are derived from the wild sea-beet *(Beta maritima)* with domestication occurring in the Mediterranean region but of unknown date. The Greek and Roman practice of using the leaves as a herb probably began the road to commercial propagation. The Romans disseminated beets throughout Europe and by the early eighteenth century sugar beet had been developed from Silesian fodder beet. Achard, a Berlin chemist who revived the earlier but unsuccessful work of his mentor Robert Marggraf, refined the chemistry necessary to extract the sugar and by 1802 the first sugar-beet factory was constructed in Kunern, Germany. Indeed, the Napoleonic wars (1800–1815) contributed to the spread of sugar beet because blockaded ports made it difficult to import cane sugar from the West Indies.

Today, beet sugar production is a major industry sustained by a crop of some 8 million tonnes grown on about 6 million hectares. (See table 1.) France, the United States, Germany, and Russia are leading producers. Modern sugar-beet varieties have a sugar (sucrose) content of about 20 percent compared with 4 percent for early varieties. Sugar beets grow best in well-drained, stone-free soils with abundant water for spring growth; harvesting is fully mechanized. Sugar beet is usually cultivated in arable rotations that include wheat, barley, and pulses. The major pests are beet-cyst nematode, several viral diseases, and storage rots, resistance to which is the focus of plant breeding and genetic modification. Improved productivity may result in some decline of hectarage but demand for sugar will remain high in the future.

Carrot

Numerous root crops are grown on a subsistence and commercial basis for use as vegetables and animal feed. Carrot *(Daucus carota* subspecies *sativus)* is one of the most important; it is widely cultivated and has a many uses, including medicinal applications. As a member of the family Umbelliferae, which includes parsnip and various species of culinary herbs as well as several poisonous plants, domestication occurred in Central Asia, possibly in what is now Afghanistan, and probably 5,000 years ago. The original domesticate was purple rather than the familiar orange. From Asia, Arab traders brought it west; the Romans consumed it as a raw or cooked purple and white root. Its details are described in Pedanius Dioscorides' *De materia medica* and many Greek and Roman scholars refer to the carrot in their texts. It was introduced to Spain by the Moors in the eighth century CE and then spread to Northern Europe. The orange version is the result of selection by Dutch growers, reputedly in recognition of the House of Orange, and was introduced to Britain in the sixteenth century when it began to replace carrots of other hues.

In 2000, about 20 million tonnes were produced worldwide from almost 1 million hectares (see table 1), mainly in the temperate areas of China (c. 30 percent), Russia, Ukraine, and the United States. Carrot cultivation favors a light, warm soil such as a loam; planting occurs in the spring and harvesting in autumn. Nutritively, carrots are about 89 percent water and 4.5 percent sugar, the remainder being starch, gluten, carotene (the source of vitamin A), pectin, malic acid, and a volatile oil. Carrot production increased by 53 percent between 1990 and 2000 and is likely to continue to increase for both animal and human consumption. Focuses of carrot biotechnology include the development of nematode and virus resistance as well as enhanced pigment expression to improve health benefits.

A. M. Mannion

Further Reading

Campbell-Culver, M. (2001). *The origin of plants*. London: Headline Book Publishing.

Crispeels, M. J., & Sadava, D. E. (2003). *Plants, genes, and crop biotechnology* (2nd ed.). Boston: Jones and Bartlett.

Graves, C. (Ed.) (2001). *The potato, treasure of the Andes: From agriculture to culture*. Lima, Peru: International Potato Center.

Persley, G. J., & MacIntyre, L. R. (Eds.). (2002) *Agricultural biotechnology: Country case studies—a decade of development*. Wallingford, UK: CABI Publishing.

Scott, G. J., Rosegrant, M. W., & Ringler, C. (2000). *Roots and tubers for the 21st century: Trends, projections and policy options*. Washington, DC: International Food Policy Research Institute and Lima: International Potato Center.

World Carrot Museum. (2002). Retrieved July 30, 2002, from http://website.lineone.net/~stolarczyk/

Rubber Tree

Many varieties of plants yield rubber latex, including sunflowers, the desert shrub guayule (*Parthenium argentatum*) of northern Mexico and southern Texas, Castilloa (Castilla) trees in Central America and western Amazonia, and most prominently Hevea species of Amazonia in South America. Prior to 1913 Latin America produced most of the world's natural rubber.

During his second voyage to the West Indies (1493–1496), Christopher Columbus (1451–1506) reported that the peoples of western Santo Domingo (Haiti) played a game with a rubber ball. The Aztec of central Mexico collected rubber as tribute from subject peoples and used it in religious ceremonies prior to their conquest by the Spanish in 1521. Centuries earlier many peoples of Mesoamerica, including the Maya, played a game using a heavy rubber ball.

European explorers and American colonists learned about rubber latex and began to experiment with its qualities of elasticity and impermeability over the next few centuries and then intensified their tinkering and experiments in the nineteenth century when industrialization made rubber a strategic commodity.

The process of heating a solution of rubber latex, lead, and sulfur to stabilize (vulcanize) rubber in 1839 and the reinvention of the pneumatic tire in 1888 made rubber for tires and tubes the biggest market for latex in the world. The bicycle craze of the 1890s and the popularity of automobiles in the United States in subsequent decades immensely expanded international and industrial demand for the rubber latex found in trees and vines in Amazonia, Africa, Asia, and Mexico.

The collection of rubber became synonymous with violent mistreatment of workers in Amazonia, Central Africa, and southeastern Asia during boom years. Slavery, torture, dismemberment, and beatings and whippings raised international scandal in the Belgian Congo (Zaire) (1897–1910) and the Putumayo/Caquetá area in northwestern Amazonia (1907–1914). High mortality rates of plantation workers in southeastern Asia raised further questions about colonialism, absentee capitalism, and imperialism. Moreover, a bonanza mentality during the Amazon rubber boom (1880–1914) destroyed rubber trees by the overaggressive tapping of high-quality *jebe fino* latex and the felling and killing of Castilloa trees to extract hundred pounds of *caucho*, a lower-quality latex. These non-sustainable collection techniques during the boom years led to great abuse of labor, disruption of the human and natural environment, and resource depletion.

Indigenous peoples of Amazonia and Central Africa were both enticed by trade goods and forced by violence to collect rubber. In the Amazon River basin, Brazilians from the poor and drought-stricken Northeast were contracted to collect rubber during the boom, as were West Indians from the Caribbean. A surprising number of Europeans and North and Latin Americans sought their fortunes during the boom, usually not realizing any great gains. The large number of migrants into Amazonia had disastrous effects, such as the introduction of epidemic disease, widespread violence, and the cultural shock of incorporation into the larger world, for tens of thousands of Amazonian natives.

The transplantation from Brazil of *Hevea brasiliensis* seeds—which yield the highest-quality rubber latex—to southern and southeastern Asia spelled doom for the rubber boom in Amazonia. Carefully planned plantations in Malaysia and Indonesia increased production, lowered costs, and improved quality. Small and more efficient rubber farms in southeast Asia now compete successfully with the neighboring older plantations.

In the 1970s and 1980s in the Brazilian state of Acre, Chico Mendes (1944–1988) and Marina Silva helped organize rubber tappers and linked them with indigenous peoples and Brazilian and international environmental organizations to protect the Amazonian rain forest from clear-cutting for cattle ranching. Mendes was assassinated in 1988, but Silva continued the work and was elected to the Brazilian senate in 1994.

Michael Edward Stanfield

Further Reading

Dean, W. (1987). *Brazil and the struggle for rubber: A study in environmental history*. Cambridge, UK: Cambridge University Press.

Hemming, J. (1987). *Amazon frontier: The defeat of the Brazilian Indians*. Cambridge, MA: Harvard University Press.

Hochschild, A. (1998). *King Leopold's ghost*. New York: Houghton Mifflin.

Mendes, C. (1989). *Fight for the forest: Chico Mendes in his own words*. London: Latin American Bureau.

Stanfield, M. E. (1998). *Red rubber, bleeding trees: Violence, slavery, and empire in northwest Amazonia, 1850–1933*. Albuquerque: University of New Mexico Press.

Weinstein, B. (1983). *The Amazon rubber boom, 1850–1920*. Stanford, CA.: Stanford University Press.

Ruckelshaus, William D.

(b. 1932)

Administrator of U.S. Environmental Protection Agency

Born in Indianapolis, Indiana, William Doyle Ruckelshaus graduated from Princeton University and Harvard Law School, and then joined his family's law firm in 1960. That same year, he was appointed deputy state attorney general for Indiana and assigned to the Indiana Board of Health. He gained direct environmental experience serving as counsel to the Indiana Stream Pollution Control Board. He also helped draft the 1961 Indiana Air Pollution Control Act, the state's first attempt to curb the problem.

Ruckelshaus won election to the Indiana House of Representatives in 1967, but lost the race for U.S. Senate in 1968. He then was selected by the incoming administration of President Richard Nixon to serve as assistant U.S. attorney general. Ruckelshaus's conscientiousness led to his appointment as administrator of the newly formed Environmental Protection Agency in December 1970.

To produce the fastest results and assure a skeptical Congress and general public of his commitment to environmental objectives, Ruckelshaus started enforcement actions immediately against polluters. The threat of bad publicity and heavy fines persuaded many of the defendants to cooperate. Ruckelshaus's approach gave the EPA instant credibility and created such a positive image of the agency and of Ruckelshaus that, in the middle of the Watergate scandal, he was asked to take over the beleaguered Federal Bureau of Investigation in April 1973 as acting director. He then became deputy attorney general in July 1973. He left his post only a few months later in what became known as the "Saturday Night Massacre," with the administration claiming that he had been fired and Ruckelshaus maintaining that he resigned. He returned to private law practice and then accepted a position as senior vice president of the Weyerhaeuser Company in 1976.

When the EPA under the administration of President Ronald Reagan ran afoul of public opinion for its environmental policies in 1983, Ruckelshaus was asked to return in order to restore confidence in the agency. He did so by bringing in experienced administrators and improving the agency's enforcement record. He had two program accomplishments during his second term. The first was an educational campaign to improve public understanding of environmental risks, so that the public could make the conscious choice about how much risk it wanted to live with. His second was the introduction of the controversial topic of acid rain to public and political debate. Though the administration chose to ignore his recommendations to reduce it, environmentalists give him credit for having the courage to broach the subject.

Ruckelshaus resigned in 1988, shortly after Reagan's reelection and returned to practicing law. That same year, he began service as chief executive officer of Browning-Ferris Industries (BFI); he served as chairman of the board of BFI until 1999. He then joined Madrona Investment Group as a strategic partner. He has remained active in environmental issues by serving on the executive boards of several different companies and environmental groups.

James G. Lewis

Further Reading

Hays, S. P. (1998). *Explorations in environmental history: Essays by Samuel P. Hays*. Pittsburgh, PA: University of Pittsburgh Press.

Landy, M. K., Roberts, M. J., & Thomas, S. R. (1990). *The Environmental Protection Agency: Asking the wrong questions*. New York: Oxford University Press.

Ruckelshaus, W. D. (1993). *U.S. EPA oral history interview 1: William D. Ruckelshaus*. Washington, DC: US EPA History Office.

USA International Business Publications. (2000). *U.S. Environmental Protection Agency handbook* (U.S. Government Agencies Investment and Business Library). Washington, DC: Author.

Williams, D. C. (1993). *The guardian: EPA's formative years, 1970–1973*. Washington, DC: US EPA History Office.

Russia and the Soviet Union

Occupying one-sixth of Earth's land area, the former Soviet Union, including Russia, occupies 22.2 million square kilometers and embraces eleven time zones. Although dominated by the European Russian and western Siberian plain, its enormous territory is variegated geologically and topographically as well as by soil type, climate, vegetation, and fauna. Major geographical subdivisions include the Arctic tundra desert, a broad belt of coniferous taiga (a moist subarctic forest dominated by conifers that begins where the tundra ends); mixed deciduous (leaf-dropping) forests; wooded steppe; steppe; extensive mountainous regions; major deserts and semideserts; and pockets of humid subtropical lowlands.

Most of this area was an immense glaciated wasteland from the late Pliocene epoch and especially the middle of the Pleistocene epoch (1 million years ago) to nearly the present (about twelve thousand years ago). By the late Neolithic period (4000 BCE), as human populations spread across this immense area with the retreat of the glaciers they learned to make their livings in the diversified environments in which they found themselves: exploitation of marine mammals and reindeer in the tundra, pastoralism in the steppe, and foraging and swidden (slash-and-burn) agriculture in the forests. Probably owing to a combination of hunting and climate change, the Siberian megafauna (animals large enough to be seen with the naked eye), whose most famous representatives included the wooly mammoth and the giant elk, disappeared at the end of the last ice age. Musk oxen held out longer, until about three thousand years ago.

As late as the early seventeenth century an unbroken grassland stretched from the Danube River to Mongolia. For centuries nomadic herders had pastured their flocks on this ocean of grass. These groups—Pechenegs, Polovtsians, Mongols/Golden Horde, Crimean Tatars, Nogais, Kazakhs, Bashkirs, Kalmyks—were often mixtures of clans and ethnicities they had defeated or absorbed.

The degree to which these groups affected steppe vegetation is the subject of an unresolved debate among ecologists and biogeographers, some of whom assert that without grazing, the fescue-feathergrass assemblage, at least in the northern part of the steppe, would have yielded to a more hydrophilic (having an affinity for water) meadow-type vegetation. During wars large tracts of the steppe were frequently burned to deprive enemies of pasture, which would have reinforced the trend toward xerophilic (thriving with minimum water) vegetation.

During the sixteenth and seventeenth centuries the Muscovite state constructed an elaborate defensive line along its southern forests bordering the steppe, consisting of abatis (barriers of cut trees) and palisades—the Belgorod line and the Orel, Smolensk, Kashira, Kaluga, and Tula abatis—to bar nomadic horsemen from invading and raiding its towns and farmsteads. Although they were no longer needed by the end of the eighteenth century, the defensive lines remained undeveloped, becoming dense islands of forest rich in wildlife amid agricultural and parklike landscapes (the Tula abatis was preserved as the *Tul'skie zaseki zapovednik*, or "inviolable" nature preserve from 1935 to 1951, when it was eliminated by the Stalin regime; the *Kaluzhskie zaseki* nature reserve was established in 1992 to protect another segment of the 16th century defensive forest line).

By the middle of the nineteenth century all of the cultivable land on the steppe had been converted to cereal farming on gentry estates. As a result the herds of European bison (*Bison bonasus L.*) and tarpan, or wild horse, disappeared (the last one died in 1877). The last *tur*, an ancestral form of the domesticated cow, was killed in 1644, and the saiga antelope (*Saiga tatarica*), once found as far west as Moldavia, was driven back eastward beyond the Don River. The steppe was cleared of beaver (*Castor fiber*) and moose (*Alces alces*) as well. The once-extensive ranges of the greater bustard (*Otis tarda L.*) and lesser bustard (*Otis tetrax L.*), common (*Grus grus L.*) and Demoiselle cranes (*Anthropoides virgo L.*), and other species of steppe avifauna (birds of a region) now contracted to isolated spots.

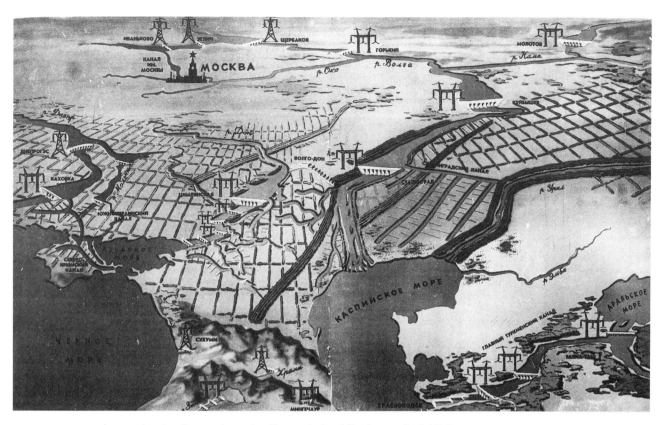

A map showing the great construction projects of the former Soviet Union. COURTESY *OKHRANA PRIRODY* AND DOUG WEINER.

The Lure of Furs

Russians originally were drawn east by the lure of furs. Expansion, first pursued by the Republic of Novgorod in the eleventh through fifteenth centuries, followed trapping grounds. After the conquest of the Kazan khanate (the state or jurisdiction of a khan) by Ivan IV, Cossacks and adventurers pushed along a northern route to the Pacific, with forts *(ostrogi)* built at Eniseisk (1619) and Yakutsk (1632). They found furs but little food and so expanded to the south, to the Amur River basin, in search of suitable growing conditions. Although the Amur region disappointed expectations, the port of Vladivostok served as a springboard for Russian whaling, sealing, and fishing in the North Pacific and for the eventual establishment of bases in Alaska and the California coast. Among the early mammalian casualties of the Russian presence in the Pacific was the Steller's sea cow, which was exterminated by 1783. By 1917 sea otter populations were also endangered, as were those of sable and beaver on the mainland.

Along with Cossacks, imperial expansion into Siberia was pioneered by convicts and exiles, who were sent to the Baikal region as early as the 1660s, as evidenced by Archpriest Avvakum. Later contingents developed the salt and gold mines at Shilka and Nerchinsk, foreshadowing greatly expanded Soviet practices. Of greater environmental impact was the construction of the Trans-Siberian railroad (1892–1916) and the great expansion of peasant migration in its wake. An estimated 7 million peasants moved to Siberia from crowded areas of European Russia in the period from 1801 to 1916. Most of these settled in western and central Siberia, in the fertile steppe of the western Altai.

Although the Russian Empire remained overwhelmingly rural, during its last half-century a remarkable process of urbanization and industrialization occurred. St. Petersburg grew from 500,000 people in 1858 to 1.5 million in 1914, and Moscow grew from 400,000 in 1858 to 1.2 million by that same year. One major environmental issue of the late imperial period was the decline of forest cover in European Russia from 213.4 million hectares (52.7 percent of the territory) in 1696 to 172.3 million in 1914 (35.2 percent). There was no single cause but rather a multitude: industrialization; railroad, home, and telegraph construction; impoverishment of the landed gentry; and, not least important, peasant land hunger.

Led by eminent field biologists, a Russian nature protection movement emerged in the 1890s. The soil scientist Vasilii Vasil'evich Dokuchaev had proposed as early as 1894 that the few remaining islands of steppe be protected to allow scientific study and to serve as baseline references (*etalons*) of what the original vegetation was like. This idea was further developed by zoologist Grigorii Aleksandrovich Kozhevnikov, who argued that representative tracts embracing all the various surviving pristine ecological communities in the Russian Empire, and later the USSR, should be protected as *zapovedniki*, or permanently inviolable nature reserves. After comprehensive scientific study of such putative (commonly accepted) closed ecological systems, he believed, appropriate uses for surrounding lands could be recommended by scientists. Because experts thought the ecological community of the *zapovednik* represented healthy nature, degraded land—that is, land altered by human economic activity—could also be restored by using the *etalon* as a model.

Kozhevnikov and other leading activists such as botanist Ivan Parfen'evich Borodin and entomologist (a biologist who studies insects) Andrei Petrovich Semenov-tian-shanskii were also concerned with ethical and aesthetic aspects of nature protection, but these arguments were downplayed in favor of scientific and utilitarian ones after the Bolsheviks assumed power in November 1917.

The institutionalization of nature protection began during the last decade of czarist rule. In 1910 the first citizens conservation group, the Khortitsa Society of Defenders of Nature, was established to save picturesque cliffs on the Dnepr River, and a year later botanist Valerii Ivanovich Taliev founded a nature protection society in Khar'kov, also in Ukraine. In 1911 as well Borodin organized the Permanent Nature Protection Commission under the auspices of the Imperial Russian Geographical Society, whose thirty-one prominent scientific and government leaders constituted an advisory body to the regime. Russia's first state nature reserve, the Barguzinskii *zapovednik*, was established in 1916 to protect habitat of sable (*Martes zibellina*). Borodin and Kozhevnikov represented Russia at the First International Conference for the Protection of Nature, held in Bern, Switzerland, in 1913.

Nature Groups Founded

In 1924 the All-Russian Society for the Protection of Nature was founded, reaching fifteen thousand mem-

bers by 1932 and publishing a bimonthly journal, *Okhrana prirody* (Protection of Nature). Led by Vasilii Nikitich Makarov, the society's leadership included prominent scientists such as Vladimir Georgievich Geptner, Aleksandr Nikolaevich Formozov, hunting specialists Frants Frantsovich Shillinger and Boris Mikhailovich Zhitkov, and lifelong activists Evdokiia Grigor'evna Bloshenko and Susanna Nikolaevna Fridman. Another strong nature protection organization was the Central Bureau for the Study of Local Regions (*Tsentral'noe biuro kraevedeniia*), established in 1925, which united sixty thousand members of local affiliates. Societies in Ukraine, Georgia, and other republics also had thousands of members.

During the 1920s Anatolii Vasil'evich Lunacharskii, RSFSR (Russian Soviet Federated Socialist Republic) people's commissar for education, created the Department of Nature Protection within that ministry, responsible for the first network of protected territories exclusively dedicated to ecological and scientific study (*zapovedniki*). The Interagency State Committee for Nature Protection, which had a mandate to assess the environmental impact of economic policies, existed from 1925 to 1931, when it was closed after opposing targets of the First Five-Year Plan. The First Five-Year Plan (1928–1932, as it was completed in four years) was the first comprehensive attempt of Soviet leaders to directly manage the entire economy, including all investment, production, and distribution. Nature protection activists bravely advanced arguments against hydropower projects, collectivization, and the "transformation of nature" (including mass acclimatization of exotics). Miraculously, the All-Russian Society for the Nature Protection and the *zapovedniki*, although attacked during the early 1930s, managed to survive as relative islands of autonomy within the Soviet state, probably owing to their extreme marginality in the eyes of the regime (although the *kraeved*, or local lore, societies, which were deeply involved in nature protection, were closed in 1937).

From the 1920s through the 1940s the *zapovedniki* were the site of much important research, including that of Vladimir Vladimirovich Stanchinskii on trophic dynamics (ecological energetics) at the Askania-Nova *zapovednik*, studies by Daniil Nikolaevich Kashkarov, Alexandr Nikolaevich Formozov, and Lev Grigor'evich Kaplanov on animal ecology, and a host of other botanical, pedological (relating to soil science), geological, and limnological (relating to the study of bodies of fresh water) studies. Many of these were published in the reserves' own individual publications or in the

Nauchno-metodicheskie zapiski Komiteta po zapovednikam (Scientific-Methodological Proceedings of the Committee for *Zapovedniki*). Control of the reserves then passed from the RSFSR People's Commissariat of Education to the VTsIK (RSFSR legislature) and then to the RSFSR Council of People's Commissars (later, Ministers), or cabinet. Other USSR republics had their own network of *zapovedniki*, and by 1951 there were 128 reserves with an aggregate area of 12.6 million hectares across the Soviet Union. That year, however, Soviet political leader Joseph Stalin signed a decree obliterating eighty-eight reserves and turning them over to logging concerns. The forty remaining "inviolable" *zapovedniki* occupied a territory of only 1.4 million hectares, barely .06 percent of national territory. Acclimatization of exotics, which had been forced on the *zapovedniki* during the 1930s, intensified, and extensive logging and afforestation began to be practiced.

With the early Soviet period came the emergence of a scientist-led field of public health and pollution control. At its core were sixteen hundred public health physicians (in 1928) and environmental chemists who actively pursued novel technical means of treating industrial wastes. Like the nature protection activists, they insisted that the regime proceed with caution in its drive to industrialize. About forty research institutes were concerned with problems of air, water, and soil quality by the mid-1930s, and the All-Union Conference for the Preservation of Clean Air was held in Kharkov in 1935. Wastewater recycling was proposed in 1934. However, in the later 1930s mass repressions of scientists, physicians, and public figures took place in this domain.

Stalin's Policies

Stalin's agricultural and industrial policies literally changed the face of the Soviet Union. Collectivization eliminated much residual variety in the landscape as monocultures were planted over enormous areas of leveled land. A network of irrigation canals was built in the arid southern steppe belt of the country and, later, in the central Asian deserts. To protect the fields from further deflation (erosion of the soil by wind), the Great Stalin Plan for the Transformation of Nature, launched in October 1948, planned a vast network of shelterbelts, similar to those planted in the United States in the 1930s. However, because, for a number of reasons (including the mandatory selection of oak) the shelterbelts were not successful, they were abandoned in 1954.

The First Five-Year Plan (1928–1932) featured the completion of a major hydroelectric power station on the Dnepr River (DneproGES) as well as the Baltic to White Sea Canal, largely hand dug by hundreds of thousands of deportees. This first gulag (Soviet penal system) project, like the Ukhta rail line that sank into the permafrost and other projects, did not have any economic or military value once completed and was destroyed during the German invasion in 1941. Later canals, such as the Moscow-Volga and Volga-Don, were used for shipping but also promoted the exchange of organisms across basins, such as the introduction of the Caspian Starred Sturgeon into the Aral Sea in 1936 which brought in the parasite *Nizschia sturionis* that killed off the endemic sturgeon. Major industrial complexes, such as the steel-manufacturing center of Magnitogorsk, the metal- and mineral-processing complexes on the Kola Peninsula, and the development of the Kuzbas coal and iron complex, rose in record time. The USSR, a country more than 80 percent rural on the eve of industrialization, had an urban majority (those living in centers of more than ten thousand) by 1959.

Reacting to programs under way in Germany and the United States, Stalin in 1942 initiated a Soviet atomic program, which was overseen by secret police chief Lavrentii Beria and led by physicist Igor' Kurchatov. An atomic bomb was exploded in August 1949, and a hydrogen bomb was tested in 1953. A year later the first atomic power plant anywhere was inaugurated at Obninsk. Atmospheric tests as well as underground ones were conducted on Novaia Zemlia in the Arctic Ocean, as well as in western Kazakhstan (Kapustin Yar) and the eastern part of that republic (Semipalatinsk area), causing large-scale, long-term damage to human health there. More than 260 sites within Russia alone are radioactively contaminated. The explosion of nuclear wastes at a secret nuclear weapons-processing plant near Kyshtym, 70 kilometers from Cheliabinsk, in September 1957 released 2 million curies (units of radioactivity). As a result, ten thousand people were evacuated, and a large area was contaminated, including the watershed of the Techa River. First deduced by the Soviet scientist Zhores Aleksandrovich Medvedev, this disaster in the Urals was admitted to by Soviet authorities only in 1989.

Other legacies of the Soviet nuclear program include the sinking of the submarine *Kursk* in 2000 and the dumping of spent nuclear fuel in the Arctic Ocean. The world's biggest single industrial accident was the 27 April 1986, explosion of nuclear reactor 4 at Chernobyl. Among the complex mix of causes was a lack of sophistication of Soviet industrial welding, which dictated a vulnerable design (RMBK–1000 graphite reactor), promoted by a politically connected scientific insider (Academy of Sciences President A. P. Aleksandrov); the increasing view among Soviet leaders that nuclear power represented a fix for a system that squandered energy against a backdrop of steeply increasing costs for extraction of hydrocarbons and coal; and a culture of fear and distorted information flow that impeded the safe testing of a retrofitted emergency cooling system. Chernobyl's consequences are still being tabulated, but it is estimated that 3.5 million people have become ill from the accident, including 1.25 million children and 300,000 cleanup workers.

Khrushchev's Campaign

In the late 1950s the Soviet leader Nikita Sergeevich Khrushchev initiated a campaign to make the Soviet Union self-sufficient in processed chemicals, especially fertilizers. The spread of chemical plants and later biochemical plants increased pollution as well. Continued military buildup also brought additional sources of pollution. The infamous pulp and paper plants at Baikal'sk and on the Selenga River at Lake Baikal were initially supposed to produce vinyl cord for air force jet tires. Later, facing hostilities with China on the countries' extensive border, Khrushchev's successors Leonid Il'ich Brezhnev and Aleksei Nikolaevich Kosygin sought to protect rail shipments across Siberia by building a new rail line, the Baikal-Amur *magistral'* (BAM), 482 kilometers north of the existing Trans-Siberian line. This "project of the century" was plagued, however, with environmental problems. A copper-refining center built along the line, Neriungri, faces frequent temperature inversions during the winter, causing dangerous air pollution for the city's workers. The railroad also led to the creation of many factories, many of them military, in the Baikal basin, where they have been a source of heavy metal pollution.

Although the All-Russian Society for the Protection of Nature survived threats to close it during Stalin's last three years in power, in the mid-1950s leadership of the society was captured by Communist Party functionaries after its merger with the All-Russian Society for the Promotion and Protection of Urban Green Plantings; despite its huge numerical growth—the All-Russian Society for the Protection of Nature had 29 million members by the early 1980s, and its Belorussian analog had 3.4 million, or 34.5 percent of that republic's population—the society played no further important role in environmental activism.

During the 1950s through the 1970s the All-Russian Society for the Protection of Nature was superseded by a number of organizations, including the Moscow Society of Naturalists (MOIP), the Moscow Branch of the Geographical Society of the USSR, and student movements that emerged in the late 1950s. Most important of these were the independent-minded Nature Protection Brigades (*druzhiny po okhrane prirody*), which appeared first at Tartu State University (Estonian Soviet Socialist Republic) and Moscow State University, with branches ultimately functioning in about 140 higher education institutions by the mid-1980s with a total of five thousand members. Some students went to the Altai during the early 1960s to organize a model sustainable forest (the Kedrograd movement). During the 1960s a powerful movement of scientists, journalists, writers, and students formed to stop the construction and operation of the pulp and paper mills at Baikal.

Other grand schemes of the Brezhnev administration, notably the construction of a gargantuan earthen-and-stone dam across the Gulf of Finland to protect the city of Leningrad (St. Petersburg) from hundred-year floods from the Baltic Sea, elicited resistance as well. Owing to protests during the Mikhail Gorbachev administration concerning the eutrophication (the process by which a body of water becomes enriched in dissolved nutrients) of the gulf, the final kilometer of the dam was never connected. Another project of unimaginable scale—the diversion of the northward-flowing rivers of Siberia and European Russia to the south to irrigate crops in the arid steppe belt to raise the level of the Caspian Sea and to stabilize the desiccating Aral Sea—was canceled by Gorbachev's premier, Nikolai Ryzhkov, after major objections from leading scientists, writers, and citizen activists.

With the freer atmosphere initiated by Gorbachev and continued by Boris Nikolaevich El'tsin in Russia, numerous outside nongovernmental conservation organizations established branches in Russia and many of the other successor states to the USSR. They include the International Crane Foundation, World Wildlife Fund, Greenpeace, International Fund for Animal Welfare, and the Sacred Earth Network. Among Russian organizations the Socio-Ecological Union, led by Sviatoslav Zabelin, has played a central role in coordinating environmental activism since 1987. Another important group is the Biodiversity Conservation Center.

Ministries Abolished

After Stalin's elimination of the State Interagency Committee for the Protection of Nature, no overarching environmental agency existed in the USSR until 1986, when the State Committee for the Protection of the Environment was established under the USSR Council of Ministers. At first headed by Fedor Morgun, an agricultural specialist, in 1989 it was placed under the leadership of Nikolai Nikolaevich Vorontsov, an eminent zoologist. When the State Committee was upgraded to a ministry in 1991, he became the first non–Communist Party member to sit in a Soviet cabinet since 1918. Under Morgun the State Committee began to publish an annual report on the state of the Soviet environment, which continued under Vorontsov until the ministry was abolished with the collapse of the USSR in December 1991. Since that time Russia and Uzbekistan have both recently abolished special ministries for environmental protection, in the Russian case merging it into the Ministry for Natural Resources, an incarnation of the former Soviet Ministry of Geology.

Environmental restoration has been pursued in a number of areas, notably on the site of the Kursk Magnetic Anomaly, a large iron deposit. During open-pit excavation, the area's topsoil was set aside and replaced after the deposit was mined out. The area has been partly revegetated. Another major success story has been the cleanup of the Moscow River.

Nevertheless, success stories are overshadowed by large-scale crises: Chernobyl, the Aral Sea, Cheliabinsk Oblast and the Urals, the Sea of Azov, the Donbas, the Kuzbas, the Black Sea and its coast, the Fergana Valley, the Kola Peninsula, Noril'sk, eastern Kazakhstan, Kalmykia, the western Siberian oil and gas fields, and Novaia Zemlia and the Kara and Barents Seas. That is just the short list. Everywhere in Eurasia dangerously toxic stockpiles of banned farm chemicals and nuclear waste in huge quantities await appropriate disposal. Foreseeing the scope of the decomposition of effective state power and the ensuing chaos, professors Igor Altshuler, Yuri Golubchikov, and Ruben Mnatsakanyan (1992, 211) have pondered, "How much collapse of the USSR is environmentally safe for the rest of the world and . . . even for mankind's survival?"

Douglas R. Weiner

Further Reading

Ahlander, A.-M. S. (1994). *Environmental problems in the shortage economy: The legacy of Soviet environmental policy*. Aldershot, UK: Edward Elgar.

Altshuler, A. I., Golubchikov, Y. N., & Mnatsakanyan, R. A. (1992) Glasnost, perestroika, and eco-sovietology. In J. M. Stewart (Ed.), *The Soviet environment: Problems, policies and politics*. Cambridge, UK: Cambridge University Press.

Bassin, M. (1999). *Imperial visions: Nationalist imagination and the geographical expansion in the Russian Far East, 1840–1865* (Cambridge Studies in Historical Geography No. 29). Cambridge, UK: Cambridge University Press.

Bater, J. H., & French, R. A. (Eds.). (1983). *Studies in Russian historical geography*. London: Academic Press.

Danilova, L. V., & Sokolov, A. K. (Eds.). (1998). *Traditsionnyi opyt prirodopol'zovaniia v Rossii*. Moscow: Nauka.

DeBardeleben, J. (1985). *The environment and Marxism-Leninism: The Soviet and East German experience*. Boulder, CO: Westview Press.

Edberg, R., & Yablokov, A. (1991). *Tomorrow will be too late: East meets West on global ecology*. Tucson: University of Arizona Press.

Ely, C. (2002). *This meager nature: Landscape and national identity in imperial Russia*. DeKalb: Northern Illinois University Press.

Goldman, M. (1972). *The spoils of progress: Environmental pollution in the Soviet Union*. Cambridge, MA: MIT Press.

Gustafson, T. (1981). *Reform in the Soviet Union: Lessons of recent politics on land and water*. Cambridge, UK: Cambridge University Press.

Gustafson, T. (1989). *Crisis amid plenty: The politics of Soviet energy under Brezhnev and Gorbachev*. Princeton, NJ: Princeton University Press.

Karimov, A. (1999, December). Russian cadastral surveys before and after Peter the Great. *The Cartographic Journal, 36*(2), 125–132.

Komarov, B. (1980). [Ze'ev Wolfson]. *Unichtozhenie prirody v sovetskom soiuze* [The destruction of nature in the Soviet Union]. Armonk, NY: M. E. Sharpe.

Lemeshev, M. (1990). *Bureaucrats in power: Ecological collapse*. Moscow: Progress Publishers.

Medvedev, Z. A. (1979). *Nuclear disaster in the Urals*. New York: W. W. Norton.

Medvedev, Z. A. (1990). *The legacy of Chernobyl*. New York: W. W. Norton.

Moon, D. (1999). *The Russian peasantry, 1600–1930: The world the peasants made*. New York: Longmans.

Organization for Economic Co-Operation and Development. (1999). *Environmental performance reviews: Russian federation*. Paris: Organization for Economic Co-Operation and Development.

Pallot, J., & Shaw, D. J. B. (1990). *Landscape and settlement in Romanov Russia, 1613–1917*. Oxford, UK: Oxford University Press.

Peterson, D. J. (1993). *Troubled lands: The legacy of Soviet environmental destruction*. Boulder, CO: Westview Press and RAND.

Pryde, P. R. (1991). *Environmental management in the Soviet Union*. New York: Cambridge University Press.

Pryde, P. R. (Ed.). (1995). *Environmental resources and constraints in the former Soviet republics*. Boulder, CO: Westview Press.

Rywkin, M. (Ed.). (1988). *Russian colonial expansion to 1917*. New York: Mansell.

Smith, J. (Ed.). (1999). *Beyond the limits: The concept of space in Russian history and culture* (Studia Historica No. 62). Helsinki, Finland: Finnish Historical Society.

Weiner, D. R. (1999). *A little corner of freedom: Russian nature protection from Stalin to Gorbachev*. Berkeley and Los Angeles: University of California Press.

Weiner, D. R. (2000). *Models of nature: Ecology conservation and cultural revolution in Soviet Russia* (2nd ed.). Pittsburgh: University of Pittsburgh Press.

Yanitsky, O. N. (2000). *Russian Greens in a risk society*. Helsinki, Finland: Kikimora Publications.

Yemelyanenkov, A. (2000). *The Sredmash Archipelago*. Moscow: IPPNW.

Sacred Places

For environmental history, sacred places are places in nature with spiritual significance. *Spiritual* means that which invokes the divine. Sacred places are important to environmental history, because many world cultures have relied on sacred places for their religious rites and shared meaning, and also because many environmental thinkers today hold that coming to see the spiritual in nature is important for developing environmental consciousness.

Sacred places have channeled and altered the currents of environmental history, too. Ancient Greek sacred places articulated the elements' meaning for humanity, allowing the roots of Western civilization to understand our home (*oikos*) as ecological. Over two thousand years later, European Romanticism rediscovered this Greek love of the elements through its own sacred places, written about in poems, which in turn inspired American transcendentalism, and so allowed many Americans to appreciate the Native American sacred places their colonization had taken from public view. Today, Native American sacred places help environmentalists protect ecological regions in the service of protecting such places, where respect for Native American culture demands respect for the land. In this way and many others, sacred places serve as points of connection for environmental history's origins, recollections, cultural translations, and protections.

Examples of Sacred Places

The following examples are not comprehensive of sacred places from around the world and across time.

Rather, they are selected to suggest comparisons between sacred places across time and the world, as well as to suggest different kinds of sacred places existing even in the same country. Almost every culture in the world has its own variety of sacred places, as the following examples suggest:

1. The Aborigines of Australia have many sacred places in their culture. In their culture, relationship with the land is as important as kinship with one's family and tribe. The land literally is part of one's *kind* (or kin). In this way, places in the land are charged with high emotional meaning and are part of the relationships making up the life of the community. For example, near Ilpili, elders take young men about to be initiated into adulthood to a rock formation on top of a hill. The place is sacred, and must be approached in silence, slowly crawling. People do not talk *about* what it is like inside, but it is a place inside which one becomes an adult.

2. Similarly, the Boy Scouts of America have an initiation into their honor core, The Order of the Arrow, named in honor of Native Americans. During this initiation, which is not spoken of publicly in detail, young men "tapped" into the Order visit a place in the woods which summons love for the earth. By visiting this place at the end of their initiation ordeal, they learn that hard work and discipline are rewarded by being *worthy* to experience the beauty in a natural place.

3. Residents of New York City have noticed over the past fifteen years that many homeless people in Greenwich Village make gardens out of whatever material they can find and on what little land they

can temporarily enjoy. These gardens are sites of intensely meaningful activity and show how the gardener's concern with the most sacred values in life are found by integrating nature and human life. Each garden is a shrine made out of found materials, such as figurines, signs, and chairs from dumpsters and curbsides. Within these built shrines, plants and even animals are encouraged to thrive. These are *urban* sacred places.

4. In Japan there are Shinto shrines within which, no matter how developed the surrounding world is, one can find the presence of wild nature, often involving trees as old as 800 years. In the inner spaces of the shrine, people can commune with a world of select, archaic wilderness.

5. Or, in fantasy, European Romanticism and the Russian Orthodox spiritual tradition combine in Andrey Tarkovsky's film *Stalker* (best translated as *Searcher*). There, people try to find "the room" in the middle of "the zone," a region where nature has taken back control from human society, and within which one's deepest dreams can come true, including the wish to end all violence.

6. Finally, consider the sacred places of the Ainu, the indigenous people who lived and still live on the islands now known as "Japan." For the Ainu, an entire ecosystem was and is a sacred place, a "field" (*iworu*), ordered by a regional animal species, such as the Great Brown Bear or the Orca, important for their way of life. These "fields" are by nature spiritual, infused with the spirit of the beings with which the Ainu are most in relationship. As such, the sacred place is not cut off from everyday life, as in a shrine or initiation site, but is *everywhere* in the circuit of everyday work and joy.

Are Sacred Places Separate from Everyday Life?

According to many environmentalists, a lot rests on whether sacred places are kept apart from or are integrated into people's lives. So the concern goes: If sacred places are apart from people's lives, they do not necessarily promote respect for nature. Take for example the Shinto shrines (example 4)—don't these exist in a society that massively redevelops land by erasing whole ecosystems? Or look at a place some Americans call sacred, the Grand Canyon. The practice of visiting the Grand Canyon involves for many a great expenditure of fossil fuel. So how does it really promote respect for nature?

Yet Aboriginal initiation sites are separate from everyday life *and still* support a culture profoundly respectful of its ecological context. Also, isolated places such as the interior of Shinto shrines or the lonely spots in the woods revered by European Romantics such as William Wordsworth may keep alive respect for nature in a culture that would otherwise completely forget it. Perhaps what matters most is whether the distinctness of sacred places points toward a background understanding that nature should be respected. This is what may make the difference when looking at the distinctness of Aboriginal sites. They accentuate a wide, cultural commitment to respecting the land, a commitment belonging to the quotidian beliefs and practices of the people.

So, many environmentalists say that cultures where sacred places are part of everyday life are cultures that support healthy respect for nature. In such cultures, such as that of the Ainu, sacred places are not isolated but integrated, as the garden shrines of the homeless in New York appear to be for the homeless (but not for New Yorkers in general). And in such cultures, the spiritual significance of nature is not apart from the meaning of life, but permeates the meaning of life. As such, sacred places emphasize the everyday meaning of life, one respectful of nature.

Accordingly, people often turn to the spirituality of Native Americans, where nature as a whole is permeated with spiritual significance and where sacred places emphasize that significance. Looking at sacred places, such as a watering hole, a place where the wind has its home, special parts of hunting areas, or a waterfall, one notices that these places endowed with spiritual intensity are often also places where some basic good or need of human life was found, fulfilled, or addressed. In this way, the meaning of the place is sacred with respect to both nature and human life, between which there is no longer a sharp distinction.

This lack of a sharp distinction between nature and humanity is emphasized even further in another way sacred places can be part of cultures. Aboriginal culture speaks of "dreamtime" and Navajo culture involves mythical time, in which sacred places arise from an origin to both the human and the natural world. For instance, some mountains are sacred for the Navajo or Dine, because Changing Woman performed important actions there in mythical time. In such a time, both the human world and nature emerge intertwined.

A hot spring in Thailand. Places that are unusual in nature are often treated as sacred.
COURTESY MARY CORINNE LOWENSTEIN.

In sum, sacred places are not found only away from society but commonly in the midst of human society. In this way, sacred places establish a link between society and nature where the work of human life can dwell within, and not just overpower, nature.

What Do Sacred Places Invoke?

Do sacred places reference gods, or God? Are they linked to general spiritual elements, such as peacefulness, beauty, or power? A popular conception of sacred places is that they directly invoke a god or gods, such as a tree god or a god of hunting. This is often so, but different spiritual traditions challenge what is meant by a "god." For instance, many Native American cultures work more in terms of spirits than transcendent gods per se, and these spirits, which may inhabit places, are part of a spiritual continuum moving through and shaping everything. Or, as in the case of many African tribal cultures, gods may dwell and interact with people, even gods who are half or more

other animal. In such cultures, gods dwell *in* sacred places, but not as creatures from another world. Rather, they are members of the "neighborhood," which includes divine places. This form of spiritual geography goes back deep into history, too. For example, the ancient Greeks frequently interacted with gods associated with special places in nature. Today, one finds small shrines across the Greek countryside devoted to gods, of the harvest, of the hunt, of the earth (to name a few). According to some philosophers, these gods found their being in the special places associated with them, such that one cannot really separate the god from the sacred and elemental place he or she inhabits.

Just so, the notion of a sacred place as a place associated with a general quality or value, but not with gods, seems to misunderstand what is at stake in sacred places. The Christian God *is* radically transcendent from the material world, but if one reconceptualizes the nature of gods and considers the divine through the notion of spirits, then the discovery of, for example, peacefulness in a natural place *can* be a way of pointing to what the divine in nature is. Such was the attitude of some of the most well known European Romantics, such as Jean-Jacques Rousseau and William Wordsworth, and, interestingly, it was also the attitude of the Christian saint Francis of Assisi, who felt closer to God in the nature of his native Italy and while talking with other animals. After all, according to his religion, they were part of Creation.

There is, however, a place for distinguishing between whether a sacred place invokes a spirit or god or something more general. Consider sacred places in many modern homes. The history of private life and of architecture shows that people often create zones in the center of their very homes where they reconnect with the heart of life's meaning. Such places are sacred, but not from invoking a particular spirit or god. Rather, they invoke *the* sacred, which might be thought of as a dimension of experience in which many different values and emotions have their home, such as peacefulness, order, passion, and love. Likewise, people can discover or make such places in nature. When they do, as when children build a tree-house back in the woods high up amidst the sunlit leaves, they may actually make a sacred place where no one god or spirit is invoked, but where the *dimension* of spirituality as such comes alive. Interestingly, such a practice opens up an unseen connection between the lives of suburban people and the lives of indigenous people marginalized through colonization. The children may be seen to be rediscovering a clue to native America.

Must Sacred Places Grow Out of Long Involvement with a Region?

According to most evidence, sacred places grow out of a life lived with the lands, seas, and/or airs they are a part of. It seems one needs to *dwell* within one's land to begin to articulate sacred places. After all, nothing sacred arises from superficial and ephemeral involvement. The sacred is deep, lasting, and the fruit of involved *relationship*. So can there be sacred places without long-lasting involvement with a region?

It may seem so. New York's homeless gardeners develop sacred places at the same time as those places are knocked down, often from one day to the next. The gardeners move nomadically from location to location. With these gardeners, the human ability and need to make sacred meaning is strong enough to be able to take root and then uproot overnight. But even such makeshift sacred places express a *wish* for long-term

involvement. Given this, sacred places require the reality or *ideal* of long-term involvement with a region.

How does such involvement come about? The history of sacred places shows they are commonly part of rituals. These rituals, in turn, reflect the historical relationship with the lands or coasts of which the places form a part. Recall how two of our examples inscribed sacred place within initiation rituals (examples 1 and 2). Even fantasies of a sacred place, such as Tarkovsky's film, involve elaborate ritual to be worthy of reaching that location (example 5). Rituals by definition are *repeated* practices performing a specific cultural function. In this way, rituals *steady* our involvement and bring us to settle on some things as more important to our lives than others. Even the homeless gardeners of New York have rituals while making their sacred and moveable sites. So one (but not the only) key to the involvement that helps places be sacred is ritualized interaction with them. Also, ritual interaction with a place can take many forms, from initiation or purification rites, to pilgrimage to that place, to making the place the subject of a story handed on across generations, to confirming a place's cosmological significance through a legend repeated from mouth to mouth.

However, there is an even more important key to what involvement goes into making a place sacred. Humans can discover and develop the sacred on relatively short notice out of a great *need* inside the human spirit to be connected to the places we inhabit. Ritual is one of the ways to realize that need. No one seems to deny that in cultures where people's lives depend upon local nature across generations, sacred places are more likely to arise and to make sense. But the homeless in New York *need* to make homes in the open air, and so are drawn close to nature out of necessity. Within their need for a home, then, they discover and create sacred places, and this fact suggests that what is really crucial to the development of sacred geography is not in the first instance long-term, ritual involvement with the land, but rather the need for a human home within the elements.

Jeremy Bendik-Keymer

Further Reading

Ariès, P., & Duby, G. (Eds.). (1989–1991). *A history of private life* (Vols. 1–5). Cambridge, MA: Belknap Press.

Balmori, D., & Morton, M. (1993). *Transitory gardens, uprooted lives.* New Haven, CT: Yale University Press.

Basso, K. (1996). *Wisdom sits in places: Landscape and language among the western Apache.* Santa Fe: The University of New Mexico Press.

Bendik-Keymer, J. (2001). Analogical extension and analogical implication in environmental moral philosophy. *Philosophy in the Contemporary World, 8*(2), 149–158.

Bonsack Kelley, K., & Francis, H. (1994). *Navajo sacred places*. Bloomington: Indiana University Press.

Cairns, S., & Olsen, W. S. (Eds.). (1996). *The sacred place: Witnessing the holy in the physical world*. Salt Lake City: University of Utah Press.

Carmichael, D. L. (Ed.). (1994). *Sacred sites, sacred places*. New York: Routledge.

Carrasco, D. (1991). *To change place: Aztec ceremonial landscapes*. Boulder: University of Colorado Press.

Epes Brown, J. (2001). *Teaching spirits: Toward an understanding of Native American religious traditions*. New York: Oxford University Press.

Gottlied, R. S. (Ed.). (1995). *This sacred earth: Religion, nature, environment*. New York: Routledge.

Harries, K. (1998). *The ethical function of architecture*. Boston: MIT Press.

Harvey, D. (2000). *Spaces of hope*. Berkeley: University of California Press.

Heidegger, M. (1975). *Poetry, language, thought*. New York: Harper & Row.

Lefebvre, H. (1991). *The production of space*. New York: Blackwell.

Park, C. C. (1994). *Sacred worlds: An introduction to geography and religion*. New York: Routledge.

Plumwood, V. (2002). *Environmental culture: The ecological crisis of reason*. New York: Routledge.

Rousseau, J. J. (1979). *The reveries of the solitary walker*. Indianapolis, IN: Hackett Publishing.

Snyder, G. (1991). *The practice of the wild*. San Francisco: North Point Press.

Tarkovsky, A. (1978). *Stalker ("Searcher")* [Motion picture]. Moscow: Mosfilms.

Tilley, C. (1994). *A Phenomenology of landscape: Paths, places, monuments*. Oxford, UK: Berg Publishing

Usner, D. (1995). *Sabino's map, life in Chimayo's old plaza*. Santa Fe: University of New Mexico Press.

Sahara

Approximately 7 million square kilometers in area, the Sahara is the largest warm desert on Earth, extending from the Atlantic coast of Africa to the Red Sea and from the mountains and coasts of the Mediterranean to the northern savannas of tropical Africa. The Sahara has played a major role in the environmental history of Africa and Eurasia. Under the force of natural climate change, it evolved from an ocean of grassland that supported pastoralism to an imposing arid vastness that separated sub-Saharan Africa from the societies that surrounded the Mediterranean Sea.

Early communities of human hunters and gatherers lived in the Saharan basin from before the sixth millennium BCE. In approximately the fifth century BCE, the hunters and gatherers' way of life was largely replaced by pastoralism, with pastoralists expanding from the Nile valley into the vast grasslands of what would later become the Sahara desert. From the middle of the third millennium BCE, the Sahara began to desiccate, and by the beginning of the second millennium BCE the Sahara as we know it today had formed.

In the first millennium CE North African peoples adopted the use of the dromedary camel, introduced from northeastern Africa. The camel made it possible for human groups both to nomadize over the extremely arid sections of the desert and to make regular crossings of the Sahara, linking North Africa with the societies to the south. Saharan camel pastoralism existed in its purest form only in the most arid regions; elsewhere pastoralists had mixed herds of camels, sheep, and goats; and toward the fringes of the desert it was possible to herd cattle as well. Camels could go for days without watering, goats and sheep had much more frequent requirements, and cattle had to be watered daily. In the desert regions with relatively abundant and accessible water supplies close to the surface, oasis communities grew up. Elsewhere, herders drew water from deep wells, often with only modest yields.

Nomadic peoples in the desert and at the desert's edge developed largely symbiotic ecological patterns of interaction with sedentary agricultural peoples along the land shores of the desert. One pattern was for desert dwellers to exchange animal products for grain with villagers who practiced rain-fed or floodplain agriculture. Along the southern shore of the Sahara, pastoralists traded salt from desert mines for grain.

Saharan traders also transported sub-Saharan slaves north across the desert. Over the long era of the trans-Saharan slave trade (c. 800–c. 1900), millions of people enslaved in interstate warfare below the Sahara were taken by Saharan traders to North African and Mediterranean markets. Saharan societies also absorbed large numbers of sub-Saharan captives, who served as slave workers in the salt mines, the oases, or the livestock sector.

A view of the Sahara Desert in Egypt in 2002. COURTESY NICOLE LALIBERTE.

During the era of European colonial conquest and rule, Saharan societies' experiences were varied, determined in part by their proximity to European settler communities or other colonial markets. During the course of the twentieth century, some Saharan regions were discovered to be rich in mineral resources such as iron ore, oil, and uranium. In the 1960s, the French set off above-ground and subterranean nuclear test explosions in the Algerian Sahara and contaminated the desert sites. In the last decades of the twentieth century, under pressure from drought, many nomads gave up pastoralism and settled in desert towns and cities. Today the Sahara remains a vast and understudied ecological region.

James L. A. Webb Jr.

Further Reading

Allan, J. A. (Ed.). (1983). *The Sahara: Ecological change and early economic history*. Boulder, CO: Westview Press.

Barrillot, B. (2002). *L'héritage de la bombe. Sahara, Polynésie (1960–2002)* [The heritage of the bomb. Sahara, Polynesia (1960–2002)]. Lyon: Centre de Documentation et de Recherche sur la Paix et les Conflits.

Cloudsley-Thompson, J. L. (Ed.). (1984). *Sahara Desert*. Oxford, UK: Oxford University Press.

Lovejoy, P. E. (1986). *Salt of the desert sun*. Cambridge, UK: Cambridge University Press.

Savage, E. (Ed.) (1992). *The human commodity: Perspectives on the trans-Saharan slave trade*. London: Frank Cass & Co, Ltd.

Webb, J. L. A., Jr. (1995). *Desert frontier: Ecological and economic change along the western Sahel, 1600–1850*. Madison: University of Wisconsin Press.

Williams, M. A. J., & Faure, H. (Eds.). (1980). *The Sahara and the Nile*. Rotterdam, Netherlands: A. A. Balkema Publishing Co.

Sahel

The term *sahel* borrowed from the Arabic for "shore" or "border", is sometimes used very broadly to refer to both the northern and southern edges of the Sahara. Generally, however, it refers specifically to the southern land shore of the western Sahara, a narrow band of territory of a few hundred kilometers in width that extends along an east-west axis from the Atlantic Ocean approximately 1,000 kilometers to the inland delta of the Niger River. The Sahel is thus situated between the fuller aridity of the Sahara, which lies to the north, and the greater humidity of the grassland savanna, which lies to the south. In a broad ecological sense, the entire Sahel is a transitional zone that by dint of oscillations in historical climate has been endowed with floral and faunal elements from both the Saharan and savanna ecological zones. The biotic composition of the Sahel has also been profoundly changed by millennia of human land-use practices, including the introduction of domesticated livestock and the use of fire for clearing agricultural fields and for eliminating the bush habitat of the tsetse fly, bearer of the parasite that carries sleeping sickness. Early human settlements developed near the flat floodplains of the Senegal and Niger Rivers and their tributaries, which flow through these semiarid lands.

At least since the introduction of the camel sometime in the second half of the first millenium CE, which allowed for mixed (camel, cattle, sheep, goat) pastoralism under arid conditions, the Sahel has evolved as a transitional cultural zone between the largely pastoral livestock economies of the western Saharan peoples and the largely agricultural (millet, sorghum, and indigenous rice) economies of the African savanna peoples. The pastoral and agricultural economies were often complementary; livestock herders traded salt from desert mines in addition to animal products (meat, milk, and hides) for cereals grown by settled cultivators. Pastoralists, however, often had the upper hand militarily and during times of duress were able to employ force to secure their access to resources. As an alternative to raiding, many pastoral groups established relationships of dominance over agricultural villages, from which they drew tribute grain.

During the precolonial era, the Sahel's principal exports into the Atlantic sector were human captives and gum arabic; during the colonial era, the principal export was peanuts; and peanuts have continued to be a staple export during the postcolonial period. During the late 1960s the Sahel suffered a severe drought, which experts at the time attributed to local human agency, alleging that the desert was expanding as a result of deforestation and the overgrazing of sahelian pastures. This perspective has been compromised by

evidence that the Sahel has historically been subject to cycles of drought and that processes of climate change such as global warming are not generated locally.

During the colonial period, the French colonial experts undertook a large-scale and unsuccessful intervention to develop the middle valley of the Niger River. The drive for large-scale development schemes remained a core theme into the early twenty-first century. In recent decades the rapidly expanding and urbanizing sahelian populations have incurred a very large cereal deficit that has been met through massive food purchases and international food aid. During the last decades of the twentieth century, some of the postcolonial sahelian states have undertaken the controversial construction of dams along the Senegal and Niger Rivers in order to harness water resources in the service of irrigated agriculture and hydropower production. These dams have altered the natural flooding patterns upon which floodplain agriculturalists have depended, and the impoundment of water and its use in irrigation has created conditions that are conducive to the increased transmission of malaria, schistosomiasis, and other diseases. These projects have also offered new agricultural options to some farmers, but the goal of sustained intensive agriculture and food self-sufficiency has remained elusive.

The Sahel continues to be subject to severe ecological stress. The sahelian farming systems have been the focus of a great deal of applied research, and most experts now seek ecological solutions that take into account the local ecological knowledge of sahelian farmers

James L. A. Webb Jr.

See also Camels; Sahara

Further Reading

Brooks, G. E. (1993). *Landlords and strangers: Ecology, society, and trade in western Africa, 1000–1630*. Boulder, CO: Westview Press.

Gritzner, J. A. (1988). *The West African Sahel: Human agency and environmental change*. Chicago: University of Chicago Press.

McIntosh, R. J. (1993). Pulse model: Genesis and accommodation of specialization in the middle Niger. *Journal of African History, 34*(2), 181–200.

Mortimore, Michael. (1998). *Roots in the African dust: Sustaining the sub-Saharan drylands*. Cambridge, UK: Cambridge University Press.

Van Beusekom, M. (2002). *Negotiating development: African farmers and colonial experts at the Office du Niger, 1920–1960*. Portsmouth, NH: Heinemann.

Watts, Michael. (1982). *Silent Violence: Food, famine and peasantry in northern Nigeria*. Berkeley: University of California Press.

Webb, J. L. A., Jr. (1992). Ecological and economic change along the middle reaches of the Gambia River, 1945–1985. *African Affairs: The Journal of the Royal African Society, 91*(4), 543–565.

Webb, J. L. A., Jr. (1995). *Desert frontier: Ecological and economic change along the western Sahel, 1600–1850*. Madison: University of Wisconsin Press.

Salinization

Salinization is a natural and human-induced process by which soluble salts accumulate in soil. Salinization has long been one of the world's major challenges for sustaining agricultural production and will continue to be so in the future. Salinization strongly regulates plant and animal communities and hydrology (the properties, distribution, and circulation of water on and below the earth's surface and in the atmosphere) in natural and managed ecosystems and affects many of the earth's major biogeochemical cycles (relating to the partitioning and cycling of chemical elements and compounds between the living and nonliving parts of the biosphere).

Salts enter soil systems mainly when they are dissolved in groundwater or irrigation water, when they are deposited from the atmosphere, and when minerals are weathered. Salts become further concentrated as water is removed from the soil via evaporation and transpiration (the uptake of water by plants).

Slow-draining clayey soils are much more susceptible to salinization than are rapid-draining sands. Salt concentrations in soils tend to increase in the direction of surface or groundwater flow, that is, from uplands to low-lying depressions or bottoms.

Chlorides and sulfates are the predominant soil salts and are generally balanced by sodium, calcium, magnesium, and potassium. Soils with elevated salts are known as "saline," and those with sodium-dominating salt composition are known as "sodic" or "natric." Sodium salts are particularly problematic for soils for physical, chemical, and biological reasons. Excess sodium can stress many plants, especially if calcium concentrations are low. Sodic soils not infrequently have high pH (above 9) and cause conditions directly injurious to plants by worsening deficiencies in nutrients such as phosphorus, copper, iron, boron, manganese, and zinc.

High sodium also adversely affects soil's physical and chemical properties, causing soil clays and organic matter to disperse into individual particles instead of remaining flocculated (i.e., attracted together in packages or aggregates of multiple particles of clay and soil organic matter). Sodium-enriched soils that are dispersed can be a near-complete barrier to water entry as dispersed clay particles block soil pores. Sodium-caused dispersion also reduces the rate of gas movement in soils. Soils that are sodium enriched readily become waterlogged and stress oxygen-demanding processes such as root and microbial activity. Only well adapted salt-tolerant plants and microbes are able to grow in salinized soils.

Plants range widely in their ability to tolerate salts in their root zone. Plants that readily accumulate or tolerate salts are called "halophytes" and include salt-tolerant grasses, herbs, and shrubs, species that are native to deserts, shorelines, and salt marshes. Most crop species are not halophytic and exhibit high sensitivity to salt; these species include many legumes, corn, rice, oats, and wheat. Crop plants that benefit from halophytic properties include beets, date palms, spinach, jojoba, and barley.

Geographical Distribution of Salt-Affected Soil

Salinization occurs chiefly in arid, semiarid, and subhumid regions. Salt-affected soils are not a widespread problem in humid regions because precipitation is sufficient to dissolve and leach excess salts out of the soil into groundwater and eventually the ocean. Some saline soils occur along humid seacoasts where seawater inundates the soil.

The significance of salinization can be expressed by the large regions throughout the world with soils that are enriched in salts. (See table 1.) Moreover, one-quarter to one-third of the world's 1.5 billion hectares currently under cultivation are saline or sodic. Salinity is most problematic in cultivated soils that are irrigated. Irrigated lands with large areas of saline and sodic soils include Australia, India, Pakistan, Russia, China, the United States, the Middle East, and Europe. In some nations, salts seriously affect more than 50 percent of irrigated lands.

TABLE 1.
DISTRIBUTION OF SALINE AND SODIC SOILS ON FIVE CONTINENTS

Continent	Saline Soils (in thousands of km²)	Sodic Soils (in thousands of km²)	Ratio of Sodic/Saline
Africa	535	270	0.5
Asia	1,949	1,219	0.6
Australia	386	1,997	5.2
North America	82	96	1.2
South America	694	596	0.9

Source: R. Naidu, M. E. Sumner, & P. Rengasamy (1995). *Australian sodic soils.* East Melbourne, Australia: CSIRO.

Reclamation of Saline and Sodic Soils

Salinization is an insidious problem, and early soil symptoms are often ignored. To control salinization and maintain irrigation-based agriculture over the long term requires soil analysis and careful monitoring of water and salt budgets (amounts) at local to river-basin scales. Such monitoring provides the technical basis for remedial action.

To diagnose soil salinity problems, a soil sample is rinsed with water, and the water's electrical conductivity is measured. The soil water's conductance is directly and linearly related to the concentration of soluble salts. The conductance at which the growth of many plant species is diminished by salts is well established. Sodium problems are diagnosed from a ratio of the soil sodium to calcium.

Leaching with high-quality (dilute) water can eventually rid a soil of its salinity problems, but the reclamation of sodic soils is not so straightforward. Because elevated sodium tends to disperse soil clays and greatly reduce the rate at which water moves through soil, the ratio of soil sodium to calcium needs to be decreased if sodium leaching is to be effective. Calcium, especially in the form of gypsum, tends to aggregate or flocculate clays, allowing sodium to be dissolved and to leach through the soil-rooting zone. Reclamation of sodic soils may, however, require large amounts of gypsum, sometimes several thousand kilograms per hectare. Gypsum additions can be costly, especially if the only sources of irrigation water have high sodium and salinity.

Reclamation of salt-affected soils requires a suitable system of disposal. In many cases the drainage is too brackish (salty) to be directly recycled. Moreover, in contemporary agricultural systems, drainage effluents also contain other constituents such as fertilizer nutrients, sediments, and pesticides, all of which amplify the importance of disposal. Nonetheless, irrigation effluents are too often simply exported to a stream or river, a practice that salinizes and pollutes the local water supply. The receiving stream will become progressively saltier, and lower reaches may become unfit as a water supply for humans, animals, or crops. Adverse effects on aquifers and estuaries are direct and potentially serious. Improving the efficiency of water and salt budgets of irrigated lands is one of the highest priorities for contemporary agronomy (the branch of agriculture dealing with field-crop production and soil management).

Salinization Historically

Salinization gravely affected the first great agricultural societies such as the Sumerian and Akkadian cultures, societies that developed on the alluvial terraces of the Tigris and Euphrates Rivers. In the southern regions of these terraces, the landscape was transformed into extensive agricultural fields irrigated for grain, forage, and palm production. Canals served as transportation routes, cities were built, and a system of writing invented. Over time the center of civilization shifted significantly northward along these rivers, a pattern frequently explained by a salinity-affected decline in agriculture in the south. Archaeological records of the Sumerian civilization in the south suggest that grain production shifted over the centuries from the much-preferred but salt-sensitive wheat to salt-tolerant barley.

The history of salinization in ancient Egypt appears to contrast greatly with that in Mesopotamia. Salt budgets and timing of annual floods along the Egyptian terraces appear to have been much more conducive to long-term management than terraces of the Tigris and Euphrates. Alluvial soils along the Nile are relatively narrow and well drained, except in the Nile's delta. The Nile's river channel is deeply incised along much of its course, ensuring that the rise and fall of the river affect a rise and fall of the groundwater under river terraces. The Nile's agricultural resources are generally considered to be nearly ideal, given the particular combination of high-quality water, relatively predictable flooding, soil fertility, nutrients, and organic matter. Salinization was never a widespread acute problem, and irrigation-based cropping along the Nile has continued for about five millennia.

Salinization has stressed other agricultural civilizations in the past. One of the largest of these developed in the Indus River valley of Asia, approximately coincident in time with ancient Babylonia. The area of the Indus irrigation systems apparently exceeded those in ancient Egypt and Sumer. Few records exist for the Indus civilizations, although several excavations partly tell their tale (at Harappan, for example). Although some archaeologists believe that catastrophic floods, earthquakes, and soil erosion devastated these ancient civilizations, salinization was also probably a major problem. In the twentieth century, salinization has greatly stressed irrigation-based agriculture which has spread across nearly 15 million hectares of the Indus River valley.

Historical patterns of salinization in Australia's enormous Murray-Darling River basin are particularly instructive, given the relatively ample documentation of the effects of land-use history on contemporary soils and agro-ecosystems. Although the basin covers about 15 percent of Australia's total area, it provides far more than this percentage of the nation's agricultural production, much of which is supported by irrigation. Since European settlement began in earnest by the mid-nineteenth century, extensive areas of deeply rooted *Eucalyptus* forests have been cut over and converted to relatively shallow-rooted annual crop systems, an ecosystem transformation that allows a significantly larger fraction of annual precipitation to infiltrate and percolate through soil and to elevate local groundwater systems. Because the underlying groundwater is saline, substantial quantities of soluble salt have been mobilized into the upper 1 or 2 meters of soil. Evapotranspiration (loss of water from the soil both by evaporation and transpiration from plants) has further concentrated these salts, and about 500,000 hectares of the Murray-Darling River basin are estimated to have saline groundwater within 2 meters of the soil surface. Australians refer to these circumstances as "secondary" salinization (i.e., human affected), reserving the term *natural salinization* to describe naturally occurring saline soils that occur in association with salt lakes in drier regions of the continent or adjacent to estuaries.

Salinization in the Future

Irrigated land today totals approximately 0.3 billion hectares of the 1.5 billion hectares of total cultivated land. About 35 percent of total crop output is currently derived from irrigated systems, a percentage that may continue to increase, given that between the 1960s and the late 1990s irrigated land increased at an incredible

rate of about 3 percent per year. Five nations account for about two-thirds of the irrigated area: China, India, Pakistan, Russia, and the United States. Numerous other nations are critically dependent on irrigated systems, particularly Egypt, Indonesia, Iraq, Jordan, and Israel. All indications are that in the future, management of water and salts in irrigated systems will be critically important because global agricultural production is increasingly dependent on such management. The challenge is, however, that contemporary management of irrigated systems is far less than optimal and in fact presents serious concerns for the future. Several examples illustrate the challenges.

A very extensive modern irrigation system has been developed along the Indus River, mainly in Pakistan, in the twentieth century. Alluvium and associated native groundwater reservoirs are deep in this great basin, which drains the western Himalaya Mountains. About 14 million hectares were under irrigation by 1993, with the length of irrigation watercourses, farm channels, and field ditches estimated to total 1.6 million kilometers. Early in the development of this massive system, saline groundwater tables were observed in the rooting zone of many fields, and by the 1960s a massive drainage project was launched that by 1992 had benefited about one-third of the entire system. Probably between 2 and 5 million hectares of the basin are adversely affected by salts. Keeping this system operational will require great continuity of effort, if only because the Indus drainage channels have such low gradient (e.g., about a 0.02 percent gradient), which must transport water many hundreds of kilometers to the ocean outlet.

In modern Egypt the challenges of controlling salinization in irrigated agro-ecosystems are similarly serious. From ancient times to the beginning of the nineteenth century, the human population of the Nile River valley totaled several million people, most of whom were supported by the river's irrigation-based agriculture. Through most of this past, Egypt was able to export enormous amounts of food, a situation that is no longer the case. Modern Egypt has now about 60 million inhabitants, a total that is expected to grow to 90 to 100 million by 2030. Along with rising agricultural imports, Egypt is placing enormous demands on its irrigated soils for domestic food production. The Aswan High Dam, constructed in the 1960s, established management control over the Nile's flood flows and thereby expanded opportunities for irrigation. On the other hand, with river flow controlled, the seasonality of river flow no longer regularly flushes soils of accumulated salt. Particularly in the alluvial soils of the great Nile delta, groundwaters have risen along with attendant salts. Future expansions of irrigation agriculture along with highly engineered drainage projects to control salts are widely contemplated.

Future problems with salinization are hardly confined to irrigated lands. Natural cycles of rainfall in arid and semiarid climates can be associated with expansion and contraction of saline and sodic soils. A celebrated and much debated example is the saline ecosystem of Amboseli National Park in Kenya at the foot of Mt. Kilimanjaro. Between the 1950s to the present, the vegetation of much of the park has markedly changed from forested savannahs with *Acacias* to a landscape more dominated by salt-tolerant grasses and shrubs with only occasional trees. A long-standing hypothesis for the ecosystem transformation has been that when regional rainfall increased through the 1960s, highly saline groundwaters rose into the root zone of *Acacia*-dominated savannas, apparently causing widespread tree decline. Whether or not the transformation of the Amboseli is explained only by salinization, the Amboseli serves as an outstanding example of how future climate change in the decades and centuries ahead may affect salt balances and salinization across wide areas and thereby the structure and function of natural ecosystems.

Daniel D. Richter Jr.

Further Reading

Allison, G. G., & Peck, A. J. (1987). Man-induced hydrologic change in the Australian environment. *Geoscience, 87,* 35–37.

Ayers, R. S., & Wescot, D. W. (1976). *Water quality for agriculture* (FAO Irrigation and Drainage Paper No. 29). Rome: United Nations.

Buol, S. W., & Walker, M. P. (Eds.). (2003). *Soil genesis and classification* (5th ed.). Ames: Iowa State Press.

Dales, G. F. (1966). The decline of the Harappans. *Scientific American, 214,* 92–100.

Hillel, D. J. (1991). *Out of the earth.* New York: Free Press.

Holmes, J. W., & Talsma, T. (Eds.). (1981). *Land and stream salinity.* Amsterdam, Netherlands: Elsevier.

Lal, R. (1998). *Soil quality and agricultural sustainability.* Chelsea, MI: Ann Arbor Press.

Naidu, R., Sumner, M. E., & Rengasamy, P. (1995). *Australian sodic soils.* East Melbourne, Australia: CSIRO.

Rengasamy, P., & Olsson, K. A. (1991). Sodicity and soil structure. *Australian Journal of Soil Research, 29,* 935–952.

Richards, L. A. (Ed.). (1954). *Diagnosis and improvement of saline and alkali soils* (Agricultural Handbook No. 60). Washington, DC: United States Department of Agriculture.

Singer, M. J., & Munns, D. N. (2002). *Soils: An introduction.* Upper Saddle River, NJ: Prentice Hall.

Soil Survey Staff. (2001). *Keys to soil taxonomy.* Washington, DC: United States Department of Agriculture.

Sparks, D. L. (1995). *Environmental soil chemistry.* San Diego, CA: Academic Press.

Western, D. (1997). *In the dust of Kilimanjaro,* Washington, DC: Island Press.

Wolman, M. G., & Fournier, F. G. A. (Eds.). (1987). *Land transformation in agriculture.* New York: John Wiley and Sons.

Yaalon, D. H. (1963). On the origin and accumulation of salts in groundwater and soils of Israel. *Bulletin Research Council Israel, 11G,* 105–113.

Salmon

Salmon are a variety of Northern Hemisphere fishes in the family Salmonidae. Most salmon are noted for great size, tasty flesh, and complex life histories. Although some species are landlocked, the archetypal salmon is anadromous, rearing in freshwater but migrating to feed off the far greater resources of the sea. All salmon species return to their natal streams to spawn, and all need clean gravel and cool, oxygen-rich environments to incubate eggs and rear juveniles. As a result, salmon are becoming a critical issue in managing rivers and lakes in developed and developing countries. Dam building and land use have warmed waters and silted spawning beds across most of the salmon's range in Asia, Europe, and North America, and both salmon and human communities have been threatened by these changes.

The term *salmon* originally referred to the Atlantic salmon *(Salmo salar),* which makes several spawning runs during its life, but, in the eighteenth century, European scientists applied the term to seven additional species in the northern Pacific basin. As ichthyologist David Starr Jordan noted, however, these species were "in strictness, not salmon at all, but something more intensely salmon than the salmon of Europe itself" (Jordan 1894, 128). Unlike Atlantic salmon, Pacific salmon developed astonishingly different physical traits during their spawning runs, such as hooked jaws, distended bodies, and vivid coloration. Pacific salmon also ceased to feed, living off their stored fat during spawning runs, and most spawned once and then died. These disparities eventually forced ichthyologists to reclassify Pacific salmon under the separate genus *Oncorhynchus*. Included in this genus are the cherry *(O. masu)*, chinook or king *(O. tshawitschwa)*, chum *(O. keta)*, coho *(O. kisutch)*, sockeye *(O. nerka)*, pink *(O. gorbuscha)*, and steelhead *(O. mykiss)*. Kokanee and rainbow trout are landlocked versions of the sockeye and steelhead, respectively, and southern European and northern Asian streams are home to a huge, landlocked species called the Danube salmon or Taimen salmon *(Hucho hucho)*, which can reach over 2 meters and 100 kilograms.

A Traditional Source of Food

Throughout their ranges, salmon are those rare animals that have both charismatic and economic importance. Their spawning runs have fascinated humans as a source of both spectacle and food. People in the Northern Hemisphere have relied on salmon for millennia for both sustenance and trade, and many societies placed the salmon at the center of their cosmological universe because of its role in maintaining life. Ancient fishers were sophisticated in their use of spears, leisters (barbed spears used to catch fish), dip nets, gillnets, seines, traps, and weirs (enclosures set in a waterway to catch fish), and many aboriginal fisheries placed intense pressure on salmon. As a result many societies held annual celebrations to honor the start of the salmon season. The Ainu of Hokkaido, Evenks in Siberia, Irish fishers, Rhine villagers, and Native Americans along both the Atlantic and Pacific coasts held "first salmon ceremonies," which featured fasting, feasts, and speeches. These were ritual expressions of dependence and veneration, but a widespread taboo against catching more salmon than could be eaten by nightfall during ceremonial periods also, if perhaps unintentionally, helped to conserve runs by enabling many salmon to escape upstream.

Folk customs were effective as long as all societies in a watershed abided by the same rules and minimally changed habitat, but customs lost efficacy with population growth and market revolutions. Salmon streams changed markedly as land-use practices intensified across Europe, Asia, and North America. Logging, agriculture, mining, damming, urbanization, and industrialization led to widespread changes in aquatic habitat. Siltation, stream realignment, inundation, and pollution thoroughly altered salmon ecology, and market fishing warped the spatial and temporal contours of harvesting with equally severe results. Folk fishers typically fished over much of the watershed and much of the year, thereby spreading their impact across all species and runs. By contrast, industrial fishers compressed fishing into ever smaller spaces, usually near the mouths of rivers, and shorter times, usually at the start of spawning runs. As a result the earliest, largest, and most marketable salmon were fished most intensively. Equipment refinements in the nineteenth century, including larger nets, traps, and fishwheels (that used the river's current to turn giant scoops that dipped salmon out of the water and deposited them onto waiting barges), and more precise electronics in the twentieth century, including bottom and location finders, exacerbated trends. The result was overfishing.

Salmon Runs Decline

In Europe salmon runs fell sharply after 1600, and industrialization accelerated problems by 1800. Some New England runs were in decline by 1750, but damage accelerated with damming, industrialization, and urbanization in the early 1800s. Angling also emerged as an elite pastime, first in Europe and England and then, in the nineteenth century, in the United States. Sportfishers posed additional pressures on fish resources but were also an early voice for conservation. Pacific salmon were the last to experience these forces. Industrial fishers moved to North America from Europe and the British Isles in the eighteenth and nineteenth century, and then to California in the 1850s. After a decade of intensive fishing and settlement began to devastate runs on the Sacramento River, fishers fled northward to the Columbia River in the 1860s and to Puget Sound, Fraser River, and Alaska in the 1870s. Everywhere they went, industrial and sportfishers spread the same problems of environmental change and unrestrained harvests. Population growth, agricultural expansion, fishing, and logging have devastated salmon runs in Japan since the 1880s and the eastern Soviet Union since the 1930s, and in the early 1960s Atlantic salmon from Canada, Ireland, and the U.K. suffered another precipitous decline when commercial fishers discovered their pelagic feeding grounds off the coast of Greenland. All across the Northern Hemisphere, habitat change and intensive harvests consumed salmon runs like a candle being burned at both ends.

Schoolchildren in Wilton, New Hampshire, take part in the Adopt a Salmon program and release endangered Atlantic salmon fry that were raised in their classroom in May 2002.
COURTESY BETH JACKSON/U.S. FISH AND WILDLIFE SERVICE.

But there is also a long history of trying to save the salmon. In the early 1800s Europeans applied ancient practices of fish culture to Atlantic salmon. By the 1850s New England investigators were reading European reports on fish culture. In the 1860s Samuel Wilmot began to cultivate Atlantic salmon, and in 1872 Livingston Stone did the same with Pacific salmon. At the behest of both sport and commercial fishers, state and federal fish commissions began to promote salmon hatcheries in Canada and the United States. The first U.S. Fish Commissioner, Spencer Baird, soon extended this work to Australia, South America, and Asia. Fish culture was politically very popular because it seemed to alleviate the need to restrict fishing, and huge bureaucracies soon developed around hatcheries in the United States and Japan, where fish culture remains the preferred tool of fishery management to this day. Actual results were usually disappointing, however, because harvests and habitat change outpaced recovery efforts and because hatcheries were plagued by disease, malnutrition, and genetic drift. The continuing decline of salmon runs unleashed a vitriolic form of conservation as different interests lobbied to exclude their rivals. Race, class, and ethnicity were often faultlines in these contests, and the most politically marginalized groups tended to suffer the greatest burdens from legislation, little of which actually effected conservation. Although most species and runs of salmon have fared poorly from these events, a few have responded well to hatchery work. By the 1960s aquaculturists had learned to pen-raise Atlantic salmon from eggs to adults. Ironically, although Pacific salmon dominated the global salmon market from the 1870s to the 1980s, farmed Atlantic salmon from Chile, Norway, Canada, and Japan now dominate that same market. Some critics worry about the impact of fish farms on pollution, disease, genetic, and employment problems, but consumers have been more interested in the low cost of farmed salmon than in their environmental and social implications.

Joseph E. Taylor III

Further Reading

Cone, J., & Ridlington, S. (Eds.). (1996). *Northwest salmon crisis: A documentary history*. Corvallis: Oregon State University Press.

Fobes, N., Jay, T., & Matsen, B. (1994). *Reaching home: Pacific salmon, Pacific people*. Anchorage: Alaska Northwest Books.

Harris, D. (2001). *Fish, law, and colonialism: The legal capture of salmon in British Columbia*. Toronto, Canada: University of Toronto Press

McEvoy, A. (1986). *The fisherman's problem: Law and ecology in the California fisheries, 1850–1980*. New York: Cambridge University Press.

Netboy, A. (1980). *Salmon: The world's most harassed fish*. Tulsa, OK: Winchester Press.

Newell, D. (Ed.). (1989). *The development of the Pacific salmon-canning industry: A grown man's game.* Montreal, Canada: McGill-Queen's University Press.

Roche, J., & McHutchison, M. (Eds.) (1998). *First fish, first peoples: Salmon tales of the north Pacific rim.* Seattle: University of Washington Press.

Shearer, W. (1992). *The Atlantic salmon: Natural history, exploitation, and future management.* New York: Halstead.

Taylor, J. E., III. (1999). *Making salmon: An environmental history of the Northwest fisheries crisis.* Seattle: University of Washington Press.

Watson, R. (2002). *Salmon, trout and charr of the world: A fisherman's natural history.* Shrewsbury, UK: Swan Hill Press.

Salt

In the year 2000 the human community produced 226 million metric tons of salt, giving a per-capita annual consumption of 45 kilograms. In addition, salt was produced spontaneously by sun, wind, and geological pressure to form saline incrustations, salt plains, and salt domes. Because the ocean, the source of all saline deposits, contains 2–3 percent salt, the amounts extracted were small in relation to the amounts available. These run to trillions of metric tons and, if extracted, would be the equivalent of a substantial landmass. On the other hand, because salt is Neptune's gift, it could be comparatively rare on a cosmic scale and constitute a terrestrial contribution to the technology and taste of a conjuncture of noospheres (the sphere of human consciousness and mental activity).

Four Ages of Salt

Although salt extraction has grown continually with time—it is an example for believers in the irreversibility of progress—it has passed through four distinct if overlapping phases. These may be characterized as the ages of primitivity, local provision, commerce and monopoly, and heavy industry. First, primitivity extends to the Neolithic revolution (when agriculture and pastoralism began). Although human physiology has minimum requirements of salt to replace losses by perspiration and urine discharge, these were easily satisfied so long as humanity was an omnivore with some intake of meat. Salt, whether gathered from the environment or produced by the boiling techniques still in use in the

Amazon River basin and New Guinea, was acquired for reasons of culture rather than nature. Presumed to have medicinal properties, especially against intestinal parasites, salt has been described as humankind's first addiction. In primitivity, however, its use was selective, small, and episodic: under 1 kilogram per capita. Second, in the classical antiquities of both East and West, salt entered civilization. Consumption rose to 2.2 kilograms per capita, but in these lands well endowed with salt sources, local provision sufficed for supply. Long-distance trade remained exceptional, and technology, whether in gathering, mining, boiling, or solar evaporation, showed no great advance over primitivity. Third, in the millennium between antiquity and modernity, two Chinese inventions, diffused across Eurasia, put the salt industry into a higher gear: successive basin solar evaporation, whereby sodium chloride was separated from calcium and magnesium contamination; and monopoly, the discovery that a state could draw a substantial revenue by interposing commercial controls between the comparatively few places of production and the relatively large number of consumers. The state, whether in China, the Italian city-states, or northern Europe, taxed but promoted long-distance commerce in salt. In countries subject to such *ordines salis* (regulatory systems), consumption of salt rose from 2.2 kilograms per capita to 4.5–6.8 kilograms, most of it in table salt but some in food preparation (soy sauce), food preservation (fisheries), and in industrial processing such as manufacturing soap, curing tobacco, and, more massively, separating silver from its ore in colonial America.

Fourth, the salt industry became the anonymous, invisible servant of the chemical revolution as raw material in the production of alkali, synthetics (aniline dyes, rayon, phenolic plastics), aluminum, and chlorinated hydrocarbons. Intermediate demand surpassed immediate demand, although road deglaciation added to the latter, and supply by solar evaporation was overtaken by supply by coal, natural gas, and electricity. Consumption per capita in advanced countries soared above 6.8 kilograms.

Salt and the Environment

The salt industry effected its environment through its links to business: backward, forward, and horizontal. First, the production of salt—in addition to brine and vessels, usually of iron, in which to evaporate it—required inputs of land, labor, and energy. Chinese administrators complained about the conversion of arable (suitable for cultivation) land to saltfields. In traditional salt industries, often part-time in character, much labor was supplied by females, so that the industrialization of production disrupted family arrangements. A major reason for medieval and early modern conversion to solar evaporation was deforestation and rising fuel costs. Salt was the first industry to base itself on renewable energy. Second, the availability of salt made possible other technologies, each with its own environmental consequences. In the days of the Le Blanc process for the manufacture of soda, chlorine waste was a major problem, but this was eliminated by the superior Solvay process, and what had been an undesired by-product eventually became a valued main product in the Castner/Kellner process. Industry indeed threatens the environment less than does agriculture. Irrigation of the Uzbek cotton fields, which absorbed most of the water of the Amu-Dar'ya and the Syr-Dar'ya Rivers, triggered the dustbowling of the Aral Sea and the widespread salt contamination that followed. Global warming, whatever its origins, may, in combination with excessive water use, threaten other salt lakes with similar disasters. Similarly, if global warming promotes the shift in civilization to the heartlands of continents predicted by early twentieth century geographers Halford Mackinder and Karl Haushofer, a side effect may be an increased use of salt in road deglaciation to meet greater transport needs with consequent multiplication of winter salt pollution. Again, higher sea levels and lower seawater salinity would mean higher inputs of energy to produce a given quantity of salt. Third, salt has partners: companions—associated with salt as an import, whether as return cargo or part of a balance of exchange—and imitators. Thus salt and alum shared Venetian shipping from the Levant; Cantonese exports of salt to Kwangsi were paired with corresponding timber imports; and sugar and petroleum borrowed technology from salt. Salt was an economic activator, an index of the level of business activity, and a clue to business structures. It became a basis for policy decisions that might affect the environment. Early Chinese policy in what is now the rustbelt region of Manchuria was strongly motivated by the imperatives of the salt administration.

In human consciousness salt has commonly carried the opposite connotations of sterility and creativity. It thus expresses the ambiguity of *Homo sapiens* in its ecosphere (the parts of the universe habitable by living organisms): the species that cannot be merely part of nature but rather must always rise above it or fall below it.

Samuel Adshead

Further Reading

Adshead, S. A. M. (1992). *Salt and civilization*. Basingstoke, UK: Macmillan.

Bergier, J. (1982). *Une histoire du sel* [A history of salt]. Fribourg: Presses Universitaires de France.

Ewald, U. (1985). *The Mexican salt industry 1560–1980*. Stuttgart, Germany: Gustav Fischer Verlag.

Kurlansky, M. (2002). *Salt: A history*. New York: Walker & Co.

Litchfield, C. D., Palme, R., & Piasecki, P. (2000–2001). *Le monde du sel* [The world of salt]. Innsbruck, Austria: Berenkampf.

Multhauf, R. P. (1978). *Neptune's gift, a history of common salt*. Baltimore: Johns Hopkins University Press.

Vogel, H. (1993). *Salt production techniques in ancient China: The Aobo Tu*. Leiden, Netherlands: Brill.

Salton Sea

The Salton Sea is California's largest inland body of water (56 by 24 kilometers), has a surface elevation of 69 meters below sea level, and was formed from 1905 to 1907 when the Colorado River flooded a portion of a depression called the "Salton Trough." Despite average annual evaporation of 1.7 meters and rainfall of only 6.35 centimeters, inflows of drainwater from the surrounding agricultural areas have sustained this desert sea east of San Diego and south of Los Angeles. Annual drainwater inputs and evaporation are currently in equilibrium at approximately 1.35 million acre-feet (an acre-foot is the volume that would cover one acre to a depth of one foot). The Salton Sea supports an abundant saltwater fishery and is California's crown jewel of avian biodiversity (biological diversity as indicated by numbers of species of animals and plants). Conflict over water threatens the continued viability of the sea as habitat for millions of birds of more than four hundred species.

The evaporative loss of surface water concentrates and leaves behind the salts present in the drainwater entering the sea. The current salinity of about 44 parts per 1,000 (ocean water is 35 parts per 1,000) will con-

The Salton Sea: A Crown Jewel of Avian Biodiversity

The importance of the Salton Sea for the conservation of avian biodiversity is far greater than a list of more than 400 bird species observed within the greater Salton Sea ecosystem. Approximately 70 percent of all bird species ever recorded within California have been observed within this ecosystem, an area that has breeding by 100 species, or more than one-third of all bird species that breed in California. Nineteen water birds use the Salton Sea ecosystem during various times of the year. Habitat loss and the strategic location of California along the Pacific flyway (a major corridor followed by migratory birds) are primary factors in the current importance of the Salton Sea. California leads the nation with a loss of more than 90 percent of its historic wetland acreage.

—Milton Friend

tinue to increase and will destroy the fishery, which is the food base for thousands of white and brown pelicans, double-crested cormorants, and other fish-eating birds that have become dependent on the sea. A joint federal-state project was initiated in January 1998 to arrest salinity, address eutrophication (the process by which a body of water becomes enriched in dissolved nutrients), and otherwise improve the environment of the sea to benefit birds, to sustain the sport fishery, and to restore the area to the prominence it had during the 1950s and 1960s as a retirement and recreation mecca.

Resolution of conflicts over the use of Colorado River water is key to whether the Salton Sea will sur-

White pelicans at Salton Sea. COURTESY MILTON FRIEND.

vive as a biologically productive ecosystem. California is mandated to reduce its current 5.2 million acre-feet use of Colorado River water to its legal allocation of 4.4 million acre-feet. Agriculture within the Imperial Valley holds historic legal rights to 3.1 million acre-feet of this allocation. San Diego and Los Angeles are seeking the transfer of 300,000 acre-feet to support their growth needs (an acre-foot is the annual average amount of water used by two families of four people each). Transfer of 300,000 acre-feet of water from agriculture to urban use will reduce irrigation drainwater flows to the Salton Sea by an equal amount. Because there are no other sources of water to offset that reduction in drainwater, the inflow-evaporation equilibrium will be destabilized, the salinity of the Salton Sea will increase sharply, and there will be a collapse of the fish and invertebrate food base for birds. The biological consequences of displacement of the affected bird populations are uncertain, but they are likely to be disastrous for some species because of other habitat losses that have occurred. The loss of the sport fishery and the abundant birdlife will have major economic impacts on local human communities and lead to further environmental degradation of the Salton Sea.

The Salton Sea is a contemporary challenge involving society's struggle to meet the increasing needs for freshwater by humans and to sustain the other species with which humans share the earth. It has been stated that this challenge is a test too important to fail but too difficult to pass. The outcome will stand in testimony to society's choices about sustaining biodiversity.

Milton Friend

Further Reading

Atkinson, S. P. (Producer). (2002). *High stakes at the Salton Sea* [Film]. Sacramento, CA: Water Education Foundation.

Barnum, D. A., Elder, J. F., Stephens, D., & Friend, M. (Eds.). (2002). *The Salton Sea*. Boston: Kluwer Academic Publishers.

Dahl, T. E. (1990). *Wetland losses in the United States 1780s to 1980s*. Washington, DC: U.S. Department of the Interior, Fish and Wildlife Service.

Dahl, T. E., & Johnson, C. E. (1991). *Status and trends of wetlands in the conterminous United States, mid–1970s to Mid–1980s*. Washington, DC: U.S. Department of the Interior, Fish and Wildlife Service.

De Buys, W., & Meyers, J. (1999). *Salt dreams: Land and water in low-down California*. Albuquerque: University of New Mexico Press.

Frayer, W. E., Peters, D. D., & Pywell, H. R. (1989). *Wetlands of the California central valley: Status and trends 1939 to mid–1980s*. Portland, OR: U.S. Department of the Interior, Fish and Wildlife Service.

Redlands Institute. (2002). *Salton Sea atlas* (University of Redlands No. P127). Redlands, CA: ESRI Press.

Scandinavia

Scandinavia is composed of five nations in northern Europe: Norway, Sweden, Denmark, Finland, and Iceland. Denmark, which lies to the north of Germany, is the only country directly connected to Europe and is separated from the Scandinavian Peninsula, made up of Norway, Sweden, and Finland, by the Baltic Sea and the Skagerrak and Kattegat Straits. Iceland lies in the northern Atlantic Ocean, approximately 1,000 kilometers west of Norway and 300 kilometers southeast of Greenland. Scandinavia's climate varies from tundra and subarctic, with parts of Norway, Sweden, and Finland lying north of the Arctic Circle, to milder temperate zones in Denmark and southern Sweden. The terrain ranges from mountainous, with peaks in Norway and Sweden rising to more than 2,000 meters, to heavily forested lake regions in Finland and flat coastal plains in southern Sweden and Denmark. Iceland possesses a unique landscape marked by treeless, grassy plains and large barren, rocky areas created by recent geological activity, and the island has several active volcanoes.

Despite their geographical separation, the five Scandinavian countries share strong linguistic, historical, and cultural ties dating back centuries. With the exception of Finland, the region speaks closely related languages, and most of the inhabitants are members of the Lutheran Church. Sweden is the most populous country in Scandinavia, with just under 9 million inhabitants, followed by Denmark (5.2 million), Finland (5.1 million), Norway (4.4 million), and Iceland (266,000). All five countries are modern industrialized societies, with some of the world's highest standards of living, characterized by high levels of state involvement in the economy and large numbers of social welfare programs. Principal economic activities include heavy manufacturing, mining, shipping, electronics, telecommunications, forestry, and fishing. And Norway possesses a large petroleum and natural gas industry based on the country's North Sea oil fields, which were first put into production in the late 1960s. Agriculture plays a relatively minor role in the Scandinavian economy, with the important exception of Denmark, much of which is intensively farmed.

Loss of Wilderness

Like other industrial countries, the Scandinavian countries face a variety of environmental problems. Compared to other regions of Europe, the region has more uninhabited wilderness, especially in Iceland and the Arctic territory in northern Norway, Finland, and Sweden. However, population growth over the last century has put pressure on the remaining wilderness areas. This is especially true in Finland, where large-scale drainage programs since the early 1900s have resulted in the loss of about two-thirds of the country's forest wetlands. Principal endangered species in Scandinavia include the Arctic fox, lynx, wolf, and wolverine. Also, the Saimaa freshwater seal, a rare species found only in one isolated Finnish lake, is all but extinct, with fewer than one hundred left in the wild.

The Scandinavian countries have also struggled with a number of pollution problems related to the development of modern industries. Air pollution is a particularly important problem, and the region was one of the first areas to recognize the threat of acid rain, which has been an increasingly troublesome phenomenon since the 1950s. Although recent efforts in Scandinavia have reduced sulfur emissions from local industries to less than half from their peak in the 1970s, pollutants from outside the region continue to effect Scandinavian forests. All Scandinavian countries are wrestling with ground and water contamination from industrial activities, especially heavy metals and chemicals. Denmark's agricultural industry has also created fertilizer and pesticide contamination problems in that country.

Given the region's long maritime tradition and the importance of fishing to the Scandinavian economies, marine pollution is also a particular concern. Pollution levels in the Baltic Sea have risen to the point that much of the fish are no longer edible, and the Scandinavian fishing industry has sharply declined since the 1970s. Oil pollution from shipping and offshore drilling has caused numerous problems, with a blowout at Norway's Ekofisk oil field in 1977 releasing 22,000 metric tons of oil into the marine environment. The leaching of fertilizers into the Baltic and North Seas has also created increasing numbers of "red tide" algae blooms, including a large bloom off the Swedish coast in 1988

that killed thousands of fish and was one of the worst cases on record.

Environmental Activism

However, Scandinavia also has some of the highest levels of environmental activism in the world. The region has a long history of protecting wilderness areas, and its first nature reserves were established in the early 1900s. Since the 1980s all Scandinavian countries have been active in creating more natural parks in order to preserve remaining wilderness. More recently Scandinavia's Arctic regions have also become important centers of environmental tourism, and Norway's hosting of the Olympic winter games at Lillehammer in 1994 has been praised for its careful planning and conservation methods. Also, most Scandinavian cities have enacted regulations to control urban growth and encourage recycling. Scandinavian countries have also led the way in the development of renewable energy sources, with Denmark investing heavily in wind turbine technology, whereas Iceland relies almost exclusively on geothermal sources for its energy supply.

Since the late 1970s green politics has become increasingly important in Scandinavia, and a majority of Scandinavians now favor environmental protection over economic growth. The Swedish Green Party (Miljöpartiet de Gröna) was formed in 1981 and enjoyed its first electoral successes in 1988, winning enough of the vote to send several members to the Swedish parliament. Also, in 1995 a member of the Finnish Green Party (Vihreä Lütto) was named Finland's environment minister. However, the green parties in Denmark and Norway have been less successful. Norway, in particular, is deeply divided over the issue of whaling because it has not agreed to accept the International Whaling Commission's call for a ban on commercial whaling and still engages in small-scale scientific whaling.

James Lide

Further Reading

Agger, P., & Utzon-Frank, T. (Eds.). (1995). *Nordic nature: Prior requirements and principles of nature conservation in the Nordic countries*. Copenhagen, Denmark: Nordic Council of Ministers.

Alanen, A. (1995). *Nordic environment: Historical and contemporary perspectives*. Madison: University of Wisconsin Department of Scandinavian Studies.

Bernes, C. (1993). *The Nordic environment: Present state, trends, and threats.* Copenhagen, Denmark: Nordic Council of Ministers.

Bernes, C. (1996). *The Nordic environment: Unspoiled, exploited, polluted?* Copenhagen, Denmark: Nordic Council of Ministers.

Munk, P. (Ed.). (1996). *Governing the environment: Politics, policy and organization in the Nordic countries.* Copenhagen, Denmark: Nordic Council of Ministers.

Scavenging

Scavenging behavior is one of several means by which a carnivorous animal may obtain meat or bone marrow. Scavenging behavior generally differs from hunting in that scavenging does not cause the death of an animal, and thus the consumer does not control when and where the food will be available. In this sense, scavenged food represents an "unearned" resource, although considerable effort may be required to find and defend the resource once it has been acquired. The most prominent sources of scavengeable meat on landscapes tend to be the carcasses of larger mammals, because they are easier to locate and decompose more slowly, due to their larger size relative to body surface area.

Scavenging opportunities may arise from the hunting activities of other predators, or from deaths from accidents, disease, or malnutrition. Many human cultures of the Industrial Age eschew the concept of scavenging, but the reality is rather different; if meat is in good condition, people willingly eat it (freshly road-killed elk, for example, or beached whales or lion-killed zebra). In the historic period, ethnographic reports of scavenging are widespread, but scavenged carcasses seldom are the dominant source of meat in human diets.

The quality and quantity of scavengeable food (meat or bone) varies tremendously with circumstance. Rates of carcass discovery and competition for carcasses depend on their relative spatial concentration on landscapes; dispersion reduces the predictability of scavengeable resources and increases the search time. Terrestrial foragers, such as humans, are often made aware of the presence of carcasses by circling raptors, sounds made by other predators, or by scent. The residual food value of a carcass depends on the extent of prior feeding by other predators and on local rates of decomposition. In warm environments, decomposition may be rapid, although bone-locked marrow may last longer. In cool environments, decomposition may be arrested temporarily by subfreezing temperatures, such that scavengeable carcasses accumulate over the winter months and become available rather suddenly with the spring melt.

Scavenging Behavior and Meat Eating Among Early Hominids

Most predatory animals that hunt are also willing scavengers. A few obligate scavengers exist within the order Carnivora (striped and brown hyenas are two examples) and among birds (vultures are a well-known example). The strategic dichotomy between hunting and scavenging among nonhuman predators is an important source of analog models for the evolution of meat-eating behavior in early hominids in Africa, including human ancestors. Scavenging opportunities are structured to a large extent by environment type, and models for arid tropical, wet tropical, and subarctic regions must differ. Of great interest are the evolutionary pathways by which human ancestors became part of large predator guilds in arid tropical savannas, groups of predator species whose diets centered on large mammals, given that impressive assemblages of large cats, hyenas, and wild dogs have existed in these environments for at least 5 million years.

Recent humans can be highly carnivorous and often depend upon the meat of large mammals in particular. This feature of human adaptations extends back to at least the Middle Pleistocene. Humans' closest living primate relatives, chimpanzees, also eat meat in the wild but in very small amounts (usually less than 5 percent of their total diet), and the meat derives almost exclusively from small animals. No modern ape has been observed to scavenge.

Early hominids of the Miocene and Pliocene are thought to have adapted originally to the consumption of large seeds and fruit, complemented by other vegetable foods and insects. The rather abrupt inclusion of large mammals in early hominid (Australopithecine) diets about 2.6 million years ago in eastern Africa is inferred from the repeated spatial associations of crude stone tools and small numbers of cut-marked ungulate bones on ancient landscape surfaces. The early evidence for hominid meat eating is clearest with respect to bone marrow acquisition. The evidence appears more mixed as to how much meat may have been present on the bones, although cut marks from primitive stone tools on bone surfaces indicate some flesh removal. Marrow removal is apparent from impact fractures from stone hammers or cobbles on the dense, compact sections of ungulate limb bones. Some of these bones are associated with large muscle masses in living prey, the sort of high quality meat seldom left behind by first-order consumers. Hence, there is controversy as to how such bones could have been obtained by hominids that possessed very limited tool kits. The competition that may accompany scavenging in habitats where other predators are common provides strong incentives for moving food away from the find site, presumably to a safer location, since processing takes time. The early cases for meat eating in the Lower Pleistocene archeological records of Africa indicate deliberate transport of food and tools to secondary locations. Models of hominids' access to carcasses include stealing leopard-stashed kills in trees, finding ravaged carcasses on the ground, and tracking other predators and displacing them from freshly killed prey by force. A related issue in research into human origins concerns the potential connection between meat eating, food transport, and food sharing at base camps, as these are essential features of recent human cultures. Models of carcass processing sites have varied from places to which nuclear family members transported food in order to share it with close kin, to quick-stop adult feeding stations where crude stone tools and bones were soon discarded.

Human Scavenging in the More Recent Past

Scavenging behavior in human cultures continues into the present, but its importance relative to other means of getting food has diminished substantially with time. The character of scavenging practices in the recent past is quite different from the evidence for scavenging by early hominids. Competing models of early hominid meat eating most often fall under the categories of confrontational and nonconfrontational scavenging. Archeological evidence suggests that both occurred in the remote past; most researchers believe that early hominids obtained meat from large animals through nonconfrontational scavenging.

Nonconfrontational scavenging is a behavior akin to the gathering of stationary foods, and it is apparent in some archeological records from the early Middle Paleolithic some 110,000 years ago onward. It clearly was a complement to hunting, and this kind of opportunism in no way reflected an inability to capture large

mammals by hunting. Confrontational scavenging, a behavior documented ethnographically, is much more akin to large-game hunting, because weapons and groups of individuals are required to displace another large predator from its kill in time to take over the bulk of the meat. This practice is almost certainly as old as large-game hunting itself, which dates back more than 500,000 years. Both nonconfrontational and confrontational scavenging have risks: In some circumstances the greatest challenge is simply locating carcasses, which may be widely scattered; in other instances, the greatest challenge is staying clear of other predators. Spurred by interspecies competition, refinements in human hunting ecology favored greater efficiency. This process was aided in large part by evolving technology, which enhanced the predictability of access to meat and nutritional returns for the effort, and also improved the means for defending food acquired. Primary access to meat raises the consumers' chances of monopolizing these precious resources, something that often is not possible for scavengers who are not also well-equipped hunters.

Mary C. Stiner

Further Reading

Aiello, L. C., & Wheeler, P. (1995). The expensive-tissue hypothesis: The brain and the digestive system in human and primate evolution. *Current Anthropology, 36*(2), 199–221.

Binford, L. R. (1981). *Bones: Ancient men and modern myths.* New York: Academic Press.

Blumenschine, R. J. (1986). *Early hominid scavenging opportunities: Implications of carcass availability in the Serengeti and Ngorongoro ecosystems* (BAR International Series No. 283). Oxford, UK: British Archaeological Reports (BAR).

Brain, C. K. (1981). *The hunters or the hunted?* Chicago: University of Chicago Press.

Brantingham, J. P. (1998). Hominid-carnivore coevolution and invasion of the predatory guild. *Journal of Anthropological Archaeology, 17*(4), 327–353.

Cavallo, J. A., & Blumenschine, R. J. (1989). Tree-stored leopard kills: Expanding the hominid scavenging niche. *Journal of Human Evolution, 18*, 393–399.

Gamble, C. (1986). *The palaeolithic settlement of Europe.* Cambridge, UK: Cambridge University Press.

Haynes, G. (1982). Utilization and skeletal disturbances of North American prey carcasses. *Arctic, 35*(2), 266–281.

Houston, D. C. (1979). The adaptations of scavengers. In A. R. E. Sinclair & M. Norton-Griffiths (Eds.), *Serengeti: dynamics of an ecosystem* (pp. 263–286). Chicago: University of Chicago Press.

Isaac, G. L. (1978). The food-sharing behavior of protohuman hominids. *Scientific American, 238*(4), 90–106.

Klein, R. G. (1989). *The human career: Human biological and cultural origins.* Chicago: University of Chicago Press.

Kuhn, S. L., & Stiner, M. C. (1998). Middle Paleolithic "creativity": Reflections on an oxymoron? In S. Mithen (Ed.), *Creativity and human evolution and prehistory* (pp. 143–164). London: Routledge.

Leakey, M. (1971). *Olduvai Gorge: Excavations in Beds I and II, 1960–1963.* Cambridge, UK: Cambridge University Press.

Morris, K., & Goodall, J. (1977). Competition for meat between chimpanzees and baboons of the Gombe National Park. *Folia Primatologica, 28*(4), 109–121.

O'Connell, J. F., Hawkes, K., & Blurton Jones, N. (1988). Hadza scavenging: Implications for Plio/Pleistocene hominid subsistence. *Current Anthropology, 29*(2), 356–363.

Potts, R. (1984). Home bases and early hominids. *Scientific American, 72*(4), 338–347.

Potts, R., & Shipman, P. (1981). Cutmarks made by stone tools on bones from Olduvai George, Tanzania. *Nature, 291,* 577–580.

Rose, L., & Marshall, F. (1996). Meat eating, hominid sociality, and home bases revisited. *Current Anthropology, 37*(2), 307–338.

Schaller, G. B., & Lowther, G. R. (1969). The relevance of carnivore behavior to the study of early hominids. *Southwestern Journal of Anthropology, 25,* 307–341.

Semaw, S. (2000). The world's oldest stone artifacts from Gona, Ethiopia: Their implications for understanding stone technology and patterns of human evolution between 2.6–1.5 million years ago. *Journal of Archaeological Science, 27*(12), 1197–1214.

Speth, J. D. (1989). Early hominid hunting and scavenging: The role of meat as an energy source. *Journal of Human Evolution, 18,* 329–343.

Stanford, C., & Bunn, H. (Eds.). (2001). *The early human diet: The role of meat.* Oxford, UK: Oxford University Press.

Stiner, M. C. (1994). *Honor among thieves: A Zooarchaeological study of Neanderthal ecology,* Princeton, NJ: Princeton University Press.

Stiner, M. C. (2002). Carnivory, coevolution, and the geographic spread of the genus *Homo. Journal of Archaeological Research, 10* (1), 1–63.

Tappen, M. (1995). Savanna ecology and natural bone deposition: Implications for early hominid site formation, hunting, and scavenging. *Current Anthropology, 36*(2), 223–260.

Wynn, T., & McGrew, W. (1989). An ape's view of the Oldowan. *Man, 24,* 383–398.

Schumacher, E. F.
(1911–1977)
German-born British economist

Ernst Fritz Schumacher wrote and worked at a time when the dominant ideology was "the bigger the better." Large institutions, multinational corporations, industrial mergers, unlimited economic growth and ever-increasing consumption were considered symbols of progress. As Schumacher said, "We suffer from an almost universal idolatry of giantism" (Schumacher 1973, 54).

In response to such idolatry, Schumacher encapsulated an alternative worldview in his seminal collection of essays, *Small Is Beautiful* (1973). Intrigued by the book, U.S. president Jimmy Carter invited Schumacher to the White House in 1977 to hear Schumacher's ideas.

E. F. Schumacher was born in Bonn, Germany. He came to England in 1930 as a Rhodes scholar to read Economics at New College, Oxford. After a short spell of teaching economics at Columbia University, New York, followed by dabbling in business, farming, and journalism, he became an economic adviser to the British Control Commission in Germany (1946–1950), followed by a long career at the National Coal Board in Britain.

It was Schumacher's involvement in the economics of developing countries that challenged and changed his economic philosophy. He realized that the Western pursuit of unlimited economic growth on a gigantic scale was neither desirable nor practicable for the rest of the world. If anything, the West itself needed to learn the simplicity, spirituality, and good sense of other cultures that were not yet in the grip of technological imperatives.

The turning point came in 1955 when he was sent as an adviser in economic development to the government of Burma (now Myanmar). He was supposed to introduce the Western model of economic growth in order to raise the living standards of the Burmese people, but he discovered that the Burmese needed no economic development along Western lines, as they had an indigenous economic system well-suited to their conditions, culture, and climate. As a result of his encounter with a Buddhist civilization, he wrote his well-known essay "Buddhist Economics" (1966). Schumacher was perhaps the only Western economist to dare to put those two words, *Buddhist* and *economics*, together. The essay was printed and reprinted in numerous journals and anthologies.

During his time in Burma, Schumacher encountered the Buddhist concept of the Middle Way (an expression of the virtue of avoiding extremes). He wanted to apply it to technology, so in 1970 Schumacher founded the Intermediate Technology Development Group (ITDG). ITDG became a practical expression of respect for cultural diversity. Complementing his interest in intermediate technology was his involvement with sustainable agriculture; he spent much time on his organic garden and became president of the Soil Association, Great Britain's leading association for organic farming.

To Schumacher it was logical and natural to produce, consume, and organize as locally as possible, which inevitably meant on a smaller scale. Therefore, to him the matter of size was an overriding and overarching principle. Beyond a certain scale people are disempowered and a bureaucratic machine takes over. For example, in a large school (say, one of 1,000 children or more), parents do not know the teachers, teachers cannot know all the children, and the children cannot know all their peers. Similarly, large hospitals, large factories, and large businesses lose the purpose of enriching human well-being and become obsessed with maintaining and perpetuating the organization for its own sake. Therefore, it could be said almost invariably that if there is something wrong, there is something too big. The same principle applied to politics for Schumacher: He believed in small nations, small communities, and small organizations. Small, simple, and nonviolent were his three philosophical precepts.

His legacy continues to be felt. Immediately after his death the Schumacher Society was established in Britain; it continues to promote the ideas of ecological economics. The Society holds annual lectures in Bristol, Liverpool, and Manchester. Some of those lectures have now been published. Schumacher Societies have also sprung up in the United States, Germany, and India.

His writings have inspired people in different disciplines. A college named after him has been established

at Dartington, Devon, in Great Britain; it explores an ecological worldview from many different perspectives, while students practice a lifestyle built around the precepts of small, simple, local, and nonviolent. *Resurgence* magazine, for which Schumacher wrote regularly, continues to examine and expound the small-is-beautiful ethos.

Satish Kumar

Further Reading

Kohr, L. (1986) *The breakdown of nations.* London and New York: Routledge & Kegan Paul. (Originally published in 1957.)

McRobie, G. (1981). *Small is possible.* London: Jonathan Cape.

Schumacher, E. F. (1973). *Small is beautiful: A study of economics as if people mattered.* London: Blond and Briggs.

Schumacher, E. F. (1989). *A guide for the perplexed.* London: Abacus, Sphere Books Ltd. (Originally published in 1977 by Green Books, Ltd.)

Wood, B. (1984). *Alias papa: A biography.* London: Jonathan Cape.

Schurz, Carl

(1829–1906)

Secretary of the U.S. Department of the Interior

Carl Schurz was born near Cologne, Germany, and attended the University of Bonn. A supporter of the failed Revolution of 1848, he fled by way of France and later England to the United States in 1852 and found work as a journalist. He married and moved to Wisconsin in 1855, passed the bar, and began practicing law. An early member of the Republican Party, his campaign work for Abraham Lincoln in 1860 was rewarded with an appointment as minister (or ambassador) to Spain. In 1862, he resigned his post and returned to serve in the Union army as brigadier general. He was promoted to major general for his performance at Second Bull Run (Manassas), and commanded troops at Chancellorsville, Gettysburg, and Brown's Ferry (Tennessee).

After the war, Schurz returned to journalism and soon became editor-in-chief of the German-language *Westliche Post* in St. Louis, Missouri. In 1869, he was elected U.S. senator from his adopted state. He broke with the administration of Ulysses S. Grant over several of its policies, including civil-service reform, and became a leader of the Liberal Republican movement. The Liberal Republicans favored removing many of the civil-service positions from political patronage and replacing patronage with merit hiring and promotion procedures. After campaigning for Rutherford Hayes in 1876, Schurz was appointed secretary of the Department of the Interior and served from 1877 to 1881. He undertook civil-service reform in the department, worked toward eliminating corruption in the Bureau of Indian Affairs, and tried to initiate a federal forestry policy.

Schurz, who had seen the benefits of scientific forestry in his native country, was outraged by the timber destruction in his adopted country. As secretary, he tried to institute a national forestry policy when the country had no professional foresters and little interest in forestry management. Schurz called for the establishment of federal forest reserves system, the initiation of reforestation practices, fees for the users of national resources, stiff penalties for the willful setting of forest fires, and vigorous prosecution of trespassers stealing timber from government land. His attempts to end political patronage and corruption in the General Land Office, which regulated activity on public lands, were thwarted by Congress and the businessmen who benefited from the system. Nonetheless, the federal government eventually adopted his policies and created the United States Forest Service in 1905 to implement them.

After leaving office, he served as coeditor of the *New York Evening Post* for two years before returning to politics to continue his promotion of civil-service reform and other causes, including forest preservation and creation of New York's Adirondack Park. In 1892, he became both president of the National Civil Service Reform League and editor of *Harper's Weekly* magazine. There he continued his reform work as an anti-imperialist (he opposed war with Spain in 1898 and the annexation of Hawaii and Puerto Rico), and supporter of civil rights for African-Americans.

James G. Lewis

Further Reading

Fuess, C. M. (1963). *Carl Schurz: Reformer; 1829–1906*. Port Washington, NY: Kennikat Press.
Schafer, J. (1930). *Carl Schurz: Militant liberal*. Evansville, WI: The Antes Press.
Schurz, C. (1887). *Life of Henry Clay* (Vols. 1–2). Boston & New York: Houghton, Mifflin and Company.
Schurz, C. (1908–1910). *The reminiscences of Carl Schurz* (Vols. 1–3). New York: Doubleday, Pate & Company.
Schurz, C. (1928). *Intimate letters of Carl Schurz, 1841–1869* (J. Schafer, Ed. and Trans.). Madison, WI: State Historical Society of Wisconsin.
Schurz, C. (1889). *The need of a rational forest policy in the United States*. Philadelphia: Spangler & Davis.
Trefousse, H. L. (1982). *Carl Schurz: A biography*. Knoxville: University of Tennessee Press.

Scientific Revolution

The Scientific Revolution occurred, in general, from the mid-sixteenth century, sparked by the publication of Polish astronomer Nicholas Copernicus's *On the Revolutions of the Heavenly Spheres* (1543), to the turn of the seventeenth century, culminating in the English physicist and mathematician Isaac Newton's *Mathematical Principles of Natural Philosophy* (1687) and *Opticks* (1706). That period brought an environmental transformation in Europe, the colonization of the New World, the rise of modern science, and the beginnings of environmental stewardship and aesthetic appreciation of nature. Several factors contributed to the environmental transformation: population growth, overseas trade, forest clearing, the rise of industry, and agricultural improvement.

Between 1350 and 1450 European society had been decimated by outbreaks of bubonic plague, but the European population slowly recovered, rising to about 90 million in 1600. By the late sixteenth century population pressure on the land was coupled with a new phenomenon, mercantile capitalism, that reshaped European land and life. An expanding market economy, which arose in the city-states of Renaissance Italy and spread gradually to northern Europe, intensified medieval tendencies toward capitalist economic forms. Stimulated by the European discovery and exploitation of the Americas, the spreading use of money facilitated population expansion, colonization, and overseas trade. Cities flourished as centers of trade and handicraft production, giving rise to a new class of entrepreneurs who supplied monarchs with the funds and expertise to build strong nation-states, authorize joint stock companies, and found New World colonies.

Between 1550 and 1700 large tracts of forested lands all over Europe were cleared for agriculture and industry. Swamps were drained, mine shafts sunk, and ore extracted. Mills and foundries produced paper, gunpowder, cannons, copper, brass, and saltpeter (used for gunpowder). The mining and metallurgical industries required vast amounts of timber to make charcoal for smelting and refining. Other uses of wood contributed to the drain on timber supplies. Wood from oak, pine, and ash was needed for houses, barns, fences, plows, casks, public buildings, fortifications, docks, bridges, barges, masts, and ship hulls in a growing mercantile economy.

Everywhere early capitalist development altered the landscape and polluted the environment. In industrial regions, coal and charcoal smoke filled the air and caused pulmonary illnesses, and mining runoff contaminated pastures and poisoned fish. In urban areas air and water pollution increased from iron manufacturing, glass making, brewing, dying, lime burning, salt and soap boiling, and other small industries that burned wood, coal, and charcoal.

Intensive agriculture and pasturing depleted the soil, and the demand for higher yields stimulated new techniques of planting and plowing. An agricultural improvement movement helped yeoman and gentleman farmers to increase their profits and status. Improved methods included draining fens (low lands covered at least partially by water), reducing bogs, regaining sea lands, planting woodlots, composting and manuring soils, planting new types of crops, vegetables, and fruit trees, warding off crows, destroying vermin, and enclosing woodlands. Books on farming methods eulogized the role of the farmer in the economy. An array of how-to books contained information on the breeding of animals, grafting of fruit trees, the art of planting, new plowing and tilling methods, means of preserving fruits and vegetables, building of fish ponds, and techniques of beekeeping. Other advice included preparing rich ground for orchards, planting and grafting fruit trees, and controlling predators. The movement initiated a new tradition of progressive scientific agriculture focused on land management for increased yields.

Experimental Science

The rise of experimental science also had implications for the use of the environment. In *The New Atlantis* (written in 1624), English philosopher Francis Bacon (1561–1626) advocated the interrogation of nature through experiment. Scientists in his utopian "New Atlantis" manipulated plants and animals for the advancement of knowledge and the human condition. They did experiments on serpents, worms, flies, fish, beasts, and birds. They bred docile animals, domesticated plants, and experimented with snow, hail, rain, water, thunder, lightning, and wind. Orchards were made to bear greater numbers of fruits, trees and flowers made to bloom earlier, and herbs and fruits made to grow larger, sweeter, and tastier. Bacon's experimental approach became a model for early European scientific societies. And other natural philosophers realized the connections between the trades, middle-class commercial interests, and the control of nature. Increasingly, they spoke out in favor of "mastering" and "managing" the earth.

The experimental method was complemented by the atomic theory of matter and the mathematical method of describing nature—approaches that likewise led to the understanding of and control over the environment. In the 1620s and 1630s the French natural philosophers Marin Mersenne (1588–1648), Pierre Gassendi (1592–1655), and René Descartes (1596–1650) revived and placed in a Christian context the ancient atomic theories espoused by the Greek pagan philosophers Democritus (460 BCE) and Epicurus (341–270 BCE) and the Roman poet Lucretius (98–55 BCE). The seventeenth-century philosophers, in contrast to the ancients, asserted that God created the atoms and put them into the cosmos at the beginning of time. The world was composed of material particles in motion that combined and separated to form the external world.

For Descartes, God sustained the created world from instant to instant throughout time. Owing to God's immutable intellect, the laws of nature were both unchanging and intelligible to the human mind. The external (extended) world of nature was described in terms of measurable quantities such as size, weight, and speed. The internal (unextended) world of the mind was the source of clear and distinct ideas that constituted the basis for truth. The logic underlying the mathematical method was the key to valid knowledge of the external world. Mathematical descriptions of the material world were the ground of certainty and yielded the laws of nature. In his *Discourse on Method* (1636), Descartes argued that through such knowledge, humans could become the masters of nature.

A Mechanical View

The assumption that nature is subject to lawlike behavior meant that phenomena could be reduced to orderly, predictable rules, regulations, and laws. Isaac Newton's three laws of mechanics and the principle of gravitation, put forward in his *Mathematical Principles of Natural Philosophy*, described the actions of the world-machine. His *Opticks* characterized matter as solid, hard, impenetrable particles and light as made up of corpuscles (grain-like particles). The mechanical worldview, fully formulated by the end of the seventeenth century, seemed to be an antidote to a society in chaos from the wars of religion, the English civil war, and the collapse of astronomer Ptolemy's Earth-centered cosmos. The experimental and mathematical methods gave humanity a measure of control and prediction over nature.

Into this mechanical view of nature, English philosopher John Locke incorporated what are now modern society's concepts of appropriation, property, cultivation, improvement, and money as rationales for subduing the earth. He asserted that human needs force people to labor in the earth and to appropriate goods from the commons, or communal land. He advocated the transformation of undeveloped nature into civilized society through labor and property ownership. His concept of property entailed active manipulation of the land, and he extended the biblical mandate of Gen. 1: 28 from merely subduing the earth to enclosing land from the commons and owning it as private property. Such ideas supported the use of nature for human benefit, an approach that nevertheless often led to the overuse of resources and to environmental pollution.

By the end of the seventeenth century some philosophers and scientists recognized the need to reduce pollution and conserve natural resources. In 1661, the English diarist John Evelyn presented King Charles II with his book *Fumifugium*, a report on air pollution. In response to the problem of burning sea-coal, a highly sulfurous coal that caused pneumatic distress among Londoners, Evelyn recommended that wood be substituted for coal by reforesting the woodlands surrounding the city. He also suggested that coke should be used for smelting, that chimney heights be increased, and that flowers be planted to offset the noxious odors of sea-coal.

In *Silva, a Discourse of Forest Trees and the Propagation of Timber in His Majesty's Dominions* (1662), Evelyn said the decline of forests could be reversed by the replanting of trees. He noted the havoc that had been wrought by the tendency to cut pristine woodlands and recommended that England's forests be conserved, trees replanted, and laws enacted to curtail tree cutting near navigable waterways. In France, Jean Baptiste Colbert, minister to King Louis XIV, warned the king in 1661 that France was in danger of decline because of the rapid disappearance of its forests. The French Forest Ordinance was passed in 1669 to reorganize the administration of the king's forests. The ordinance divided forests into equivalent sections to be harvested every twenty years, whereas stands of large timber needed for shipbuilding were to be harvested every 120 years.

A Designed Universe

The evolution of a conservation consciousness was supported by a new image of a designed universe, with God as a wise conservator and humans as caretakers of nature. In *The Wisdom of God Manifested in the Works of the Creation* (1691), the English theologian John Ray argued that God expects people to use nature's bounty to glorify their Creator, even as they use that bounty to increase trade and prosperity throughout the globe. The abundance of life and resources on Earth were evidence of the wisdom of God in designing a spacious, well-furnished world, whose "natural advantages" were available to those willing to develop its vast supply of minerals, metals, animals, and plants. Gold and silver existed in just the right abundance to use as money for commerce and trade. In *Physico-Theology* (1713), the British theologian William Derham accepted the idea of a designed Earth in which humans are stewards over creation. God made men in his own image as wise conservators whose mission is to glorify God and improve the human condition. Just as God is the caretaker, steward, and wise manager of the natural world, so humans have a responsibility to imitate that mandate.

Other writers found beauty in nature and expressed an appreciation of the majesty of mountains, sunsets, waterfalls, and oceans. In England, writers such as the poet John Dennis (1657–1734), the essayist Anthony Ashley Cooper (third earl of Shaftesbury, 1621–1683), and the playwright Joseph Addison (1672–1719) wrote of the sublimity of nature. For Dennis, God's works evoked feelings of delight and joy, and Shaftesbury praised a nature that was both diverse and abundant and extolled the experience of viewing wild scenes created by God. In *Pleasures of the Imagination* (1712), Addison wrote of the appreciation of a sublime nature that could be grasped by the human imagination.

In conclusion, the Scientific Revolution was a period of environmental transformation sparked by the growth of European populations, the exploration of the New World, the rise of mercantile capitalism, and the emergence of the experimental and mathematical methods as ways of understanding and controlling the natural world. Although many of these developments were positive for much of the Western world, others had negative impacts on nature.

Carolyn Merchant

See also Tragedy of the Commons

Further Reading

Koyré, A. (1958). *From the closed world to the infinite universe.* New York: HarperCollins.

Merchant, C. (1980). *The death of nature: Women, ecology, and the scientific revolution.* San Francisco: HarperCollins.

Nef, J. U. (1966). *The rise of the British coal industry.* Hamden, CT: Archon.

Nicholson, M. H. (1977). *Mountain gloom and mountain glory: The development of the aesthetics of the infinite.* Seattle: University of Washington Press.

Oelschlaeger, M. (1991). *The idea of wilderness: From prehistory to the age of ecology.* New Haven, CT: Yale University Press.

Ponting, C. (1991). *A green history of the world: The environment and the collapse of great civilizations.* New York: St. Martin's Press.

Turner, B. L., Clark, W. C., Kates, R. W., Richards, J., Mathews, J. T., & Meyer, W. (Eds.). (1980). *The earth as transformed by human action: Global and regional changes in the biosphere over the past 300 years.* New York: Cambridge University Press.

Webster, C. (1975). *The great instauration: Science, medicine, and reform, 1626–1660.* London: Duckworth.

Sea Turtle

Sea turtles are among the oldest reptiles on Earth, predating the dinosaurs and swimming the temperate and tropical oceans for more than 100 million years. Sea turtles share many characteristics, including extremities that are relatively nonretractile, skulls that are extensively roofed, and limbs that are modified into paddle-like flippers. They are long-lived animals and relatively large in size, weighing between 35 and 500 kilograms and having carapace (shell) lengths ranging from 60 to 170 centimeters. Although sea turtles spend the vast majority of their time at sea, all must return to lay eggs on land. Females often aggregate at preferred nesting beaches. After the eggs hatch, the young turtles migrate across the beach to the ocean. Although marine turtles lay thousands of eggs throughout their life, very few sea turtles reach adulthood due to high natural rates of predation of eggs and juveniles.

Sea turtles are made up of two families consisting of seven species. Chelonidae, or the hard-shelled sea turtles, can be identified by their flattened, streamlined shells covered with epidermal scutes, or enlarged scales. As adults, all chelonids, except the olive ridley (*Lepidochelys olivacea*), tend to be residents of near-shore or continental-slope habitats. The leatherback (*Dermochelys coriacea*), the only member of the family Dermochelyidae, is the largest turtle on Earth and is identified by its broad, streamlined shell and lack of epidermal scutes. Leatherbacks are unique among reptiles because they have the ability to generate and conserve body heat even in cooler waters. The body heat is generated by muscular activity and conserved by a large surface area-to-body ratio, highly insulated oil-laden skin, and other physiological adaptations that help to reduce heat loss. Leatherbacks are highly migratory, potentially crossing entire ocean basins in pursuit of jellyfish blooms and other soft-bodied marine organisms.

Casual observations by early European explorers usually describe sea turtle populations as being extremely plentiful when compared to today's populations, but little historical data exists that can be statistically compared. Green sea turtles were found to be extremely abundant on and around the Cayman Islands in the early 1500s. Over the next century, explorers began to sporadically harvest turtles and in the 1650s, the wholesale commercial harvest of the turtles began. By the late 1700s, the Cayman Island rookeries were no longer a commercial source for turtle meat due to the dwindling population, and by the early 1900s, no green sea turtles nested on the Cayman Islands. Sea turtle populations around the world have experienced local extinctions due to other overexploitation pressures.

The six species found in U.S. waters are listed as endangered or threatened under the Endangered Species Act. Sea turtles are also internationally recognized as endangered. All species of sea turtles are listed on Appendix 1 by the Convention on International Trade in Endangered Species (CITES) of wild flora and fauna. This listing makes international trade in sea turtle parts or products illegal under the CITES agreement. The species survival commission of the International Union for Conservation of Nature and Natural Resources (IUCN) also lists all sea turtle species as either vulnerable, endangered, or critically endangered.

Relationship with People

The overexploitation of breeding adults and the harvesting of eggs are largely responsible for the current status of sea turtles. Green sea turtles (Chelonia mydas) have been overharvested for their eggs and meat since European explorers and settlers traveled to the Western Hemisphere and Asia. Green sea turtle meat continues to be a favorite food item in parts of Mexico, the Caribbean, and South America. Loggerhead (Caretta caretta) meat is favored in the Mediterranean, Africa, and South America. Leatherbacks are eaten in Peru and the Caribbean. In various Caribbean and coastal Central American societies, sea turtles were a significant source of protein. For example, the green sea turtle provided up to 70 percent of the animal protein intake for the Miskito Indians of coastal Honduras and Nicaragua prior to commercial harvesting. Sea turtle eggs are also harvested in many parts of the world. Most countries prohibit the taking of eggs, but poaching is rampant due to poor law enforcement.

Many products of economic and cultural importance are made from marine turtles. Hawksbills (Eretmochelys imbricata) have been exploited for thousands of years for their highly coveted thorny scutes. Hawksbill scutes are used for making tortoiseshell jewelry, art, and other objects of cultural importance. Despite the protection granted to the hawksbill, tortoiseshell products are still highly sought after, and illegal trade continues. The hides of sea turtles are also used for leather. Boots and other articles of clothing are commonly made from leather of the green sea turtle, leatherbacks, loggerheads, and ridleys. Young marine turtles are also caught, stuffed, and sold to tourists in many parts of the Caribbean. The oil-laden skin of leatherbacks is used for treating boat timbers in India and Arabia.

While persistent overexploitation for human sustenance and turtle-related products has greatly reduced sea turtle populations from historic levels, other anthropogenic (human-caused) pressures also have continued to deplete the sea turtle population. Captures in commercial shrimp trawling nets have been responsible for more sea turtle mortality than any other form of incidental capture. Although incidental catches associated with shrimp trawling occur in all near-shore areas of the world, they occur most often in the waters of the Caribbean and the eastern North America. For example, in the late 1980s, it was estimated that fifty-five thousand marine turtles died annually off the coast of the eastern United States from shrimp trawling activities. Other commercial fishing devices, such as longlines, shoreline set nets, driftnets, and seines, also result in the death of thousands of marine turtles each year.

Habitat degradation of the nesting beaches also has reduced marine turtle populations. Many nesting beaches have been lost to urban development. The modifications associated with urbanization have increased beach erosion, which decreases the available nesting sites. The presence of vehicles and people on the beaches has disrupted adult nesting and increased the mortality of hatchlings. Artificial lighting, such as streetlights and building lights, on beaches is also problematic to sea turtles. Hatchlings use visual cues based on light to find the sea. Prior to artificial lighting, the ocean would always be brighter than the land due to reflection from the stars and the moon. However, artificial light disorients hatchlings and results in thousands of deaths.

The current state of the marine environment also poses threats to sea turtles. Oil, pollutants, and damage to coral reefs endanger foraging grounds, dispersal routes, and crucial habitats. Plastic debris, confused with jellyfish, squid, or some other food sources, can be ingested. The debris can also cause a number of physiological problems, such as blocking the digestive tract, which results in starvation and eventually death.

Conservation

In addition to the CITES listing, a number of conservation measures have been implemented to preserve marine turtles. Many countries, like Costa Rica, the United States, and Australia, have established preserves on nesting beaches and near-shore habitats, which protect the eggs and adults from poachers. Some sea turtles are born and raised in captivity for up to a year before being released. This process, known as headstarting, is thought to protect young sea turtles against high rates of natural predation that would have occurred in their early months of life. The effectiveness of headstarting is a controversial issue among marine turtle biologists. Turtle excluder devices (TEDs) are currently being used to reduce the number of juvenile and adult fatalities associated with commercial shrimp trawling. TEDs allow for the capture of shrimp and other small organisms and exclude larger animals such as sea turtles. TEDs are currently mandatory in many areas of the United States; unfortunately, many commercial shrimpers have yet to fully accept TEDs. Changes in the placement and type of lights is reducing the impact on turtle nesting beaches. Some sea turtle populations have increased in areas that have received protection. Despite the efforts to conserve sea turtles, populations continue to decline globally.

Steven J. Price

Further Reading

Allen, W. H. (1992). Increased dangers to Caribbean marine ecosystems. *Bioscience, 42*(5), 330–335.

Bjorndal, K. A. (Ed.). (1995). *Biology and conservation of sea turtles* (Rev. ed.). Washington, DC & London: Smithsonian Institution Press.

Bjorndal, K. A., Bolton, A. B., & Lagueux, C. J. (1993). Decline of the nesting population of hawksbill turtles at Tortuguero, Costa Rica. *Conservation Biology, 7*(4), 925–927.

Carr, A. F., Jr. (1952). *Handbook of turtles: The turtles of the United States, Canada, and Baja California.* Ithaca, NY: Cornell University Press.

Carr, A. F., Jr. (1987). The impact of nondegradable marine debris on the ecology and survival outlook of sea turtles. *Marine Pollution Bulletin, 18*(6b), 352–356.

Frazer, N. B. (1992). Sea turtle conservation and halfway technology. *Conservation Biology, 6*(2), 179–182.

Henwood, T. A., & Stuntz, W. E. (1987). Analysis of sea turtle captures and mortalities during commercial shrimp trawling. *Fisheries Bulletin, 85*(4), 813–817.

Lutz, P. L., & Musick, J. A. (1996). *The biology of sea turtles.* Boca Raton, FL: CRC Press.

Marquez, M. R. (1990). Sea turtles of the world: An annotated and illustrated catalogue of sea turtle species known to data. *FAO Fisheries Synopsis, 125*(11), 1–81.

National Research Council. (1990). *Decline of the sea turtles: Causes and prevention.* Washington, DC: National Academy Press.

Rudloe, J., & Rudloe, A. (1989, December). Shrimpers and lawmakers collide over a move to save the sea turtles. *Smithsonian, 20* (9), 44–55.

Salmon, M., & Witherington, B. E. (1995). Artificial lighting and sea finding by loggerhead hatchlings: Evidence for lunar modulation. *Copeia, 4*(4), 931–938.

Witherington, B. E., & Bjorndal, K. A. (1991). Influences of artificial lighting on the seaward orientation of hatchling loggerhead turtles *Caretta caretta. Biological Conservation, 55*(2), 139–149.

Zug, G. R., Vitta, L. J., & Caldwell, J. P. (2001). *Herpetology: An introductory biology of amphibians and reptiles* (2nd ed.). San Diego, CA: Academic Press.

Seton, Ernest T.
(1860–1946)
Writer, artist, and naturalist

Ernest Thompson Seton was among the twentieth century's most popular proponents of the idea that communion with nature is an antidote to the ills of industrial civilization. Born in England and originally named Ernest Thompson, in 1866 he moved with his family to Canada. The young Thompson chafed under his father's overbearing manner and strict adherence to conservative Calvinist doctrine; he often sought solace in wild lands near Toronto, where he found a harmony unavailable in his unhappy home. As a teenager Thompson began to produce paintings of the natural world, and his family encouraged his burgeoning artistic abilities. He also began adding "Seton" to his name, acting on a family legend that claimed a direct lineage from the seventeenth-century Scottish earl George Seton. After a brief stint at London's Royal Academy of Art, in 1882 Thompson joined his brother Arthur at his homestead in western Manitoba. The wilderness near his new home inspired Seton's creativity; by 1885 he left the homestead and began publishing nature stories and illustrations in popular magazines. He also accepted commissions for wildlife drawings from such organizations as the American Ornithologists Union and the U.S. Biological Survey.

In 1898 Seton collected several of his magazine articles into the book *Wild Animals I Have Known.* The book was an instant best-seller; four printings sold out within the year. Seton's stories were entirely sympathetic to the natural world and overtly moralistic in their portrayal of animal nobility in wild nature. This sentimental attitude ensnared Seton in the "nature faker" controversy in which Seton and other popular writers were charged with producing "sham" rather than scientific natural history. Seton recoiled from the charges and attempted to buttress his scientific credentials through the writing of texts such as the four-volume *Lives of Game Animals,* which became a classic of American mammalogy. Seton believed that communion with the natural world would teach people honor, physical courage, self-reliance, and spiritual harmony. To that end Seton founded, in a 1902 series of articles in *Ladies' Home Journal*, the Woodcraft League, a youth organization that taught children spiritual discipline and woodcraft skills through direct contact with the outdoors. The Woodcraft League was modeled on the lives and practices of Native Americans, whom Seton revered as examples of people living in physical and spiritual harmony with nature. Soon there were over 200,000 of Seton's Woodcraft "Indians." The organization attracted the attention of Robert Baden-Powell, whom Seton met on a 1906 lecture tour of England, and the two men collaborated in the creation of the Boy Scouts. When the Boy Scouts of America was incorporated in 1910, Seton was chief scout and author of its first handbook. Yet Baden-Powell's militarism and relative lack of interest in woodcraft drove a wedge between the two men, and Seton resigned from the Boy Scouts in 1915. Seton continued his Woodcraft League and continued to publish nature stories and to produce landscape and wildlife paintings until his death.

Kevin C. Armitage

Further Reading

Anderson, H. A. (1986). *The chief: Ernest Thompson Seton and the changing West*. College Station: Texas A&M University Press.

Lutts, R. H. (1990). *The nature fakers: Wildlife, science and sentiment*. Golden, CO: Fulcrum.

Wadland, J. H. (1978). *Ernest Thompson Seton: Man and nature in the Progressive Era, 1880–1915*. New York: Arno.

Sheep

The ancestor of domestic sheep was the mouflon (*Ovis orientalis*), which may still be found wild in mountainous regions of Sardinia, Cyprus, and other islands of the Mediterranean. Several varieties of sheep, however, have never been domesticated, primarily because they cannot easily be herded. Among these is the American bighorn sheep (*Ovis canadensis*) found in the Rocky Mountains, which, though untamed, provides wool used by the Navajo and other Native American tribes in intricately woven and brightly colored blankets.

Sheep—together with goats, their close relatives—became the first herd animals to be domesticated, originally in Asia Minor and Iraq, by about 8000 BCE. The domestication of sheep was a gradual process that probably grew out of efforts of hunters to manipulate stampeding herds. By the third millennium BCE, captive herds of sheep had become common throughout the Near East, central Europe, and western Asia.

As human population increased and people were compelled to abandon the lives of hunter-gatherers, a rivalry between herders and agriculturalists arose. This rivalry is commemorated in the biblical story of brothers Abel and Cain. Abel was a shepherd and offered a sacrifice of a sheep to Yahweh (God), whereas Cain tilled the soil and offered up fruits and vegetables. When Yahweh looked with favor only on the sacrifice of Abel, Cain became angry and killed his brother (Genesis 4).

Social Organization

One consequence of the domestication of animals for food was that it enabled people to store up considerable amounts of wealth, which led to increased social differentiation. Herds of animals are often mentioned in the Old Testament of the Bible and other books of the ancient world as a measure of riches. The earliest coins, from Lydia in the seventh century BCE, were stamped with pictures of food animals, and their value was measured in livestock.

The Hebrews were a nation of herders, especially of sheep, and important biblical figures, including Abraham, Jacob, Moses, and David, were shepherds. The relationship of a shepherd to his flock provides an important metaphor for benevolent leadership in many biblical passages. A good example is Psalm 23, which begins:

> Yahweh is my shepherd
> I lack nothing
> In meadows of green grass he lets me lie.
> To the waters of repose he leads me. . . . (Ps. 23:1–
>   4, Jerusalem translation)

The society of the Hebrews, as described in the Bible, did indeed have some organizational resemblance to that of sheep. In both there was generally a single leader, but otherwise membership was comparatively egalitarian. Anthropologists have observed that this pattern is generally characteristic of semi-nomadic herders, in contrast to societies of agriculturalists with their complex gradations of status and power.

The metaphorical importance of sheep continues in the New Testament. On seeing Jesus for the first time, John the Baptist says, "Look, there is the lamb of God that takes away the sins of the world" (John 1:29). In the Book of Revelation, "the Lamb" is repeatedly used to refer to Christ.

Industrial Society

Large forests throughout the Near East and Europe were cut down to provide grass for sheep and other herd animals. Overgrazing drastically reduced the fertility of the soil in the Mediterranean region, contributing to the decline of ancient civilizations such as those of Greece and Mesopotamia. In a similar way, the forests that once covered most of central Spain were later cut down to make way for the prized merino sheep, a breed introduced to the region by Moors in the twelfth century. Rains then washed the topsoil away, doing enormous damage to Spanish agriculture.

Scholars often consider the beginning of farming during Neolithic times and the Industrial Revolution starting around the eighteenth century as the two great revolutionary changes in human society, and sheep played an important role in both changes. Modern animal husbandry began when the English farmer Robert Bakewell (1725–1795), an expert on sheep, developed scientific methods of breeding. This enabled people to produce sheep that would yield greater amounts and varieties of wool. In 1764, the spinning jenny was invented by the Scotsman James Hargreaves (c. 1720–1778). This machine helped people to exploit the wool, in a mechanized textile industry, which provided a model for mass production that was soon extended to many other kinds of manufacturing.

The new technologies created a demand for wool in unprecedented quantities, which, in turn, led to massive changes in the traditional societies of Britain and continental Europe. To clear the land for herding of sheep, many tenant farmers in Britain were forced off their ancestral lands in the late eighteenth and early nineteenth century in what is often known as the "tragedy of the commons." This, in turn, led to rapid urbanization, as well as increased emigration to the Americas.

A Romantic Image

Shepherding has always been celebrated by poets for the closeness it provides to nature and the opportunity it allows for contemplation. Around the middle of the eighth century BCE, the Greek poet Hesiod told how

the Muses had inspired him as he was tending sheep. In early modern times growing urbanization created a nostalgic longing for rural life, and the shepherd became a favorite figure of poetic literature. At the end of the novel *Don Quixote* by the Spaniard Miguel de Cervantes (1547–1616), the dreamy hero, disillusioned with the life of chivalry, decides to become a shepherd. The French queen Marie Antoinette (1755–1793) would dress and act the role of a shepherdess on a bucolic farm where she went to escape the intrigues of the French court. But the idealized image of the shepherd or shepherdess cherished by aristocrats was far from the reality of people who depended on sheep for a living.

As synthetic fabrics have become more widely available, the wool industry has become considerably less significant economically. Nevertheless, sheep became an important part of yet another potential upheaval in human society in 1996, when a sheep named Dolly (1996–2003) became the first mammal ever to be successfully cloned.

Boria Sax

Further Reading

Attenborough, D. (1987). *The first Eden: The Mediterranean world and man*. Boston: Little, Brown.

Caras, R. A. (1996). *A perfect harmony: The intertwining lives of animals and humans throughout history*. New York: Simon & Schuster.

Clutton-Brock, J. (1999). *A natural history of domesticated animals*. New York: Cambridge University Press.

Fournier, N., & Fournier, J. (1995). *In sheep's clothing: A handspinner's guide to wool*. Loveland, CO: Interweave Press.

Rifkin, Jeremy (1991). *Biosphere politics: A new consciousness for a new century*. New York: Crown.

Shinto

Shinto is one of Japan's major religions and it has played a key role in shaping Japanese attitudes toward the environment. Before the importation of Buddhism in the sixth century, Japanese worshiped the myriad *kami* (deities) who inhabited the Japanese Islands. They viewed *kami* as the divine manifestation of an animate universe, where trees and flowers, clouds and sky, mountains and forests, rivers and streams, and even the abundant wildlife possessed a sacred dimension. Over time, *kami* worship developed into a form of reverence shown toward all natural phenomena at simple shrines built in remote forests or villages. Through such shrines and their forested precincts, Japanese came to see the natural world as bubbling over with a mysterious and incomprehensible power, and worshiping and beseeching these *kami* became a way of trying to understand the environment. If Shinto can be said to have a theology, it would be embodied in the behavior of the *kami* and the notion that their worship helped Japanese cope with seasonal cycles and natural change.

History and Origins of Shinto

In the eighth century, after Japan imported Buddhism and other forms of East Asian culture from the continent, the ruling elite sought to formalize *kami* worship, and so they gave it a name, calling it Shinto (or sometimes Kannagara), meaning the "way of the *kami*," and *kami* worship became part of the "state religion" of the Yamato state (300–710 CE). Many scholars now believe that Japanese actually borrowed the word "Shinto" from an eighth-century Chinese word for Taoism. The Northern Zhou dynasty had manipulated Taoism to persecute Buddhism and bolster its power in late sixth-century China, and the Yamato state, persuaded by such models, transformed the study of the "way" into part of its state orthodoxy. In the eighth century, the Yamato state requested that Taoist priests travel to Japan from China, and in time the entire Japanese conception of empire and even the cult of the emperors themselves took on a Taoist flavor. Nonetheless, early Japanese probably did not identify, isolate, and categorize Shinto as their "religion." Rather, for a people who lived close to nature on a wild and mountainous archipelago, Shinto probably constituted everything they knew and sought to know about the natural world. There are several types of Shinto in Japan today, including folk Shinto, shrine Shinto, imperial-household Shinto, and state Shinto; but folk and shrine Shinto most directly shaped Japanese attitudes toward the environment.

To this day, two groups in Japan debate the exact origins of Shinto. Scholars tied to the Shinto establishment, such as those associated with Kogakkan and Kokugakuin universities (the two institutions that train official Shinto priests), maintain that Shinto is the indigenous religion of Japan. These scholars argue that Shinto has continued in an unbroken line since the earliest times to the present, and that the unique relationship with nature expressed in Shinto serves as one of the foundational pillars of traditional Japanese culture. By contrast, other scholars argue that the notion that Shinto is Japan's indigenous religion is the invention of the Meiji state (1868–1912 CE), and that Buddhism and Taoism are Japan's only real religions. These scholars argue that what we identify as Shinto is in fact a modified form of Taoism. They emphasize that Japan did more than just borrow the name "Shinto" from China in the eighth century, it borrowed the basic teachings and political worldview of Taoism. Eventually, Taoism destroyed or appropriated what remained of any earlier "indigenous" Japanese religion, and even Shinto icons, such as mirrors and swords, resonate with Taoist symbolic meanings.

Shinto and Japan's Imperium

In the seventh and eighth centuries, the Yamato clan, progenitors of Japan's imperial family and architects of Japan's first polity (called the Ritsuryo state), wielded Shinto as a tool with which to make sacred their expanding political authority. In some respects, the Ritsuryo state became a kind of Shinto-Buddhist theocracy, wherein the "way of the *kami*" legitimized the Yamato claim to political rulership throughout the central part of the Japanese Islands. Yamato officials even called political affairs *matsuri-goto*, a word that exemplifies the unity of religion and politics because *matsuri* are also sacred ceremonies and events. It was also at this juncture that the importation of East Asian culture and institutions compelled Japanese to canonize Shinto theology, much like Chinese had Taoism and Buddhism, and the earliest written Shinto prayers and genealogical mythologies emerge out of the historical mist of the eighth century. These prayers expose the two primary concerns of early Shinto: worship of the *kami* and the central place of the imperial family in Japanese political and spiritual life.

Shinto prayers or spells, called *norito*, provide a window into the sacred world of early Japan. Originally chanted by priests, *norito* celebrate fecundity, rice harvests, and powerful Shinto deities such as Amaterasu Omikami, the "sun goddess" and legendary progenitor of all Japanese people; but they also celebrate seasonal cycles and natural phenomena. *Norito* also expose the role of *kotodama* in Shinto chants, or the sacred power of certain words. Shinto mythologies, such as those contained in the *Nihon shoki* (720), even provide explanations for certain natural phenomena, such as the fertility of the soil and the richness of the forests. In one myth, the Shinto deity Tsukiyomi killed another deity named Ukemochi, and from the decaying remains of Ukemochi's body the five cardinal grains sprouted. Myths also tell of the deity Itakeru, who, after descending from the High Plain of Heaven with tree seeds, decided to plant them all in Japan. Later, the deity Susano-o pulled out hairs from his beard, scattered them, and they eventually grew into Japan's majestic ancient cedars.

Mountain Worship

Over the centuries, Shinto became even more deeply intertwined with Buddhism, Taoism, and Chinese yin-yang cosmologies. Still, many folk religions in Japan retained an emphasis on worshiping *kami* and revering the sacred nature of the natural environment and the creatures who inhabit it. Take Shugendo, or the practice of mountain asceticism, which can be traced to the ninth and tenth centuries, and which retained a strong Shinto flavor. Shugendo viewed certain mountains in Japan as sacred, and mountain ascetics, called *shugenja* or *yamabushi*, traveled deep into these mountains during harsh winter months to commune with the otherworldly *yama no kami*, or mountain deities. One sacred mountain, Mt. Sanjo in the Omine Mountains, remains so sacred that the Shugendo tradition prohibits women from climbing it, because Shinto views women's menstrual cycles as a form of pollution. (Indeed, Shinto abhors blood in general.) The most important sites in the Shugendo tradition, however, remain the three shrines at Mt. Kumano. Once mountain ascetics enter the supernatural realm of mountains such as Kumano, they perform various rituals and austerities, cast spells and recite incantations, all designed to purify themselves and worship the mountain deities, who often take both Buddhist and Shinto forms. Shugendo and

The Fushimi Inari Shrine in southeastern Kyoto at the site where the Inari deity was first worshiped. Japanese worshipers offer prayers and money at the main shrine as they summon shrine deities by ringing the *suzu* bells. The building is flanked by statues of the fox messenger. COURTESY BRETT WALKER.

other forms of folk Shinto also held rivers to be of particular importance, because in the spring, at about the same time the mountain deity entered villages to became the *ta no kami*, or field deity, tributaries from the mountains brought fresh water and fertility to the agrarian communities of Japan's lowlands. Mountain ascetics, drawing on Shinto mythologies that held rivers to be sources of purification, often cleansed themselves in these waters, letting waterfalls cascade over their heads in a practice called *misogi*.

Forest Worship

Nature worship in the Shinto tradition often referred to not only the external environment, but also a more inherent cosmology and spirituality created by nature, animals, and the people living in a particular region. Shinto could be highly localized and its view of nature decidedly cultured. In the eighth and ninth centuries, the view that certain local landscapes were sacred compelled the Yamato state to adopt early environmentalist policies. Historians point out how the construction of Shinto shrines and Buddhist temples led to deforestation and erosion in the Nara basin. Not wanting to offend the deities who lived in these forests (not to mention cause sediment build-up in important waterways), the emperor issued edicts in 821 prohibiting the felling of trees that bordered watersheds. By contrast, orders from 841 sought to protect sacred sites, such as the forest precincts of the Kami Mountains and the Kasuga Shrine in Nara Prefecture, by prohibiting hunting and cutting trees in that region. Highlighting the important place of trees in Shinto theology, originally the Japanese probably read *jinja*, the word for shrine, as *kamu tsu yashiro*, referring to a sacred forest or grove of trees. The place of Shinto worship—the shrine—might have been the forest itself at one time. To this day, Shinto priests adorn some large trees in shrine precincts with *shimenawa* ropes to signify their sacred status.

The Fox Messenger

If folk Shinto viewed mountains as a liminal space between this world and the other world, and trees as sacred, then the animals who inhabited these mountains and forests, from foxes to the now extinct Japanese wolf, took the form of otherworldly deities. Take Inari worship in Japan. Like Shugendo, Inari is highly syncretic, drawing on Shingon Buddhism, Chinese yin-yang cosmologies, and animistic notions of mountains as otherworldly realms and animals as otherworldly deities. Scholars believe that Japanese have worshiped the Inari deity and its fox messenger since at least the eighth century. Similar to debates surrounding the origins of Shinto, some scholars argue that Inari might be of Korean descent.

In the Shinto pantheon, the main deity of Inari belief is Inari. Its Buddhist incarnation, however, is called Dakiniten. The symbol of Inari worship is the fox, an animal that, in Japanese folklore, possesses shape-shifting powers which it uses sometimes to change itself into women in order to seduce men. Foxes can also possess people, and like most *kami*, foxes wield both *nigimitama* (benign spirit) and *aramitama* (dangerous spirit). Foxes could possess people; but some Inari worshipers also viewed these canids as protectors of rice crops. To show respect to the fox messenger, Inari worshipers sometimes make offerings of fried tofu and red beans to foxes. If the fox does not accept the offering, worshipers interpret this as an inauspicious sign. In northeastern Japan, Inari and its fox messenger also became associated with fishing *kami* and bountiful catches, while urbanites brought home *ofuda*, or talismans, from Inari shrines such as Fushimi and Toyokawa (the two largest Inari shrines), with images of foxes, designed to protect their homes from the ever-present danger of fire. Inari worship also tapped into the sacred power of mountains. Inari Mountain is located east of Kyoto at the southern end of the Higashiyama Range, and like Kumano and other Shugendo sites, mountain ascetics traveled there to commune with the Inari and other mountain deities.

The Wolf Messenger

By contrast, the Mitsumine Shrine, in Saitama Prefecture, holds the Japanese wolf as its divine messenger. Tucked among the peaks of Kumotori, Shiraiwa, and Myohogatake, Mitsumine was also a favorite haunt of mountain ascetics. One tributary of the river Aragawa that descends from Mitsumine has a purification waterfall, for example, marked by a traditional Shinto *torii*, or shrine archway. Mythology related to the shrine explains that in ancient times a white wolf deity helped the mythical unifier of Japan find his way after he had become lost in the mountains. At the entryway to the Mitsumine Shrine, rather than the traditional Yadaijin and Sadaijin statues (two deities who watch over the shrine precincts), two wolf statues guard the shrine instead. *Ema*, or wooden votive amulets, distributed by Mitsumine Shrine, also picture the guardian wolves with pups, iconography designed to signify agrarian and human fertility. Other shrines that used the wolf as a messenger, such as Yamazumi Shrine in Shizuoka Prefecture, also distribute talismans with images of wolves, iconography designed to protect people from theft and disease. In Japan's seventeenth and eighteenth centuries, peasants often placed such talismans with images of wolves around the perimeter of their grain fields, a gesture designed to ward off the sharp hooves and ravenous appetites of wild boar and deer.

Annual Shrine Ceremonies

To this day, Shinto shrines and their ceremonies stand at the center of community life in Japan. There are some 100,000 Shinto shrines throughout Japan (the largest and most splendid being the Ise, Izumo, and Yasukuni shrines), and about 75 percent of Shinto shrines are registered with the Jinja Honcho, a shrine organization located in Tokyo. The Shinto establishment claims to have some 110 million Shinto practitioners, some 90 percent of the total Japanese population. These Shinto shrines and their practitioners have created a certain degree of uniformity in their worship practices: worshipers rinse their mouths and wash their hands at the *temizuya* before entering under a *torii* archway and into the shrine precincts, and they summon shrine deities by ringing the *suzu* bell. Annual events at shrines, such as those documented at the Suwa Shrine in Nagasaki, include the Great Purification rituals of June and December, the festival of New Rice in November, and New Year celebrations. In purification rituals, Shinto priests wave branches from the *sakaki* tree, native only to Japan, to frighten away evil spirits and pollutants. Today, such purification rituals are even performed to cleanse newly purchased automobiles, whereas in the *jichinsai* ceremony, Shinto priests purify and revere the *kami* of the earth by blessing ground that is to be broken during construction projects.

Controversies

Ironically, despite Shinto's historical reverence toward the environment, Japan boasts one of the worst environmental records. In the twentieth century, Japanese paved over much of their once splendid landscape with useless concrete, littered beaches with even more useless erosion-prevention devices called "tetrapods," and blackened the sky and poisoned the waterways with industrial garbage. Still, even in the face of such damage, some Shinto priests, such as the High Priest of the Tsubaki Shrine in Mie Prefecture, have tried to turn Shinto into a modern form of environmentalism designed to save the world from industrial pollution and the overexploitation of resources. The High Priest Yamamoto Yukitaka has turned to Shinto to articulate a new relationship with the natural world, one with ancient roots in *kami* worship. Yamamoto explains, "The cosmic process called Great Nature, the collective reality we call the universe, is honored even by those *kami* that brought it into being. Within the vast compass of Great Nature, therefore, together, things that exist are given life and thus human beings become able to enjoy the happiness of truth and sincerity. This is the principle that binds heaven and earth, which is called Kannagara, the Way of the Kami. The way known as Kannagara can be understood as the character that lies at the foundation of the existence of all humanity, the principle of mutually cooperative peaceful coexistence" (Picken 2002, 2000).

Even in Japan's industrial age, folk and shrine Shinto continue to emphasize ties between human beings, the myriad *kami*, and the divine nature of the natural environment. To date, however, Shinto's power has failed to stem the tide of Japan's looming environmental crisis.

Brett L. Walker

Further Reading

Breen, J., & Teeuwen, M. (Ed.). (2000). *Shinto in history: Ways of the kami*. Honolulu: University of Hawai'i Press.

Nelson, J. K. (1996). *A year in the life of a Shinto shrine*. Seattle: University of Washington Press

Picken, S. D. B. (2002). *Shinto: Meditations for revering the earth*. Berkeley, CA: Stone Bridge Press.

Shrimp

While there are various crustacean species that are commonly referred to as shrimp, this term usually refers to small marine decapod crustaceans that are closely related to lobsters and crabs. Like lobsters, their bodies are laterally compressed and have ten pairs of jointed thoracic legs and abdominal swimming appendages called swimmerets. Some marine shrimp are predators that live in novel environments such as deep sea vents or in sea anemones, but most economically important species are detritivores (consumers of organic debris) living near coastlines, where tides and estuaries provide a reliable food source. Some species live in brackish and freshwater habitats. Many freshwater shrimp are becoming increasingly rare, and four species are on the U.S. endangered species list.

Many coastal species migrate in the spring to the open ocean to reproduce. Females typically lay hundreds to thousands of eggs. Upon hatching, larvae drift as plankton back coastward, arriving at high-nutrient habitats such as wetlands and estuaries. Very few larvae survive to adulthood, but they are an important food source for other organisms.

Shrimp have been an important human food source since prehistoric times. Shrimpers today exploit wild populations using trawl nets dragged along the ocean bottom or farm shrimp by clearing coastal wetlands to form enclosures. Although there are many species of marine shrimp, the bulk of the world's wild and farmed shrimp are large bodied species in the family of Penaeidae. Most are harvested or cultivated near coastlines, but there is also an associated offshore fishing industry. Nearly every coastal nation hosts a shrimp industry, but Thailand, Ecuador, Mexico, India, China, and Indonesia are the major shrimp exporters. Currently harvests exceed 3 million metric tons per year, although there is concern in many areas about recent declines in catch.

Like other fisheries, the shrimp industry has expanded rapidly over the last twenty years. More boats are trawling the waters, particularly near coastlines. Problems associated with mortality of by-catch (organisms accidentally caught in nets) is high. Turtle mortality led to the requirement to use turtle-excluding devices in some fisheries, but far more important is the mortality of fish species such as herring, crab, mullet, flounder, and tuna. By-catch of finfish by shrimpers exceeds the finfish industry harvest each year by 20 percent.

Worldwide, many shrimp populations are overharvested. The U.N. Food and Agriculture Organization (FAO) has stated that the current world shrimp industry is harvesting two times the estimated long-term sustainable limit. In some areas, decreases in catch have led to violent confrontations between competing boats. In Brazil, poor fishermen in canoes are increasingly in the way of trawlers that must now fish close to shore. In Texas, increasing numbers of immigrant-owned boats are seen as competition by the established industry.

Since the 1970s, declines in wild catches have led to a boom in shrimp aquaculture. Because it is difficult to breed shrimp in captivity, young wild shrimp are sequestered in shallow water often by clearing vegetation in wetlands such as mangrove swamps, or by flooding rice fields. Approximately 1.3 million hectares have been converted in this way, mostly in Southeast Asia and China. Growing shrimp in confined areas increases the risk of disease, so aquaculture relies on antibiotics, algicides, pesticides, and fertilizers to maximize production, with negative consequences for the environment.

Environmentalists are divided over what to do about the shrimp industry. Shrimp are a high-value export product and an important source of income for many developing countries, but profits come at an extremely high cost to the environment. Seventy percent of the world's shrimp catch is exported to the United States and to Japan. Nongovernmental organizations have been pressuring the industry to encourage consumers to purchase shrimp labeled as sustainably harvested, although the World Trade Organization has claimed such labeling violates free-trade practices. Nongovernmental organizations such as the FAO, the World Bank, the Global Aquaculture Alliance, and the World Wildlife Fund (WWF), as well as shrimp producers, traders, and retailers are developing guidelines for sustainable shrimp aquaculture. One goal is to promote smaller, lower-density aquaculture, where fertilization and antibiotics are reduced because shrimp are less crowded, healthier, and forage on wild foods. Nigeria, Thailand, and other developing countries are passing laws to protect mangroves and limit development of inland, high-intensity shrimp farms.

Vicki Medland

Further Reading

Ahmed, F. (1997). *In defence of land and livelihood: Coastal communities and the shrimp industry in Asia.* Ottawa, Canada: Consumers' Association of Penang, CUSO, Inter Pares, & Sierra Club of Canada.

Browdy, C. L., & Jory, D. E. (Eds.). (2001). The new wave. *Proceedings of the Special Session on Sustainable Shrimp Culture, Aquaculture 2001.* Baton Rouge, LA: The World Aquaculture Society.

Durrenberger, P. E. (1996). *Gulf coast soundings: People and policy in the Mississippi shrimp industry.* Lawrence: University of Kansas Press.

Gulland, J., & Rothschild, B. J. (Eds.). *Penaeid shrimps: Their biology and management.* Farnham, UK: Fishing News Books.

Mohan, C. V. (1996). *Health management strategy for a rapidly developing shrimp industry: An Indian perspective.* Rome: Food and Agriculture Organization. (Food and Agriculture Organization of the United Nations Fisheries Technical Paper No. 0 (360) 75–87).

Sierra Club

Founded in 1892, the Sierra Club has consistently advocated the protection of national parks and many wilderness areas. The Sierra Club was the brainchild of Robert Underwood Johnson (1853–1937), editor of the influential *Century* magazine. He came west in the early 1890s to persuade John Muir (1838–1914), the pioneering wilderness preservationist, then involved in fruit farming, to resume writing his articles about the wilderness. He pledged to publish Muir's writings in the *Century*. Muir, in turn, asked Johnson to lobby in his magazine for the establishment by Congress of a new national park at Yosemite in California. This new park was established in 1890, and it later incorporated portions of the smaller state park of the same name.

Muir, however, drew Johnson's attention to the fact that no national organization to protect Yosemite and Yellowstone parks existed in the early 1890s. Johnson's suggestion of a "defense association" led a group of Californians to form the Sierra Club in June 1892. In the words of Holway R. Jones, the Club "devoted itself to the study and protection of national scenic resources, particularly of mountain regions." Muir, characterized by a contemporary as a person "who lacked the social instincts of the average man," nonetheless accepted the Club's presidency, a post he held for twenty-two years until his death. Muir himself hoped to "be able to do something for wilderness and make the mountains glad."

In its early years, the Club was instrumental in bringing about the creation of Mount Rainier (1899) and Glacier (1910) National Parks. An early test for the Club came when some San Francisco developers determined to provide new sources of water for their city following the 1906 earthquake. They advocated a dam on the Tuolumne River in the Hetch-Hetchy Canyon of Yosemite. The majority of the Club felt strong opposition to the project. Their effort was spearheaded by attorney William Colby (1875–1964), then its secretary and a longtime Club director. Muir took the position, in the words of one friendly critic, "Me and God

and the Rock where God put it," a viewpoint with which most members seemed to agree. But some conservationists, notably Gifford Pinchot, favored the project. The issue split the Club, and some dam supporters resigned. After a seven-year struggle (1906–1913), the dam was approved by President Wilson in 1913, and Muir died, a broken man, the next year. Thereafter, the Club tended to oppose economic development in national parks but not everywhere else. The group consistently pressed Congress for the establishment of a national park service, which was achieved in 1916, and for new and expanded national parks in the West. Other early Club leaders included Joseph Le Conte (1823–1901) and his son Joseph Nisbet Le Conte (1870–1950), University of California professors. The younger Le Conte succeeded Muir as president and held other Club offices between 1898 and 1940. William Colby succeeded J. N. Le Conte as president (1917), and was a director for forty-nine years. He initiated the Club's "high trips" into mountain regions in 1901 and led them until 1929. He was also first chair of the California Park Commission (1927–1936).

The Middle Years

Club membership rose modestly, from 1,000 in 1908 to around 10,000 in the mid-1950s. During the 1920s, 1930s, and 1940s, the Club primarily concerned itself with the exploration, protection, and enjoyment of wilderness, the responsible use of natural resources, and with the publication of many environmental books, reports, and other informational and educational materials. In 1949, the Club sponsored a High Sierra Wilderness Conference, which was to be the first of fourteen biennial wilderness conferences. David Brower (1918–2000), an active Club member since 1935, and a board member from 1941, was appointed the Club's first paid executive director in 1952. He had been a publicity director at Yosemite in the late 1930s, and as an Army officer, had helped to train American mountain troops during World War II.

Mid-Twentieth Century to the Present

During Brower's tenure (1952–1969) the Club entered a more militant phase. Among many other initiatives, it opposed government efforts to build dams in Glacier National Park in Montana, King's Canyon in California, Glen Canyon in Arizona, the Grand Canyon, and Dinosaur National Monument in Utah. Most of these dams were never built. It endorsed Congressional establishment of a national wilderness system, which finally came into being in 1964. But the Club's increasing political activism caused the Internal Revenue Service to take away its tax-deductible status. Brower found himself increasingly out of step with the Board, which requested his resignation in 1969. In that year, the Club had nearly 70,000 members. Brower later organized Friends of the Earth and the Earth Island Institute.

Western Canada, the first Club chapter outside the United States, was organized in 1972. The Club was involved in the first conference on the International Environment in Stockholm (1972), and sponsored the International Earthcare Conference in New York (1975). In 1972, a Club lawsuit led to a ban on the domestic use of the pesticide DDT. During the final decades of the twentieth century, the Club continued to press for the establishment of more national parks and monuments and the protection of existing ones. It vigorously supported efforts by Congress to improve the nation's environment and air quality. In 1980, it gave strong support to federal superfund legislation, intended to clean up toxic waste dumps, and has since backed the periodic reauthorizations of those enactments. In 1984, the Club won a lawsuit that required the Environmental Protection Agency to regulate radioactive pollutants. At the end of the 1990s, some consideration was being given to dismantling the dam at Hetch-Hetchy. By the year 2000, approximately 700,000 Sierra Club members belonged to 58 chapters in the United States and Canada, which in turn were subdivided into nearly 500 smaller groups.

Keir B. Sterling

Further Reading

Cohen, M. P. (1988). *The history of the Sierra Club, 1892–1970*. San Francisco: Sierra Club Books.

Fox, S. (1981). *John Muir and his legacy: The American conservation movement*. Boston: Little Brown.

Jones, H. R. (1965). *John Muir and the Sierra Club: The battle for Yosemite*. San Francisco: Sierra Club Books.

Pierson, B. E. (2002). *Still the wild river runs: Congress, the Sierra Club, and the fight to save the Grand Canyon*. Tucson: University of Arizona Press.

Turner, T. (1991). *Sierra Club: 100 years of protecting nature*. New York: H. N. Abrams in association with the Sierra Club.

Sierra Nevada Mountains

The Sierra Nevada Mountains are a mountain chain, 400 miles long and between 30–50 miles wide located in the United States in the northern two-thirds of the state of California. Within their 5 million acres lie 3 National Parks, 6 National Forests, 14 major rivers, 7 of the highest mountain peaks in North America, thousands of species of plants, and numerous species of birds, mammals, and amphibians.

It is generally agreed that 100 million years ago, the Sierra Nevada pluton was formed and, since then, various tectonic and gradational processes have resulted in its present complex geomorphology. The most recent tectonic processes involve volcanism, which occurred around 730,000 years ago, and are associated with the still seismically active Long Valley Caldera. Remnants of the volcanism are exhibited in numerous cinder cones and ancient basaltic flows such as the Devil's Postpile and the Mammoth Mountain volcano, all located on the tectonically active east side of the Sierra Nevada Mountains.

The present shape of the Sierra Nevada Mountains is a result of geologic uplift along its eastern length as recently as 5 million years ago. It is this vertical displacement eastward along its length that gives rise to Mt. Whitney, which at 14,494 feet is the highest mountain peak in the coterminous United States. In addition, 7 peaks surrounding Mt. Whitney reach up over 14,000 feet, allowing for spectacular vistas of the High Sierra. In this alpine region, hardy hikers can observe where Pleistocene glaciations once covered present-day alpine meadows, as examples of glacially carved features such as arêtes, cols, and cirques exist alongside hundreds of small remnant glaciers. In contrast, the western slope of the Sierra Nevada Mountains is gentle and, because it faces moist, prevailing winds from the Pacific Ocean nearly a hundred miles away, it contains the drainage basins of more than 14 major rivers. The largest trees in the world, the giant Sequoia Redwoods, are located in Sequoia National Park. Also located on the western slope is Yosemite National Park, one of the earliest and most visited national parks in North America. Yosemite Valley presents a spectacular example of a glacially carved valley and exhibits examples of other weathering processes, such as Half Dome, a huge granite face worn by exfoliation.

Prior to European settlement, several Native American tribes occupied territory in the Sierra Nevada Mountains. During this time the total Native American population in California numbered 300,000 and included small groups, which clustered in the foothills and river valleys throughout California. Because of the diversity of the Sierra Nevada mountain environment, regionalization of Native American tribes occurred, resulting in several distinct tribal groups, each occupying a specific area. Such tribes included the Konkow, Washo, Nisenan, Miwok, Paiute, Monache, Shoshone, Foothill Yokuts, Tubatulabal, Kawaiisu, and Kitanemuk. As California became attractive for European settlement, thousands of Native Americans died as a result of European diseases to which they had no natural protection. The discovery of gold in the Sierra Nevada Mountains spurred Spanish settlement, further reducing the Native American presence and pushing them farther into less desirable areas.

Since the discovery of placer gold in 1848 at Sutter's Mill, the western flank of the Sierra Nevada mountains has experienced increasing human settlement. Many present-day towns along these western foothills were founded to accommodate the early miners and their needs. After California gained statehood, these towns flourished, and today they serve as historical sites drawing tourists from around the world. Beside gold, lumbering and livestock ranching economies developed to support a growing permanent population.

Declaring the Sierra Nevada Mountains "the range of light" because of its spectacular mountain vistas, John Muir founded the Sierra Club in 1892 and a dialogue about conservation of the Sierras began. In the last half-century this dialogue has increased to include the Federal Sierra Nevada Ecosystem Project, the Mountain Resources Defense Council, the Sierra Business Council, the Nature Conservancy, and even prominent California senators, each agency expressing concerns regarding the preservation of the Sierra Nevada ecosystem. The focus is presently on sustainability in light of the need for economic activities to exist alongside the natural beauty of these mountains. Everyone agrees that this area is unique and deserves our best effort at preserving its integrity. Eighty-five percent of the Sierra's ancient trees have been logged, 200 of its plant species have become rare or endangered, and 69 species of fauna are at risk of extinction because of habitat loss from logging, mining, livestock ranching, and urbanization. On the Sierra Nevada's western slopes, auto congestion and smog have resulted in some of the worst air quality readings in North America. Today, many inhabitants of the area, as well as environmentalists and nature conservationists worldwide, would like to see these economic activities controlled or even stopped.

Carol Ann DeLong

Further Reading

Adler, T. (1996, June 15). A plan for the struggling Sierra Nevada. *Science News, 149,* 375.

At work in the range of light. (1994, March–April). *Sierra, 79,* 127.

Bean, W., & Rawls, J. J. (2000). *California: An interpretive history.* New York: McGraw-Hill.

Forstenzer, M. (1997, March–April). What's wrong in the Sierra? A look at an ecosystem in trouble. *Audubon, 99,* 14.

Hornbeck, D. (1983). *California patterns: A geographical and historical atlas.* New York: Mayfield.

King, P. B. (1977). *The evolution of North America.* Princeton, NJ: Princeton University Press

Polster, S. (1998). Status of the Sierra Nevada. *Planning, Sierra Business Council, 6*(4), 20.

Selby, W. A. (2000). *Rediscovering the golden state.* New York: John Wiley & Sons.

Shedding light on John Muir's "range of light." (1996, Spring). *The Amicus Journal, 18,* 51.

Sierra Nevada plan unveiled. (2001, Spring). *The Amicus Journal, 23,* 43.

Wuerthner, G. (1993, Winter). Dimming the range of light. *Wilderness, 57,* 10.

Silk and Silkworm

Silk is secreted from glands in the mouth of certain moth caterpillars and from the tail spinnerets of spiders. It is a complex protein substance made up of a tough elastic protein, fibroin, which forms an inner core, and a gelatinous protein, sericin, which coats it with a sticky covering. Although spider silk is of tremendous ecological importance in catching insect prey in spider webs and as silken "parachutes" for the aerial dispersal of spiderlings, it is too thin and sticky for use in fabrics. About twenty moth species from several families are used worldwide for commercial silk production, and the gypsy moth (*Lymantria dispar*) was introduced into the United States to be tested as a possible source of silk, only to become a notorious forestry pest defoliating large areas of trees. However, the oriental silkworm (*Bombyx mori*), wholly domesticated and unknown in the wild, dominates what is now a major international industry.

Silk production, especially rearing the silkworms, is a laborious process. A silk moth female, bloated and with shriveled wings incapable of flight, lays 350–500 eggs. After a short dormant period, the tiny caterpillars (silkworms) hatch and are reared, in captivity, on freshly harvested mulberry leaves, usually laid on trays. Because of the limitations of harvesting this natural foodplant, which is deciduous and produces leaves only during the growing season, a synthetic food material is also being increasingly used, especially in Japan. After about three weeks the caterpillars have reached full size (as large and fat as a thumb) and pupate. Each caterpillar now takes two or three days to wrap itself in a single white strand of silk 500–2,000 meters long and about 30 microns (thousandths of a millimeter) in diameter. In nature the silk cocoon of a moth caterpillar protects the hard pupa (chrysalis) in which metamorphosis into the adult moth takes place.

Only a small number of cocoons are kept for rearing the next generation of moths; they are sorted by weight to identify males and (heavier) females, and the remainder of the cocoons are graded by size and shape for use in thread production. Immersion in boiling water for a few minutes dissolves the sericin, which acts as a natural glue to stick the silk strands together, and the cocoons begin to unravel. Placed on spindles, the silk cocoons can now be unwrapped by machine, usually twisting several strands together, and this becomes the raw silk thread for dying and weaving.

Ancient China

The origins of sericulture (silk production) are shrouded in the mists of prehistory, but the first records from China date to about 2600 BCE. China is the natural center for the silkworm and its foodplant, the white mulberry tree (*Morus alba*). The Chinese Empress Hsi Ling-Shi (also known as Te-ling-she), the principal princess of Emperor Hwang-te, is credited by some as the discoverer of silk's potential as a fiber for weaving in about 2640 BCE. Legend has it that when a silk moth cocoon was dropped into a cup of hot tea, it unraveled into a single silk strand. The oldest known silks are threads and embroidery estimated at being forty-five hundred years old.

Silk was one of the earliest recorded commodities shipped across the globe, from China to Japan, India, the Middle East, and Europe. The Silk Road was a famous overland trade route out of China, but it was not a single route, and many other items were transported along it. Metals, ivory, precious stones, and glass moved eastward while ceramics, jade, bronze, lacquer,

and silk moved west. The various routes left the cultural capital of China, Changan (now Xian), skirted the Gobi and Taklimakan Deserts to Kashgar, branched south to India and east to Tashkent, Samarqand, the Caspian Sea, and thence to the Mediterranean. Although silk was known to the Romans from about 50 BCE, and after that there was always a trickle of silk into the West, major trade along the Silk Road to the Roman Empire did not begin until the early centuries of the Christian era. At the height of the Silk Road's importance, in the seventh and eighth centuries, Changan was one of the largest cities in Asia, with a population of nearly 2 million.

Despite the high monetary value of burgeoning trade along the Silk Road, arguably the most significant commodity to be transported was not silk, but rather religion and philosophy. Buddhism went to China from India, bringing immense artistic and cultural changes in its wake. Later Christianity made inroads, following the Church of Rome's outlawing of the Nestorian sect in 432 CE.

For many centuries the Silk Road was a thriving elongated community of towns stretching across central Asia. But it declined during medieval times because of increasing political instability in the area. Many settlements were lost under the shifting sands of China's Taklimakan Desert until they were rediscovered by archeologists and explorers in the nineteenth century. Silk continued to be traded in greater and greater quantities, but long-distance trade between East and West became increasingly maritime as Western ship-building techniques and seamanship improved.

China maintained a monopoly on silk production for over twenty-five hundred years, safeguarding its silk industry by threat of the death penalty. But in about 150 BCE silk moth eggs were smuggled out to India and later to Persia (Iran), Turkey, and beyond. Silk is now produced worldwide, but the market is still dominated by China and Japan.

The Cloth of Kings

Silk thread and the cloth woven from it are light, strong, flexible, and hard-wearing but have a luxurious sheen much sought after for the production of clothes, tapestries, and other fabric goods. Despite the costly process of making silk, it has always been prized and has commanded high prices. Although silk originally was the cloth of kings and emperors, used only for the highest-quality robes and hangings, modern commercial production has brought the price of silk down to the point that it is accessible to most, at least in the richer Western developed world. But silk is still revered for its high quality and is an important fabric for special occasions and formal clothes. Japan is currently the largest consumer of silk, particularly in the manufacture of richly decorated dress kimonos.

Today the word *silk* has been misappropriated by marketing departments and advertising companies to promote anything from cigarettes and chocolates to paint and cosmetics. Despite the wide availability of relatively cheap silk, it remains a potent byword for wealth and luxury. Sadly, even a basic knowledge of its creation by lowly worms is not nearly as widespread as its consumption by a fashion-hungry populace.

Richard Jones

Further Reading

Feltwell, J. (1990). *The story of silk*. London: Alan Sutton.
Hopkirk, P. (1980). *Foreign devils on the Silk Road*. Oxford, UK: Oxford University Press.

Silver

Silver is a shiny, white metal. It is a chemical element, atomic number 47 in the periodic table of the elements, and has an average atomic weight of 107.87 atomic mass units. Silver is similar in physical properties to gold and copper and has many useful qualities. It is a very malleable and ductile metal. Silver is the best conductor of heat and electricity of all the metals. It is resistant to both acids (with the exception of nitric acid) and oxidation—making silver one of the noble (unreactive) metals. Silver does tarnish in the presence of sulfur compounds. Some silver compounds are highly sensitive to light.

Silver is a relatively uncommon element in the earth's crust, with an average crustal abundance of .07 parts per million. It is the sixty-seventh most abundant element in the earth's crust. The geological processes of the earth have created small but scattered deposits of silver that are far more concentrated than the average crustal abundance implies. As a result, small amounts of silver have been readily available throughout history in many parts of the world.

Uses of Silver

Silver can be found in some deposit sites in its native (elemental) form or in an easily processed mineral form. Since silver is easy to process and work with, it has a long history of human use. The earliest documented use of silver was in Europe and the Mediterranean region around 4000 BCE. For much of human history, silver has been used mainly as currency and for decorative purposes (as jewelry and silverware, for example). Pure silver is very soft, and it is often alloyed with copper to make it harder. In the modern era, decorative silver is usually in the form of sterling silver. Sterling silver is 92.5 percent silver and 7.5 percent copper. The demand for silver has changed in modern times as the traditional uses of silver have been surpassed by uses that depend more on its chemical properties.

In 2000, only 33 percent of the world's consumption of silver was in traditional products like jewelry, silverware, and coins. Over 40 percent was in industrial applications. This category is very broad, but the largest area of consumption is in electrical and electronics products. Silver's properties of high electrical conductivity and resistance to oxidation make it an ideal material for use in these types of products. Photography needs accounted for another 25 percent of the total consumption. Silver salts are the active ingredients on film and printing papers used to create negatives. Silver also has small but important uses in the chemical and medical industries.

The United States consumed 22 percent of the world's silver in 2000. The sectors of silver use in the United States were proportioned differently than that for the world as a whole, with photography needs accounting for more than 50 percent of the total consumption of silver. Industrial applications accounted for nearly 20 percent of the total consumption. The traditional uses of silver in jewelry and silverware accounted for less than 10 percent.

Sources of Silver

There are four potential sources of silver available to meet consumption needs. Silver can be mined from the earth, recycled from old scrap material, obtained from government sales of official silver stocks, or obtained from sales by private investors. Silver production from mining accounted for over 60 percent of the world's annual silver supply in 2000. The recycling of silver accounted for nearly 20 percent, and net sales (sales minus buying) from governments and investors added another 20 percent to the world's supply of silver. In some years, buying by governments and investors exceeds their sales, with the result being greater demand for and less availability of silver.

The primary source of silver is from mining ores. The mining industry provides silver in two ways. Ores that consist of native silver and silver sulfides are mined primarily for the silver. These types of operations accounted for about 25 percent of mined silver production in 2000. The majority of mined silver, however, is obtained as a by-product of lead or zinc mining (40 percent), copper mining (24 percent), and gold mining (15 percent). The prominence of by-product silver has arisen because of the continuing improvement in technologies that make possible metal concentration and separation.

Mine sources of silver are scattered around the world, with the Americas being the leading region of production. The countries with the most productive silver mines in 2000 were, in order of production, Mexico, Peru, Australia, the United States, China, Canada, Chile, and Poland. Silver is mined in a number of states in the United States. Eleven mines accounted for 80 percent of U.S. production in 2000, and about half of the total output was from primary silver ore sources. Nevada and Idaho lead in silver production.

Recycled silver is obtained from photographic waste, the recycling of catalysts, and electronic scrap. The recovery of silver from photographic waste is very inefficient, with only about 20 percent of the potential silver values being recovered. The primarily sources of silver scrap are the United States, Japan, and Europe.

Silver and the Environment

In its elemental form, silver is not hazardous to the environment. However, the presence of excessive silver in a person's diet over time can lead to a disfiguring skin condition called argyria, in which the skin turns a gray-blue color. Silver's major negative environmental impact has been caused by its mining and processing. Silver minerals and their associated minerals contain sulfur. The mining and processing of silver can expose the sulfur to water and air and be a cause of acid mine drainage and acid rain. The processing of gold-silver ores often uses cyanide, which means there is always a potential risk of dangerous cyanide spills. All of these potential environmental hazards can be safely avoided with proper procedures, but those procedures are not always followed.

Gary A. Campbell

Further Reading

Craig, J. (1998). Silver. In M. S. Coyne, & C. W. Allin (Eds.). *Natural Resources*: *Vol. 3*. (pp. 732–736). Pasadena, CA: Salem Press.

Gold Fields Mineral Services. (2001). Silver. In *Mining Annual Review 2001*. London: The Mining Journal.

Hilliard, H. E. (2000). Silver. In *Minerals Yearbook*. (pp. 70.1–70.13). Washington, DC: U.S. Geological Survey.

Slovakia

(2002 est. pop. 5.4 million)

Slovakia was established on 1 January 1993 after the peaceful split of the former Czech and Slovak Federative Republic. The capital is Bratislava. The territory of Slovakia is 49,035 square kilometers.

Slovakia is a parliamentary democracy. It is in a period of transition from a centrally planned economy to a market economy. Its prevailing industrial activity, inherited from its socialist past, is heavy industry (metallurgy, heavy machinery, chemicals, power generation).

The State and Development of the Slovak Environment

Intensive human activities, a preference for highly polluting heavy industry as well as industrial agriculture, lack of the environmental legislation and institutions, and relatively limited environmental awareness among the population has resulted in much environmental damage in Slovakia's recent past. On the other hand, Slovakia is a country with great natural and landscape diversity, protected in nine national parks and about six hundred nature reserves.

Since the overthrow of the Communist regime in 1989, most environmental indicators have been improving, some of them quite rapidly. In part, this is because industrial activity and related pollution peaked at the end of 1980s, followed by a period of economic slowdown brought about by systemic changes after 1989. In particular, the old reliance on heavy industry and industrialized agriculture has been reduced. A partial improvement in the field of eco-efficiency has also been recorded during 1990s. Last but not least, environmental legislation, programs, and institutions were adopted, created, and improved.

The biggest environmentally relevant questions in the recent period are how to develop the Danube river region (with some favoring a technocratic solution, such as developing hotels, parking lots, and stadiums and others a national park; some supporting big dams and others integrated water management), how to solve energy problems (the debate being between nuclear power and sustainable energy), where to invest (in highways and shopping malls, or in nature-oriented projects), and how to develop (with some advocating direct and indirect support of heavy industry and other environmentally unfriendly activities and others supporting more environmentally friendly, conservation-oriented sustainable development).

Environmentally Relevant Acts and Documents

The Constitution of Slovakia commits the nation to building a socially and ecologically oriented market economy. In 1992 the General Environmental Act was passed. Among other important documents that can be mentioned are the Strategy, Principles and Priorities of the State Environmental Policy (adopted by the government in Resolution 619 in 1993), the National Environmental Action Programme I (1996) and II (1999), the National Sustainable Development Strategy (2001) and *Toward a Sustainable Slovakia: National Study* (1995), a report compiled by a nongovernmental organization (NGO) called Society for Sustainable Living in the Slovak Republic.

International Relationships, Controversies, and Cooperation

The biggest recent environmentally relevant bilateral controversies with neighbor countries are the dispute involving two dams on the Danube River where the river creates a natural border between Hungary and Slovakia and the dispute between Slovakia and Austria over the continued operation of one nuclear power plant (Jaslovske Bohunice, about 60 kilometers from the Austrian boundary) and the completion of a second (the Mochovce Nuclear Power Plant, about 120 kilometers from the border).

The Hungarian and Czechoslovak governments started the Danube dam project in 1977, with support from the Soviet Union. Opposition to the dams on environmental grounds started in both Hungary and Czechoslovakia in the early 1980s, and Hungary later suspended its contribution and subsequently decided to withdraw from the project. For their part, Slovak environmentalists were also active in their opposition. At the time of Czechoslovakia's dissolution, public opinion (especially in Hungary) was that the dams would mean that farmland, forests, and wetlands would be lost and freshwater damaged, while an earthquake might precipitate a major flood disaster. The Slovak government, pressured by business lobbies and nationalists, took the opposite position and completed the project, which diverted water into an artificial channel only on Slovak territory. The project destroyed more than 30 square kilometers of floodplain woodland and created an artificial river system that now needs permanent energy input for its management. Hungary challenged Slovakia through the International Court of Justice and, although the Court ruled that Slovakia should not have proceeded unilaterally, it also upheld the legality of the original agreement. Dispute over the interpretation of the Court decision continues.

As for the nuclear power plant controversy, the energy sector lobby, which favors the plant, has prevailed. However, environmental NGOs have submitted an alternative energy policy, based on a combination of energy savings, improved energy efficiency, and utilization of renewable energy resources. Moreover, pressure from antinuclear Austria has had a positive impact with regard to improving nuclear security. In addition to these controversies, there are several positive examples of good bilateral or multilateral cooperation, such as common national parks (especially with Poland), water management (with Austria), and support of international environmental NGOs.

Mikulas Huba

Further Reading

Huba, M. (1997). Slovak Republic. In J. Klarer & B. Moldan (Eds.), *The environmental challenge for central European economies in transition*. New York: John Wiley & Sons.

Institute for Public Affairs (1996–2001). *Slovakia: Global reports on the state of the society* (1995–2001). Bratislava, Slovakia: Institute for Public Affairs.

Ministry of the Environment of the Slovak Republic. (1993–2001*). Report on the state of the environment in the Slovak Republic* (1993–2000). Bratislava, Slovakia: Ministry of the Environment

Statistical Office of the Slovak Republic. (1993–2001). *Statistical yearbook of the Slovak Republic* (1993–2001). Bratislava, Slovakia: Statistical Office.

Smelters

Smelters (or smelteries) are facilities or works where smelting takes place. Smelting is the pyrochemical process that heats ore to the molten or liquid state so that a desired metal may be separated from non-desired minerals, called gangue. Materials called fluxes are usually added to the ore during smelting to aid in the separation of metal from gangue.

Metals exist in two states in nature: either in their pure or native state, or chemically bound with other elements to form mineral compounds. If a mineral deposit is rich enough in a particular metal to make extraction of the metal practicable, the mineral deposit is classified as an ore. Humans first used metals found in the native state, but at least seven millennia ago people had learned to extract metals from ore using metallurgical processes in crude smelters.

Although the narrow definition of smelting entails bringing ore to the liquid state, smelting also more broadly encompasses several sequential steps by which heat is used to separate the desired metal or metals from the other elements in a given ore. There are generally three such steps: 1) roasting or calcining, in which heat is used, short of the melting temperature, to drive off volatile materials; 2) smelting, in which heat is used to bring material to the melting temperature, at which point chemical and physical changes take place causing a further separation of metal from other elements; and 3) refining, in which heat is used to treat the often impure product of smelting and to produce a pure (or nearly pure) metal.

Each step in the smelting process produces a product and one or more by-products, which may be further processed but which generally are discharged into the environment as waste products. The by-product of all three stages of smelting is smoke. In addition to whatever conventional smoke may be given off by the fuel used, smelting produces metallurgical smoke consisting of volatile substances and dust. For example, many metals exist in nature as sulfide minerals—they are bound chemically with sulfur and perhaps other elements. Thus, galena is the sulfide of lead and pyrite is the sulfide of iron. A purpose, then, of both roasting and smelting is to drive off the sulfur, which historically was discharged into the atmosphere as sulfur dioxide. Smelter smoke also carries considerable quantities of dust composed of the metals and other elements present in the ore and fuel. A by-product of the smelting and refining stages of the process is slag, which contains nondesired elements such as silicon,

calcium, aluminum, or iron that are separated from the desired metal during the molten phase (less than economically recoverable amounts of aluminum or iron are often present in the ores of other metals, such as copper, and so are considered gangue in those cases). Tailings are a by-product not of smelting but of the processes of milling and concentrating, which are purely mechanical processes that often precede smelting.

The first metal known from archaeological evidence to have been used by humans was copper, but analysis of these artifacts, dating from about 9,000 years ago in the Anatolian region of what is now Turkey, shows that they were made from native copper. The oldest objects known to have been made from smelted metal are of lead that was smelted from galena. They date from about 7,000 years ago in Anatolia and Mesopotamia. Shortly thereafter, archaeological evidence shows, people also learned to smelt copper. Since then, people have smelted other metals as well, notably iron. Smelting skills sometimes migrated from region to region and sometimes arose independently. By the time of the Industrial Revolution, metallurgical skills were practiced throughout the world, and industrialization gave people the means to smelt metals at scales of operation far greater than anything practiced previously. Yet it was not until the late nineteenth century that metallurgists began to understand scientifically the processes they were employing. Prior to that, smelting practice was shrouded in myth and mystery.

By smelting ores for seven millennia, humans have discharged by-products that have changed the environment. Primitive smelters may generate pronounced effects only locally, but recent studies show that once smelting began in Anatolia the winds began carrying lead in the form of dust over great distances. Since the Industrial Revolution, giant smelters have caused impacts over much broader areas. For example, SO_2 in smelter smoke has denuded hundreds of thousands of acres of forests near some smelters. Arsenic, which is present in many ores, is volatilized during roasting and discharged with the smelter smoke. Once in the atmosphere, the arsenic condenses as a fine powder, and then settles on vegetation downwind, killing wildlife or livestock that may graze on the vegetation. Lead in the particulate component of smelter smoke also settles on the landscape, leading to high lead levels in the blood of humans and other animals. Elements in smoke and slag find their way into streams and rivers, changing the biological regime both physically and chemically and perhaps rendering the waters unfit for human use. In the early twentieth century, as smelters grew to huge proportions and the damage they were causing increased proportionally, smelting companies began to try to recover by-products and find marketable uses for them. Absent such marketable use, however, smelters did little to curtail the discharge of by-products into the environment.

Smelters have always been unpleasant neighbors for humans, with smoke and dust exacerbating respiratory ailments and damaging property. Smelters have therefore been at the center of a variety of social conflicts between industry, which has used environments as "sinks" for industrial wastes, and other groups, such as city dwellers or farmers, who have wanted to use those same environments for alternative purposes, such as residence or agriculture. Smoke from the Anaconda Copper Mining Company's smelter in Montana, for example, led to some monumental lawsuits filed in the early twentieth century by farmers and the U.S. government against the mining company, and in the 1920s, smoke from the lead smelter at Trail, British Columbia, caused complaints by farmers in the state of Washington, leading to a diplomatic conflict between the United States and Canada. Only in the second half of the twentieth century, with the advent of the abstract concept of "the environment" as something that it is in the public interest to protect, have smelters come under the regulatory umbrella of governments. This has led to a global shift in the location of smelters away from countries such as the United States and either toward countries such as Japan, which are willing to make the investment in environmental controls, or toward developing countries, which as yet do not have a strong regulatory infrastructure. Metallurgists also continue to find new non-pyrochemical processes that allow the recovery of metals from ores while discharging few, if any, by-products into the environment.

Fred L. Quivik

Further Reading

Day, J., & Tylecote, R. F. (Eds.). (1991). *The industrial revolution in metals*. London: The Institute of Materials.

Maddin, R. (Ed.). (1988). *The beginning of the use of metals and alloys*. Cambridge, MA: The MIT Press.

Tylecote, R. F. (1992). *A history of metallurgy*. London: The Institute of Materials.

Wirth, J. D. (2000). *Smelter smoke in North America: The politics of transborder pollution*. Lawrence: University Press of Kansas.

Snail Darter

This three-inch bottom-dwelling minnow that resembles a perch is found in the upper Tennessee River drainage in southeastern Tennessee, northeastern Alabama, and northwestern Georgia. It is a mottled brown percid (belonging to the genus *Perca*) with little known value for economic or recreational purposes, yet it became famous in the 1970s as a result of the controversy surrounding the construction of the Tellico Dam.

The Tennessee Valley Authority (TVA) conceived the Tellico Dam in the late 1930s, but it did not fund it until 1967. The project's goal was to create higher residential land values and recreational opportunities, including a new community of 50,000, as a result of a 6,400-hectare reservoir over part of the Little Tennessee River. In the process, it would eliminate Tanasi (capital city of the Cherokee nation), other cultural sites, and about six hundred family farms on prime agricultural land. It would also change the ecology of the river from a shallow, fast-moving stream with excellent trout fishing to a deep reservoir roughly 48 kilometers in length. In 1971, the governor of Tennessee requested that the project be abandoned given its adverse effect on the recreational benefits of the natural river, but it was evidently ignored by the TVA.

In 1973, a few months before the Endangered Species Act (ESA) passed Congress, zoologist David Etnier found the previously unknown snail darter while snorkeling in the river. Over the next two years it was determined the snail darter had distinct biological differences from other species. Consequently, it received an emergency listing as an endangered species whose critical habitat was limited to a 30-kilometer reach immediately below the dam on the Little Tennessee River. Although the dam was nearly complete, the project was stopped by a Supreme Court decision in 1978 as required by the ESA.

The case ultimately went to the Supreme Court, where the TVA argued the project should be exempt from the ESA because it had begun before the law was passed. The court ruled against the TVA (*Tennessee Valley Authority v. Hill*, 1978). In early 1978, at the urging of Senator Howard Baker of Tennessee, Congress created the Endangered Species Committee (dubbed the God Committee), which could provide exemptions to the ESA. After reviewing the facts, this committee unanimously rejected the TVA's request for an exemption in January 1979.

In the interim, the House had passed a bill exempting the dam in October 1978. The Senate, which waited on the decision of the God Committee, rejected the exemption in June 1979. The following day, John Duncan, the congressman from the Tellico district, added the exemption to a Public Works Appropriation bill that immediately passed the House. The Senate initially passed only the appropriation bill, but the conference bill including the exemption amendment passed both houses in November 1979. President Carter, who opposed the Tellico Project, did not have the political will to veto the entire appropriation bill. Thus, the dam was completed and the reservoir filled.

Two years earlier, in an attempt both to comply with the ESA and complete the dam, TVA biologists successfully transplanted snail darter specimens from the Little Tennessee River to form new populations in the Hiwassee River and other nearby habitats. Transplantation met with limited success, and the snail darter was later found living in several other locations. In 1984 it was downgraded from an endangered to a threatened species.

Louis P. Cain

Further Reading

Hargrove, E., & Conklin, P. (Eds.). (1983). *TVA, fifty years of grass-roots bureaucracy*. Urbana: University of Illinois Press.

Mann, C. C., & Plummer, M. L. (1995). *Noah's choice: The future of endangered species*. New York: Alfred A. Knopf.

Wheeler. W. (1986). *TVA and the Tellico Dam, 1936–1979*. Knoxville: University of Tennessee Press.

Court Cases

Tennessee Valley Authority v. Hill, 437 US 153, 194 (1978).

Socialism and Communism

The terms *socialism* and *communism* are often used as equivalents to refer both to a model of social organization based on the principles of common ownership and collective control over the economy and to the working-class political movement that seeks to bring about that model of social organization and replace the capitalist system. Although the socialist intellectual tradition has provided invaluable contributions to the scientific debates about environmental problems and environmental history, the work of socialist authors has been criticized for being antiecological, anthropocentric (human centered), and largely oblivious to the environmental problems caused by the material progress that they celebrated as one of the biggest achievements of modern society. However, recent work on the environmental underpinnings of the socialist intellectual tradition has led to an increasing recognition that some of these criticisms have been ill founded because, in fact, these authors made significant contributions toward the scientific understanding of the interweaving relationship between humans and the natural environment.

Socialism or Communism?

The historical record of modern socialism goes back to the English Civil War (1642–1652) and includes important actors from the French Revolution such as François Noël Babeuf (1760–1797), early nineteenth-century English and French utopian socialists (pre-Marxist thinkers prior to the 1848 European revolutions, who were called 'utopian' because of their belief in the possibility of social progress without class struggle or proletarian revolution), including Robert Owen (1771–1858), François-Marie-Charles Fourier (1772–1837), and Claude-Henri de Rouvroy, Comte de Saint-Simon (1760–1825), and the English Chartist movement (roughly 1838–1850). In particular, utopian socialism provided a framework for what later would be established as the main tenets of socialist thinking. These authors believed that the capitalist form of industrialization, driven by private accumulation of profits, competition, and exploitation of workers, was a source of social disintegration and conflict. However, they also shared a fascination with the possibilities offered by a rationalized, ordered industrial organization and sought to develop a new science of society tailored after the model of the physical sciences with the objective of bringing about social harmony and cooperation by means of social reforms.

German political philosopher Karl Heinrich Marx (1818–1883) and German socialist Friedrich Engels (1820–1895), the most prominent socialist theorists, adopted the concept of "communism" to differentiate themselves from utopian socialists. Among other issues, they tried to avoid rooting their critique of capitalist society on romanticized visions of a pristine natural environment that would have been enjoyed by precapitalist societies, a view that was widely held among critical thinkers of the time. Rather than reverting to an idealized feudal past, they argued for the

Russian Communist leaders Lenin and Stalin planning "In the Name of Communism." COURTESY *OKHRANA PRIRODY* AND DOUG WEINER.

need of a new social order, communism, that would be superior to capitalism and that would be based on the principles of free association and rational government of human-nature relationships. Their *Communist Manifesto*, first published in 1848, is considered the foundation stone of the modern socialist movement, which illustrates the often-interchangeable use of the two terms.

The Russian Communist leader Vladimir Lenin (1870–1924) further elaborated on these two concepts and provided a clearer distinction whereby *socialism* came to refer to the first phase of a postcapitalist society as described by Marx, whereas *communism* would refer more specifically to what Marx had called "the higher stage of communist society" (Marx 1970, Section I) that would eventually follow. Ever since, there has been a historical tension between the two terms, especially with regard to the means by which the working class seeks to achieve the abolition of private property and class divisions and the establishment of the new social order. With the Russian Revolution (1917), and in particular after the Third International (also called

the "Communist International" or "Comintern," an organization launched in Moscow by the Bolsheviks in 1919 seeking to replace the Second International, the socialist workers' international association that had collapsed with the First World War in 1914) that took place that year, *communism* adopted the more specific meaning of a working-class political movement seeking to overthrow the capitalist system by means of a violent revolution. In turn, *socialism* came to refer mainly to political movements that seek the replacement of the capitalist system through peaceful means and constitutional reform, as illustrated in the approach adopted by social democratic parties. With the consolidation of the Soviet Union, especially during the period of power (1929–1953) of Soviet political leader Joseph Stalin (1879–1953), the term *communism* became associated with the actual political regime adopted, which was based on the centralized control of the economy and the abolition of electoral competition, with political rule concentrated in the Communist Party. By extension, during the twentieth century the term *communism* came to refer mainly to the countries that adopted this type of political regime, which included about one-third of the world population during much of the past century.

Notwithstanding this historical differentiation between the two terms, many authors continue to use *socialism* and *communism* indistinctly. Also, *socialism* is widely used for referring to the intellectual legacy of socialist thinkers independently of their preferences for political action.

Socialism and the Environment

Critics coming from different perspectives, including deep ecology (a radical version of environmentalism promoting a shift from an anthropocentric to a biocentric perspective in environmental values, developed mainly in the United States), sociological theory, and political ecology, have criticized classical socialist thinkers for being antiecological and anthropocentric and for justifying the environmental depletion caused by capitalist society in the name of a particular notion of progress derived from the ideals of the Enlightenment (the intellectual and scientific European movement that sought to overcome medieval "darkness" and ignorance through the use of reason and systematic empirical observation, challenging the authority of the Church and postulating the feasibility of continuous human progress through scientific development and education, specially characteristic of the seventeenth and eighteenth centuries). Among other criticisms being made, Marx and Engels would have been key advocates of the Promethean approach (from Prometheus, the Greek god that gave the gift of fire to humans, thus enhancing human capacity for controlling nature and unleashing human inventiveness and productivity; the Promethean approach implies a human-centered relationship with the natural environment) to human relationships with the natural environment, whereby nature's subjugation to human will is predicated on the assumption of the primacy of technological progress over ecological considerations. Thus, although they paid central attention to the capitalist exploitation of human beings, they would have been oblivious to the limitless exploitation of nature characterizing the capitalist system. As they had shared to the full the nineteenth-century celebration of industrial organization, rationality, and visions of unstoppable human progress, they would have also uncritically accepted the main tenets of the classical political economy of the time, especially the conception that natural resources do not play a role in the creation of value

during the production process. Thus, following the tradition of liberal economic thinkers such as the Englishmen David Ricardo (1772–1823) and Thomas Malthus (1766–1834), Marx and Engels endorsed the view that the production of value depends entirely on human labor, whereas nature was conceived as a free gift in relation to the production process. Not only would these and other obstacles to the adoption of a more ecocentric approach have marked the work of the classical socialist thinkers, but also their antiecological legacy would have inspired some of the worst ecological tragedies in history.

In this connection, a crucial factor behind some of these criticisms of socialism's environmental credentials is undoubtedly the fact that the twentieth-century communist regimes, especially after World War II, adopted development practices that were largely oblivious to environmental concerns. Communist countries maintained for decades that they had a moral superiority over the capitalist world in relation to the treatment of both human beings and the natural environment and continued to deny the existence of environmental problems in their territories well into the 1980s. However, with the collapse of the communist regimes in the former Soviet Union and eastern Europe since the late 1980s, it became evident that most of these countries had been affected by large-scale environmental degradation, which in some cases amounted to what some analysts have termed "ecocide." Other communist countries such as China and Cuba have also suffered large-scale environmental damage, although the nature of the problem differs from that in the former Soviet Union and eastern Europe in important aspects, mainly owing to their lower degree of industrialization. Not surprisingly, some critics have contended that there exists a direct association between socialist thinking and the practices of the countries that claimed to be organized around socialist/communist principles.

Socialism and Environment Revisited

Recent work on the engagement of the socialist intellectual tradition with environmental issues has led to an increasing recognition that some of these criticisms have been ill founded because in fact socialist authors made significant contributions toward the scientific understanding of the interdependence characterizing socio-natural processes. In this connection, Marx anticipated some of the principles developed in the historical sociology of ecological regimes and in coevolutionary theory, which postulate the existence of an evolving and mutually binding process between humans and the natural environment. For instance, he identified the key environmental problems affecting nineteenth-century capitalist society, in particular the large-scale degradation of soil fertility caused by industrial agriculture and the long-term environmental implications of the extensive use of artificial fertilizers that was taking place at the time. He also discussed other crucial environmental problems, such as the pollution of air and water in urban areas and the depletion of forests and mineral reserves, and provided a rationale for the scientific treatment of such issues as environmental justice and environmental sustainability.

Marx's contributions in this field ranged from arguments in favor of implementing recycling practices for dealing with industrial and urban waste to the elaboration of embryonic notions of sustainability and intergenerational justice. In this regard, one of his most important developments was the concept of socio-ecological metabolism, which refers to the intertwining between human activity and nature through the material and energetic flows that constitute the process of labor. For him, labor is the process through which humans adapt the materials of nature to meet their own needs, but in the process human nature itself is transformed in the metabolic interaction, which is framed by the conditions imposed by nature on the human capacity for technological development. Far from negating the importance of nature, the concept of metabolism highlighted the interweaving of the natural and the social in the production of value through the labor process, which is governed both by physical-natural laws and by the social norms and institutions of the time.

Another important contribution of classical socialist thinkers concerned the analysis of the environmental impact of modernization. Thus, drawing on the advanced knowledge of soil chemistry that was available in the second half of the nineteenth century, Marx analyzed the problems of soil fertility affecting farmland in countries like England and the United States. He addressed the case of large-scale agriculture, in terms similar to industrialization, as a process marked by internal contradictions that would have to be overcome by the future communist society that he envisaged. In particular, he argued that the escalating depletion of natural resources driven by the requirements of an intensified agricultural production, especially the depletion of soil nutrients, was destroying the material base on which the whole process was dependent. He also

conceptualized this process as an exploitation of the natural wealth of the countryside by the city and pointed out that the process was already acquiring international character through the expansion of trade, which implied the appropriation of the natural wealth of entire countries by the industrialized world centers.

In addition to these specific topics related to social-natural interactions, it is worth noting that Marx and Engels's vision of a communist society introduced in embryonic form concepts such as environmental sustainability and intergenerational environmental justice, which acquired international currency only in the late twentieth century. For instance, one of the key principles of what Marx and Engels called the "communist social order" would be the abolition of the private property of natural resources, which would then be possessed in common by humans not as owners but as temporary beneficiaries. Moreover, they argued, society would have the duty to preserve and hand over natural resources in an improved state to future generations.

After Marx and Engels, environmental concerns continued to play a crucial role in the work of socialist thinkers. For instance, both the German Marxist theorist Karl Kautsky (1854–1938) and Lenin argued about the exploitative relationship imposed on rural areas by urban centers with its negative impact on the natural environment. Following Marx's insights on the topic, they elaborated on the need to reverse the loss of soil fertility caused by increased agricultural production to supply the growing urban population by implementing the recycling of organic elements and thus reducing the need for artificial fertilizers. Also, the Russian Communist leader Nikolai Ivanovich Bukharin (1888–1938) further explored Marx's concept of socio-ecological metabolism and conceived the relations between humans and the natural environment as being in a state of unstable equilibrium, which was susceptible of regression and decline. Drawing on the concept of "biosphere," coined by the Soviet scientist Vladimir Ivanovich Vernardsky (1863–1945) in the 1920s, Bukharin understood the process of socio-ecological metabolism as a constant adaptation of human society to the natural environment, an approach that was shared by other socialist authors of the time.

Unfortunately, the early development of socialist thinking about environmental issues suffered an impasse after the adoption of accelerated industrialization and collectivization policies by the Soviet Union after the late 1920s. As mentioned, the actual practices of communist countries throughout the twentieth century, and particularly after World War II, were in open contradiction with classical socialist thinking in relation to the environment. This was reflected in the fact that, apart from some isolated exemptions, the tradition of socialist environmental thinking was virtually ignored until the 1970s.

A Living Debate

The controversy about the relationship between socialist/communist intellectual tradition and practices and the natural environment goes on. However, in the light of current international debates, the legacy of classical socialist thinking in this field remains highly relevant. It is especially important with regard to dealing with the problems of sustainability, environmental justice, and intergenerational rights and with regard to developing a coevolutionary approach to the development of the relations between human beings and the natural environment.

José Esteban Castro

Further Reading

Bookchin, M. (1980). *Toward an ecological society*. Montreal, Canada: Black Rose Books.

Bukharin, N. (1925). *Historical materialism: A system of sociology*. New York: International Publishers.

Eckersley, R. (1992). *Environmentalism and political theory: Toward an ecocentric approach*. Albany: State University of New York Press.

Foster, J. B. (1999). Marx's theory of metabolic rift; classical foundations for environmental sociology. *American Journal of Sociology, 105*(2), 366–405.

Giddens, A. (1985). *A contemporary critique of historical materialism*. Cambridge, UK: Polity Press.

Goudsblom, J. (1992). *Fire and civilization*. London: Allen Lane.

Grundmann, R. (1991). *Marxism and ecology*. Oxford, UK: Oxford University Press.

Harvey, D. (1996). *Justice, nature, and the geography of difference*. Cambridge, MA: Blackwell.

Leiss, W. (1972). *The domination of nature*. New York: Braziller.

Lenin, V. I. (1961). The agrarian question and the "critics of Marx." In *Collected works: Vol. 5. Moscow* (pp. 103–222). Moscow: Foreign Languages Publishing House. (Original work published 1901)

Martínez-Allier, J. (1987). *Ecological economics*. Oxford, UK: Basil Blackwell.

Marx, K. (1976). *Capital*. New York: Vintage. (Original work published 1867)

Marx, K., & Engels, F. (1967). *The communist manifesto*. Harmondsworth, UK: Penguin. (Original work published 1848)

Marx, K., & Engels, F. (1970). Critique of the Gotha Programme. In (Vol. 3) *Selected Works* (pp. 13–30). Moscow: Progress Publishers.

Moore, S. (1980). *Marx on the choice between socialism and communism*. Cambridge, MA: Harvard University Press.

O'Connor, M., & Spash, C. (Eds.). (1999). *Valuation and the environment: Theory, methods and practice*. Cheltenham, UK: Edward Elgar.

Parsons, H. (Ed.). (1977). *Marx and Engels on ecology*. Westport, CT: Greenwood.

Redclift, M., & Benton, T. (Eds.). (1994). *Social theory and the global environment*. London: Routledge.

Rubin, I. I. (1972). *Essays on Marx's theory of value*. Montreal, Canada: Our Generation Press. (Original work published 1928)

Schmidt, A. (1971). *The concept of nature in Marx*. London: New Left.

Soil

Soil is the top 1 or 2 meters of the earth's surface, which is tremendously abundant with life. No subject is more central to the environment than soil. It is the ultimate ecosystem, combining all the elements of other ecosystems and carrying out the critical ecosystem function of decomposition for most other ecosystems. Befitting this centrality, many disciplines study aspects of soil, but generally students of soil come from the geosciences, agronomy (a branch of agriculture dealing with field-crop production and soil management), and ecology. The branches of soil science (pedology) include genesis and classification, geography, fertility and crop productivity, chemistry, microbiology, physics, and erosion and conservation. Taken together, the disciplines study soil from at least three perspectives: geologically as a part of the earth's surface, ecologically as an ecosystem, and agronomically as a medium for plant growth.

Because soil is the geological layer and ecosystem that humans contact first, it bears the strong imprint of humanity. Indeed, the more soils are studied around the natural world, even in the Amazonian wilderness, the more anthrosols, the soils of strong human influence, are found. Today humans cause more geomorphic change than any other single Earth surface process (e.g., rivers, wind, and glaciers); the largest human agent of landscape change is soil erosion.

Soils in the Environment

The pedosphere (soil sphere) derives from and interacts with the lithosphere (the outer part of the solid Earth composed of rock essentially like that exposed at the surface), biosphere (the part of the world in which life can exist), hydrosphere (the aqueous envelope of the earth including bodies of water and vapor in the atmosphere), and atmosphere. Every biogeochemical (relating to the partitioning and cycling of chemical elements and compounds between the living and nonliving parts of an ecosystem) cycle has a major sink (a body or process that acts as a storage device or disposal mechanism) and many transformations through soil. Soil's role is paramount in the nitrogen, potassium, and phosphorous cycles, and ecosystem productivity would be greatly decreased without soil nitrogen-fixing bacteria. In an era of global warming with carbon dioxide as the chief anthropogenic (human caused) contributor, it should be remembered that the soil holds two times more carbon than the atmosphere and nearly three times more than land plants. Land-use changes can accelerate the transfer of soil carbon into atmospheric carbon dioxide and also sequester it from the atmosphere. Therefore, the role of soil in both causing and preventing global change is important and sometimes overlooked.

The functions that soil plays in the hydrologic cycle (the sequence of conditions through which water passes from vapor in the atmosphere through precipitation upon land or water surfaces and ultimately back into the atmosphere as a result of evaporation and transpiration) and water filtration are equally as important. Water infiltrates soils, where it serves as the main reservoir for plant water use, and water percolates through soils into groundwater. In this cycle many processes filter and purify water. These properties have led humans to use soils as natural water treatment plants to remove a myriad of contaminants. Peat is one type of wetland soil, known as Histosol, that performs such ecosystem functions worth billions of dollars a year free to the taxpayers of the world. Unfortunately, Histosols and the wetlands in which they form are rapidly disappearing around the world as humans find more convenient land uses.

Soil Definitions and Formation

In some senses soil is simply the cover of mineral and organic aggregates that cover much of the continental surface of the earth. However, most of the large expanses of glaciers, shifting desert sands, and rock pavements don't grow plants and are not really soils. Soil has texture (sand, silt, and clay particles), structure (how these textures adhere together in aggregates called "peds"), organic matter (dead plant and animal material), gases and water in micropores and macropores, and an incredible myriad of life-forms that parallel above-ground ecosystems but with more emphasis on decomposers. These soil ecosystems are still the least understood in nature.

A host of processes—weathering, particle translocation, and organic matter addition or removal over time—act upon the soil medium to produce horizons, or soil zones differentiated horizontally by color, texture, structure, and chemistry. Generally, through a soil profile, from the top down, soils can have O, A, E, B, and C horizons. The O horizon occurs especially in forest and wetland soils and indicates a layer dominantly made up of partly decomposed plant matter. The A horizon in most soils is the uppermost mineral horizon with high amounts of organic matter, structure that enhances aeration and infiltration, and high fertility. The E horizon is a zone of removal, where leaching of nutrient ions and organic matter occurs, whereas a B horizon is a lower zone of addition or transformation of clay and weathered minerals. Finally, a C horizon is the soil's parent material altered by mineral weathering. A soil could have all of these horizons or just one and still be soil, such as a Histosol or peat made up predominantly of O horizons.

Soils have diverse and complicated morphologies (the forms and structures of phenomena or any of their parts), and scientists analyze and classify them based on these morphologies and on genesis, that is, their constituents are the product of the geomorphic (relating to the form or surface features of the earth) processes that formed the medium, chemical and biological weathering, and the history and time lapsed since the medium formed. In this sense, it is useful to conceptualize soil as a living ecosystem controlled by its factors of formation: $S = f$ (cl, o, r, p, t, . . .), where soil (S) is a function (f) of climate (cl), organisms (o), relief (r), parent material (p), and time (t). The dots signify other possible factors. This factorial method considers soil as a part of the whole ecosystem, and it recognizes that soil evolves over time.

The factors of soil formation allow people to study sequences of soils that vary by only one of the five factors, such as relief. For example, a series of soils across a slope is known as a "catena" or "soil toposequence," and soils along it would range from the crest of the slope downward to the shoulder, back, foot, and toe of the slope. The cause for soil variation on this slope is the slope gradient and position, and the results of this would be differences in erosion, deposition, water drainage, and weathering. These topographic and other sequences, together with the horizontally varied layers of soil, give a range of characteristics that groups of soils tend to have. This range provides baselines to estimate change in soils such as sediment burial of topsoils and truncation of topsoils by erosion.

Soil Classification

Classifying soils has an ancient history, and most agricultural societies, including the Romans, Greeks, Aztecs, and Maya, have had soil taxonomies (classifications). Farming people depend on the soil landscape, and successful farmers differentiate regions where crop yields are good or where they lag after a period of time. The Maya of the Yucatan Peninsula, for example, use a folk soil taxonomy that is a panoply of potential cropping areas. The taxonomy includes seven principal arable (suitable for cultivation) land taxa (classes) and many other modifying taxa. These taxa names usually refer to a soil characteristic of topography, texture, or color, but folk soil taxa have significance that transcends mere descriptions. Each taxon is richly meaningful about the crops that work best for a particular soil, especially maize varieties.

Many contemporary soil taxonomies had their origins in the genetic classification of the Russian school of the later nineteenth century led by V. V. Dokuchaiev. The underlying idea is that soils are unique bodies formed by the major factors and many pedogenic (relating to the formation and development of soil) processes. This idea passed through K. D. Glinka in Germany to C. F. Marbut, who introduced the idea in the United States in the 1920s. Two of the classifications used most are those of the United States Department of Agriculture (USDA) and the United Nations Food and Agriculture Organization (FAO), although many nations have their own classifications. The USDA classifies the world's soils in twelve general orders based on a variety of soil characteristics related to the five main soil-forming factors.

Most observers can relate to such soil orders as Entisols, Inceptisols, Aridisols, Andisols, Gelisols, and Histosols because they have straightforward definitions. Entisols are juvenile soils, whereas Inceptisols are more developed but still immature. Both form in recent deposits such as floodplains, steep, active slopes, or beaches and together make up more than 25 percent of the earth's soil surface. Aridisols form in arid environments and make up nearly 12 percent of the earth's soil surface. They have buildups of salts or carbonates and, where not yet salinized, often salinize quickly with irrigated agriculture. Many of the first hydraulic civilizations (irrigated-agriculture-based societies) farmed on Aridisols and Entisols. Andisols are soils formed in recent volcanic materials and cover less than 1 percent of the earth's soil surface. Gelisols have dark, organic surfaces and form in permafrost; these cover almost 9 percent of the earth's soil surface, including most of Alaska. Histosols are peat and muck, forming from organic matter; they cover only about 1 percent of the earth's soil surface.

The other soil orders are almost as easy to understand. The world's richest soils are nutrient-rich and organic matter-rich Mollisols, and they form in some tropical limestone terrains but predominantly in the world's prairies and steppes in the midwestern North and South America and central Eurasia. Mollisols make up about 7 percent of the earth's soil surface but more than 21 percent of the U.S. soil surface. Because they are so fertile, cultivation covers most of their land area, although urban sprawl is spreading over notable areas of these prime agricultural lands. Alfisols generally form under temperate and mixed deciduous (leaf-dropping) forests and make up almost 10 percent of the earth's soil surface. These are also fertile soils that have both nutrient and clay enrichment in subsoils but lack the dark, organic topsoils of Mollisols. Ultisols make up about 8 percent of the earth's soil surface and are similar to Alfisols with their enriched clay subsoils, but more intense and longer weathering makes them more acidic and lower in organic matter and nutrients. Alfisols occur in pockets all around the world, but the redder, more leached Ultisols occur more in subtropical climates such as the southeastern United States, southern China, and India. Mediterranean climates often have "terra rosa" soils, which are usually Alfisols and Ultisols. Spodosols are another acidic forest soil, but they tend to form in sand plains of the subtropics (e.g., Florida) or under coniferous boreal (northern) forests (e.g., Siberia). These are the most colorful of soils, with black organic topsoils that overlie pale, sandy horizons, which in turn overlie red and yellow, iron-rich and aluminum-rich horizons. They make up only about 2.5 percent of the earth's soil surface, but six U.S. states, including Alaska and Florida, have declared them their state soils. Vertisols make up about 2.5 percent of the earth's soil surface. They are the most dynamic soils because they are dominated by highly expansive clays that self-plow and shrink and swell with dehydration and hydration. They occur in extensive clayey pockets around the world in India, Central America, Africa, and the United States. Oxisols are usually red, clay-rich soils that are composed of highly weathered iron and aluminum oxides. These cover about 7.5 percent of the earth's soil surface but only in the tropics or as remnant soils of ancient tropical climates in temperate latitudes. Oxisols predominate in tropical rain forests such as Amazonia, southeast Asia, and central Africa.

Soil Fertility

Soil is a medium of growth for nearly all plants on Earth. Soil fertility is thus vital, and many characteristics contribute to soil fertility, including nutrient availability, lack of toxic elements, texture, structure, and a healthy microbial ecosystem. Plants need six macronutrients in higher quantities from soil: nitrogen, phosphorus, potassium, calcium, magnesium, and sulfur. Plants also need eight micronutrients at smaller quantities: iron, manganese, copper, zinc, boron, molybdenum, chlorine, and nickel. These nutrients come from the weathering of minerals in the soil's parent material, from recycling of other plants, and some from atmospheric deposition, wind-eroded particles, and tephra (solid material ejected into the air during a volcanic eruption).

Within the soil, clays and organic matter are the storehouses of soil nutrients. These store and release nutrients with weathering and mineralization, and they hold nutrient ions at and near their surfaces in solution. Uptake of these nutrients by plants occurs most effectively where soils harbor rich ecosystems. Most important of all are soil fungi called "mycorrhiza," which develop mutualistic relationships with plants, increasing plant uptake of nutrients and requiring only some carbon compounds in return. Plentiful mycorrhiza, for example, allow the important tropical crop of cassava to prosper in soils low in phosphorous.

Some elements and nutrients, such as aluminum or magnesium, can be at levels that are too high. For example, serpentine is a type of rock that can weather out toxic levels of magnesium and produce barrens or spotty plant communities resistant to high levels of this macronutrient.

Soil Degradation

The causes of soil degradation are numerous. They include all the causes of other forms of environmental degradation. One obvious cause of intensifying degradation is intensifying land use: more plowing, more plowed area, more irrigation, generally more cultivation of more marginal lands, and more toxic chemical use and oil exploitation. Greater chemical use, especially nitrogen fertilizer, has led to higher yields, but large areas of polluted soils have also developed, especially from metal smelting, petroleum, and a stew of other toxic wastes. The expansion of these processes occurred especially after World War II and spread to the developing world with heavy industry in the 1970s.

United Nations Agenda 21 (a global partnership adopted at the United Nations Conference on Environment and Development at Rio de Janeiro in 1991) underscores the problems of land degradation and the need for conservation. Several studies in the 1990s estimated that 23 percent of global arable land had been degraded to an extent that limited its productivity. One report ranked the following causes of soil degradation by importance of their impact: water erosion at 58 percent, wind erosion at 28 percent, chemical degradation at 12 percent, and physical degradation at 4 percent. However, degradation is often a combination of processes and factors. For example, desertification is the product of complex factors that has caught international attention in the U.N. Convention to Combat Desertification, which more than one hundred nations have signed. The other complex processes that degrade soils are nutrient removal, salinization, water logging, pollution, and land development (urban and suburban sprawl). Essentially each process either removes or limits soils from agricultural production or other ecosystem functions such as soil's ability to sequester carbon dioxide, filter polluted air, provide habitat, and function in the nitrogen, hydrologic, and other biogeochemical cycles.

One type of degradation is land conversion or development, which affects only about 1 percent of the earth. In the United States developed land is about 40 million hectares. More than 8 million hectares, including 242,812 hectares of prime farmland, are developed each year. Of this loss, about 24,000 hectares per year are wetland, which is often the most ecologically rich land. China has recently been urbanizing at a faster pace, but even in the period from 1987 to 1992 China lost about 4.8 million hectares to urbanization. Urban and industrial pollution has degraded another 2 million hectares.

Most types of degradation are natural processes, but human activity speeds them up. Rates of water and wind erosion depend on some combination of vegetative cover, conservation technique, wind or rainfall intensity, soil's inherent resistance to erosion, and steep and long slopes. Natural soil erosion is not necessarily a negative process but rather a complex of processes acting to sculpt the land over different temporal and spatial scales. Human-induced erosion is often many times faster and can produce changes that render upland soils unusable for agriculture and downstream floodplains glutted with sediment. Some studies report the rate of human-induced erosion as two to three times faster than the background rate, but this fails to convey the point that accelerated erosion over the short period of European settlement around the world has cleaved off significant parts of the most fertile topsoils that took millennia to form. Accelerated erosion sets off a cascade of problems: nutrient and organic matter depletion, decreased infiltration, increased impacts of floods and droughts, and degradation of wetlands and waterways.

Salinization, and often associated waterlogging, is another natural form of degradation greatly accelerated by irrigation, raised saline groundwater, and salt water intrusion. One estimate is that 5.6 million hectares of U.S. land and about 10 billion hectares of world land are influenced by salt and that salinization causes 10 million hectares to be deserted each year. Moreover, several studies have implicated salinization in the decline of at least three ancient societies: the Sumerian, Harappan, and Hohokam. Iraq, the modern home of ancient Sumer, is still afflicted today, with 71 percent of its irrigated land salinized.

History of Erosion

One model by which to understand the history of human-induced soil erosion is in three great waves. The first wave started as humans expanded out of their floodplains in Bronze Age China, the Middle East, and south Asia about 2000 BCE. The second wave started with the fifteenth-century European expansion around the world, pioneering new lands that Old World farmers had never before encountered. Soil erosion coursed through these colonial and other newly plowed lands because the settlers had developed their practices in the milder climates and gentler slopes of Europe. The third wave started after World War II with the tremendous expansion of agriculture onto marginal lands, especially in the tropics, where intense rain and steep slopes combined to produce some of the world's highest rates of erosion. The three waves were similar in one respect: Pioneer farmers moved onto lands that they did not understand and that were usually more erodible than lands with which the farmers were familiar.

Old World Antiquity

An environmental history of soil might be said to begin when people noticed that some lands produced better crops or pastures than other lands or when they noticed that land had eroded or become buried by erosion from somewhere else. People manipulated these soils toward further degradation, greater productivity, or sustainability. The recording of the history of agriculture plausibly began in Mesopotamia with the first writing as cuneiforms on clay tablets, which were fired and preserved. Appropriate for intensive agricultural societies, many of these clay tablets concerned agriculture and evidence of its decline.

One dominant theme in soil history has been soil erosion and degradation of soil resources. The Greek philosopher Plato's *Critias* probably gives the best-known early recognition of soil erosion and degradation: "the earth has fallen away all round and sunk out of sight . . . all the richer and softer parts of the soil having fallen away, and the mere skeleton of the land being left" (*Critias*, 360 BCE). Some writers have taken such "ancient wisdom," with the reports of sedimentation around ancient Greek harbors such as Ephesus and Pergamon, as clear evidence of human-induced soil erosion. Studies in Greece and the Mediterranean have recognized that much of the soil erosion and sedimentation evident in denuded and buried landscapes was indeed human induced and began long before the Romans. Even within the dominant view that humans accelerated soil erosion increasingly after the agricultural revolution there are disagreements: Some experts ascribe high Roman-era erosion to intensive land use, whereas others ascribe it to the breakdown of Roman terraces after the collapse of Rome. Some, looking at delta and coastal plain progradation (building out), see a dominant hand of nature in rivers adjusting steadily to the 125-meter sea-level rise that occurred after ice age glaciers melted.

The major soil questions of the ancient world concerned ways to produce more crops from the soil and ways to solve the major problems: soil erosion, salinization, desertification, and fertility declines. Producing more crops is more complex than it seems, and it relies on irrigation, fertilizers, pest control, timing, and sunlight. As agriculture became the dominant way of life in these places in the third millennium BCE, the first urban civilizations arose with surpluses of food. Fertile alluvial soils combined with canal irrigation that delivered life-giving water and fertile silt, both of which began the decline of agriculture in Mesopotamia but not in Egypt. In Mesopotamia larger but shorter floods carried more silt, but the water subsided faster. The silt clogged waterways and elevated channels and thus increased flooding. The water running into arid fields accelerated salinization there. Over time salinization ruined large expanses of land and caused farmers to shift to more salt-tolerant crops, evident in cuneiform accounts of more production of salt-resistant barley than wheat over time. Some studies connect salinization in southern Mesopotamia with its decline relative to northern Mesopotamia, which was less prone to salinization. In contrast, along the Nile River in Egypt more flood water for a longer time flushed salt, and its slower, steadier flow carried less silt to clog canals. Hence, irrigated agriculture has continued along the Nile to the present.

Shards from broken vessels in fields in the Near East point to ancient fertilization. Many Greek and Roman writers recognized the need for fertilization. They wrote of manure (even of canals for delivering human sewage to crops), green manures (several kinds of legumes), marl, ashes, and saltpeter (potassium nitrite) being used on soil. Most of the Romans who wrote of agriculture wrote about soils, and the Roman writer Columella even wrote a book on soils.

Ancient Americas

Most soil research in the ancient Americas has focused on the Maya lowlands, the highlands of central Mexico, the southwestern United States and northern Mexico, the Andes, and the Amazon. One important lesson from this research is that pre-Columbian cultures intensively used, altered, managed, and, in some places, damaged their soils. Impacts in a few places, such as central Mexico and the Maya lowlands, were greater in pre-Columbian times than in post-Columbian times.

The great areas of South American soil research are anthrosols in Amazonia, agricultural terracing and soil manipulation through the Andes and foothills, and wetland raised-field agriculture, especially of the Lake Titicaca basin. Research teams in Amazonia have recently recognized widespread anthrosols called *terra preta* (black earths). These fertile, black soils occur in tropical rain forests, which are usually stereotyped as having infertile, acidic, red soils. These black soils cover up to 10 percent of Amazonia and have the strong imprint of long and intensive human use. Contemporary farmers still seek them out. Such soil evidence shows the long impact of human activities on the world's greatest wilderness with the highest biodiversity (biological diversity as indicated by numbers of species of animals and plants).

Similarly spectacular are the agricultural terraces and raised and irrigated fields of South America. All of these soil-management techniques are common in several parts of the Andes but nowhere more so than at the Lake Titicaca basin. There raised fields, sunken gardens, channels, and terraces produce a dominantly anthropogenic landscape, showing long and continuous uses.

The Maya civilization (1500 BCE to its ninth-century CE collapse in Guatemala's Petén and later devolution in the northern Yucatán) developed a complex of soil-management techniques—still visible in the landscape—that was appropriate to the varied environments of the region. The Maya developed wetland fields, canals, and terraces that maintained soil thickness, fertility, and moisture. However, these impressive techniques for farming tropical hillslopes had some environmental impacts. In the depressions, lakes, and valleys of the Maya lowlands, a thick clay covers the old soil (paleosol) that the first Maya encountered. This clay is often called the "Maya clay" because it represents soil eroded by Maya activities such as forest clearing and farming. Maya clay occurs over a broad region and shows the wide impacts of the Maya on the soil landscape. Perhaps terracing and other conservation measures were "too little too late" in a degrading environment, but the evolution and diffusion of complex soil- and water-management features across the lowlands during the Classical period (250–830 CE) argue more against an environmental cause for the Maya collapse.

Soil Erosion and U.S. History

The United States provides another example of soil-erosion history. European settlement eroded soil profiles in the uplands and the sediment-clogged channels in the lowlands. Soil erosion truncated upland soils and inundated reaches of the Chesapeake Bay, the Mississippi River valley, the Piedmont and coastal plain watersheds, and many other parts of the United States. From the mid-nineteenth to early twentieth century a whole town was buried by streams carrying eroded soils in Minnesota, and a whole canyon in Georgia, known as "Providence," was eroded nearly 50 meters deep, 1,500 meters long, and 100 meters across. In the late-nineteenth century, hydraulic mining in California had even more acute impacts, leading to a loss of soil equal to about a thousand years of Mississippi River sediment loads. Wind erosion may not have been as important, but its dramatic dust clouds and regional impacts in the Dust Bowl years and afterward have been an obvious reminder of what human-induced soil erosion can do.

Americans came to recognize soil erosion from a series of inventories that started with President Theodore Roosevelt's Conference of Governors in 1908, when he called soil erosion: "the most dangerous of wastes now in progress" (Harbough 1993, 96). However, Hugh Hammond Bennett, the so-called father of soil conservation, brought the threats of soil erosion to the fore in the early twentieth century with many publications, such as *Erosion: A National Menace* (1928), that detailed U.S. and world soil erosion. As head of what came to be the U.S. Soil Conservation Service (SCS) and later the Natural Resources Conservation Service he also turned soil conservation into a national effort during the Dust Bowl years. Since that time the SCS (later the NRCS) has helped spread the gospel of soil conservation around the United States and conducted a series of erosion inventories; however, soil-erosion rates remain higher than soil-formation rates in several parts of the United States that produce large amounts of food, such as the spring wheat belt of eastern Washington State and the corn belt of the upper Mississippi River valley. As of 1997 nearly one-third of U.S. farmland was experiencing excessive erosion.

This point is ironic: Soil degradation is high in productive areas. Hence, does degradation matter if the land is still productive? Some areas with wind-blown loess (an unstratified silty deposit), which is rich but erodible, can remain productive even with high rates of soil loss, whereas other areas start to lose productivity fast. However, soil erosion is still a problem in both areas because of the downstream or offsite impacts on rivers, wetlands, and estuaries.

Another controversial aspect of soil erosion is the costs projected in some studies. For example, one study estimated the total cost of onsite and offsite soil erosion to be $44 billion per year in the United States, where soil conservation has been active since the 1930s. Some critiques have argued that this estimate is too high or too low, but soil erosion has decreased, though less than desired, through many traditional and newer conservation approaches—such as the Conservation Reserve Program (CRP)—that subsidizes farmers not to grow crops and to plant natural vegetation on marginal lands. In 2002 about 14 million hectares of land were enrolled in the CRP with a government outlay of $1.6 billion.

Soil has the most central role in the earth's ecosystems. Soil is unique to the earth, as far as is known, because life is also unique to the earth. Soil is an ecosystem itself and is a part of all but the most extreme of other ecosystems on Earth. Soil contains ecological niches, habitats, ecosystem functions, trophic levels, symbiosis, and untold biodiversity. Soil is also the storehouse of fertility and water for plants, supplying the necessary nutrients, moisture, and physical medium for plants to grow. Moreover, soil does more for decomposition than do other ecosystems. Its role in removing contaminants from infiltrating water is enormously important, and humans have harnessed this role for wastewater treatment.

The great diversity of soil on Earth reflects its neglected biodiversity. Science defines thousands of different soils and twelve main orders in the U.S. classification system. Mollisols are the most fertile soils on Earth; they make up only about 7 percent of Earth's soil surface, but in the United States they are the most extensive soils.

Since the dawn of agriculture soil has been degraded by erosion, salinization, waterlogging, pollution, desertification, and land-use changes. Soil is becoming more and more altered by human activities, but scientists know that soil degradation is both ancient and pervasive because anthrosols are found even in what were assumed to be pristine areas. Indeed, people now recognize that ancient cultures altered many soils for the better. Ironically, however, human impacts on degradation, especially soil erosion, are ancient and devastating. Soil erosion is now the largest single geomorphic agent on Earth, with impacts as large at downstream and offsite locations in rivers and wetlands as at onsite locations where detached particles and dissolved nutrients start their cascading impacts. All of this erosion occurred as crop yields and agricultural production increased significantly in the twentieth century. In developed nations fertilizers, made with the use of fossil fuels, and hybrid seeds have compensated for erosion on uplands, but these same fertilizers have compounded the damage to eroded soils downstream in channels, wetlands, lakes, and estuaries. Channels have built up, floods and dredging have increased, ecosystem functions have been reduced, and waters have eutrophied (become enriched in dissolved nutrients).

All of the processes of soil degradation started insidiously, but several became noticeable by at least classical antiquity, and all increased dramatically after the Industrial Revolution. The obvious aspects of soil degradation—for example, gullies and salinization—catch people's attention, but the insidious aspects—sheet and rill erosion and nutrient removal—are more important because they go unnoticed by most people. Some farmers and consumers have become concerned about environmental impacts of soil degradation, which has led to a small but growing sustainable agriculture movement, especially in the developed world. This movement, along with the billions of government dollars spent on soil conservation, will determine if, like the poor, soil degradation will "always be with us."

Timothy Beach

See also Agribusiness; Agriculture; Dust Bowl; Organic Agriculture; Salinization

Further Reading

Amundson, R., Harden, J., & Singer, M. (Eds.). (1994). *Factors of soil formation: A fiftieth anniversary retrospective* (Special Publication No. 33). Madison, WI: Soil Science Society of America.

Beach, T. (1994) The fate of eroded soil: Sediment sinks and sediment budgets of agrarian landscapes in southern Minnesota, 1851–1988. *Annals of the Association of American Geographers, 84*(1), 5–28.

Beach, T. (1998) Soil catenas, tropical deforestation, and ancient and contemporary soil erosion in the Petén, Guatemala. *Physical Geography, 19*(5), 378–405.

Bennett, H. H., & Chapline, W. R. (1928). *Soil erosion: A national menace* (USDA Circ. No. 33). Washington, DC: USDA.

Birkland, P. W. (1998). *Soils and geomorphology* (3d ed.). New York: Oxford University Press.

Buol, S. W., Hole, F. D., McCracken, R. J., & Southard, R. J. (1997). *Soil genesis and classification* (4th ed.). Ames: Iowa State University Press.

Butzer, K. (1976). *Early hydraulic civilization in Egypt.* Chicago: University of Chicago Press.

Dunning, N. P. (1992). *Lords of the hills: Ancient Maya settlement in the Puuc Region, Yucatan, Mexico* (Monographs in World Archaeology No. 15). Madison, WI: Prehistory Press.

German Advisory Council on Global Change. (1994). *World in transition: The threat to soils: Annual report.* Bonn, Germany: Economica Verlag.

Harbough, W. (1993). Twentieth-century tenancy and soil conservation: Some comparisons and questions. In D. Helms & D. Bowers (Eds.), *The history of agriculture and the environment* (pp. 95–119). Berkeley and Los Angeles: University of California Press.

Hillel, D. (1991). *Out of the earth: Civilization and the life of the soil.* Berkeley and Los Angeles: University of California Press.

Hooke, R. L. (2000). On the history of humans as geomorphic agents. *Geology, 28,* 843–846.

Hughs, J. D. (1994). Sustainable agriculture in ancient Egypt. In D. Helms & D. Bowers (Eds.), *The history of agriculture and the environment* (pp. 12–22). Berkeley & Los Angeles: University of California Press.

Jenny, H. (1941). *Factors of soil formation.* New York: McGraw-Hill.

Lowdermilk, W. C. (1953). Conquest of the land through seven thousand years (Agricultural Information. Bulletin No. 99). Washington, DC: USDA.

Mann, C. C. (2002). 1491. *The Atlantic, 289*(3), 41–53.

McNeill, J. (2000). *Something new under the sun: An environmental history of the twentieth-century world.* New York: W. W. Norton.

National Research Council. (1993). *Soil and water quality.* Washington, DC: National Academy Press.

Pimentel, D., Harvey, C., Resosudarmo, P., Sinclair, K., Kurz, D., McNair, M., Crist, S., Shpritz, L., Saffouri, R., & Blair, R. (1995). Environmental and economic costs of soil erosion and conservation benefits. *Science, 267,* 117–123.

Plato. (2000). *Critias.* (B. Jowett, Trans.). Retrieved February 25, 2003, from http://classics.mit.edu//Plato/critias.html. (Original work published 360 BCE)

Reich, P., Eswaran, H., & Beinroth, F. (2003). Global dimensions of vulnerability to wind and water erosion. Retrieved February 14, 2003, from http://www.nrcs.usda.gov/technical/worldsoils/landdeg/papers/

Soil Survey Staff. (1998). *Keys to soil taxonomy* (8th ed.). Washington, DC: USDA Natural Resources Conservation Service.

Tanji, K. K. (1990). The nature and extent of agricultural salinity problems. In K. K. Tanji (Ed.), *Agricultural salinity assessment and management* (American Society of Civil Engineers Manuals and Reports on Engineering Practice No. 71) (pp. 1–17). New York: American Society of Civil Engineers.

The twelve soil orders. (n.d.). Retrieved February 14, 2003, from http://soils.ag.uidaho.edu/soilorders/index.htm

United Nations Food and Agriculture Organization. (1996). *Our land, our future*. Rome: United Nations Food and Agriculture Organization and United Nations Environment Programme.

United Nations Food and Agriculture Organization. (1998). *World reference base for soil resources*. Rome: United Nations Food and Agriculture Organization and International Society of Soil Science.

Van Andel, T. H. (1998). Paleosols, red sediments, and the old Stone Age in Greece. *Georchaeology, 13*(4), 361–390.

Wild, A. (1993). *Soils and the environment: An introduction*. Cambridge, UK: Cambridge University Press.

Yaalon, D. H. (2000, September 21). Why soil—and soil science—matters? Millennium essay. *Nature, 407*, 301.

Soil Association

The Soil Association is the United Kingdom's leading campaigning and certification organization for organically produced food and farming. Its organic symbol is the United Kingdom's most recognizable trademark for organic produce—food produced and processed to strict and rigorous environmental and animal welfare standards.

The organization was founded in 1946 by a group of farmers, scientists, and nutritionists. They wanted to direct attention to the effects of farming practice on plant, animal, human, and environmental health. In many ways they demonstrated great foresight. Many problems that they spotlighted have only become really obvious in recent decades. The 1930s dust bowls on the American plains had made clear the dangers from soil erosion. However, pollution and other forms of environmental degradation were linked in most minds with industry, not agriculture, even though the latter activity has done far more to change the face of the earth over the course of human history. Indeed many ancient civilizations collapsed because they undermined that most basic building block of the real wealth of nations: soil.

The immediate catalyst behind the formation of the Soil Association was the publication of *The Living Soil* by Lady Eve Balfour, a farmer and conservationist, in 1943. She presented the case for an alternative, sustainable approach to agriculture that today is generally known as organic farming.

The Association has sought to draw attention to loss of soil through erosion and nutrient depletion, the decreased nutritional quality of intensively produced food, the maltreatment of animals in intensive livestock units (for example, hens in battery cages—massed units of tiny cages that do not permit hens room to stand), and the general impact of large intensive farming systems on the countryside and wildlife.

These negative effects are not just environmental. Modern farming has also emptied the countryside of people, as machinery has increasingly replaced human labor. Intensive farming is also very expensive and dependent on huge government subsidies, perhaps the most notorious example being the subsidies provided through the Common Agricultural Policy of the European Union.

The work of the Soil Association has included the management of demonstration farms to show that there is a better way of producing food. In the early 1970s it set up a certification system to provide an independent audit and tracking system from the individual field through to the final packing. Most organic food in the United Kingdom is now certified by the Association. The Association also does a great deal of general education work about food supply systems.

Nevertheless, the number of organic farmers in the United Kingdom remained small until the launch in 1995 of the Organic Aid Scheme, through which the government began to help farmers through the difficult process of converting from conventional farming to organic farming. Organic land still accounts for less than 0.5 percent of all agricultural land, whereas in nearby Denmark 5 percent of the land is farmed organically. Both figures show how far there is to go to put agriculture on a more sustainable footing.

An important development in recent years has been the growth of Local Food Link schemes supplying food direct from producers to consumers. Demand for organic food has grown so fast that much is imported from abroad, the environmental impact of long-distance food transportation being one negative factor.

Sandy Irvine

Further Reading

Lampkin, N. (1991). *Organic farming*. Alexandria Bay, NY: Diamond Farm Book Publishing.

Litchfield, C. (Ed.). (2001). *The organic directory*. Dartington, UK: Green Books.

Thirsk, J. (1997). *Alternative agriculture: A history*. Oxford, UK: Oxford University Press.

The Soil Association. (2002). The Soil Association home page. Retrieved May 28, 2002, from http://www. soilassociation.org/SA/SAWeb.nsf/!Open

Solar Energy

Solar radiation is powering photosynthesis that yields all of our food (directly as plants, indirectly as animal tissues) and that produced the fossil fuels whose combustion is the energetic foundation of modern civilization. No less importantly, solar radiation powers the atmospheric circulation and heats oceans and continents, thereby producing distinct climates. Every civilization is thus utterly dependent on solar energy for its very existence. But the subject of this entry is solar energy that is seen much more narrowly as a set of techniques designed either to improve the use of incoming radiation for space and water heating or to use for the generation of electricity.

More effective passive solar space heating began in antiquity with proper orientation of houses built with south- or southwest-facing courtyards and windows. However, traditional architectures were much better in designing buildings for passive cooling in warm climates than for passive solar heating in cold regions. Glass windows, introduced by the Romans during the first century CE, made that task easier, but in most parts of the world they did not become common until the nineteenth century. Glass, and later also plastics, made it possible to build solar water heaters whose ownership became eventually widespread in California, Japan, and Israel. Today's best passive solar houses combine proper orientation and shading with windows that are coated with a very thin layer of material that transmits or rejects certain frequencies of radiation and with thick wall and roof insulation. Depending on the climate and construction, such measures can reduce the heating and/or cooling requirements commonly by 15–30 percent.

Solar Thermal Power

The first solar electricity projects to be connected to commercial grids were central solar power (CSP) systems that use troughs, towers, or dishes to focus sunlight in order to generate superheated steam for conventional turbogenerators. Peak solar-to-electric conversion efficiencies range from just over 20 percent for troughs, 23 percent for power towers, and 29 percent for dishes but annual rates are considerably lower, ranging 10–18 percent for troughs, 8–19 percent for towers, and 16–28 percent for dishes. In spite of their relatively poor ratings, parabolic troughs are the commercially most mature technique, and until the late 1990s the nine plants operating at three sites in the Mojave Desert near Barstow in California accounted for more than 90 percent of the world's thermal solar capacity. These plants were built between 1984 and 1990 and their total installed capacity is 354 megawatts with unit sizes between 14 and 80 megawatts. Other trough CSP projects include small plants in Egypt, Iran, Morocco, Spain, Greece, and India and much larger trough facilities are planned for Iran, Northern Morocco, Egypt, Mexico, and Rajasthan in India.

Photovoltaics

In 1839 Edmund Becquerel found that electricity generation of an electrolytic cell made up of two metal electrodes increased when exposed to light. Little work was done on this photovoltaic (PV) effect until the 1870s, when the discovery of the photoconductivity by selenium made it possible to make the first PV cells whose efficiencies were too low for any practical application. In 1918 Czochralski demonstrated how to grow large silicon (Si) crystals but the decisive technical breakthrough came only in 1954 when a team at the Bell Laboratories produced Si cells that were 4.5 percent efficient, and raised that performance to 6 percent just a few months later. By March 1958, when *Vanguard I* became the first PV-powered satellite, Hoffman Electronics had cells that were 9 percent efficient. In 1962 *Telstar*, the first commercial telecommunications satellite, had 14 watts of PV power, and just two years later *Nimbus* rated 470 watts.

During the last four decades of the twentieth century, PV cells became an indispensable, and spectacularly successful, component of rapidly expanding satellite industry as PV arrays have come to power scores of communication, meteorological, Earth-observation, and spy satellites. But land-based applications remained uncommon even after Carlson and Wronski at RCA Laboratories fabricated the first amorphous silicon PV cell in 1976. PV cells have obvious advantages for electricity generation. They have no moving parts (and hence low maintenance requirements), operate silently at atmospheric pressure and ambient tempera-

The sun, with all those planets revolving around it and dependent on it, can still ripen a bunch of grapes as if it had nothing else in the universe to do.

—Galileo

The use of solar energy has not been opened up because the oil industry does not own the sun.

—Ralph Nader, quoted in *Loose Talk* (Linda Botts, Ed.), 1980.

ture with a minimal environmental impact, and they are inherently modular. Photovoltaics could be translated into commercial terrestrial applications only after (1) the cells reached conversion efficiencies close to, and in excess of, 10 percent, and (2) as the average price of PV modules (typically made up of 40 PV cells) and arrays (made up of about 10 modules) was reduced by nearly an order of magnitude, which took place between 1975 and 1995.

Large efficiency gaps remain between laboratory and field performances, as well as between high-purity single crystals, polycrystalline cells, and thin films. Thin PV films are made of amorphous Si or of such compounds as gallium arsenide or cadmium telluride. Theoretical single-crystal efficiencies are 25–30 percent, with more than 23 percent achieved in laboratories. Lenses and reflectors can be used to focus direct sunlight onto a small area of cells and boost conversion

This Massachusetts home uses a passive solar design including a true south orientation and a three-story sunroom to maximize heating efficiency. COURTESY CATHLEEN FRACASSE.

1139

efficiencies to more than 30 percent. Stacking cells sensitive to different parts of the spectrum could push the theoretical peak to 50 percent, and to 30–35 percent in laboratories. Actual efficiencies of new single-crystal modules are now just 12–14 percent, and they may drop to below 10 percent. Thin-film cells convert as little as 3–7 percent after several months, and multijunction amorphous Si cells convert at least 8 percent.

As the efficiencies rose so did the annual worldwide shipments of cells and modules. During the 1990s they increased from about 43 peak megawatts to 288 peak megawatts as the typical price fell by 25–30 percent. The largest PV cell and module producers in 2000 were BP Solarex in the United States, Japan's Kyocera and Sharp, and Germany's Siemens. Installed capacity in the year 2000 amounted to about 500 peak megawatts in the United States and almost 1 peak gigawatts worldwide, the latter total being less than 0.05 percent of more than 2.1 terawatts in fossil-fueled generators. Grid-connected modules have finally surpassed telecommunication industries to claim the single largest share of the PV market. Other markets include recreational uses (mainly camping and boating), home solar systems (remote generation preferable to expensive hookups to distant grid, and village generation in poor countries), and water pumping.

Recent growth of PV capacity at 15–25 percent a year has led to many optimistic forecasts. The U.S. Department of Energy aims at 1 million rooftop PV systems with about 3 peak gigawatts by 2010 (compared to just 51,000 installations and 80 megawatts in 2000) and Japan plans to install annually ten times as many rooftop units by 2010 as it did in 1999. PV cells under development include photoelectrochemical devices based on nanocrystalline materials and cheap conducting polymer films that allow them to capture light from all angles and be fashioned into electricity-producing windows. Whatever their eventual progress may be, the key fact remains: PV conversions of solar radiation harness the largest renewable source of energy and their affordable mastery would revolutionize the terrestrial supply of electricity no less than it has already done in space applications. The hope is, as with many other techniques in a relatively early stage of development, that continuing improvements in the net energy gain and durability of PV cells and declines in their unit cost will make them a leading choice for a variety of household and industrial uses in a not too distant future.

Vaclav Smil

Further Reading

Butti, K., & Perlin, J. (1980). *A golden thread: 2500 years of solar architecture and technology*. Palo Alto, CA: Cheshire Books.

Dracker, R., & Laquill, P. D. (1996). Progress comercializing solar-electric power systems. *Annual Review of Energy and the Environment, 21*, 371–402.

Goetzberger, A., Knobloch, J., & Voss, B. (1998). *Crystalline silicon solar cells*. Chichester, UK: John Wiley.

Perlin, J. (1999). *From space to earth: The story of solar electricity*. Ann Arbor, MI: Aatec.

South Africa
(2000 est. pop. 40 million)

South Africa, located at the southern tip of the African continent, became an independent nation in 1910. During the nineteenth century the region was populated by independent African kingdoms, such as the Zulu and Sotho, lesser chiefdoms, and settler states (in the nineteenth century, European settlers controlled two colonies; the Cape of Good Hope; and two independent republics, the South African Republic and Orange Free State). South Africa was the only part of sub-Saharan Africa to attract a substantial number of European settlers, beginning in the seventeenth century. But people defined as white never exceeded 22 percent of the total population. Black African people predominated in a population that rose from 6 million in 1910 to 40 million by the year 2000.

After a long history of white minority rule, which culminated in the oppressive apartheid period beginning in 1948, South Africa held its first nonracial democratic election in 1994, and an African National Congress government took power.

Environmental issues and policies in South Africa have been deeply affected by the heritage of segregation along racial lines. Africans were restricted in their access to land and other natural resources such as woodland and wildlife.

Three linked environmental issues have been central in South Africa over the long term: the preservation of its rich wildlife; the conservation of pastures; and the condition of the African reserves.

Wildlife Protection

Hunting was a major pursuit of both white settlers and Africans; Boer (South Africans of Dutch or Huguenot descent) frontiersmen, and British visitors were profligate hunters of elephants for ivory, of antelope for subsistence, and of predators to protect their livestock. By the late nineteenth century some hunters began to lament the demise of the prey; increasing scientific interest provided regulatory muscle for new preservationist concerns. The government, following the U.S. model of national parks and the British imperial ideas of forest reserves, set aside land for game reserves in which hunting was disallowed. Kruger National Park, founded in the 1890s, was named after an Afrikaner (a South African of European descent whose native language is Afrikaans) leader in new legislation in 1926. It is one of the largest game reserves in the world.

After World War II new ecological ideas and concerns about habitat led to a wider variety of national parks being set aside, including coastal and desert areas, to protect water birds and rare plant species. The system was managed by the National Parks Board; protected areas under provincial and local authorities also proliferated. Beginning in the 1950s South Africa was a pioneer in wildlife farming on private land. In some areas diverse species were stocked for tourism and game lodges; elsewhere, the emphasis was on venison production and commercial hunting of antelope. Overall, however, the quantity and diversity of wildlife in the country by the early twenty-first century are far greater than they had been for at least one hundred years.

Pastures

Over 60 percent of South Africa is semiarid, receiving less than 500 millimeters of rainfall; part of the rest of the country is mountainous. In both the semiarid and mountainous areas, and among many rural African people, livestock were at the heart of agriculture. Between 1800 and 1930 the number of sheep and goats in South Africa increased from fewer than 2 million to almost 60 million. Cattle also increased sharply in the first few decades of the twentieth century as veterinary controls were established. Most of the small stock were farmed by white landowners who specialized in wool, angora/mohair, and mutton production. South Africa became the second-largest producer of fine merino wools. Livestock farming was largely dependent on the veld (natural pastures). As production became more intensive, some farmers and experts perceived that livestock were degrading the veldt. Serious soil erosion in pastures and some arable (suitable for cultivation) lands was evident by the 1920s and 1930s.

South Africa experienced a dust bowl of sorts in the pastoral districts at much the same time as did the United States.

Conservationist concerns articulated at this time formed the basis for widespread propaganda and far-reaching intervention, such as the 1946 Soil Conservation Act (which borrowed from the United States). Intervention in this sphere was spearheaded by a rhetoric of progressive agriculture and scientific management. A central plank in state policy was to abolish trekking or transhumance (long-distance seasonal movement of people and animals to pastures) as well as kraaling (daily movement of animals from central corrals to distant pastures). With millions of animals involved, these practices were seen to worsen pasture degradation through daily and seasonal tramping; they also spread disease. The official ideal was for farmers to use fenced rotatable paddocks, in which animals could be left undisturbed. This entailed large investments and environmental control: fence construction, extermination of predators, water provision in the form of small dams and boreholes (wells); by 1950 more than fifty thousand boreholes had been sunk. This project was largely achieved on the white-owned farms in the second half of the twentieth century, contributing to the social as well as the technical transformation of the countryside. It was part of a broader process in which farms became larger, and some African tenants and workers—many of whom continued to live on white-owned farms—were ejected. Opinions are divided on how far these changes have contributed to a long-term recovery of agricultural land. There is some evidence that pastures have stabilized or even improved in some areas; game reserves and the switch to game farming may be one factor.

Reserves

About 10–13 percent of the country was reserved for sole occupation by Africans. Much of this was in the heartlands of the old African chiefdoms, in the wetter zones of the country, and 40–50 percent of Africans lived in these reserves or homelands until the late twentieth century. A significant number of rural Africans maintained small-scale production of crops (especially maize) and livestock (especially cattle). Increasingly dense settlement and agriculture placed great pressure on timber, water, and land. The government had difficulty regulating resource use in scattered African settlements. About the time of World War II the government decided to make radical interventions:

concentrating settlements into villages, grouping arable plots, and fencing grazing land along the lines pursued on the white farms. This was an ambitious policy that involved moving millions of African people. It caused great social disruption and triggered widespread rural protests.

By the 1980s, when implementation largely stopped, such "rehabilitation" was by no means complete. Its results were widely criticized. Environmental ills, already concentrated in these poor and densely settled African areas, were often worsened in new villages and towns with little piped water, sanitation, or electricity. Animals were also congregated around these settlements, compounding their problems.

During the late twentieth century environmental justice movements took up a wide range of issues that resulted from the legacy of apartheid, dispossession, rapid population increase, and urbanization. Black communities were largely segregated into poorer areas on the fringes of major cities. These, especially burgeoning informal settlements from the 1980s, were unsanitary and inadequately serviced and suffered from pollution caused by the use of cheap coal for heating. The mining industry had been a major source of South Africa's industrial wealth, and activists highlighted industrial diseases resulting from asbestos, mercury waste, and mining dust. All of these, however, have been overshadowed by the scourge of HIV/AIDS, which, although it has had a disproportionate impact on people in poor urban and rural environments, is not essentially an environmental disease.

William Beinart

Further Reading

African environments: Past and present. (2000). Special edition of *Journal of Southern African Studies, 26*(4).

Beinart, W. (1984). Soil erosion, conservationism and ideas about development: A southern African exploration, 1900–1960. *Journal of Southern African Studies, 11*(1), 52–83.

Beinart, W. (2003). *The rise of conservation in South Africa: Settlers, livestock and the environment, 1780–1950.* Oxford, UK: Oxford University Press.

Beinart, W., & Coates, P. (1995). *Environment and history: The taming of nature in the United States and South Africa.* London: Routledge.

Carruthers, J. (1995). *The Kruger National Park: A social and political history.* Pietermaritzburg, South Africa: University of Natal Press.

Clarke, J. (2002). *Coming back to Earth: South Africa's changing environment.* Johannesburg, South Africa: Jacana.

Delius, P. (1996). *A lion amongst the cattle: Reconstruction and resistance in the northern Transvaal.* Oxford, UK: James Currey.

Dovers, S., Edgecombe, R., & Guest, B. (2002). *South Africa's environmental history: Cases and comparisons.* Claremont, CA: David Philip.

MacDonald, D. A. (Ed.). (2002). *Environmental justice in South Africa.* Athens: Ohio University Press.

MacKenzie, J. (1988). *The empire of nature: Hunting, conservation and British imperialism.* Manchester, UK: Manchester University Press.

The Politics of conservation in southern Africa. (1989). Special edition of *Journal of Southern African Studies, 15*(2).

Southern Cone

The "Southern Cone" refers to the cone-shaped area of South America located south of the Tropic of Capricorn. Although geographically this includes part of southeastern Brazil, in terms of political geography the Southern Cone has traditionally comprised Argentina, Chile, Paraguay, and Uruguay. Starting in the 1990s, and especially since the creation of the Southern Common Market (SCM) in 1991, the term is often used to refer to a larger area also including Brazil and Bolivia. This usage has created some confusion, to the point that SCM is sometimes incorrectly understood to signify *Southern Cone Common Market* (The Columbia Electronic Encyclopedia 2002). The following discussion uses the term in its traditional, political–geographical sense.

The Region's History

The countries of the Southern Cone achieved independence from Spain (from Portugal in the case of Brazil) in the early nineteenth century, and by the 1870s the populations of most of them had doubled or even tripled. Starting in the mid nineteenth century, Argentina, Chile, Uruguay, and Brazil attracted large-scale immigration, with Argentina alone receiving around six million European immigrants between the 1870s and 1930. However, until the 1870s the region was characterized by ongoing civil war and sporadic border wars. Only in the last two decades of the nineteenth century did most of these countries develop into stable nation states with clear territorial control, although border disputes among Southern Cone countries still persist.

Although the Southern Cone as a whole was characterized by highly unstable politics during much of the twentieth century, becoming particularly notorious for brutal military dictatorships in the 1970s, the histories of the individual countries vary considerably. While Argentina has faced almost continual institutional disruption and cyclical economic instability since the 1930s, Chile and Uruguay have maintained greater institutional stability. Since the 1980s, the return to democracy in the Southern Cone, and the promotion of regional integration through the creation of the Southern Common Market in 1991, have created new possibilities for achieving political and economic stability in the region.

Main Geographical Characteristics

Ecoclimatic diversity characterizes the Southern Cone. The subtropical Andean region reaches its highest point at Aconcagua Mountain (6959 meters) in Argentina; the Atacama Desert in Chile is one of the driest places in the world; forests in Argentina and Chile range from the subtropical to the subantarctic; large fertile plains (the pampas) stretch across southern Brazil, Uruguay, central-eastern Argentina, and the Patagonian steppes. The climatic spectrum is broad, with clearly defined seasons and high regional variability in the annual precipitation from a low 100 millimeters in Patagonia to about 5,000 millimeters in Chile's Valdivian forest.

The Río de la Plata is the largest drainage basin in the region. Comprising the complex systems of the Paraná, Paraguay, Pilcomayo, Bermejo, Uruguay, and Río de la Plata rivers, it is the second-largest drainage basin in the subcontinent and the fifth-largest in the world. The basin contains the most densely populated areas of the whole subcontinent, including large portions of Brazil, Bolivia, Paraguay, Argentina, and Uruguay, and including megalopolises and industrial centers such as São Paulo and Buenos Aires. The economic activities sustained by the basin account for about 70 percent of the combined GDP of its constituent countries. The basin has undergone large-scale transformation, especially through construction of massive dams such as Itaipú Dam, located on the border between Brazil and Paraguay. This is the site of the world's largest operating hydroelectric plant, supplying around 25 percent of Brazil's energy needs and over 90 percent

of Paraguay's. The Yaciretá Dam, another large hydroelectric dam on the Paraná River, is located on the border between Argentina and Paraguay.

Environmental Issues

The region's ecosystems have suffered extensive degradation and loss of biodiversity as a result of long-term anthropogenic transformations. Particularly serious are deforestation and resultant soil erosion and desertification caused by farming and overgrazing, construction of large-scale hydraulic works, and industrial and urban pollution of soil, air, and water. The massive dams in the region are thought to contribute to climatic change and play a part in the recurrent floods affecting Paraguay and northeast Argentina in recent decades. Extensive agriculture and forestry has drastically transformed the landscape. This has led to the decline of much indigenous flora and fauna, notably the virtual extinction in large areas of the most valuable timber species, and indigenous fish and large mammals.

Although the region has a long record of environmental protection and has contributed to scientific understanding of environmental processes and their history, environmental concerns rank low among government priorities. Although there has been change in this area since the 1980s, and environmental policy has become mainstream in Brazil, most policy decisions related to environmental issues are still driven mainly by considerations such as geopolitical strategy or are subordinated to powerful economic and political interests. Recent reports by environmental agencies such as the United Nations Environment Programme have highlighted the urgent need for action on a number of fronts, especially in the designation and enforcement of protected areas to reverse ecosystem degradation and loss of biodiversity.

José Esteban Castro

See also Argentina; Chile

Further Reading

Columbia Electronic Encyclopedia. (2002). Southern Cone Common Market. In *Columbia Electronic Encyclopedia*. Retrieved January 31, 2003, from http://www. bartleby.com/65/st/SthrnCnCmM.html

Crosby, A.W. (1986). *Ecological imperialism: The biological expansion of Europe, 900–1900*. Cambridge, UK: Cambridge University Press.

Instituto, H. L. (1997). *MERCOSUR: Un Atlas Social, Cultural y Económico* (MERCOSUR: A Social, Cultural, and Economic Atlas). Río de Janeiro & Buenos Aires: Manrique Zago Ediciones.

Redford, K. H., & Eisenberg, J. F. (1992). *Mammals of the neotropics: Vol. II. The Southern Cone: Chile, Argentina, Uruguay, Paraguay.* Chicago: University of Chicago Press.

National Museum of Natural History. (2002). *South America: Centres of plant diversity and endemism, VIII Southern Cone.* Retrieved January 31, 2003, from http://www.nmnh.si.edu/botany/projects/cpd/sa/sa-viii.htm

United Nations Environment Programme. (2000). *The GEO report for Latin America and the Caribbean—environment outlook 2000.* Mexico City: UNEP.

United Nations Environment Programme. (2002). Past, present and future perspectives. *Global Environment Outlook 3.* Nairobi: UNEP-Earthscan.

Soviet Union *See* Asia, Central; Asia, Central – Ancient; Russia and the Soviet Union

Soybeans

The soybean belongs to the family Leguminosae (leguminous, nitrogen-fixing plants). The cultivated form, named *Glycine max* (L.) Merrill, grows annually. Its plant is bushy, with height ranging from 0.5 to 1.2 meters. Soybean seeds are spherical to long oval. Most are yellow, but they can also be green, dark brown, purplish black, or black. On an average, dry soybeans contain roughly 40 percent protein, 20 percent oil, 35 percent carbohydrate, and 5 percent ash. Thus, soybeans have the highest protein content of all the cereal and legume species, and the second-highest oil content among all food legumes after peanuts.

Historical and geographical evidence indicates that soybeans originated in northern China, and soybean cultivation in the region started approximately 5,000 years ago. The soybean (then known in Chinese as *shu*, now as *da dou* or *huang dou*) was repeatedly mentioned in later records; it was considered one of the five sacred grains, along with rice, wheat, barley, and millet. The Chinese gradually developed various tasty and nutritious foods derived from soybeans, including tofu, soymilk, soy sprouts, soy paste, soy sauce, and more. Thus, the soybean has made a significant contribution to Chinese culture and civilization.

Soybean cultivation and methods of preparing soy-derived foods were gradually introduced to Japan, Korea, and other Asian countries about 1,100 years ago. Peoples in these countries accepted the Chinese way of preparing soy foods and added innovations of their own, incorporating the soybean into their cultures and traditions. Japanese *natto* and Indonesian tempeh are two such examples.

The soybean was first introduced to Europe and North America in the eighteenth century. However, large-scale official introduction into the United States did not occur until the early 1900s. Thousands of new varieties were brought in, mostly from China, during this period. Until 1954, China led the world in soybean production. Since then the United States has become the world leader.

During the twentieth century, the soybean emerged as one of the most important agricultural commodities in the world, with a steady increase in annual production. In the early twenty-first century, global production is estimated at 150 million metric tons, with major producers being the United States, Brazil, Argentina, China, and India. There are several reasons for this rapid growth. First, soybeans produce the highest amount of edible protein per hectare of land. Second, because soybeans have the ability to fix nitrogen, they are a good rotational crop: Land that has been depleted of nitrogen by previous crops can be sown with soybeans, which will return nitrogen to the soil. Soybeans can also adapt to a wide range of soil and climate. Finally, soybeans have many possible end uses. Broadly speaking, soybeans can be used as human food, animal feed, and industrial material. At present, the majority of the annual soybean production is crushed into oil for cooking and defatted meal for animal feed.

In recent years there have been some breakthroughs in soybean research. Biotechnological advances in the field of genetic engineering have permitted the development of new soybean varieties with increased herbicide tolerance, pest resistance, and altered chemical composition. Medical discoveries have linked the consumption of soy to the prevention and treatment of such chronic diseases as heart disease, certain cancers, and bone diseases; further biotechnological research has focused on new ways of producing nutraceuticals (functional foods; foods, mainly isolated food ingredients that deliver specific non-nutritive physiological benefits that may enhance health, in addition to their nutritional values) and industrial material from soybeans. In the world of the twenty-first century, the soybean may well be the most important protein source for both humans and animals and an important renewable source of industrial material.

Keshun Liu

Further Reading

ISPUC-III. (2000, October). *Proceedings of the Third International Soybean Processing and Utilization Conference.* Conference held in Tsukuba, Japan.

Kauffman, H. E. (Ed.). (1999, August). *Proceedings of World Soybean Research Conference VI.* Conference held at the Global Soy Forum, Chicago.

Keshun L. (1997). *Soybeans: Chemistry, technology, and utilization.* Gaithersburg, MD: Aspen Publishers, Inc.

Wang, X., et al. (1997). *Zhong guo da zhi ping* [Chinese soybean products]. Beijing: Zhong Guo Qing Gong Ye Chu Ban She [China Light Industry Publisher].

Space Exploration

Space exploration, although initially driven by Cold War politics of the twentieth century, ultimately had the goal of understanding the nature of space. This goal was expressed by the U.S. television program *Star Trek* (1966–1969): "To explore strange new worlds, to seek out new life and to boldly go where no one has gone before." People have always been fascinated by the nature of space and have wanted to understand their relationship with a cosmos that transcends earthly cultures.

This desire to understand the cosmos is shown by the development of astrology and eventually astronomy in ancient cultures. Although rooted in religious philosophy, people's relationship with their largest environment, the cosmos, was the crux of Western civilization's debate over the geocentric (Earth-centered) philosophical and scientific worldview advocated by the Greek philosopher Aristotle and Danish astronomer Tycho Brahe, versus the heliocentric (sun-centered) worldview of the Italian astronomer Galileo Galilei, the German astronomer Johannes Kepler, and the English physicist Isaac Newton. The heliocentric Galilean and Newtonian worldview eventually prevailed and became critical to making exploration of

space possible. Historians generally credit Galileo's observations of the moon by telescope for transforming this worldview. His observations revealed a celestial body with an incredible array of mountains and craters. According to the historian David West, Galileo's work *Siderius nuncius* (Starry Messenger) radically transformed humankind's vision of the cosmos from a perfect and flawless celestial environment to one in which "The Moon was not an abstraction. It was a place" (Reynolds 2002, 17). Space exploration became feasible only after the invention of modern rocket technology, which was based upon Galilean and Newtonian physics. This technology would also have major environmental effects for humans as they moved into space.

History of Space Exploration

Rocket technology is based on the scientific principles of mass, inertia and momentum, projectile motion, and energy and combustion. However, the technology that became the underpinning of modern rocketry—gunpowder and rocket artillery—emerged in the thirteenth century in China. Through the centuries many tales would be told about space exploration; among the most realistic was the book *From the Earth to the Moon* in 1865 by French science-fiction writer Jules Verne. According to the U.S. archeologist David Reynolds, Verne's tale is about members of the Baltimore Gun Club attacking "the problem of launching a Moon rocket with straightforward calculations rather than dreamy musings. In a few short meetings, the Baltimore Gun Club determines the necessary force of the explosive power, the size of the gun they will need to build and the size of the projectile, all using basic physics" (Reynolds 2002, 16). Reynolds says that Verne's work was the inspiration for the pioneers of rocketry and a prologue for space exploration.

Modern rocketry emerged during the first half of the twentieth century and is credited to scientists from around the world such as the Russian theorist Konstantin E. Tsiolkovsky, who, after reading Verne's book, produced in his 1903 work *Exploring Space with Reactive Devices* the mathematical calculations and design concepts that became the foundations of liquid-fueled rocketry. Also influential was the Romanian physicist Herman Oberth, whose works such as *The Rocket into Interplanetary Space* (1923) and film *Frau im Mond* (Woman in the Moon) popularized rocket science in Europe. Especially influential was the U.S. experimentalist Robert H. Goddard, who is considered to be the "father of modern rocketry." The U.S. National Aeronautics and Space Administration historian Roger D. Launius points out in his book *NASA and the Exploration of Space* that Goddard, despite a lack of public support in the United States, explored the use of liquid rocket propulsion and argued that rockets could be used to explore the earth's upper atmosphere. Launius states that Goddard's work culminated "in the launching of history's first successful rocket on March 16, 1926, near Auburn, Massachusetts. Although it rose only 184 feet, the feat heralded the modern age of rocketry" (Launius, Ulrich, & Glenn 1998, 19). Goddard, with the financial support of the philanthropist David Guggenheim, developed systems to steer rockets, gyroscopes to maintain rockets' proper position, and rudders to deflect rockets' exhaust gases. Goddard's work led to the development of the Curtiss-Wright XLR25-CW-1 rocket engine, which was used to help break the sonic barrier in 1947. The development of rocket technology was also heavily influenced by the work of Frank J. Malina of California Institute of Technology (and eventually the Jet Propulsion Laboratory) and Wernher von Braun after he came to the United States from Germany. Malina and his engineers developed the WAC (without any control) *Corporal* rocket, which was first launched on 11 October 1945. This rocket had an 11-kilogram payload and an altitude of 30 kilometers. Von Braun is credited with developing the V-2 rocket for Germany during World War II. The rocket was first tested on 13 June 1942, on the Baltic Sea coast at Peenemunde. After further testing the V-2 rocket was used as a devastating weapon (even though it was more of a prototypical space rocket than an artillery rocket) against Allied targets in France, Belgium, and England, resulting in large-scale annihilation of both human life and the environment. "Traveling at speeds in excess of 3,500 miles per hour, the rockets delivered 2,200 pound warheads" (Launius 1998, 21). More than eleven hundred V-2 rockets were launched against England, and sixteen hundred were launched against continental targets such as Antwerp, Belgium. Von Braun voluntarily surrendered the V-2 technology to U.S. forces after his arrest by the German government for wasting its wartime money on space technology. Von Braun would transform the V-2 rocket into the Redstone rocket, "a missile with a 200-mile range like the V-2 but with improved guidance and the ability to carry a four ton payload" (Reynolds 2002, 25). These developments would be critical to space exploration because they would be used to launch the first spacecraft in the United States' Mercury, Gemini, and Apollo projects.

Motivations for Space Exploration

Although by 1947 Americans had sent into space a rocket carrying a camera that took pictures of the earth, historians consider the 1 October 1957, launch of the first satellite, *Sputnik I*, by the Soviet Union as the beginning of space exploration. The development of *Sputnik*, although driven by the intense political, social, and technological competition between the two Cold War superpowers, was inspired by a scientific desire for more information about the earth's environment. *Sputnik* emerged in response to the international scientific community's International Geophysical Year (IGY). The IGY, which was the period between 1 July 1957 and 31 December 1958, encouraged international participation in the development of satellites that would study geophysical phenomena (such as solar activity) expected to occur during that period and map the earth's surface.

Sputnik I was launched from the Soviet Union's rocket-testing facility in a desert in the Kazakh Republic. During its brief life (1 October 1957 to 4 January 1958) the satellite traveled around the earth every ninety-six minutes in an elliptical orbit, verifying exact locations on the earth's surface. By 3 November 1957, the Soviet Union took another major stride on its second space mission when it demonstrated that life is possible in space. *Sputnik II* launched the first living being into space—a dog named Laika. *Sputnik II* was in orbit for almost two hundred days.

To Boldly Go Where No One Has Gone Before

Not to be outdone (and humiliated) by the launch of the *Sputnik* satellites by the Soviet Union, the U.S. Congress within a year passed the National Aeronautics and Space Act, which was signed by President Dwight D. Eisenhower on 29 July 1958. This act began the U.S. space program by creating the National Aeronautics and Space Administration (NASA) effective 1 October 1958. NASA had three primary goals: development of robotic missions to the moon and planets in the solar system, deployment of communications satellites, and human exploration of space beyond the earth's atmosphere. NASA accomplished all three goals within eleven years through Project Mercury, Project Gemini, and Project Apollo. Project Mercury was developed to determine whether a human could withstand the space environment. The *Mercury* spacecraft was launched into space using Redstone and Atlas rocketry. During a sixteen-minute flight on 31 January 1961, Project Mercury demonstrated that higher life-forms, specifically a chimpanzee named Ham, can withstand the space environment. This flight was followed by the first human space flight—of just one orbit—by the Soviet cosmonaut Yuri Gagarin on 12 April 1961, aboard the spacecraft *Vostok I*. Gagarin was followed in less than a month by the first American in space, Alan Shepard, on 5 May 1961. He was in flight for fifteen minutes. The goal of Project Mercury was to keep humans in space for several days, and on 15–16 May 1963, astronaut Gordon Cooper circled the earth twenty-two times in thirty-four hours. NASA also considered Project Mercury a success because it provided information about the impact of microgravity on humans and about other biomedical issues of space flight in addition to exploring aspects of tracking and control. Human exploration of space was furthered by the U.S. mission to the moon conducted in Project Gemini and Project Apollo. The objectives of Project Gemini were to determine whether humans could work outside the spacecraft and in the space environment, to connect with other spacecraft in the space environment, and to collect more physiological data about human response to extended space flight. The *Gemini* spacecraft was designed to hold two astronauts for two weeks and was launched by the Titan II rocket, which was designed as a ballistic missile. Project Gemini consisted of ten successful missions that increased the flight and mission times of astronauts. On 23 March 1965, the Gemini 3 mission launched U.S. astronauts Gus Grissom and John Young into space for five and one-half hours. In June 1965 astronaut Edward H. White II took the first EVA (extravehicular activity) space walk during the Gemini 4 mission, which lasted four days. In August 1965 the Gemini 7 mission lasted two weeks with astronauts Frank Borman and Jim Lovell. In addition to increasing the human capacity to survive the space environment, the missions provided information about weightlessness, biomedicine, and the use of extravehicular activity needed for the Project Apollo moon missions. The Gemini 11 mission on 12 September 1966, with astronauts Dick Gordon and Pete Conrad, gave the world its first view of the earth as a sphere.

Within eight years of the inception of Project Apollo, which was announced before a joint session of Congress by President John F. Kennedy on 25 May 1961, humankind's understanding of its own environment and its relationship to the cosmos was changed forever in a way that could never have happened without space exploration. Within three years of the last Gemini mission the U.S. space program put the first humans (Edwin E. "Buzz" Aldrin and Neil Armstrong) on the moon on 16 July 1969, on its Apollo 11 mission. This was the first time that humans had a direct encounter with another environment in their solar system. Unlike their own "blue planet" teeming with life, the moon that the astronauts observed had a barren, desert-like surface that ranged in color from dusty gray to light tan. U.S. astronauts did not claim the moon for the United States but rather placed a plaque and a U.S. flag on its surface to state that they had come in peace for all humankind. The moon landing was only the first of many space exploration firsts for humans. During the Apollo 8 mission, astronauts Frank Borman, James A. Lovell, and William A. Anders "became the first humans to pass out of Earth's gravitational control and into that of another body in the solar system" (Launius 1998, 89). The Apollo 8 mission was also the first time that humanity was able to see how unique its own home planet is: "a lovely and seemingly fragile blue marble hanging in the blackness of space" (Launius 1998, 88). The NASA historian Launius states that Project Apollo galvanized the modern environmental movement by "a new perception of the planet and the need to protect it and the life it supports" (Launius 1998, 105).

Risks of Space Exploration

Project Apollo also brought the first loss of human life connected with the U.S. space program and the first environmental hazards posed by space technology. On 27 January 1967, three astronauts—Gus Grissom, Ed White, and Roger Chaffee—asphyxiated in the command module during a mock launch sequence for *Apollo 1* after a fire erupted (consuming pure oxygen) from a short circuit in the electrical system. This was not the first time that humans died during space exploration. The U.S. science historian Antony Milne points out in his book *Sky Static: The Space Debris Crisis* that one of the worst space exploration accidents occurred in 1960 when several dozen Soviet scientists were incinerated at the launch pad after being ordered by Soviet leader Nikita Khrushchev to test the rocket before it was ready. Twenty years after that Soviet accident, "in 1980, 50 Soviet technicians were killed when a booster rocket engine blew up while being fueled" (Milne 2002, 15). On 28 January 1986, seven U.S. astronauts died during the launch of the space shuttle *Challenger* (STS–51L) seventy-three seconds into its flight. An explosion was caused by a leak in one of the craft's two solid-fuel rocket boosters, which ignited its main liquid-fuel tank. The *Challenger* disaster occurred less than five years after the first flight of the first space shuttle, the *Columbia*, on 12 April 1981. Seventeen years later seven international astronauts died when *Columbia* disintegrated while descending on 1 February 2003. One possible cause of the *Columbia* disaster being investigated is space debris, which has been accumulating like a flying junkyard during the more than forty years of space exploration.

Human Impact on the Space Environment

Starting with Project Gemini and Project Apollo, humans began to alter the space environment by polluting it and collecting its resources. During its final mission *Apollo 17* brought back 110 kilograms of lunar material. In addition to removing material astronauts have used the space environment as a dumping ground. According to Milne's study over eight thousand spacecraft have been launched since 1957, and "mission-related rubbish is generally reckoned to account for more than 1,000 known objects" (Milne 2002, 74). This debris includes training shoes, toothbrushes, spanners and cameras lost on space walks, sensor covers, altitude control devices, clamp bands and explosive bolts, human feces and urine, and garbage. In addition are rockets and satellites that were lost because they were knocked out of orbit after a collision with other space debris, because they lost their power sources and began to decay from their orbit, or because they had mechanical failure. This debris poses risks to humans both on Earth and in space. If the debris collides with a spacecraft, it can pierce the thin metallic skin that covers such pressurized crafts, resulting in explosive ruptures. Milne points out that in the U.S. space program "on 54 missions flown from June 1992 to November 2000, 43 suffered debris impacts" (Milne 2002, 75). Given the reentry speed of debris, if debris deorbits into the earth's atmosphere, it can have devastating impacts on life-forms and on ecosystems. The most insidious possibility of deorbiting debris is the dispersal of nuclear materials, which have been used throughout the history of space exploration. Nuclear power sources were used aboard the *Thor, Apollo, Pioneer, Viking, Voyager,* and *Ulysses* spacecrafts. In 1996 Russia's nuclear-powered *Mars-96* probe contained 200 grams of plutonium-238. The probe failed to gain its trajectory toward Mars and fell back to Earth, resulting in nuclear material being dispersed among unsuspecting residents of Chile in spite of attempts to warn

the Chilean government. This incident was followed by one of the most controversial space missions using nuclear power sources. The U.S. *Cassini* spacecraft was launched in 1997 on a Titan 4 rocket (after the *Challenger* and *Mars-96* disasters) with 32 kilograms of plutonium-2138 dioxide as a power source for its instruments, "which is about 280 times more radioactive than plutonium-238, the material in atomic bomb fallout" (Milne 2002, 45). The radioactive power source for *Cassini* was placed in the most dangerous of places for the mission: directly above the fuel tanks of the second stage used to propel the craft into orbit. Like all spacecraft, if the *Cassini* did not exit the gravitational pull of the earth it would become essentially a satellite and eventually lose power and plunge into the earth's environment.

Because 120 spacecraft are launched annually the environmental risks from ever-increasing space debris continue to escalate. NASA has begun to address this problem; however, the problem will be abated only with the development of technologies that can make space debris harmless upon reentry into the earth's atmosphere or that can jettison space debris farther in space.

Sylvia Hood Washington

See also Cosmology; Technology

Further Reading

Atwill, W. D. (1994). *Fire and power: The American space program as postmodern narrative.* Athens: University of Georgia Press.

Barbour, J. (1969). *Footprints on the moon.* New York: Associated Press.

Byrnes, M. E. (1994). *Politics and space: Image making by NASA.* New York: Praeger.

Challoner, J. (2000). *Space.* London: Channel–4 Books.

Davies, J. (1992). *Space exploration.* Edinburgh, UK: Chambers.

Dick, S. J. (1996). *The biological universe: The twentieth-century extraterrestrial life debate and the limits of science.* New York: Cambridge University Press.

Irvine, M. (1989). *Tele-satellites.* New York: Gloucester Press.

Launius, R. D., Ulrich, B., & Glenn, J. (1998). *NASA and the exploration of space.* New York: Stewart, Tabori & Chang.

Mellberg, W. F. (1997). *Moon missions: Mankind's first voyages to another world.* New York: Ian Allan.

Milne, A. (2002). *Sky static: The space debris crisis.* Westport, CT: Praeger.

Reynolds, D. W. (2002). *Apollo, the epic journey to the moon.* New York: Tehabi Books.

Urias, J. M., DeAngelis, I. M., Ahern, D. A., Caszatt, J. S., Fenimore G. W., III, & Wadzinski, M. J. (1998). *Planetary defense: Catastrophic health insurance for planet Earth.* Springfield, VA: National Technical Information.

Verschuur, G. (1996). *Impact: The threat of comets and asteroids.* Oxford, UK: Oxford University Press.

Wilford, J. N. (1969). *We reach the moon.* New York: Bantam.

Spain and Portugal

(2001 est. pop. 50 million)

Spain and Portugal are located on the Iberian Peninsula of southwestern Europe, bordered by the Mediterranean Sea to the south and east, the North Atlantic Ocean to the west, and the Pyrenees Mountains to the north. Portugal also includes the Madeira and Azores Islands in the Atlantic Ocean; Spain, the Balearic Islands in the Mediterranean and the Canary Islands in the Atlantic. The Iberian Peninsula is made up of a series of great plateaus, separated from each other and bounded by ranges of mountains on the north, west, east, and south. These plateaus slope gently from east to west and lie at elevations of between 150 and 1,050 meters above sea level. Coastal Portugal and northern Spain have a temperate humid, or maritime, climate, whereas the rest of the peninsula has a Mediterranean climate: hot toward the coast, colder in the interior, humid in the mountains, and dry elsewhere.

Iberian Institutions

Spain and Portugal are predominantly Roman Catholic (Spain, 99 percent; Portugal, 94 percent), with a population totaling about 50 million (Portugal, 10,066,253 [July 2001 estimate]; Spain, 40,037, 995 [July 2001 estimate]). Dictators ruled the two countries for long periods of time during the twentieth century. The death of Antonio de Oliveira Salazar in 1968 in Portugal and of General Francisco Franco in Spain in 1975 led eventually to democratic rule. During Salazar's and Franco's regimes, protectionist policies retarded economic growth and industrialization. Both countries were among the first wave to join the European Union (EU) and have grown considerably in the years since. To meet EU strictures, each country has embraced a series of neoliberal reforms to increase its competitiveness in world markets. Spain and Portugal will have to further reduce unemployment and adjust to monetary and other economic policies of an integrated Europe in the years to come.

Early Modern Environmental Conflict and Management

Many of the mountain ranges of Spain and Portugal are geologically young. With often torrential rainfall in the fall and spring, they are at considerable risk for erosion. This risk has been well studied in the Alpujarra, a region on the southern slopes of the Sierra Nevada in southern Spain. Syrian tribes introduced irrigation and agricultural terracing into the region, and villages prospered through the sixteenth century, growing a wide range of horticultural crops and cultivating silkworms. The effort by Christians to drive the Muslims out of Spain wrought havoc with the Alpujarra population and the irrigation infrastructure. Following a three-year rebellion that began in 1568, most of the surviving population of the Alpujarra was deported and Christian settlers brought in. Christians came in insufficient numbers, though, and lacked experience with intensive irrigation. They preferred to sow wheat and raise sheep: the pattern of the plateaus of central Spain. But wheat cultivation and sheep grazing were ill adapted to the mountain slopes. Deforestation to provide the land needed for this system brought widespread erosion. The introduction of maize and potatoes in the eighteenth century helped increase agricultural productivity, but the region never fully recovered from deforestation.

Modern environmental history has its origins in a series of administrative reforms driven by liberal intellectual currents in the nineteenth century and designed to bring Spain and Portugal into a new era. The impact of these reforms on land, forests, and water was substantial. Land held communally by townships or by the church and mortgaged out was considered to be underused and capable of being made more productive through subjection to market forces. To this end, much land moved into private hands through auctions. By the end of the nineteenth century, approximately 15 percent of the national territory of Spain had passed from control by the church and townships to control by individuals.

Public woodlands also came under scrutiny. Since the mid-eighteenth century their functions had shifted from providing firewood, pasture, and construction materials for subsistence to meeting commercial and industrial ends. In the nineteenth century the state began to actively pursue forest management, subjecting public woodlands increasingly to market forces. Millions of hectares of public woodlands were sold to private parties. Much had never been cultivated because of steep slopes or shallow soils. The new owners put it to the plow, resulting in widespread erosion.

Irrigation has always played an important role in the agriculture of the dry, semiarid interior of the Iberian Peninsula. Many Iberian irrigation systems have an extraordinary history, dating to the Roman (208 BCE–409 CE) and Islamic (711 CE–1492 CE) presence. In the late nineteenth century Spain began to intervene vigorously in water policy. A comprehensive water law in 1879 brought all running water into the public domain except for the surface water rising from streams on one's land. One could obtain a use right to such water by putting it to some productive use. Property owners were also allowed to pump water be-

neath their land and use it as a private good. Until then, it was considered in the public domain. The 1879 Water Law also included a procedure for organizing groups of irrigators into corporate irrigation communities, which could petition for permanent rights to the water they shared. Provincial officials were given an increased role in water management until their eclipse in 1926 with the creation of watershed management authorities.

The origins of modern environmental conflict in Iberia also date to the late nineteenth century. The mines of Río Tinto in southwestern Spain were of strategic importance, the world's largest deposits of iron disulfide, used in the manufacture of sulfuric acid, basic to the chemical and fertilizer industries. The mines also exploited large deposits of copper, indispensable to the expansion of electricity. The mines employed a system to aid mineral extraction by calcination, the heating of large piles of minerals. The process took place in the open, and toxic fumes affected the nearby fields of Zalamea la Real. Public outcry led to the creation of the

A view of the Sierra de Gredos, which separate Spain and Portugal, from Jaraiz de la Vera in Spain. COURTESY SARAH CONRICK.

first environmental organization in Spain: the Liga Antihumos de la Provincia de Huelga (Antismoke League of Huelva Province). On 4 February 1888 national police opened fire on a concentration of miners and their families who were protesting the fumes. Two hundred people are estimated to have been killed.

Modern Environmental Conflict and Management

The Franco and Salazar dictatorships followed similar paths in quelling environmental conflict. Neither regime accorded natural resources special treatment. This was to change. The deaths of Salazar and Franco were followed by elections and new constitutions and eventually a modern era of environmental concern. The return to democracy opened up political space for new actors and new issues long held in abeyance in resource management arenas.

The modern environmental movement in Spain can be traced to the formation of the Asociacion Española para la Ordenación y el Medio Ambiente (AEORMA; Spanish Association for Planning and Environment) in 1970. AEORMA in 1974 issued the *Manifiesto de Benidorm (Benidorm Manifesto)*, an important expression of environmental problems and principles to follow in resolving them. The *Benidorm* statement brought public attention, often for the first time, to urban pollution in large cities, the degradation of hydraulic infrastructure in regions of intensive irrigated agriculture, the presence of nuclear centers in the Cantabrian Coast, the Ebro, and the Coasts of Tarragon, water transfers from water-surplus to water-deficit regions, and the degradation of fisheries by excessive harvesting and industrial pollution. Tourism, a major source of income, rose substantially in the aftermath of the *Benidorm* statement and has come to represent a substantial source of pollution in the coastal areas. Many national and regional environmental organizations became active during the 1970s. The strongly political Asociación para la Defensa de la Naturaleza (ADENA; Association for the Defense of Nature) and the Federación de Amigos de la Tierra de los Pueblos de España (FAT; Federation of Friends of the Earth of the Peoples of Spain), a federation of groups affiliated with the World Wildlife Fund, have been of particular importance. The environmental movement in each country worked hand in hand with nongovernmental organizations. By the year 2002, 761 environmental nongovernmental organizations were operating in Spain.

The European Green Party has had less success in the environmental movement in Iberia. The Portuguese Green Party, Partido Ecologistica-Os Verdes, was founded in 1982. Os Verdes is represented in the national parliament, where in 2002 it held 2 of 230 seats. On the local level it has a total of 35 seats. It is also represented on the National Elections Council and the National Council of Education. Linguistic complexity and the regional division of Spanish politics (four languages and over ten nationalist parties) have made it difficult for Spanish Greens to push their cause. A complicating factor has been the strength of the left-wing party, Izquierda Unida, which has maintained close ties with the environmental movement despite its generally old-left ideology. A conservative party, the Partido Popular, is now in power, and Izquierda Unida's ties with the ecological movement have been weakened. In May 2001 the Greens got a considerable boost with the constitution of the Federación Los Verdes–Izquierda Verde (Greens–Green Left)—an act of affiliation—at a meeting of over six hundred delegates from all over Spain. This new broad-based green-left federation offers the best chance so far for putting environmental issues on the national political agenda.

The European Union

The entry of Spain and Portugal into the European Union had dramatic long-term implications for environmental management. Member countries are required to adopt environmental legislation emanating from the European Union to maintain their status. This legislation included a wide range of directives in the areas of industrial waste management, environmental impact assessments, the implementation of water quality standards, minimum levels for rivers to maintain biotic diversity, and many other environmental "best practices." The EU also took on the task of coordinating the agricultural sector of member countries through a common set of policies. A major reform of the Common Agricultural Policy in 1992 incorporated measures to compensate farmers for using less-intensive farming methods (converting arable land to meadows and pastures, preserving habitats and biodiversity, practicing afforestation, and practicing long-term set-aside) and promoted organic agriculture. Increased production is now but one of several goals, including environmental concerns, of agriculture in the European Union.

In response to these directives, each country has had to compile a corpus of environmental legislation and to expand government bureaucracies to apply it. The Ministry of Environment in Spain now has separate agencies to address environmental quality, coastal waters, freshwater resources, watershed management associations, nature conservation, and national parks.

Environmental Issues

Many environmental issues confront Spain and Portugal as they enter the twenty-first century. Coastal zones experienced an increase of urbanization from 1975 to 1990, and nearshore and offshore water became polluted from raw sewage and effluents from the offshore production of oil and gas. Air pollution caused by industrial and vehicle emissions has been a serious problem, growing in sync with urbanization. Spain and Portugal are among the countries in the world with the greatest increase in ownership of vehicles: Spain went from 239 vehicles per thousand people in 1980 to 467 in 1998, an increase of 95 percent; Portugal from 145 to 347, an increase of 139 percent over the same period. Lisbon, the capital city of Portugal, exceeded the World Health Organization's levels for nitrogen dioxide during 1990–1995. Excessive ozone concentrations in Spain have been a problem in regions near petrochemical plants. And Barcelona has been plagued with excesses of sulfur dioxide, nitrogen dioxide, and suspended particles in its air.

In 1985 Spain's new Water Law was implemented to correct deficiencies of the earlier law and to adjust water policy to the creation of regional autonomous communities in the 1978 Constitution. The 1985 Spanish Water Law contains environmental components that synthesize five EC (European Community) directives linking surface and underground water together as part of the public domain. The 1985 Water Law distinguishes water renewed through the hydrological cycle and subject to state ownership from nonrenewable water capable of being privatized. The use of groundwater, relatively unfettered under the 1879 Water Law, became highly circumscribed by the state. Watershed management authorities have been reorganized to administer large territorial divisions rather than small rivers flowing into large rivers, as under the 1926 legislation that created watershed management authorities. Watershed management authorities now control watersheds exceeding the territorial boundaries of the autonomous communities created in the 1978 Constitution.

The 1985 Water Law charged a newly created National Water Council with overseeing the drafting of a National Water Plan and balancing the interests of regional autonomous communities and the central government. When a draft plan was released in 1993, it triggered a national debate over whether to pursue a traditional course of increasing water supply by constructing dams and transferring water from water-surplus basins to water-deficit basins or a new course of instituting measures to manage demand and save water. The controversial measures under debate included the application of standardized volumetric measures, tariffs levied on water consumed in excess of an optimum threshold, sanctions for water wastage, and water pricing prioritized by use.

Natural resources and protected areas take on special significance in Iberia. Geographically isolated from the rest of Europe by the Pyrenees, the Iberian Peninsula's plant life developed relatively independently of the rest of the continent, with spectacular results: Of about six thousand species of flora in the Iberian Peninsula, about one-quarter occur nowhere else in the world. Portugal has more than twenty protected areas, ranging from the vast Parque Natural da Serra da Estrela to the tiny Reserva Natural do Paúl de Arzila, a bird sanctuary not far from Coimbra. More than one-half the bird species of Europe are found in Doñana National Park bordering the estuary of the Guadalquivir River in southern Spain on the Atlantic coast. Doñana lies along a major migration route from western Europe to western Africa, and five of its bird species are threatened. The United Nations Educational, Scientific, and Cultural Organization (UNESCO) recognized Doñana as a biosphere reserve in 1980, and it is Europe's largest nature reserve. In April 1998 a dam containing toxic effluents from a zinc mine burst, releasing 5 million cubic meters of contaminated sludge and water over a 45-square-kilometer area. The sludge spread 40 kilometers downstream into the Guadalquivir River system, seriously damaging Doñana National Park and the protected adjoining wetlands. The Doñana disaster has been a rallying point for a new environmental consciousness in Spain as the country moves into the twenty-first century.

David Guillet

Further Reading

Bentley, J. (1989). Bread forests and new fields: The ecology of reforestation and forest clearing among small-woodland owners in Portugal. *Journal of Forestry 33*(4), 188–195.

Brouwer, R. (1995). *Planting power: The afforestation of the commons and state formation in Portugal*. Netherlands: Eburon

Gallego Martinez, D., Jiménez Blanco, J., Sebastián Amarilla, J., Zambrana Pineda, J., & Zapata Blanco, J. (2000). Forest Policy and Public Forest Production in Spain, 1855–1936. In M. Agnoletti & S. Anderson (Eds.), *Forest history: International studies on socio-economic and forest ecosystem change, Report No. 2 of the IUFRO Task Force on Environmental Change*, (pp. 313–320). Wallingford, UK: CABI Publishing.

García Latorre, J., Andrés Sánchez, P., & García Latorre, J. (2001). The man-made desert: Effects of economic and demographic growth on the ecosystems of arid Southeastern Spain. *Environmental History, 6*(1): 75–94.

García Latorre, J., García-Latorre, J., & Sanchez-Picón, A. (2001). Dealing with aridity: Socio-economic structures and environmental changes in an arid Mediterranean region. *Land Use Policy* 18:1: 53–64.

Glick, T. F. (1979). *Islamic and Christian Spain in the Early Middle Ages*. Princeton, NJ: Princeton University Press

González de Molina, M. (2001). The limits of agricultural growth in the nineteenth century: A case study from the Mediterranean world. *Environment and History* 7(4), 473–499.

González de Molina, M., & Martínez Alier J., (Eds.) (1993). *Historia e ecologia* [*History and Ecology*]. Madrid: Marcial Pons

Grove, A. T., & Rackham, O. (2001). *The nature of Mediterranean Europe: An ecological history*. New Haven, CT: Yale University Press

Guillet, D. (2002). Co-management of natural resources: The long view from northwestern spain. *Environment and history*, 8(2), 217–236.

McNeill, J. R. (1992). *The mountains in the Mediterranean world: An environmental history*. New York: Cambridge University Press.

Pridham, G. (1994). National environmental policy making in the European framework: Spain, Greece and Italy in comparison. In S. Baker, K. Milton, & S. Yearley (Eds.), *Protection the periphery: Environmental policy in the peripheral regions of the European Unions* (pp. 80–101). London: Frank Cass

Silvers, G. M. (1991). The natural environment in Spain: A study of environmental history, legislation, and attitudes. *Tulane Environmental Law Journal* 5(1), 285–316.

Varillas, B. (1981). *Para una historia del movimiento ecologista en España* [Toward a history of the environmental movement in Spain]. Madrid, Spain: Miraguano.

Vassberg, D. E. (1984). *Land and society in golden age Castile*. New York: Cambridge University Press.

Sparrow *See* House Sparrow

Spinoza
(1632–1677)
Dutch philosopher and writer

Baruch Spinoza was a Dutch philosopher and writer on religion whose writings encouraged a new view of the relationship of nature and humankind. By drawing attention to the historical character of the Pentateuch, the first five books in the Bible, he introduced doubts about the "dominion" that humans assumed had been given them over nature. Spinoza's conception of God and God's relationship to nature was quite different from that which both Christians and Jews claimed to draw from the Scriptures. For Spinoza, God and nature are not quite identical but rather inseparable. In his philosophy the contemplation of nature is inherently meritorious and a true source of happiness for humans.

Spinoza, also known as Benedictus (Latin) or Bento (Portuguese), was born in Amsterdam to a family of Jewish merchants whose members had moved to the Netherlands to escape the religious persecution of their native Portugal. Baruch's father provided a rabbinical education for his son but allowed him also to study Latin, classical literature, and the sciences, a situation that was not approved by the Jewish community. Spinoza was publicly excommunicated by his synagogue in 1656. Many scholars consider this event politically motivated, however, a matter of the Jewish community not wanting to be considered a source of subversion in Protestant Netherlands.

Spinoza lived modestly by tutoring and by grinding lenses, a task at which he became quite proficient. He also received small gifts from supporters and friends. He published only two works in his lifetime. One of these, the *Tractatus Theologico-Politicus*, contained Spinoza's thoughts on the Pentateuch as a collection of historical documents, arguing against a literal interpretation of the events described and for full freedom of opinion in religion. Spinoza is regarded by theologians as one of the founders of the so-called higher criticism, the analysis of the Scriptures as a reflection of the culture that produced them.

Spinoza's most important work, the *Ethics*, was published posthumously by his friends. The book actually deals with metaphysics and psychology as well as ethics. The arguments in the book are set out in the manner of mathematical proofs, as in Euclid's *Elements* in geometry, because in Spinoza's view they follow logically from a very few metaphysical assumptions. The most important of these is that there is really one substance—the divine substance—in existence. Thus individuals and objects do not have existence in themselves but rather as components of the divine. It follows, to Spinoza at least, that nothing is truly evil from the standpoint of God and that free will is an illusion. The main cause of human suffering is humans' attachment to passionate emotions, their emotional investment in things beyond their control. Finally, human happiness is possible in a commitment to God, a commitment to all that is in nature because all nature is of the same substance as God.

Spinoza spent his adult life living in rented rooms in the Netherlands. Following his excommunication he moved to a country house, then near to Leiden, and eventually to the Hague. He died of tuberculosis at the age of forty-five.

Donald R. Franceschetti

Further Reading

Jaspers, K. (1974). *Spinoza*. New York: Harcourt Brace Jovanovich.

Russell, B. (1945). *A history of Western philosophy*. New York: Simon & Schuster.

Wild, J. (Ed.). (1958). *Spinoza selections*. New York: Scribner's.

Sports

Sport and the environment coexist in an uneasy relationship. On the one hand, some sports depend for their existence on environmental features such as wind (e.g., sailing) and precipitation (e.g., skiing). On the other hand, some sports seem to seek to neutralize the environment, seeing it as a factor that interferes with the ideal milieu in which they should take part. For example, turf science seeks to improve on the natural environment in the construction of sports sites for football, cricket, and golf courses. In track and field the turf surfaces upon which competitions take place has, over the course of a century, been replaced by totally synthetic surfaces where the vagaries of the natural surface are neutralized. Additionally, some sports, such as badminton, take place only in fully enclosed buildings. The tendency to "improve on nature" is said to be central to sport. So, too, is the use of the environment by the most apparently benign sports.

The fact that nature is used in the playing of sport suggests that at a deep structural level sport is in some way antinature. Ecologist Johann Galtung suggests that sport is a "carrier of deep culture and structure." He adds that

> sporting events decreasingly take place in natural surroundings, and increasingly in special places made for this purpose, with an overwhelming amount of concrete rather than just pure, unmanipulated nature. The sports palace and the stadium, Olympic or not, are anti-nature and have to be because of the near-laboratory settings in which the unidimensionality of competitive sports can unfold itself under controlled conditions. Pure nature has too much variation in it, too much "noise." (Galtung 1984, 14

The "pure nature" that Galtung alludes to can be exemplified by the tennis court. Ideally, it should consist of a flat, smooth surface. It should be a prescribed size, each court being exactly the same size. The markings on the court have standardized, geometric markings. In few other cultural activities is one place so much the same as another. But if this were not so, sport as it is known could not exist.

Even sailing and yachting use starting and finishing lines and buoys as markers, a subtle yet symbolic demonstration of human power. In such a case, human dominance can hardly be said to be malignant. Many sports environments can be likened to gardens where the humanization of the environment, while being a reflection of human dominance, is also one of affection. It is, as Chinese-American geographer Yi-Fu Tuan would have it, dominance with a human face. The groundsman lovingly tends the grass surface of a lawn tennis court or cricket field. "Tending" implies a benign form of dominance. Extreme dominance over nature can occur when a natural surface is totally re-

Sports Stadiums and Their Affect on the Community

Based in Britain, the Federation of Stadium Communities exists to "improve the quality of life of communities which exist in the shadow of sports stadia." The Federation's website lists more than twenty-five common issues and complaints that have been made about stadiums in various communities. Below are the environmental issues cited by the Federation.

Air pollution

Children unable to play outside

Congested and delayed public transport

Despoliation of open space

Dirt and litter

Floodlighting intrusion

Loss of daylight and/or sunlight

Loud noise especially from PA system

Massive overshadowing structures

Traffic queues, controls and delays

Unattractive visual appearance

Source: Federation of Stadium Communities. Retrieved March 10, 2003, from http://www.f-s-c.co.uk/background.htm

moved and when the natural environment is repeatedly degraded.

The domination of the landscape by sports has assumed basically two forms. The first is enclosure; the second is artificialization.

Containing Space and Transforming the Land

A fundamental dimension of the laws of virtually all sports is that they possess precise spatial limits. The human construction of a sports environment has resulted in highly geometric places. Lines, arcs, circles, and rectangles typify the modern sports site. So, too, do the rigid spatial limits that define their extent. Such confinement reflects the power of human territorialization. However, the geometries of sport are more than matched by artificialization. For sports to take place in their optimal environment, nature had to be improved upon. The flat plane and the smooth surface must prevail over the roughness and irregularity of nature. Plastic comes to replace grass. As noted, sports require a standardized milieu that permits international comparisons. Were it not for such standardization, local, national, and international sports events could not take place, and sports records would be meaningless.

In the case of some sports events, environmental impact may be restricted to the local scale; in the case of other sports events, environmental impact may be regional. In some cases, as in orienteering (a cross-country race in which each participant uses a map and compass to navigate between checkpoints along an unfamiliar course), the environmental impact is modest, almost nonexistent; in other cases, sport's environmental is extensive.

Swimming, cricket, golf, and skiing are sports that have had a significant, if not profound, influence on the physical environment.

Swimming

Water as part of the natural environment has been controlled for sporting uses in many ways. Early swimming races usually took place in natural water courses—river, lakes, or a sea. The swimming events of the 1896 Olympics in Greece were held in the Piraeus and those of 1900 in the River Seine in France. For purposes of comparative record keeping, however, such courses were unsatisfactory. Swimmers were invariably affected—positively and negatively—by currents; in other cases the waters were polluted. An early improvement of such environments was to enclose a segment of water and provide changing rooms and other facilities close by. Rectangular, indoor pools came later but by the mid-twentieth century were commonplace. Natural water had been eliminated, and recycled chlorinated water became the norm.

Cricket

The image of English cricket is one of naturalness. However, the norms of cricket require nature to be drastically improved upon. Traditionally, the management of the cricket ground was undertaken by sheep, but an improved field was necessary for the emergence of the game in its modern form. With the legalization of over-arm bowling (the ball being bowled over the shoulder of the bowler, rather than the less aggressive 'under-arm' method) in the mid-nineteenth century, a closely mowed and rolled playing area became a necessity in the interests of safety and skill.

Two factors strongly affected the natural milieu in which cricket was played: science and technology. Science was represented by the groundsman, an expert in horticulture. The first groundsmen were former gardeners, experts in dominating nature—but with nurturing care. The landscape of cricket was the object of "turf science." The turf of the cricket field was affected by technology. The heavy roller, introduced in the 1870s, further served to standardize the playing surfaces, and the late nineteenth century brought the growth of specialized cricket equipment to aid the gradual leveling and equalizing of the cricket landscape.

Implicit in the ethos of many modern sports is that the physical environment should be eliminated as far as possible. In cricket the playing surface was covered during wet weather. In 1982 a motorized cover was introduced. It covers almost all the playing area and at the flick of a switch can be rolled to the edges of the playing area when rain threatens. In some countries indoor cricket has been introduced, converting the game from the rural idyll to an industrialized pleasure zone.

Golf

In Scotland, widely regarded as the home of modern golf, golf has colonized a wide variety of environments. Although early courses were found on the coastal links (sand dunes), the demand for the sport was so great that a wide variety of physical environments were sculptured into simulations of the coastal dunes. In the United States golf courses have colonized environments of desert and coniferous forest. Huge amounts of water are required to maintain courses in Arizona and other arid states. As with cricket and lawn tennis, the human dominance expended on the landscape has traditionally been of a relatively benign nature, the turf being lovingly tended and manicured.

More recently, however, the construction of golf courses has led to considerable controversy and encouraged ecological activism. U.S. courses use an average of 680 kilograms of pesticide a year—about seven times the amount used by farmers. Rainwater runoff from golf courses has contaminated nearby groundwater, lagoons, lakes, and wetlands. Golf is growing most rapidly in east Asia, notably Japan and Korea. Whereas there were only seventy-two courses in Japan in 1956, the figure is now nearer three thousand. Dominance over nature in this context has led to pollution and despoliation. Golf ideally needs undulating land near cities that is neither built on nor given over to agriculture. With no such land available, golf development has accelerated forest clearance. Developers have used tons of herbicides, fungicides, pesticides, germicides, coloring agents, and organic chlorine and other fertilizers, including some that are carcinogenic or cause other health abnormalities. Water draining into rivers and lakes has resulted in widespread damage to animal and human life. In Korea it has been found that pesticides spread on golf courses can be absorbed into the human body through inhalation or skin contact. In the 1980s the Japanese Ministry of Health found that water quality had been harmed by golf course development in 950 places.

Such as been the impact of golf on the environment that local activist groups often emerge to oppose golf course development. Global concern is reflected in the Global Anti-Golf Movement, based in Japan.

Skiing

Arguably, the sport that has attracted most environmental concern is skiing, a space-extensive sport that requires substantial infrastructure that changes the natural landscape and environment. Skiing assumes several forms, and differing ski sports have different environmental impacts. Cross-country skiing, for example, has minimal direct effects on the environment. Downhill and slalom skiing and ski jumping, however, cause considerable reshaping of the environment. Major sports events such as the Olympics can lead to catastrophic changes in environment, both directly through the impact on the land surface and indirectly through increased traffic, noise, and congestion.

The natural landscape is changed in two ways to satisfy the demands of serious skiing. First, earth- and rock-moving equipment changes the profiles of slopes in order to make them "suitable" for downhill skiing. Second, for ski-jumping events, new structures are erected. Ski jumps have become longer and taller over the last century, and the long profile of the slope has been gradually steepened. Where the surface geology is neither eroded by machines nor built upon in the interests of skiing, the vegetative landscape is often removed in order to create suitable pistes (downhill ski trails). It has been estimated that in some parts of the Swiss Alps, as much as 15 percent of the surface area has been harmed ecologically by the development of ski facilities.

Sports have had such significant environmental impacts that several movements have contested the hosting of large sports events in their areas. In 1972 Denver, Colorado, turned down the offer to host the 1976 winter Olympics. However, such opposition focuses not only on the winter games. Opponents of the Toronto bid for the 1996 summer Olympics successfully argued that the negative environmental (as well as social) impacts should be taken into account. Likewise, in 1997 environmental groups in Italy campaigned to undermine Rome's Olympic bid on the grounds that the city could not cope with the influx of tourists.

The Olympics pose formidable environmental challenges. Waste management, energy consumption, transportation, materials recycling, and major constructions all need to be accommodated in the face of a growing awareness of environmental ethics. Winter Olympics are regarded as more serious because they affect relatively isolated areas that have not previously experienced activities on such a scale.

Consideration of golf and skiing should not divert attention from the environmental effects of sports in smaller places. Weekly stadium-based events can cause environmental harm that is unwillingly borne by residents near the stadiums. In Britain this environmental harm has been researched. A major feature of spectator sports is that a substantial proportion of spectators travel by car for much of their journey to spectate, hence adding to emissions of noxious gases in the urban environment. However, congestion, parking, and the antisocial behavior of fans also cause harm. Additional environmental harms are noise and light pollution. All of these negative consequences of sports impose hidden costs on those living near stadium-based events. At the local level, activism against new stadium developments is reflected in Britain by the Federation of Stadium Communities, which seeks to assist local groups in resisting such developments.

John Bale

Further Reading

Bale, J. (1994). *Landscapes of modern sport*. London: Leicester University Press.

Galtung, J. (1984). Sport and international understanding; sport as a carrier of deep culture and structure. In M. Illmarinen (Ed.), *Sport and international understanding*. (pp. 12–19). Berlin: Springer Verlag.

Horne, J. (1998). The politics of sport and leisure in Japan. *International Review for the Sociology of Sport, 33*(2), 171–182.

Tuan, Y.-F. (1984). *Dominance and affection: The making of pets*. New Haven. CT: Yale University Press.

Sprawl

Possibly no other landscape form has had its image transformed as quickly as sprawl has since 2000. In just a few years, sprawl has gone from a model of successful economic development to a model of poor community planning that lacks foresight and good taste. Today, sprawl includes nearly all landscape transformation related to economic development, including roadways, shopping areas, and suburbs. The landscape becomes sprawl when it prioritizes the automobile over other considerations.

The United States is the world's capital of sprawl; however, nations around the world face similar challenges with the arrival of American-inspired economic development. As the United States and many other developed nations look for a new landscape beyond sprawl, many less-developed nations view sprawl as a link to jobs and economic advancement.

Communities and Spatial Preference

Sprawl is a development pattern in the United States only after World War II. Sprawl is based on the decentralizing of the human population. Stylistically, it also ignores historical or ecological precedent and human experience. Although sprawl may sound unappealing, it has come to dominate nations such as the United States simply because of convenience.

From concentrated towns and cities, suburban development has led middle-class residents to construct satellite areas that are now referred to as "sprawl." Until recently this pattern was largely absent from the rest of the world. Throughout human history, most communities were centered about a common area, possibly a market, a central structure, or an open area. Most habitation grew outward from this center and created urban areas.

Agriculture was the most common activity outside of the urban or town center. A great deal of early agriculture grew outward from these central areas on land owned and tended commonly. Societies structured around private property ownership began systematic changes to this community structure. Most commonly, agriculturalists constructed homes in outlying areas where they could also tend their own land. Such shifts rarely meant true decentralization. Markets still kept rural inhabitants intimately involved with the town. On the whole, living near the central town in many societies before 1800 was a mark of status; residences more distant were most often relegated to the poor.

Most of these spatial dynamics continued for much of the Industrial Age, when workplaces located themselves within a downtown business district. The growth of more-defined middle and upper classes combined with a growing desire for a cleaner, simpler residential environment to propel Europeans to country estates and summer homes. By 1850 Romanticism and other cultural developments had contributed to an aesthetic appreciation of more rustic and primitive living. This intrigue of some wealthy residents stimulated a larger shift in spatial preferences. Ultimately this shift led many nations to suburbanize by the late 1800s. The effort to link suburbs with necessary services led to the creation of sprawl on the landscape.

Transportation and Suburbia

Sprawl grew out of the increasing decentralization that accompanied suburbanization after 1900. Transportation served as the most important tool for this shift. By prioritizing transportation corridors, the United States led the way toward today's landscape of sprawl. Early examples of suburbanization were seen in "green cities" in Britain and France. Such plans rarely incorporated sprawl; instead, their priorities lay in green spaces and rustic style. Providing shelter remained the primary goal of housing, but setting and aesthetics became crucial components of many homes.

By 1930 some suburban planners had begun to look for inspiration less in nature and more in technological solutions. Planners in Germany helped to create the International style (style that prioritizes simplicity and function over ornamentation) of the 1920s, and their Modernist designs influenced architecture throughout the twentieth century. Although Modernism was most evident in skyscrapers, the ideas inherent in style pioneered by European architects could also be seen in everything ranging from roadways to home design.

As the United States adopted this pattern by 1920, planners and developers combined the impulse to move outward with transportation infrastructure and prefabricated home design. The result was the unprecedented rapid development of suburban areas outside of major cities. Initially, such developments followed railroad and streetcar corridors. However, after automobiles became widely affordable, many land developers and other businesses began marketing a single vision of the American Dream: owning one's own single-family house on a large lot in the suburbs. This marketing appeal resonated with many consumers, who saw the suburbs as an opportunity to escape the noise, crowds, and social problems of the city and to raise children in a safe, clean environment.

American suburbanization was spurred by a number of social and political factors. Through the Federal Housing Administration (FHA) and Veterans Administration (VA) loan programs, the federal government provided mortgages for 11 million new homes after World War II. With the surge in American population that is called the "baby boom," a new American ideal was born: a new single-family home in an outlying suburb. Policies of FHA and VA programs discouraged the renovation of existing houses and turned buyers away from urban areas.

Planners created home styles that allowed them to develop one site after another with the automobile linking each one to the outside world. The ticky-tack world of Levittown, New York (the first of which was constructed in 1947), involved a complete dependence on automobile travel. This shift to suburban living became a hallmark of the late twentieth century, with

ITS NOW OR NEVER...
OUR LAST CHANCE!!!

FINAL PLANNING BOARD HEARING TO APPROVE/DISAPPROVE BURNING TREE DEVELOPMENT

ATTENTION: All residents of the Castle Hill, Hollenbeck, Lake Mansfield, Christian Hill and Division Rd. neighborhoods (i.e. the traffic corridor linking Great Barrington and surrounds to the proposed BURNING TREE development on Christian Hill Rd.

Thursday, November 14
Great Barrington Town Hall

Public comments will be heard <u>first</u> starting at **7:30**

COME BAND TOGETHER
the sheer number of residents in attendance will be our strongest statement!
LET'S PACK THE ROOM

This handbill announces a meeting to consider the building of a major subdivision in a rural area. The protest was evidently successful since the plan was scaled down from over 100 to 15 homes.

over half of the nation residing in suburbs by the 1990s. The planning system that supported this residential world, however, involved much more than roads. The services necessary to support outlying, suburban communities also needed to be integrated by planners.

Instead of the Main Street prototype, the auto suburbs demanded a new form. Initially, American planners such as Jesse Clyde Nichols devised shopping areas such as Kansas City's Country Club District, which appeared as a hybrid of previous forms. Soon, however, the "strip" evolved as the commercial corridor of the future. These sites quickly became part of suburban development in order to provide basic services close to home. A shopper rarely arrived without an automobile; therefore, the car needed to be part of the design program. Signs were the most obvious architectural development of this new landscape. Integrated into the overall site plan would be towering neon advertisements that identified services. Also, parking lots and drive-through windows suggest the integral role of transportation in this new commerce. In short, sprawl had arrived.

During this period of massive home construction, federal and local subsidies also spurred the construction of roads—including a 66,000-kilometer interstate highway system. The scale of this construction will likely stand as one of the great building feats of human history. Between 1945 and 1954, 9 million Americans moved to suburbs and became entirely reliant on roadways for their everyday life. Between 1950 and 1976, central city population in the United States grew by 10 million while suburban population grew by 85 million. Housing developments and the shopping/strip mall culture that accompanied decentralization of the population made the automobile a virtual necessity.

The automobile proved to be the ultimate tool for decentralizing the landscape. With satellite communities constructed miles from downtown resources and shopping, developers seized the opportunity to develop the arteries connecting suburbs to cities. With little thought to livability or other priorities, suburbs incorporated shopping and service areas that would evolve into forms on the American landscape. The common link between each portion of the landscape became the automobile.

These developments culminated in the shopping mall, which quickly became a necessary portion of sprawl. By the 1970s developers' initiatives clearly included regional economic development for a newly evolving service and retail world. Incorporating suburbs into such development plans, designs for these pseudocommunities were held together by the automobile.

Strip malls, which open on to roadways and parking lots, were installed near residential areas as suburbs extended farther from the city center. Developers then perfected the self-sustained, enclosed shopping mall. Try as they might, such artificial environments could never re-create the culture of local communities. Shopping malls became the symbol of a culture of conspicuous consumption that many Americans began to criticize during the 1960s. Many Americans began to ask: Have we given up our ties to genuine community?

Questioning Sprawl

Peter Blake's seminal work *God's Own Junkyard* in the early 1970s helped to ask critical questions of the automobile-inspired landscape. Blake and others referred to the landscape as "blight," largely from its lack of a design program or architectural style. Robert Venturi and others set out to consider the auto strip as a viable architectural form, but few architects agreed. Inspired and organized by consumption and not living, they argued, sprawl is a horrific symbol of the most decadent and wasteful aspects of twentieth-century life.

Although many critics described sprawl as "tasteless," few scientists had applied new lines of thought such as ecology to suburban planning. In the late 1960s Ian McHarg published *Design with Nature*, which urged architects to consider the ecology of a site when devising a plan. Beginning in the 1970s critics such as Jane Jacobs and Jim Kunstler, writing for a more general reader, identified an intrinsic bias on the American landscape. (Kunstler, for example, writes: "Main Street persists in our cultural memory . . . though the majority of Americans have moved into the new model habitat called Suburban Sprawl" [1998, 37].)

Such an idea remained foreign until the late 1970s. The modern environmental movement asked hard questions of American consumption. In the 1970s this movement resulted in new responsibilities for the federal government, including the Environmental Protection Agency (EPA). The EPA's regulative authority brought new demands on developers. Environmental-impact statements, particularly as suburban plans affected watersheds, became a standard part of planning during the 1980s. Sprawl still happened, but a great deal of the planning had to funnel through EPA regulators.

The 1990s closed with the unfolding of the new politics of urban sprawl. "I've come to the conclusion," explained Vice President Al Gore on the campaign trail in 1998, "that what we really are faced with here is a systematic change from a pattern of uncontrolled sprawl toward a brand new path that makes quality of life the goal of all our urban, suburban, and farmland policies" (Egan 1998, para. 6).

Gore and others had seen the future not in the United States but in Europe, especially in nations such as Finland, Norway, and the Netherlands. The international planners were well ahead of American designers. The green movement in Europe had spurred significant changes in land planning in many nations. A great deal of this planning was inspired by Postmodernism. This intellectual approach called for abandoning the rigid rules of architectural Modernism and showing greater sensitivity to history and local context and for allowing diverse voices, such as minorities, to be heard. The blend was tailored for European communities with a long history but an interest in modernizing.

Designing beyond Sprawl

The American version of these plans has come in the form of New Urbanism, one of a handful of responses to sprawl's shortcomings. Instead of single-use developments, New Urbanist communities provide mixed uses within a walkable neighborhood. Additionally, housing options are varied, and the automobile becomes an unnecessary part of everyday living. Some examples of New Urbanist communities include Seaside, Florida; Celebration, Florida; and Kentlands, Maryland. Many European towns and cities were already structured around such preautomobile models. New Urbanists single out Capri, Florence, and Barcelona as cities that have maintained connections to ideals of these new models of town planning.

Internationally, sprawl has become an issue wherever population density combines with American-inspired residential development. With shopping centers and the spatial organization that they bring, many nations have found that economic development means sprawl. However, efforts are being made by the U.N. and other international agencies to disseminate the ideas of planning and particularly New Urbanism.

These ideas are generally included in the U.N.'s broad mandate to spur sustainable development. Specific programs, such as the U.N.'s Center for Human Settlements–Habitat, seek to link urban planning with environmental understanding all over the world. Also, the U.N. runs its Sustainable Cities Program (SCP).

Currently the SCP operates twenty main demonstrations and twenty-five replicating cities around the world, including cities in China, Chile, Egypt, Ghana, India, Kenya, Korea, Malawi, Nigeria, the Philippines, Poland, Russia, Senegal, Sri Lanka, Tanzania, Tunisia, and Zambia. Activities are planned in Bahrain, Cameroon, Iran, Kenya, Lesotho, Rwanda, South Africa, and Vietnam. Some critics argue that nations must be free to develop strategies of their choice—particularly those that are less costly than urban planning. However, projects such as this one make certain that the information is available for nations desiring it.

Sprawl continues to be the end product when communities allow development to unfold without a plan. However, more and more communities are using new ideas in planning and design to construct a positive human environment and control sprawl.

Brian Black

Further Reading

Belasco, J. (1979). *Americans on the road*. Cambridge, MA: MIT Press.

Calthorpe, P. (1993). *The next American metropolis*. New York: Princeton Architectural Press.

Clark, C. E., Jr. (1986). *The American family home*. Chapel Hill: University of North Carolina Press.

Duany, A., Plater-Zyberk, E., & Speck, J. (2001). *Suburban nation: The rise of sprawl and the decline of the American dream*. New York: Northpoint Press.

Egan, T. (1998, November 14). Dreams of fields: The new politics of urban sprawl. *New York Times*. Retrieved January 7, 2003, from http://www.cprproject.org/news/1998/nytimes_1114.html

Flink, J. J. (1990). *The automobile age*. Cambridge, MA: MIT Press.

Gugler, J. (1996). *The urban transformation of the developing world*. New York: Oxford University Press.

Hart, J. F. (Ed.). (1991). *Our changing cities*. Baltimore: Johns Hopkins University Press.

Jackson, K. T. (1985). *Crabgrass frontier*. New York: Oxford University Press.

Jacobs, J. (1961). *The death and life of great American cities*. New York: Vintage Books.

Kay, J. H. (1997). *Asphalt nation*. Berkeley: University of California Press.

Kunstler, J. H. (1993). *The geography of nowhere*. New York: Touchstone Books.

Kunstler, J. H. (1998). *Home from nowhere: Remaking our everyday world for the twenty-first century*. New York: Touchstone Books.

Lewis, T. (1997). *Divided highways*. New York: Penguin Books.

Liebs, C. H. (1995). *Main Street to miracle mile*. Baltimore: Johns Hopkins University Press.

McShane, C. (1994). *Down the asphalt path*. New York: Columbia University Press.

Relph, E. (1987). *The modern urban landscape*. Baltimore: Johns Hopkins University Press.

Wright, G. (1992). *Building the dream*. Cambridge, MA: MIT Press.

Stalin, Joseph

(1879–1953)

Leader of the Soviet Union

Joseph Vissarionovich Stalin, born Iosif Vissarionovich Dzhugashvili in Georgia in the Russian Empire, was the leader of the Soviet Union from 1929 until his death. He presided over rapid industrialization, collectivization of agriculture, and modernization of the military. Many of the programs adopted by the Communist Party during his reign had a significant impact on the environment. They included the operation of huge industrial enterprises such as steel mills and petrochemical plants with little filtering or safety equipment; construction of canals, hydroelectric power stations, and irrigation systems; and vigorous exploitation of ore, coal, oil and natural-gas deposits.

Stalin had an early interest in the subjugation of nature that he expressed in a fascination with irrigation and electrification. In the late 1920s Stalin pursued large-scale projects as the centerpiece of an officially proclaimed "Great Break" with previous policies to transform the country politically, socially, and geophysically. He pursued industrialization at a breakneck pace and forced peasants into collective farms, in part to serve as a source of investment capital for industrialization. During collectivization, builders irrigated millions of hectares of land and built impoundments (artificial lakes), reservoirs, and canals to improve municipal water supply and transport. Collectivization involved creating massive farms out of small, inefficient private peasant plots, and expanding land under cultivation through mechanization and heavy use of chemical pesticides and fertilizers.

The human costs of the Great Break were significant: Millions died of famine or perished at the hands of the secret police. Victims included engineers and managers whose projects failed to reach targets. The secret police accused them of "wrecking" plans when they suggested a slower, more environmentally sound pace. The Stalinist prison labor camps were a source of labor for many of the nature transformation projects, including mining and lumbering activities in the far north and Siberia.

Economic development under Stalin centered on such so-called hero projects as the Baltic-White Sea Canal ("Belomor"), the Dniepr Hydroelectric Power Station, and the Magnitogorsk Steel Mill, all of which were completed in the 1930s. The projects were inefficiently organized and poorly planned. Some engineers pointed out that the projects did not meet technical requirements. Stalin seems to have cared little if the projects were poorly built and designed, or if they led to the deaths of slave laborers: Symbolic meaning was more important than physical function.

The Communist Party held back the development of ecology as a discipline and interfered in the activities of such professional organizations as the Russian Society for the Conservation of Nature, which was founded in 1924. Such societies fell under attack for attempting to protect nature preserves from economic development and protesting the pace and scale of some projects.

Under Stalin, officials ultimately determined that nature and climate were "enemies of the people." They believed "capricious" nature could be forced to operate according to plan. In concert with this belief, in October 1948 the Communist Party unanimously endorsed the Stalinist Plan for the Transformation of Nature. The plan called for straightening rivers and shoals, dredging, and building huge dams to hold water for irrigation, electricity, and municipal uses. It authorized the planting of thousands of kilometers of "forest belts" to protect the land from hot, dry winds largely in the steppe region of the Lower Volga River basin

Much of the 1948 plan came to an end after the death of Stalin on 6 March 1953. But construction of canals and hydropower stations continued. The result of Stalinist environmental policy was extensive damage to ecosystems, pollution, haphazard disposal of waste, destruction of fish spawning areas, and clearcutting of forests.

Paul R. Josephson

Further Reading

Graham, L. (1997). *The ghost of the executed engineer*. Cambridge, MA: Harvard University Press.

A photo of Joseph Stalin overlooking a map of Russia and commenting, "And we will defeat drought as well!" COURTESY *OKHRANA PRIRODY* AND DOUG WEINER.

Josephson, P. (2002). *Industrialized nature*. Washington, DC: Island Press.

Weiner, D. (1988) *Models of nature: Ecology, conservation, and cultural revolution in Soviet Russia*. Bloomington: Indiana University Press.

Steiner, Rudolf

(1861–1925)
Founder of anthroposophy

Rudolf Joseph Lorenz Steiner was the founder of anthroposophy, which is based on the esoteric philosophy of theosophy (a belief system combining elements of several mystic and Asian religions that focus on rediscovering the mental abilities of humans) and aims to explore the nature of man and the paranormal world. Based on Steiner's thoughts, an extensive subculture of anthroposophical institutions emerged and encompassed medicine, pharmaceutical and beauty companies, agriculture, and education. Most notable among the institutions initiated by Steiner are the Waldorf schools, therapeutic pedagogy (a form of education to aid the development of mentally or physically handicapped people), eurhythmy (a system of harmonious body movements to the rhythm of spoken words) as a new art form, and biodynamic agriculture (agriculture that does not use artificial fertilizers and pesticides).

Steiner was born in Kraljevec, Hungary (now Croatia). Because of his interest in combining philosophy and the natural sciences he was appointed editor of the German writer Johann Wolfgang von Goethe's natural-scientific works from 1882 to 1896. In 1893 Steiner's magnum opus *Die Philosophie der Freiheit* (Intuitive Thinking as a Spiritual Path: A Philosophy of Freedom) was published. Steiner joined the Theosophical Society in 1902 and started working on the concepts of anthroposophy. Although Steiner shared the theosophical fascination with Eastern religious concepts like karma and reincarnation, he focused more on occidental philosophical and religious traditions like Goethe's pantheist concept of nature, the philosophy of German

A Selection from the Writings of Rudolf Steiner

If we do not develop within ourselves this deeply rooted feeling that there is something higher than ourselves, we shall never find the strength to evolve to something higher. The initiate has only acquired the strength to lift his head to the heights of knowledge by guiding his heart to the depths of veneration and devotion. The heights of the spirit can only be climbed by passing through the portals of humility. You can only acquire right knowledge when you have learnt to esteem it. Man has certainly the right to turn his eyes to the light, but he must first acquire this right. There are laws in the spiritual life, as in the physical life. Rub a glass rod with an appropriate material and it will become electric, that is, it will receive the power of attracting small bodies. This is in keeping with a law of nature. It is known to all who have learnt a little physics. Similarly, acquaintance with the first principles of spiritual science shows that every feeling of true devotion harbored in the soul develops a power which may, sooner or later, lead further on the path of knowledge.

Source: Steiner, Rudolf. (1986). *Knowledge of the Higher Worlds and Its Attainment.* Hudson, NY: Anthroposophic Press, pp. 7–8. (Originally published in 1947)

idealism, the German philosopher Friedrich Nietzsche's individualism, and a new interpretation of Christianity. Steiner saw anthroposophy as a scientific way to obtain insight to one's nature. He also saw it as a way to get in contact with the world of supernatural beings.

Steiner left the Theosophical Society in 1913 and founded the Anthroposophical Society, whose center became the Free University of Arts (Goetheanum) in Dornach, Switzerland. In 1919 the Waldorf schools were established in Stuttgart, Germany, as an alternative to the highly authoritarian, class-based state schools. Steiner also held training courses on a broad variety of subjects. His agricultural training course (1924) became the starting point of biodynamic agriculture. Steiner viewed each farm as a living organism. According to Steiner, fertility of the soil should be promoted not by using synthetic fertilizers or pesticides but rather by bringing the forces of nature and the cosmos into balance. This could be achieved by careful timing of each activity with cosmic rhythms, compost manure, and special preparations made of medicinal herbs, minerals, and cow dung added to the fertilizers in homoeopathic (extremely high) dilutions.

Steiner's ideas soon became popular. By 1931 more than one thousand farms in Germany worked according to biodynamic principles as an alternative to industrial agriculture. In the 1930s biodynamic agriculture spread to Switzerland, the Netherlands, Austria, England, Sweden, Norway, and New Zealand. The biodynamic association Demeter, founded in Germany in

1932, today is the biggest provider of organic goods worldwide. Other anthroposophical institutions have grown considerably over the last thirty years as well—especially the Waldorf schools with 855 schools worldwide in 2002—as more people have demanded a sustainable or spiritually more fulfilling lifestyle. Membership of the Anthroposophical Society reached over sixty thousand in the late 1990s, the German branch with more than twenty thousand members being the most influential. However, Steiner and the principles of anthroposophy remain controversial. Especially in Germany, parts of his concept of humanity have been criticized as racist and misogynistic; the esoteric character of his work has been called scientifically unsound.

Ute Hasenöhrl

Further Reading

Hemleben, J. (2001). *Rudolf Steiner: An illustrated biography.* Hudson, NY: Anthroposophic Press.

Lippert, S. (2001). *Steiner und die Waldorfpädagogik: Mythos und wirklichkeit* [Steiner and Waldorf pedagogy: Myth and reality]. Berlin, Germany: Luchterhand.

Steiner, R. (1993). *Agriculture: Spiritual foundations for the renewal of agriculture.* Kimberton, PA: Bio-Dynamic Farming and Gardening Association.

Steiner, R. (1995). *Intuitive thinking as a spiritual path: A philosophy of freedom.* Hudson, NY: Anthroposophic Press.

Tummer, L., & Lato, H. (2001). *Rudolf Steiner and anthroposophy for beginners*. New York: Writers and Readers.

Sturgeon

Sturgeons are ancient, bottom-feeding fishes with peculiar, armor-plated bodies. Like salmon, sturgeons are anadromous, migrating to the sea but reproducing in freshwater. Some species live for more than a hundred years, and their fossils date back 250 million years.

Humans have coveted sturgeon for many centuries. The earliest record of eating caviar comes from Batu Khan, a grandson of Genghis Khan, in the thirteenth century. By the sixteenth century Russia's Ivan the Terrible had made caviar a staple of his table, and in 1704 Peter the Great of Russia extended czarist control over the Caspian Sea sturgeon fisheries. Other European monarchs soon followed to protect their own fisheries, but widespread consumption of caviar only began in the late nineteenth century, when French gourmands first imported Russia caviar in large quantities. Some species of sturgeon are also harvested for their tasty flesh, and sturgeon air bladders were once made into isinglass (a type of gelatin). Unfortunately, sturgeon's slow growth, delayed maturity, and dependence on bottom environments make it vulnerable to intensive fishing and habitat alteration.

There are many Asian species, but the species of the Caspian Sea are particularly important because the beluga *(Huso huso)*, Russian *(Acipenser gueldenstaedtii)*, stellate *(A. stellatus)*, and Persian *(A. persicus)* sturgeons formed the backbone of a world market in caviar. The beluga is the largest of the species, reaching 1,740 kilograms, but intensive fishing, rising sea levels, and the end of the Soviet Union's control over most of the Caspian Sea have threatened fish populations. Only the Iranian fishery in the southern Caspian is still effectively controlled. The Amur *(A. schrenckii)*, Sakhalin *(A. mikadoi)*, and Japanese *(A. multiscutatus)* sturgeons also support commercial fisheries, but these suffer from similar pressures. Urbanization, agriculture, and dams imperil many wild species, including the sterlet *(A. ruthenus)*, Siberian *(A. baerii baicalensis)*, Lena River *(A. baerii stenorrhynchus)*, dwarf *(Pseudoscaphirhynchus hermanni)*, Amu Dar'ya *(P. kaufmanni)*, and Kaluga *(H. dauricus)* sturgeons in Asian rivers, the Baikal sturgeon *(A. baerii baerii)* of Lake Baikal, Syr Dar'ya *(P. fedtschenkoi)* and thorn *(A. nudiventris)* sturgeons of the Aral Sea, and Yangtze *(A. dabryanus)* and Chinese *(A. sinensis)* sturgeons of China and the northwestern Pacific. In Europe the sturgeon of the eastern Atlantic *(A. sturio)* and the Adriatic sturgeon *(A. naccarii)* in the Mediterranean are also threatened by harvests and habitat loss. Efforts to sustain some species with hatcheries have fared poorly because of genetic drift (chance changes in small gene pools) in brood stocks.

In North America the Atlantic *(Acipenser oxyrinchus oxyrinchus)* and shortnose *(A. brevirostrumon)* sturgeon of the east coast, and the lake sturgeon *(A. fulvescens)* in northern waters, were staples for some Native American groups. Commercial fisheries began on the

The Atlantic Sturgeon. COURTESY DUANE RAVER/U. S. FISH AND WILDLIFE SERVICE.

Great Lakes and Lake Winnipeg in the mid-1800s but declined sharply by 1900. Fisheries in the Manitoba and Nelson Rivers began later but suffered similar fates, imperiling important subsistence fisheries. The pallid sturgeon (*Scaphirhynchus albus*) and the stickleback or shovelnose sturgeon (*S. platorynchus*) of the Missouri and Mississippi Rivers, and the Alabama (*S. suttkusi*) and Gulf (*A. oxyrinchus desotoi*) sturgeons of the Gulf of Mexico are endangered or vulnerable due to development. Ranging from Monterey Bay to the Aleutian Islands, the white sturgeon (*A. transmontanus*) is the largest species indigenous to North America at up to 720 kilograms. The smaller green sturgeon (*A. medirostris*) ranges from Ensenada to the Aleutians. Both were intensively fished, but restrictions aided recovery until dam building posed new problems, including isolating some populations on the middle Columbia and Snake Rivers.

Joseph E. Taylor III

Further Reading

Birstein, V. J., Waldman, B., Waldman, J. R., & Bemis, W. E. (Eds.). (1997). *Sturgeon biodiversity and conservation*. Dordrecht, Netherlands: Kluwer Academic Publishers.

Harkness, W. J., & Dymond, J. R. (1961). *The lake sturgeon: The history of its fishery and problems of conservation*. Toronto, Canada: Ontario Department of Lands and Forests, Fish and Wildlife Branch.

Newell. D., & Ommer, R. E. (Eds.). (1999). *Fishing places, fishing people: Traditions and issues in Canadian small-scale fisheries*. Toronto, Canada: University of Toronto Press.

Taylor, S. (1997). The historical development of the caviar trade and the caviar industry. *Occasional Papers of the IUCN Species Survival Commission, 17*, 45–53.

Suburbanization

The development of suburbs is often thought of as a uniquely U.S. tradition. In fact, Americans came late to the spatial redefinition that fueled suburbanization in the twentieth century. U.S. suburbs, though, helped to integrate cultural and design forms that have contributed to global trends. As international critics of suburbanization have become more vocal at the start of the twenty-first century, much of the criticism is directed toward the larger cultural impacts that relate to U.S. suburbanization. However, critics since the 1960s have noted that wherever suburbs occur, they carry with them a massive disruption of regional ecology and the substitution of nonindigenous species and habitats.

In the twentieth century many developed nations redefined an age-old understanding of spatial organization. Communities, villages, and towns had long been organized around utilitarian ideas. Those residing outside of urban areas were normally involved in agriculture. By the late 1800s country estates in many European countries had become a conspicuous mark of the wealthy. Transportation revolutions, though, beginning around 1900 allowed humans to entertain a new framework of residential organization: The suburb was born.

Upper- and middle-class Americans had begun moving to suburban areas in the late 1800s. Initially, upper-class urbanites followed the model of the French and British and constructed elaborate country residences. Eventually, though, some of these residences became full-time homes. In addition, taste makers such as the U.S. landscape architects Andrew Jackson Downing and Frederick Law Olmsted linked Romanticism (a literary, artistic, and philosophical movement originating in the eighteenth century and characterized by a reaction against neoclassicism and an emphasis on the imagination and emotions) to the designs for living environments—particularly parks and homes. With such influence, the spatial preferences of many Americans had changed considerably by the late 1800s.

The first suburban developments, such as Llewellyn Park, New Jersey (1856), followed railroads or the corridors of other early mass transit. "Streetcar suburbs" took shape around most U.S. cities by the mid- to late 1800s. Each one followed a model grown from British roots, particularly the London area. The U.S. suburb began its unique development when it linked itself to one form of transportation above others: the automobile. The automobile allowed access to vast areas between and beyond these corridors. Suddenly the suburban hinterland around every city compounded.

On the Road

Integrating such communities into urban corridors relied almost completely on the automobile after 1930. As early as the 1910s planners began perfecting ways of further integrating the car into U.S. domestic life. In the early twentieth century many homes of wealthy

Americans soon required the ability to store vehicles. Most often these homes had carriage houses or stables that could be converted. Soon, of course, architects devised an addition to the home and gave it the French name: *garage*. From this early point, housing in the United States drew a direct link to the integration of the auto and roads.

As early as 1940 about 13 million people lived in communities beyond the reach of public transportation. Due to these changes, suburbs could be planned for less-wealthy Americans. Modeled after the original Gustav Stickley homes or similar designs from *Ladies Home Journal* and other popular magazines, the houses in middle-class suburbs appealed to working-class and middle-class Americans. The bungalow became one of the most popular designs in the nation, even sold through major retailers such as Sears Roebuck and Montgomery Ward. The construction halt of the Great Depression set the stage for more recent ideas and designs, including the ranch house.

Auto suburbs spread quickly before 1940, but post–World War II growth dwarfed anything previous. The world had never before seen a spread in the middle-class standard of living like that in the United States after 1945. The symbol of such change was the community of Levittown, New York, built in 1947. Replica communities spread across the United States.

Standardization was the term that governed the Levittowns. Prefabricated construction allowed for thousands of homes to be constructed in a matter of months. As the economy expanded after the war, suburbs could be planted almost immediately in order to provide uniform shelter and community to inhabitants. No doubt, though, a great deal was lost in the race to house the baby boom.

In 1950, 33 percent of the U.S. population lived in urban areas, 23 percent in suburban areas, and 44 percent in rural areas. By 2000, over 50 percent of Americans lived in suburban areas. Suburbs and the transportation systems that support them require the subordination of natural elements to those best suited to rapid site preparation. Throughout the twentieth century the economics of planning and development fueled the standardization of landscape and environment. Whether woodland, prairie, or farmland, the suburban development cleared the land and reshaped it with heavy equipment. In addition, regional ecologies throughout the nation had been significantly altered. In their place builders installed residential human environments, adorned with nonnative turf grass and ornamental trees. Natural habitats and re-gional ecologies can rarely be reinstalled, regardless of the "green" intentions of any developer.

A World Symbol

Massive suburbanization damaged the ecological integrity of countless locales and placed residential pressures on many regions such as Los Angeles, California, that were ill suited for such development. However, U.S. suburbs became an enviable symbol for much of the world. In the famous "kitchen debate" of 1957 Vice President Richard Nixon used the model American home constructed in Moscow as a symbol that democracy and capitalism represented the world's fastest route to happiness and comfort. This symbol had great resonance to leaders around the world for more than a half-century.

Standards of living, of course, did not rise uniformly around the world after World War II. Decolonization helped to create vast areas more concerned with starvation than turf grass maintenance. The suburb became one of the great international symbols of the gap between rich and poor nations. The private "palaces" of the U.S. middle class struck many international observers as decadent and wasteful.

As urban areas in Asia, Mexico, and Africa became the most densely populated regions on Earth, planners and human rights agencies searched for sustainable urban plans. Suburbanization requires that residents have a certain level of capital and that developers be free to make homes affordably. Also, open space and transportation links are essential. For many nations this model of development is impossible. Other nations want to follow an urban design pattern that wastes fewer resources. Much of the world, however, will live with the lifestyle of suburbia for decades to come.

Brian Black

Further Reading

Duany, A., Plater-Zyberk, E., & Speck, J. (2001). *Suburban nation: The rise of sprawl and the decline of the American dream.* New York: North Point Press.

Fishman, R. (1987). *Bourgeois utopias: The rise and fall of suburbia.* New York: Basic Books.

Jackson, K. T. (1985). *Crabgrass frontier: The suburbanization of the U.S.* New York: Oxford University Press.

Jacobs, J. (1961). *The death and life of great American cities.* New York: Vintage Books.

Kunstler, J. H. (1993). *The geography of nowhere: The rise and decline of America's man-made landscape.* New York: Simon & Schuster.

Olmsted, F. L. (1997). *Civilizing American cities: Writings on city landscapes*. New York: Da Capo.

Rome, A. (2001). *The bulldozer in the countryside: Suburban sprawl and the rise of American environmentalism*. New York: Cambridge University Press.

Schuyler, D. (1986). *The new urban landscape: The redefinition of city form in nineteenth-century America*. Baltimore: Johns Hopkins University Press.

Warner, S. B., Jr. (1962). *Streetcar suburbs: The process of growth in Boston*. Cambridge, MA: Harvard University Press.

Succession

In ecology, succession is the change in plant communities and ecosystems that occurs as all the organisms in the ecosystem respond to and modify that ecosystem. Successional models, as theoretical frameworks for describing and interpreting the development of plant communities and ecosystems, have had profound impact on how humans interpret and manage the land. The classic model posits that soils, plants, and the animals associated with them go through various stages of development until they reach a stable equilibrium with their physical environment. This final stage is termed a climax state, achievable in the absence of disturbances that set the community or ecosystem back. The classic illustration of primary succession begins with a volcanic eruption and fresh lava that eventually weathers. Plant seeds brought in by wind or animals take root. Soils form, and a predictable succession of plant communities or ecosystem states from grass and shrubs to forest ensues. Canopy closure shades out the pioneering plant species, and the old-growth forest eventually reaches a stable state of equilibrium.

According to this view, secondary succession happens after less traumatic events or disturbances, as when a forest is burned or cut down and then recovers, progressing from grass and shrubs back to trees. The environmental characteritistics and species interactions at each site determine the community at the endpoint, whether forest or desert scrub. The different stages of plant community succession at a site, referred to as a successional sere, may provide habitat for distinct wildlife species. For example, the spotted owl of California, believed to depend on an old-growth forest habitat, is often described as a climax species. Various attempts have been made to correlate maximum biodiversity and other features with climax stages. Evaluation of the condition of an ecosystem or plant community based on how close its current state is to the predicted climax, though considered an invalid method of assessment by today's ecologists, is still practiced by some observers and land managers.

The ecologist Frederick Clements, studying plowed fields in the Midwest and building on ideas developed around 1900, was a major force in the application of the linear, deterministic succession model to describe vegetation response to human disturbance; hence "Clementian Succession," which is sometimes used to refer to the model. In the decades following his work, ecologists debated the particulars of the model, whether succession follows from the organic development of ecosystems, the individual characteristics of plants, or the initial floristic composition on the site. More recently the linear deterministic model has been challenged by the recognition that ecosystems are normally subject to unpredictable disturbance, and that many ecosystems may never consistently remain in a state of equibrium. Non-equilibrium ecology, an alternative to the classic view, holds that ecosystem characteristics may be influenced more by external disturbance than by the biotic interactions that are argued to explain the linear pattern of classic succession. In this view models for change in the plant community should recognize multiple pathways and stable ecosystem states, as well as the role of disturbance in ecosystem function. Models are being modified to accommodate the role of stochastic or chaotic processes in ecosystem change, and to avoid the value-laden interpretations that are so easily derived from the linear deterministic model.

In classic succession, any force that drives an ecosystem away from climax is considered detrimental. This idea has influenced the way ecologists, resource managers, and environmental historians have interpreted landscapes, and has provided a rationale for suppressing indigenous patterns of natural-resource management and use. The effect of humans on the ecosystem, seen as a form of disturbance, has often been assumed necessarily to be detrimental to the ecosystem's condition by moving the ecosystem further from a climax state. Twentieth-century professional forest managers in the western United States treated natural and man-made fire as a detrimental disturbance for decades, and only recently have begun to accept fire as a shaper of New World forests. Protection from this "disturbance" has vastly changed forest ecosystems. The scholars James Fairhead and Melissa Leach argued in a 1995 article in the journal *World Development* that environmental historians misinterpreted a landscape in Africa because they assumed that human actions, inherently degrading to ecosystems, would cause a loss rather than a gain of forest cover. Underlying this misinterpretation is the classic succession model, largely rejected by ecologists but still widely influential.

Lynn Huntsinger and James W. Bartolome

Further Reading

Begon, M., Harper, J. L., & Townsend, C. R. (1996). *Ecology: Individuals, populations, and communities* (3rd ed.). Cambridge MA: Blackwell Science.

Clements, F. E. (1916). Plant succession: An analysis of the development of vegetation. (Carnegie Institution of Washington Publication No. 520). Washington, DC: Carnegie Institution of Washington.

Connell, J. H., & Slatyer, R. O. (1977). Mechanisms of succession in natural communities and their role in community stability and organization. *American Naturalist, 111,*1119–1144.

Egler, F. E. (1954). Vegetation science concepts. I: Initial floristic composition, a factor in old-field vegetation development. *Vegetatio,* 4, 412–417.

Fairhead J, & Leach, M. (1995). False forest history, complicit social analysis: Rethinking some West African environmental narratives. *World Development, 23*(6), 1023–1035.

Odum, E. P. (1963). *Ecology.* New York: Holt, Rinehart & Winston.

Tillman, D. (1985). The resource-ratio hypothesis of plant succession. *American Naturalist, 125*(6), 827–852.

Wiens, J. A. (1984). On understanding a non-equilibrium world: Myth and reality in community patterns and processes. In D. R. Strong, D. Simberlong, K. G. Abele & A. B. Thistle. (Eds.). *Ecological communities: conceptual issues and the evidence.* Princeton, NJ: Princeton University Press.

Sugar and Sugarcane

Sugarcane was in all likelihood first domesticated in New Guinea, from which it spread gradually to India, the Philippine Islands, and perhaps Indonesia. Texts in Sanskrit, the first known written language, mention sugar in the context of other foods as early as 400–350 BCE, but not in its granular form. In 327 BCE Alexander the Great's armies took note of a reed that yielded a sweet nectar found growing from the Indus River to the Euphrates and this was probably sugarcane. However, evidence of sugar manufacture, that is crystallization, does not appear in historical documents until around 500 CE and this was first observed, appropriately, in Hindu religious texts. There are also descriptions of sugar manufacture around Baghdad in the early seventh century with references to the product's Indian origins.

Spread of Sugar and Sugarcane

Sugar's westward movement was linked to Islamic expansion across the Mediterranean during the seventh and eighth centuries. Cane cultivation took root in Syria, Palestine, and Egypt, and then moved through the Nile Valley, and across North Africa. As Arab armies expanded through the Mediterranean, sugar was introduced to Cyprus, Crete, Sicily, Morocco, and during the early eighth century to Iberia along the southern Spanish coast. Yet, even prior to these direct contacts sugar had been imported and distributed to European societies by Venetian merchants who traded widely with North Africa and the Middle East, although it was an expensive commodity confined to upper-class consumption. The Crusades of the eleventh century were another factor that placed northern Europeans in contact with sugar. The first notices of sugar in England appeared around 1100 CE.

Sugarcane cultivation entered the Atlantic world due to Portuguese exploration of the West African littoral during the fifteenth century. The subsequent conquest and colonization of various island groups in the Atlantic—Madeira, the Cape Verde Islands, São Tomé, and the Canaries—were accompanied by sugarcane's introduction. Sugar manufacture was also developed in the Canary Islands by Spanish colonizers after 1475.

Development of Sugar Plantations

Slave labor was closely associated with sugar production at least from the Mediterranean phase of expansion, although slaves were not derived from racially or ethnically specific cultures, and forced labor was only one part of a complex mosaic of labor systems. Slavery, thus, did not stand out as a labor mechanism in any pronounced way, and this was the case in both the early Madeira sugarcane fields, and in the Canary Islands as well.

The development of the sugar economy of São Tomé during the sixteenth century opened a new phase in productive methods. Here the Portuguese established the first real plantation forms of sugarcane cultivation. These were economies of scale that required large labor inputs. The African slave-based sugar plantations that would emerge in the Brazilian northeast during the late sixteenth century, and later in English-dominated Barbados in the mid-seventeenth century, had their origins in the Portuguese-developed São Tomé sugar industry.

Sugarcane was introduced to the New World by Columbus on his second voyage and planting ensued in Hispaniola, which became the first important plantation zone in the Americas. Cane was grown and ground in small quantities from early settlement, but it was mostly to produce for the limited local market and to supply *aguardiente*, or cane brandy, and rum to settlers. But, the lucrative export market always beckoned and by the 1550s exports to Europe were significant—although by the late 1580s Hispaniola's role as an important supplier of sugar to world markets had ended.

It was northeastern Brazil, however, which would become the first large-scale New World slave-based sugar plantation society. Beginning in the 1520s on a small scale and until the 1570s, Brazilian sugar production, centered in Pernambuco and Bahia, was based largely on indigenous slave labor. For numerous reasons, including death, flight, and resistance, the use of Indian slaves became economically unviable, and emulating their experiences in São Tomé the Portuguese turned to the African slave trade for labor supplies. Sugar and African slavery were closely associated in Brazil until slavery was abolished in 1888.

Vying for Dominance

The geography of American sugar production changed drastically from the mid-seventeenth century on with the entrance of the Dutch, English, and French into the world of sugar production. The Dutch were the first to challenge the Portuguese near-monopoly on slaving and sugar production attacking and successfully occupying Pernambuco, Brazil, from 1630 through 1654 after several failed attempts in the 1620s. During the same period the Dutch, as well as the English and the French, were occupying eastern Caribbean islands, the Leewards, and beginning to establish sugarcane plantations and construct mills. The most important early producer was Barbados, settled in the late 1620s

by England, and developed into one of the world's greatest sugar economies in the mid-seventeenth century. Not only was Brazil's near monopoly on sugar production broken, but the African slave/plantation model was reintroduced to the Caribbean (Spanish Hispaniola was the first attempt) and this would become the future organizational schema for the plantation economies of Jamaica and French St. Domingue during the eighteenth century, and later in nineteenth-century Cuba.

Toward the same objectives the French occupied Martinique, Guadeloupe, and at the end of the seventeenth century their greatest prize, the western side of Hispaniola, was ceded by the Spanish in a 1697 treaty and became French St. Domingue. The Dutch took control of Surinam, Curação, Aruba, and Bonaire converting Surinam into a major sugar-producing zone.

All of the preceding set the stage for the development of the three greatest slave/sugar Caribbean plantation economies: English Jamaica and French St. Domingue during the eighteenth century, and Spanish Cuba in the nineteenth century. Until the 1720s Barbados continued as the largest Caribbean sugar producer but thereafter Jamaican and St. Domingue production dwarfed that of all other Caribbean producers, and for that matter, world producers, of sugar. In 1791, on the eve of the Haitian slave revolt that ended St. Domingue's role in world sugar markets, the British and French Caribbean colonies combined produced approximately 76 percent of the world's sugar output.

In British Jamaica sugar continued to be produced in significant quantities even after the abolition of slavery in 1833, but the dramatic rise of Cuba as the world's leading sugar exporter and the Caribbean's only large-scale slave importer by the 1830s, opened a new cycle in the history of sugar production. By 1820 Jamaica still out-produced Cuba, and there had been a significant revival of Brazilian production. But by 1840 Cuba's sugar production was twice that of Brazil, while Jamaican production had fallen to relative insignificance for the world market.

Cuba clearly emulated the British and French models of sugar development, but by the middle of the nineteenth century technological innovations such as the railroad, the steam engine, and vacuum pan evaporators made Cuba one of the most productive sugar-producers in the world. Yet, despite technological sophistication in transportation and manufacturing, the Cuban sugar economy relied heavily on slave labor until the institution was finally abolished in 1886.

During the nineteenth century, sugar production for export developed in other areas of the Americas that had not been significant producers earlier in the colonial period. Louisiana became a major producer before the U.S. Civil War and continued to produce sugar after slave emancipation. Toward the end of the nineteenth century certain Mexican regions, such as the state of Morelos, became important producers of sugar; and coastal regions of Peru also entered the world of sugar production and export on an intense scale. Brazilian sugar exports also continued to be a significant factor in world markets. Yet, on the eve of the Cuban War for Independence in 1894, Cuba's cane sugar production dwarfed that of other countries.

Toward the end of the nineteenth and beginning of the twentieth centuries, new sugarcane producing zones emerged on a significant scale in Hawaii, the Philippine Islands, Puerto Rico, and the Dominican Republic, largely because of U.S. corporate investments. Additionally, Asian producers began to have a small impact on world sugar markets, especially Taiwan, which was developed by Japanese investors to satisfy market needs there, and Java where the industry was developed by the Dutch who had a long history of sugar production dating from the seventeenth century. Sugarcane and sugar production also expanded in India, where it was originally produced in antiquity, as well as on mainland China. Another important producer by the early twentieth century was Australia, where cane cultivation was developed along the northeastern coast in New South Wales and Queensland. Australia became a major sugar exporter during the twentieth century.

Sugar produced from beets challenged cane-derived sugar on world markets during the nineteenth century. The process for manufacture was known from the mid-eighteenth century, but it was during the Napoleonic Wars of the early nineteenth century, when cane sugar had difficulty entering European markets, when production grew significantly in France, the German states, and in Russia. Later beet sugar was produced on a significant scale in the United States. By the 1880s it is estimated that as much sugar was produced by beets as by cane, although cane sugar dominated international trade as beet-derived sugar was usually produced for domestic consumption by the producing nations.

Environmental Consequences

The production of cane sugar had a devastating impact upon the ecological conditions of producing nations, especially in the eighteenth and nineteenth centuries, primarily because of extensive deforestation and accompanying soil erosion. This was not only because virgin forest lands had to be cleared for cane planting, but also because of the extensive, and often exclusive, use of wood as fuel to power the mills which processed cane into sugar. Until coal, and later natural gas, oil, and electricity, powered mills in the late nineteenth and twentieth centuries, mills had to be located in relative proximity to forest reserves. Accordingly, sugar industries usually moved gradually toward frontier regions, and this exacerbated the destruction of forests and led to declining soil fertility until the widespread utilization of natural and chemical fertilizers primarily in the twentieth century.

At the turn of the twenty-first century world sugar production stood at approximately 128 million tons. India was the world's largest single producer of sugar followed by the combined output of the European Union nations, Brazil, the United States, and China. The largest sugar exporters were Brazil, the European Union nations, Australia, and Thailand, since Indian and Chinese sugars are produced principally for domestic markets. Indeed, approximately three-quarters of world sugar output is consumed in the domestic markets of producer nations. About 70 percent of the world's sugar supply is derived from sugar cane, the remainder from beets.

Laird W. Bergad

Further Reading

Deerr, N. (1949–1950). *The history of sugar*. London: Chapman & Hall.

Galloway, J. H. (1989). *The sugar cane industry: An historical geography from its origins to 1914*. New York: Cambridge University Press.

Mintz, S. W. (1985). *Sweetness and power: The place of sugar in modern history*. New York: Viking Penguin.

Tracy, J. D. (Ed.). (1990). *The rise of merchant empires: Long distance trade in the early modern world, 1350–1750*. New York: Cambridge University Press.

Summer Camps

Summer camps—overnight camps attended by children without their parents—were first established in the 1880s in North America, fueled by Victorian con-

A boy must learn to sleep under the open sky and to tramp ten miles through the rain if he wants to be strong. He must learn what sort of men it was who made America, and he must not get into this fuss and flurry of our American civilization and think that patent leather shoes and white kid gloves are necessary for the salvation of his life.

—Edward Everett Hale. Quoted in *Camping for Boys*. New York: (1913). Association Press, p. 38.

victions about nature's moral and physical benefits, as well as newer concerns about degeneracy and falling birth rates. In the twentieth century, the summer camp idea became an international phenomenon, supported by organizations with varied social, political, religious, and pedagogical agendas. In short, summer camps have become an increasingly important means for immersing children in nature.

The earliest camps were private camps for boys, developed in response to growing concerns about the emasculating tendencies of what was called "overcivilization." Catering to the sons of elite families, many of these camps were located in the woods of northern New England, far from the temptations of city life and the refinements of the feminized home. Among the earliest were Chocorua (in operation between 1881 and 1889), Asquam (founded as Camp Harvard in 1885 and renamed in 1887), and Pasquaney (established in 1895), all located on or near Squam Lake in New Hampshire. Highly rustic in character, these camps consisted of permanent buildings with unhewn timbers supporting the roofs of wide piazzas, in railings, and as siding battens.

A camp-building boom in the 1890s brought camping to a wider audience, including poor slum dwellers (who attended camps organized by religious organizations, social settlements, and other social welfare agencies) and middle-class boys served by the YMCA (the Young Men's Christian Association, which established its first boys' camp, later known as Camp Dudley, in 1885). By 1901, the YMCA estimated that it served 5,000 boys each summer, a number that grew to 23,300 by 1916. Unlike elite camps, these early YMCA camps tended to mimic military encampments with sleeping tents pitched around a square parade ground where campers enacted reveille, morning inspection, calisthenics, and taps. While these military trappings allowed boys to experience an all-male environment that contrasted sharply with the feminized home, they also insured that these camps sat lightly on their natural sites, a particular advantage for camps held on borrowed land. In the early twentieth century, Native American motifs became increasingly popular, thanks in part to the Woodcraft Indians, a precursor to the Boy Scouts of America, another organization that encouraged summer camping for boys after 1910.

Camps for girls were established in the early twentieth century to foster a new, more self-reliant generation of young women. Among the earliest were private camps (like Camp Kehonka in New Hampshire and the Wyonegonic Camps in Bridgton, Maine, all founded in 1902), although the Camp Fire Girls (established in 1911) and Girl Scouts of the U.S.A. (established in 1912) soon started camps for middle-class girls. By 1925, there were some three hundred Girl Scout camps in the United States.

Whether serving boys or girls, camps fostered an active engagement with the natural world through nature study classes (often held in the Nature Museum, a building type introduced to the camp landscape in the 1920s) and through other activities that encouraged a contemplation of nature's spiritual power. Calling upon a long-standing conviction that a natural setting enhances religious feeling (something already practiced at camp meetings attended by adults and family groups), many camps featured a forest chapel, fitted out with rustic furniture and a wood or stone altar, framed by a lake view.

By the 1920s, this sense of nature's spiritual associations prompted many religious groups to move beyond their early charitable camping endeavors into religious-based camping for the children of middle-class and elite families. In addition to Catholic camps and Protestant Bible camps, Jewish camps enjoyed a surge of popularity between the 1920s and the 1950s, as they sought to maintain ethnic practices threatened by modernization and assimilation. The approach to Jewish identity varied widely at such summer camps, some of which (like Camp Ramah in Wisconsin) were explicitly religious in orientation, others (such as Massad Hebrew Camps) also Zionist, and still others (like Cejwin

Camps at Port Jervis, New York) emphasizing secular Jewish cultural practices.

In other parts of the world, turn-of-the-century experiments with charitable camps gave way to a wider range of camping endeavors in the 1920s. In New Zealand, camps were closely associated with rebuilding the health of delicate children. Established in 1919, the first health camp used Army surplus tents provided by the Defense Department at a nominal rate. By the 1930s, nine health-camp associations had instituted camps, including Canterbury's Sunlight League, which emphasized sunbathing as prescribed by the new science of heliotherapy. In the late 1930s, health camps came under government regulation, resulting in a new emphasis on permanent, year-round facilities. By the 1950s, increasingly stringent government standards forced many summer-only camps to close.

In other settings, the 1920s and 1930s saw the rise of summer camps of a political bent, including a range of left-wing camps in the United States (including twenty-seven Communist camps in New York state by 1956), Communist camps in France, Germany, and Austria, Fascist *colonie* in Italy, and camps to sustain Polish culture on the contested border between Poland and Germany. Unlike radical camps in the United States which differed little in physical form from other American camps, French *colonies de vacances* established by Communist-governed municipalities (like Ivry-sur-Seine) were instituted in part to secure party loyalty and thus served large audiences. The *colonie* at Les Mathes opened in 1929 near Royan on nineteen hectares of pine woodlands; supplementing old farm buildings were five new dormitories (each with a capacity of one hundred children) and a refectory/ kitchen serving eight hundred. Equally massive were the *colonies* established in Fascist Italy to aid in the cause of political indoctrination; they housed children in large, austere, modern buildings adjoining vast, unplanted terraces for mass sunbathing and calisthenics.

Just before World War II, North American campplanning ideas were transformed as professional experts lent their advice to camp directors (themselves newly professionalized since the formation of the American Camping Association in 1935). The findings of child psychologists prompted the introduction of the unit plan (which divided the camp landscape into age-based living units), and the construction of elaborate sleeping quarters (including socializing space to facilitate closer camper-counselor interaction). Watersafety experts at the American Red Cross suggested improved waterfront designs with lifeguard towers, check-boards, and carefully demarcated areas for nonswimmers, beginners, and swimmers. Camp planning experts (many of whom had worked for the National Park Service under the aegis of the New Deal designing camps in thirty-four federal Recreation Demonstration Areas) advocated master planning as an important means of renewing natural resources once assumed to be inexhaustible. Camp planners also applied picturesque planning principles to the entire camp landscape, disguising the extent to which human intervention shaped the experience of nature offered at camp. Codified in camp planning manuals published in the 1940s by the YMCA, the Girl Scouts, and the Camp Fire Girls, this advice guided the postwar camp-building boom that paralleled the baby boom.

In the postwar period, camps for children with special needs became increasingly common, as did skillbased camps teaching foreign languages, music, and computer programming. At the end of the twentieth century, however, the traditional, rustic, characterbuilding summer camp enjoyed renewed popularity.

Summer camps, then, contribute to environmental history by highlighting the impact of cultural attitudes on attempts to bring children into contact with nature. At the same time, camps speak to a growing irony in this relationship: throughout the twentieth century, the so-called natural environment offered to campers has been increasingly produced by human intervention.

Abigail A. Van Slyck

Further Reading

De Martino, S., & Wall, A. (Eds.). (1988) *Cities of childhood: Italian* colonies *of the 1930s*. London: Architectural Association.

Downs, L. L. (2002). *Childhood in the promised land: Working-class movements and the* colonies de vacances *in France, 1880–1960*. Durham, NC: Duke University Press.

Joselit, J. W., & Mittelman, K. S. (Eds.). (1993). *A worthy use of summer: Jewish summer camping in America*. Philadelphia: National Museum of American Jewish History.

Kohlstedt, S. G. (1985). Collectors, cabinets and summer camp: Natural history in the public life of nineteenth-century Worcester. *Museum Studies Journal, 2*(1), 10–23.

Macleod, D. I. (1983). *Building character in the American boy: The Boy Scouts, YMCA, and their forerunners, 1870–1920*. Madison: University of Wisconsin Press.

Maynard, W. B. (1999). "An ideal life in the woods for boys": Architecture and culture in the earliest summer camps. *Winterthur Portfolio, 34*(1), 3–29.

Mechling, J. (2001). *On my honor: Boy Scouts and the making of American youth.* Chicago: University of Chicago Press.

Mishler, P. C. (1999). *Raising Reds: The Young Pioneers, radical summer camps, and Communist political culture in the United States.* New York: Columbia University Press.

Tennant, M. (1996). Children's health camps in New Zealand: The making of a movement, 1919–1940. *Social History of Medicine, 9*(1), 69–87.

Van Slyck, A. A. (2002). Housing the happy camper. *Minnesota History, 58*(2), 68–83.

Van Slyck, A. A. (2002). Kitchen technologies and mealtime rituals: Interpreting the food axis at American summer camps, 1890–1950. *Technology and Culture, 43*(4), 668–682.

Sustainability *See* Brundtland Commission

Sweet Potato

Sweet potato is a very important food crop in parts of the tropics and subtropics. The edible tuber is the most important part of the plant. The leaves are also eaten in some places. It is a highly productive crop and returns a large amount of food energy for the labor expended in growing it. Large quantities are fed to pigs in many countries. It is the seventh most important food crop in the world, after maize, rice, wheat, potato, cassava, and barley. As well as being a significant source of food energy, the tubers are rich in Vitamins A and C. It is culturally important in societies as diverse as Japan, southern United States, and New Guinea.

Sweet potato grows in a wide range of environments: from sea level up to 2,800 meters (near the equator); from about 40° north to about 40° south (in New Zealand); under a wide range of soil moisture conditions; in locations with a mean annual rainfall from 750 to over 5,000 millimeters; and on a wide range of soil types. In the western Pacific, long-term cultivation of sweet potato at the same site often results in a change in vegetation from forest to a mix of woody regrowth and grass, or even to grasslands. Soil fertility is also reduced by long-term continuous cultivation. In low intensity agricultural systems—where the cropping period is short and the fallow period long—these changes do not occur.

Sweet potato was domesticated thousands of years ago in tropical America, in either Central America or western South America. Polynesian voyagers took it from its South American homeland to the Pacific Islands about one thousand years ago. It became an important food at the extremities of Polynesia in Easter Island, Hawaii, and New Zealand before the era of European exploration. Christopher Columbus brought it back to Europe from the Americas in 1492. Portuguese travelers then took it to Africa, India, and to Southeast Asia in the sixteenth century. It was spread from eastern Indonesia (Maluku) into New Guinea by local travelers.

Sweet potato arrived in the New Guinea highlands about 350 years ago. The new crop had a major impact there, allowing greater human and pig populations and occupation of high-altitude locations (2,200–2,800 meters in altitude), as well as probably resulting in a revolution in economic and social organization.

World production is now dominated by China where some 85 percent of tubers are grown. Another 10 percent of world production occurs in Uganda, Papua New Guinea (PNG), Nigeria, Vietnam, Indonesia, Rwanda, and Japan. Sweet potato is a significant food in three regions where consumption by people and pigs is high. These regions are the western Pacific (Solomon Islands, Papua New Guinea, and Papua [Indonesian New Guinea]); southern China; and east Africa (Rwanda, Burundi, Uganda, and Tanzania). It was also a significant food item in parts of East Asia until the 1960s or 1950s, particularly in Taiwan and Japan. However consumption has decreased in East Asia and sweet potato is associated with poverty and harsh wartime conditions there.

In the western Pacific, the quantity produced per person has expanded greatly since the 1940s. It is the main staple food in the Solomon Islands, parts of lowland Papua New Guinea, and all of the New Guinea highlands (both in PNG and Papua). In PNG, sweet potato now provides 63 percent of food energy from locally grown foods, compared with 45 percent in the 1960s. The expansion of sweet potato, and other new crops from the Americas, has facilitated a significant intensification of land use in the western Pacific and has allowed two generations of a rapidly increasing population to be fed with minimal disruption.

R. M. Bourke

Further Reading

Bourke, R. M. (2001). Intensification of agricultural systems in Papua New Guinea. Special issue: Agricultural Transformation and Intensification. *Asia Pacific Viewpoint, 42*(2–3), 221–237.

FAO (2002). FAOSTAT Agricultural Data. Food and Agricultural Organization of the United Nations, Rome. Retrieved September 3, 2002, from http://apps.fao.org/page/collections

Villareal, R. L., & Griggs, T. D. (Eds.). (1982). Sweet Potato. *Proceedings of the First International Symposium*. Tainan, Taiwan: Asian Vegetable and Research and Development Corporation.

Yen, D. E. (1974). Sweet potato and Oceania. *Bishop Museum Bulletin 236*. BP Bishop Museum, Honolulu, Hawaii.

Switzerland

(2000 est. pop. 7.2 million)

Switzerland is a small country (41,000 square kilometers) in the heart of Europe. It falls into three physiographical zones: In the south are the Alps; in the north is the Jura, an array of low ridges; and between the two mountain zones is the central plateau, where most people live. The population has an annual growth rate of .6 percent, resulting mainly from immigration. Four official languages—German, French, Italian, and Rhaeto-Romanic—are spoken. Switzerland is among the richest nations on Earth.

The Swiss federal constitution implemented in 1848 was partly modeled on that of the United States. It provided the right to vote for men; women, however, had to wait until 1971 to get the right to vote. Direct democracy is a key element of Swiss political culture: The 1848 constitution enshrined the obligatory constitutional referendum at the federal level. The revised constitution of 1874 began a new stage of direct democracy: Any nonurgent law could be challenged in a nationwide referendum. Finally, the constitutional initiative for partial revision of the Federal Constitution was introduced at the federal level in 1891. Since then most controversial issues have been decided by ballot.

Before 1800 environmental degradation in Switzerland was limited to local effects because mining was negligible and population growth was moderate. Subsequently, population grew at a faster pace. Cheap labor and growing demand for food allowed improvements in the efficiency of the agricultural system. Whereas the growing population could be fed, the demand for firewood could be met only by using unsustainable methods of forest management. As a result, many mountainous regions had become deforested by 1850. At the same time the frequency of severe floods grew at an alarming rate. Increasingly disastrous floods were blamed on deforestation. Finally, a law was passed in 1876 to prohibit deforestation in mountainous areas and to provide federal subsidies for reforestation. However, recent research has demonstrated that the high frequency of floods between 1830 and 1880 was caused by increased precipitation. Migration from the peripheries of the country to the center and the importation of coal for the railways relieved the pressure to exploit mountain forests. On the other hand, the importation of coal via the railways allowed the mass manufacturing of drainage pipes, which would have been too expensive to manufacture on the basis of firewood. This promoted the drainage of wetlands in the central plateau. Until 1970 most of the wetlands had been converted to pasture, in particular as a result of food shortages during the world wars.

Scenic Stereotypes

Travelers, artists, and writers discovered and praised the wilderness and grandeur of the alpine environment beginning in the eighteenth century. Their propaganda laid the basis for the development of tourism in the nineteenth century. After that time, alpine landscapes and stereotypes were also increasingly utilized as patriotic symbols in the process of nation building in Switzerland, which could not draw on a common language and culture.

The main phase of the Industrial Revolution resulted in rapid modifications in the countryside. Between the 1890s and 1914 large parts of the alpine environment were opened up to the public through a network of electric rack rails and hotels. This tourism boom also threatened symbolic landscapes and summits. In order to safeguard sites such as the Matterhorn from rack rail fever, the League for the Conservation of Picturesque Switzerland was created in 1905. After 1906 natural scientists, engineers, and foresters worked together in the Swiss League for the Protection of Nature. In 1914 they created the Swiss National Park in lower Engadine, which has remained the only Swiss

This view of the central Swiss Alps shows the impact of centuries of deforestation in response to the need for more pasture as local populations were exceeding the carrying capacity of the times. COURTESY JACK D. IVES.

National Park. In 1954 the league unsuccessfully initiated a referendum against the creation of a hydropower station in Rheinau (northern Switzerland).

Until the 1950s Swiss society still lived widely according to the principles of sustainability. Up to that time wages did not offer large surpluses, residential areas were situated within the range of local public transportation, and agricultural production was close to today's concept of "biodynamic farming" (a method of organic agriculture designed to enhance soil fertility or recycling of organic wastes). On the other hand, many people still had to perform hard physical work for moderate wages, and individual behavior was socially controlled.

With the transition to mass consumer society beginning in the late 1950s the scope of individuals was greatly enlarged, and the physical environment was modified profoundly. As in other countries of western Europe this involved the introduction of Fordism (sytem of mass production and consumption characteristic of highly developed economies during the 1940s–1960s), a rapid rise of incomes, suburbanization, and mass motorization. One of the key issues was the long-term decline in the price of fossil fuel in relation to the price of other goods, services, and wages. This scissor effect promoted the substitution of human labor (wages) by fossil fuel-driven technology and thus promoted energy-intensive forms of production, distribu-

tion, and consumption as well as manifold forms of environmental pollution.

Air Pollution

The quest for environmental protection gained rapid acceptance after the late 1960s, at first in the German-speaking areas. Federal subsidies for sewage treatment plants were raised substantially in 1971. As a consequence, a nationwide network of such plants was built in the 1970s. Air pollution was put on the agenda by government in 1983 with the demonstration of "Waldsterben" (forest death, forest decline). The resulting shock speeded up the adoption of a federal law on the environment (1983). The subsequent debate on the role of auto-produced air pollution in forest disease promoted the implementation of the catalytic converter for motor vehicles. On the other hand, the debate eroded the credibility of scientific experts. The series of annual surveys carried out since 1984 show neither the predicted steep rise in the degree of damage in the 1980s nor a progressive shift of the proportion among the damage classes from the lower to the higher damage classes and, finally, to death. In fact, there was no increase in mortality and no substantial extra cut was necessary.

In November 1986 a fire broke out at the Sandoz chemical plant at Schweizerhalle, near Basel. The water that firefighters used to put out the fire flushed huge amounts of insecticides and pesticides into the Rhine River, sparking an ecological catastrophe. As a consequence, public pressure was put on manufacturers to take tougher action against pollution. In September 2000 a referendum was held on the introduction of a levy on nonrenewable energy and an ecological tax reform. However, a rise in fuel prices prior to the referendum contributed to its defeat. The defeat of the referendum will slow down the government's once-ambitious environmental program.

Christian Pfister

Further Reading

Haefeli, U. (2001). Umweltschutz [Environmetnal protection]. In *Historisches Lexikon der Schweiz [Historical encyclopedia of Switzerland]*. Retrieved December 23, 2002, from http://www.snl.ch/dhs/externe/protect/textes/D24598–1–974.h tml

Pfister, C. (1998). The "syndrome of the 1950s" in Switzerland: Cheap energy, mass consumption and the environment. In S. Strasser, C. McGovern, & M. Judt (Eds.), *Getting and spending: European and American consumer societies in the twentieth century* (pp. 359–378). New York: Cambridge University Press.

Pfister, C. (1999). *Wetternachhersage: 500 Jahre Klimavariationen und Naturkatastrophen 1496–1995 [Climate retrodiction: 500 years of climatic variations and natural disasters 1496–1995]*. Bern, Switzerland: Paul Haupt.

Pfister, C., & Messerli, P. (1990). Switzerland. In B. L. Turner, et al. (Eds.), *The earth as transformed by human action: Global and regional changes in the biosphere over the past 300 years* (pp. 641–652). Cambridge, UK: Cambridge University Press.

Walter, F. (1990). *The evolution of environmental sensitivity 1750–1950*. In P. Brimblecombe & C. Pfister (Eds.), *The silent countdown: Essays in European environmental history* (pp. 231–247). New York: Springer.

Taiga

Taiga, also known as "boreal forest" and "northern coniferous forest," is a forested biome (a regional-scale unit of the biosphere defined by specific flora, fauna, and climate) characterized by evergreen, needle-bearing, coniferous trees, low temperatures and precipitation, and a short growing season. The word *taiga* is derived from a Russian word meaning "land of little sticks," which probably refers to the northern tree line where taiga meets tundra and trees are small and scattered.

Geography

Taiga, the world's largest biome, comprises about 18 million square kilometers and is restricted to the Northern Hemisphere. Largely subarctic and circumpolar in distribution, taiga has obscure boundaries. To the north, the tree line may extend into tundra for over 350 kilometers in sheltered valleys, reaching 72°N in Siberia and 69°N in North America. The tree line is dynamic, shifting in response to climatic changes. The 10°C isotherm, at which tree growth greatly declines, is a good predictor of its northern limit. To the south, taiga merges with deciduous forest, reaching 45°N in North America.

Climate

Cold, dry continental air masses dominate taiga during most of the year. Mean temperatures during summer range from 12° to 15°C. Winter temperatures can drop below −30°C, especially in mountainous eastern Si-beria, where a low of −71°C has been reported. The growing season for taiga ranges from fifty to one hundred days. Day length during the growing season ranges from sixteen hours in the south to twenty-four hours north of the Arctic Circle. Annual precipitation is low, ranging from 40 to 50 centimeters, falling mainly in summer. Cool summer temperatures—a result of the low angle of the sun at high latitudes—minimize evaporative losses. Thus the region appears wet, with numerous ponds, lakes, and bogs.

Soils

Taiga soils are relatively young spodosols—a soil order (or level of soil classification) that consists of highly leached, acidic, and nutrient-poor soils that form under coniferous vegetation. The soil profile consists of a thick organic layer—humus—overlaying a grayish-white, sandy, mineral horizon. Most taiga soils are thin, developed from bedrock exposed by recent glaciation. Cool summer temperatures and a short growing season slow decomposition and cause organic matter, particularly conifer needles, to build in a coarse layer. As much as 60 percent of total ecosystem carbon in taiga occurs in soil organic matter and debris. Water percolating through this organic layer leaches out organic acids and becomes acidified, with a pH range of 3.5–4.5. Acidified water leaches out cations—positively charged nutrients—as it infiltrates the soil. Thus most taiga soils are relatively infertile.

Organic soils, consisting of nondecomposed sphagnum moss and other organic matter, often develop in poorly drained areas—such as the muskeg bogs of North America. Permafrost (permanently frozen ground hundreds of meters thick and a few decimeters from the soil surface) is sometimes present in taiga, especially at high latitudes and high elevations (e.g., eastern Siberia) and under organic soils that warm and cool slowly. Seasonal freeze-thaw cycles result in significant movement of the soil's surface layers, creating hummocks (rounded knolls) up to 0.5 meters tall. Soil movement can dislodge shallow-rooted trees, causing them to uproot or lean, creating a haphazard arrangement of tree trunks whimsically called "drunken forest."

Flora and Fauna

Taiga is dominated by conifers of relatively few species, particularly spruce (Picea) and fir (Abies). Dominant trees include black spruce (Picea mariana), white spruce (Picea glauca), balsam fir (Abies balsamea), and tamarack (Larix laricina) in North America, Norway spruce (Picea abies) in Europe, and Siberian spruce (Picea obovata), larch (Larix sibirica), stone pine (Pinus sibirica), and Siberian fir (Abies sibirica) in Siberia. Deciduous, broad-leaved trees may occur with conifers in taiga, especially where soils are deep and the climate is less extreme or following disturbance such as fire. In North America deciduous trees like paper birch (Betula papyrifera) and quaking aspen (Populus tremuloides) dominate taiga sites after fire, eventually to be replaced by conifers. In Siberia burned sites dominated by deciduous trees are called "white taiga." Dwarf shrubs, particularly heaths (family Ericaceae), mosses, and some herbs and grasses, form a ground layer in taiga, especially where the forest canopy is sparse, light is abundant, and humus is thin.

Taiga can be divided into three structural classes that vary in forest canopy closure: forest-tundra ecotone (a transition area between two adjacent ecological communities), open lichen woodland, and closed forest. The forest-tundra ecotone, scattered patches of woodland and individual trees, lies north of the tree line in tundra. Trees are often less than 2 meters tall, depending on exposure, but may be hundreds of years old. Open lichen woodland occurs south of the forest-tundra ecotone. Trees are widely and regularly spaced, with lichens, shrubs, and other plants forming a patchy ground layer. Closed forest, in which the canopy is nearly continuous, is the southernmost of taiga structural classes. Shaded by dense canopy, few plants—largely shade tolerant—occur in the ground layer of closed forest.

The animal life of taiga includes both migratory and resident species. Large herbivores include caribou and reindeer (Rangifera tarandus) that winter in taiga and summer in tundra, and moose (Alces alces), a year-round resident. Small herbivores in North America include voles (Microtus species), snowshoe hare (Lepus americanus), and porcupine (Erethizon dorsatum). Predators include large species such as brown bear (Ursus arctos) and wolf (Canis lupus), medium to small species such as wolverine (Gulo gulo), lynx (Felis lynx), marten (Martes americana), and fisher (Martes pennanti). Many Neotropical (relating to the region south, east, and west from the central plateau of Mexico) migrant birds, including special concern species (species that are threatened, endangered, or declining in abundance in all or part of their range) such as Swainson's warbler (Lymnothlypis swainsonii), nest in North American taiga during summer and overwinter in the tropics. Resident birds include spruce grouse (Dendragapus canadensis) in North America and the circumboreal raven (Corvus corax).

Human Influences

Humans have a long history of living in the taiga. For centuries seminomadic hunter-gatherers in Eurasia and North America hunted taiga animals for food, clothing, and shelter—especially herds of caribou and reindeer—and collected abundant berries produced in summer and fall. By or before 800 CE, northern Europe's Sami evolved reindeer hunting into reindeer herding, a way of life now threatened by changes in land ownership. Sparsely populated today, taiga is valued by some as a vast resource for forest product extraction—pulp, lumber—and oil and gas development, largely for export to the developed world. Others value taiga as undeveloped "frontier forest," where vast areas can be conserved to ensure that the taiga's unique flora and fauna and ecosystem services (e.g., carbon storage) will persist into the future. The long-term integrity of taiga may be threatened by global warming, which could increase the frequency of fire. Some scenarios predict that taiga will decline from 40 to 60 percent in area in the next thirty to fifty years and release 1.5–3.0 metric gigatons of carbon annually, more than is currently being emitted by tropical deforestation.

Charles E. Williams

Further Reading

Archibold, O. Q. (1995). Ecology of world vegetation. New York: Chapman and Hall.

Bailey, R. G. (1998). *Ecoregions: The ecosystem geography of the oceans and continents.* New York: Springer-Verlag.

Barbour, M. G., Burk, J. H., Pitts, W. D., Gilliam, F. S., & Schwartz, M. W. (1999). *Terrestrial plant ecology.* Menlo Park, CA: Benjamin/Cummings.

Bryant, D., Nielsen, D., & Tangley, L. (1997). *The last frontier forests: Ecosystems and economies on the edge.* Washington, DC: World Resources Institute.

Daily, G. C. (Ed.). (1997). *Nature's services: Societal dependence on natural ecosystems.* Washington, DC: Island Press.

Montaigne, F. (2002). Boreal: The great northern forest. *National Geographic, 201*(6), 42–65.

Mulvaney, K. (2001). *At the ends of the Earth: A history of the polar regions.* Washington, DC: Island Press.

Perry, D. A. (1994). *Forest ecosystems.* Baltimore: Johns Hopkins University Press.

Peterken, G. F. (1996). *Natural woodland: Ecology and conservation in northern temperate regions.* Cambridge, UK: Cambridge University Press.

Smith, R. L., & Smith, T. M. (2001). *Ecology and field biology* (6th ed.). San Francisco: Benjamin/Cummings.

Vankat, J. L. (1979). *The natural vegetation of North America.* New York: John Wiley and Sons.

Tailings

Tailings are the waste or by-product of the process of milling ore to extract minerals and metals. Although minerals and metals may sometimes be mined at a level of purity that allows their use after a minimum of treatment, often the desired mineral or metal is found in the earth mixed with other material and must be milled to separate the desired product from the undesired material, called "gangue." Milling of ore broadly encompasses two processes: (1) crushing and grinding to reduce the particle size and perhaps to expose metal or mineral particles encased in gangue and (2) separating the desired metal or mineral from the gangue. The desired metal or mineral is then sent to the market or elsewhere for further processing, and the gangue is discarded as a waste product in the form of tailings. If milling serves as an intermediate step between mining and a more complex and costly metallurgical process such as smelting, then the mill is often called a "concentrator," and its product is called "concentrate." Concentration is never 100 percent effective,

so some of the desired metal or mineral is lost to the tailings.

The term *tailings* is sometimes mistakenly applied to waste rock from a mine, but only material that has been discarded by a mill or concentrator (or by a piece of equipment in a mill or concentrator) fits the definition of *tailings*. Because tailings are the by-product of a mechanical process, they are also distinct from metallurgical by-products such as smoke and slag, which are generated by smelting, a pyrochemical process. Humans learned to smelt ores to yield metal at least seven thousand years ago. The direct smelting of ores (smelting without prior concentration) reigned for at least four thousand years before miners developed crude concentrators, which allowed them to eliminate much of the gangue prior to smelting and therefore to reduce the overall cost of treatment.

Early concentrators were often powered by water, and their operators also learned that a stream of water could effectively carry the ore through the crushing equipment and then carry the crushed ore, called "pulp," through the concentrating apparatus. For that reason, concentrators have usually been located along flowing streams. Because milling is a continuous process, it is necessary to constantly convey tailings away from the mill so that ever more ore can be treated. As a consequence, those same streams also historically served as disposal sites, intended to carry the tailings away. Not until the Industrial Revolution and the rapid improvement of methods of milling and concentration did mining and smelting companies begin to intentionally store their tailings, recognizing that future technological improvements would most likely make it possible to reprocess the tailings and recover the metals initially lost to waste.

Tailings pollute streams, soils, and groundwater in a number of ways. The particle size of tailings varies, depending on the ore being treated and the processes being used, from gravels and sands to a very fine size called "slimes." Coarse tailings and slimes each have varying effects on the hydraulic characteristics of streams and lakes. Crushing and grinding of ore expose more surface area of a given volume of rock to the process of weathering, which may in time convert insoluble minerals to soluble ones. Tailings in streams, therefore, may greatly increase the amount of heavy metals in solution. Zinc in solution, for example, is poisonous to fish. Harmful minerals or chemicals in tailings may leach down into the ground, contaminating groundwater systems. Tailings may also alter the acidity of streams. As a consequence, tailings discharges have led to conflicts between the mining industry and other segments of society. In the early twentieth century, for example, farmers along the Coeur d'Alene River in Idaho filed a series of lawsuits against some of the United States' largest lead and silver mining companies, which were dumping their tailings directly into the river and its tributaries. At the beginning of the twenty-first century tailings disposal is heavily regulated in the United States, but old tailings deposits continue to pose cleanup problems.

Fred Quivik

Further Reading

Agricola, G. (1950). *De Re Metallica* [Concerning mining] (H. C. Hoover & L. H. Hoover, Trans.). New York: Dover. (Latin edition published 1556; original translation published 1912)

Morrissey, K. G. (1999). Mining, environment, and historical change in the inland Northwest. In D. D. Goble & P. W. Hirt (Eds.), *Northwest lands, Northwest peoples: Readings in environmental history* (pp. 479–501). Seattle: University of Washington Press.

Smith, D. A. (1987). *Mining America: The industry and the environment, 1800–1980*. Lawrence: University Press of Kansas.

Tanaka Shozo

(1841–1913)
Pioneer Japanese environmentalist

During the decades 1890–1910 Tanaka Shozo played a leading role in the political struggle to halt severe downstream pollution caused by operations at the Ashio copper mine and smelter complex, which was located in narrow valleys about 100 kilometers north of Tokyo. Decades later, when industrial pollution grew into a harsh national issue, he came to be viewed as a pioneer environmentalist.

A brusque, rough-spoken, and stubbornly tenacious man, Tanaka grew up in the household of a village headman in what is now southwestern Tochigi Prefecture, some 30 kilometers and a high mountain range away from Ashio. In 1860, at age nineteen, he succeeded to his father's role as headman, later left the post, and in 1879 established a prefectural newspaper through which he continued to speak vigorously in defense of local interests. A year later he was elected to the prefectural legislature, where he soon collided with the governor, a Tokyo appointee, and was temporarily jailed for his conduct. When a national legislature, the Imperial Diet, was opened in 1891, he entered it as the elected representative from Tochigi.

The Ashio mine had been a modest source of copper for centuries, but during the 1880s a new owner, the entrepreneur Furukawa Ichibei (1832–1903), equipped it with up-to-date mining, smelting, and refining machinery. Furukawa's men located additional veins of ore and during that decade rapidly expanded Ashio's output, transforming the mine into Japan's largest and most productive. This escalation in copper output yielded commensurate tailings, led to sharply expanded deforestation of adjoining hillsides, which provided mine timbers and fuel wood, and through greatly increased air pollution killed off most of the surviving vegetation. The result was intensified erosion and flooding, and, especially after downpours in 1890, severe pollution of downstream rivers and floodplains with a witch's brew of sulfuric acid, arsenic, copper sulfate, and other poisons.

By 1891 the pollutants had destroyed upwind forests, downstream fisheries, and the livelihood of thousands. They had ruined over 1,500 hectares of arable land, poisoned several villages, and produced poverty, illness, and death, much of it in Tanaka's electoral district. That year he demanded in the newly opened Diet that the mining be stopped and remedial actions taken. However, because Furukawa had good political connections, because his copper exports generated badly needed foreign currency, and because the ideal of rapid industrial modernization was deeply held by the Japanese leadership, his protests and demands were brushed aside.

During the 1890s Tanaka and a slowly growing group of legislators and others continued to protest the lack of effective government action. Not, however, until 1896—when disastrous floods killed hundreds, ravaged some eighty-eight villages, transported poisons to the very edge of Tokyo, and spurred outraged villagers to organize, overwhelm local police, and march on the city—did Japan's political and intellectual elites finally address the issue. Over the next few years, new legislation forced Furukawa to modify his procedures, and by the time of Tanaka's death in 1913 the rate of pollution had dropped substantially. During the next few decades most of the villages recovered, the social damage was gradually repaired, and much of Japan went on to forget the affair.

During the 1960s, however, when the country was convulsed by a new siege of pollution and antipollution activism, his name was invoked as a champion of the cause. He and the Ashio incident then acquired their present stature as emblems of Japan's entrance into the age of industrialism, industrial pollution, and the people's struggle against it.

Conrad Totman

Further Reading

Pyle, K. B., Notehelfer, F. G., & Stone, A. (1975). Symposium: The Ashio Copper Mine pollution case. *Journal of Japanese Studies*, 1(2), 347–407.

Strong, K. (1977). *Ox against the storm: A biography of Tanaka Shozo, Japan's conservationist pioneer*. Tenterden, UK: Paul Norbury.

Ui, J., (Ed.). (1992). *Industrial pollution in Japan*. Tokyo, Japan: United Nations University Press.

Taoism

Western philosophy has been criticized for perpetuating ideas, such as dualism and reductionism, that promote distance from, if not outright antagonism toward, the environment. Chinese philosophy offers an alternative approach by advocating ideas, such as holism and nondualism, which encourage living in harmony with the environment. Chinese philosophy is commonly summarized in the expression *tianren heyi* ("nature and humanity unite as one") (*tian* is usually rendered as Heaven, which represents the natural world). Nondualism is the philosophical notion that opposites are not independent dualities, but interrelated and interpenetrating, such that the universe and people form a united whole.

Confucianism, Taoism (in pinyin romanization, Taoism) and Buddhism are the three major philosophies of China. Confucianism advocates humans living in harmony with nature, but its main focus is social, moral, and political philosophy. Imported from India, Buddhism also promotes harmony with nature, but its primary concern is liberating people from suffering by means of meditation and enlightenment. Taoism has its own moral, social, and political philosophy, and its own practices of meditation and interpretation of awakening, but Taoism goes beyond the other philosophies in its emphasis on living in harmony with the natural environment. In this sense, Taoism is China's foremost environmental philosophy, in that it makes living in harmony and unity with the natural environment its ultimate goal.

Brief Historical Background

Some Taoists claim that the ideas, masters, and texts of Taoism were originally generated by the *Dao* (or Tao, meaning "Way," the ordering and creative principle of the universe) in the primordial chaos of undifferentiated, pure potentiality of existence (*hundun*) from which all things are generated. Historians believe that Taoism had its conception in the ecstatic vision quests of the ancient shamans of southern China from about the tenth to fifth centuries BCE. Some see Taoism developing out of the individualistic thought of hermits like Yang Zhu (c. sixth–fifth century BCE), who believed the world formed an organic whole, such that he would not remove one hair from his shin to benefit the world (that is, he thought that each and every thing was so interconnected that one could not save the whole world by destroying any part, even a tiny hair). Most commonly, however, the origin of Taoism is usually attributed to Laozi (or Lao-tzu, meaning literally "the old master"; he is believed to have lived sixth–fifth century BCE), who is the alleged author of the book that bears his name as its title, and which is also known as the *Daodejing* (or *Tao Te Ching* in English, Classic of the Way and Its Power).

The second major figure in Taoism is Zhuang Zhou (or Zhuangzi, c. fourth–third century BCE), who is believed to have written the first seven, or inner, chapters of the text that bears his name as its title. The impact of the *Zhuangzi* on Taoist philosophy and religion cannot be overstated. Whether or not Zhuangzi advances the teaching of Laozi—as opposed to being simply an independent thinker in a similar vein—is currently under debate. The expression Lao-Zhuang, referring to the teachings of both thinkers, was first used in the preface to another Taoist work, the *Huainanzi* (139 BCE), and it was especially popular to discuss Lao-Zhuang teachings during the Wei Jin period of Chinese history (220–420 CE).

In the Later Han dynasty (25–220 CE), Laozi underwent a process of apotheosis and became a celestial god. He was deified by 165 CE as Taishang Laojun, the Most High Lord Lao. This led to the development of Taoism as a religion. Zhang Daoling, a small landowner, proclaimed a new order based on revelations that he said the god Laozi made to him in 142 CE. He advocated the rule of the Three Heavens, which would deliver the world from an age of decadence and establish a perfect state for the chosen "seed people." Zhang's movement began in Sichuan under the name of Wudoumi dao (Way of the Five Baskets of Rice, a name taken from the tax levied on followers), and later became known as Tianshi dao (Way of the Celestial Masters). The teachings and practices of this religion and related alchemical and meditative practices underwent a complex process of change and development during the ensuing centuries. Taoism is still practiced today both in and outside of China.

Taoist Ecology

Because the early Taoist texts criticize Confucian virtues and morality, some scholars wrongly assert that Taoism lacks a morality. The early Taoist texts do in fact advocate moral ideas, proposing that the best way to live is by modeling the forces of nature and living in harmony with nature. Laozi tells us that the best people are like water, and Taoists try to emulate the virtues of water. They celebrate its softness, flexibility, and frictionless traits, its ability to erode mountains, its murky and chaotic condition when agitated, and its depth and clarity when calm. To go with the flow, literally and metaphorically, is the Taoist key to proper living.

Zhuangzi develops Taoist environmental philosophy. Some scholars postulate that Zhuangzi may have been the warden of a forest reserve. He certainly was familiar with local flora and fauna. Zhuangzi advocates a type of perspectivism: He states that each creature is limited in its understanding by the perspective from which it experiences the world. He gives numerous examples of how different creatures find different habitats and foods pleasing. He maintains that there is no single correct or privileged perspective; rather, each perspective has its unique benefits and traits. Though not the highest ideal, Zhuangzi proposes that a person should aspire to be "a companion of nature/heaven" (Watson 1968, 56–57).

One area in which Taoism can assist modern ecology and environmental ethics is in human transformation. Many people propose that humans must change how they think about the environment and especially how they behave toward it. Taoists have developed various ideas and methods to help people embrace natural and personal transformation. Embracing change as a natural fact allows one to think and act more profoundly than does simple conservationism. Instead of conservationism, Taoists seek to love in harmony in the face of rapid change. For example, selective burning or removing of dead trees would be allowed, if that enhanced human harmony with the forest. People are also changing; we need to transform ourselves to become even in harmony with nature. Taoists advocate cutting loose (jie) from the restrictions of social custom, psychological feelings, and divisive ideas. Cutting loose helps Taoists break free from social conventions that encourage people to exploit natural resources.

The ultimate goal for Taoists is to return to the primordial oneness of *Dao*, or the way of nature. They employ a number of metaphors to express this union with nature. For example, Taoists talk about riding the wind, riding a dragon, entering water without getting wet or fire without getting burned, and living like a hermit in the mountains, only consuming dewdrops. Zhuangzi expressed this union aptly: "Heaven and earth were born at the same time I was, and the ten thousand things are one with me" (Watson 1968, 43). Taoism can awaken us to a deeper understanding of and relationship with the environment.

James D. Sellmann

Detail of Taoist monastery on Mt. Qingcheng in Sichuan Province, China. COURTESY JAMES MILLER.

Further Reading

Addiss, S., & Lombardo, S. (1993). *Tao te ching (Lao Tzu)*. Indianapolis, IN: Hackett Publishing Co.

Ames, R. T. (1989). Putting the te back into Taoism. In J. B. Callicott & R. T. Ames (Eds.), *Nature in Asian traditions of thought: Essays in environmental philosophy* (pp. 113–144). Albany: State University of New York Press.

Graham, A. C. (1981). *Chuang-tzu: The inner chapters*. Channel Islands, UK: Guernsey Press Co.

Lau, D. C., & Ames, R. T. (1998). *Yuan Dao: Tracing Dao to its source.* New York: Ballantine Books.

Rowe, S., & Sellman, J. D. (2000). Ecological feminism and Taoism. *Asian Culture Quarterly, 28*(4), 11–25.

Watson, B. (1968). *The complete works of Chuang Tzu.* New York: Columbia University Press.

Taro

With a distribution that extends from West Africa to India, East Asia, and Oceania, taro *(Colocasia esculenta)* was the world's most widely distributed food plant before the modern era of international transport and rapid plant dispersal that began with the European age of exploration (late fifteenth century–sixteenth centuries CE). Taro is a starchy root crop with very small, easily digested starch granules located in underground storage organs called corms. These organs are actually swollen stems, not roots, but other root crops do store starch in roots. Taro now grows in tropical to temperate regions, on all continents and innumerable islands, and there are hundreds of different cultivated varieties (cultivars).

When harvested, the corms range in weight from a few grams (the side, or child, corms) to one or two kilograms (the central, or parent, corms). The number, shape, color, and eating qualities of corms vary greatly, and many cultivars also have edible, nutritious leaf stems and leaf blades. Preparation methods vary according to cultivar, part eaten, and local food styles, but the corms are always peeled and cooked (or cooked and peeled) to remove acridity. All taros are acrid to some degree, and acridity is strongest in wild-type taro (the natural, wild form of taro). Although irritating to the human skin, mouth, and throat, acridity helps protect taro against herbivores. The crop is thus well suited for organic farming.

In most regions, taro is only a minor food source alongside starchy cereals and legumes. In Oceania, cultivated cereals and legumes were generally absent in the past, and taro was an important staple on many islands, alongside other aroids (members of the Araceae family, the family to which taro belongs) and other root crops or tree crops. The main edible aroids are *Colocasia gigantea* (a leaf vegetable known as *hasuimo* in Japan), *Alocasia macrorrhizos, Amorphophallus paeoniifolius, Amorphophallus konjac, Cyrtosperma chamissonis,* and *Xanthosoma sagittifolium.* The last species originated in tropical America, is similar to taro in appearance and uses, and has replaced taro in many other tropical areas. Many aroids are grown as ornamental plants, and taro is also used as an ornamental in Australia, Japan, Italy, and elsewhere.

Archaeological records for taro are scarce because the plant is a soft herb with no hard parts. The oldest clues are soil erosion and earthworks that may or may not reflect taro cultivation, 6,000 years ago or earlier in highland New Guinea, and starch granules that are possibly from taro, on stone tools dated to approximately 28,000 years ago in the Solomon Islands. In wild and apparently natural habitats by swamps, streams, and waterfalls, wild-type taro is distributed from northeastern India to southern China, Southeast Asia, Australia, and New Guinea. Genetic studies indicate that domestication occurred independently in more than one region.

Although wild taros in tropical climates produce abundant flowers and seed, cultivated taros are always grown vegetatively from corms and corm tops. Many cultivated taros can also produce flowers and seed, but the seed is not used for propagation by farmers. The earliest stages of domestication of this crop must have involved selection of preferred plants from among naturally variable wild populations. Subsequent domestication may have involved selection and vegetative propagation of plants produced by crosses between wild and cultivated taros in natural and disturbed habitats, active gardens, and fallow gardens. In some regions, this complex and understudied process is likely to be continuing.

P. J. Matthews

Further Reading

Bayliss-Smith, T. (1996). People-plant interactions in the New Guinea highlands: Agricultural hearthland or horticultural backwater? In D. R. Harris (Ed.), *The origins and spread of agriculture and pastoralism in Eurasia* (pp. 499–523). London: UCL Press.

Bown, D. (2000). *Aroids: Plants of the arum family.* (2nd ed.). Portland, OR: Timber Press.

Chandra, S. (Ed.). (1984). *Edible aroids.* Oxford, UK: Clarendon Press.

Loy, T. H., Spriggs, M., & Wickler, S. (1992). Direct evidence for human use of plants 28,000 years ago: Starch residues on stone artifacts from the northern Solomon Islands. *Antiquity 66,* 898–912.

Matthews, P. J. (1995). Aroids and the Austronesians. *Tropics 4*(2), 105–126.

Matthews, P. J. (1997). Field guide for wild-type taro, *Colocasia esculenta* (L.) Schott. *Plant Genetic Resources Newsletter*, 110, 41–48.

Mayo, S. J., Bogner, J. & Boyce, P. C. (1997) *The genera of Araceae.* Kew, UK: Royal Botanic Gardens.

Wang, J.-K. (Ed.). (1983). *Taro: a review of* Colocasia esculenta *and its potentials.* Honolulu: University of Hawaii Press.

Tea

Humans consume more tea than any other substance except air and water. It is the most important medical plant on the planet, and its effects have been enormous. There are several varieties of tea, but they all derive from a species of camellia *(camellia sinensis)*. Green and black tea are from similar leaves but are processed in different ways.

The tea bush originated in the area where India, China, and Myanmar (Burma) meet in the hot, wet, mountainous regions of the eastern Himalayas. It was originally eaten and drunk by tribal groups in that area. Over two thousand years ago it was used as a medicine and an aid to concentration in China, its use being inspired by the expansion of Buddhism. By the eighth century CE it was widely drunk throughout most of China. In the thirteenth century it spread to Japan and by the fifteenth century had become a central part of Japanese life, particularly in the tea ceremony. During the same period it spread through Central Asia. As "brick tea" (compacted lumps) it became the most important trading object and absolute necessity to the Tibetans, Mongolians, and Manchurians.

Rumors of tea reached the West in the sixteenth century, but it began to be imported in any quantity only in the middle of the seventeenth century. Its importation took off in the 1720s when the direct clipper ship trade to China was established by the Dutch and British. Although it had early success in much of northwestern Europe, it was in Britain that it became the main drink. By the later eighteenth century it was drunk throughout Britain and by all social groups. It was drunk both in the home and in tea houses and gardens. As the British Empire grew, tea was reexported and became the favorite drink of many parts of the empire, although after the Boston Tea Party in 1773, when tea chests were thrown into the harbor as a pro-test against taxes, trade from Britain to the United States diminished. India itself took to tea drinking only when it was introduced by the British in the first half of the twentieth century. The growth of tea drinking continued so that by the late twentieth century tea was the main drink of the inhabitants of the three-quarters of the globe who lived in eastern Asia, the former British Empire, Russia, and much of the Middle East.

Domestication

Tea originally grew wild. When it was domesticated it was grown as a peasant product. The manual labor was intensive and based on the family. The leaves were picked, dried, rolled, and crushed. Failures to introduce the bush into the West led the Dutch (in Java) and the British (in Assam State in India and then in Sri Lanka) to experiment with tea production. By the later nineteenth century the application of industrial methods, capitalistic funding, and rigid discipline had created the tea plantation system. Huge profits were made by the British and Dutch. The laborers on the tea estates suffered enormously, with horrendous conditions and high mortality rates. Yet, the system was so efficient that it undercut the Chinese production and destroyed the Chinese export trade in tea by 1900. In fact, China had already been weakened by the Opium Wars of the 1840s, which had also been linked to the British desire for tea, which the British had increasingly been able to purchase only by selling opium to the Chinese.

Much of Chinese and Japanese life has been influenced by tea drinking, most famously in the aesthetics and rituals of the ornate tea ceremonies, with their influence on ceramics, furniture, architecture, gardening, and literature. Similarly in the West, the introduction of tea gave a great boost to the consumer revolution of the eighteenth century, in particular the development of pottery and porcelain, furniture, and tableware. Through the development of tea gardens in the West, tea drinking encouraged new forms of sociality that stimulated music, literature, and garden design. It also added greatly to the influence of Asian civilizations on European cultures in the eighteenth century.

Tea has altered the relations between social classes, relations between the sexes, and relations within the family. For example, it gave a new role to women as tea mistresses and encouraged family meetings over tea. It changed the patterns of eating, altering the nature of breakfast and allowing the evening meal to be eaten later as afternoon tea and cakes would stave off hunger. It encouraged the growth of clubs and social recreations outside the home. It led to the elaboration of a great deal of social ritual around its serving.

The Business of Tea

The trade in tea created the first large-scale global market, and the promotion of tea in the West was the first example of modern consumer marketing. It made the fortunes of Dutch and British merchants and in particular the East India Company. In fact, ironically, without Chinese tea it is doubtful whether the British would have absorbed India into their empire. The extra energy supplied by tea with sugar and milk helped sustain the enormous effort needed to create the first industrial revolution in Britain between 1750 and 1850. In Asia the effects were no less great because tea provided the energy needed for the grueling work of intensive wet rice cultivation in China and Japan.

Tea was originally recommended for its health benefits. It contains substances (polyphenols and caffeine) that kill waterborne bacteria, and its preparation encourages the boiling of water. So it has had a massive effect on dysentery, typhoid, and other waterborne diseases. Recent research has indicated that it also has beneficial effects on other diseases such as cancer, heart disease, stroke, muscular problems, tooth decay, and influenza.

In the beginning the growing of tea did not have a large effect on the environment because tea was grown alongside other crops on the hillsides of China and the hedgerows of Japan. But when the British and Dutch applied industrial production methods to tea growing and processing in the nineteenth century, the effect on the environment became dramatic. The new tea growers carved out great plantations in Assam, Ceylon, Indonesia, and later Africa and South America. Vast tracts of forest were leveled and countless animals destroyed to make way for the orderly rows of tea bushes. A monoculture, based on the methods of the West and the plant of the East, was established.

It is not difficult to argue that this apparently small and insignificant plant has had more impact on human happiness and misery than any other. In turn, its cultivation has changed the ecology of the considerable areas of Asia, Africa, and South America where it has been grown.

Alan Macfarlane

Further Reading

Hardy, S. (1979). *The tea book.* London: Whittet Books.

Harler, C. R. (1958). *The culture and marketing of tea.* Oxford, UK: Oxford University Press.

Hobhouse, H. (1985). *Seeds of change: Six plants that transformed mankind.* London: Macmillan.

Macfarlane, A., & Macfarlane, I. (2003). *Green gold: The empire of tea.* London: Ebury Press.

Ukers, W. H. (1935). *All about tea.* New York: Tea and Coffee Trade Journal Company.

Technology

A history of technology as it relates to the environment is a history of human production as a way of manipulating the environment and its impact on the global ecosystem. Technology historians Melvin Krantzberg and Carol Pursell point out in *Technology in Western Civilization* that "technology is man's efforts to cope with his physical environment—both that created by nature and that created by man's own technological deeds, such as cities—and his attempts to subdue or control that environment by means of his imagination and ingenuity in the use of available resources" (Krantzberg & Pursell 1967, 4–5). Humankind's development has always been measured by its technological innovations, which allowed people to change their way of life through the control of nature. Hence the progression of human civilization has classically been assigned to stages of technological developments, such as the Stone Age, Bronze Age, Iron Age, Atomic Age, and Computer Age. Environmental costs and benefits were linked to each technological stage of human evolution. In each of these stages technological developments and innovations brought about significant changes in the quality of air, water, and land by causing dramatic changes in the numbers of humans in the ecosystem and by producing waste products that altered natural resources.

The greatest environmental impacts on a global scale arose from technological developments that occurred during the Industrial Revolution and exponentially during the twentieth century. Environmental historian John R. McNeill asserts that "The technologies of the twentieth century, intertwined with related changes in energy and economy, powerfully determined the rates and kinds of environmental changes"

Three Quotes on the Limits of Technology

Western society has accepted as unquestionable a technological imperative that is quite as arbitrary as the most primitive taboo: not merely the duty to foster invention and constantly to create technological novelties, but equally the duty to surrender to these novelties unconditionally, just because they are offered, without respect to their human consequences

—Lewis Mumford

The system of nature, of which man is a part, tends to be self-balancing, self-adjusting, self-cleansing. Not so with technology.

—E. F. Schumacher

For a successful technology, reality must take precedence over public relations, for Nature cannot be fooled.

—Richard P. Feynman

(McNeill 2000, 306). During this period of technological development humans faced a myriad of potentially devastating global environmental issues, ranging from acid rain produced by the use of fossil fuels in combustion technologies to global warming as a result of massive deforestation by agricultural technologies to the potential for global annihilation by nuclear technologies.

Numerous technologies have been produced by humans since their emergence more than 25 million years ago if the concept of technology includes tools (however primitive) used to alter humans' interaction with the environment. The first tools were, in fact, humans' hands and teeth, but these were eventually replaced by stones, bones, sticks, and other materials to help humans interact with their environment more effectively.

Early People and Fire: Burning Desires for Control

One of humans' earliest technological conquests was fire. During Paleolithic times (the old Stone Age, which lasted about a million years to 8000 BCE) in Europe and Asia humans discovered the percussion method for fire production. This early technology consisted of striking together lumps of flint and pyrites to release sparks in the presence of tinder, straw, or other inflammable fuel to generate light and fire. Early humans soon learned how to develop fire technologies to preserve or initiate fire because it proved to be a critical resource to their relationship with their environment.

According to Franz J. Broswimmer, research specialist at the Globalization Research Center at the University of Hawaii at Manoa, "Learning to manage fire represented a remarkable technical and cultural advance for anatomically pre-modern hominids. It brought the possibility of warmth and light and therefore a double extension of the human environment into the cold" (Broswimmer 2002, 17). Once discovered, fire became a precious resource for early people, who carried it around with them and shared it only with their clan members. The critical need for early humans to have "portable" fire produced the early fire technologies because fire was usable only if it could travel to locations where it was needed (i.e., for warmth, for hunting, and for light). This was especially true for communities who early in their histories had not learned how to start a fire, as had the Australian aborigines, Tasmanians, and Andaman Islanders, and thus carried firesticks. The three fire technologies that prevailed among early people, as environmental historian Stephen J. Pyne points out, were the "fire drill, the fire piston, and the fire striker" (Pyne 2001, 122). The fire drill technology also included fire plows and saws and drills proper. This class of pyrotechnologies was based on the principle of vigorously rubbing combustion materials to generate enough heat friction to result in the kindling of tinder. The fire piston functioned similarly to a diesel engine by the quick plunging and then rapid release of a tinder-draped piston into a small chamber. These actions produced a rapid buildup of heat and a sudden release into oxygen, causing ignition. The fire striker used a multitude of

---

Plato on the Deforestation of Attica, Circa 400 BCE,
What now remains compared with what then existed is like the skeleton of a sick man, all the fat and soft earth having wasted away, and only the bare framework of the land being left.

---

instruments that showered sparks onto tinder, causing ignition.

Early humans' discovery of fire, however, radically changed their relationship to their environment by allowing them to obtain more secure living shelters in the forms of caves, which they could now acquire by driving away cave-dwelling animals with fire. Fire also allowed humans to advance their other technologies, such as spears, which could now be hardened and made more useful by applying fire. Early mastery of fire technologies contributed to the development of cooking, which radically changed the nutritional and dietary patterns of prehistoric people. Cooking allowed people to digest foods that had been previously indigestible; seeds and bitter foods became more palatable through cooking. John McNeill points out that "When humankind occupied caves and began to burn fuel wood for heating and cooking, indoor pollution made its debut. Many caves inhabited millennia ago retain a patina of smoke on their walls, and cave dwellers presumably suffered lung and eye ailments derived from exposure to smoke. Blackened lungs are common among mummified corpses from Paleolithic times" (McNeill 2000, 55).

The discovery of fire also had an impact on big-game hunting by humans and eventually on agricultural development as land that was cleared by cutting tools was also burned to prepare the soil for planting. Hunting and agricultural practices radically changed humans' ecosystem by contributing to the extinction of other humans, plants, and animals. Fire would be used by early humans to alter their environment in a variety of ways that made it more habitable. Humans used fire to create potash (a source of potassium) for fertilizers to boost agricultural production, to produce cement from limestone, and to produce glass from sand and ceramics from clay. Humans also used fire in naval industries (e.g., shipbuilding) by slow cooking pine to produce tar, pitch, and turpentine and in mining to burn land to expose rock to gain excess to mineral ores and also to produce tunnels, forge, and smelt. Stephen Pyne describes an early treatise (c. 1556 CE) by

German scholar Georgius Agricola that detailed the use of fire by early miners prior to the Industrial Revolution. The treatise points out that "Where the (mining) veins resisted their iron picks, hardrock miners lit fires to shatter the stone sufficiently to pry out ore. This was dangerous work, requiring that mines consider ventilation; but miners already relied on fire to illuminate the shafts, and it was only a matter of degree to put their torches to the stone directly" (Pyne 2001, 132).

Prehistoric humans produced fire mainly with primitive fuels: dead branches, dry wood, and shrubs. In some parts of the world (especially the East) these fuels would eventually be supplemented by straw and farm animal refuse.

As humans evolved over time and developed industries that required large-scale uses of heat, wood as a fuel was replaced by charcoal. Historians and archaeologists estimate that charcoal burning began in 4000 BCE primarily for use in metal smelting and was critical to the emergence of the Bronze and Iron Ages. Large quantities of charcoal then and now were produced by the controlled and incomplete combustion of wood. The wood was heated with fire, but the amount of air (oxygen) was controlled to allow for a slow burn. This incomplete combustion released the by-products of water vapor in the form of steam, carbon dioxide, and volatile environmental pollutants such as tar, oils, and naphtha. The product, charcoal, consisted of a solid black residue containing 30 percent carbon, 10 percent hydrogen, and 5 percent oxygen and mineral ash with trace elements of potassium, sulfur, and nitrogen. The kiln technology was developed to produce massive quantities of charcoal for industrial use. The Romans used vast quantities of charcoal to make weapons and used the by-products (slag) from their charcoal furnaces to build roads. The large-scale use of charcoal for ancient industries contributed to the massive deforestation of areas around the world. Historian of technology R. J. Forbes points out that deforestation was a real concern in antiquity, so much so that "the Greek Philosopher Plato (427–347 BCE) deplored the disappearance of the many forests of Athens due to charcoal-burning and ship building" (Krantzberg & Pursell 1967, 16).

Cutting Edges of Extinction

Critical to humankind's development was an ability to cut down what they perceived to be their environmental adversaries, which included other humans, animals, and plants. As Krantzberg and Pursell point out, "man as we know him, surely would not have evolved or survived without tools. He is too weak and puny a creature to compete in the struggle with beasts and caprices of nature with only hands and feet" (Krantzberg & Pursell 1967, 7). Cutting tools throughout human history have been used to alter the environment (such as in clearing lands for agriculture and in hunting prey) and have led to massive deforestation and extinctions.

Spears, Axes, and Early Extinction

The first stone tools produced by humans were eoliths (crudely chipped flint) during the early Stone Age and were provided by the environment. They were naturally shaped stones picked up from riverbeds. Shortly after this time humans learned how to shape stones from other stones and produced standardized cutting tools for chopping and hunting. Around one hundred thousand years ago humans began to make pear-shaped hand axes, scrapers, knives, and pointed stones. Around forty thousand years ago humans began to produce cutting tools, which included spears and axes that were thin and had parallel-sided blades from the core. Between twenty-three thousand and twenty thousand years ago humans began to produce small, light blades that could be used as projectiles and advanced their hunting capacity with the invention of the bow and arrow, snares, and nets. All of these technological advances contributed to the extinction of mammals and fish and to deforestation. Overhunting facilitated by these advances in hunting tools was believed to have caused the extinction of the bison in North America and the near extinction of the sea otter on the Aleutian Islands. People had hunted the sea otter for almost one thousand years using primordial hunting tools until around 500 BCE. On the Hawaiian Islands, within one thousand years of human settlement thirty-nine species of land birds became extinct due in large part to hunting. In Australia aboriginal people are believed to have been instrumental in the extinction of 86 percent of large animals over the last forty thousand years by using similar types of primor-

dial hunting tools. In South America the loss of 80 percent of animal life is believed to have been caused by the same hunting technologies.

Chain Saws

European settlement in the New World, particularly the Americas and Australia, resulted in massive deforestation facilitated by cutting technologies. For the most part these technologies were used to clear land for agricultural production. Haiti, whose name means "green island" in the local language, has only 10 percent of its original forests. In the United States by 1850 about 40 percent of the original 2.6 million square kilometers of ancient forests had been destroyed, and by 1930 only 13 percent of the original forests remained. In Australia approximately one-half of the original forests were destroyed after its initial settlement in the late eighteenth century, and this amount included three-quarters of the rain forest. New Zealand lost at least one-half of its original forests after colonization.

Environmental impacts would reach new levels, however, with development of the chain saw, which was patented in 1858 and first manufactured in 1917. The chain saw had its first substantial impacts on the environment after World War II. By 1958 chain saws had replaced all other forms of lumber technology (such as bucksaws and axes) in North America.

John McNeill points out that the chain saw "allowed men to cut trees 100 or 1,000 times faster than with axes. Without the chain saw, the great clearance of tropical forests would either not have happened, have happened much more slowly, or have required 100 or 1,000 times as many laborers" (McNeill 2000, 308).

By the 1980s an estimated 11.3 million hectares a year were being cleared. Chainsaw technology has had its greatest environmental impact in Third World countries. About two-thirds of the total loss of forest in the world has been in Africa—the Ivory Coast, Nigeria, Liberia, Guinea, and Ghana.

Agricultural Technologies and Deforestation

As people evolved and developed agricultural societies, cutting tools proved instrumental in creating their new lifestyle. Axes were used to remove unwanted vegetation and to plant crops. As environmental scholar Clive Pointing points out, land clearing radically disrupts the ecosystem because, "When vegetation cover is removed, solar energy, instead of being partly absorbed is reflected from the bare ground, increasing temperatures, drying the soil, creating dust in the atmosphere and helping to stop rain clouds forming" (Pointing 1991, 258). Effects are usually seen after about 260,000 square kilometers of land have been cleared. Scholars believe that such land clearing resulted in the formation of the Sahara Desert and contributed to the collapse of many agriculture-based ancient societies such as Mesopotamia. Mesopotamia collapsed because its irrigation systems led to salinization, which created agricultural problems, but also because Mesopotamia cut down its forests to acquire wood with which to build ships and buildings and to use in its bronze and pottery industries. By the early twenty-first century in western Africa, four times the amount of land specified by Pointing has been cleared, resulting in twenty-three years of aridity. This area of Africa has experienced one-third less annual rainfall than it did one hundred years ago.

Land under cultivation increased by at least 809 million hectares beginning around 130 years ago. A significant percentage of this increase was due to the clearing of natural forests. In China it is estimated that natural forests originally covered 75 percent of the land but now cover only 5 percent. China is believed to have lost around 20 million hectares due to deforestation between 1950 and 1980.

Industrial Revolution: Energy Technologies and Global Disruption

The environmental impacts of combustion and pyrotechnologies on the world's ecosystems increased during the Industrial Revolution. Human impact on the environment (both good and bad), although significant prior to the Industrial Revolution, became exponential. During this period human societies began to produce massive quantities of materials for consumption and trade not merely for subsistence but also for power, wealth, and improved standards of living. The control and use of natural resources, especially heat and fire (e.g., combustion), were at the heart of the Industrial Revolution because many of the industrial technologies relied on natural resources such as coal, oil, gas, and timber and on biomass (the amount of living matter). Environmental historian J. Donald Hughes points out that "The inventions that did the most to shape the modern age were those that allowed the application of new sources of power, especially, fossil fuels, to the production process. These machines became the instruments of the industrial revolution" (Hughes 2001, 110). The technologies that arose during the Industrial

Revolution allowed societies to replace human power with mechanical power and increased the output of production exponentially. Mechanical power was initially supplied by the natural resources of water and air. The Dutch during the early period of the Industrial Revolution obtained additional agricultural land by opening up their low-lying areas by controlling water using dikes and dams. They also ran mills by harnessing mechanical power from the air with the use of windmills. These windmills drew on ancient pump technologies, such as the Archimedes screw, which was developed by the ancient Greek philosopher Archimedes in Sicily. Over time, however, mechanical power demands in the Industrial Revolution were met primarily by the energy supplied by combustion, and this process relied heavily on fossil fuels to power engines and pumps. The use of fossil fuels had severe consequences for global ecosystems. Hughes points out that "With the manipulation of immense amounts of energy made possible by technology, the human use of resources became increasingly exploitative and . . . ushered the massive exploitation of nature's resources to drive the machines of production" (Hughes 2001, 110). The growth in the use of fossil fuels is reflected in the increases in the production of coal beginning in the nineteenth century. Production rose from 500 million metric tons in 1890 to 2.6 billion metric tons in 1960. The production level of coal was exceeded by that of petroleum, diesel, and natural gas.

Europe, the center of the Industrial Revolution, drew massive amounts of raw materials initially from itself to feed its engines of production. Eventually Europe and other areas that came to be industrialized (such as the New World and its colonies) began to use and degrade the energy capital of ecosystems abroad. As a result the laissez-faire doctrine emerged and was advocated by European economic thinkers such as the Scotsman Adam Smith and the Englishman John Stuart Mill. This doctrine stated that unchecked natural resource exploitation occurring globally and at the expense of other human populations and the biosphere (the part of the world in which life can exist) for the economic growth of industrialists is the order of nature and should not be regulated. This doctrine created enormous environmental inequalities for human and nonhuman communities across the world and helped lead to large-scale destruction of ecosystems.

The technologies of the Industrial Revolution radically improved the production output of many industries but especially that of the agricultural industry, which was critical in altering population levels. The human population explosions, which started during the Industrial Revolution and have continued to today, have been a result of technological and scientific innovations or discoveries such as the mechanization of agriculture, new sources of fertilizers, and the construction of large-scale irrigation systems. The increases in consumption and waste products caused by increases in the human population had major impacts on the environment. Between 1700 and 1900 Europe's population increased from 122 million to 421 million (despite a 40-million emigration to the Americas and globally); China's population increased during the same period from 150 million to 436 million; India's doubled to 290 million, and sub-Saharan Africa's almost doubled (despite losses caused by the slave trade and the tsetse fly) as it went from 61 to 110 million. Early ecological and environmental philosophers, such as the Englishman Thomas Robert Malthus (1766–1834) believed that without outside interference this population explosion would become self-correcting. In his "Essay on the Principle of Population" the Malthusian principle made its debut and stated that the rapid rise in population would be checked by a diminishing food supply, as was the case in the Irish famine of the 1840s. Technological innovations, however, in the agricultural industry during this time were key in undermining a worldwide Malthusian crisis.

Nineteenth-Century London: Technology and the Environment

Throughout the nineteenth century London was the largest city in the world. It grew from a population of 1 million in 1801 to 2.3 million in 1854 to 6.6 million in 1901. People left behind low-paying agricultural jobs in the countryside for marginal increases in their standard of living and higher-paying factory jobs. The growth of London was an early example of the "treadmill of production" phenomenon. According to the "treadmill of production" model, as pointed out by Broswimmer,

> "Investors and managers are driven to accumulate wealth and expand their operations in order to prosper within a globally competitive milieu. For the vast majority of the world's people, the commitment to the treadmill is more limited and indirect; they simply need to obtain jobs at livable wages. However, to retain these jobs and to maintain an acceptable standard of living it is necessary to run faster and faster in order to stay in the same place." (Broswimmer 2002, 93–94)

London thus became an industrial center (made possible by rapidly evolving technologies) that continued to grow exponentially and was unparalleled in its number of manufacturing workers. These workers were employed in a multitude of industries such as clothing, shoes, musical instruments, furniture, machinery tools, jewelry, and beer. The majority of London factories and homes were powered by fossil fuels, which polluted the city's air, land, and water. Hughes points out that "Industries and homes switched to coal for heat and gas for lighting. By 1880 there were 600,000 homes in the central part of the city with 3,500,000 fireplaces, virtually all burning coal" (Hughes 2001, 120).

This massive consumption of fossil fuels to operate combustion technologies in both the residential and manufacturing sectors resulted in London's infamous "smog" (a term coined by Dr. H. A. Des Voeux in 1905 to describe the mixture of fog and noxious smoke). The London smog caused massive amounts of environmental deaths and health problems during the nineteenth and early twentieth centuries. The deadliness of the London smog lay in the fact that the city was prone to fog because of its location low in the Thames River basin. People walked or stumbled into the river if smog conditions were severe. The smog suffocated residents who already had lung problems. Between one hundred and seven hundred deaths above the normal rate were reported in January 1880 during one smog incident.

The chemicals needed for industries or produced as by-products went into the water system of London. Industrial wastes, coupled with the massive levels of human wastes (sewage), killed most of the fish and mammals in the water ecosystems of the Thames River. Waste water pouring into the Thames River did not always reach the North Sea as intended. At high tides the waste water would back up, and the solid wastes would precipitate out, fouling the air. In 1858 this phenomenon became so bad that it caused the "Great Stink," which resulted in Parliament adjourning for a week because the stench of the air was intolerable.

Sewage problems resulting from population explosions also caused cholera and typhoid epidemics that killed thousands in London and Chicago, Illinois, and similar cities around the world.

The environmental degradation that nineteenth-century London industry produced continued into the next century and served as a model for the relationship between industrial production and the environment. Environmental sociologist Allan Schnaiberg introduced the concept of a relationship between industrial production and the environment in 1980. According to Schnaiberg and his students, the modern factory in the twentieth century became capital intensive, requiring even higher levels of energy to fuel exponentially increasing levels of production, and as a result "ever-greater levels of withdrawals from ecosystems were required. These ecological withdrawals led to one set of environmental problems, natural resource depletion" (Schnaiberg, Pellow, & Weinberg 2002, 23–24).

Technology and Environmental Consequences in the New Millennium

The environmental consequences of technology in the twenty-first century (deforestation and air, land, and water pollution) were carried forward from technological developments of the Industrial Revolution and especially of the twentieth century. As a result of these environmental consequences, environmental regulations at the local, national, and international levels emerged during the twentieth century. For instance, starting in the 1970s the United States put into force its National Environmental Policy Act, Clean Air Act, Clean Water Act, Resource Conservation and Recovery Act, and Toxic Substance Control Act. The United States and other industrialized countries also witnessed the rise of city and environmental planning that sought to optimize land-use development by taking into account the environmental consequences of technological processes used in industries. Regulations have benefited the integrity of the environment by mandating that industrial waste be monitored and regulated. These regulations have been effective largely because of the emergence of environmental technology innovations to control polluters such as electrostatic precipitators, waste-water retention pond technologies, opacity monitors, and groundwater-monitoring technologies. In the future the impact of technology on the environment will be determined at least in part by the environmental technologies and planning that are used to curtail harm to the global ecosystem.

Sylvia Hood Washington

See also Automobile; Industrial Revolution; Oil; Space Exploration

Further Reading

Broswimmer, F. J. (2002). *Ecocide: A short history of the mass extinction of species.* London: Pluto Press.

Diamond, J. (1997). *Guns, germs and steel: The fates of human societies.* New York: W. W. Norton.

Drachman, A. G. (1967). The classical civilizations. In M. Krantzberg & C. Pursell Jr. (Eds.), *Technology and Western civilization: Vol. 1.* (pp. 47–65). New York: Oxford University Press.

Forbes, R. J. (1967). The beginnings of technology and man. In M. Krantzberg & C. Pursell Jr. (Eds.), *Technology and Western civilization: Vol. 1.* (pp. 11–25). New York: Oxford University Press.

Forbes, R. J. (1967). Mesopotamia and Egyptian technology. In M. Krantzberg & C. Pursell Jr. (Eds.), *Technology and Western civilization: Vol. 1.* (pp. 26–46). New York: Oxford University Press.

Goudie, A. (2000). *The human impact on the natural environment* (5th ed.). Cambridge, MA: MIT Press.

Hughes, J. D. (2001). *An environmental history of the world: Humankind's changing role in the community of life.* New York: Routledge.

Hughes, J. D. (Ed.). (2000). *The face of the Earth: Environment and world history.* Armonk, NY: M. E. Sharpe.

Krantzberg, M., & Pursell, C., Jr. (1967). The importance of technology in human affairs. In M. Krantzberg & C. Pursell Jr. (Eds.), *Technology and Western civilization: Vol. 1.* (pp. 3–10). New York: Oxford University Press.

Krantzberg, M., & Pursell, C., Jr. (Eds.). (1967). *Technology and Western civilization. Vol. 1.* New York: Oxford University Press.

McNeill, J. R. (2000). *Something new under the sun: An environmental history of the twentieth-century world.* New York: W. W. Norton.

Melosi, M. V. (2000). *Sanitary city, urban infrastructure in America from colonial times to present.* Baltimore: Johns Hopkins University Press.

Merchant, C. (1980). *The death of nature: Women, ecology and the scientific revolution.* San Francisco: Harper & Row.

Merchant, C. (1992). *Radical ecology: The search for a livable world.* New York: Routledge.

Pointing, C. (1991). *A green history of the world: The environment and the collapse of great civilizations.* New York: St. Martin's Press.

Pyne, S. J. (1995). *World fire: The culture of fire and earth.* New York: Holt.

Pyne, S. J. (2001). *Fire, a brief history.* Seattle: University of Washington Press.

Schnaiberg, A. (2002). *Globalization and energy policy: The critical role of the state and its constituencies.* Evanston, IL: Northwestern University.

Schnaiberg, A., Pellow, D. N., & Weinberg, A. S. (2002). The treadmill of production and the environmental state. In A. Mol & F. Buttel (Eds.), *The environmental state under pressure* (pp. 15–32). Kidington, UK: Elsevier Publishing.

Simmons, I. G. (1989). *Changing the face of the Earth: Culture, environment and history*. Oxford, UK: Blackwell.

Sponsel, L., Headland, T. N., & Bailey, R. C. (Eds.). (1996). *Tropical deforestation: The human dimension*. New York: Columbia University Press.

Worster, D. (1977). *Nature's economy: A history of ecological ideas*. San Francisco: Sierra Club Books.

Worster, D. (Ed.). (1988). *The ends of the Earth: Perspectives of modern environmental history*. Cambridge, UK: Cambridge University Press.

Terracing and Field Ridging

Soil erosion was the first legacy of human manipulation of steep land, but terracing was probably fast on erosion's heels. Terracing started with the first intensive agriculture in the Fertile Crescent (the area from the southeastern coast of the Mediterranean Sea around the Syrian Desert north of the Arabian Peninsula to the Persian Gulf), and it remains an effective technique today for soil conservation, water management, and maintaining a planting surface on steep slopes. Terracing in some form probably started during the Holocene epoch (the last eleven thousand years); most sources mark its earliest dates to around four thousand years ago in the Middle East. It may well have started much earlier, but its earliest traces may be long lost in the archaeological record by generations of reconstructing the terraces with new and old materials, slope wash (erosion by surface runoff), and organic decomposition of vegetative terrace dams.

Terracing is significant in at least three aspects of environmental history: geomorphology (the study of the form or surface features of the Earth), conservation and development, and indigenous agriculture. First, geomorphic terraces are once active floodplains, formed by running water but left as old benches along valley sides because their parent stream has cut down farther into its valley. Geomorphic terraces can tell people much about the chronology and processes of valley formation, and some are linked to human-induced environmental change. Indeed, some geomorphic features can look like agricultural terraces and diversions; perhaps these geological features were the model for the initial agricultural terraces. At least two natural forms can be difficult to differentiate from cultural features: tree-fall or root-throw mounds, formed when a tree is uprooted, and later deposition behind them and layer–cake-like horizontally stratified sedimentary rocks. Second, resource managers have built terraces all over the world for soil conservation and development, but their effectiveness has varied from actually causing more erosion to creating sustainable planting surfaces. Third, terraces have a long and rich history in prehistorical and indigenous societies around the world.

Terrace Studies

Because terraces cover such a large area, the future of many steeply terraced lands could be in jeopardy. The terraces of Portugal, the Mediterranean, and the Philippines come to mind. Some of these terraced lands are in danger of eroding away with misuse or disuse. In many landscapes terraces require high initial labor and long-term maintenance. Yet, in many places terraces remain intact after millennia. Many researchers have studied terraces for these practical reasons of sustaining agriculture, developing, and protecting against erosion, but others have been interested more in how people adapted terraces, how they affected erosion history, how the technology diffused, and what terraces can tell people about past cultures, that is, do they imply some kind of centralized control?

Types and Functions of Terraces

Why did and why do farmers build terraces? In modern terms terraces are one of the main types of soil and water conservation features. All soil conservation features attempt to decrease slope gradient and length and decrease the impact of raindrops and flowing water. For example, contour plowing slows water down and decreases its kinetic energy; cover crops and mulches protect soil from raindrops and divert flow, and vegetative berms and waterways slow overland flow, often in critical areas.

Farmers often use terraces on the steepest slopes, where land is scarce and labor is cheap, because building them is a laborious task. For example, the U.S. Natural Resources Conservation Service has a land-capability classification system that grades land into eight classes, from "one," prime agricultural land, to "eight," where steepness makes the landscape soils limited to nonagricultural uses. However, terracing all over the world makes class-eight soils into vineyards or plots for other high-value crops.

The Middle Mountains of Nepal where the entire natural landscape has been modified by generations of peasant toil so that everything down to the last tree or shrub is "anthropogenic." COURTESY JACK D. IVES.

Terraces have at least six propable functions: to create planting surfaces, to improve soil conditions, to improve soil moisture conditions by facilitating infiltration and minimizing evaporation, to control erosion by slowing water flow, to divert water from downstream fields or springs, and to control water flow along terrace plots. Some terraces also have gravel beds that may act to drain intense flows. Field terraces may also link to habitation terraces, which in turn could have been used for kitchen or house gardens.

There are at least six types of terraces: check dams, dry slope or contour, step terraces, footslope, box terraces, diversions, field walls for maintaining planting platforms, and rock or vegetation berms. Indigenous farmers built most of these terraces by removing the soil from rock strata (or at natural outcrops) and by constructing rubble rock walls (often with extremely large boulders) on top of the bedrock. For some terraces, such as contour ones, however, farmers incrementally adapted them to moderate slopes. These may have been formed into planting platforms by constructing walls and then allowing upslope soil erosion to fill in behind them. Several studies of ancient and contemporary terracing describe this type of adaptation, frequently evolving with little planning.

Check dams (also known as "weir terraces" and "cross-channel terraces") are worldwide and range greatly in their environmental context, size, and construction. These terraces occupy smaller valleys and run across channels. In most places, dry slope or contour terraces are the most common type of terrace. These are often small features that are hard to detect in landscapes. They occur on less-steep slopes and are comparable to contour ridges. Step terraces are the stereotypical forms. These create stair-stepped valley slopes and can be curved, linear, boxed, or irregular in form. They consist of walls of stones, with any of a variety of support architecture that dam usually level soil platforms. Footslope terraces or valley floor terraces are often long and lie at the base of steep (20° to 30°) slopes. These tend to be built of large retaining walls that act to collect erosion and mass wasting at the slope's base. The walls are commonly two parallel walls built of boulders and cobble with a fill of smaller stones and earth. Ancient farmers may also have built footslope terraces to build up and reclaim soil beds away from adjacent wetlands. Lastly, box terraces are subtle, rectangular features usually located near residences, and they may have functioned as beds for seedlings that would be replanted.

Terraced landscapes have diverse functions but they may leave little trace of their existence. One of the most important functions is to divert water through diversion channels used to direct runoff onto or away from downhill fields or supplies of freshwater. Likewise field walls, which mark property or plot divisions, may be associated with any of the types of terraces and may be eccentrically shaped and their function indiscernible. These terrace dams could also be built from earth or living or dead vegetation and erode or decompose, thus leaving little or no trace after abandonment.

Field Ridging

Another category of agricultural land manipulation is field ridging, which means building up linear ridges with plows or by hand. There are at least four functions for such ridges: contour ridging perpendicular to slopes to inhibit flowing water erosion, contour ridges perpendicular to the general direction of wind to inhibit wind erosion, building up fields above water tables to grow crops, and building up fields to allow the coldest air to drain away from plants. Contour ridging is one of the most common types of soil conservation around the world on moderate slopes. Ridging is different from contour terracing only in that it builds up soil into ridges.

Raised or drained fields are subjects of considerable research in archaeology, conservation, and development studies. The main purpose of these fields is to reclaim wetlands for cultivation, which implies building some areas up and allowing drainage canals in between. This combination of canals and fields also creates a potential for soil water maintenance, fertilizer maintenance from canal dredge, stabilized soil microclimates, and increased solar radiation along canal edges. The best known of these fields are the historical *chinampa*s of the basin of Mexico; others occur in the Maya lowlands, but as impressive as *chinampa*s were the ancient fields of South America from Venezuela to Argentina. Several studies report similar raised field systems in New Guinea, China, and Africa.

Ridged fields, built for planting beds that drain cold air away, have a significant literature and wide geography. Indeed, cold air drainage is only one of several possible reasons for building such fields. Ridged fields also are built because they increase fertility and soil depth of mounded organic rich materials, allow easier cultivation, inhibit pests, and, of course, alter soil moisture conditions. Archaeological evidence suggests numerous ridged field systems in aboriginal North America in such places as Florida, Wisconsin, and Michigan and in indigenous circumstances in the highlands of New Guinea.

Terracing in Mesoamerica

In Mesoamerica and other parts of the world the highland mountainous slopes often have heavy rains and high rates of erosion, thus making terracing a necessity for cultivation. The Maya lowlands provide one particularly interesting region of terracing because of the large area of terracing preserved for at least twelve hundred years. The remains of ancient Maya terraces are preserved soils, stone walls, and artifacts that date to the Classic period (250 to 830 CE). Remnants of ridged field agriculture occur in many perennial wetlands around the Maya lowlands. This region has three main areas of widespread and complex terracing: northern to central Belize from about the Three Rivers region south through the Vaca Plateau, the Rio Bec of Mexico, and the Petexbatún of Guatemala. The Vaca Plateau was the first recognized region of ancient Maya terracing, and it has at least 400 square kilometers of terraces, including the extensive terracing around the important site of Caracol and many other sites southward to the Maya Mountains. In some drainages the ancient Maya built several types of terraces, dams, and diversion weirs, indicating complex whole watershed engineering and some level of corporate control. Because terraces are still well preserved in this region, many have speculated on reusing them and redeveloping conservation agriculture based on this indigenous legacy from antiquity.

Terracing in the Andes

The great terraces that surround Machu Picchu in Peru help make this site one of South America's greatest attractions and a United Nations Educational, Scientific, and Cultural Organization (UNESCO) World Heritage Site. Much of the Andes Mountain region required terracing because of the extremely steep slopes. Hence, terracing allowed for higher population densities throughout prehistory because it maintained soils and soil moisture for high production of potatoes, other tubers, quinoa, and corn. Similarly, wetland agriculture in a variety of types of ridged fields was especially developed in the Andean region in prehistory. The apparent success of terracing and wetland agriculture across the Andean region has led to attempts to rebuild and maintain these ancient techniques.

Terracing in East Asia and Oceania

The terraces in East Asia and Oceania (islands of the Pacific Ocean) are among the world's most picturesque. An example is the rice terraces (such as Banaue) of the Philippine mountains, which farmers started to build about two thousand years ago. These terraces, which stretch over 800 meters of slopes, attract tourists, and UNESCO lists them as a World Heritage Site. These intensive plots have supported one thousand people per hectare through multiple crops and high

labor requirements. The last chapter in this testament to intensive agriculture tells of their destruction by abandonment, earthquakes, and erosion.

The vast rice terraces of Bali provide another example of a populous and beautifully terraced mountain landscape. Written records indicate organized irrigation of terraces by 300 BCE. Hindu priests in the water temples (religious temples that also serve to manage water) interspersed through the terraces have managed elaborate irrigation flow with their own traditional *subak* (water board) system over these terraces, and several studies show that their indigenous management proved more efficient than recent government attempts at terrace-water management.

Terracing developed much later in Hawaii for taro (a tropical plant grown for its edible rootstock) because the first Polynesians arrived about 400 CE. Terracing there took a number of forms from bench terraces to pond or flooded terraces, which were irrigated by canals through complex water rights. Several projects have maintained and rebuilt ancient terraces, and the National Register of Historic Sites lists Waikane Valley, an important area of taro terraces.

Terracing in the Middle East

The Middle East covers an enormous area, and terracing covers steep slopes throughout this region. The Arabian Peninsula appears to have been the first home of terracing in the third millennium BCE, but dating terracing is notoriously difficult. Many scholars date terraces from the architecture of related structures, which, as these scholars know, can be unreliable but is the only available information. The Negev of Israel is one zone of ancient terracing that also depended upon manipulating a whole watershed to harvest enough water for agriculture. There a variety of systems collected runoff and diverted onto terraced fields to produce crops in a region generally too arid for rainfed agriculture. Some researchers have been able to transfer this system of ancient indigenous water harvesting and terracing to other arid regions such as Paktia Province in Afghanistan. Moreover, the Israelis have even reconstructed an ancient terraced landscape for research and tourism at Sataf in the Judean Hills.

Level, dryland terracing occurs all across this region from Yemen to the Maghreb, but erstwhile farmers are abandoning terraces to migrate for other jobs. For example, near the oldest terracing on Earth in the Haraz Mountains of Yemen nearly 1 million have abandoned their terraced landscapes to migrate to oil-rich regions.

Terracing in Europe and the Mediterranean

Terracing also occurs over the steepest agricultural land of Europe, especially for vineyards, from France and Spain through the Mediterranean to the Caucasus. UNESCO has named two such areas in Europe as World Heritage Sites: Portugal's Alto Douro wine region and Germany's upper-middle Rhine River valley. Herein ancient rock terraces hold vineyards onto steep hillslopes. Little archaeological evidence exists for dating these terraces, but they must have been common in antiquity from the Levant to Spain. Terracing may predate the Mycenaean period (1600–1100 BCE), but little firm evidence exists for terraces before the middle Bronze Age (c. 1500 BCE). Dendrochronology (the science of dating events and variations in environment in former periods by comparative study of growth rings in trees and dead wood) can date some terraces because trees have grown over segments of the terrace. One case probably dates to the Hellenistic period, although most such cases are much later. Researchers have been interested in the role of terraces in the erosion record, their cultural significance (e.g., if they were associated with impoverished areas), and the environmental significance of the large area of abandonment.

Terracing in Africa

Development programs constructed hundreds of thousands of hectares of terraces all over Africa in the twentieth century, but, unfortunately, terracing has actually increased erosion in several countries. In too many cases, local people have had no say in these terraces, and thus they have rarely maintained them. In other cases, terraces were made incorrectly or against the wishes of local people who had developed their own appropriate agricultural techniques. Sedimentation, gullying, and terrace bursting occurred in a number of cases. After independence Kenyans, for example, even ripped out terraces that had been forced upon them by colonial administrators.

Terracing in the United States

Indigenous terracing occurred in many areas of the southwestern United States and adjacent Mexico, where terracing and irrigation were the most complex in aboriginal North America. Modern terracing started in the nineteenth century, but large-scale terracing occurred only after the 1930s with the advent of the Soil Erosion Service (later Soil Conservation and Natural Resources Conservation Service) under the leadership of Hugh Hammond Bennett. Bennett did more for soil conservation than any other American, and terracing spread to many steep lands in the United States.

In the contemporary United States farmers still use terracing, especially for high-value and highly erodible crops, such as wine grapes. Grapes are so erodible because they are row crops that have little natural cover for the soils that lie between rows. Hence, vineyards are famous for terracing and erosion in the United States, as they have been in Europe's wine regions such as Tuscany.

Terracing is a valuable, simple, and ancient form of soil and water conservation. In some places it developed into a complex manipulation of entire watersheds for irrigation and cultivation. In its simplest form, it implies building walls perpendicular to slopes to decrease soil erosion and create and maintain planting platforms. However, terracing grew in complexity to include a variety of forms in different kinds of landscapes to conserve soil moisture and manipulate water flow, as well as conserve soil. Also related to this are the several forms of field ridging to conserve soil and provide appropriate moisture and temperature conditions for crops.

The diverse terracing and ridging that started in antiquity have led many to propose and a few to start rebuilding ancient terracing and experiment with integrated landscape complexes of ancient agriculture. In some places such as Israel and South America this has been successful, but in many parts of Africa this has been an abject failure. To maintain terraced landscapes in some regions requires much labor, connection to the land, and expert knowledge. However, several problems have led to the failure of terracing. In some ancient terraced lands such as the Philippines and Yemen, the migration of rural farming populations to cities has drained indigenous knowledge and labor, which has led to significant degradation of terraces and elevated soil erosion and sedimentation. In some cases in Africa, especially, colonialism led to terracing that local people rejected after independence, and poorly made terraces actually increased erosion. An important and increasingly more obvious lesson from this development history is that not involving local people in development often leads to long-term problems. Such a conclusion from the twentieth century has important implications for how people should read the terraced landscapes of the past.

Timothy Beach

Further Reading

Beach, T., & Dunning, N. P. (1995). Ancient Maya terracing and modern conservation in the Petén rain forest of Guatemala. *Journal of Soil and Water Conservation, 50*(2), 138–145.

Beach, T., Luzzadder-Beach, S., Dunning, N., Hageman, J., & Lohse, J. (2002). Upland agriculture in the Maya lowlands: Ancient conservation in northwestern Belize. *The Geographical Review, 92*(3), 372–397.

Denevan, W. (1998). Cultivated landscapes of native Amazonia and Andes. Oxford, UK: Oxford University Press.

Donkin, R. (1979). *Agricultural terracing in the aboriginal new world* (Viking Fund Publications in Anthropology No. 56). Tucson: University of Arizona Press.

Doolittle, W. (2000). *Cultivated landscapes of Native North America.* Oxford, UK: Oxford University Press.

Dunning, N. P., & Beach, T. (2000). Stability and instability in pre-Hispanic Maya landscapes. In D. Lentz (Ed.), *Imperfect balance: Landscape transformations in the pre-Columbian Americas.* New York: Columbia University Press.

Hudson, N. W. (1987). *Soil and water conservation in semi-arid areas.* Rome: United Nations Food and Agricultural Organization.

Hurni, H. (1988). Options for conservation of steep lands in subsistence agricultural systems. In W. C. Moldenhauer & N. W. Hudson (Eds.), *Conservation farming on steep lands* (pp. 32–44). Ankeny, IA: Soil and Water Conservation Society of America.

Lansing, J. S. (1991). *Priests and programmers: Technologies of power in the engineered landscape of Bali.* Princeton, NJ: Princeton University Press.

Lentz, D. (Ed.). (2000). *Imperfect balance: Landscape transformations in the pre-Columbian Americas.* New York: Columbia University Press.

Lewis, L. A. (1992). Terracing and accelerated soil loss on Rwandan steeplands: A preliminary investigation of the implications of human activities affecting soil movement. *Land Degradation & Rehabilitation, 3,* 241–246.

National Academy of Sciences. (1995). *Regenerating agriculture: Policies and practice for sustainability and self-reliance.* Washington, DC: National Academy Press.

Spencer, J., & Hale, G. (1961). The origin, nature, and distribution of agricultural terracing. *Pacific Viewpoint, 2*(1), 1–40.

Turner, B., II.(1974). Prehistoric intensive agriculture in the Mayan Lowlands. *Science 185* (4146), 118–124.

Theophrastus

(372–288 BCE)
Greek writer and botanist

Theophrastus of Eresus is of all ancient writers the one who made the most advances in the field of ecology. He was born in Eresus on the island of Lesbos. He became a colleague of Aristotle, and succeeded him as head of the Lyceum, Aristotle's school in Athens. In the Lyceum's garden, Theophrastus tended specimens sent from India by Alexander the Great. He traveled through Greece collecting plants and making observations of natural phenomena.

Among his works are *Enquiry into Plants* (often titled in Latin, *De historia plantarum*) and *Causes of Plants* (*De causis plantarum*). These works constitute the first careful treatment of botany (Aristotle had written on zoology). His philosophical work is *Metaphysics*, which criticizes Aristotle's doctrine that all things have as a final cause the service of human beings. Theophrastus maintained that the nature of each living thing aims at its own goal, and the goal of a plant is not to feed us or give us wood, but to produce seed for the perpetuation of its species. Aristotle would not have denied this, but made it a subsidiary cause in his hierarchy of nature. For Theophrastus it is the main point.

Theophrastus anticipated later ecological discoveries. He always discussed a plant in the context of the environment: sunshine, soil, climate, water, cultivation, and other plants and animals. He observed that the nature of a plant (what modern biologists might call its genotype) may or may not find its immediate environment favorable. A plant prefers an environment where it may fulfill its own purpose. He calls that environment the "appropriate locale" (*oikeios topos*), which modern ecologists might call its niche. Among the factors determining the nature of a place he included soil, moisture, temperature, exposure, winds, and elevation. Especially in mountains, he noted, these vary over short distances, producing what modern ecologists call microhabitats. Theophrastus also observed that plants growing near each other affect each other, and catalogued effects of animals on plants.

Theophrastus investigated the influences of human intervention on plants, which succeed if planted in a locale that "their nature requires," but fail when planted "against their nature." Therefore environment is more important than human cultivation. But he also saw cases where human activity such as clearing forests changed the climate of a region. He had much to say about forestry.

Theophrastus also wrote on physics, geology (including rocks and fossils), meteorology, and human physiology. In his most famous writing, *Characters*, he sketched human personality types, giving as much care to their description as he did to plants in his botanical works.

Theophrastus was an admirable writer and scientist. Where he differed from his teacher, Aristotle, it was because he was more dependent upon observation and less ready to make universal statements of principle unsupported by perceptible facts. He was a forerunner of ecology, viewing species not as isolated phenomena but as interacting with their physical environment and other species.

J. Donald Hughes

Further Reading

Einarson, B., & Link, G. K. K. (Trans.). (1976, 1990). *Theophrastus: De Causis plantarum.* 3 vols. London: William Heinemann & Cambridge, MA: Harvard University Press. Loeb Classical Library.

Hughes, J. D. (1987). Theophrastus as ecologist. In W. W. Fortenbaugh & R. W. Sharples (Eds.), *Theophrastus as natural scientist, and other papers* (pp. 67–75). New Brunswick, NJ: Transaction Books. Rutgers Studies in Classical Humanities, vol. 3.

Rubner, H. (1985). Greek Thought and Forest Science. *Environmental Review, 9*(4), 277–295.

Third World *See* Africa; Africa, Central; Africa, East; Asia, South; Asia, Southeast—Insular; Asia, Southeast—Mainland; Indigenous Peoples

Thoreau, Henry David
(1817–1862)
American writer, naturalist, and philosopher

Henry David Thoreau, prophet and patron saint of the American environmental movement, was born in Concord, Massachusetts, and except for brief periods lived there his whole life. He was one of four children born to John Thoreau, a pencil-maker, and Cynthia Dunbar Thoreau, a lively woman active in the Concord Anti-Slavery Society. He attended Harvard College (1833–1837), receiving a bachelor's degree. Afterwards he taught grammar school, worked as a land surveyor, and helped run his father's pencil and plumbago manufactory. All these jobs were secondary to his main career as a writer and to his exploration of the woods, fields, lakes, and streams of his beloved Concord countryside. He never married, living with his family for most of his adult life.

Thoreau's main intellectual influence came from his close friendship with Ralph Waldo Emerson (1803–1882), America's most important nineteenth-century thinker and Thoreau's neighbor in Concord. In his great work "Nature," Emerson had written: "Nature is the opposite of the soul, answering to it part for part . . . the ancient precept, 'Know thyself,' and the modern precept, 'Study nature,' become at last one maxim." Thoreau dedicated himself to living this idea, exploring nature in every way possible: fishing and picking huckleberries, writing poetry and nature essays, counting trees rings and studying forest succession. In the process, he found his own voice and his place in the universe. Few writers are so thoroughly identified with their local landscape.

Thoreau is best known for two pieces of writing that had their genesis in 1845, when he was twenty-eight years old. In that year, he was arrested and sent to jail for refusing to pay his poll tax, his protest against state support for slavery and the Mexican-American War. In the essay "Resistance to Civil Government," Thoreau makes the case that slavery and imperialism are such terrible injustices that citizens have a moral duty to oppose them. He goes on to argue the superiority of the moral law to mere statutory law and the supremacy of individual conscience over personal comfort and social conformity. Thoreau's positions have been hotly contested; it should be noted that he explicitly states that civil disobedience should not be undertaken for trivial reasons, but rather as a response to gross, systemic injustices. "Resistance" has exerted great influence over the years: both Mahatma Gandhi and Martin Luther King Jr., cite Thoreau as an important inspiration for their political philosophies of nonviolent resistance to injustice.

Also in 1845, Thoreau began a two-year sojourn at Walden Pond, a mile and a half from the center of Concord village. There this "self-appointed inspector

The Voice of Thoreau

Our village life would stagnate if it were not for the unexplored forests and meadows which surround it. We need the tonic of wildness,—to wade sometimes in marshes where the bittern and the meadow-hen lurk, and hear the booming of the snipe. . . . At the same time that we are earnest to explore and learn all things, we require that all things be mysterious and unexplorable, that land and sea be infinitely wild, unsurveyed and unfathomed by us because unfathomable. We can never have enough of Nature. (*Walden* 1854)

What are the natural features which make a town-ship handsome—and worth going far to dwell in? A river with its water-falls—meadows, lakes—hills, cliffs or individual rocks, a forest and single ancient trees—such things are beautiful. They have a high use which dollars and cents never represent. If the inhabitants of a town were wise they would seek to preserve these things though at a considerable expense. ("Huckleberries," c. 1862)

The kings of England formerly had their forests "to hold the king's game," for sport or food, sometimes destroying villages to create or extend them; and I think that they were impelled by a true instinct. Why should not we, who have renounced the king's authority, have our national preserves, where no villages need be destroyed, in which the bear and panther, and some even of the hunter race may still exist, and not be "civilized off the face of the earth," our forests, not to hold the king's game merely, but to hold and preserve the king himself also, the lord of creation,—not for idle sport or food, but for inspiration and our own true recreation? (*The Maine Woods* 1864)

---

of snow storms and rain storms" built a sturdy one-room shack, cleared a few acres of forest to grow potatoes and beans, walked, fished, watched the seasons come and go, and began to write an account of his stay at the pond. Over nine years and eight revisions, this work became *Walden*, one of the most important and enduring books written in America during the nineteenth century.

Walden describes a life devoted to personal development and enriched experience, centered on the pursuit of knowledge of self and nature. It advocates ethical, intellectual, and creative striving. In a key passage, Thoreau writes: "I went to the woods because I wished to live deliberately, to front only the essential facts of life, and see if I could not learn what it had to teach, and not, when I came to die, discover that I had not lived . . . I wanted to live deep and suck out all the marrow of life . . . to know it by experience, and be able to give a true account of it in my next excursion."

Much more than a literal account of Thoreau's two years in the woods, *Walden* is among other things a transcendentalist self-help manual, encouraging its readers to live simpler, saner, more focused lives (Neufeldt 1989). Part of the book's success lies in its seamless blending of seemingly disparate aims and elements. It combines personal honesty and outrageous tall tales; ethical idealism and direct, affectionate engagement

with the material world; accurate natural history and poetic descriptions of nature; no-nonsense techniques for dealing with life's minutiae and soaring, transcendental flights into the ether.

While *Walden*'s literary brilliance has ensured it a place in the American canon, it has also become a sort of Bible to many environmentalists. Thoreau's keen observations and affection for nature have appealed to many, as has his ability to blend scientific and poetic experience, and knowledge and enjoyment of nature. Also important has been his demonstration that a life "simple in (material) means" can be "rich in (cultural and spiritual) ends." Thoreau makes a strong case that lives dedicated to exploring and enjoying nature are better than lives devoted to piling up material wealth or to gross material consumption.

Simple living and low consumption make up one half of Thoreau's environmental philosophy. The other half centers on his appreciation and advocacy for wild nature. Thoreau's writings are filled with detailed descriptions of the local flora and fauna. He explored his native country with the intelligent curiosity of a scientist and the creativity and large heart of a poet. "We can never have enough of Nature," he wrote in *Walden*.

This love for wild nature and appreciation for what it contributes to human life led Thoreau to propose many practical conservation measures. He argued that every village should preserve wild forests, river walks, and other places of natural beauty, for public enjoyment and education. His realization that many wild species retreat as human settlement advances led to one of the first proposals for a system of "national preserves," that would protect the full complement of native species and keep some lands unmanaged and unmodified by human beings.

In the few years left to him following the publication of *Walden*, Thoreau's life and writings took a decidedly scientific turn. He spent thousands of hours botanizing in the fields and forests around Concord, paying particular attention to the details of phenology, seed dispersal, and forest succession. In 1859, when John Brown was captured after the abortive attack on Harpers Ferry, Thoreau, almost alone among prominent abolitionists, rushed to his defense, in speeches that helped sway public opinion.

In 1862 Henry Thoreau died of tuberculosis, aggravated by a cold he caught counting tree rings during a winter storm. A short time before his death, a clergyman dropped by for a visit. To the question of whether, so near death, he had any intimations of the life to come, Thoreau responded: "One world at a time."

Philip Cafaro

Further Reading

Harding, W. R. (1992). *The days of Henry Thoreau: A biography*. Princeton, NJ: Princeton University Press.

Neufeldt, L. N. (1989). *The economist: Henry Thoreau and enterprise*. New York: Oxford University Press.

Richardson, R. D., Jr. (1986). *Henry Thoreau: A life of the mind*. Berkeley: University of California Press.

Thoreau, H. D. (1993). *Faith in a seed: The dispersion of seeds and other late natural history writings*. Washington, DC: Island Press.

Thoreau, H. D. (1981–). *Journal* (multiple volumes). Princeton, NJ: Princeton University Press.

Thoreau, H. D. (1980). *The natural history essays*. Salt Lake City, UT: Gibbs-Smith Books.

Thoreau, H. D. (1973). *Reform papers*. Princeton, NJ: Princeton University Press.

Thoreau, H. D. (1971). *Walden*. Princeton, NJ: Princeton University Press.

Thoreau, H. D. (1983). *A week on the Concord and Merrimack Rivers*. Princeton, NJ: Princeton University Press.

Walls, L. D. (1995). *Seeing new worlds: Henry David Thoreau and nineteenth-century natural science*. Madison: University of Wisconsin Press.

Tiger

The tiger *(Panthera tigris)* is found in a variety of habitats around Asia, from the tropical evergreen and deciduous (leaf-dropping) forests of southern Asia to the coniferous forests of Siberia. Although tigers once inhabited these areas in great numbers, their numbers are threatened by loss of habitat, poaching, and population fragmentation.

Evolution and Life History

Tigers evolved from miacids, which were long-limbed, carnivorous, civet-like mammals that lived more than 60 million years ago during the age of dinosaurs. Over millions of years the miacids developed into many species, including cats, bears, dogs, and weasels. Approximately thirty-seven of these early cat species exist today, including the largest of them all, the tiger. Fossil records show that tigers evolved in southeastern Asia during the late Pliocene/early Pleistocene epochs. Between 1.3 and 2.1 million years ago tigers lived in Java. They moved through the central Asian woodlands to the west and southwest, giving rise to the Caspian tigers. Tigers from China also moved to southeastern Asia, the Indonesian islands, and then westward to India.

Modern-day tigers have distinctive gold coloring with black stripes, although their coloring can range from yellow and brown to even white and black. They have life spans of ten to fifteen years. They are carnivorous and stalk their prey, consuming sometimes more than 18 kilograms of meat in one sitting. Adults—with the exception of mothers with cubs, who stay with their mothers for two years—generally live alone and do not share their territory, which extends from 20 to 388 square kilometers, depending on the habit and availability of prey.

The estimated five thousand to seven thousand wild tigers that exist today are divided into five subspecies. Amur (or Siberian) tigers *(Panthera tigris altaica)*, whose numbers hover between 360 and 410, live in the wild in northeastern China and southeastern Russia. Approximately five hundred live in captivity in zoos in scientifically managed tiger conservation programs. Amur tigers live in coniferous, scrub oak, and birch woodlands and are the largest of all tigers. The males can grow to almost 3.3 meters in length and weigh up to 294 kilograms. The female is smaller, measuring only 2.6 meters from head to tail and weighing between 90 and 158 kilograms. The Amur tiger's characteristic orange stripes are paler than those of other tigers, and it has a white fur ruff around its neck. The Amur tiger moves seasonally and preys on elk and wild boar.

Unlike the Amur tiger, with its relatively stable population, the South China tiger *(Panthera tigris amoyensis)* is the most critically endangered of all tiger subspecies. Only twenty to thirty exist in the wild, and fifty live in captivity in Chinese zoos. The South China tiger is smaller than its relatives, measuring approximately 2.4 meters from head to tail and averaging 149 kilograms in weight. Females are slightly smaller. Because of its small population, less is known about the South China tiger.

Indochinese tigers *(Panthera tigris corbetti)* number 1,200 to 1,750 in the wild and 60 in zoos across Asia and the United States. The wild tigers live primarily in Cambodia, China, Laos, Myanmar, Thailand, Vietnam, and peninsular Malaysia. They range along the forested borders of southeast Asian countries, where human access is often restricted. They eat wild pig, deer, and cattle.

The Bengal tiger *(Panthera tigris tigris)* ranges across India, Bangladesh, Bhutan, Myanmar, and Nepal. Its population numbers 3,100 to 4,700 in the wild and 330 in captivity, mostly in Indian zoos. White tigers are a color variant of Bengal tigers, but they are rarely found in the wild. The Bengal tiger lives in a variety of habitats—from the cold, coniferous Himalayan mountains to the warm and humid mangroves of the Sunderbans and the dry hills of the Indian peninsula. It preys primarily on wild deer and cattle.

The Sumatran tiger *(Panthera tigris sumatrae)* lives only on the Indonesian island of Sumatra, in lowland and mountain forest. Its population is approximately four hundred in the wild and two hundred in captivity in Sumatra's parks. The Sumatran tiger has the darkest coat and is the smallest of all tiger subspecies. The tiger is listed as one of Sumatra's endangered species, and illegal hunting and logging continue to threaten its population. More than 80 percent of its natural habitat has disappeared.

Extinction

In the early 1900s more than 100,000 tigers roamed Asia. Yet, only a century later the tiger population is estimated at fewer than 8,000 worldwide. Many factors, including poaching, loss of habitat, and population fragmentation, threaten the existence of tigers.

Poaching, or the illegal trafficking of tigers, is one of the gravest threats. In some cultures tiger parts are valuable. Traditional Chinese medicine uses the bones, whiskers, and tail as medicine for maladies from toothaches and paralysis and also as an aphrodisiac. Estimates claim that one tiger a day is killed in India for medicinal and religious purposes. Most of the trade occurs with China, Japan, Korea, and Taiwan.

Over the past century three tiger subspecies have become extinct: the Caspian, Javan, and Bali. The Caspian tiger *(Panthera tigris virgata)* ranged across Afghanistan, Iran, Turkey, Mongolia, and central Asia before it became extinct in the 1950s. The Javan tiger *(Panthera tigris sondaica)*, last seen in the late 1970s, lived in Java. The Bali tiger *(Panthera tigris balica)*, was last seen in Bali in the late 1930s.

Approaches to Conservation

Since the 1970s governments and nongovernmental organizations have sought to preserve tigers and their diverse habitats. The Chinese government has worked to protect its native tiger. It passed the Wild Animal Protection Law in 1988 and has worked extensively with the IUCN (the World Conservation Union) to evaluate its wildlife management programs. Thailand developed a master plan for the support of tigers in captivity in 1995 and is expanding its captive management program. In India zoos have bred the Bengal tiger since 1880 and have achieved great success in their breeding programs.

The IUCN brings together nine hundred governments, government agencies (such as the U.S. Environmental Protection Agency), and nongovernmental organizations to develop wildlife conservation management plans for the tiger. CITES (the Convention on International Trade in Endangered Species of Wild Fauna and Flora) has, since the early 1970s, regulated and monitored illegal wildlife trade. The United States in particular has developed legislation to protect tigers, including the Rhinoceros and Tiger Conservation Act of 1994. Despite such programs, habitat for tigers is still shrinking, and their future is uncertain.

Jessica B. Teisch

Further Reading

Colinvaux, P. (1990). *Why big fierce animals are rare.* New York: Penguin Books.

Miller, S. D., & Everett, D. D. (Eds.). (1986). *Cats of the world: Biology, conservation, and management.* Washington, DC: National Wildlife Federation.

Rathore, F. S., Singh, T., & Thaper, V. (1983). *With tigers in the wild*. New Delhi, India: Vikas Publishing House.

Sankhala, K. (1993). *Return of the tiger*. New Delhi, India: Lustre Press.

Seidensticker, J., Jackson, P., & Christie, S. (Eds.). (1999). *Riding the tiger: Meeting the needs of wildlife and people in Asia*. Cambridge, UK: Cambridge University Press.

Tilson, R. L., & Seal, U. S. (Eds.). (1987). *Tigers of the world: The biology, biopolitics, management and conservation of an endangered species*. Park Ridge, NJ: Noyes Publications.

Tilapia

Tilapia is one of the most important fish raised in aquaculture, providing a cheap and rapidly breeding source of protein. Tilapia includes several genera of the family Cichlidae that are native to Africa. Large-scale aquaculture of tilapia, rapidly developing since the middle of the twentieth century, is limited almost exclusively to three species: *Oreochromis niloticus*, *O. mossambica*, and *O. aureus*. Tilapia was farmed more than three thousand years ago in Egypt and is also known as "St. Peter's fish" because it is thought to have been the fish that was caught and fed to the multitudes in the New Testament story.

Tilapia is able to grow and reproduce in water of poor quality and can eat a diversity of food: phytoplankton, macroalgae, fish, and even biodegraded (composted) organic material. Unusual for fish, tilapia is able to digest the cell walls of bacteria. Tilapia is also known for incubating and hatching its eggs in its mouth. Due to its ability to grow quickly in poor conditions, achieving growth rates of 2 percent of body weight per day, tilapia deserves the nickname "the aquatic chicken." It can gain 1 kilogram for every 1.5 kilogram of food when fed a high-protein feed. Tilapia is marketed at 600–700 grams at six months of age and produces a mild, soft, white fillet of great nutritious value. The meat has a slightly sweet taste.

Ponds are by far the most common method of tilapia aquaculture. But a major problem of this method is excessive reproduction, which results in overcrowding. To solve this problem, a monosex male culture was invented in which the fry are treated with male hormones. This culture also increases the harvest because males grow almost twice as fast as females. One of the risks of tilapia cultivation is that the fish is car-

nivorous, eating the eggs and young of its own species and other species. This has led, for example, to depletion of the Guapeta, a fish indigenous to Costa Rica.

Tilapia is farmed in more than eighty-five countries, with an annual harvest of 720,000 metric tons, which is second only to the carp harvest among farmed freshwater fishes. The main tilapia-producing areas are China, India, southeastern Asia, Latin America, Israel, and African countries around Lake Victoria. In many countries tilapia is cultivated in rice fields, maximizing water use and assisting in pest control. Tilapia also has been cultivated in power station cooling ponds in Great Britain, Germany, Russia, and the United States. Much of the tilapia produced is sold in domestic markets, but it also is exported to the United States and Europe. However, consumer awareness of tilapia in these areas is still low, and there is considerable room for expansion of the market.

Julia Lajus and Dmitry Lajus

Further Reading

Beveridge, M. C. M., & McAndrew, B. J. (Eds.). (2000). *Tilapias: Biology and exploitation*. Boston: Kluwer Academic Publishers.

Costa-Pierce, B. A., & Rakocy, J. E. (Eds.). (1997, 2000). *Tilapia aquaculture in the Americas*. Baton Rouge, LA: World Aquaculture Society.

Fitzsimmons, K. (Ed.). (2000). *Tilapia in the 21st century: Proceedings of the fifth international symposium on Tilapia in aquaculture*. Rio de Janeiro, Brazil: Ministry of Agriculture.

Stickney, R. R. (Ed.). (1993). *Culture of non-salmonid freshwater fishes*. Boca Raton, Florida: CRC Press.

Stickney, R. R. (1996). *Aquaculture of the United States: A historical survey*. New York: John Wiley & Sons.

Timber *See* Agroecology and Agroforesty; Forests, Temperate; Forests, Tropical; Logging; Wood

Tobacco

The tobacco plant is a member of the family Solanaceae and the genus *Nicotiana*. It is a coarse, large-leaved perennial that grows in warm climates and rich, well-drained soils. Tobacco's defining feature for people is its nicotine, which composes 2 to 7 percent of the leaf. In concentrated form, nicotine is used as an insecticide and drug. It acts primarily on the human autonomic nervous system and, in small doses, imparts feelings of alertness and pleasure. Nicotine is physiologically addicting, which is perhaps one of the major reasons for tobacco's global spread.

Early History

Tobacco (Nicotiana tabacum) was first grown by natives in the pre-Columbian Americas. It is thought to have first been cultivated in the Peruvian Andes, where it was used for medicinal and ceremonial purposes. From there it spread throughout the continent. Evidence shows that the Aztecs smoked tobacco leaves stuffed in hollow reeds and that Central and North American natives smoked thick bundles of tobacco wrapped in palm leaves and maize husks. Because tobacco was a medium that connected the natural and supernatural worlds, shamans used large quantities of it in religious ceremonies and healing rituals. In order to alleviate certain illnesses, for example, shamans placed tobacco on patients' skin, eyes, gums, and tongue or boiled the leaves in water and fed it to patients as a liquid.

Although tobacco was introduced from Mesoamerica to North America about 200 CE, Europeans did not come into contact with it until many centuries later. Christopher Columbus became aware of tobacco when he visited the West Indies, where he had seen the Cuban natives smoking small cigars (tabacos) through their nostrils. He brought a few tobacco seeds and leaves with him back to Spain. At first, because tobacco was a rare commodity, smoking signified social status and wealth. Most Europeans did not get their first taste of tobacco until the mid-1500s, when travelers and diplomats like English Sir Walter Raleigh and the French Jean Nicot (for whom nicotine is named) popularized its use. By the early 1600s tobacco had spread throughout most of South America, Europe, the Caribbean, and the North American colonies.

Tobacco in the American South

Tobacco soon became an important commodity in Europe but an even more important commodity for the American colonies. Virginia, Maryland, and North Carolina's eighteenth- and early nineteenth-century economies depended almost entirely on tobacco, which was harvested as a cash crop and sent to European and North American colonial markets. Indeed, tobacco was the single greatest factor in the development of the southern colonies' economic, political, and social life.

The Englishman John Rolfe, who observed local Native Americans growing different strains of tobacco, cultivated the first successful commercial crop of Nicotiana tabacum in Virginia in 1612. In fact, the Native American princess Pocahontas was the first "poster girl" of tobacco, and her marriage to Rolfe assured that native peoples would not attack the Jamestown colony or destroy the new cash crop. By the 1620s tobacco had become Virginia's major crop.

Virginia's fledgling tobacco industry created great demands for land and labor. Because tobacco quickly depleted the land by removing nitrogen and potash from the soil and depositing toxic elements, farmers seldom planted more than three or four crops on the same plot of land before they abandoned it to corn or wheat. Thus colonial planters constantly cleared forest to make room for more tobacco lands and began to establish large plantations deeper in the interior.

For the next two centuries, tobacco cultivation, which was labor intensive, fueled the demand for labor, particularly imported African slave labor. To start a crop, seeds were sown in beds in late spring. Plants had to be carefully weeded and cut. In early fall, ripe plants were cut and hung on pegs in a ventilated tobacco house to cure for a month or more. The leaves were then cut from the plant, tied into bundles, and shipped to England and the other colonies. At first, planters relied on indentured servants imported from England for this labor. But after 1700 tobacco plantations employing several dozen imported African slaves or more were common, and, by the 1790s, more than 650,000 slaves worked on tobacco plantations. By the time of the Civil War, the South's agricultural economy rested on the labor of more than 4 million African slaves.

By the 1830s, however, the instability of the tobacco market, combined with soil exhaustion, had created unfavorable conditions for tobacco expansion. Many farmers in the old tobacco-growing regions of Virginia, Maryland, and North Carolina shifted to other crops, and the center of tobacco cultivation moved westward. In the mid-nineteenth century, while the North experienced dramatic economic growth, the South remained primarily agrarian. Short-staple cotton replaced tobacco as the region's dominant agricultural commodity by the late 1800s.

Cigars, Cigarettes, and Cancer

Tobacco was initially cultivated for pipe smoking, tobacco chewing, and snuff dipping. Cigars became common in the early 1800s, and cigarettes became popular in the 1860s, although they had existed in crude form since the early 1600s. The spread of "Bright" tobacco, a yellow leaf grown in Virginia and North Carolina, combined with the invention of the cigarette-making machine in the late 1880s, created new markets for cigarettes. Improvements in cultivation and processing likewise reduced the acid content in tobacco, making cigarette smoking more appealing to the masses.

The harmful health effects of tobacco were not initially known. In fact, many physicians, who looked at Native American uses of tobacco, recommended the leaf for medicinal uses. But by the early twentieth century, scientists and physicians began to address the harmful health effects of tobacco. In 1930 German researchers statistically correlated cancer and smoking. The next decade the American Cancer Society linked smoking and lung cancer. A *Reader's Digest* article published in 1952 outlined the dangers of smoking and had tremendous impact on the smoking community. Tobacco sales subsequently declined. The tobacco industry countered claims that linked nicotine and cancer but nonetheless introduced "healthier" lines of cigarettes, including filtered cigarettes with low-tar formulas. By the 1960s, however, the formation of the Surgeon General's Advisory Committee on Smoking and Health again threatened big tobacco by showing that the average smoker was ten times more likely to develop lung cancer than was the nonsmoker.

Since then, the tobacco industry has been engaged with the government and citizens' groups in battles over the proper labeling, advertising, and sales of tobacco. In 1971 all broadcast advertising was banned, and the days when one heard a famous soprano declare, "I protect my precious voice with Lucky Strikes" ended. The first major legal challenge to the tobacco industry came in 1993, when Rose Cipollone, a smoker dying from lung cancer, filed suit against Liggett Group, claiming that the company had failed to warn her about tobacco's health risks. She won a $400,000 judgment against the company, but the judgment was later overturned. In 1994 the state of Mississippi filed the first of twenty-two state lawsuits seeking to recoup millions of dollars from tobacco companies for smokers' Medicaid bills. Today, however, tobacco production has not declined. The United States produced 765 million kilograms of tobacco in 1997, about one-tenth of world production. China, India, Brazil, Turkey, and Zimbabwe are the other chief producing countries, and Russia, Japan, and Germany are the major importers.

Jessica Teisch

Further Reading

Breen, T. H. (1985). *Tobacco culture: The mentality of the great Tidewater planters on the eve of revolution.* Princeton, NJ: Princeton University Press.
Craven, A. O. (1965). *Soil exhaustion as a factor in the agricultural history of Virginia and Maryland, 1606–1860.* Gloucester, MA: Peter Smith, Publishers.
Daniel, P. (1985). *Breaking the land: The transformation of cotton, tobacco, and rice cultures since 1880.* Urbana: University of Illinois Press.
Gately, I. (2001). *Tobacco: The story of how tobacco seduced the world.* New York: Grove Press.
Glantz, S. A. (1992). *Tobacco, biology & politics.* Waco, TX: Health Edco.
Goodman, J. (1993). *Tobacco in history: The cultures of dependence.* London: Routledge.
Prince, E. E. (2000). *Long green: The rise and fall of tobacco in South Carolina.* Athens: University of Georgia Press.
Wilbert, J. (1987). *Tobacco and shamanism in South America.* New Haven, CT: Yale University Press.

Tourism

Historically, tourism has involved travel for pleasure or culture; it has been the opposite of work. The tourist has been a temporarily leisured person who voluntarily visits a place away from home for some esoteric purpose. Tourism became a significant widespread activity, with far-reaching social, economic, and environmental implications, only after the emergence of a consumer culture; the development of reliable and reasonably priced transportation; the knowledge that another region contained culturally significant or naturally scenic features; positive local inducements for visiting another region; and the expansion of classes with adequate income and leisure time to travel. To date, the world's most industrialized nations have generated the greatest percentage of tourists. Tourism has never existed universally.

Antecedents to Tourism

Many authors note tourism's association with industrial or modern society because a necessary cause was a level of productivity sufficient to sustain leisure. Nonetheless, modern tourism finds its antecedents in various preindustrial institutions. In ancient Greece, citizens with leisure time enjoyed traveling for pleasure, health, and spirituality. Ancient Romans constructed country villas. Although it is difficult to isolate leisure within hunting and gathering societies, perpetual religious migrations of the Australian aborigines perhaps constituted a form of early tourism. In medieval Europe, students joined pilgrims in overcoming difficult and dangerous obstacles to travel.

During the Renaissance, Europeans developed a new consciousness—a belief that truth could be discovered outside the body and mind. Oceanic explorations in the fifteenth and sixteenth centuries aroused intellectual curiosity. By the seventeenth century, aristocrats and other wealthy people traveled around Europe seeking old historical truths. During the next century, elite classes in England launched the Grand Tour with its cultural, educational, and political motivations. Yet, before the nineteenth century, the discomforts of travel and the widespread absence of disposable income and leisure time discouraged all but the wealthiest members of society or the hardiest adventurers from participation.

The Growth of Tourism

The Industrial Revolution provoked changes that led to a nineteenth-century boom in tourism. In addition to prompting scientific exchanges, trade, and imperial expansion, industrialization gave rise to a romanticism that ennobled the search for sublime nature. In the nineteenth century bourgeoisie travel supplanted the elites' grand tours. New modes of transportation and new political arrangements made travel safer and less expensive for an emerging and widening class of consumers. Across the globe, railroads soon changed the tourist landscape. Scenic wonders and cultural attractions became more accessible as railroads promoted tourism as a means of increasing profits. Early train travelers tended to be middle-aged and prosperous. Other visitors sought winter refuge in more temperate climates. In an effort to monopolize all aspects of travel, some railroads constructed resorts to attract the wealthiest tourists, but as the century progressed, these entities offered less-expensive cars and sleeper accommodations. With the increasing affluence of greater numbers of consumers in industrialized nations and more expansive cultural notions of what constituted worthwhile sights, the travel market expanded.

Displaced from cultural and historical centers in Europe and the Far East, elites pioneered a new tourism that later became a product of mass consumption as well. They annually left home for health and recreation, taking the "cure" at spas in places such as Bath, England, or Baden-Baden, Germany. Glamorous Mediterranean and Adriatic rivieras housed aristocracy and the idle rich until World War I minimized the importance of the ruling families who fueled the lifestyle and opened these places to more middle-class visitors.

Widespread use of automobiles for long-distance travel coincided with an interest in scenic wonders and affordable tourism that reached across class lines. In 1910, for example, an estimated 200,000 people visited U.S. national parks. With the wide-scale use of automobiles, park attendance jumped to almost 3 million in 1930. By 2000, more than 125 million visitors explored these parks annually. Automobiles changed the tourist landscape. Less-expensive motels sprang up along the concrete highways built by governments to address the new demands of their constituents. Other global travelers increasingly used the automobile for travel, although given the more thorough public transportation systems in other nations, they did so to a lesser extent.

There was phenomenal growth in tourism around the world after World War II, although again tourists from the most industrialized nations tended to dominate the ranks of travelers. In 1950 international tourists numbered 25 million; by 1990, estimates approached 430 million. Tourist destinations developed at different times and at different rates, but this economic sector emerged significantly in most parts of the world. In 1967, for example, the Soviet Union hosted 1.8 million visitors and sent 1.5 million of its own citizens abroad. In the same era, the small island of Majorca, Spain, home to fewer than 400,000, welcomed more than 2 million visitors each year. Growth in mass tourism is attributable to numerous factors, including increased paid vacation time and greater disposable income in developed countries; the arrival of commercial jets in 1958; relatively less-expensive oil; and the entry of multinational corporations in the tourism industry. In the postwar era, Europe emerged as the primary host region, followed by the Americas, East Asia and the Pacific, Africa, South Asia, and the Middle East, although the relations between these regions remained fluid. Tourism developed first and most strongly in destinations that provided natural amenities in combination with historic sites or exotic cultures.

Forms of Tourism

Leisure activities chosen by tourists have differed over time and from place to place. Historical tourism catered to education-oriented tourists. Situated in or near large cities, an institutionalized tourist industry serviced large numbers of travelers who sought glories from the past at the Parthenon in Greece, the pyramids of Giza, or Machu Picchu high in the Peruvian Andes. Cultural tourism included the "nostalgic" or "picturesque," vestiges of vanishing lifestyles within easy distance from more modern resorts, that is, visits to Native American reservations from dude ranches in the western United States. Promoters marketed the closely related ethnic tourism to consumers curious about "authentic" customs of indigenous and often exotic peoples, such as the San Blas Indians of Panama or the Toraja in Indonesia. This type of tourism frequently involved traveling to difficult-to-reach locations, participating in local rituals, or shopping for souvenirs that possessed intrinsic rather than monetary value. These travelers often attempted to get close to "Nature" through people once considered primitive, instinctual creatures.

Recreational tourism involved sand, sea, or snow and stimulated development in mountain and seaside resorts across the world. Other recreational tourists eschewed luxury hotels, preferring more active encounters with nature through backpacking, hiking, rafting, rock climbing, and extreme sports. Often the expectations of metropolitan centers prompted the development of once-alien regions as recreation centers. Before the 1950s and the production of a John Huston film, *The Night of the Iguana* (1964), there, Puerto Vallarta was a relatively isolated, ethnically picturesque fishing village; with the publicizing of its unblemished character through the movie, it emerged as one of Mexico's prime tourist destinations, losing much of its mystique in the process. With entertainment tourism, best represented by Las Vegas, people indulged in gambling, sexual practices, and other activities that they might have avoided or minimized at home.

Historically, nature tourism displayed many manifestations. For nineteenth-century romantics, the land, sea, and sky provided spiritual and physical renewal. Nature did not convey a symbolic meaning; humans assigned nature both aesthetic and utilitarian values according to their own social structures and cultures. In the more extreme expressions of nature tourism, the absence—or limited presence—of humans became a factor. In supposedly pristine wildernesses across the globe, people found sublimity. Other travelers attempted to understand human-nature relationships and thus observed Ceylonese tea-processing facilities; Japanese pearl farms; French vineyards and wineries; or nineteenth-century Chicago meat-processing plants. Machines and human work were displaced and displayed as products of nature. In the last decades of the twentieth century, with ecological tourism or ecotourism, tourists tried to leave as little effect as possible on the places visited. Alternatively, with traditional hunting, another form of nature tourism, limited thought was given to effect, and some souvenirs were brought home. Yet, more recently, seasonal hunting under state supervision helped maintain sustainable populations of various animal species.

Impacts of Tourism

The major stimulus for fostering tourism has always been economic. For underdeveloped areas worldwide, tourism has been viewed as a developmental tool. Boosters have emphasized the financial enhancement of local economies from the influx of expenditures, particularly with the introduction of currency from those industrialized nations that tend to supply the majority of the travelers. The German mark, Japanese yen, Swiss franc, U.K. pound, or the U.S. dollar have provided important foreign exchange with which residents have purchased food, medicine, machinery, and other items needed for their survival or development. Some economists highlight the "multiplier effect" by which funds have recirculated through local economies in several exchanges and thus even benefited businesses not directly related to tourism. Certain indigenous peoples have actively participated in creating tourist landscapes as investors and as cultural brokers. Nonetheless, early studies of tourism suggested that foreign investors initially siphoned money back to the source of their capital rather than vitalizing local businesses. Unfortunately, certain less-developed nations have experienced similarly exploitive patterns in other industries as well. In Korea, for example, almost 50 percent of the profits in the electronics industry was siphoned back to the source of foreign capital. Other commentators suggested, however, that as the tourism sector became more integrated into the domestic economy, the degree of "leakage" declined. Tourism often reinvigorated traditional industries by providing new, enlarged markets for the consumption of native products.

In tourist areas across the globe, great discrepancies between hosts and guests often placed the cost of living beyond the means of the hosts, contributing to a stratified labor system and the potential for crime against travelers unfamiliar with the social milieu. Over time, contacts between hosts and guests also changed. The first visitors were novelties, studied by the hosts, and because tourism was new, job opportunities were limited. As local inhabitants developed usable job skills, local employees obtained positions of greater responsibility. Yet, economic strains frequently appeared due to the seasonality of much tourism, which left hotels empty and employees idle. Moreover, as the terrorism of 11 September 2001 illustrated, tourist travel vacillated in accordance with variables over which neither local hosts nor their visitors exercised control.

Tourism also proved culturally stressful. Production for the tourist market has been perceived as the "trinketization" of indigenous aesthetics. Tourism facilitated the appreciation of diverse cultures and landscapes, but servicing tourists became a monotonous, repetitive business. When the economic goals of mass tourism were realized and the few initial visitors were replaced by a steady influx of consumers, guest identities blended into stereotypical ethnic or national images. Tolerated for economic gain, "dehumanized" guests, in turn, looked upon their hosts with curiosity and objectification. As early as 1870, Francis Kilvert, a British minister, captured sentiments common to residents of frequently visited destinations: "Of all the noxious animals, too, the most noxious is a tourist" (Plomer 1969).

Although the environmental implications of mass tourism still merit substantial investigation, tourists clearly generated physical as well as social impacts. Every tourist activity relied on environmental resources. Some offbeat travelers avoided crowds or sought the heightened excitement of doing something unusual and perhaps dangerous, generally adapting somewhat or fully to local norms and thus limiting, but not removing, their impact. Mass tourism, on the other hand, provoked a continuous flow of people who inundated certain places, such as Hawaii, year around, and other areas, such as the European summer resorts, the Caribbean, and coastal Mexico, seasonally. Built upon middle-class income and values, mass tourism demanded modern cultural amenities, and its sheer numbers required infrastructure improvements. As

the numbers of tourists progressively increased, more facilities were needed. Many of these mass tourists sought the supposed romance of nature, but through the pane of an air-conditioned bus or the porthole of a cruise ship where they were assured of workable plumbing and safe food and water. These tourists generally imposed the greatest impact on the host's culture and ecosystem by virtue of their greater numbers and demands for extensions of their home environments for which they are willing to pay handsomely.

Increasingly commentators have focused on the relationship between tourism and sustainability. *Our Common Future* (1987), from the World Commission on Environment and Development, defined sustainable development as "development that meets the needs of the present without compromising the ability of future generations to meet their own needs" (13). This focus necessitates examining the true environmental costs of actions and contemplating greater equity between, and empowerment of, all stakeholders. Industrial mass production demanded massive supplies of raw material and energy from global sources. There were parallels in the way that nature was packaged, sold, and consumed in mass tourism, whether on a ski slope in the Alps, a safari in east Africa, or a snorkeling adventure at the Great Barrier Reef. Tourism, like other industries, was an agent of development and change. It always was consumptive, the level of consumption determined by the scale and style of tourism.

Some mass tourist resorts overwhelmed local environmental systems and the capacities of local societies to manage them; thus, such resorts appeared to be the antithesis of sustainable tourism. The great diffusion of tourism in the post-World War II era generated more travel and brought more local systems under threat, but there is also a need to distinguish between the impact of massive numbers of tourists in particular regions such as the Costa del Sol in Spain and their concentration in large, isolated resorts such as Ocho Rios in Jamaica. Mass tourism imposed very different environmental implications according to how it was implanted within regions and according to the contingencies of space and place. Moreover, mass tourism coincided with more individualized, and thus more difficult to track, forms of tourism. And it often has been difficult to distinguish the damage from tourism and that associated with other forms of development. Nonetheless, there remain some telling historical incidents.

The European Alps provide a well-known example of the large-scale destruction of an ecosystem through vegetation removal to accommodate tourist facilities. Ski slopes, lifts, gondolas, pylons, buildings, and access roads replaced hundreds of square kilometers of forest, making the hillsides less able to retain water and causing increased susceptibility to soil erosion, flood, landslides, and avalanches. By the 1970s Swiss ski lifts accommodated as many as 250,000 riders each hour during the high season, but the evacuation of tourists became a regular occurrence due to avalanches associated with deforestation. Mudslides and floods in Tyrol, Austria, in July 1987 left more than sixty people dead and another seven thousand homeless following the destruction of fifty towns.

In other places, seasonal tourism coincided with animal breeding, and the ecological impact of tourists became an issue of contention. Some Mediterranean beach resorts of Greece and Turkey provided rare turtle populations with breeding grounds where they laid their eggs in chambers dug out of the sand. In certain resorts, conservationists distributed leaflets warning tourists not to place towels on the sand, not to use umbrellas, and not to light evening bonfires, activities that could destroy egg clutches or disorient hatchlings trying to reach the sea. The conservationists' efforts met with limited success. Even ecotourism, which strives to respect and benefit protected areas as well as their peoples, has proven damaging. The disappearance of the golden toad in the 1980s from Costa Rica's Monteverde Cloud Forest Reserve coincided with the substantial growth of ecotourism there. By 1980 poorly controlled tourists at the Galapagos Islands threatened habitats of unique ecological and historical value. The tourists collected shells, rocks, and plants, often venturing beyond designated areas. They disturbed plant and animal life, leading to concerns about animal migration. Other species became overly reliant on tourists as a source of food, a development disadvantageous over time.

In Africa some plant and animal species declined due to pressures from hunting or wildlife tourism. Their disappearance in countries such as Senegal due to the manufacture and marketing of trophies, gifts, and souvenirs led to ecological imbalances even where animals were protected by law. General disturbances by even the relatively small number of tourists at Tanzania's Serengeti National Park hurt the cheetah population. Vehicles crushed vegetation in some of Kenya's national parks and wildlife reserves. Yet, other studies confirmed that despite these types of damage, interest in animal viewing and photographic safaris resulted in the creation or continuation of national parks, fisheries,

and wildlife reserves in developing African nations. Wildlife tourism and controlled hunting represented less-intensive forms of exploitation in such countries than previously existed. Reserves in Kenya benefited greatly from tourist expenditures and the associated publicity, ensuring within limits both habitat protection and job opportunities.

The natural environment also has been a major focal point in selling Asia to tourists in the post-World War II era. Romantic images of pristine environments and exotic cultures stand at the forefront of perceptions of the "orient" in Western eyes. Yet, because their development patterns paralleled each other, it has been difficult to distinguish the impacts of tourism from the effects of other exploitive industries such as logging and fishing or of agriculture and urban sprawl. Some commentators believe that to focus on the negative impacts of tourism on the natural environment misses the far greater environmental problems facing the region from global warming, rising sea levels, deforestation, a loss of biodiversity, and overpopulation. These environmental problems have intensified at substantial costs; the World Bank estimated that $30 billion a year would be needed in the twenty-first century to restore the region's ecosystems.

Of all the economic activities that occurred in the coastal zones of the Asia-Pacific region during the last four decades of the twentieth century, none increased with the volume, diversity, or rapidity of tourism. By the 1990s this sector grew to such a magnitude that it became a factor in the development plans of most national governments. At the same time, almost all coastal and oceanic issues affected tourism directly or indirectly. Clean water, white sand beaches, bountiful marine resources, and safety were fundamental to successful tourism. Sustainable long-term tourism required security from risks associated with natural coastal hazards such as storms, flooding, hurricanes, and tidal waves. Coastal tourism also necessitated the construction of cultural amenities such as hotels, restaurants, and second homes, plus the infrastructure to support them—access roads, retail businesses, and marinas. All of these activities, along with the introduction of the millions of tourists over the decades, increased pressure on the coastlines just as many of these areas faced concentrated uses from agriculture, urban settlement, commercial fishing, and industrialization.

The coincidental impact of tourism and these other economic activities on sand cays, for example, has been well documented. The extensive removal of near-shore vegetation led to sea storm erosion and decreased plant material decomposition on beaches. Resort hotels and the expanded coastline populations necessitated extensive and excessive tapping of fresh groundwater resources, draining them faster than they could be replenished and causing the intrusion of salt water. Local residents joined tourists in producing sewage that overwhelmed shallow waters, and reefs built up nutrients and prompted algal growth that killed coral. Seawalls designed to protect hotels or second homes from high waters unintentionally impaired seasonal sand distribution, reducing the landmass of many islands.

Nonetheless, it remains difficult to distinguish the historical and ecological implications of tourism from those of other developmental activities, although most observers acknowledge that both have impacts. At the same time, the interdependence of tourism and the state of the environment became all the more evident. In the 1980s a budding interest in ecotourism in Thailand, for example, was matched by rapid industrialization and the commensurate environmental degradation, particularly the overlogging of native forests. From the perspective of the tourist trade, poor planning and uncontrolled urban and industrial growth diminished resort destinations and beaches. Pattaya, once billed as the "queen" of Southeast Asia's resorts, was rapidly transformed from a tranquil village to a destination that caters to 3 million or more visitors a year, losing much of its original charm within two decades. Environmental considerations were neglected in favor of economic interests, but in the end, these decisions hurt the tourist trade.

The relationship between tourism and the state of the environment was brought into sharp focus in 1997 when much of Southeast Asia was covered by smoke from Indonesian forest fires, purposefully started by loggers under the government's catastrophic land-clearance policies. Drought conditions exacerbated the fires. The fires and the smoke they generated damaged tropical forests and indigenous wildlife, such as the orangutan, and dramatically diminished the number of visitors to the region. In the wake of this environmental crisis, European travel markets rarely distinguished between Indonesia and other nations such as Malaysia and Thailand, and the number of leisure travelers to the region in general declined substantially. One significant development that emerged from this tragedy was the confirmation of the idea that international efforts were required to prevent future disasters. The internationalization of environmental issues be-

came apparent in the plethora of regulations and protocols from international bodies, regional coalitions, nation-states, and local governments, although tourism tended to be covered within general environmental and planning laws rather than claiming its own specific agenda.

Yet how these laws were enacted and implemented over the last two decades varied from one global region to another. In Europe, where the majority of people are urbanized and where industry was the main engine of economic growth, the concept of nature as a resource to be enjoyed by urban consumers was understandable. Participation in a new postindustrial economy has only enhanced this appreciation of natural landscapes. In Africa, however, where the majority of people depended for their subsistence on agricultural production, the concept of nature was very different. The land and its wildlife were not sources of aesthetic enjoyment but rather resources to be managed so that people survived. For many Africans the land was not an arena for leisure but rather a means of livelihood and survival.

Tourism as an economic and environmental phenomenon has been the subject of serious study for only a few decades. Given the growing magnitude of tourism during the twentieth century, the great complexity of motivations and expectations from both guests and hosts, and the diversity of cultural and ecological responses to tourist activity, this study offers only a glimpse into the social, economic, and environmental implications of its historical applications. That tourism harmed the physical environment has become well recognized within the travel literature. At present, the historical links between specific forms of tourism, other economic and social activities, and the environment is inadequately developed. Tourism and sustainability remain areas for investigation.

Kathleen A. Brosnan

See also Ecotourism

Further Reading

Blackford, M. G. (2000). *Fragile paradise: The impact of tourism on Maui, 1959–2000.* Lawrence: University Press of Kansas.

Hall, C. M., & Page, S. (2000). *Tourism in South and Southeast Asia: Issues and cases.* Boston: Butterworth Heinemann.

Honey, M. (1998). *Ecotourism and sustainable development: Who owns paradise?* Washington, DC: Island Press.

Hunter, C., & Green, H. (1995). *Tourism and the environment: A sustainable relationship?* New York: Routledge.

MacCannell, D. (1999). *The tourist: A new theory of the leisure class* (Rev. ed.). Berkeley & Los Angeles: University of California Press.

Mowforth, M., & Munt, I. (1998). *Tourism and sustainability: New tourism in the Third World.* New York: Routledge.

Plomer, W. (Ed.). (1969). *Selections from the diary of the Rev. Francis Kilvert* (Rev. ed.). London: Cape.

Rothman, H. K. (1998). *Devil's bargains: Tourism in the twentieth-century West.* Lawrence: University Press of Kansas.

Smith, V. L. (Ed.). (1989). *Hosts and guests: The anthropology of tourism* (Rev. ed.). Philadelphia: University of Pennsylvania Press.

Williams, A. M., & Shaw, G. (Eds.). (1998). *Tourism and economic development: European experiences* (Rev. ed.). New York: J. Wiley.

World Commission on Environment and Development. (1987). *Our common future.* Oxford & New York: Oxford University Press.

Toxicity

Toxicity is the property of toxic chemicals (also known as "toxins") that renders them harmful to living organisms. Toxicity can cause acute (immediate) harm or chronic harm (over an extended time) due to longer-term exposure. Chronic toxicity is the case, for example, with carcinogens (chemicals that cause cancer) and xenoendocrines (chemicals that harm the endocrine or hormone system, often leading to birth defects, immune system failure, and other delayed diseases). Of the eighty thousand chemicals in commercial production, approximately 2 percent are toxins capable of causing damage at low levels of exposure. Among these are heavy metals and their salts, known since ancient times, such as mercury, lead, and arsenic. Organic (carbon-containing) substances may also be toxic. The Greeks, for example, employed the toxic properties of certain animals and plants, such as hemlock, used to execute Socrates (399 BCE), while ancient Chinese literature, as early as 2700 BCE, referred to experiments with the poisonous properties of fish and salamanders.

There are many classification schemes for toxins, such as those based on effect, origin, physical state, chemical structure, mechanism of action, and potential to poison an organism. Numerous organic compounds—principally derivatives of petroleum or natural tree resins, such as benzene, toluene, and turpentine—have been isolated over the past two centuries. By far the largest category of toxins (both in number and mass circulating in the environment) is the halogenated organic compounds formed by combining halogens—such as bromine, fluorine, and, most significantly, chlorine—with hydrocarbon (combinations of carbon and hydrogen). Discovered and manufactured principally since World War II, most organochlorines (chlorinated hydrocarbons) are anthropogenic (human created). They are constituents of pesticides, cleaning solvents, pharmaceuticals, plastics, and many other products of modern life. Responsible for over one-fourth of world output, the United States experienced a remarkable increase in organochlorine production from the birth of the industry during World War II to more than .9 metric ton per capita today.

Toxicology

Toxicology is the study of toxins and their impact on living organisms. The subfield eco-toxicology has grown with recent demonstration that wildlife impact is often a good indicator of potential human impact, particularly with endocrine disrupters. As a formal field, toxicology is relatively young, embracing an understanding both of chemistry and biology, although, since medieval times, alchemists and other self-styled chemists were already experimenting with various chemicals, trying to ascertain their relative toxicity. Even earlier, aboriginal peoples understood the poisonous qualities of certain plants, with some anthropologists and geographers now suggesting that the first plants were domesticated over ten thousand years ago for medicinal and poisonous properties (useful for hunting), rather than for food. Indeed the very term *toxic* derives from the ancient Greek word *toxikon*, referring to arrow poison.

The Swiss-born alchemist and physician Paracelsus (1493–1541) is reputed to have come up with the basic principle for toxicology, "the dose makes the poison." Thus every chemical, even oxygen and salt, is harmful at high enough concentrations. At the other extreme, even a single molecule of a toxin may be capable of causing cell damage, although this possibility is proportionately diminished as the concentration of the toxin approaches zero. With controlled human data hard to come by, toxicologists rely upon megadose (high-level) exposure in laboratory animals, typically rats, with extrapolation back to human levels of exposure when determining the toxicity of various substances. Regulators use these dose-response curves to set human exposure limits under a wide variety of state and federal laws dealing with environment and workplace exposure to pesticides, occupational hazards, air and water pollutants, and even cleanup of contaminated sites. Although fraught with difficulty due to the extrapolation required, megadose testing is considered necessary. This is because the impact of many chemicals at typical exposure levels is so low that thousands of test animals would be needed to uncover a statistically significant impact where the impact rate may be only one or two additional premature deaths per 100,000 population.

Risk Analysis

Most risk analysis relies on cancer as the most sensitive disease, at least for those chemicals that are also carcinogenic. Recent research suggests, however, that many xenoendocrines, belonging to the same family of organochlorines as carcinogens, display impact at background levels of exposure in the environment. This challenges the need for megadose testing with interspecies extrapolation to set exposure limits. Moreover, this research demonstrates that with xenoendocrines the timing of exposure may be more important than the actual dose, particularly because these endocrine disrupters have a narrow window of opportunity to disrupt fetal development at specific periods during pregnancy when sexual differentiation occurs or organs develop. With major technical advances now allowing identification at parts per billion and beyond at the levels necessary to detect background exposure to xenoendocrines, regulatory agencies, such as the U.S. Environmental Protection Agency, are reassessing their traditional reliance on megadose testing for cancer, and linear dose-response curves, as the model used for setting exposure limits.

Other difficulties with traditional risk assessment for toxins include an inability to model and quantify complex synergistic (relating to an interaction of discrete agents or conditions such that the total effect is greater than the sum of the individual effects) reactions among any number of chemicals that individuals are exposed to in a busy industrial area or at a waste site; the lack of full human health exposure assessments for the vast majority of chemicals in commercial production; an inability to deal with the problem of bioaccumulation over time; and insufficient attention to age,

gender, ethnic, and other genetic differences among the exposed population.

Concluding that too often risk assessment is more politics than science, many environmental activists are pushing for toxic use reduction and risk elimination rather than managed release of toxins into the environment based upon questionable assumptions regarding the assimilative capacity of the environment and human bodies. The environmental organization Greenpeace, for example, is leading a worldwide campaign to have chlorine phased out of production because it is the keystone chemical in the production of many of the listed toxins and responsible for their toxic properties. Although powerful vested interests decry such a phase-out as economic lunacy and technically impossible given human dependence on organochlorines, it should be noted that toxic use reduction is already considered the best way to deal with toxins as outlined in federal and state waste management hierarchies. Germany, Sweden, and several other European countries have recently moved to eliminate the use of chlorine for bleaching paper, producing polyvinyl chloride plastics, and for many other nonessential products or services. In the United States, Massachusetts and New Jersey are leaders with state attention to toxic use reduction.

Michael K. Heiman

Further Reading

Colborn, T., Dumanoski, D., & Myers, J. (1996). *Our stolen future.* New York: Dutton/Penguin.

Crosby, D. (1998). *Environmental toxicology and chemistry.* New York: Oxford University Press.

Hughes, W. (1996). *Essentials of environmental toxicology.* Washington, DC: Taylor & Francis.

Stine, K., & Brown, T. (1996). *Principles of toxicology.* Boca Raton, FL: Lewis.

Thornton, J. (2000). *Pandora's poison: Chlorine, health, and a new environmental strategy.* Cambridge, MA: MIT Press.

Traditional Environmental Knowledge

Traditional environmental knowledge (TEK) is knowledge of the environment possessed by indigenous people. Traditional environmental knowledge is sometimes called "indigenous knowledge" (IK), "traditional ecological knowledge," "local environmental knowledge," "ethnoecology," "ethnobiology," or "folk biology." Traditional environmental knowledge derives for the most part from indigenous culture but also reflects novel cultural categories of nonindigenous people and embraces introduced animals and plants along with native species. Tradition is assumed to be rooted in the past even though admittedly open to influence and at times even invented anew by succeeding generations. Also, the concepts of the environment, nature, and the natural world require careful consideration for their applicability in specific cultures. Traditional environmental knowledge is often contrasted with Western scientific knowledge of the natural world.

Indigenous people who have been living for generations in a particular environment develop intimate familiarity with it, render it culturally sensible, and encode it linguistically. They also distinguish proper from improper thoughts about and behavior toward the natural world. Indigenous people possess a keen awareness of the natural world. They name birds that they hear or see; vines, trees, and plants that they encounter; and reptiles, mammals, fish, and insects that they use for food or that attract their attention. Often the depth of knowledge is formidable: For example, in their dense, dimly lit, misty forests, the West Papuan Ketengban are able to distinguish—on the basis of song, behavior, posture, and silhouette—similar species of distant canopy-flitting birds whose recognition bedevils Western ornithologists.

The total body of indigenous environmental knowledge can also be remarkable. It is reflected in language, in the labels that people use for elements of the natural world. One measure of its extent is in the labels given to kinds of things that are perceived to be distinct from other kinds of things. The smallest perceived discontinuities are at the level of, and take their names from, the biological species and genus. Some experts argue that the genus reflects the most fundamental perceptual discontinuities. So-called generics are often monotypic, that is, they often contain no further specific distinctions. Some people, especially those who live in environments rich in biodiversity (biological diversity as indicated by numbers of species of animals and plants) or who engage in both gathering and subsistence farming, list hundreds, if not more, generics. One Tzeltal Maya botanical collaborator, for example, distinguished 485 ethnobotanical generics in Chiapas, Mexico. The Philippine Hanunóo distinguish over nine hundred generic plant types and over seventeen hundred specific plant types. They are near the upper

limit. The average number of labeled generic categories is less: 200 plant categories among noncultivators, 500 among cultivators, and 390 animal categories among indigenous people. Some experts suggest that the average of approximately five hundred generics in major classes of living things (such as plants or animals) represents one measure of the capacity of memory of ethnobotanical or ethnozoological categories. Impressive as these numbers of named categories are, however, they are fewer than would be distinguished in an inventory in Western science.

Names in the Natural World

There is a long-running debate over why certain things are named and others not, over whether indigenous people name and classify the natural world because of intellectual or gustatory and other practical interests. Indeed, in many instances, things that are unperceived because of such factors as size or behavior are not selected for naming, and things that are practical or utilitarian—because they are used for food, clothing, ornamentation, or some other obvious practical purpose or because they are noxious or tabooed or because they are important in ritual or narrative—*are* selected for naming. Yet, also named are things that have no discernible utility in the senses suggested. It seems that neither intellectual nor practical reasons alone account for the presence or absence of names for the natural world.

Generics are related to one another in classifications or taxonomies, which in theory can have as many as five or six levels of inclusion from most to least inclusive categories (scientific analogues are class, order, family, genus, species, and subspecies). In actuality indigenous taxonomies of the natural world are often relatively shallow, with only two or three levels. The greatest correspondence with Western scientific classification is with generics and specifics, with which there is often a one-to-one correspondence. Yet, even on these levels some people might use different names for males and females in species in which they differ greatly in appearance or use the same name for two or more similar and closely related species. The least correspondence with Western taxonomy is found in levels higher or lower than generics and specifics. For example, the Itzaj Maya sort birds first according to their edibility or inedibility, and then according to their habitat and habits, as fish-eating water birds, edible fruit-eating ground birds, edible fruit-eating tree birds, inedible flesh-eating birds, inedible fruit-eating birds, and inedible blood-sucking birds (bats).

Traditional environmental knowledge is not just vast but also ecological. That is, it is systemic, relational, and attentive to interdependencies—it shows the hallmarks of ecological thought. It is also, of course, cultural and therefore premised on, for example, theories of animal behavior (ethology) or ideas about habitat locations or the presence of other-than-human beings specific to particular cultural systems. Therefore, indigenous ecological thought—the culturally based comprehension of ecological systems—varies culturally; ecology is ethnoecology.

It is commonly assumed that actions that proceed from traditional environmental knowledge are more respectful of the environment and sustainable than those that proceed from assumptions rooted in Western science. The assumption is romantic if not rash. Indigenous people have managed their environments through fire and other means to ensure that the plants and animals identified as important in subsistence, material culture, well-being, or other cultural domains continued to be present. Although many actions of indigenous people have had less impact than those of nonindigenous people, especially ones in industrial society, and although the actions of indigenous people have resulted in biodiversity where the actions of many nonindigenous people have not, subsistence and material needs keyed to the size of the population, to human mobility or sedentariness, and to work and leisure cycles have determined environmental impact, not environmental knowledge. Moreover, respect for the natural world, present in many ideologies and expressed ritually, is again cultural, and culture-specific beliefs like reincarnationhave brought about behavior antithetical to conservation. Knowledge by itself does not therefore translate into kinder and gentler ways of behaving in the natural world; lifestyles sustainable over time most likely resulted from the demand for food or fuel and the interest in the accumulation of material property both remaining within the capacity of environmental resources. Today there is conservation potential in local ideologies of conservation, but the key is harnessing them to behavior.

Threats to Knowledge

In any indigenous society traditional environmental knowledge varies by family history, gender, age, occupation, involvement in curing or ritual activity, degree of exposure and commitment to nonindigenous cul-

ture, interest and curiosity, and other factors. If indigenous people are removed from their traditional environments for such factors as formal education, if their relationships with their environments change, if the environments themselves undergo alteration from deforestation or the depletion of animals near settlements, or if a new language displaces the indigenous language with its encoded categories, then the collective and transgenerational basis for knowledge is threatened, can change, and might even disappear. Thus today the preservation of traditional environmental knowledge is seen as urgent before it vanishes forever.

Such preservation is far from straightforward. There are striking ethical and legal dilemmas unless the preservation is controlled by those who possess such traditional environmental knowledge. Indigenous people—according to the United Nations, 300 million indigenous people live in five thousand groups in over seventy countries—increasingly think of safeguarding their knowledge as critical. They are threatened by multinational companies prospecting for biogenetic resources in hope of discovering useful plants for the next generation of pharmaceuticals. Indigenous people increasingly voice their concern over what they regard as biopiracy and their right to control knowledge. Some invoke the concept of intellectual property rights, which would need broadening to be applicable in law. The issues are complex, without clear-cut solution. Nonprofit organizations designed as partnerships to share profits and control with indigenous people have started to evolve. In the meantime, scholars interested in recording traditional environmental knowledge, especially of an ethnobotanical nature, risk being regarded by indigenous people as exploiters unless theirs is research of, by, and for the people.

Shepard Krech III

See also Genetic Piracy; Medicinal Plants

Further Reading

Berlin, B. (1992). *Ethnobiological classification: Principles of categorization of plants and animals in traditional societies.* Princeton, NJ: Princeton University Press.

Gragson, T. L., & Blount, B. G. (Eds.). (1999). *Ethnoecology: Knowledge, resources and rights.* Athens: University of Georgia Press.

Krech, S., III. (1999). *The ecological Indian: Myth and history.* New York: W. W. Norton.

Medin, D. L., & Atran, S. (Eds.). (1999). *Folkbiology.* Cambridge, MA: MIT Press.

Minnis, P. E. (Ed.). (2000). *Ethnobotany: A reader.* Norman: University of Oklahoma Press.

Nazarea, V. D. (Ed.). (1999). *Ethnoecology: Situated knowledge/located lives.* Tucson: University of Arizona Press.

Stepp, J. R., Wyndham, F. S., & Zarger, R. K. (Eds.). (2002). *Ethnobiology and biocultural diversity.* Athens: University of Georgia Press.

Tragedy of the Commons

As popularized by the human ecologist Garrett Hardin in a 1968 essay for *Science*, the tragedy of the commons is a metaphor describing the use and fate of common resources. It is based on a theory suggesting that individuals, each acting in their own self interest, will overuse and ultimately cause the collapse of collectively owned resources. Conceived in neoclassical economics as the "prisoner's dilemma," the "tragedy" is portrayed by Hardin as the inevitable result of rational behavior when the gain to be had from increased use of a common resource outweighs the individual's share in the collective loss from additional use. Privatization of the common resource, while desirable, is not possible when boundaries cannot be established or access denied. As a result, Hardin suggests "mutual coercion, mutually agreed upon"(Hardin 1968, 1247) as the practical way to control a common resource—precisely the approach taken today: Use of a common resource is typically regulated by democratically accountable government agencies, and under international agreements.

Hardin's popular essay is arguably the most reprinted ever to appear in the environmental literature. The metaphor employed involves herdsmen sharing a common pasture. Here each herder is compelled to increase his herd for to do otherwise would be "self-eliminating," as the herder suffers the consequence of decreased resource availability while others maximize their own individual gain. The metaphor has been applied to a wide variety of dilemmas involving resource use, including whaling and marine fisheries, firewood gathering, access to national parks, Antarctic mineral exploration, outer-space satellite placement, and, as with air and water contamination, pollution itself when an individual gains from putting something into the commons instead of extracting a resource.

Written primarily as a critique of the then-popular idea that improved access to voluntary family planning would suffice to limit Third World population growth rates, Hardin's contribution was to apply the theory of the commons to family size decisions and demonstrate that appeal to voluntary self-restraint could could not work if there was a material advantage in having a larger family. However, the actual anticipation of a tragedy inherent in common resource use was not new. Hardin popularized an idea that already had intellectual roots in an observation by Aristotle (384–322 BCE) that "what is held in common by the largest number of people receives the least care." (paraphrased in Aristotle 1998, 28). This idea was picked up by the British philosopher Thomas Hobbes (1588–1679) in *Leviathan*, in which he suggested that the commons should be regulated by the "Leviathan," or state, toward which each citizen must submit in the collective interest of peace and social order. In 1833 the English essayist William Lloyd came up with the simple mathematical model of common pasture use applied by Hardin.

Critiques of the Metaphor of the Tragedy of the Commons

The metaphor of the tragedy of the commons has been criticized as historically inaccurate, while the logic of the theory and proposed solution have been characterized as ideologically limiting. Historians have pointed out that the eighteenth- and early nineteenth-century collapse of common resource use in England was not due to any intrinsic structural flaw with the commons itself, nor with critical overuse of the resource base. Rather it occurred through the concerted efforts of the landed class, backed by Parliamentary decree, to forcibly enclose common lands. As a result subsistence peasant and tenant farmers were driven toward industrial wage labor and the land given over to commercial agriculture in a growing capitalist society.

Over time, there have been a wide variety of decentralized indigenous institutional solutions to common resource use short of privatization or external centralized regulation. In England, for example, prior to the rise of a capitalist market economy, there was little pressure to produce more than what the farmer could directly consume or was demanded by the landlord for rent. In practice, environmental destruction through overgrazing and deforestation actually increased under privatization. In India and Thailand common forests, as research findings of U.S. political scientist Elinor Ostrom show, once protected and sustainably managed by local villages as sacred groves, came

Individual Property and Community Blight

The following extract is dialogue from Edward Bellamy's novel, *Looking Backward; 2000–1887*, written in 1898. The novel sets forth Bellamy's vision of a cooperative world, free of economic competition and this passage concerns the effect of individualism on the city.

"In general," I said, "what impresses me most about the city is the material prosperity on the part of the people which its magnificence implies."

"I would give a great deal for just one glimpse of the Boston of your day," replied Doctor Leete. "No doubt, as you imply, the cities of that period were rather shabby affairs. If you had the taste to make them splendid, which I would not be so rude as to question, the general poverty resulting from your extraordinary industrial system would not have given you the means. Moreover, the excessive individualism which then prevailed was inconsistent with much public spirit. What little wealth you had seems almost wholly to have been lavished in private luxury. Nowadays, on the contrary, there is no destination of the surplus wealth so popular as the adornment of the city, which all enjoy in equal degree."

Source: Bellamy, Edward. (2000). *Looking Backward, 2000–1887.* New York: Signet Classic, p. 28. (Originally published 1898)

---

under increased pressure when taken over by central governments, as underpaid wardens succumbed to bribes from poachers and loggers.

The Tragedy of the Commons and Capitalism

Turning to the ideological underpinning of the tragedy argument, Hardin's essay, in practice, is a defense of the capitalist state when it is called upon to help protect the conditions necessary for continued private accumulation. With "the alternative of the commons too horrifying to contemplate," (Hardin 1968, 1247) Hardin considers only privatization or state intervention as solutions to avoid collapse. Moving beyond an historical record demonstrating that common resources can be managed locally for collective gain—even under conditions of high population density, as existed in aboriginal communities on islands and in the Amazon prior to European market penetration—one has to question just what it is that makes the commons inherently tragic. One can argue that it is the private appropriation of the commons for individual gain—a condition furthered under capitalist market conditions—that creates the tragedy. Following Hardin's metaphor, the tragedy may lie with the existence of private cattle rather than in the structure of the collective commons, for were the cattle themselves communalized, there would be less incentive for individual gain at communal expense.

In summary, the tragedy of the commons serves as a powerful metaphor applicable to a wide variety of situations. It describes common resource use under historically specific conditions of private appropriation within the framework of capitalist market relations. As a metaphor, we must be careful not to assume that the motivations and conditions it describes are universal. Taken out of context, the solutions proposed can undermine preexisting, and often sustainable, resource allocation regimes with resulting violence both to the affected populations and to the resource base they depend upon.

Michael Heiman

See also Hardin, Garrett

Further Reading

Aristotle. (1998). *Politics* (C. Reeve, Trans.). Indianapolis, IN: Hackett.

Buck, S. (1998). *The global commons: An introduction.* Washington, DC: Island Press.

Hardin, G. (1968). The tragedy of the commons. *Science, 162,* 1243–1248.

Hobbes, T. (1991). *Leviathan* (R. Tuck, Ed.). Cambridge, UK: Cambridge University Press. (Originally published 1651)

Lloyd, W. (1977). On the checks to population. In G. Harden & J. Baden (Eds.), *Managing the commons* (pp.

8–15). San Francisco: W. H. Freeman. (Original essay published1833)

Neeson, J. M. (1993). *Commoners: Common right, enclosure and social change in England, 1700–1820.* Cambridge, UK: Cambridge University Press.

Ostrom, E. (1990). *The evolution of institutions for collective action.* Cambridge, UK: Cambridge University Press.

Trans-Alaska Pipeline

In January 1968 the largest oil field in North American history was discovered at Prudhoe Bay on Alaska's North (Arctic) Slope. Various proposals were suggested for moving the oil to refineries and markets in the continental United States—including ice-breaking supertankers, nuclear submarines, specially reinforced jumbo jets, and a pipeline via Canada's Mackenzie Valley to the Chicago area. But the proposal backed by the oil companies involved was a 1,284-kilometer buried pipeline south to Valdez, North America's northernmost ice-free port. The Trans-Alaska Pipeline was the most ambitious construction project in American history. By thrusting the fate of Alaska's wilderness and wildlife to the forefront of the nation's environmental agenda, the pipeline proposal spawned a public debate (1969–1973) unprecedented in American environmental history.

Because the pipeline route mostly traversed public lands, the consortium of oil companies had to apply to the government for construction permits. Because permafrost underlay much of the route, federal officials indicated that a lot of the pipe needed to be raised (above ground). Marine oil spills after tankers left Valdez presented another potential problem. So did intrusion into a region—north of the Yukon—increasingly celebrated as America's "last great wilderness." Native Alaskan land claims further complicated matters. Lawsuits filed by Alaska Natives and environmentalists in the spring of 1970 were upheld, raising three obstacles to authorization: Alaska Native land claims, the maximum pipeline corridor width provisions of the Mineral Leasing Act of 1920, and the recent National Environmental Policy Act's (NEPA) requirement for an environmental-impact statement (EIS). Congress settled Alaska Native claims in December 1971, and the government's draft EIS (January 1971) endorsed the project. But many people remained unconvinced that Alyeska (the formal corporate entity now behind the project) could build a reliable pipeline, some preferring the "Canadian alternative" in the Mackenzie Valley route. Others felt that *any* pipeline, regardless of quality, involved a desecration of sacred wilderness values. Nevertheless, the final EIS (March 1972) restated the desirability of such a pipeline. In August 1972, the injunction based on noncompliance with NEPA was dissolved. But in February 1973 a court sustained the charge that construction violated the Mineral Leasing Act. The stalemate was broken only by the energy crisis of 1973; Vice President Spiro Agnew used his tie-breaking power in the Senate to release from further court-ordered delay a project that became the flagship of President Richard Nixon's drive to reduce American dependence on foreign oil supplies. Final congressional authorization came in November 1973, construction began in April 1974, and the first oil flowed toward Valdez in 1977.

Four years of environmentalist pressure had vastly improved a project that could have been an environmental disaster and that turned out to be the most expensive private engineering project in world history. For example, fears that the raised sections of pipeline might interfere with caribou movements, delaying their arrival at coastal breeding grounds, were addressed by specially designed animal crossings.

The pipeline is a central feature of Alaska's landscape but remains controversial through its connection with the most sensitive environmental issue in America today: the oil industry's campaign to penetrate the Arctic National Wildlife Refuge.

Peter Coates

Further Reading

Berry, M. C. (1975). *The Alaskan Pipeline: The politics of oil and Native land claims.* Bloomington: Indiana University Press.

Coates, P. (1993). *The Trans-Alaska Pipeline controversy.* Fairbanks: University of Alaska Press.

Coates, P. (1995). The crude and the pure: Oil and environmental politics in Alaska. In R. Lowitt (Ed.), *Politics in the postwar American West* (pp. 3–21). Norman: University of Oklahoma Press.

Strohmeyer, J. (1993). *Extreme conditions: Big oil and the transformation of Alaska.* New York: Simon & Schuster.

Worster, D. (1993). *Under western skies: Nature and history in the American West* (pp. 154–224). Oxford, UK: Oxford University Press.

Transport Systems

As early humans began to explore and utilize their environment, their need to move more efficiently across the terrain gave rise to various forms of transport. Activities that used natural resources (or the transfer of goods arising from such use) and demanded transport usually involved agriculture and trade. The first form of transport was, of course, people's own legs, but eventually people began to use animate and inanimate forms of locomotive power such as slaves, horses, rafts, canoes, ships, trains, cars, and airplanes.

Water's Role in Early Forms of Transport

Transport systems remained primitive even as human beings advanced during the Neolithic period (8000–5500 BCE) and entered into the first "urban revolution" by creating the first cities because of their abilities to produce and trade surplus food and luxury items. Most of the early societies during this time relied on simple water transport systems to move their trade items from trade center to trade center. Simple rafts (which were sometimes modified using skins), large high-rimmed baskets, and dugout canoes were the primary water transport systems used by the Mesopotamians. Early civilizations worked with natural resources of the environment in the employment of their transport systems. Historian of technology R. J. Forbes points out that the Mesopotamians "had learned to avail themselves of the propulsive power of the wind, and their little wooden ships circled Arabia and penetrated the Red Sea, where rock pictures show them to have had square sails. Such ships later inspired the Phoenician ship-builders and became the prototype of the Aegean galley" (Krantzberg & Pursell 1967, 23). Egyptian water transport systems along the Nile River during this period used primarily rafts, canoes, and eventually wooden boats, which were initially made of reeds because of the scarcity of timber.

The heavy reliance on water transport systems had severe ecological impacts on societies (especially maritime societies) for thousands of years because the building of boats with wood caused massive deforestation across the world. This deforestation had already started in early societies such as Greece and Mesopotamia. Environmental scholar Franz J. Broswimmer points out that the militaristic culture of ancient Greece, which was highly dependent on ships, was critical to Greece's ecological decline. According to Broswimmer "the seemingly unending Peloponnesian War between Sparta and Athens consumed large quantities of wood for the construction of warships. The result was the severe deforestation of mainland Greece and Asia Minor. Large areas of countryside were transformed into relatively barren wastes, and there are indications that much-increased soil erosion and flooding resulted" (Broswimmer 2002, 40). Environmental historian J. Donald Hughes has a similar assessment of the causes of ecological decline in ancient Greece but emphasizes that the massive use of wood leading to deforestation was caused not only by military use but also by construction of "merchant ships and other means of transport, and in construction (even marble temples had wooden roof supports)" (Hughes 2001, 63). Greece's heavy reliance on wooden ships caused it to exploit "the resources of the land it could dominate along its frontiers, and its tentacles of trade and economic power reached outward to draw valued materials of many kinds from lands located overseas or across mountain barriers. Places around the Aegean Sea were deforested in response to Athens's demands for fuel and shipbuilding" (Hughes 2001, 65).

This pattern of laying waste to forests to support water transport systems continued across the centuries and across the world even as societies became more urban and industrialized. Hughes points out that demands for shipbuilding (and for fuel) caused England to lose numerous forests, including the famous Sherwood Forest, and to have "proportionately less woodland than any other European country at the beginning of the nineteenth century" (Hughes 2001, 123). By 1864 the last of the oak trees in England's Forest of Dean were used to build ships.

Whales and Water Transport

Water transport systems played a critical role in the near extinction of whales by the commercial whaling industry. Whaling for subsistence began around 3000 BCE, and global whaling began during the first centuries CE in Japan and southeastern Asia. Europeans, specifically the Norwegians and the Basques, however, were the first to engage in commercial whaling around 800 to 1000 CE. Their early commercial whaling was concentrated around the Bay of Biscay on the Atlantic Ocean around 900 CE. This whaling was seasonal and conducted from small boats on which whalers used a harpoon attached to a coiled rope to capture whales. Although these activities were small scale they had severe ecological impact because whaling in this area led to the near extinction of Biscay right whales, forcing the industry to move by the fifteenth century to the

Newfoundland area. Despite this move, by the sixteenth century the Biscay right whales were extinct as a result of the European whaling industry. According to environmental scholar Clive Pointing, by the end of the eighteenth century the European whaling industry had in its employment about ten thousand men and several hundred vessels and was slaughtering 2,000–3,000 right whales every season.

By the seventeenth century the whaling industry had spread to the Americas and reached its height by the mid-nineteenth century. By 1840 U.S. whalers employed more than seven hundred vessels, which operated in the Pacific and occupied every whaling ground from 88°N to 55°S. The overharvesting of whales caused a decline in the industry by the later half of the nineteenth century. These ships made it possible for whalers to stay at sea longer and increased dramatically the number of whales that whalers could hunt and process. Two other technological advances in water transport in the nineteenth century were critical to the extinction of whales: the steam engine (and eventually the internal combustion engine), which let ships travel faster, and the explosive harpoon, which detonated inside the body of a whale. By the first half of the twentieth century technological advances and modifications to whaling ships such as the stern slipway (in 1925) resulted in whaling ships becoming floating whale-processing factories, and this also increased the level of slaughter. The slaughter of twenty-nine thousand blue whales from 1930 to 1931 was directly related to technological changes in the water transport industry. This number grew to an average of forty thousand per year later in the 1930s. Two million large whales were slaughtered between 1946 and 1985 by commercial whaling, and this level of activity was reduced only with the reduction in profit in whaling. The severe ecological impact of technological advances in water transport systems in whaling is reflected by the fact that today there are only about 300 right whales in the North Atlantic and only 250 in the North Pacific. "A species related to the right whale, the bowhead whale, was hunted to extinction in the Atlantic Ocean but still exists in the North Pacific" (Broswimmer 2002, 69).

Land Transport Systems

Land transport for thousands of years was confined to what humans or their domesticated animals could carry, and this was usually limited to short-distance transport. Humans carried other humans, usually as status symbols, in rickshaws, sedan chairs, and palanquins (enclosed litters borne on the shoulders of people by means of poles). Humans and beasts of burden in earlier societies (and even today in less-developed countries) were used to draw carts and to take their loads to nearby bodies of water for long-distance transport. This changed slightly around 1000 BCE with the domestication of the camel, which allowed long-distance travel across the hostile environment of deserts and made possible shortened trade routes between Mesopotamia, Egypt, and Palestine.

Domestication of the horse, however, had the greatest impact on the environment of any land transport system besides the automobile. The horse was domesticated around 4000 BCE in Ukraine and may have been instrumental in the transfer of the Indo-European languages throughout the Western Hemisphere (these languages replaced all others in this area with the exception of Basque).

Horses as Military Transport Systems

The initial value of horses as a form of transport for humans was in war. Horses were pivotal in the emergence of the war chariot and the cavalry as effective tools of war. Environmental scholar Jared Diamond points out that Eurasia's horses' "military role made them the jeeps and Sherman tanks of ancient warfare on that continent" (Diamond 1997, 91). Horses as war transports allowed Spanish explorers Hernan Cortes and Francisco Pizarro to overthrow Aztec and Inca Empires with only a small band of men. After people learned how to optimize the use of horse power with

Men and women travel by bicycle on a downtown street in Shanghai, China, in August 2002. Bicycle travel in China is becoming more difficult due to the rapid increase in the use of automobiles. COURTESY KAREN CHRISTENSEN.

the use of yokes, horses ushered in a revolution in warfare technology. Warfare in the Near East, the Mediterranean, and China changed radically after the invention of horse-drawn battle chariots around 1800 BCE. Horses as transportation facilitated the conquest of horseless Egypt by the Hyksos in 1674 BCE. By 1500 BCE the Egyptians adopted the horse-drawn war chariot.

The conquests of Asia and Russia were due in large part to horse transport used by the Mongols in the thirteenth and fourteenth centuries. These conquests were part of a longer history that began with the Huns' terrorization of the Roman Empire. The Huns' attacks were made possible by horsemen who could travel long distances and maneuver difficult terrain after the invention of saddles and stirrups. By 1130 CE England bred specialized warhorses that were used for transport of supplies and for military assault. By the fourteenth century armies employed around three thousand to five thousand horses. The critical use of horses for military purposes peaked in the eighteenth and nineteenth centuries but continued into the twentieth century. Not until World War I were horses replaced by tanks and trucks as the fastest form of war transport; despite this fact they continued to be used in war. The British army used 1.2 million horses in World War I, and in World War II the German army used twice as many horses as it did in World War I (2.7 million, despite the fact that the army had a mechanized Panzer armored division).

Diamond also makes the point that horses were part of the original germ warfare used by people. He asserts: "Of equal importance in wars of conquest were the germs that evolved in the human societies with domestic animals. Infectious diseases like smallpox, measles, and flu arose as specialized germs of humans, derived by mutations of ancestral germs that had infected animals" (Diamond 1997, 92). The germs from domesticated animals, such as the horse, initially claimed many lives among the humans who possessed them. Over time the human communities that domesticated these animals developed some immunity to the germs; however, when people of these communities came into contact with their military opponents, who had had no previous exposure to the germs, epidemics resulted, killing up to 99 percent of the opponents. The extinction or near extinction of indigenous populations by European conquest and occupation of lands around the world was greatly facilitated by the use of the horse as a military transport. For example, in the fifteenth century the Hispaniola native population declined from 8 million to zero after the European invasion be-

ginning with Columbus (1492 to 1535); one-quarter of the population of Fiji was lost to measles after one of its chiefs returned from European-occupied Australia in 1875; and the native Hawaiian population, after European occupation, was decimated from 500,000 to 84,000 between 1779 and 1853.

Horses as Civilian Transport Systems

Lynn White, historian of technology, points out that improvements in horse transport technologies such as the harness (along with the heavy plow, open fields, and three-field rotation) were critical to the agricultural revolution in northern Europe that led to a new agrarian system between the sixth and ninth centuries. This new agricultural system produced food surpluses that led to a steady population increase well into the thirteenth century. The harness appeared around 800 CE in the Carolingian realm (areas under the rule of Charlemagne [742–814], the king of Franks and the Emperor of the Holy Roman Empire). The harness consisted of a rigid padded collar that rested on the horse's shoulders and permitted the horse to breathe. It also had lateral traces or shafts placed to make traction effective. As White points out, "With this new harness a team of horses could pull four or five times the load they could draw with a yoke harness. Hitherto the horse had been valued for its speed; the new harness made horse power available in conjunction with speed" (Krantzberg & Pursell 1967, 74). The harness allowed people to use the horse for hauling as well as plowing; however, other technological advances, such as nailed horseshoes (invented simultaneously around 890 CE in Siberia, Byzantium, and Germany) and the whiffletree (a pivoted swinging bar to which the traces of a harness are fastened and by which a vehicle or implement is drawn) (eleventh century CE), had to emerge before the horse could be used to haul heavy loads and people. By the twelfth century the *longa caretta* (large cart), the first horse-drawn cart that could transport heavy loads of people or goods, was invented. Eventually road transport employing horses was more efficient, more comfortable, and faster with the development first of the springed and eventually the suspended carriage around the fourteenth century. Because of these advances in horse transport technology, horses began to steadily replace oxen as haulers in the fifteenth and sixteenth centuries and would become the dominant form of land transport for at least three more centuries.

The decline of horses as the dominant form of land transport was not threatened by the introduction of railways, although railways did cause a decline in stagecoach use. Clive Pointing asserts: "By generating more traffic, railways actually increased the demand for horses and their numbers reached a peak in both Europe and North America at the end of the nineteenth century" (Pointing 1991, 273). This assertion is supported by the dramatic increase in the number of privately owned carriages during this time in Great Britain (which had the largest railway system in the world). Carriage ownership increased from 15,000 in 1810 to 40,000 in 1840 to 120,000 in 1870. Horses used for both private and business purposes in towns increased from 350,000 in 1830 to 1.2 million; by 1913, 88 percent of London's traffic goods were carried by horses. The six-thousand-year dominance of the horse as the main form of land transport continued in the nineteenth century despite German engineer Nikolaus Otto's invention of the gas engine in 1866 and the use of steam-powered railroads for several decades. The Otto engine was weak and awkward (over 2.1 meters tall) and could not compete with the horse as an alternative land transport system. The dominance of the horse is also reflected in its worldwide numbers at the turn of the twentieth century: 3.5 million horses in Britain and France and 20–30 million in the United States. That many horses exacted a commensurate environmental cost. By 1900 Great Britain's horses consumed around 3.6 million metric tons of oats and hay each year. This consumption level required the use of 6 million hectares of land, and in the United States crops for horse feed took up about 36 million hectares of land. The only way Great Britain could sustain its horse population by 1900 was to use cheap imports because it also had to feed its human population.

The ecological costs of using horses for transport were reflected in the diseases caused by the huge volume of waste that horses generated. A large percentage of pollution in cities before industrialization was caused by the feces and urine of horses. Dried horse droppings produced noxious dust particles, and the droppings that didn't dry attracted flies, which helped transfer diseases to humans. Cities employed street sweepers to remove wastes so that humans could move about more freely. The majority of horse manure was not recycled by farms and usually rotted in the streets, eventually entering sewers and poisoning natural water resources and contributing to outbreaks of typhoid fever. The streets of Britain had 2.7 million metric tons of rotting manure in 1830, and by 1900 this amount had increased to 9 million metric tons. The large-scale use of horses for transport also resulted in

their inhumane treatment; their life span was reduced to two years in urban areas. Horses died on the streets of London, New York, and Chicago from overuse and maltreatment. By 1900 New York was clearing fifteen thousand dead horses per year from its streets, and by 1912 Chicago was clearing ten thousand per year. Historian Donald Miller states that "in Rochester, New York, health officials estimated that the fifteen thousand horses on the city's streets in 1900 produced enough organic waste a year to create a one-acre-wide, 175 foot high mountain of manure capable of breeding 16 billion flies" (Miller 1997, 267).

Motor Vehicles

Motor vehicles were slow to replace the horse as transport. Horse-drawn street railways were the first to be replaced by motor transport (specifically electric railways), and they became obsolete by 1888. The rapid elimination of horses in this form of transport is reflected by the fact that investment in horse railway systems declined from $150 million in 1882 to less than $2 million in 1902. Historian of technology Harold I. Sharlin points out that the conversion to electricity had a significant environmental impact on cities because "The electric street railway eliminated the huge stables, the army of stablemen, the relay station, and the danger from costly horse diseases" (Krantzberg & Pursell 1967, 574). The electric railway systems and their infrastructure demands, however, could not keep up with the demands of urban sprawl as cities continued to grow. These demands eventually were met by an individualized form of motor transport, the mass-produced automobile. However, even with technological innovations automobiles were expensive for the average civilian to buy in 1905. They would replace the horse as a civilian transport system only after the U. S. military and military lobbyists launched a campaign to convince civilians to replace horses with cars after World War I. As environmental historian John McNeill points out, the spread of the car worldwide occurred in three stages. The first stage occurred in the United States during the 1920s after assembly line technology made cars more affordable to the average consumer; the second stage occurred in western Europe between 1950 and 1975; the third stage occurred in eastern Asia (led by Japan) from 1960 until today. In 1910 there were fewer than 1 million cars worldwide, but this number grew, according to McNeill, to "about 50 million in 1930, surpassed 100 million by 1955 and 500 million by 1985. In 1995 the world tallied

777 million cars, trucks, and motorbikes" (McNeill 2000, 60).

By the 1940s people around the world in industrialized cities such as Los Angeles lodged public complaints about the environmental nuisances created by cars and trucks. By the mid-1940s public officials in Los Angeles began to suspect a connection between cars and environmental health problems. They observed that most citizen complaints about eye irritations stemming from smog came from areas where there was a high density of automobile traffic. The fact that cars are the principal cause of smog was not established until the late 1940s by the Dutch-born American biochemist Dr. Arie Haagen-Smit. Dr. Haagen-Smit's experiments revolving around the chemistry of Los Angeles air showed that it contained organic peroxides that could come only from petroleum. He eventually demonstrated that the formation of cloud pollution identical to Los Angeles smog came from the combination of gasoline vapors and ozone. As historian Scott Hamilton Dewey points out, Haagen-Smit and his colleague Dr. Frits Went showed that the eye tearing and stinging (lachrymation) in the Los Angeles area were caused by peroxyacetl nitrate (PAN), which is a "by-product of the reaction of unburned gasoline hydrocarbons with nitrogen dioxide in the presence of sunlight" (Dewey 2000, 48). Public health problems stemming from smog occurred across the world. As late as 1987, two thousand people in Athens, Greece, died from smog after car ownership rose after 1975, causing ozone levels in the late 1980s to double from levels of the period between 1900 and 1940. Likewise, Mexico, especially Mexico City, suffered severe environmental consequences from the adoption of cars as the primary form of land transport. The number of cars in Mexico City increased from 100,000 in 1950 to 2 million in 1980 and exceeded 4 million by 1994. McNeill points out that car pollution became so severe that at one point "in 1985, birds fell out of the sky in mid-flight onto the Zocalo, Mexico City's great plaza" (McNeill 2000, 78).

In addition, cars polluted the air with lead emissions and combustion by-products such as carbon monoxide and carbon dioxide (which accounted for one-fifth of the total amount added to the atmosphere). Many scientists believe that these emissions have contributed to the greenhouse effect (warming of the surface and lower atmosphere of the Earth caused by conversion of solar radiation into heat) and global warming.

Suburban sprawl and its environmental consequences were tied to the emergence of the car as the dominant form of land transport. Donald Miller states that "with the coming of the automobile, urban transportation corridors became escape ways from the city, not linkages, as they had briefly been, between two separate but interpenetrating social worlds . . . giving rise to the formless Spread City of highways and strip malls" (Miller 1997, 293–294). This sprawl had many environmental consequences, particularly on human, ecological, and economic resources. From an ecological point the use of cars demanded infrastructural support in the form of roads, fueling stations, and parking spaces. Environmental historian J. Donald Hughes asserts that the population patterns of the rapidly expanding suburbia were such that "the density of residence was less than nearer the centers (urban), so that they occupied proportionately more land. Roads, parking lots, and fuel supply facilities began to use more space in the cities than residences, other businesses and green space" (Hughes 2001, 142). A vast amount of some of the richest agricultural land in cities was eventually covered by asphalt and concrete to provide the infrastructure requirements demanded by motorized transport systems.

Suburban sprawl also caused tremendous population losses in cities, leading to the loss of both public and private services for the poor who remained behind. This remaining population was responsible for contributing to the development of marginalized and sometimes unsustainable communities. By the 1960s Britain's inner cities had lost 500,000 jobs. New York City is an example of a major city whose sustainability was harmed by suburban sprawl. New York City lost 11 percent of its employment between 1969 and 1975. By the early 1990s, 25 percent of the city's population was below the poverty line, 90,000 people were homeless, and 500,000 were drug addicts. Cities became plagued with crime and urban decay as they continued to lose populations and economic resources to suburbia and exurbia (a region that lies outside a city and usually beyond its suburbs). They also became the locus of the most severe sources of pollution because polluting industries initially had located in cities because of their original natural resources (e.g., water and land). The rise of environmental inequalities is also tied to motorized transport because only some of the workers (those who could afford transportation) and most of the employers were able to flee the cities and gain access to cleaner green spaces in suburbia. The advent of motorized transport, especially the car, is therefore critical to understanding how the brunt of environmental health effects from industrial pollution would be borne disproportionately by poor and minority communities.

Transport systems, although critical to the rise of civilizations, have carried significant environmental costs for global ecosystems for many millennia. From weapons of war to inadvertent weapons of ecological destruction, technologies of transportation have allowed humans to dominate themselves and their environment in ways unforeseen by their inventors. Societies across the world and across the centuries, however, have made efforts through regulation and technological innovation to mitigate the costs of transport systems.

Sylvia Hood Washington

Further Reading

Broswimmer, F. J. (2002). *Ecocide: A short history of the mass extinction of species.* London: Pluto Press.

Dewey, S. H. (2000). *Don't breathe the air: Air pollution and U.S. environmental politics, 1945–1970.* College Station: Texas A&M University Press.

Diamond, J. (1997). *Guns, germs and steel: The fates of human societies.* New York: W. W. Norton.

Drachman, A. G. (1967). The classical civilizations. In M. Krantzberg & C. Pursell Jr. (Eds.), *Technology and Western civilization. Vol. 1.* (pp. 47–65). New York: Oxford University Press.

Forbes, R. J. (1967). The beginnings of technology and man. In M. Krantzberg & C. Pursell Jr. (Eds.), *Technology and Western civilization. Vol. 1.* (pp. 26–46). New York: Oxford University Press.

Forbes, R. J. (1967). Mesopotamia and Egyptian technology. In M. Krantzberg & C. Pursell Jr. (Eds.), *Technology and Western civilization. Vol. 1.* (pp. 11–25). New York: Oxford University Press.

Goudie, A. (2000). *The human impact on the natural environment* (5th ed.). Cambridge, MA: MIT Press.

Hughes, J. D. (2001). *An environmental history of the world: Humankind's changing role in the community of life.* New York: Routledge.

Hughes, J. D. (Ed.). (2000). *The face of the Earth: Environment and world history.* Armonk, NY: M. E. Sharpe.

Krantzberg, M., & Pursell, C., Jr. (1967). The importance of technology in human affairs. In M. Krantzberg & C. Pursell Jr. (Eds.), *Technology and Western civilization. Vol. 1.* (pp. 3–10). New York: Oxford University Press.

Krantzberg, M., & Pursell, C., Jr. (Eds.). (1967). *Technology and Western civilization. Vol. 1.* New York: Oxford University Press.

McNeill, J. R. (2000). *Something new under the sun: An environmental history of the twentieth-century world.* New York: W. W. Norton.

Melosi, M. V. (2000). *Sanitary city: Urban infrastructure in America from colonial times to present.* Baltimore: Johns Hopkins University Press.

Merchant, C. (1980). *The death of nature: Women, ecology and the scientific revolution.* San Francisco: Harper & Row.

Merchant, C. (1992). *Radical ecology: The search for a livable world.* New York: Routledge.

Miller, D. L. (1997). *City of the century, the epic of Chicago and the making of America.* New York: Simon and Schuster.

Pointing, C. (1991). *A green history of the world: The environment and the collapse of great civilizations.* New York: St. Martin's Press.

Pyne, S. J. (1995). *World fire: The culture of fire and earth.* New York: Holt.

Pyne, S. J. (2001). *Fire, a brief history.* Seattle: University of Washington Press.

Simmons, I. G. (1989). *Changing the face of the Earth: Culture, environment and history.* Oxford, UK: Blackwell.

Sponsel, L., Headland, T. N., & Bailey, R. C. (Eds.). (1996). *Tropical deforestation: The human dimension.* New York: Columbia University Press.

Williams, T. I. (1982). *A short history of the twentieth-century technology, c. 1900–c. 1950.* New York: Oxford University Press.

Worster, D. (1977). *Nature's economy: A history of ecological ideas.* San Francisco: Sierra Club Books.

Worster, D. (Ed.). (1988). *The ends of the Earth: Perspectives of modern environmental history.* Cambridge, UK: Cambridge University Press.

Trees *See* Dutch Elm Disease; Eucalyptus; Redwoods; Wood

Tundra

Tundra is a biome (a regional-scale unit of the biosphere defined by specific flora, fauna, and climate) characterized by short-stature vegetation and cold temperatures. The word *tundra* is derived from the Finnish *tunturia,* meaning "treeless plain" or "open barrens," and refers to the lack of trees in this biome. Tundra consists of two types: arctic tundra—common in the circumpolar north—and alpine tundra that occurs on high-elevation temperate and tropical mountains.

Geography

Arctic tundra comprises about 25 million square kilometers, largely in North America, Europe, and Asia. Alpine tundra comprises about 9.5 million square kilometers in the Northern Hemisphere, primarily in central Asia and western North America, and about 1 million square kilometers in the Southern Hemisphere, including mountainous regions of South America, eastern Africa, Indonesia, and New Zealand. The northern limit of Arctic tundra occurs in Greenland at 83.5°N. Canada's cold continental climate allows tundra to reach a southern limit along Hudson Bay at about 55°N. Arctic tundra can be divided at 72–73°N into two climatic and vegetation zones: northern high Arctic tundra and southern low Arctic tundra. In Antarctica extensive ice sheets have limited development of tundra-like vegetation to small areas of the Antarctic Peninsula.

Climate

Climate details vary for Arctic and alpine tundra, but low temperatures and short growing seasons are typical. In Arctic tundra, temperature during the growing season is usually less than 10°C; the growing season ranges from fifty to ninety days. Minimum temperatures during winter can exceed −50°C. The growing season for temperate alpine tundra ranges from fifty to ninety days to year around in the tropics. Day length is a key difference between Arctic and alpine tundra environments. During the year, day length ranges from zero to twenty-four hours and from four to twenty-two hours in high and low Arctic tundra, respectively, and from six to twenty hours and from ten to fourteen hours in temperate and tropical alpine tundra, respectively. Day lengths are shorter during the growing season in alpine tundra than in Arctic tundra. Intense radiation during the day and rapid heat loss during the night—intensified by thin alpine air—cause daily temperatures to fluctuate greatly in alpine tundra. Frost, lacking in Arctic tundra during the growing season, is common in temperate alpine tundra and occurs nightly in tropical alpine tundra.

Cold, dry continental air masses dominate Arctic tundra during most of the year. Moist air enters the region in summer when sea ice begins to melt. Annual precipitation in Arctic tundra ranges from 10 to 50 centimeters a year but is generally less than 25 centimeters a year, with 60 percent falling as snow. High Arctic tundra, often classified as polar desert, receives less than 10 centimeters of precipitation a year. Annual precipitation for alpine tundra ranges between 100 and 200 centimeters a year. Despite low precipitation, Arctic tundra is moist during the growing season; ponds, lakes, and bogs are common. Cool summer temperatures lower evaporation, and low topographic relief and restrictive permafrost minimize runoff and soil drainage, respectively. Alpine tundra soils are drier during the growing season than Arctic tundra soils because drainage is greater, and steep slopes increase runoff.

Soils

Arctic tundra soils include two orders—histosols and entisols—within the Tundra Great Soils Group (Great Soil Groups include major soil types of a specific terrain and vegetation). Histosols are wet organic soils. Poor drainage slows decomposition and creates anoxic (oxygen-poor) conditions; thus histosols consist of a layer of muck or peat overlaying a dense, strongly gleyed mineral horizon (a horizon with blue or grey deposits created by the reduction of iron to ferrous compounds under anoxic conditions). Entisols—young soils with little soil profile development—are mixed by annual freezing and thawing. The topsoil—talik—is brown, coarse-textured, and ranges from 15 to 60 centimeters in depth. A major characteristic of Arctic tundra is permafrost—permanently frozen ground hundreds of meters thick and a few decimeters from the soil surface. Permafrost restricts soil drainage and root growth but provides a summer water source in dry soils when its upper surface melts. Alpine tundra soils are diverse in origin; most are coarse textured and of two orders—entisols and inceptisols. Entisols occur on ridges where erosion is common; inceptisols—mineral soils just beginning to develop a distinct soil profile—have a well-developed organic layer and occur on gentle slopes. Permafrost may be present at high elevations in northern latitudes.

Tundra soils are dynamic and unstable; cryoplanation (the molding of a landscape by frost action) dominates landscape processes. Solifluction (the down-slope movement of saturated soil) is common, especially over permafrost. Freeze/thaw cycles produce patterned ground such as symmetrical frost polygons, a characteristic feature of Arctic tundra. Patterned ground forms when fine, saturated soil materials freeze and expand, then thaw and contract. Coarse materials are pushed up and outward by this action, forming patterned surfaces.

Flora and Fauna

The flora of Arctic tundra, geologically young and not particularly diverse, first appeared during the late Tertiary period (c. 3–4 million years ago). Many Arctic tundra plants, circumpolar in distribution, also occur in northern alpine tundra. Grasses, sedges, dwarf shrubs, and mosses are characteristic plants of Arctic and alpine tundra; herbaceous perennial species are dominant. Short, cushion-like or rosette growth forms are common in tundra plants. Low stature allows plants to escape abrasion by windborne snow and ice and increases the probability of cover by sheltering snow during winter. Net primary productivity is low, with biomass (the amount of living matter) concentrated below ground in roots.

Most animals of Arctic tundra are circumpolar in distribution. Herbivores are common and include caribou or reindeer (*Rangifera tarandus*), musk oxen (*Ovibos moschatus*), and Arctic hare (*Lepus arcticus*). The dominant herbivore of Arctic tundra is the lemming (*Lemmus species*), a small rodent that undergoes cyclic peaks of abundance. Important predators include Arctic wolf (*Canis lupus*), Arctic fox (*Alopex lagopus*), and snowy owl (*Nyctea scandiaca*). Many migratory bird species nest in Arctic tundra during summer, such as Arctic tern (*Sterna macrura*), plover, and sandpiper, but year-round residents, like ptarmigan (*Lagopus mutus*), are few. Insects are abundant in summer, particularly blood-feeding mosquitoes, blackflies, and deer flies. Few animals are characteristic of alpine tundra. These include herbivores such as pika (*Ochotoma princeps*, a mammal related to rabbits), bighorn sheep (*Ovis canadensis*), and mountain goat (*Oreamnos americanus*) in western North America, chamois (*Rupricapra rupricapra*) and moufflon (*Ovis aries*) in Europe, and argali sheep (*Ovis ammon*) and tahr goat (*Hemitragus jemlahicus*) in Asia.

Human Influences

Tundra is a fragile biome. Until recently human impacts on Arctic and alpine tundra have been minimal. Indigenous Arctic peoples—like North America's hunter-gatherer Inuit and northern Europe's reindeer-herding Sami—traditionally maintained low-density populations and were seminomadic, spreading their impacts across the landscape. Alpine tundra is used for grazing in many regions; intense grazing, especially by sheep, reduces vegetation and increases erosion.

Mineral extraction, especially oil drilling, is a threat to Arctic tundra. Tundra recovers slowly from oil spills and road building: Impacts may persist for decades. Atmospheric deposition of pollutants from industrial nations, global fallout, and fallout from the Chernobyl nuclear accident in 1986 have caused accumulation of toxins and radioactivity in tundra soils, animals, and humans. Perhaps the greatest threat to tundra is global warming, which could increase seasonal temperatures and alter precipitation patterns, disrupting the climatic regimen that defines the structure and function of the tundra biome.

Charles E. Williams

Further Reading

Archibold, O. Q. (1995). *Ecology of world vegetation*. New York: Chapman and Hall.

Bailey, R. G. (1998). *Ecoregions: The ecosystem geography of the oceans and continents*. New York: Springer-Verlag.

Barbour, M. G., Burk, J. H., Pitts, W. D., Gilliam, F. S., & Schwartz, M. W. (1999). *Terrestrial plant ecology*. Menlo Park, CA: Benjamin/Cummings.

Flaherty, T. H., Jr. (Ed.). (1985). *Grasslands and tundra*. Alexandria, VA: Time-Life Books.

Lopez, B. (1986). *Arctic dreams: Imagination and desire in a northern landscape*. New York: Scribner.

Marchand, P. J. (2001). Arctic fires. *Natural History* 110 (5), 72–74.

Mohlenbrock, R.H. (2000). Excursion to the Arctic Circle. *Natural History* 109(6), 20–22.

Mulvaney, K. (2001). *At the ends of the Earth: A history of the polar regions*. Washington, DC: Island Press.

Smith, R. L., & Smith, T. M. (2001). *Ecology and field biology* (6th ed.). San Francisco: Benjamin/Cummings.

Vankat, J. L. (1979). *The natural vegetation of North America*. New York: John Wiley and Sons.

Zwinger, A. H., & Willard, B. E. (1972). *Land above the trees: A guide to American alpine tundra*. New York: Harper and Row.

Turkey *See* Wild Turkey

Turtle *See* Sea Turtle

Ukraine

(2000 est. pop. 49.7 million)

Ukraine is an independent nation in eastern Europe. Formerly a member nation of the Soviet Union, it is now a member of the Commonwealth of Independent States. Ukraine is situated in the center of Europe and shares borders with Poland, Slovakia, Hungary, Romania, Moldavia, Russia, and Belarus. It is bordered by the Black and Azov Seas on the south. Ukraine encompasses 603,700 square kilometers and administratively is divided into twenty-four regions, one autonomous republic (Crimea), and two urban centers (Kiev and Sevastopol).

About 73 percent of the population is Ukrainian and 21.2 percent Russian. The remainder is divided among 110 ethnic groups such as Jews, Belarusans, Moldavans, Bulgarians, Poles, Greeks, Hungarians, Crimean Tatars, Armenians, Germans, and Gypsies. Ukrainian is the official language and Christian Orthodoxy the dominant religion.

About 95 percent of the Ukraine correlates with east European flatland, of which about 70 percent is lowlands. Ukraine is divided by its main river, the Dnipro, into two sections: Right Bank Ukraine (Volyns'ko-Podil's'ka highland, eastern Carpathy, Polyssia) and Left Bank Ukraine (Dnipro lowland, Donets'ka highland). The Black Sea lowland is situated at the south. The two major mountain ranges are the Crimea Mountains and the Carpathians (the highest point in Ukraine is Mount Goverla at 2,061 meters). The most important rivers are the Dnipro, Pivdenny Bug, Dniester, and Danube (all of which empty into the Black Sea) and

their tributaries, including the Psel, Goryn, Desna, and Ingulets. Natural lakes are concentrated in Ukrainian Polyssia and in the lower Danube region; along the Black Sea coast there are numerous semisalt estuaries. *Chernozem* (rich humus) is the most widespread soil type.

Ukraine has more than thirty thousand natural floral species and about forty-five thousand natural faunal species. The four main geographical zones are forest (average afforestation level is 14 percent; mixed forests dominate), mixed forest-steppe, steppe (arid and semiarid, about 40 percent of the territory of Ukraine), and the Crimea Mountain zone.

The climate is moderate, warm, and continental, at the southern part of Crimea littoral-subtropical one. Average temperatures in January are $-°$ C in northeastern Ukraine and 4° C in Crimea; in July, 17° C in northwestern Ukraine and 23° C in southern Ukraine. Average annual precipitation is 300–500 millimeters in the Black and Azov Seas region, 600–700 millimeters in northeastern Ukraine, 1,000–1,200 millimeters in the Crimea Mountains, and more than 1,500 millimeters in the Carpathians.

Combustible mineral resources (hard coal, oil, natural gas), metals (iron, manganese, uranium, titanium, mercury), ores, and nonmetallic mineral sources (graphite, fireclays, rock salt, building materials) create a natural resource base and determine the direction of international trade and national production development.

Environmentally, Ukraine is known for the 1986 Chernobyl nuclear power station accident, which contaminated 21 percent of the territory of Ukraine as well as neighboring nations with cesium isotopes. Since the

АСКАНІЯ-НОВА — Зоологическій садъ, Ф. Э. Фальцъ-Фейнъ.
ASKANIA-NOVA — Zoologischer Garten von F. E. Falz-Fein.

The Askania-Nova Nature Reserve. COURTESY DOUG WEINER.

end of the 1990s the Danube estuary problem has become acute. Issues of natural environment protection, water pollution, and air pollution are discussed by representatives of the Ukrainian Ecological Association "Green Light" and by members of Ukrainian Green Party. The Green Party was represented in the Ukrainian Parliament after the elections of 1998; it failed to gain seats in the 2002 elections. Since independence in 1991 the problem of insufficient energy sources has become acute because of restrictions on the generation of nuclear power as well as external relations with former Soviet Union republics.

Olena V. Smyntyna

Further Reading

Naulko, V. I. (1998). *Khto i vidkoly zhive v Ukrayini* [Who and since what time lives in Ukraine]. Kyiv: Golovna Spezializovana Redakcia Literatury Movamy Natzionalnyh Menshin.

Popov, V. P. (Ed.). (1968). *Fiziko-geographicheskoye rayonirovanie Ukrainskoi SSR* [Natural geographic demarcation of Ukraine SSR]. Kiev, Ukraine: Naukova Dumka.

Smoliy, V. A. (Ed.). (1998). *Ukraina kriz' viky* [Ukraine throughout the centuries]. Kyiv: Alternativy.

United Kingdom and Ireland

(2000 est. pop. 62 million)

The conglomeration of islands on the northwestern periphery of the continent of Europe, known collectively as the United Kingdom and Ireland, has wielded a disproportionate influence over the human history of the planet. As a result, one could argue that it has wielded a disproportionate influence over the environmental history of the planet as well. The British Empire, which once boasted control over one-fifth of the Earth's land surface, helped to stimulate, directly or indirectly, the exploitation of natural resources on an unprecedented global scale. This in turn led to industrialization, a process that has fundamentally altered the ability of humans to harness the Earth's resources and caused the removal of most of the inhabitants of these islands from a rural, predominantly agricultural environment into an urban, industrialized one. At the same time, that rural environment—or perceptions of what it had once been—became associated with a nostalgic sense of identity that partly informs contemporary environmentalism within the United Kingdom. This view of the past also influences such diverse aspects of public policy as planning, forestry, recreation, and the allocation of resources to agriculture.

Raw Materials

If the United Kingdom and Ireland drifted across the Atlantic and ended up off the eastern coast of North America, the northernmost limit of these islands (Shetland) would be on a level with Labrador and the southernmost limit (Isles of Scilly) with Newfoundland. Fortunately, however, most of the islands share the temperate climate of the European mainland and also benefit from the warming effects of the North Atlantic drift (the warm ocean current flowing from Northwest Mexico towards northwest Europe under the influence of prevailing winds), which allows even palm trees to grow on the northwest coast of Scotland.

Within the main islands of the United Kingdom and Ireland is a significant east-west divide in terms of rainfall. The west endures increasing amounts of warm, wet weather throughout the year, perhaps as a result of global warming, whereas the east can struggle with periods of drought in summer. Some parts of the country, particularly the mountainous regions of Scotland, northern England, Wales, and Ireland, are at the limits of cereal cultivation. However, they are not inherently marginal, given that the ability to maintain large numbers of animals, the vagaries of climate change, the existence of significant mineral resources, and participation in international trade over the last millennia have all contributed to a complex and varied history.

In terms of resources in general, the mountains, plains, rivers and seas of the United Kingdom and Ireland have played host to a plethora of valuable—and exploitable—assets, from gold to salt to herring to sheep to oil and much in between. Most of the human history of the United Kingdom and Ireland encompasses determined efforts to extract and utilize these resources, which may have seemed limitless at one time. Unfortunately, this has not proved to be the case. However, having recently recognized the human con-

tribution to the degradation of these resources, sometimes to the point of extinction, parts of the United Kingdom are finally making strenuous efforts to harness the power of renewable resources. These include technology related to both wind and wave power, which these areas have in abundance.

As ever, the underlying geological structure determines the soil type, which in turn affects the vegetation cover and hence the animal and bird species that live there. As with climatic conditions, there is considerable variation across the main islands of the United Kingdom and Ireland. These essential ecological conditions have continually interacted with the cultural attributes of the human populations who live within them to create the environmental histories of these islands.

The precise nature of what happened in the past is never either predictable or uniform: comparable environmental conditions do not produce the same histories because groups of humans behave differently within them. This is in part a result of the fact that the networks of human interaction throughout most of the earliest consistent period of historical knowledge (since the last ice age, about ten thousand years ago) have extended far beyond the immediate surroundings of the individual groups. The ability of humans to transfer and adapt knowledge has meant that humans have also had a long-standing ability to divert nature to their own ends well beyond their numeric strength. However, despite the rhetoric of the medieval Western Christian church in particular, which asserted that humans have dominion over nature, much of this human history has also been characterized by a long-standing struggle against indifferent environmental conditions.

A traditional small English garden outside a seventeenth century stone farmhouse near Bath, England, in 1994. COURTESY KAREN CHRISTENSEN.

From Tundra to Farming

The great glaciers that pressed down on the landmasses of northern Europe during the last ice age, gouging out many of the landforms still evident today, also wiped out most of the traces of human history prior to that date. There are only a few such traces in the United Kingdom and Ireland, all in the east of England. In the first millennia after the retreat of the ice, environmental conditions dictated the course of history, even after the arrival of the first humans. Temperatures continued to rise, causing the replacement of the tundra landscape of boulders, light soils, and scrubby plants such as juniper with warmth-loving trees. Birch arrived first (around 8000 BCE), followed by Scotch pine, to be joined in turn by oak and other deciduous (leaf-dropping) trees.

This was a gradual process, and there were also environmental limits to the changes taking place. Deciduous forest did not spread beyond the highland line (a geological fault cutting across Scotland from the southwest to the northeast and effectively dividing the country into a mountainous highland region to the northwest and lowland plains to the southeast of it). Equally, with the expansion of the deciduous trees, pine and birch were largely restricted to north of the highland line. However, by 7000 BCE most of the United Kingdom and Ireland was covered in forest of one kind or another.

With the arrival of trees, many of the great animals of the tundra, such as reindeer and wild horse, disappeared. The transition from birch and pine to oak forest also provided a better environment for some animals over others, although the fact that different parts of the country had different types of tree cover ensured some diversity. Red and roe deer, wild pig, and beaver were all particularly at home in the oak forests.

These are essentially the environments that the newly arrived human populations found as they spread across the land bridge that attached mainland Britain to Europe until about 6000 BCE. Many settled around the coasts, supplementing the more unreliable hunting of animals with the collection of berries and other vegetation and the extremely healthy fruits of the rivers and seas. The fact that these peoples seem to have operated over comparatively large areas, taking advantage of the products of the changing seasons, indicates that they could not (or would not), as yet, manipulate the environment to any great degree. This would have enabled them to stay closer to somewhere that might now be called "home." However, archaeologists debate whether these early peoples used fire to clear spaces in the trees to attract larger numbers of animals that would thus be easier to kill or whether they just took advantage of natural glades. Given the human capacity to learn and adapt, it is likely that the former developed out of the latter.

But one of the most important innovations in the whole of environmental history was soon to occur. Around 3500 BCE the peoples of these islands became aware of the techniques associated with a rather different way of life. Farming had finally made its way across Europe from the Middle East. Now humans began to have a much more direct impact on the environment, manipulating species to create domesticated cereals and animals, dividing land into field systems and designated areas for animal husbandry, developing permanent settlements, and constructing visible symbols of their existence and relationship with the universe.

First Enclosed Farmland

One of the best examples of the impact of prehistoric human predecessors on the visual appearance of the landscape comes from the Céide (pronounced kayje) Fields in County Mayo in the west of Ireland. They represent the oldest enclosed farmland discovered in the Western world (older than the Egyptian pyramids), built about five thousand years ago. Mosaics of stone walls criss-cross a huge area, dividing it into fields. They would not have looked out of place to the improvers who advocated the enclosure of land in the eighteenth century. This is certainly not the story of a consistent increase in human impact on the environment from the last ice age to modern times.

The move to settle down (which took many millennia) probably had the greatest effect on the forest as large swaths were chopped down to make way for agriculture. Environmental historians in the United Kingdom and Ireland have devoted much attention to woodland history because there is so little forest left, but the blame for much of the reduction must lie at the feet of prehistoric human ancestors, rather than more recent entrepreneurs. Purely environmental factors were still causing change—a decrease in temperatures and an increase in precipitation, for example, may have been responsible, at least in part, for the reduction in tree cover because of the expansion of waterlogged soils, leading to the creation of peat. However, the debate over which was the chicken and which the egg—human action or climate change—rages on.

The increasing evidence for the activities of these prehistoric farmers, particularly the great monuments related to the dead, lets one see how they viewed themselves as part of a bigger picture. The heavens played a key role in their belief systems, perhaps not surprisingly considering that so many sources of difficulty seemed to relate to the skies, whether it was too much or too little rain or an eclipse, which was often viewed as a portent of disaster such as disease. Many tribes also adopted particular animals or birds as symbols of the tribe, and offerings were made to sacred sites, such as bogs and lakes. All this suggests that these early peoples saw themselves as part of the environment that they occupied and were well aware of the need to placate nature, which had the power of life or death.

The great ritual sites of the pre-Christian era also indicate that considerable power was given to those who proved most able to understand, and therefore, to some degree, to control the elements. Nevertheless, one suspects that, for most people, the vagaries of nature were still largely incomprehensible and greatly to be feared. Any innovation that eased life pitted against the environment was most welcome.

Although a hierarchy in society had evolved long before the arrival of the Romans to conquer Britain in 43 CE, the newcomers showed the natives of parts of these islands (mostly England—Ireland, Wales, and most of Scotland were not conquered) just what could be achieved with the centralization of power. The harnessing of the empire's resources, including human slaves, provided wealth for its citizens and the environment in which to develop the technology that brought about the famous bathhouses, aqueducts, road systems, and basic central heating. However, one shouldn't believe everything the Romans said. For example, they blamed their failure to conquer the Caledonians in the north of Britain on an impenetrable Great Wood of Caledon, which experts now believe was more myth than reality. Nevertheless, the Great Wood, or at least its disappearance, is now an icon of Scottish environmentalism, representing all that is bad about the impact of humans on the natural world.

As one empire began to decline, another—technically of a spiritual rather than a secular nature—began to rise. Christianity arrived in Britain in the sixth century CE, taking various routes and various forms. However, it was the reformation of the Roman Catholic version of Christianity from 1000 onward that led to the dominance of the view that humans are masters on Earth, based on Gen. 1:26. The medieval chroniclers of that later period continued to interpret the activities in the skies as portents of disaster or retribution for bad behavior here on Earth, but they had little to say about the environment in general.

Church Innovation

The post–1000 church in the British Isles was also responsible for considerable innovation in agriculture and the exploitation of natural resources generally. The development of the moldboard plow a few centuries earlier had been important because the plow created a furrow in the soil, burying the seed deeper and increasing the impact of arable (suitable for cultivation) production on the environment. The new monastic orders, imported to the United Kingdom and Ireland from Europe after 1100, were determined to employ whatever measures they could think of to make the most of the considerable landholdings that the elites of the United Kingdom and Ireland were keen to give them. Most particularly, they engaged heavily in the production of wool, which supplied the extremely successful cloth manufacturers of the Netherlands. Thousands of sheep were grazed on the hills, and although they were often smaller breeds than their modern successors, the impact of their hungry mouths on the vegetation must have been significant.

By the later Middle Ages, also, the regulation of access to resources, from the rights of the tenantry to take wood, peat, and other essentials of existence to the privilege of the nobility to hunt for deer and game in specially designated areas known as "forests" (which did not explicitly mean trees), was long established. Salt and coal extraction, the mining of metals such as tin and even gold, the harnessing of rivers by means of waterwheels—a whole host of activities attested to the practical abilities of humans to increasingly control the environment. Even the great cathedrals of this period stretched their vast walls upward toward heaven in an apparent attempt to overcome even gravity.

However, disease, affecting humans, animals, and crops, was also a major aspect of the Middle Ages, with plague only one type, devastating though the repeated bouts of it from 1348 onward undoubtedly were. Pollution was already affecting some of the denser populations, especially in London, thanks to the burning of coal. Also, the period before 1300—when the population had expanded well beyond the carrying capacity (the population that an area will support without deterioration) of existing settlements, prompting the conversion to agriculture of "unproductive" land such as woodlands and heaths—had shown the basic effect that demographics had on the course of environmental history.

Throughout the historic period the United Kingdom and Ireland have never been closed systems, totally self-sufficient and completely isolated. Trade brought in luxury and essential goods, as well as ideas. The peoples of these islands were also prone to travel, as well as to accommodate incomers, willingly or unwillingly. However, the early modern period witnessed a new expansion of horizons with the discovery of the New World far to the west. The British Empire was beginning.

At the same time, science was advancing in all directions, challenging religious versions of how the world had come about, how it operated, and where it might be going. This led to the Age of Enlightenment, and British scientists and thinkers were at the forefront of it.

The Goal of Improvement

The drive for rationality, rather than a reliance on traditional assumptions, spilled over into almost every aspect of life, and agriculture was not immune from the microscope. Improvement was the practical expression of enlightenment thinking and involved the application of scientifically established principles to farming. Higher productivity was achieved through fertilizers, primarily manure but also marl, lime, and chalk on acidic soils. New crops, such as turnips and clover, also improved yields.

Like the monastic orders before them, the devotees of improvement understood that, to effect the changes that they believed were absolutely necessary for progress, as much land as possible needed to be brought under their full control. During the eighteenth century this meant common land, which had housed the animals of the peasantry for centuries but which was regarded by landowners as "waste" because they could not do what they liked with it. The process of enclosure, which had begun in England under the direction of individual landowners as early as the sixteenth century, was now sanctioned by Parliament in the eighteenth century as absolute property rights became more clearly enunciated in law. As a result, the open systems of the Middle Ages gave way to the hedged and fenced fields that are more familiar today.

The draining of the fens (low lands), a constant refrain of the history of southeast England, continued, but experiments took place elsewhere, most particu-

larly in the *carse* (river) lands around the river Forth near Stirling, which were transformed from a peat bog into productive arable land. Interestingly, the remnants of this bog at Flanders Moss are now a National Nature Reserve. One era's wasteland is another era's prime ecological conditions.

The process of improvement took place at different times and in slightly different ways in the various parts of the United Kingdom and Ireland. However, in some parts—most notably the western parts of Ireland and the northwestern part of Scotland—improvement was often also associated with a time when the land was unable to meet the basic dietary needs of the expanding population. The famines of the eighteenth and nineteenth centuries caused immense psychological damage to the people involved and their successors. However, more serious investigation is needed before a judgment is made about whether the blame lay with the environment itself or the management of it.

The result of these difficult conditions in both areas was an exodus of people, partly to the growing urban centers of England and lowland Scotland and partly to transatlantic emigration. The places they left behind, often still containing poignant relics of past settlement, are now regarded as some of the best wilderness in the country. However, to the successors of those involved, the peace and quietness of these depopulated areas, so much in demand in today's busy times, stand as an indictment of past policies by both government and landowners. It seems fitting, somehow, that the last wolf in Britain was shot during the eighteenth century.

Industrialization

However, the transformation of Britain did not end with depopulation. The entrepreneurialism that thrived within the empire with its plethora of cheap resources, when combined with scientific and technological innovation, brought about something radically new: industrialization. This is not meant to imply that there had been no industry before. Mining of coal, salt, and tin was already centuries old, and it could be argued that the sheep ranching of the later Middle Ages was industrial in scale, even before the domestic cloth industry, especially in England during the same period, is mentioned.

However, this modern industrialization was different because now, finally, mechanization began to supplant human muscle power. After that had happened, the unending circle of output and consumption encompassing the acquiring and consuming of sufficient food to fuel directly the range of activities that humans needed to engage in to ensure that they produced enough food and so forth was finally broken. Humans had transcended the life sentence, handed out to Adam and Eve when they were forced out of Eden, for most of the population to till the soil. Although humans still had to work, they could now sign up to an ever-increasing range of jobs, develop new skills that differentiated them from others, and, eventually, embrace a new set of activities associated with the concept of leisure time. However, not yet.

The first major industries revolved around textiles, with cotton grown in the colonies—by slaves taken in British ships from Africa—shipped over to the United Kingdom to be worked into cloth. Those who operated the spinning jenny (an early fiber-spinning machine) and other mechanized aids to industry often still lived within the rural environment. However, their direct connection with the land had been broken because the material they finished was not grown there.

The implications of this triumph of machine over muscle also had serious implications for the impact of human activity on the environment. Thanks to improvement, the land began to produce more food of better quality and greater reliability. Eventually industrialization, albeit through the exploitation of humans and resources in other parts of the world, meant that wages generally began to increase, and, more importantly, so did disposable incomes, which technology hastened to accommodate with the production of a myriad of goods, large or small, useful or otherwise. The demand for more and more products, using larger amounts of raw materials and more and more energy to produce and transport them, emphasized both the human ability to transcend almost any restrictions that nature might provide and an increasingly inventive talent for destruction.

By the nineteenth century the population began to rise beyond any previous scale, placing unprecedented pressure on, for example, housing space, water supplies, food production, and the transport infrastructure. Human ingenuity and initiative overcame many of these problems, particularly the supply of clean water which reduced the occurrence of diseases such as cholera. However, the impact on catchments (the area of land bounded by watersheds draining into a river, basin, or reservoir) as clean water was sought higher and higher in the hills, is only now being measured. The serious flooding of recent years has made it clear that diverting river flows and reclaiming flood-plains over the last few centuries have not been without serious consequences.

As industrialization began in earnest, with the creation of factories and the rapidly expanding urban environment to go with them, coal emissions began to become both visible and deadly. Although coal emissions were associated with every major industrial city, London's "peasoupers" (a dense, dirty yellow fog) in particular gave considerable added atmosphere to many literary works of the period. However, the power of the industrialists ensured that legislation to curb industrial emissions was slow in coming, though progress was made after the Alkali Act of 1863. Nevertheless, domestic emissions, a far greater source of pollution, were not curbed through the law until 1956 and 1968. Here cultural inbreeding played its part: The British refused to ditch their inefficient, polluting, open coal-burning hearths in favor of closed continental ones simply because British was bound to be best.

Artistic Community

The profound changes to the landscape and way of life associated with industrialization affected the artistic community as well as everyone else. Some, such as writer Emily Brontë in *Wuthering Heights*, although celebrating the wildness of preindustrial rural England, also saw the potential for change for those sections of the population trying to eke out a living from difficult conditions. However, belief in the all-encompassing benefits of progress were also seriously challenged. Admittedly those who did so had mixed motives: poet William Wordsworth and other writers enamored of the Lake District in northwest England lamented not only the criss-crossing of the country by the railways with their infernal racket and ungodly appearance by the middle of the nineteenth century. They were also concerned that the ability of the lower classes to move around under the railway's steam might mean an influx of insensitive souls to such rural idylls. Not everyone had sufficient sensibility to appreciate the poetry in these wildernesses.

Ironically, the success of these writers has frozen the Lake District into an image of dry-stone walls, neat fields, and sheep, as well as daffodils—a perfect improver's landscape and illustrative of a comparatively recent history. Nevertheless, it is an icon of English identity, and woe befall anyone trying to change it, from the Forestry Commission that attempted to grow plantations of trees there in the 1930s to the force of nature itself, decried eloquently by one farmer during the 2001 foot-and-mouth disease crisis, who predicted that, if all the sheep were culled, there would be scrub within five years and trees within ten. It was clear that, unlike in Scotland, the restoration of trees was most unwelcome.

Concern for the environment was not restricted to those of an artistic bent. Experience out in the colonies led to the first direct appreciation of the power of nature to hit back and led to theories about deforestation, climate change, and desiccation as early as the mid-eighteenth century. These theories were then imported back to Britain, where, even if they were not directly applicable, at least they generated discussion about the potential impacts of the exploitation of resources.

The twentieth century brought perhaps the greatest impact of human activity on the environment in absolute terms. Ironically, however, the twentieth century also brought a huge upsurge in concern for the environment, associated in part with the rise of democracy and grassroots movements from the 1960s. For some, the pressures of twentieth-century life, the inescapable everyday symbols of the never-ending human capacity to use up fossil fuels and other irreplaceable resources, forged a sense of a past golden age, when humans and nature lived in harmony. The truth, inevitably, is far less simple.

Another potentially positive aspect of the twentieth century was the growth of the state's willingness and ability to intervene, both in the United Kingdom and in Ireland (which became a separate state in 1921), often thanks to pressure from conservation organizations. In particular, the 1947 Town and Country Planning Act, followed by the National Parks Act of 1949, provided the legislative basis for regulation of both the built and the natural environment within the U.K.

However, despite some positive trends, the twentieth century also brought the increasing globalization of economies and therefore the globalization of the impact of human activity, particularly by industrialized nations such as the United Kingdom. This has sometimes meant that policies designed to clean up Britain's environmental record have been achieved at the expense of the continuing exploitation of someone else's resources: The move to restore seminatural woodlands while still importing large amounts of softwoods from Canada and Scandinavia is a case in point. The United Kingdom is also no longer the world's leading industrial nation, although it has been called the "Dirty Man of Europe" because of its continuing pollution.

Adjustment to the new world order in the twenty-first century also means understanding how the environments contained within these islands have evolved. There has been almost no point during the last ten thousand years when humans have not had an impact, and that is something that must be accepted as intrinsic to the human relationship with the rest of the natural world. However, the human role as master of technology has proved to be as double-edged as that of human nature itself. Millions of people in the United Kingdom and Ireland have been lifted out of the physical hardship and drudgery of subsistence living into the psychological difficulties of a world containing weapons of mass destruction and the knowledge of their own responsibility for the degradation of the planet that sustains them. These islands northwest of the European continent have experienced a full, rich, and varied environmental history. It is vital that people learn from the past so that the future can also be full, rich, and varied.

Fiona Watson

See also British Empire

Further Reading

Aalen, F. H. A., Whelan, K., & Stout, M. (1997). *Atlas of the Irish rural landscape*. Cork, Ireland: Cork University Press.

Allanson, P., & Whitby, M. (Eds.). (1996). *The rural economy and the British countryside*. London: Earthscan.

Andrews, M. (1989).*The search for the picturesque: Landscape aesthetics and tourism in Britain, 1760–1800*. Stanford CA: Stanford University Press.

Bell, J. (1992). *People and the land: Farming life in nineteenth century Ireland*. Belfast, Northern Ireland: Friar's Bush.

Brimblecombe, P. (1987). *The big smoke: A history of air pollution in London since medieval times*. London and New York: Routledge.

Bunce, M. (1994). *The countryside ideal: Anglo-American images of landscape*. London and New York: Routledge.

Chambers, J. D., & Mingay, G. E. (1966). *The agricultural revolution 1750–1880*. London: Batsford.

Clapp, B. W. (1994). *An environmental history of Britain since the industrial revolution*. Harlow, UK: Longmans.

Coleman, D., & Salt, J. (1992). *The British population: Patterns, trends and processes*. Oxford: Oxford University Press.

Cook, H. F., & Williamson, T. (1999). *Water management in the English landscape: field, marsh and meadow*. Edinburgh, UK: Edinburgh University Press.

Dodghson, R. A. & Butlin, R. A. (1990). *An Historical geography of England and Wales*. London: London Academic.

Edwards, K. J., & Smout, T. C. (2000). Perspectives on human-environment interactions in prehistoric and historical times. In G. Holmes & R. Crofts (Eds.). *Scotland's environment: The future*, pp. 3–29. East Linton, UK: Tuckwell Press.

Evans, E. E. (1992). *The personality of Ireland: Habitat, heritage and history*. Dublin: Lilliput.

Foster, S., & Smout, T. C. (Eds.). (1994). *The history of soils and field systems*. Aberdeen, UK: Scottish Cultural Press.

Fraser Darling, F. (Ed.). (1955). *Weset highland survey: An essay in human ecology*. Oxford: Oxford University Press.

Grove, R. (1995). *Green imperialism: Colonial expansion, tropical island Edens and the origins of environmentalism 1600–1860*. Cambridge, UK: Cambridge University Press.

Grove, R. (1997). *The evolution of the colonial discourse on deforestation and climate change, 1500–1940*. Cambridge, UK: Cambridge University Press.

Hassan, J. (1998). *A history of water in modern England and Wales*. Manchester and New York: Manchester University Press.

Howell, D. W. (1978). *Land and people in nineteenth century Wales*. London and Boston: Routledge and Kegan Paul.

Huckle, J., & Martin, A. (2001). *Environments in a changing world*. Harlow, UK: Pearson Education Ltd.

Johnson, J. H. (1994). *The human geography of Ireland*. Chichester, UK, and New York: Wiley.

Lamb, H. H. (1988). *Weather, climate and human affairs*. London and New York: Routledge.

Linnard, W. (1982). *Welsh woods and forests: History and utilization*. Cardiff: National Museum of Wales.

Mackenzie. J. M. (1997). *Empires of nature and the nature of empires. Imperialism, Scotland and the environment*. East Linton, UK: Tuckwell Press.

Mitchison, R., & Roebuck, P. (1988). *Economy and society in Scotland and Ireland 1500–1939*. Edinburgh, UK: John Donald.

O'Flanagan, P., Ferguson, P., & Whelan, K. (Eds.). (1987). *Rural Ireland 1600–1900: Modernization and change*. Cork, Ireland: Cork University Press.

Parry, M. L. (1978). *Climatic change, agriculture and settlement*. Folkestone: Dawson.

Perry, R. (1978). *Wildlife in Britain and Ireland*. London: Croom Helm.

Peterken, G. F. (1996). *Natural woodland: Ecology and conservation in northern temperate regions*. Cambridge, UK: Cambridge University Press.

Rackham, O. (1976). *Trees and woodland in the British landscape*. London: Dent.

Rackham, O. (1986). *The history of the countryside*. London: Dent.

Roberts, N. (1989). *The Holocene: An environmental history*. Oxford: Blackwell.

Rose, C. (1991). *The dirty man of Europe. The Great British pollution scandal*. London: Simon & Schuster.

Sheail, J. (2002). *An environmental history of twentieth-century Britain*. Basingstoke, UK: Palgrave.

Simmons, I. (2001). *An environmental history of Britain*. Edinburgh, UK: Edinburgh University Press.

Smout, T. C. (1993). *Scotland since prehistory*. Aberdeen, UK: Scottish Cultural Press.

Smout, T. C. (2000). *Nature contested: Environmental history in Scotland and Northern England since 1600*. Edinburgh, UK: Edinburgh University Press.

Smout, T. C. (Ed.). (2002). *People and woods in Scotland. A history*. Edinburgh, UK: Edinburgh University Press.

Stephenson, T. (1989). *Forbidden land: The struggle for access to mountain and moorland*. Manchester, UK: Manchester University Press.

Thirsk, J. (1997). *Alternative agriculture: A history from the black death to the present day*. Oxford: Oxford University Press.

Thirsk, J. (Ed.). (1967–2000). *The agrarian history of England and Wales*, vols. 1–8.

Thomas, K. (1983). *Man and the natural world: Changing attitudes in England 1500–1800*. London: Allen Lane.

Trinder, B. (1987). *The makine of the industrial landscape*. London: Phoenix.

Wheeler, D., & Mayers, J. (Eds.). (1997). *Regional climates of the British Isles*. London and New York: Routledge.

Whyte, I., & Whyte, K. (1991). *The changing Scottish landscape, 1500–1800*. London and New York: Routledge.

Woodell, S. R. J. (Ed.). (1985). *The English landscape: Past, present and future*. Oxford: Oxford University Press.

Wrigley, E. A. (1988). *Continuity, chance and change: The character of the industrial revolution in England*. Cambridge, UK: Cambridge University Press.

United Nations Environment Programme

The United Nations Environment Programme (UNEP), established in 1972, encourages sustainable development through sound environmental practices. Its activities cover a wide range of issues, from atmospheric and terrestrial ecosystems and the promotion of environmental science and information to an early warning and emergency response capacity to deal with environmental emergencies.

UNEP's priorities include (1) environmental information, assessment, and research, including environmental emergency response capacity and strengthening of early warning and assessment functions; (2) enhanced coordination of environmental conventions and development of policy instruments; (3) freshwater; (4) technology transfer and industry; and (5) support to Africa.

UNEP is headquartered in Nairobi, Kenya, and has offices in Paris, Geneva, Osaka, the Hague, Washington, New York, Bangkok, Mexico City, Manama (Bahrain), Montreal, and Bonn.

After World War I, the scale of death and destruction wrought by the war led world political leaders to search for ways of preserving the peace. Out of this search came the League of Nations. The failure of the League of Nations deterred renewed attempts to preserve the peace after World War II. However, the advent of nuclear weaponry and the increasing lethality of conventional warfare gave renewed impetus to finding ways of preserving the peace. Thus the United Nations (U.N.) was founded in 1945. New York City was chosen to be its home.

Although the goals of the U.N., like the League of Nations, are peace and security, the U.N.'s responsibility and area of activity is much wider. Through a host of specialized agencies, the U.N. also seeks to solve problems in many areas of global society. These problems include hunger (via its Food and Agriculture Organization), disease and other health problems (via the World Health Organization), displaced peoples (via the U.N. High Commission for Refugees), and human rights abuses and crime (via the International Court of Justice).

The disastrous bouts of inflation and mass unemployment in the years between the world wars also encouraged the U.N. to seek ways of preventing renewed economic instability while furthering economic growth (the World Bank and the International Monetary Fund). The U.N. Educational, Scientific and Cultural Organization (UNESCO) similarly promotes greater understanding between peoples and general social development.

Challenges for the U.N.

The prospects for the fledgling U.N. were quickly compromised by the growing East-West tensions of the

Cold War, when the United States and the USSR faced each other in an arms race in which fear of the consequences of actual conflict acted as a deterrence.

Occasionally the Cold War broke out into actual fighting. However, fighting did not occur at a global level as in the two world wars but rather occurred as civil wars and rebellions in what became known as the "Third World." The superpowers aggravated these conflicts by backing local rivals. Nations such as Korea, Vietnam, and Cambodia (Kampuchea) were devastated in these conflicts. Civilians have formed an ever-larger proportion of those killed and wounded in modern wars. Since 1945 the number of people, both military and civilian, who have been killed in the 140 or so wars has surpassed the total number of people killed in World War II.

The U.N. was unable to prevent these wars, and in cases such as the violent breakdown of the former Yugoslavia or the invasion of Kuwait by Iraq, the U.N. played a somewhat marginal role as the world's strongest power, the United States, largely determined the response of the international community.

Indeed, critics of the U.N. increasingly argued that its very structures—including the Security Council headed by the United States, United Kingdom, Russia, China, and France—effectively marginalized the world's many smaller or less-developed countries, especially those in what increasingly became known as the "South." This new terminology reflected growing awareness that the world's real divide lay not between East and West but rather between the rich countries of the "North" (with Australia and New Zealand as added members) and the largely poor countries in the "South" (i.e., Central and South America, southern Asia, and especially Africa).

Some critics went further and argued that, through its agencies, the U.N. was pushing models of development that had proved to be unsustainable in already industrialized countries and that would be equally unsustainable in poorer countries. Furthermore, the models were deemed to be irrelevant to the basic and most immediate needs of the world's estimated 1 billion people living in grinding poverty. Specific developments—such as large-scale hydroelectric and irrigation programs like the Aswan Dam in Egypt—as well as more general developments seeking to replicate the industrialized farming systems of the United States and western Europe were particularly attacked.

Particular criticism was directed at the U.N. economic agencies. These, it was argued, served to impose one economic model via so-called market reforms and free trade—a model that, apart from its social and environmental costs, merely served the interests of the huge transnational corporations. The austerity programs imposed by the International Monetary Fund were singled out for their severe social costs, which were borne by those people least able to bear them—the poor. The growth of the antiglobalization movement has amplified such criticism.

Birth of UNEP

Although UNESCO played a part in creation of the International Union for the Conservation of Nature, environmental issues did not play a major part at the United Nations until the late 1960s. Rising concern during that period led the U.N. to convene the international Conference on the Human Environment in Stockholm, Sweden, in 1972. This conference led to creation of the United Nations Environment Programme. UNEP's mission is to provide leadership and encourage partnership in caring for the environment by inspiring, informing, and enabling nations and peoples to improve their quality of life without compromising that of future generations.

Subsequent conferences—often referred to as "Earth Summits"—were held in 1992 in Rio de Janeiro, Brazil, and in 2002 in Johannesburg, South Africa. The Rio summit was at the time the largest international gathering ever, with 108 heads of state represented. The attendants generated several significant documents, including the Rio Declaration on Environment and Development, Agenda 21, the Framework Convention on Climate Change, and the Convention on Biological Diversity. At such Earth Summits official attendants are joined by thousands of representatives of nongovernmental organizations and activist groups, with considerable debate between developed and developing countries over international protocols and between the United States and much of the rest of the world over responses to global warming. Antiglobalization activists are an increasing presence.

Much of UNEP's work is the circulation of environmental information, assessment, and research. The monitoring and assessment role includes the Global Resource Information Database (GRID); the International Register of Potentially Toxic Chemicals (IRPTC); and the United Nations Environment Network website (www.unep.net), which offers access to environmental information. A series of annual reports, *Global Environment Outlook*, summarizes UNEP's latest findings. The development of "early warning" systems to anticipate

environmental problems before they grow worse has been a particular focus.

Critics of UNEP mainly focus on its weakness in challenging other U.N. agencies that, they argue, are committed to environmentally destructive policies. They also claim that UNEP is failing to spotlight other agents of global environmental destruction, especially transnational corporations and indeed the whole system of the so-called world market. Critics also argue that UNEP has paid insufficient attention to the problems posed by human population growth.

Sandy Irvine

Further Reading

Dodds, F. (Ed.). (2001). *Earth Summit 2002: A new deal*. London: Earthscan.

French, H. (1995). *Partnership for the planet: An environmental agenda for the United Nations*. Washington, DC: Worldwatch Institute.

Irvine, S. (1992, Summer). What went unsaid at UNCED. *Real World, 1*, 4–6.

McCoy, P., & McCully, P. (1993). *The road from Rio*. Oxford, UK: Jon Carpenter Publishing.

Retallack, S. (1997). Kyoto: Our last chance. *The Ecologist, 27*(6), 229–236.

Sitarz, D. (Ed.). (1993). *Agenda 21, the Earth Summit strategy to save the Earth*. Boulder, CO: Earth Press.

Ward, B. (1972). *Only one Earth*. Harmondsworth, UK: Penguin.

United States—Midwest

The environmental history of the Midwest of the United States is essentially a history of the states of the Great Lakes (Illinois, Indiana, Michigan, Ohio, and Wisconsin) and the states of the Great Plains (Iowa, Kansas, Missouri, North Dakota, and South Dakota) and is critical to understanding the early, modern, and postmodern environmental history of the entire country and the world. The human activities in this region, known as the U.S. "heartland," have radically changed not only the region's environment, but also that of the globe since the seventeenth century, when Europeans came to the Midwest. The environmental changes were dramatic after Europeans arrived because they began to exploit the region's natural resources on a large scale, not for subsistence but for economic gain to satisfy international trade demands—initially in Europe and North America but eventually across the world. Over time Anglo-American activities have produced in many parts of the region unsustainable ecosystems and have led to the near extinction of indigenous wildlife by early fur trappers, deforestation by logging and land clearing for agricultural development, eutrophication (the process by which a body of water becomes enriched in dissolved nutrients) of the Great Lakes by shipping and industrial development, and global warming and acid rain production by emission of combustion products from industrial power plants and automobiles.

Environmental changes in the region also evolved with the large-scale movement of people into the Midwest after it became the industrial center of the country. The human migrations beginning in the late nineteenth century would forever change the air and water quality of the region and lead to the disruption of numerous ecosystems.

Early Environmental History of the Great Plains

The terrain of the Great Plains was shaped by glacial movements during the Pleistocene epoch (beginning 1.6 million years ago), but unlike the Great Lakes area, the Great Plains was more intemperate. "Droughts and other disasters common to low-moisture regions affected both the Plains environment and the humans dependent on it throughout time, but the evidence suggests that the climate never became severe enough to force its inhabitants to abandon the area. To the contrary there is a record of continuous human inhabitation (since the Clovis culture) on the Great Plains for the past 11,500 years" (Wood 1998, 1). As U.S. archaeologist Marvin Kay points out in his study of the central and southern Plains Archaic (10,000–2500 BCE), a prevailing hypothesis is that the Clovis (based on artifacts found near Clovis, Texas, in the early 1930s) culture was "derived from the technology of adventurous bands of hunters who migrated across the Bering Land Bridge in search of mega fauna" (Kay 1998).

Prehistoric Native American Great Plains farmers and nomads lived in the heart of the North American continent in an interior grassland that extended from the Gulf of Mexico north to central Canada. The area was dominated by perennial grasses and a multitude of burrowing and grazing animals, including millions of roaming bison.

Archaeological evidence shows that farming communities existed in the Great Plains several hundred years before nomadic communities arrived in late prehistoric and early modern times. There was, however, little difference between the material culture of farming and nomadic communities outside of the fact that the farming communities had specialized architecture for earth lodges, pottery, and gardening tools. Both communities were subsistence cultures, and both engaged in some level of hunting to sustain their members. Hunting provided the essential food sources for the northwestern and northern Plains Archaic cultures, especially in open grasslands. Gathering in the early cultures became critical in areas that did not support large herbivores.

Evidence shows that early extinctions of mammals in the Great Plains ecosystems were caused by the hunting of the Clovis and later Paleo-Indian (early American hunting people of Asian origin living in the late Pleistocene epoch) groups. According to scholars, these extinctions were not caused by "overkill" but rather by reduced habitat diversity and less-nutritious foliage, increased biological stress, and competition among herbivores, especially the many nonruminant (nonhoofed) ones that died out. The early agricultural inhabitants of the midwestern portion of the Great Plains lived along the Missouri River and its tributaries (mainly in western Iowa and Missouri) beginning in the eleventh century. Agricultural villages reached their peak in the thirteenth century in Kansas, especially along the Kansas River and its tributaries: the Republican, Solomon, Smoky Hill, and Saline Rivers. During the thirteenth century the central Great Plains would undergo a major population expansion and the beginning of major migrations into the northern Great Plains, the Platte River valley in Nebraska, and along the Missouri River in northeastern Nebraska and southeastern South Dakota. After two centuries of population expansion and movement this region experienced a major population decline because of dry and colder climates produced by the Little Ice Age in the fifteenth century.

The lifestyle of hunters remained fairly constant until the introduction of the horse by Spanish settlers in the fifteenth century. Many scholars equate the magnitude of the environmental impact on the Great Plains Native Americans by the introduction of the horse with that of the diseases that were introduced by Europeans. The Great Plains pedestrian lifestyle became extinct because the horses became an essential component to Native American lifestyles, especially those of the Arapahos, Cheyennes, Comanches, Assinboins, and Dakotas.

Early Environmental History of the Great Lakes Region

Geologically speaking, the Midwest is new; its bodies of water (the Great Lakes) and their surrounding landscape were formed during the Pleistocene epoch by the advance and retreat of ice during four glacial epochs. The first of these glacial epochs was the Nebraskan epoch (1,000,000 to 950,000 years ago), which was followed by the Kansan epoch (475,000 to 425,000 years ago); then the Illinoian epoch (300,000 to 250,000 years ago) and finally the Wisconsin epoch, which covered Canada as well as sections of the United States from 65,000 to 3,500 years ago. Each time glacial ice advanced over this landscape, moving southward and melting, it deposited valuable minerals and soils, shaped and reshaped landforms, and created lakes, rivers, and other geographic features. The once-rolling and low landscape that characterized the region—grassland, desert, or forest—was leveled by the advance of glacial ice. U.S. Environmental historian William Ashworth points out in his study of the Great Lakes that prior to the Ice Age, "there was a broad branching network of river valleys, following the courses laid out for them by the Superior Syncline [a trough of stratified rock in which the beds dip toward each other from either side] and the Michigan Structural Basin" (Ashworth 1991, 19). The final advance of ice around twelve thousand years ago left behind craters hundreds of kilometers across and 400 meters deep that filled with water to become today's Great Lakes: Lake Erie, Lake Michigan, Lake Superior, Lake Huron, and Lake Ontario. The Great Lakes acted as a drainage system that extended deep into the North American continent and flowed east to the Atlantic Ocean. Three of these Great Lakes (Huron, Michigan, and Superior) would be formed from crustal rebound (when the earth's crust expands upward after the removal of ice glaciers that had created the downward movement of the earth's crust from intense pressure) and the drainage of a more ancient Great Lake, the three-lobed Lake Nipissing, which covered the entire Upper Lakes area. The Upper Lakes area includes the area north of current day states Illinois, Ohio, Indiana, and Wisconsin and contains the lakes: Duluth, Stanley, Chippewa, Early, Erie, and Early Ontario. These lakes would become known as "America's fifth coast" and would be critical water routes for travel and trade in North

American history. Their environmental degradation by humans would also transform the environmental history of the region.

The glaciers also left behind moraines (ridges along the margins of the glaciers) that were up to 160 kilometers long and 152 meters thick. They also left behind rich agricultural soil 60 to 90 meters deep, natural filtration systems for groundwater, and abundance of raw materials (such as coal, iron, wood , salt, and copper) for future industrial and commercial operations.

Human activities also changed the land during this time. Early human inhabitation of the region is believed to have begun at the latest around the time of the Great Lakes formation. Ashworth points out that "artifacts have been found beneath glacial deposits associated with the final southward thrust of ice—known as the Valders Advance—and a cave on an Ohio River tributary in western Pennsylvania, the Meadowcroft Rock Shelter near Eldersville, contains cultural remains dating back at least as far as 14,000 B.C.E." (Ashworth 1991, 13). These people were Paleo-Indians, and archaeologists believe that they migrated into the area from the Great Plains region. These people (believed to be of no relation to modern Native Americans) hunted mastodons and barren-ground caribou along the ice margins using the Clovis (chipped-stone) spearhead. They would be succeeded by the Aqua-Plano culture, the Boreal Archaic culture, the Old Copper culture (4000 to 1100 BCE), and the Mound Builders culture (1000 BCE to 700 CE). The activities of the last two cultures would transform the environment and ecosystems of the region.

Old Copper Culture

The first humans to exploit the natural resources in the region for more than just subsistence were members of the Old Copper culture. U.S. Environmental writer Russell McKee points out that the Old Copper Indian culture was believed to have been very large, encompassing areas that stretched north to Lake Superior, west to the Mississippi, east to Ontario and northwest to central Manitoba. Members of the Old Copper culture, as their name implies, were extensive users of metals and were the first miners in the region. They hunted deer, domesticated the dog, buried their dead in cemeteries, built boats (and may have invented the birch-bark canoe), and began to experiment with agriculture, but most importantly from an environmental standpoint they began to exploit on a massive level the copper resources of the region by mining copper amygdales—copper pieces contained in holes of volcanic rocks. The volcanic rocks would be cracked open to extract the copper pieces, and if this method proved too difficult the rocks would be heated and then quickly cooled with cold water to facilitate breakage. These people sought out metallic resources that were exposed at ground level and cleared away rocks to gain access to other sources by cutting into bedrock where copper was exposed. Archaeologists have found hundreds of shallow mine pits on Isle Royale of Lake Superior, where it is believed that mining was conducted at an extensive level. The copper would then be worked to create knives, spear points, and jewelry, and many scholars believe that the metal-hunting tools produced by this culture were partially responsible for the demise of both the mammoth and the mastodon. The demise of the Old Copper culture around 1100 BCE was also the demise of the exploitation and extensive use of copper for several centuries in the region.

Mound Builders

The Mound Builder culture arose at the close of the Old Copper culture around 1000 BCE. Scholars are uncertain about the origins of this culture, but a common belief is that it came from the Mississippi and Illinois River valleys and moved eastward along the Ohio River valley. By 800 BCE permanent groups of Adena mound builders had settled in Illinois, Indiana, and Ohio. A few centuries later another mound building group, the Hopewell-Adenas, would settle in the Ohio River valley. This group is credited with the long-term transformation of the environment in the Midwest by introducing agriculture into the Great Lakes region. As a result of their successful agricultural practices, mound builders were able to create permanent settlements because of the food supplements they could provide to their communities over and above that obtained from traditional hunting, fishing, and gathering. Mound builders grew corn, beans, gourds, squash, melons, and tobacco and farmed along rivers and in well-watered areas. Their ability to control the environment allowed them to transform their society. They were the first human inhabitants in the region to develop socially stratified small cities, religious ceremonies, complex burial routines, and a trade economy. Archaeologists have found that these mound-building societies used weapons of flint, argillite, obsidian, copper, sheet mica, and other precious stones. The presence and use of these materials could be obtained only with skills of mining and collecting as well as a knowledge of how to transform

raw materials. After the demise of the Mound Builder culture (700 CE) a period referred to as the "Native American Dark Ages" existed that spanned between 800 and 1600 CE. By 1600, fifteen years before the arrival of "the father of New France," French explorer Samuel de Champlain, 100,000 Native Americans were living in the Great Lakes region, representing 10–15 percent of all Native Americans living in North America north of New Mexico. The introduction of permanent European settlement would bring the extinction of both native peoples and natural resources in the Midwest.

Environmental Consequences of European Exploration and Settlement

The arrival of Europeans in the Midwest and particularly in the Great Lakes region was not happenstance but rather the direct result of a concerted and systematic search by Old World explorers for the Northwest Passage to the South Sea (the Pacific Ocean), which would lead them to the legendary riches of Cathay (China). The first recorded European encounter with the Great Lakes region occurred in 1615, the year Champlain came into the North Bay Gap. This area was proximate to Ottawa, Mattawa, and the Old Chippewa Stanley Outlet channel. Instead of finding the South Sea, Champlain found a large freshwater body of water, which was the first of the Great Lakes—Lake Huron. Other French explorers, such as Etienne Brulé and Jean Nicolet, continued to search for the Northwest Passage in the region, and within fifty years of Champlain's discovery of Lake Huron, all of the Great Lakes were discovered. With hopes for finding passage to the famed Cathay dashed Europeans began to realize that money could be made by exploiting the abundant natural resources of the Great Lakes region. Great Britain and France sought to capitalize on these resources and were critical to the environmental transformations of the region.

Fur Trading

Beavers were the first natural resource of the Midwest to be exploited by Europeans for the fur trade, and their exploitation created the beginning of the environmental decline of the region. The fur trade, also known as the "Beaver mine," lasted for 150 years and was dominated by the Company of New France and Great Britain's Hudson Bay Company. Both companies received considerable support and participation from Native Americans. Beavers were hunted and trapped for their fur to the point of near extinction by Native Americans and Europeans alike because the fur was a highly valued luxury commodity in the Old World. In the Old World beavers had been exploited to produce luxury clothing, and the demand for such clothing had resulted in the virtual disappearance of beavers in Europe by the sixteenth century. By the 1520s beavers had disappeared from England. In the U.S. Midwest prior to their massive and long-term exploitation, beavers had served as the perfect flood-control system for the environment. The beavers' small dam systems were instrumental in protecting against soil loss and preserving groundwater quality and the habitats of fish and fowl. However, the level of hunting was too high for beavers reproductively to keep up with. With their population decline came flooding, increases in siltation, the widening of riverbeds, increases in river flow speeds, and the destruction of spawning beds. The decline of the beaver population heralded the beginning of widespread destruction of ecosystems and environments in the Midwest that would continue for hundreds of years and that still has not completely abated.

Population Booms

The wars between France, Great Britain, Native Americans, and the newly emerged United States in the region focused on the control and ownership of the region's natural resources but were over after the War of 1812. With wars behind them the New Americans (non-aboriginal Americans) began to settle the region around the middle of the nineteenth century. This permanent settlement had a tremendous impact on the environment because it necessitated destroying forests for farming, filling in wetlands, dredging bars and harbors, constructing breakwaters, and paving soils. All of these activities removed or destroyed some of the richest and most diverse ecosystems in the region. Dredged bars and harbors resulted in the loss of aquatic vegetation that acted as gigantic water filters that percolated out harmful bacteria and suspended solids. Lumber and sawmills were critical in land clearing for permanent settlement. In 1850 sawmills lined both sides of the Saginaw River for several miles upstream. By the mid-1890s there were one thousand mills, and the cut had peaked at over 1 billion board-feet a year. By the early part of the twentieth century the lumber business had died down. The mills had contributed not only to deforestation but also to the destruction of the Great Lakes ecosystems. Because most of the mills were situated along rivers and lakes, lost lumber and waste sawdust fell into these bodies of water, destroying spawning beds and the feeding grounds of fish and other aquatic life. This waste also led to an increase in water temperatures because of the decay of the organic materials (wood). As a result many fish and other aquatic life-forms became extinct.

The massive population boom also generated huge levels of waste products from humans, horses, and activities required to carry out societal functions and needs. The fastest growth in the Midwest occurred in Chicago beginning in the 1830s. Ashworth points out that "at the beginning of the decade, the same 12 families were still living by themselves on the banks of 'Checago Creek.' Three years later the number of residents had risen to 500 and four years later to 5,000. . . . By 1900 Chicago had reached the two million mark" (Ashworth 1991, 56). Human, animal, and industrial waste poured into the Chicago River and found its way to Lake Michigan, creating a public health nightmare from cholera and typhoid fever because the lake was used to obtain drinking water. The environmental stress and the consequences of the population boom in Chicago were two reasons for the widening of the Illinois Michigan Canal and the creation of the Chicago Sanitary and Ship Canal.

Mining

Beginning in the 1840s the mining of minerals, such as coal, copper, and iron ore, was critical in the development of the Midwest as the major industrial center in the United States and consequently as one of the most polluted regions in the world. Glacial action in the region had produced massive deposits of coal and iron ore and potential critical water routes in the form of the Great Lakes and rivers. In 1835 industrial development was made easier with the opening of the Ohio Erie Canal. The canal provided a cheap route for bringing iron ore from the Lake Superior district and coal from mines in the Ohio River valley; this proved instrumental in the development of the steel mill industries of the Midwest, especially in Cleveland, Ohio. The steel mills would have devastating environmental impacts on the Midwest ecosystems. Pig iron production yielded environmentally harmful products such as ammonia, coal, tar, and methane gas. Likewise, the process of making steel alloys produced poisonous waste products of molybdenum, chromium, vanadium, and nickel. Although less complicated, the smelting process for copper began to employ a sulfuric acid wash.

Most of these by-products went into the waterways and killed off numerous aquatic life-forms and eventually the life-forms that depended on them for survival. Unlike the beaver and lumber exploitation, mining persists in the region.

The steel industry was critical in the development of other industries in the region because they relied on steel products. All of these industrial operations, particularly their waste-disposal processes, until the last quarter of the twentieth century were virtually unchecked. Massive amounts of chemicals were poured into the air, water, and soil. It would take the burning of the Cuyahoga River, on 22 June 1969, in the steel mill flats of Cleveland to create an environmental wake-up call for the nation about the environmental costs generated by industrial operations. Ashworth points out in his first study of the Great Lakes that "several linear miles of the Cuyahoga in the industrial section of Cleveland—a smoky wasteland of factories and dumps and slag heaps known as 'the Flats'—went massively up in flames, and the fireboat Anthony J. Celebrezze had to rush up stream from its berth in the city's wharf district and put out the river" (Ashworth 1991, 143). This event made Cleveland a national laughingstock for years and helped motivate passage of the National Environmental Policy Act (NEPA) in the same year by the U.S. Congress, which declared NEPA a "national policy which will encourage productive and enjoyable harmony between man and his environment" (NEPA, 1970).

Sylvia Hood Washington

Further Reading

Ashworth, W. (1991). *The late Great Lakes: An environmental history.* Detroit, MI: Wayne State University Press.

Ashworth, W. (2000). *Great Lakes journey: A new look at America's freshwater coast.* Detroit, MI: Wayne State University Press.

Cronon, W. (1991). *Nature's metropolis: Chicago and the great West.* New York: W. W. Norton.

Frison, G. C. (1998). The northwestern and northern Plains Archaic. In W. R. Wood (Ed.), *Archaeology on the Great Plains* (pp. 140–172). Lawrence: University of Kansas Press.

Garland, J. H. (Ed.). (1955). *The North American Midwest, a regional geography.* New York: John Wiley and Sons.

Kay, M. (1998a). The central and southern Plains Archaic. In W. R. Wood (Ed.), *Archaeology on the Great Plains* (pp. 173–200). Lawrence: University of Kansas Press.

Kay, M. (1998b). The Great Plains setting. In W. R. Wood (Ed.), *Archaeology on the Great Plains* (pp. 16–47). Lawrence: University of Kansas Press.

McKee, R. (1966). *Great Lakes country.* New York: Thomas Y. Cromwell.

Washington, S. H. (2000). *Packing them in: A twentieth-century working-class environmental history.* Unpublished doctoral dissertation, Case Western Reserve University, Cleveland, Ohio.

Wood, W. R. (Ed.). (1998). *Archaeology on the Great Plains.* Lawrence: University of Kansas Press.

United States—Northeast

The Northeast is composed of two distinct regions, the Mid-Atlantic states of New York, Pennsylvania, and New Jersey and New England. New England is composed of the states carved out of the original Puritan colonies of Massachusetts, Rhode Island, Connecticut, New Hampshire, Vermont, and Maine on the northeastern coast of the United States. Like much of the rest of the United States, the Northeast has drawn its population from around the world so that the ancestors of today's New Englanders came from England, Scotland, Ireland, France by way of Canada, the Azores Islands, Scandinavia, Germany, Poland, Italy, Greece, Russia, southern and southeastern Asia, the Caribbean, Mexico, Latin America, China, and Japan.

New York at the mouth of the Hudson River is the country's largest city dominating the nation's commercial and financial services. It was the entry point for a majority of immigrants to America and a nurturing ground for immigrant enterprise. Philadelphia, along the Pennsylvania shore of the Delaware River with a rich hinterland of fertile farmland began the nineteenth century as the nation's leading city, but fell behind New York City's more aggressive commercial activity. The completion of the Erie Canal through the Mohawk River Valley, the only natural passageway through the Appalachian Mountain Chain into the rich and productive farmlands of the Great Lakes region solidified New York's position as the nation's highest ranked city. Pittsburgh at the convergence of the Monongahela and Allegheny Rivers to form the Ohio River expanded from a trading post serving travelers into the interior to a major iron and glass manufacturing center utilizing local iron ore and silica deposits, lumber for charcoal and potassium, and coal and natural gas. Newark

Cape Cod National Seashore

In the early 1960s New England attempted to control some of the development along the eastern edge of Cape Cod by setting aside land in a national park. The Cape Cod National Seashore was not a wilderness preserve. It included homes. It allowed for some development, but it did attempt to limit development and set aside land for public appreciation. The success of the national seashore has led to other similar parks in other coastal regions, but the park is not the answer to the crisis of land use along the coast of New England. As more and more people crowd into a limited space—summer residents, retirees, and people making their living off of them—the fragile ecosystem becomes ever more threatened. Freshwater supplies are quickly being depleted, and salt infusion is a real concern. Increased population densities also pressure water purity along the coast. Private septic systems and public treatment facilities are being overloaded, and nitrate concentrations are increasing in coastal waters. Dangerous levels of contamination are close at hand. The economics of tourism, like the economics of most industries, is growth based. Builders, developers, real estate agents, restaurateurs, and shop owners make money with more construction, people, and sales. These people have a long-term interest in development. Their livelihoods are at stake, and their interests are voiced in the public arena. A question that writer Henry David Thoreau asked almost a century and a half ago is still relevant today: "Who speaks for the fish?" or, more broadly, who speaks for the fragile ecosystem?

New England's coast is at a turning point. Much is protected, but there is a growing awareness that something must be done to maintain the vitality of the coastal ecosystem. Fishers went to sea for generations, harvesting cod from the rich ocean banks in boats driven by sail. They worked with dinghies and hand lines. In the twentieth century they moved to steam-driven and then diesel-driven fishing boats and abandoned hand lines for large dragnets. Still, these were small, four- or five-person operations. But increasingly in the later half of the century New England and Canadian fishers confronted foreign factory ships working massive nets. In response, the U.S. and Canadian governments passed legislation restricting foreign ships from the rich northwestern Atlantic fishing grounds, but the governments did not restrict the building and equipping of Canadian and American fishers with bigger and more efficient boats. By the end of the century the cod population on the banks had collapsed. The richest fishing grounds in the world were in crisis. Fishing was cut back, but at this point it is unclear whether the cod population will ever recover

John T. Cumbler

and Trenton, New Jersey, built industries from communities of local skilled artisans into major enterprises serving both regional and national markets. Rochester, New York, milled grain from the rich Mohawk River valley and shipped its produce east through the Erie Canal to east coast traders and bakers. Buffalo, New York, at the western terminus of the Erie Canal gathered produce from the upper Midwest for processing and shipping east and sent out manufactured good to the expanding farms of the west. Albany at the juncture of the Erie Canal and the Hudson River serves not only as the state capital but also as an important commercial and trading center for upstate New York.

Boston, the city facing Cape Cod Bay on the Atlantic coast, dominates New England, but the cities of Providence, Rhode Island, and New Haven, Connecticut, to the south, Hartford, Connecticut, and Springfield, Massachusetts, to the west, Portland, Maine, to the north, and Worcester, Massachusetts, in the center of that state are all important regional cities, and the cities of Lowell, Massachusetts; Manchester and Concord, New Hampshire, are significant old industrial centers.

The first people to alter the New England countryside were the Native Americans who occupied the region twelve thousand years before the first Europeans set foot upon its shores. One has to look hard to see the remnants of their world, but they are still there. The occasional arrowheads dug up by farmers and gardeners tell of a people who hunted the game of the region. Rocks with the grooves of thousands of sharpening strokes reflect a place where arrowheads, hatchets, and spears were made. Because these early American inhabitants walked lighter on the land than did the later Europeans, there is much less to see of how they altered the land. The early Anglo settlers noticed the imprints in clearings in forests where Native Americans had burned out ground cover to scare up game and larger clearings for settlement or farming. The selection of game that early European settlers found available to them was also a product of Native American activity. The mammoths, which roamed the region in the previous millennium, were hunted out of existence by the first paleo-hunters who followed the retreating glaciers into New England, but the animals that came to reside in New England after the large mammals were hunted out ten thousand years ago were those adapted to the world of hunter and hunted. Fleeter, smaller animals flourished. And those that met the needs of the hunters for clothing, food, and bedding were encouraged through a system of conscious and unconscious husbandry.

An Altered Environment

But the region was already an altered environment when the Native Americans arrived. Three major geological forces created the modern Northeast. The rise of the Appalachian Mountain range, which finds its northern terminus in New England, gives the region its picturesque mountains, hills, and valleys. The Green Mountains run up the western spine of New England and link to the Taconic Range in western Massachusetts. A second mountain range to the east of the Green Mountains, the White Mountains, runs from central Massachusetts up through western Maine to the Canadian border. From the Appalachian plateau flow the major rivers of the region. In the western part of the region the Connecticut River, which separates the Green Mountains from the White Mountains, spills out of a series of marshy lakes between the United States and Canada and runs south into an ever-widening valley until it spills into Long Island Sound. The high plateau of the White Mountain range gives rise to the Merrimack River, which runs south along the eastern face of the range until it flows out into the coastal plain of southern New Hampshire and northern Massachusetts. The White Mountains also are the origin of the

Sacco River, which flows south through southern Maine, the Kennebec, which cuts southeast through central Maine, and the Penobscot, which flows out of the northern reaches of the White Mountain range. To the west of the Green Mountains and separated from them by the upper reaches of the Hudson River and Lake Champlain lie the Adirondack Mountains, and to the south of the Adirondacks are the Catskill Mountains. Between these two mountain ranges flows the Mohawk River and the Erie Canal. The upper Delaware River separates the Catskills from the Pocono Mountains of northeastern Pennsylvania. The Susquehanna River breaks the Pocono Mountains from the Allegheny Front and Plateau of central and western Pennsylvania.

Far more recently the Northeast was reshaped by as many as five successive glaciers. As the glaciers moved south they scraped over the mountains and hills of northern New England, pushing down the land and gathering up into itself rocks, boulders, sand, and dirt. The moving glaciers dug out gorges in some places and deposited hills of its accumulated diggings in others. About sixteen thousand years ago the Earth began to warm, and the last glacier began to break up and melt off its southern edge. Glacier melt began to flow, taking with it the rocks, boulders, sand, and dirt that it had gathered up on its way south. The melting of the glacier and its leaving of deposits transformed the countryside anew. The deposits created Long Island, New York, and Cape Cod, Martha's Vineyard, and Nantucket in Massachusetts. The sandy, marshy, pond-littered region of southern Massachusetts and Rhode Island was created by the scatterings of glacial till, the material plowed up by the glacier as it slowly pushed across the countryside. Water from the glacier eroded out riverbeds and streambeds and filled in lakes. Remaining ice chunks covered with gravel, sand, and soil slowly melted, creating small ponds, called kettle ponds. Everywhere the glacier left behind rocks scraped from the mountains that it crossed over on its way through the northern Northeast. Those rocks were the bane of early farmers whose every shovel turned a stone. With no place else to put them, New England farmers piled them along the edges of their fields, where they remain today in suburban backfields and uphill forests, reminders of a distant agricultural past. Melting glacier waters raised the level of the oceans, covering the broad coastal plain, but when the weight of the glacier was removed from the region's shoulders the land rose as well, separating it from the sea. As the glacier melted, water and alluvia flowed southward carving out valleys and depositing wash. Southeast of the Hudson and Delaware Rivers sand filled in the Jersey shore while the retreating seas left behind an expanding coastal plain of rich fertile soil that made up central New Jersey and eastern Pennsylvania.

Abundant Fish and Game

Off the Northeast coast, warm ocean currents moving up from the south collide with colder currents flowing down from the Arctic in the waters. These colliding currents stir up nutrients from the ocean depths. Plankton and other small marine life thriving over the long Artic summer days move south with the flowing currents. These nutrient-rich waters wash over the several banks of New England. These banks, particularly the Georges and Grand, provided, until recently, some of the richest fishing in the world, especially for cod, a fish particularly suitable for storing.

When the Europeans landed in the Northeast they found an abundance of lumber and game animals. The Europeans brought with them other animals—horses, cows, sheep, chickens, and pigs—and diseases. The diseases took a heavy toll on the Native Americans, quickly reducing their population to a fraction of its previous size. The animals helped the Europeans transform the land. Forests were cut and, with the aid of oxen and horses, stumps removed and broad, plowable fields opened up. Game animals were killed and predators such as the wolf driven from the land. Pigs, cows, horses, sheep, and chickens became more plentiful in the region than the game that Native Americans hunted. But through the first two and a half centuries of European settlement, the rivers and oceans remained bountiful and were harvested aggressively.

The rich alluvial soil of the Hudson River Valley, central New Jersey, and southeastern Pennsylvania provided farmers with bountiful harvests of fruits and grains while the expanding markets of the coastal cities guaranteed good prices for their crops. By the early nineteenth century these farmers were rotating crops to maintain the land's fertility and choosing crops for each rotation according to prices they were liable to get at harvest time. Unlike early settlers who let their livestock wander the woods, these nineteenth century farmers kept their animals fenced and under close supervision. They fattened their cattle in barns over the winter and drove them to market heavy from a winter of rich hay feed. Manure from the barn would be spread on fields to increase productivity. The rapidly growing cities of New York and Philadelphia absorbed

a good proportion of these farms' surpluses while the excess went into overseas' markets, particularly the West Indies. With the crisis of food shortage in Ireland and England due to the failure of the potato crop and the repeal of the English Corn Laws in 1846, trade in food staples also increased between America and Great Britain. Grain from the fertile farm land of the region's river valleys and southeastern Pennsylvania not only flowed into the new market streams, but the surpluses coming out of the rich Midwestern farms traveled through east coast ports on their way to the ovens and tables of the Atlantic world. Agricultural produce needed to be processed, packed, barreled, stored, and shipped. Warehouses needed to be built, barrels manufactured, boats loaded and unloaded, and paperwork maintained. Philadelphia, New York, Providence, and Boston expanded with carpenters, haulers, coopers, clerks, and sailors. Homes crowded in close to the harbor. Wagons and carriages moved goods and people and horses filled the streets and deposited their wastes. Farmers wanted manufactured farm tools and implements to work expanded farms, and farm wives wanted finished cloth. With prosperity they wanted books, pianos, and furniture and soon cities' side streets were filling with small artisan shops producing goods to send back out to the countryside. These were walking cities closely packed together. They were also dirty cities threatened with disease. In 1793 yellow fever struck Philadelphia carrying off one in twelve residents. In response the city built the nation's first major waterworks that with its expansion in 1823 was pumping clear water from the Schuylkill River up to the Fairmount Hill reservoirs and then down to the city by gravity feed. New York built its water system in 1842 and Boston began its expanded system in 1845. By the post Civil War period most large urban centers had municipal waterworks.

If the soil and climate of the south central part of the region was conducive to rich harvests, the glaciers' legacy haunted the farmers of the region's northern sections. Stones broke their shovels, plows, and scythes. The thin, acidic soil frustrated their harvests, and the short growing seasons plagued them with late and early frosts. They had plenty of rain but not enough good soil to take full advantage of it. Except for the river valleys, the northern Northeast was a poor place to practice European agriculture, and that was the only agriculture the Europeans knew.

Finding a virtue in a reality, New Englanders turned to their streams, forests, and the ocean for salvation. In the ocean they found cod and whales that they fished and hunted and traded away. From their forests they got timber to build the boats that they took to sea to fish, whale, and trade. From their streams they found power. Initially New Englanders dammed their streams for gristmills and sawmills to process the products of the land. But the marginal harvests encouraged them to look for other uses for waterpower.

Water-driven machines soon became New England's financial salvation. Woolen mills, cotton mills, paper mills, woodworking mills, and machine shops all began to utilize the power of flowing waters. Mills were built along fault lines where rivers flowed downward quickly, and not just in New England. Water flowing across the falls of the Passaic River in New Jersey and the Delaware at Lambertville, New Jersey, and New Hope, Pennsylvania, and other rivers and streams was tapped to power machinery throughout the region. Mill workers gathered to live in nearby boardinghouses and then tenements. First they came from the rural countryside, but by the second half of the nineteenth century they came from the Irish, then the Canadian, and then the European countryside. They gathered in dense concentrations, and they worked in dense conditions. They worked in mills that were powered by the water that was backed up by dams. The fish that yearly migrated up the streams were now blocked from their spawning grounds. The cotton, wool, paper, woodwork, and machinery of the mills that were powered by the flowing waters generated massive amounts of wastes. Organic wastes from processing raw wool, cotton, rags, pulp, and lumber had to be disposed of. Processing acids and other chemicals also had to be disposed of. Flowing water offered a convenient way to externalize the problem of waste disposal. With the acquiescence of the legal system, manufacturers systematically dumped hundreds of tons of industrial wastes into the streams that flowed by their mills. Water flowing downstream from the larger manufacturing enterprises was foaming and discolored for miles below. The traditional rural outhouse could no longer accommodate the high concentrations of people working and living in the growing mill towns and cities. Human wastes were added to those of the mills as the water flowed downstream.

Downstream Pollution

People living downstream confronted foul-smelling streams without fish and were afraid to let their animals drink the water. Urban residents drawing drinking and bathing water from sources contaminated by upstream water experienced increased mortality from diarrhea, cholera, dysentery, and typhoid, especially among the young. Although municipal waterworks provided urban areas with clear water, they did not necessarily guarantee safe water. Before the acceptance of the germ theory in the late nineteenth century most urbanites assumed if their water lacked smell and looked clear it was safe to drink. The work of Massachusetts' scientists and public health officials in the late nineteenth century finally convinced municipal work systems that they needed to filter or chemically purify their water if they hoped to reduce urban diseases. Filtered and purified water dramatically reduced urban death rates, but sewage and industrial wastes continued to be dumped into the closest available stream well into the twentieth century.

Although waterpower was vital to the growth of the region's manufacturing, steam soon supplanted water as the major source of energy. Increasingly after 1850, coal-driven steam engines and coal-driven trains powered machinery and moved people and goods. Although by European standards America was a nation of trees, wood for fuel for powering machinery, smelting iron, and heating homes was becoming scarcer and more expensive by the second half of the nineteenth century. The discovery of hard high carbon content anthracite coal northwest of Philadelphia and southwest of Boston provided a cheaper alternative fuel for manufacturing and increasingly in the late nineteenth century for home heating. Canals were dug to move the heavy bulk coal to market centers in New York and Philadelphia. Anthracite burnt clean, but was buried deeper in the earth than softer high sulfur content bituminous coal. Soon bituminous coal was shipped east from the rich fields of central and western Pennsylvania. Bituminous coal was cheap but it burned dirty. The air of cities filled with partially combusted coal soot. People living along the coast had the advantage of ocean breezes to displace the sooty air, but all suffered from its irritation. Dirty water depleted of fish and dirty air prompted residents to embark on a century-long campaign to clean up and restore their rivers and air. Finally, with the help of federal legislation during the 1960s and 1970s and with the decline of traditional industries, the region's water and air are recovering.

Farms abandoned as hopeless in the nineteenth century are taking on new value as summer residences for urban citizens looking for peace and quiet. Rural farm families find themselves employed to look after summer homes, maintaining wells, building additions, and plowing driveways rather than plowing wheat fields. Others have found new markets for rural produce in the resorts and in local farmers' markets catering to summer residents. The rural Northeast increasingly is selling its past as its produce. For now, the countryside seems to be able to maintain a balance between its new economy and its ecology.

Coastal New England is not so fortunate. The fragile coastal region offers spectacular views and unique and intriguing scenery. The glacial wash that created Long Island, Cape Cod, Martha's Vineyard, and Nantucket is a delicate gathering of sand with limited sources of freshwater and shallow estuaries facing the stormy Atlantic. It is a fabulous place to vacation or, for the lucky few, to own a home. But the very fragility of the landscape that makes it so alluring to visitors is put at risk by those very visitors. Each new home represents a new well and septic system or drains upon existing ones. Each visitor means more feet on delicate sand dunes. Homes, restaurants, shops, stores, gas stations, roads, driveways, parking lots, and highways mean more trees and brush cleared, more boats and bobbers in the water, and more waste on the land.

Northeast residents for centuries have lived off the environment in one form or another. Doing so changes the environment and takes a toll, no matter how carefully it is done. The more careful and aware the region's citizens are when they use the environment, the more likely it will be that future generations will be able to enjoy the region as a rich and beautiful place.

John T. Cumbler

Further Reading

Cronon, W. (1983). *Changes in the land: Indians, colonists, and the ecology of New England.* New York: Hill and Wang.

Cumbler, J. T. (2001). *Reasonable use: The people, the environment, and the state, New England 1790–1930.* Oxford, UK: Oxford University Press.

Foster, C. H. W. (1985). *The Cape Cod National Seashore: A landmark alliance.* Hanover, NH: University Press of New England.

Foster, D. R., & O'Keefe, J. F. (2000). *New England forests through time: Insights from the Harvard forest dioramas.* Cambridge, MA: Harvard University Press.

Judd, R. W. (1997). *Common lands, common people: The origins of conservation in northern New England.* Cambridge, MA: Harvard University Press.

Kurlansky, M. (1997). *Cod: A biography of the fish that changed the world.* New York: Walker and Comp.

Lemon, J. (1972). *The best poor man's country: A geological study of early southeastern Pennsylvania.* Baltimore: Johns Hopkins University Press.

Merchant, C. (1989). *Ecological revolutions: Nature, gender, and science in New England.* Chapel Hill: University of North Carolina Press.

Muir, D. (2000). *Reflections in Bullough's Pond: Economy and ecosystem in New England.* Hanover, NH: University Press of New England.

Raymo, C., & Raymo, M. E. (1989). *Written in stone: A geological history of the northeastern United States.* Old Saybrook, CT: Globe Pequot.

Steinberg, T. (1991). *Nature incorporated: Industrialization and the waters of New England.* Cambridge, UK: Cambridge University Press.

Wallace, A. F. C. (1972) *Rockdale: The growth of an American village in the early industrial revolution.* Boston: Alfred A Knopf.

Warner, S. B. (1968). *The Private City: Philadelphia in Three Periods of Its Growth.* Philadelphia: University of Pennsylvania Press.

Warner, S. B. (2001). *Greater Boston: Adapting regional traditions to the present.* Philadelphia: University of Pennsylvania Press.

United States—Overview

The environmental history of the United States from European settlement to the present is a history of land and resource use based on the exploitation of forests, wildlife, soils, grasslands, and minerals followed by conservation and resource management. Although native peoples had used the land for thousands of years prior to European colonization, the rapid growth of population over the first three hundred years of European settlement took a toll on many resources. By the late nineteenth century depletion sparked the conservation and preservation movements, which sought to manage resources for the greatest good of the greatest number for the longest time and to set aside lands as national parks and to preserve wildlife and wilderness. By the end of the twentieth century the environmental movement focused on environmental quality and the regulation of industrial pollution and urban development.

1247

Men still live who, in their youth, remember [passenger] pigeons. Trees still live who, in their youth, were shaken by a living wind. But a decade hence only the oldest oaks will remember, and at long last only the hills will know. . . . To love what was is a new thing under the sun, unknown to most people and all pigeons. To see America as history, to conceive of destiny as a becoming, to smell a hickory tree through the still lapse of ages—all these things are possible for us, and to achieve them takes only the free sky, and the will to ply our wings.

Source: Leopold, Aldo. (1949). "On a Monument to the Passenger Pigeon." In *A Sand County Almanac*, pp. 109, 112.

Through time science has played an integral role in shaping the environment. It was initially appropriated to exploit natural resources, starting with forests, but the conservation movement engaged science as a tool for efficiently developing them. The twentieth-century environmental movement used sciences not only to manage resources but also to justify not developing them at all.

Natural Resource Exploitation

Forests were the first natural resource exploited and then brought under management in the United States. Raphael Zon, one of the first American foresters, observed, "No other economic and geographical factor has so profoundly affected the development of the country as forests" (Williams 1989, 4). Although forests provided nearly everything needed by European settlers, until the 1820s forests were looked upon as hindrances to be removed for agriculture. In a subtle shift in attitude, the growing demand for wood by mid-nineteenth century led business people, land speculators, and even the federal government to view forests as just another agricultural commodity to be bought, sold, and harvested. Changes in saw technology and manufacturing made increased production possible. By 1850 the lumber industry had become the second-largest industry and remained among the top five industries until 1920. Census figures showed that lumber production had been rising swiftly over the last half of the nineteenth century.

Forests provided more than timber. They also held essential game animals that provided meat for settlers and Native Americans alike and valuable skins and pelts for trade with European merchants. As early as 1604 French and British explorers began trading with Native Americans in exchange for knives, glasses, combs, hatchets, kettles, and food. Several tribes in New England soon became dependent upon European traders for food and European tools needed for subsistence, which accelerated the rate at which animals were killed. Between 1700 and 1775 the beaver composed over half of England's total fur imports, and eight other animals totaled 40 percent. As the beaver and its habitats disappeared from the New England states, so did other associated species. The white-tailed deer was exterminated in all of New England (except Maine) by 1890, and buffalo, the American elk, caribou, and moose had largely disappeared from the region by then, too. The pattern of exploitation and extermination was repeated in other regions with other animals used for trade purposes, including otter (West Coast), buffalo (the Great Plains), and deer (Southeast).

Agriculture also contributed to environmental problems. In the South, early dependence upon commercial crops created a vicious cycle: Because tobacco and cotton quickly rob the soil of nutrients, land had to be rehabilitated by being enriched with fertilizer or by being left fallow for several seasons, or new land had to be acquired. Impatient growers who were focused on immediate profits instead of long-term planning moved on to new land instead of developing environmentally beneficial practices. Commercial production led to the wasteful clearing of forests as farmers continually moved on to new lands. Land cleared of ground cover created soil erosion problems, such as silt clogging waterways and vital topsoil being lost.

The Conservation Movement

Just as forests were the first resource exploited, they were the first protected. The dramatic increase in lumber production during the late 1800s, coupled with the visual evidence of how lumbering altered the landscape, created fear of a timber famine among some

A first day of antiair pollution stamp and envelope by the U.S. postal service on 28 October 1970.

citizens. The conservation movement of the late nineteenth century was a direct response to that fear. In the 1860s and 1870s a small group of American scientists and political leaders, including George Perkins Marsh, Charles S. Sargent, and Carl Schurz, spoke out against the rapid deforestation, as well as the depletion of water, minerals, and soil. They deplored the unregulated exploitation of natural resources and called for government action on public land. Many favored conservation, or the sustained yield of renewable resources, such as water, trees, and game animals, and the careful, scientific management of nonrenewable resources on a permanent basis. They conducted research and petitioned Congress to take action.

After years of such agitation Congress responded by passing the Forest Management Act in 1897, but decisive action came during Theodore Roosevelt's presidency (1901–1909). Roosevelt's administration made scientific exploitation accepted policy. But federal conservation measures protected only public lands. Clearing land for agriculture remained the biggest factor in altering the environment. Forest removal had caused flooding, soil erosion, and loss of wildlife and their habitat on land and in waterways, sometimes causing permanent changes. Nonetheless, faced with the twin crises of the Great Depression and environmental overexploitation, especially in the Great Plains, President Franklin Roosevelt's administration in the 1930s expanded state-controlled management. Soil conservation became a major priority to combat the Dust Bowl in the Great Plains during the mid-1930s. Through programs such as the Civilian Conservation Corps and the Tennessee Valley Authority, the government tried to use science to reverse environmental damage on both private and public lands.

Wilderness Preservation and Environmentalism

Wilderness preservation and protection had grown along with the conservation movement, but they largely remained a secondary priority until the 1960s. Until then, scientific research provided a rationale for subduing the wild for the benefit of humankind. Federal and state governments built roads and lodging facilities in their parks and forest recreation areas to make wilderness more accessible to the masses. They supported systematically eliminating wolves and other predators from grazing areas and parks. The federal government responded to the unprecedented demands for natural resources during World War II and the postwar era by relaxing regulations on public lands and cooperating with industry. The environment suffered proportionate injury from the increased extraction activities such as mining and lumbering, from the introduction of chemical pesticides in agriculture, and from the discharge of industrial waste into waterways and landfills.

The Dust Bowl had exposed the weakness of unlimited scientific exploitation. Conservationists' focus on efficient development of natural resources no longer provided all the answers. Ecologists began explaining how human activity affects the environment and how humans are part of the environment, not separate from it. In the early 1950s the general public's growing interest in outdoor activity in a more natural environment fused with the science of ecology to create the environmentalism movement.

All sides in the debate over the environment deployed scientific arguments to support their causes. Some scientists favored responding to ecological problems with increased human intervention, whereas others favored a reduction. Industry used its own scientific findings to support the status quo or the removal of regulations. But when information about ecological damage reached the general public it instead generated a passionate desire to reduce human intervention. Private organizations such as the Wilderness Society or the Sierra Club expressed a desire to limit or halt development in public wilderness areas and set them aside for protection on behalf of the general public. Demands to protect nature became a major factor in the debate over the environment.

Congress responded in the 1960s with legislation permanently preserving wilderness and wild and scenic rivers. From that point forward, government policy prized resources for both their aesthetic value and commercial value. Emboldened, environmental groups pushed for curbs on pollution—first for air and water in the 1950s and 1960s and toxic chemical waste in the 1970s. They sought local, state, and federal laws to protect drinking water, clean up the air and waterways, and contain the spread of toxic chemicals. Environmentalists moved from reacting to a problem to preventing it through government regulation. If the government failed in its duty, environmentalists filed lawsuits to compel enforcement.

This shift has left environmentalists at odds with industry leaders and quite frequently with the government agencies in charge of enforcing environmental regulations. Policymakers continually find themselves in difficult situations. They must balance the economic needs of industry and the local populations dependent upon them with the ecological requirements of the land and with the aesthetic and material needs of taxpayers. Because scientific research is used by all involved to support their respective arguments, science, which had once provided the answer, has now become part of the problem.

James G. Lewis

See also Army Corps of Engineers; Audubon Society; Brower, David; Carson, Rachel; Civilian Conservation Corps; Conservation; Dewey, John; Douglas, Marjorie Stone; Douglas, William O.; Environmental Protection Agency; Friends of the Earth; Ickes, Harold; Izaak Walton league; Jefferson, Thomas; Johnson, Lyndon; Leopold, Aldo; Manifest Destiny; Marsh, George Perkins; Muir, John; National Park Service; National Wildlife federation; Nature Conservancy; Nixon, Richard; Roosevelt, Franklin Delano; Roosevelt, Theodore; Ruckleshaus, William; Schurz, Carl; Sierra Club; Watt, James; Wilderness Society

Further Reading

Bowler, P. J. (1993). *The Norton history of the environmental sciences.* New York: W. W. Norton.

Cohen, M. P. (1988). *The history of the Sierra Club.* San Francisco: Sierra Club Books.

Graham, F., Jr. (1971). *Man's dominion: The story of conservation in America.* New York: M. Evans.

Hays, S. P. (1959). *Conservation and the gospel of efficiency: The progressive conservation movement, 1890–1920.* Cambridge, MA: Harvard University Press.

Limerick, P. N. (1987). *The legacy of conquest: The unbroken past of the American West.* New York: W. W. Norton.

Merchant, C. (1989). *Ecological revolutions: Nature, gender, and science in New England.* Chapel Hill: University of North Carolina Press.

Mitchell, L. C. (1981). *Witnesses to a vanishing America: The nineteenth-century response.* Princeton, NJ: Princeton University Press.

Petulla, J. M. (1977). *American environmental history: The exploitation and conservation of natural resources.* San Francisco: Boyd & Fraser.

Reisner, M. (1986). *Cadillac desert: The American West and its disappearing water.* New York: Viking Penguin.

Udall, S. (1963). *The quiet crisis.* New York: Holt, Rinehart and Winston.

Williams, M. (1989). *Americans and their forests.* Cambridge, UK: Cambridge University Press.

United States—South

The history of the South of the United States has been influenced by several environmental factors. Although climate varies locally throughout the South, the region experiences mild winters and hot and humid summers compared to the rest of the nation. Its generally mediocre soil quality once forced farmers to continue using traditional methods long after they had become outdated. And like the climate, the impact of technology has varied from locality to locality, but it has created problems that afflict the region universally.

Geography

The geography of the South is more diverse than simply the "upper" and "lower" South previously used to describe the Confederacy. In addition to the eleven states of the Confederacy (Alabama, Arkansas, Florida, Georgia, Louisiana, Mississippi, North Carolina, South Carolina, Tennessee, Texas, and Virginia) the states of Delaware, Kentucky, Maryland, Missouri, and West Virginia should also be considered when discussing the geography and environment of the South. Its two dominant physical features, the Coastal Plains and the Appalachian Mountains, have influenced human activity to a greater extent than is often recognized. In fact, they have left the region divided rather than unified. Of the two, the Coastal Plains are the more dominant feature, comprising about one-third of the South's land. Runoff from the Coastal Plains flows to the coastline, which is over 4,800 kilometers long. A major feature of the Coastal Plains is the Mississippi River valley, which has long been a conduit for commerce and travel, as well as a physical barrier and environmental threat through flooding. Cotton, rice, and sugarcane once dominated the economy and landscape of the Coastal Plains. Historically, the Coastal Plains link the South with the Atlantic Seaboard both culturally and economically.

The crescent-shaped Coastal Plains envelop the Piedmont Plateau, which extends from central Alabama northward through Maryland. The Appalachian Mountain system, which extends from central Alabama to Newfoundland in Canada, forms the plateau's western border. The southern section is formed by the Appalachian system, which is composed of two parallel mountain belts, including the Appalachian Mountains themselves, and the Blue Ridge Mountains. The Appalachians historically have been linked more directly to the Northeast and helped differentiate that region culturally from the Coastal Plains. The Central Lowlands, which have long been linked to the Midwest and Southwest, compose the western and northwestern boundary of the South, which is found in part of the upper South and east Texas. It is a vast plain stretching from the Appalachians to the Rocky Mountains, broken up by an area called the "Interior Highlands" in northern Arkansas and southern Missouri.

Although the South is geographically diverse, the soil and other natural resources have unified the region. Because the last Ice Age did not reach the region, the soil largely lacks minerals such as nitrogen, phosphorus, potassium, and sulfur, which were ground up by the ice and can be found in other regions. With annual rainfall greater than most of the nation, southern soil has also been further depleted of its nutrients, leaving large deposits of clay. Consequently the region has low- to medium-grade soils, subject to erosion because of the slope of the land. The land is rich in timber and other resources, including coal, oil, gas, bauxite, copper, phosphates, and other ores used by industry. The region also possesses a series of excellent waterways that allows inland navigation.

Agriculture, Economics, and the Environment

Cotton is traditionally considered the South's most important crop. The story of how cotton transformed the South is a familiar one—of how, by the close of the eighteenth century, cotton growing dominated the region and left it economically dependent upon one crop and shaped southern culture. But this story focuses

too narrowly on one aspect of southern agriculture. It ignores the broader context of environmental and economic history.

A climate favorable to growing commercial crops such as tobacco and cotton encouraged dependence upon an agricultural economy until the early to mid-twentieth century. Planters in the Coastal Plains practiced mixed farming and stock raising on a limited basis because the long, hot summers made growing shallow-root crops and feed crops difficult; the summers also limited the combination of livestock and food crops that usually makes small farms profitable. With access to good transportation routes, growing the leading commercial crops—cotton, tobacco, rice, and sugarcane—proved highly profitable. In the Appalachians, the opposite was true. Mixed farming dominated but rarely proved profitable because the mountainous terrain made transporting goods expensive.

But the favorable climate also worked against the growers. Cotton requires a growing season of two hundred frost-free days, a condition that can be duplicated in few areas outside the South. Rice and sugarcane also require lengthy growing seasons, and their growers depended on slave labor to succeed. Sugarcane, grown in much of Louisiana near the lower Mississippi and Red River valleys and on the terraces above them created during the last Ice Age, required frequent fertilizing to compensate for the rapid depletion of potassium caused by the cane. As in the rice lands of coastal Georgia and the Carolinas, production required great numbers of slaves on large plantations to carry out the complex growing and refining process. Growing rice presented its own unique problems. The plant required flooding during part of its development, and the stagnant waters became breeding grounds for malaria-carrying mosquitoes. Indigo, a plant grown for its dye in the Carolina coastal areas and heavily dependent upon slave labor, was an important commercial crop until the industry collapsed after the American Revolution because of Britain's postwar protective policy. Many of its growers switched to Sea Island, or black-seeded, cotton and remained trapped in shaky economic circumstances. Dependence upon commercial crops created a vicious cycle: It meant that growers focused on immediate profits instead of long-term planning and contributed to the dependence upon slave labor, which in turn led to a need to grow more commercial crops in order to support the slave labor.

Growing little besides commercial crops also wreaked havoc on the soil. Because tobacco quickly robs the soil of nutrients, its commercial production led to the wasteful clearing of forests as farmers continually moved on to new lands. Either farmers had no knowledge of the harm they were inflicting through their planting activity, or they displayed little concern over that harm while new land was available. The switch to less "demanding" crops, such as wheat, and the use of fertilizers eventually improved farming in the Tidewater Virginia area, where commercial tobacco planting began. But soil erosion and exhaustion remained a chronic problem throughout the Piedmont Plateau from both tobacco and corn cultivation. The South—specifically the tobacco-growing areas of Maryland, Virginia, and North Carolina—had the dubious honor of experiencing the nation's first large-scale soil erosion problem.

Soil erosion also became a problem in the "Cotton Belt," which stretched from the Carolinas eventually to east Texas. Soil easily wore out and eroded from years of growing the same crop on the same land. Erosion left behind tens of thousands of gullies, with some in Georgia as deep as 45 meters. Although larger planters were guilty of abusing their lands, smaller landholders operating under the tenant and share-cropping systems may have done more damage because they had less land in reserve for rotation or lying fallow.

The continued use of fire as an agricultural tool caused other environmental problems. European settlers had adopted Native American burning practices to prepare farm sites, to generate potash for fertilizer, and to dispose of debris. Smaller farmers forced onto less productive land used fire to keep pine trees from overtaking their land. Stripping land of ground cover accelerated soil erosion problems. Historian Stephen J. Pyne has observed, in *Fire in America*, that "the confluence of economic, social, and historical events that worked to sustain this pattern of frontier economy long after it disappeared elsewhere in the United States" created a "socioeconomic environment for the continuance of woodburning." Thus reliance on burning kept farmers from investigating other potentially healthier practices.

Despite all these problems, cotton growing remained the most important commercial activity in the South until the 1940s. The introduction of soil conservation techniques, fertilizer, pesticides, and mechanization, coupled with a shift to other crops like soybeans and peanuts in rotation, spelled the end of cotton's domination, but helped bring agricultural productivity back to the South.

Timber Conservation

Prior to European settlement, largely unmodified, uninhabited forests stretched from the Mississippi River to the Atlantic Coast with few exceptions, such as in Virginia, where there was a sizable Native American population. The forests, a mix of deciduous (broadleaf) trees and evergreens, still make up approximately 40 percent of the nation's commercial forests, including the largest portion of its hardwood reserves.

After European settlement, wood was of critical importance in everyday life. Settlers used wood for nearly everything in the home: Wood furniture rested on hardwood floors inside of clapboard houses with wood-shingle roofs surrounded by wooden fences. Tools, utensils, storage containers such as barrels and boxes, and transportation vehicles (wagons, ships, and carriages) were also made of wood. The abundance of timber led to the establishment of a handful of large commercial lumbering operations. They managed to produce enough timber for export, but most was produced for local or regional consumption. From the 1830s until the outbreak of the Civil War, the naval-stores industry (the harvesting of tar, pitch, and wood for shipbuilding) rivaled the cotton industry. In areas too poor for cotton farming, farmers slowly turned to working in the lumber industry. In the Appalachians, subsistence farmers supplemented income by selling lumber to the coastal lowlands. Early attempts at forest preservation failed because of the abundance of timber in the mountains.

Commercial logging did not become widespread in the South until the 1880s. Extensive logging in the Northeast and the Great Lakes region dominated until then, but after the best stands were cut, lumbermen turned to the southern forests. New railroad lines opened up the Appalachians to logging. Improved saw technologies, both in the sawmills and in the forests, increased production to meet rising demand for inexpensive lumber. Clearcutting left behind devastated lands that were not capable of natural regeneration.

A reluctance to give up fire as an agricultural tool contributed to the slow acceptance of forest conservation measures by southerners. Although the South was home to the first forestry school in the nation (the Biltmore Forest School, opened in North Carolina in 1898), ironically the federal government did not inaugurate scientific forestry management in the region until two years after the school closed in 1909. In 1911 Congress passed the Weeks Act, which provided for the acquisition of eastern lands for national forests to protect watersheds and to restock forests and encouraged cooperative fire control programs with state forestry bureaus. In addition, the Clark-McNary Act of 1924 championed fire suppression as a management policy. In another twist, the ecological problems created by fire suppression led the U.S. Forest Service to develop the technique of prescribed burning, or the setting of controlled fires to reduce fuel buildup in the forest and reduce the incidence of disastrous fire, first in the South to improve the land and to regenerate longleaf pine and other species.

In the 1930s the development of chemical processes that allowed the pulp industry to utilize southern pines accelerated conservation activity and encouraged private fire control. Although industrial logging had largely destroyed the First (virgin) Forest by the 1930s, pine plantations for pulp production led to the creation of the Second and then the Third Forests, the latter of which is now being harvested and regenerated. Major lumber companies, in cooperation with state and federal land management bureaus, have taken an active role in fire protection, land management, and regeneration.

The Civil War, Industrialization, and Urbanization

The South suffered more than the loss of lives during the Civil War. The economic and environmental destruction that resulted from the war is often overlooked. Southern cities lay in ruins, their industrial capabilities destroyed. Railroads no longer had lines to run their cars, factories and mills were destroyed, and crops and homes burned. Much of the region's infrastructure was gone. Bridges, trestles, and roads were destroyed along with telegraph lines, making movement and communication difficult. Forests sprang up in the abandoned countryside where they had not grown for years; in other cases, forests were destroyed as a result of battle or foraging. As historian John Brinckerhoff Jackson has noted, in *American Space*, the rebuilding effort required "the almost total reorganization of the Southern landscape—an undertaking scarcely less arduous than the creating of a brand-new landscape in the West."

The devastation of war gave the South the opportunity to modernize as it rebuilt. Although industrial growth lagged behind that of other regions, it served as a bridge between the agriculture activity of the past and the mixed economy of agriculture and industry in the present. Until the 1870s the South's economy was based on the production of raw materials such as cotton or timber for manufacturers in the Northeast or England. Until then southern industrial output was largely limited to tobacco processing, textiles, and iron production. Industrial growth became evident after 1880, but not on the scale seen in the Northeast. Most activity centered on the timber and mining industries and the manufacture of iron and steel. Although the change would not be fully apparent for several generations, the slow evolution away from agrarianism toward a mixed economy had begun.

In the 1930s two developments significantly altered the southern landscape and the way southern people interacted with the land. In the upper South, construction by the Tennessee Valley Authority (TVA)—a series of dams and improved waterways in the Tennessee River basin that covers parts of seven states—began as part of President Franklin Roosevelt's New Deal. The TVA not only modernized the region by introducing electricity and other amenities to homes, but also opened the region to new levels of exploitation, chiefly in coal, construction material, grain, petroleum, chemicals, and forest products. The TVA brought urbanization and higher standards of living but also all kinds of pollution and land degradation. Large companies with few or no historical ties to the land soon dominated regional lumber and agricultural operations.

Arguably, the introduction of air conditioning created the greatest changes in the South. Air conditioning has made adapting lifestyles to the climate a moot point. Although air-conditioned movie theaters and railway cars had become common in the South during the 1930s, it was not until after World War II that air conditioning became widespread in office buildings and public transit vehicles and then in homes and automobiles by the 1950s. Now tractors and lumber equipment are air conditioned to make workers more productive. This helped reverse the outmigration by the 1960s and sparked the growth of "the Sunbelt," as the South has become known. Air conditioning has played a key role in the industrialization and urbanization of the region. New factories, businesses, and housing complexes have increased urban sprawl and pollution as people have flocked to the region for work, vacation, or retirement. As a result the South has also lost much of its cultural uniqueness and its connection to the land.

Technology has allowed southerners to shift from adapting to the environment to altering the environment itself. Industrialization and urbanization made possible by the TVA, air conditioning, and other inventions have accelerated the rate of alteration while further diminishing the region's agrarian legacy. By keeping pace with other regions of the country, the South has increasingly come to resemble those regions.

James G. Lewis

Further Reading

Clark, T. D. (1984). *The greening of the South: The recovery of land and forest.* Lexington: University Press of Kentucky.

Cobb, J. C. (1984). *Industrialization and southern society, 1877–1984.* Lexington: University Press of Kentucky.

Cobb, J. C., & Namorato, M. V. (Eds.). (1984). *The New Deal and the South: Essays.* Jackson: University Press of Mississippi.

Cowdrey, A. E. (1983). *This land, this South: An environmental history.* Lexington: University Press of Kentucky.

Fite, G. C. (1984). *Cotton fields no more: Southern agriculture, 1865–1980.* Lexington: University Press of Kentucky.

Goldfield, D. R. (1982). *Cotton fields and skyscrapers: Southern city and region, 1607–1980.* Baton Rouge: Louisiana State University Press.

Jackson, J. B. (1972). *American space: The centennial years, 1865–1876.* New York: W. W. Norton.

Pyne, S. J. (1982). *Fire in America: A cultural history of wildland and rural fire.* Princeton, NJ: Princeton University Press.

United States—Southwest

New Mexico, Arizona, and most of Utah, Nevada, and Colorado constitute the Southwest region of the United States. Aridity primarily defines the region's environment. Explorers once described the Colorado plains as the "Great American Desert" because they receive less than 50 centimeters of precipitation a year. West and south of the southern Rocky Mountains, deep canyons, tall mesas, the country's highest plateau (the Colorado Plateau), and four deserts (Mojave, Sonora, Chihuahua, and Great Basin) receive even less precipitation. Sporadic vegetation dots these areas, the isolated peaks interrupting the plateau, and the mountains rimming the Great Basin. The more heavily forested southern Rockies extend from northern New Mexico into Colorado, reaching heights of 4,200 meters and capturing snow and rain that feed the Southwest's two major rivers and their tributaries. The Colorado River and the Rio Grande provide much of the region's cherished water. These and other rivers have dictated living patterns through three overlapping eras of human habitation: Native American, Spanish and Mexican, and American.

Native American Habitation

Despite limitations imposed by the difficult environment, the Southwest experienced extensive human settlement and agricultural development prior to the arrival of Europeans. Communities existed well before 1000 BCE, but around this time, Mogollan people along the southern Arizona–New Mexico border adopted systematic farming to grow maize, squash, and beans. Well into the thirteenth century CE they erected permanent settlements on mountain streams and dug pithouses (mud homes dug into the earth) to deal with extreme temperatures. Migrant people from Mexico called the "Hohokam" similarly settled along the Salt and Gila Rivers in Arizona, where they maintained the region's first irrigation system. A series of brush dams diverted water through earthen canals to fields lining central Arizona's river terraces. The descendants of the Hohokam, the Pima, worked fields based on this irrigation system.

In the Four Corners area, where Colorado, Arizona, New Mexico, and Utah meet, increased aridity in the eighth century CE forced the Anasazi culture to enhance its cultivation techniques with more extensive irrigation and terraced fields. The Anasazi shifted from long-established pithouses to aboveground, multistoried masonry structures. More intensive farming allowed for weaving and ceramics production, influenced religious ceremonies related to weather, and extended Anasazi villages over an area larger than contemporary California. A densely populated, cooperative society, Anasazi culture employed complex water distribution systems running from springs and side canyons. In the late thirteenth century CE, drought, soil salinity and erosion, deforestation from pueblo construction, damaged watersheds, and hostile nomadic tribes contributed to the Anasazis' decline. Some migrated south to become ancestors of the Hopi and Zuni; others migrated east to the Rio Grande Valley and emerged as modern Pueblos.

Relative latecomers to northern New Mexico and Arizona, the Navajo probably moved from the Great Plains between the thirteenth and sixteenth centuries. Originally nomadic hunters, they foraged and raided villages of the Pueblos before they emulated the latter's

Water flows uphill towards money. (Anonymous saying in the American West)

cultivation systems. Other migrants from the Great Basin and Great Plains, the Apaches, continued to hunt and raid. When the Spanish first entered the Southwest in 1539, they encountered a land populated by these and other Native Americans.

Spanish and Mexican Habitation

The first Spanish settlers assumed that this arid region was most fit for grazing by cattle, sheep, and horses based on their experience with water-scarce landscapes in Spain and Mexico. Concluding that water was too limited for individual management, they created community rights to preserve it for the common good, established cooperative agricultural villages, and constructed distribution systems. The Rio Grande Valley offers the most enduring legacy of Spain's colonial desert occupation. Its first settlements appeared as early as 1598, but they grew little before the Pueblo Revolt of 1680, a violent quest for freedom on the part of Native Americans due to stress from drought, starvation, Apache raids, and Spanish persecutions. The successful, albeit bloody *Reconquista*, or reconquest of the Pueblos by the Spanish, prompted greater Spanish expansion. During the Spanish era, however, approximately 99 percent of the New Mexican population, including the Spanish, the Native Americans, and people of mixed blood, occupied only 1 percent of the land centralized in three Rio Grande villas: Santa Fe founded in

The ruins of stone cliff dwellings of the Anasazi in Mesa Verde, New Mexico. COURTESY DAVID LEVINSON.

1610, Santa Cruz in 1695, and Albuquerque in 1706. This habitation pattern reflected both limited water resources and intermittent threats posed by nomadic tribes.

Most Spanish colonists engaged in a subsistence economy. Self-reliant local production for local consumption involved the broad utilization of the entire ecosystem. With salinization from irrigation, deforestation, overgrazing, and gradual population growth, the villas exceeded their carrying capacity near the end of the eighteenth century. In the long run, perhaps the most significant environmental impact of the Spanish proved to be their introduction of alien species, such as apples, peaches, wheat, and grazing animals. The Apache, for example, quickly adapted to the horse and used it to facilitate raids on the Spanish and the Pueblos, forcing uneasy alliances between these two societies. The Apache brought the horse to the southern plains, where the Kiowa and the Comanche and later the Cheyenne and Arapaho adopted it. There, by 1850, a combination of ecological factors (drought, competition from other grazers, bovine diseases) and market forces (Native American overhunting and cow selectivity) contributed to the near extinction of the bison and the decline of plains Native American cultures.

Despite the duration of Spanish colonization and the continuation of its resource management policies during twenty-five years of Mexican control, Spain's limited territorial expansion left a relatively large, relatively stable Native American population until American occupation. Encounters with the Spanish had not necessarily eroded community identity. Indeed, some Native Americans easily incorporated Spanish grazing animals, plants, and technology into their production systems. The Pima of the Gila River flourished until the arrival of numerous Americans in the second half of the nineteenth century. On the other hand, the fragmented Pueblos, who participated in some Spanish legal and religious systems, tried to reestablish communities in an effort to avoid absorption first by Spain and later by Mexico.

American Habitation

Official American occupation of the Southwest began with the Treaty of Guadalupe Hidalgo between the

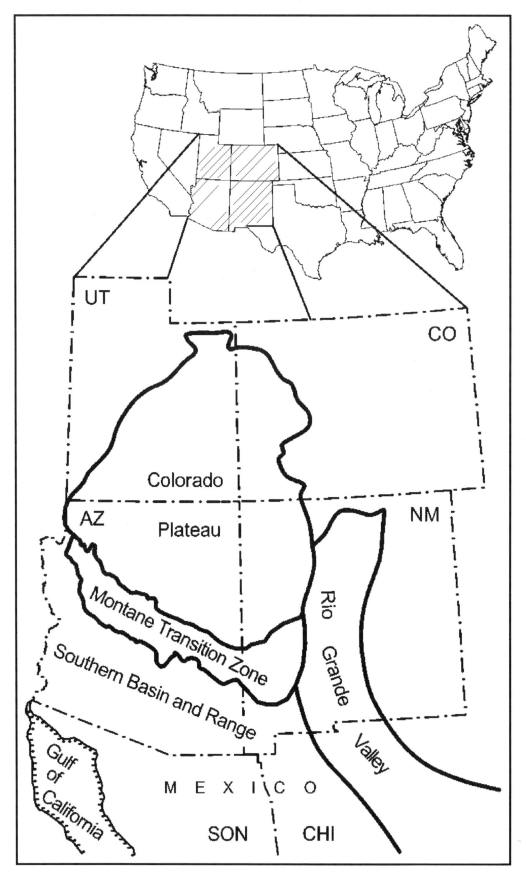

The Prehistoric American Southwest. COURTESY MICHAEL DIEHL/DESERT ARCHAEOLOGY, INC.

United States and Mexico in 1848, although trappers and traders had participated in the regional economy since Mexico opened its borders to trade in the 1820s. Although only 150 years in duration, the American era of habitation has proved the most dramatic in terms of environmental change. Americans in the arid West rejected, for the most part, the Hispanic model of cooperative agriculture and water management. Mormons in the desert wilderness of Utah, searching for spiritual freedom and economic independence, proved an exception. Their scarce resources belonged to the religious community. Hydraulic technology ensured the equitable distribution of water. Mormons used community water law to limit outside investors and settlement by nonmembers. As the nineteenth century drew to a close and Utah's economy became increasingly integrated into the nation's, the state moved from a centralized authority dominated by the Mormon Church to a more secular system of localized and dispersed canal districts responsive to immediate crises.

Mining formed a significant aspect of the Nevada, Colorado, and Arizona economies during the late nineteenth and early twentieth centuries. Ecologically destructive techniques developed at Nevada's Comstock Lode were transported to other regional mines. "Square-set" (wooden support structures within mines) timbering contributed to excessive deforestation, taking as much as 40 percent of Colorado's forests by 1900. Pollution from mines and refining plants blackened skies and killed the small amounts of vegetation that remained. Tunnels were cut through mountain sides to remove excess groundwater or to ventilate shafts; subsidences, or depressions on the surfaces, were common. Piles of tailings (residue) dotted slopes and filled streams, clogging waterways and killing fish. Animals disappeared due to these changes and overhunting. In isolated areas, hydraulic mining introduced water cannons that washed aside entire hillsides.

Other Americans who moved into the Southwest initially committed to the concept of individual family farms on privately owned land. As the nineteenth century drew to a close, however, they realized that traditional solutions did not work. Private capital, personal initiative, and individual state action failed to overcome the region's aridity. Westerners asked the federal government to provide substantial waterworks while the nation's taxpayers paid the bill.

Congress passed the Newlands Reclamation Act in 1902 and mandated that the Bureau of Reclamation, founded the following year, serve small family farmers by providing irrigation water. This act, commentators suggest, was as important as the Homesteading Act in Americans' development of the Southwest. Sales of western lands by the federal government were intended to provide the money to fund reclamation construction projects. During its first thirty years, the Bureau of Reclamation built twenty-two dam projects, primarily in states and territories with greater land sales. In one of the early projects, the bureau constructed the Roosevelt Dam on the Salt River, the principal tributary of the Gila, the master stream of central Arizona and a Colorado River feeder. At present, with a series of dams, little water from the Salt reaches the Gila.

Problems plagued the reclamation project during its first three decades. Conflicts over water rights, slow land sales, premature settlement, high levels of private debt incurred by small farmers, and more specific agricultural problems such as drainage and salinity limited successful farming under reclamation. When President Franklin Roosevelt made reclamation a cornerstone of his New Deal for the Southwest, however, the Bureau of Reclamation found its solutions. The construction of Hoover Dam on the Colorado River ushered in a new era of water management through mammoth multipurpose dams. In 1922 the seven states that make up the river basin signed the Colorado River Compact to distribute water equitably among themselves and to allow a small amount for Mexico. However, because the compact based its distribution amounts on a flood year, the river now ran at a deficit by human standards. With Hoover Dam and subsequent dams, the bureau sought to rectify the deficit through technology so that southwestern rivers might provide irrigation water for farmers, electrical power for cities and industries, and flood control. Booming economic development in the Southwest after World War II depended upon the control of water and the financing of these projects primarily by the general federal treasury rather than the reclamation fund.

Dams Change Natural Environment

By 2000 more than thirty thousand significant dams plugged rivers across the American West. Construction of these dams has also meant a concrete and steel network of roads, railroads, cement factories, diversion tunnels, irrigation canals, quarries, and power plants that have usurped natural environments. Ten dams on the Colorado River have prompted greater urban growth and agricultural production in the nation's most arid region. With such dams, salinity has destroyed farmland, downstream wetlands have disappeared, bird habitats have dried up, upstream canyons and their archaeological treasures have been lost, people have been dispossessed, and silt has filled reservoirs, diminishing their capacity and destroying aquatic life that adapted over millennia.

The Central Arizona Project (CAP) carries water from the Colorado River more than 535 kilometers to Phoenix and Tucson, desert cities that boomed during the 1940s due to the federal investment in reclamation and military-industrial facilities. Environmentalists subsequently criticized CAP because 50 percent of its water is lost in evaporation and because it illustrates the bureau's abandonment of the small farmers in favor of large agribusiness. Phoenix sits in a natural bowl that captures heat and pollution. CAP and other projects that drain the Gila River made life tolerable there by powering air conditioners, filling swimming pools, and watering golf courses. Yet, at the same time, Arizonans pulled 80 percent of their water from underground aquifers, an overdraft of 8,000,000,000 square meters of water each year.

Through all these changes, the Southwest remains home to a substantial Hispanic population and the largest concentration of Native Americans and Native American-controlled land in the United States. The Navajo are the largest group, whereas the Pueblo people are among the most cohesive Native American cultures. Hispanic community grants and Native American rights, increasingly given greater recognition in U.S. courts, have influenced and continue to complicate legal controversies over natural resource usage in the region.

In the late nineteenth and twentieth centuries enterprising entrepreneurs concluded that the region's less tangible natural elements held economic value and set a course for twenty-first-century resource usage debates. These entrepreneurs marketed magnificent natural scenery to tourists seeking sublimity and aridity and altitude to wealthy consumptives seeking health. Colorado Springs, Santa Fe, Salt Lake City, and Denver acquired wealth from such enterprises. Las Vegas boomed after 1945 with Hoover Dam, federal military expenditures, and its exploitation of Nevada's gambling laws. At the end of the twentieth century, these and other cities centered a service economy based on outdoor recreation and high-tech industries. Their emergence prompted new arguments for the allocation of more water to urban and recreational uses over the agrarian and extractive industries that claim the lion's share. As Americans entered the twenty-first century, they moved into the Southwest in greater numbers, occupying cities that acted as oases while reaching farther into the desert and taxing its limited resources.

Kathleen A. Brosnan

Further Reading

Alexander, T. G. (1995). *Utah, the right place: The official centennial history.* Layton, UT: Gibbs Smith.

Gutierrez, R. (1991). *When Jesus came, the corn mothers went away: Marriage, sexuality, and power in New Mexico.* Stanford, CA: Stanford University Press.

Iverson, P. (1993). Native peoples and native histories. In C. Milner, C. A. O'Connor, & Sandweiss, M. A. (Eds.), *The Oxford history of the American West.* (pp. 13–44). New York: Oxford University Press.

Lamar, H. R. (2000). *The far Southwest, 1846–1912: A territorial history* (Rev. ed.). Albuquerque: University of New Mexico Press.

Miller, C. (Ed.). (2001). *Fluid arguments: Five centuries of western water conflict.* Tucson: University of Arizona Press.

Moehring, E. P. (2000). *Resort city in the Sunbelt: Las Vegas, 1930–2000.* Reno: University of Nevada Press.

Reisner, M. (1993). *Cadillac desert: The American West and its disappearing water* (Rev. ed.). New York: Penguin.

Sherow, J. E. (Ed.). (1998). *A sense of the American West.* Albuquerque: University of New Mexico Press.

Weber, D. J. (1993). The Spanish-Mexican rim. In C. Milner, C. A. O'Connor, & Sandweiss, M. A. (Eds.), *The Oxford history of the American West.* (pp. 45–78). New York: Oxford University Press.

Wescoat, J. L., Jr. (1990). Challenging the desert. In Michael P. Conzen (Ed.), *The making of the American landscape.* (pp. 186–203). Boston: Unwin Hyman.

Worster, D. (1985). *Rivers of empire: Water, aridity, and the growth of the American West.* New York: Pantheon Books.

United States Fish and Wildlife Service

The U.S. Fish and Wildlife Service (FWS) is the primary agency responsible for wildlife conservation in the United States. The FWS is a hybrid of two earlier agencies that divided the natural world between aquatic and terrestrial wildlife. The first was the U.S. Commission of Fish and Fisheries, which was established on 9

February 1871 under the Department of Commerce and renamed the Bureau of Fisheries on 1 July 1903. The commission's first director was Spencer Fullerton Baird (1823–1887), an important nineteenth-century American naturalist who helped create the Smithsonian Institution's scientific research program. Baird established the commission as a center for federal fisheries science and propagation, creating a network of national fish hatcheries and scientific centers, including the fisheries lab at Woods Hole, Massachusetts. The Bureau of Fisheries successfully propagated a number of sport fishes (for example, trout and salmon) in the nation's waterways.

The second was the Office of Economic Ornithology and Mammalogy, which was established on 3 March 1885 under the Department of Agriculture to oversee conservation of birds and mammals. In 1896 it was renamed the Division of Biological Survey and in 1905 renamed again the Bureau of Biological Survey. The Biological Survey's first director was Clinton Hart Merriam (1855–1942), an explorer, naturalist, and leader in bird protection who moved the new agency's mission away from studying the effects of birds on agriculture to studying the natural history and "life zones" (similar to biomes [major ecological community types]) of North American wildlife. In 1939, as part of New Deal conservation efforts, the Bureau of Biological Survey and the Bureau of Fisheries were merged and transferred to the Department of Interior, and in 1940 the name of the two bureaus was officially changed to the U.S. Fish and Wildlife Service. One of the rising young employees of the new agency was

Paul Kroegel at Pelican Island the first National Wildlife Refuge (est. 1903). COURTESY THE UNITED STATES FISH AND WILDLIFE SERVICE.

Rachel Louise Carson (1907–1964), who came to work for the Bureau of Fisheries in 1936 as a junior aquatic biologist and rose to become editor-in-chief for all FWS publications by the time she retired in 1952. In her years with the FWS Carson honed her ability to make complex scientific issues accessible to the public, a talent that served her well through her marine biology books and *Silent Spring* (1962). In 1956 the FWS was again divided into two bureaus: the Bureau of Commercial Fisheries and the Bureau of Sport Fisheries and Wildlife. In 1970 the Bureau of Commercial Fisheries was moved permanently to the Department of Commerce and renamed the National Marine Fisheries Service. The Bureau of Sport Fisheries and Wildlife remained in the Department of Interior, reclaiming its U.S. Fish and Wildlife Service name in 1974.

Although the agency has been managed by three diverse departments and endured many name changes, its mission has remained the protection of the nation's wildlife. In at least three areas the FWS has been a pioneer in the American conservation movement. First, the FWS has been the primary federal wildlife law enforcement agency since the Lacey Act of 1900 prohibited the interstate shipment of illegally taken game and importation of injurious species. These tasks were expanded under the Migratory Bird Treaty Act (1918), the Bald Eagle Protection Act (1940), and the Endangered Species Act (1973). Second, the FWS manages a significant habitat base through the National Wildlife Refuge System. The refuge system began in 1903 when President Theodore Roosevelt set aside a 2-hectare island on Florida's coast as a federally protected bird reservation. The system subsequently grew to over 530 refuges encompassing more than 37 million hectares in all fifty states, a vast natural experiment to protect enough habitat for North America's wildlife to survive and thrive. Third, since 1973 the FWS has been the lead agency in implementing the Endangered Species Act—a revolutionary piece of legislation attempting to prevent species extinction. The FWS is responsible for listing species and implementing recovery plans for endangered wildlife such as the California condor, bald eagle, and gray wolf.

Mark Madison

Further Reading

Cameron, J. (1929). *The Bureau of Biological Survey.* Baltimore: Johns Hopkins University Press.

Dolin, E. (1989). *The U.S. Fish and Wildlife Service.* New York: Chelsea House Publishers.

Laycock, G. (1965). *The sign of the flying goose.* Garden City, NY: Natural History Press.

Reed, N., & Drabelle, D. (1984). *The United States Fish and Wildlife Service.* Boulder, CO: Westview Press.

United States Forest Service

The U.S. Forest Service was one of the first government service agencies to conserve and promote efficient, rational use of American natural resources. Under the popular banner of what would become known as "conservation," Congress authorized the creation of forest reservations in the 1891 General Land Revision Act. It enabled the president to "proclaim" forest reserves on public lands, most of which were in the mountainous regions of the western United States covering an area of 191 million acres. Pressures for government forestry reserves came from new professional and scientific organizations (e.g., the American Forestry Association, organized in 1882), alarming articles in the press about an impending "timber famine," and calls to protect watersheds for urban and agricultural water supplies.

Purpose and Philosophy

In the Department of Agriculture's Forestry Division, research occurred under the direction of Bernhard E. Fernow linking "forest influences" to climate moderation and the storage of water. From these investigations emerged the phrase "favorable flows of water" meaning a gradual release of water from forested lands over the spring and summer seasons into streams flowing to lower elevations for agricultural and urban uses. The investigations shaped the 1897 Forest Organic Act that clarified management goals for the reserved forest lands: (1) to achieve favorable flows of water; (2) to provide a continuous supply of timber. By declaring for a use-oriented management, Congress pacified westerners who feared prohibitions on resource use and development.

Another trained forester, Gifford Pinchot, succeeded Fernow. Pinchot advocated conservation, which for him meant the economic use of resources or the avoidance of wasteful resource exploitation that ultimately translated into the more formal policies of "sustained yield." He was a skilled publicist from a wealthy family and not without influential political connections. Most of all he was a man with a cause—the promotion of forest conservation in the United States. Despite these advantages Pinchot faced a major problem from his position in the Department of Agriculture. He desperately wanted to apply forestry principles to the new forest reserves, but they were under the Department of Interior.

When Theodore Roosevelt became president after the assassination of President McKinley in 1901, Pinchot's opportunity appeared. His friendship with Roosevelt and like-mindedness on conservation policies brought support for the 1905 Transfer Act that placed the management of forest reserve lands under the Department of Agriculture. A new U.S. Forest Service emerged from the Transfer Act and the Secretary of Agriculture named Pinchot as Chief Forester to direct it. Pinchot was now in a position to implement his utilitarian conservation policy: "the greatest good of the greatest number in the long run." The Forest Service issued new management rules in book form significantly called the *Use Book* to forest rangers in the various reserves, now renamed National Forests.

Resource Regulation Problems

The Forest Service's regulation of timber, forage, water power sites, and minerals left little room for the promotion of aesthetic or recreational values until the 1920s when it designated "primitive areas" for wilderness experiences such as hiking and camping comparable to the undisturbed landscapes of the national park system. Also, it did not assert its ownership of water in the forests or the wildlife, preferring to defer to state laws. It did see the forests linked to the quality and quantity of water running in the streams and by the last decade in the twentieth century tried to assert "instream" water rights in opposition to diversion by water users. While the Forest Service operated primarily from a western land base, the 1911 Weeks Act expanded its presence into the eastern U.S. with the acquisition of exhausted, often abandoned agricultural lands for purposes of watershed protection.

In the first two decades of the twentieth century, the Service faced challenges from the western grazing industry. In 1906, it instituted a system of grazing fees based upon animal unit months (AUMs) or a count of animals grazing on forest ranges. The fee system came with a permit or grazing privilege granted to graziers. Most stock interests initially opposed permits and fees, but the U.S. Supreme Court in several cases by 1911 affirmed the regulatory authority of the Service.

An antipollution brochure distributed by the U.S. Forest Service.

Beyond the force of law, the Forest Service sought the authority of science. Range experts in the Forest Service advanced the estimate of "carrying capacity" to determine numbers of stock allowed each year on individual forests. The estimate required botanical investigations or an appeal to the authority of science to justify restrictions on use. Similarly, it applied forest science or silviculture to its timber-cutting decisions making "scientific conservationism" an essential element in its policy decisions. Yet there was little applica-

tion. Before World War II the National Forests supplied only about 2 percent of the demand for milled lumber.

Budget restrictions and new emergency duties blunted Forest Service plans to extend its rules of forest harvest and management to private forest land during Great Depression. The Civilian Conservation Corps (CCC) in the 1930s played a major role in building forest roads, trails, campsites, and upgrading of winter sport areas.

Multiple Use and Environmentalism

During World War II the Forest Service tried to avoid the mistakes of excessive use of its resources that had occurred during World War I. But in the postwar decades the exhaustion of private forest lands and an expanding economy increased demand. The 1960 Multiple Use Act made formal policy out of management of diverse resources, succeeding the vague guidelines of the 1897 Forest Management Act that only acknowledged water and timber resources. Although the Forest Service pioneered conservation and innovative administration sensitive to local needs, it fell out of step with a changing American society during the 1960s. With the decline of federal budget appropriations beginning with the Vietnam War, the Service hastened "to get out the cut" to maintain its revenue base. It resisted the formal creation of wilderness and roadless areas, cut old growth timber, and continued scientifically defensible policies of clearcutting.

By the 1970s, the Forest Service strove to conform to the rules of the new National Environmental Policy Act (NEPA), but came under trenchant criticism for spawning an institutional culture that embraced a false optimism about its flawed conservation and environmental record. Criticism came from without and from within its own ranks for its failure to protect resources; also from traditional use advocates who saw it in an opposite light—the tool of environmentalists, especially when it sought to enforce the Endangered Species Act to protect the spotted owl in the far western forests. To counter criticisms of environmental shortcomings, the Service by the 1990s hoped to combine science and policy to achieve its historic goals of protecting resources and allowing prudent use in a newly announced "ecosystem management" policy.

William D. Rowley

Further Reading

Hirt, P. W. (1994). *A conspiracy of optimism: Management of the National Forests since World War II*. Lincoln: University of Nebraska Press.

Rowley, W. D. (1985). *U.S. Forest Service grazing and range-lands: A history*. College Station: Texas A&M Press.

Steen, H. K. (1976). *The U.S. Forest Service: A history*. Seattle: University of Washington Press.

Urbanization

The term *urbanization* has two contrasting meanings. The first involves settlement patterns: Urbanization occurs when a population moves from a state of lesser concentration to one of greater concentration. The second involves culture and lifestyle: Urbanity and civic culture, the hallmarks of civilization, are said to originate in major cities and to diffuse from them to smaller places and to rural areas. The usual indicator of urbanization in the first meaning is the percentage of the population living in urban areas. In the second meaning, the indicators are those that chart cultural evolution.

Urban Origins

The world's first cities emerged as secondary consequences of the formation of the state. There were several areas of primary urban generation: lower Mesopotamia in southwestern Asia, where Sumerian cities such as Ur, Uruk, Kish, Lagash, and Umma appeared 5,000 years ago; the Indus River valley of Asia 4,500 years ago; the northern China plain 3,000 years ago; Mesoamerica 2,500 years ago; the central Andes and Peruvian coast 2,000 years ago (although recent evidence places the age of the pyramids at Caral in Peru at 4,600 years); and the Yoruba territories in western Africa 500 years ago and beginning at the same time in Zimbabwe and the lower Congo River valley. Diffusion of institutions from already urbanized societies also stimulated the rise of cities in a number of other areas: Japan, the Indian Deccan region, southwestern Asia, the eastern Mediterranean, and the western Mediterranean and Europe. Beyond these areas, in the New World in particular, urbanization came as a consequence of colonial expansion and imposition, often with explicit planning guidelines, as in Spain's sixteenth-century Law of the Indies.

The characteristic sequence of cultural evolution in each of the zones of primary urban generation began with domestication of plants and animals and the emergence of class-based societies, followed by the formation of military and religious elites who gathered clans into states and used their power to extract surpluses from village agriculturalists. In such states hierarchies of specialized institutions developed and exercised authority over territory and maintained order within their populations. At the core of these states were monumental complexes, the focal points around which capital cities evolved as concentrated settlements and the *axes mundi* (the places where heaven, Earth, and the underworld were believed to connect) at which leaders were thought to be able to maintain contact with the gods and to ensure that stability and harmony with the universe prevailed. Within the settlements resided specialists who began as temple and palace functionaries and later evolved into producers for the market. Similarly, the merchants who conducted long-distance trade evolved from the networks of tribute that had earlier been secured by military action. Astronomy was important in the regulation of the rhythms of agriculture and also in the physical plans of the capital cities, which included astronomical orientations and cardinal (usually north-south and east-west) street alignments. The social geography of the cities was predominantly centripetal: The higher the status, the closer a resident lived to the center, but within often-walled "quarters" within which different ethnic groups were clustered.

Most classical capital cities were small and compact. Levels of urbanization never exceeded 10 percent, including any secondary centers that developed, and these were few and small. As late as 1700 there were probably no more than fourteen cities in the world with populations exceeding 200,000 (in China, Beijing 650,000, Hangchow 300,000, and Guangzhou [Canton] 200,000; in Japan, Yedo 680,000, Osaka 380,000, and Kyoto 350,000; in the Mughal empire, Ahmedabad 380,000 and Aurangabad 200,000; in Persia, Isfahan 350,000; in the Ottoman Empire, Constantinople 700,000; and in Europe, London and Paris both over 500,000 and Amsterdam and Naples both just over 200,000). Perhaps another fifty cities exceeded 50,000. They created local environments that were both exhilarating and problematic, and they produced rings of environmental modification in surrounding regions.

In her dramatic description of London in 1700, M. Waller captures the contrasts that were present in the capital cities of the time:

> London in 1700 was the most magnificent city in Europe. . . . The capital dominated the kingdom to an extent that it has never done before or since. It was home to at least 530,000 people—one in nine of

Self-Reliance and Citizen Involvement in the Developing World

In most developing countries between one-fourth and one-half of the economically active urban population cannot find adequate, stable livelihoods. With few jobs available in established businesses or government services, people have to find or create their own sources of income. These efforts have resulted in the rapid growth of what has been termed the "informal sector," which provides much of the cheap goods and services essential to city economies, business, and consumers.

Thus, while many poor people may not be officially employed, most are working—in unregistered factories and construction firms, selling goods on street corners, making clothes in their homes, or as servants or guards in better-off neighbourhoods. Most of the so-called unemployed are in fact working 10–15 hours a day, six to seven days a week. Their problem is not so much underemployment as underpayment.

Most house building, maintenance, or upgrading in the cities of developing countries is done outside official plans and usually in illegal settlements. This process mobilizes untapped resources, contributes to capital formation, and stimulates employment. These informal-sector builders represent an important source of urban employment, in particular for low and unskilled labour. They are not capital- or technology-intensive, they are not energy-intensive, and as a rule they do not impose a drain on foreign exchange. In their way, they contribute their share to attaining some of the nation's major development objectives. Moreover, they are flexible in responding to local needs and demands, catering in particular to poorer households, which usually have nowhere else to turn. Many governments have begun to see the wisdom of tolerating rather than quashing their work. Large-scale bulldozing of squatter communities is now rarer, although it still happens.

Source: World Commission on Environment and Development. (1987). *Our Common Future*. Oxford, UK: Oxford University Press, p. 248–249.

the entire population—while the second city, Norwich, had a population of 30,000. Not only did so many of William III's subjects live in London, but the city impinged on the lives of many more. It was a magnet to all classes. Aristocracy and gentry flocked to London to be seen at court, to attend Parliament, to settle their legal affairs, to enjoy the season and arrange marriages for their children, and to shop. London was a shopper's paradise, a great emporium of goods for its hungry consumers. The booming newspaper industry in Grub Street found a ready market in London's coffee-houses where everything was up for discussion. London was the centre of a lively publishing trade, the theater and music. Visitors absorbed its ideas and culture and disseminated them to all parts of the kingdom.

But this great city could not sustain itself. The mortality rate was higher than it had been a century previously. In any year there were more burials than christenings. One in three babies died before the age of two. Only one in two of the survivors passed the

age of fifteen. Adults in their twenties and thirties, often family breadwinners, were particularly vulnerable. The streets were open sewers, the drinking water was contaminated, the stink of decaying refuse and overflowing graveyards was pervasive: houses did not have the conveniences of running water or flush lavatories—and anyway, there was no understanding of basic hygiene. The atmosphere was thick with sulphurous coal smoke belching out of thousands of domestic and industrial fires, begriming the inhabitants and stultifying the gardens.

Tuberculosis was widespread and a particularly virulent strain of smallpox cut a swathe through the densely packed population. Medicine was largely helpless in the face of disease and a broken limb could be the harbinger of infection and death. It is not surprising, therefore, that native-born Londoners were chronically sick and of poor constitution, and the metropolis needed a constant influx of more robust migrants from the provinces. About 8,000 young people from all parts of the kingdom and as far away as

Ireland poured in every year, attracted by the promise of wages 50 per cent higher than anywhere else. (Waller 2000, 1–2)

There also were distinct regional effects. Despite their small size, capital cities served as the focal points of distinct city-centered "world economies," economically autonomous sections of the planet able to provide for most of their own needs. Each was surrounded by an immediate core region that was called on to provide foodstuffs and migrants and within which modification of the Earth was greatest, a modestly developed middle zone exploited for transportable resources and products, and a vast and relatively untouched periphery. The core contained the concentration of everything that was most advanced and diversified, lying at the heart of the middle zone, the settled area of the state.

Break with Classical Patterns

The first break with these classical patterns came in the late seventeenth and the eighteenth centuries in the Low Countries (Netherlands, Belgium, and Luxembourg). Exploiting new maritime technology—deepbellied cargo vessels that significantly changed seagoing goods-carrying capacity and costs—Amsterdam had become the warehouse of the world, and the United Provinces were its middle zone. In this zone, urbanization levels rose to more than 30 percent. The areas surrounding Amsterdam developed a high degree of market-based specialization in cash crops for both the urban consumer and the industrial market. Agriculture intensified, and ingenious new methods

The Pudong financial district in Shanghai, China, in August 2002. A center for global trade, the district is built on what were poor neighborhoods and farmland. COURTESY KAREN CHRISTENSEN.

of crop rotation soon transformed the English agricultural landscape. New technologies enabled the Netherlands to create cultivable polders (farmlands below sea level, protected by dikes and kept free of water by pumping) by draining swampland. Later, Dutch engineers brought their technology to England and enabled the Fens area to be settled. And a new middle-class spirit of Protestantism linked to capitalism was fostered, carrying with it associated ideas of humans' dominion over nature and the godliness of engaging in production and trade for profit. The closer to Amsterdam, the greater the degree of cash-crop specialization and the greater the extent of environmental modification. The farther from the United Provinces, the more likely it was that regions were still composed of selfsustaining agricultural villages lodged within feudal societies.

The second break with classical patterns came in eighteenth-century Britain as that country's navy and trading companies established their ascendancy and a global empire was built. Radiating outward were waves of clearance, drainage, conversion, and extraction, with the extent of environmental modification patterned by gradients of accessibility to London, by now the largest city in Europe. Its demand for food radically changed the agricultures of the English core. Its wealthy merchants bought country estates and hired landscape gardeners who created a new kind of designed rural landscape. The wealthy merchant classes became the principal dissenters who set in motion Europeans' drive to master the North American wilderness. Britain's urbanization levels reached 30 percent by 1800, but in the rest of the world there was little change from 1700. The number of cities with greater than 500,000 population increased only from five to six, and the number of cities exceeding 100,000 increased from only thirty-five to fifty. Predominantly rural societies within the new trading empires were dominated by only a few large trading centers. In contrast to the monumentally centered capital cities of earlier states, these new centers focused on their ports, docks, and warehouses. Predominantly "walking cities," they had little separation of land uses, of workplaces and homes, or of social classes and races.

Enter Industrialization

Yet, by 1800 new forces were at work that were to radically redraw the world map of urbanization. In England urban growth was already accelerating outside London, with the main burst of expansion occurring

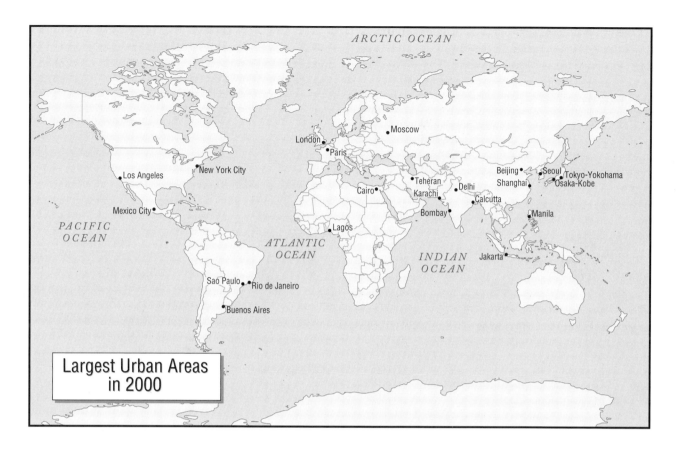

Largest Urban Areas in 2000

in the last quarter of the century in such cities as Manchester, Liverpool, Birmingham, and Glasgow, and a second echelon of urban areas in the range of 20,000 to 50,000 that included Leeds, Sheffield, Newcastle, Stoke, and Wolverhampton. The English share of European urban growth had been 33 percent in the seventeenth century, but it was more than 70 percent in the second half of the eighteenth century. This increased share was concentrated outside London in the newly industrializing North. The precipitating factor was the initial wave of the Industrial Revolution, brought about by major advances in the cotton and iron industries, the first flush of factory building, and significant improvements in waterborne transportation with the building of canals and the dredging of rivers. The new urban centers that emerged were either mill towns in which the workers resided within walking distance of the factory, cities such as Birmingham that had at their cores specialized industrial districts, or centers of control and finance of the new economy such as Manchester. Demand for labor was fed by rural-to-urban migration or by workers displaced from such occupations as hand spinning and hand-loom weaving by the new factory production.

Nineteenth-Century Industrial Urbanization

Building upon this break with the past, accelerating technological change brought a new kind of city between 1800 and 1900, built on productive power, massed population, and industrial technology. By the end of the century, this new kind of city had been credited with the creation of a system of social life founded on entirely new principles, not only in Britain, but also elsewhere in Europe, in the United States, and in pockets elsewhere across the globe. By 1900 the level of urbanization had reached 80 percent in Britain, exceeded 60 percent in the Netherlands and newly industrializing Germany, 50 percent in the United States, and 45 percent in France. Sixteen cities in the world exceeded 1 million in population, and 287 exceeded 100,000, and the world economy was shaped around two great urban-industrial core regions in western Europe and the northeastern United States, with a third emergent in Japan.

Contemporary observers recognized that something dramatic had happened. Adna Weber, a chronicler of the changes, wrote in 1899 that the most remarkable social phenomenon of the nineteenth century was

1265

the concentration of population in cities. The tendency toward concentration (or agglomeration), he said, was all but universal in the Western world. The change involved a process whereby, as societies modernized, their market mechanisms expanded in scope and influence. The size of production units increased, as did the number and complexity of production decisions. Increased division of labor and increased specialization, which accompany increased productivity, became forces promoting population concentration in cities. Associated with this population shift was the shift in the occupational structure of economies from agriculture and from unskilled occupations in primary production to more skilled clerical and higher-level occupations, largely in the secondary (manufacturing) and tertiary (service) sectors in urban concentrations. New institutions were created, and old institutions were radically altered. This was particularly true in the case of financial and market institutions, which, in turn, contributed to a massive accumulation of social and economic overhead in cities, making further high-level productivity increases possible and the modern institutions more effective. Cities grew as dense concentrations around their central business districts, which housed the headquarters of their corporations and centers of finance, together with agglomerations of downtown business, in locations that offered maximum accessibility to the surrounding population. The new urbanism became a new way of life as the increasing size and density of cities and the increasing heterogeneity of their immigrant populations produced definable social consequences: greater individual freedoms and opportunities for social and economic advance, but also the inequality, alienation, and deviance that produced unhappiness, unrest, and revolution. The new cities also dramatically changed their local environments through the unrestricted discharge of effluents into their air and waters and onto the land.

Twentieth-Century Urban Growth

During the twentieth century the urbanization level in economically advanced nations leveled off at around 80 percent, but additional bursts of technological change brought accelerating urban growth to most other parts of the world. By 2000 no part of the globe was less than 40 percent urbanized, 440 cities exceeded 1 million population, and 1,800 exceeded 100,000. At least a dozen "megacities" exceeded 10 million.

The new technologies also brought change in the spatial pattern of urban growth. The concentrated industrial metropolis had developed in the nineteenth century because centrality and proximity meant lower transportation and communication costs for those interdependent specialists who had to interact with each other frequently or intensively under horse-and-buggy conditions. But shortened distances meant higher densities and costs of congestion, high rents, loss of privacy, and the like. In contrast, virtually all the technological developments of the twentieth century had the effect of reducing the constraints of geographic space and the costs of concentration, making it possible for each generation to live farther apart and for information users to rely upon information sources that were spatially distant. As a result, decentralization and declining overall densities moved to the fore as dominant spatial processes, producing far-flung metropolitan regions and emptying out the higher-density cores.

As these changes unfolded, researchers began to codify the modifications of the physical environment produced by this rapid urban growth and transformation. These modifications occurred at three geographic scales:

1. Locally, by altering the nature of the surface of the Earth: the replacement of the natural surface of soil, grass, and trees by the urban surfaces of brick, concrete, glass, and metal at different levels above the ground. These artificial materials change the nature of the reflecting and radiating surfaces, the heat exchange near the surface, and the aerodynamic roughness of the surface.

2. Regionally, by generating large amounts of heat artificially and by altering the composition of the atmosphere via emission of gaseous and solid pollutants. At certain times of the year in midlatitude cities, artificial heat input into the atmosphere by combustion and metabolic processes may approach or even exceed that derived indirectly from the sun. The heat island that results serves as a trap for pollutants.

3. Globally, potentially, by making urban contributions to sulfur and carbon dioxide levels in the atmosphere and thus to the greenhouse effect, to global warming, and to sea-level changes, which are likely to be of greatest consequence for major coastal cities.

One of the principal local effects is via land-use changes that affect the hydrologic regime (the system of rivers and streams and the patterns of runoff):

TABLE 1.
EFFECTS ON ENVIRONMENT

Element		Compared to Rural Environs
Contaminants	Condensation nuclei (particles that serve to attract condensation)	10 times more
	Particulates (e.g., soot)	50 times more
	Gaseous admixtures (mixtures of polluting gases)	5–25 times more
Radiation	Total on horizontal surface	0–20% less
	Ultraviolet, winter	30% less
	Ultraviolet, summer	5% less
	Sunshine duration	5–15% less
Cloudiness	Clouds	5–10% more
	Fog, winter	100% more
	Fog, summer	30% more
Precipitation	Amounts	5–15% more
	Days with less than 5 mm	10% more
	Snowfall, inner city	5–10% more
	Snowfall, lee of city	10% more
	Thunderstorms	10–15% more
Temperature	Annual mean	0.5–3.0 °C more
	Winter minimums (average)	1–2 °C more
	Summer maximums	1–3 °C more
	Heating degree days	10% less
Relative Humidity	Annual mean	6% less
	Winter	2% less
	Summer	8% less
Wind Speed	Annual mean	20–30% less
	Extreme gusts	10–20% less
	Calm	5–20% more

changes in peak-flow characteristics (the scale and speed of runoff after storms); changes in total runoff; changes in water quality; and changes in hydrologic amenities (the desirability of water bodies for recreation). After urbanization, runoff occurs more rapidly and with a greater peak flow than under nonurban conditions. Urbanization increases the impervious land area, and the urban area may be served by storm sewers. Both increase the peak discharge: Maximum sewerage and imperviousness result in peak discharges that are more than six times greater than those in unurbanized conditions. In turn, sharper peak discharges increase flood frequencies and the ratio of overbank flows. Urbanization, then, increases the flood volume, the flood peak, and the flood frequency, and the flushing effect increases turbidity (the mixing of sediments in the water) and pollutant loads, although sediment loads may fall, and the channel response will therefore shift from aggradation (build-up of sediment deposits) to bank erosion. Water pollution changes the quality of downstream resources, the ecology of the riverine environment, and the amenity value of the river bank or estuary. The effects become pronounced downstream of larger cities, where natural flushing is incapable of preventing long-term damage.

At the metropolitan scale, H. E. Landsberg has summarized the major effects of urbanization on the environment. (See table 1.)

Perhaps the most dramatic effect of metropolitan growth is the creation of the urban heat island, which serves as a trap for atmospheric pollutants. Other things being equal, the temperature difference between the city core and the rural periphery, increases with city size; the difference is small and ephemeral in cities of 250,000 or less population but is substantial and longer-lasting in larger cities. The heat island expands and intensifies as the city grows, and stronger and stronger winds are needed to overcome it. Wind speeds of 5 m/sec^{-1} (12 mi/hr) can eliminate the heat island in a city of 250,000, but speeds of 10m/sec^{-1} (22 mi/hr) are required for 1 million, and 14 m/sec^{-1} (32 mi/hr) for 10 million. Yet, the surface roughness of the city serves to reduce wind speeds and inhibit this ventilation: Average wind speed may be reduced as much as 30 percent by a big city. In cities over 10 million, the mean annual minimum temperature may be as much as 2.5°C higher than that of the surrounding rural periphery. This difference is much greater in summer than in winter.

The causes are twofold, both of which are seasonally dependent: (1) In summer, the tall buildings, pavement, and concrete of the city absorb and store large amounts of solar radiation, and less of this energy is used for evaporation than in the country because of the high runoff. The stored energy is released at night, warming the urban air. (2) In winter, human-made energy used for heat and light produces the warming, yet the blanket emissions reduce incoming solar radiation by as much as 20 percent (a phenomenon known as heat rejection). When the Boston-Washington megalopolis reaches a population of 50–60 million, it will be characterized by heat rejection of 65 cal/cm^2/d. In winter, this is 50 percent, and in summer 15 percent, of the heat received by solar radiation on a horizontal surface. In Manhattan, the heat produced by combustion alone in winter has been estimated to be two and one-half times the solar energy reaching the ground. This energy is trapped by the blanket of pollutants over the city, including particulates, water vapor, and carbon dioxide, and is reemitted downward to warm the ambient air.

In addition to the heat island, other climatic effects of urbanization—all increasing with city size—include greater cloudiness, fog, dust, and precipitation, but lower humidity. And as wind dissipates the heat island, a downwind urban heat plume is detectable in the atmosphere. Along this plume, there are increased precipitation, thunderstorm, and hail probabilities, often quite distant from the city. Beyond such regional-scale consequences, urban activities are a major source of carbon dioxide and of the fluorocarbons that, in combination, may affect future global climates and sea levels.

All of these effects are intensifying as more than 50 percent of the world's 6 billion population has moved into the cities; the list of cities with more than 1 million population is expected to increase from four hundred in 2000 (in 1950 there were only eighty-six) to six hundred by 2020, and the number of megacities (urban agglomerations of 10 million or more), which totaled only one in 1950 and sixteen in 2000, is expected to rise to more than twenty by 2020.

Brian J. L. Berry

Further Reading

Berry, B. J. L. (1982). *Comparative urbanization: Divergent paths in the twentieth century.* Basingstoke, UK: Macmillan.

Berry, B. J. L. (1990). Urbanization. In B. L. Turner II, W. C. Clark, R. W. Kates, J. F. Richards, J. T. Mathews, & W. B. Meyer (Eds.), *The Earth as transformed by human action: Global and regional changes in the biosphere over the past 300 years* (pp. 103–119). Cambridge, UK: Cambridge University Press.

Berry, B. J. L., & Horton, F. E. (1974). *Urban environmental management: Planning for pollution control.* Englewood Cliffs, NJ: Prentice Hall.

Chandler, T. (1987). *Four thousand years of urban growth: An historical census.* Lewiston, ME: St. David's University Press.

DeVries, J. (1981). Patterns of urbanization in preindustrial Europe: 1500–1800. In H. Schmal (Ed.), *Patterns of European urbanization since 1500* (pp. 77–109). London: Croom Helm.

Eisenstadt, S. N., & Shachar, A. (1987). *Society, culture and urbanization.* Beverly Hills, CA: Sage Publishing.

Hall, P. (1999). *Cities in civilisation: Culture, innovation and urban order.* London: Phoenix Orion.

Knox, P. L. (1994). *Urbanization.* Englewood Cliffs, NJ: Prentice Hall.

Landsberg, H. E. (1981). *The urban climate.* New York: Academic Press.

Leopold, L. B. (1968). *Hydrology for urban land planning* (Geological Survey Circular No. 554). Washington, DC: US Government Printing Office.

Sassen, S. (2001). *The global city* (2nd ed.). Princeton, NJ: Princeton University Press.

Short, J. R., & Kim, Y.-H. (1999). *Globalization and the city.* London: Longman.

Waller, M. (2000). *1700 scenes from London life.* London: Hodder and Stoughton.

Weber, A. F. (1899). *The growth of cities in the nineteenth century: A study in statistics.* New York: Macmillan.

Wheatley, P. (1971). *The pivot of the four quarters.* Chicago: Aldine.

Wolman, M. G. (1967). The cycle of sedimentation and erosion in urban river channels. *Geografisker annaler, 49A,* 285–295, 355.

Wrigley, E. A. (1987). *People, cities and wealth.* Oxford, UK: Basil Blackwell.

Uruguay *See* Southern Cone

Utopianism

For as long as humans have existed they have created images of ideal societies. Utopian dreaming is the way by which people conceive corrective measures for the problems in the world they have built for themselves. The process is no different for environmental problems than for social problems—utopias are tools that people use to describe and experiment with both the logical consequences of proceeding heedlessly and the many alternative paths that people might choose from.

Utopian dreaming came by its name through the writings of English statesman Sir Thomas More, whose 1516 account of a visit to a fictional country, Utopia, initiated the literary genre. In More's classless agrarian society, people work equal hours at whatever they do best and enjoy equal rights and rewards. Clothing is plain, simple, and practical, not unlike that of today's Mennonites, Amish, and the Hutterites, who began building utopian communities in Moravia in 1528. More's Utopians exchange homes every few years (as do some traditional Mormons in Utah and Arizona) and eat in common dining halls (as do residents of kibbutzim [communal farms] in Israel and co-housing settlements [communities in which multiple houses are oriented around a common open area and a common building] in North America and Scandinavia). Hereditary distinctions are unknown, and children live within the household of their choice. Consumerism is discouraged. If a surplus is produced, a holiday is declared.

Utopia has most often been viewed through a social lens, but More's vision was also ecological:

> [River water] is carried in earthen pipes to the lower streets; and for those places of the town to which the water of that river cannot be conveyed, they have great cisterns for receiving the rainwater, which supplies the want of the other. . . . They cultivate their gardens with great care, so that they have vines, fruits, herbs, and flowers in them; and all is so well ordered, and so finely kept, that I never saw gardens anywhere that were both so fruitful and so beautiful as theirs. (More 1901, Book II)

More's fictional account compares remarkably to a vision for Melbourne, Australia, that the executive director of the Australian Conservation Society sketched in 1990: an urban village surrounded by forest and wetland, its human population harmlessly integrated with native species of plants and animals. In this future Melbourne, residents generate their own energy from sunlight, and buildings are designed to heat and cool themselves passively.

The utopian tradition may have originated with the Greek philosopher Plato (427–347 BCE) and his *The Republic*, which provided a detailed model for an ideal

society as a way of elucidating the shortcomings of contemporary culture. After More in the sixteenth century, prominent eco-utopias (utopias with a particular focus on living in ecologically and environmentally sound ways) included those described in Italian philosopher Tommasso Campanella's *Città del Sole* (City of the Sun) (1602), British philosopher Frances Bacon's *New Atlantis* (1627), Welsh philanthropist Robert Owen's *A New View of Society* (1813), French socialist Henri de Saint-Simon's *Catéchisme Politique de Industriels* (Industrial Political Catechism) (1824), U.S. writer Henry David Thoreau's *Walden* (1854), British naturalist William Hudson's *A Crystal Age* (1877), U.S. writer Edward Bellamy's *Looking Backward* (1888), British poet William Morris's *News from Nowhere* (1891), Russian philosopher Peter Kropotkin's *The Conquest of Bread* (1892) and *Fields, Factories and Workshops* (1899), British reformer Ebenezer Howard's *Garden Cities of Tomorrow* (1902), U.S. psychologist B. F. Skinner's *Walden Two* (1948), British writer Aldous Huxley's *Island* (1962), U.S. writer Ernest Callenbach's *Ecotopia* (1975), U.S. feminist Marge Piercy's *Woman on the Edge of Time* (1976), and U.S. social anarchist Murray Bookchin's *The Ecology of Freedom* (1982) and *Remaking Society* (1990). There is also a genre of frightening anti-utopian or "dystopian" novels that includes works such as English writer Samuel Butler's *Erewhon* (1872), Russian novelist Yevgeny Zamyatin's *We* (1923), Aldous Huxley's *Brave New World* (1932), English writer George Orwell's *Nineteen Eighty-Four* (1949), and U.S. writer Ray Bradbury's *Fahrenheit 451* (1972). If benevolent utopias can be carried to their most paradisiacal extremes, the dangerous consequences of a utopia turning against itself can also be imagined.

Revolutions

The revolutions of the late eighteenth century introduced the possibility that utopian thought could intervene in human affairs. Thomas Jefferson in the U.S. Declaration of Independence (1776), Niquet le Jeune in the *Déclaration des droits de l'homme et du citoyen* (Declaration of the Rights of Man, 1786), and other revolutionaries moved utopian idealism into national government charters.

The nineteenth century brought the proliferation of utopian communities, both religious and secular. In 1799 Robert Owen purchased the cotton spinning mills of New Lanark, Scotland, reduced the workday, and gave his employees low-rent housing, free medical care, low-cost education, reduced prices on food and other household supplies, and free access to social and recreational facilities, gardens, and parks. Although Owen's experiment at New Lanark was a success on many levels, he did not believe that it was the ideal community in which to establish his "New Moral World." In 1824 he purchased the community of Harmony, Indiana, and nine hundred of his followers moved there to start over as New Harmony.

After a failed experimental settlement in Texas, the French socialist Etienne Cabet relocated 275 of his followers to the town of Nauvoo, Illinois, in 1849 and there built the Icarian Society, which practiced a communal economy. Members of the community received free schooling from age four until adulthood.

At the same time the Shakers (United Society of Believers in Christ's Second Appearing) believed that they could set an example of the perfect life and established several model settlements in the eastern United States. Their requirement of celibacy dwindled their numbers, but the perfection in their designs for furniture, buildings, villages, and music endures.

In the early 1870s U.S. social reformer John Humphrey Noyes led his Oneida, New York, community to found successful enterprises in the production of steel traps, silk thread, and fruit preserves and later the manufacture of silver and stainless steel dinnerware. By 1881 disagreements over leadership and widespread criticism from the outside world over the practice of a form of free love in which all members were married to each other led to the dissolution of the community and the formation of a joint business corporation that survives today.

Many of these communities believed that they had found the answer to all human ills, and they presented themselves as exemplars to the rest of the world. But far more influential were German political philosopher Karl Marx and German socialist Friedrich Engels, whose *Communist Manifesto* in 1848 retold history as a series of class struggles. The Paris Commune revolt in March 1871 established a worker state in Paris, with a revolutionary calendar, a ban on religion, and better working conditions. After two months, government troops attacked the barricades around Paris, killing 20,000, arresting 38,000, and deporting 7,000. However, Marx's doctrine soon found even larger followings in Russia and China. More people live in communist societies today than lived on Earth when Marx put pen to paper.

In 1892 William Morris wrote *News from Nowhere; or, an Epoch of Rest. Being Some Chapters from a Utopian Romance.* Morris's protagonist, William Guest, awakens one morning after a troubled sleep to find himself in a place completely unlike his own Victorian London. He discovers instead a society of youthful people whose members are happy, energetic, free from want, and, most important, engaged in work for the pure pleasure of serving others and expressing their own creativity. Morris's *Nowhere* depicts a utopia that is devoid of class, governmental structures, money, poverty, crime, and industrial pollution.

The first decade of the twentieth century brought the birth of futurism, an attempt to see the future, not as it should be, but as it likely will be. The Italian writer Filippo Marinetti, in his *Manifesto tecnico della letteratura Futurista* (Technical Manifesto on Futurist Literature) of 1912, declared the liberation of words from traditional grammar and syntax.

The word *robot*, derived from the Czech word *robota*, meaning "drudgery or forced labor," was used for the first time in 1920 in *R.U.R.* (Rossum's Universal Robots), a play by Czech writer Karel Čapek. Set on an island where labor-emancipating robots are manufactured on assembly lines, the play provides a critical look at the use of machines to replace humans and presciently gives a warning against genetic manipulation.

A History of Extremes

The history of utopias is a history of extremes. In the twentieth century the world witnessed large-scale attempts to improve society, and when some of those attempts failed, consequences were devastating. Most such attempts were carried out in the name of progress, liberation, justice, and equality. Every aspect of human life and society—human genes, food supply, families, communications, settlement patterns, weather, exploration of outer space—was pushed to new limits in the name of social virtue. Although many benefits were in fact achieved, no aspect was entirely free of unexpected and negative results.

If there is today a hotbed of utopian experiments, it is the United States. Since the earliest experiments at Plymouth Colony, Bohemia Manor, and Ephrata Cloister, the United States has never been without communal utopias. At times concurrent experiments have numbered more than five thousand in the United States. Many have been eco-utopian in their outlook, attempting, like More's Utopians, to balance human needs with the renewable capital that nature provides.

Fruitlands, Fellowship Farms, Little Landers, School of Living, Camphill, Emissaries, the Farm, Tolstoy Farm, Drop City, Twin Oaks, and Arcosante were among the more notable efforts to get back to the land in an ecological way. The shared intention was to reconstruct society from a simple egalitarian social contract.

Some of these experiments were strongly influenced by utopian fiction, for example, Twin Oaks by Skinner's *Walden Two*, the Farm by U.S. writer Isaac Asimov's *Foundation* trilogy, New Harmony by Owen's *A New View of Society*. Others sprang from parallel wellsprings but without any explicit literary inspiration.

The United States does not have a monopoly on such communities, however. The kibbutz movement that regreened the deserts of Palestine in the twentieth century was Zionist (relating to an international movement originally for the establishment of a Jewish national or religious community in Palestine and later for the support of modern Israel) in outlook at inception but developing a restorative ecology rationale at the end of the century, with the Green Kibbutz Network leading the young toward a new set of goals. In Germany the *ökodorf* movement began in the early 1980s, finding followers among utopian idealists after German reunification. At the same time permaculture communities (which are consciously "cultivated" to have the diversity, stability, and resilience of natural ecosystems) in Australia (e.g., Crystal Waters, Kookaburra Park, and Jarlanbah) pioneered easy paths to more environmentally sensitive lifestyles for the middle class. In Scandinavia co-housing, which sprang from social and economic objectives, gave birth to ecovillages, which added a filter of energy and materials choices to new settlement design. The Eco-Village Network of Denmark (Landsforeningen for økosamfund, or LøS) was among the first to create a coalition of ecovillages, but it was soon followed by the Ecovillage Network of the Americas and the Global Ecovillage Network (GEN). By the end of the century GEN claimed more than fifteen thousand utopian communities as members on six continents.

Influenced by philosophers such as Ralph Borsodi, Aldo Leopold, John Muir, Helen and Scott Nearing, and J. R. Rodale of the United States, Bill Mollison and John Seed of Australia, Rudolf Steiner of Austria, and Arne Naess of Norway, ecovillagers endeavor to address the social, environmental, and economic dimensions of sustainability in an integrated way, with human communities as part of, not apart from, balanced ecologies. As environmental scientist William J. Metcalf first observed, any real solutions to the global environmental crises of the present era begin with changes in lifestyle.

Environmental Consequences

People have imagined ideal societies existing in the real world, in the imaginary world, and, most recently, in cyberspace. All too often, however, these societies are grandiose and impractical. Although proclaiming themselves as formulas for a better world, they often contain the seeds of their own undoing. Perhaps utopianism is best realized in small increments, with damages fully assessed before moving along to the next increment. The environmental lessons of nuclear energy, chemical farming, biotechnology, nanotechnology (the art of manipulating materials on an atomic or molecular scale), and climate-altering energy systems are still to be widely accepted, but the scale of their industrial adoption has assured that the consequences will be neither benign nor easily ignored.

People are what they have dreamed they would be. Sometimes they are even a little more. The aboriginal saying is, "Ngaantatja apu wiya, ngayuku tjamu—This is not a rock, it is my grandfather. This is the place where the dreaming comes up." Modern civilization is the product of the dreams of ten thousand generations. A Nubian slave dreamed that his children would have the wealth of the pharaohs. Perhaps not all of his children yet do, but more people have greater wealth today than the pharaohs could have imagined, and more have attained pharaoh-like wealth than there were people on the Earth when the pyramids were raised. That this level of extravagant consumption is based upon, and may already have exceeded, the capacity of Earth's regenerative abilities has yet to sink in.

What comes tomorrow will depend on what people dream today.

Albert Bates

Further Reading

Bellamy, E. (1999). *Ecological utopias: Envisioning the sustainable society.* Utrecht, Netherlands: International Books.

Bellamy, E. (2000). *Looking backward 2000–1887.* New York: Penguin Putnam. (Original work published 1888)

Christensen, K., & Levinson, D. (Eds.). (2003). *Encyclopedia of community.* Thousand Oaks, CA: Sage.

Fogarty, R. (1990). *All things new: American communes and utopian movements 1860–1914.* Chicago: University of Chicago Press.

Metcalf, W. J. (1977). *The environmental crisis: A systems approach.* St. Lucia, Australia: University of Queensland Press.

Miller, T. (1998). *The quest for utopia in twentieth-century America: Vol. 1. 1900–1960.* Syracuse, NY: Syracuse University Press.

More, T. (1901). *Utopia.* New York: Ideal Commonwealths. (Original work published 1516)

Pitzer, D. E. (1997). *America's communal utopias.* Chapel Hill: University of North Carolina Press.

Ross Jackson, J. T. (2000). *And we are doing it: Building an ecovillage future.* San Francisco: Reed Publishers.

Sargent, L. T. (1988). *British and American utopian literature, 1516–1985: An annotated, chronological bibliography.* New York: Garland.

Toyne, P. (1991). Creating an ecologically sustainable Australia for 2001. *Social Alternatives, 10,* 2.

Vegetarianism

Vegetarianism, the term used to describe a diet that excludes the flesh of animals, has a long, complex and often tumultuous history. Many of the world's religions and philosophies have praised it as the ideal diet, but vegetarians have also been condemned and killed for their refusal to eat meat. The choice to eat or not eat flesh foods has typically reflected deeply ingrained philosophical and religious beliefs. Foremost among these has been the idea of human kinship with the nonhuman world. While the underlying motives for vegetarianism differ widely throughout different cultures and historical periods, certain themes predominate. These include: the idea of transmigration of souls, compassion for nonhuman animals, asceticism, purification of the body and soul, health benefits, the dehumanizing effects of meat-eating, environmental considerations, and the unnaturalness of eating flesh foods. Some of the additional underlying themes include the association of meat with class, caste, and gender.

Definition

Most of the world's populations have usually eaten a predominantly plant-based diet. The word *vegetarian*, however, is generally reserved for the self-conscious decision to abstain from flesh foods, based upon philosophical, ethical, metaphysical, scientific, or nutritional beliefs. The term first appeared in the 1840s and was derived from the root word *vegetus*, signifying the idea of "whole and vital." Although the word refers to those who abstain from eating flesh, there is disagreement about what constitutes flesh, and some people who call themselves vegetarian consume chicken and fish. Most vegetarians, however, believe that the term should be retained for those who avoid all forms of animal flesh. The most common types of vegetarian are: lacto-ovo vegetarians, who include eggs and dairy products in their diet; lacto-vegetarians, who include milk; ovo-vegetarians, who include eggs; vegans, who exclude all animal products; natural hygienists, who eat a nonprocessed, plant-based diet; raw fooders, who eat only raw foods; and fruitarians, who eat only fruit.

Origins in the East

Vegetarianism has two major philosophical roots in the ancient world, Jainism in the East and Pythagoreanism in the West. Both schools of thought arose in the sixth century BCE at approximately the same time, and scholars continue to speculate on the cross-fertilization of ideas between the East and West.

The Jains' notion of *ahimsa* refers to the desire not to cause injury to other living beings and the concomitant idea of compassion for all living beings. Jains argue that all life goes through a series of incarnations, with the highest incarnation belonging to humans who have attained enlightenment or nirvana. By eating flesh foods humans attract negative karma to their soul (*jiva*), and impede their chances of attaining enlightenment. They also risk dining on their next of kin from a previous life. Jains believe that one can only contact the god within by conquering the "animal passions" that lead one to acts of violence and self-indulgence, including the eating of flesh foods. Jains also condemned the practice of animal sacrifice, intimately connected to meat-eating in the ancient world.

Buddhism also contains the ideas of *ahimsa*, transmigration of souls and compassion for animals. Buddhism helped to spread vegetarianism throughout Asia, and influenced the development of a strong vegetarian tradition in Hinduism.

Origins in the West

Pythagoras is regarded as the greatest influence on vegetarian thought in the Western world. The Pythagorean sect was founded at the end of the sixth century BCE in Croton, Italy, in Magna Grecia. The basic precepts of Pythagoras's school included a refusal to eat meat or to offer blood sacrifice. Pythagoras believed that the human soul could transmigrate to humans or other animals after death but the ultimate goal was to free the soul from the earthly rounds of existence to reunite with its divine origins. This was accomplished through a series of strict, ascetic rules for purifying the body.

Most of the modern arguments against meat eating can be found among Ancient Greek as well as Roman philosophers. Plutarch (c. 350–433 BCE) believed that this "barbaric vice" was unnatural for humans and engendered violence. Other ancient philosophers who advocated vegetarianism include Theophrastus (360–287 BCE), Empedocles (c. 495–c. 435 BCE), and Porphyry, who made one of the first ecological defenses of vegetarianism. According to Porphyry it was not necessary to kill animals to curb the problem of animal overpopulation, since nature would find a balance by itself.

Early Jewish and Christian Vegetarians

There were several early Jewish Christian sects that are believed to have adhered to a strict vegetarian diet. Among these were the Essenes, the Ebionites, and the Nazoreans, considered by many to be the first Christians. The early ascetic Jewish Christian sects were a minority tradition in the first-century ancient world. Nonetheless, scholars have argued that Jesus counted among their numbers and was himself a vegetarian.

The early Church fathers believed that meat was a powerful sexual stimulant, so it was appropriate for those in holy orders to refrain from eating it in order to curb their sexual desires. However, abstaining from meat was acceptable only as part of a practical exercise in subduing the "animal passions."

From the third to the thirteenth century the Church engaged in a vigorous campaign against a number of heretical Gnostic sects. Ranging from the Balkans in the Byzantine Empire to Southern France, they included the Manicheans, Cathars, Paulicians, Montanists, Masslians, Apostolics, and Bogomils. The refusal to eat meat was viewed by Church authorities as evidence of heresy.

Middle Ages to Renaissance

Support for vegetarianism went into a long dormancy during the Middle Ages. In the early Renaissance, due to late-thirteenth century food shortages, the vast majority of the population, particularly the poor, ate primarily vegetarian food. It was at this time that the emphasis on meat-eating as desirable and necessary for one's health became an article of faith, particularly for men. A small number of dissidents protested against cruelty to animals and meat-eating, including Sir Thomas More (1478–1535) who blended concern over animal suffering with the first environmental critique of the large amounts of land used to produce meat. Other dissidents included Erasmus (1467–1536), Montaigne (1533–1592), and Leonardo Da Vinci (1452–1519), although Da Vinci was the only one of the three to become vegetarian.

Seventeenth Century: Cartesian Thought

In the seventeenth century, Rene Descartes (1596–1650) developed the Christian belief that animals lacked souls or spirit with devastating consequences for nonhuman animals. He contended that since animals lacked spirit, and hence the capacity to understand, they could not feel pain. Their anguished cries were in all probability merely mechanical responses. Cartesian philosophy sanctioned the widespread practice of vivisection in the seventeenth century as well as the confinement of animals on factory farms.

Despite this setback to the status of nonhuman animals, the seventeenth century simultaneously witnessed the growth of a greater sensitivity to nonhuman animals. Ironically, this was due in part to animal studies, which showed the structural similarities of their nervous systems to those of humans, suggesting the commonality in their experience of pain. In addition, as the threat from nature receded, people began to have greater empathy for nonhuman animals. Most advocates for vegetarianism, including Thomas Tryon (1634–1703), one of the foremost advocates for vegetarianism of his age, still framed their calls for compassion in religious terms. Other proponents of vegetarianism during the seventeenth century include John Ray, John Evelyn, and Margaret Cavendish, duchess of Newcastle.

Eighteenth to Nineteenth Century

The eighteenth century gave rise to humanist philosophy and to the notion of natural rights, based on the belief in the inherent dignity of humans. Due in part to Evangelical religion's emphasis on concern for the oppressed, and the Lockean idea of human beings' innate capacity for benevolence, there was an increasing sensitivity to animal suffering.

As the century progressed, public attention began to focus upon a wide range of social issues, including prison reform, child welfare, care for the poor, sick, and elderly as well as opposition to slavery. A growing number of people viewed concern for nonhuman animals as a logical extension of these social movements. While compassion for nonhuman animals was the foremost concern of these animal advocates, they also pointed to the harmful effects of meat-eating on human moral character. Joseph Ritson (1752–1803), John Oswald (1730–1793), Percy Bysshe Shelley (1792–1822), and Jean-Jacques Rousseau (1712–1778) all linked meat-eating with interhuman violence, including war.

The emphasis on the harmful effects of meat-eating on human moral and spiritual character continued into the nineteenth century. There was an increased focus, however, on the wrongfulness of animal suffering in and of itself. Acknowledging the moral significance of animal suffering was an integral part of Jeremy Bentham's (1748–1832) utilitarian theory. According to Bentham, "the question is not, can they reason?, Nor can they talk? But, can they suffer?"(Bentham, 1780).

Arguments for vegetarianism were also increasingly being linked to land use practices. As a result of the enclosures, the common land was being seized by rich land owners who were using it to grow fodder crops to feed their cattle. The philosopher and priest, William Paley (1743–1805), Shelley, and Dr. William Alcott (1798–1859) all inveighed against the inefficiency of feeding fodder to animals instead of directly to human beings.

Food Reform Movement

The food reform movement began in Germany in the 1820s and 1830s as a reaction to the growing ties between the food industry and science and technology. In the 1830s, vegetarians became a vocal minority within the radical wing of the food reform movement. Many of the food reformers, including Sylvester Graham (1794–1851), Bircher-Benner (1867–1939), and John Harvey Kellogg (1852–1943), combined health and ethical arguments, focusing on the purifying effect, both spiritual and physical, of a vegetarian diet. Meat-eating was typically condemned for its over-stimulating effect. Indeed for Graham, stimulation was the root of all disease. Meat-eating was also linked to overindulgence in sex. Kellogg maintained that meat-eating caused undue pressure on the male organ and that vegetarianism was the cure.

The success of the food reform movement and the vegetarian cause is largely attributable to the support of women. Some of these women included Catherine Harriet Beecher Stowe (1800–1878) and Harriet Beecher Stowe (1811–1896) in the U.S., and Luise Otto-Peters (1819–1895) and Lina Morgenstern (1830–1909) in Germany.

A number of feminists promoted vegetarianism, often connecting it with the themes of peace and nonviolence. The contemporary author Carol Adams sees in their writings the beginnings of a feminist, vegetarian, pacifist tradition. Some of these women include Charlotte Despard (1844–1939), Charlotte Perkins Gilman (1860–1935) and Agnes Ryan (1878–1954), and Susan B. Anthony (1820–1906) as well as the theosophists Annie Besant (1847–1933) and Anna Kingsford (1846–1888). Kingsford maintained, "universal peace is not possible to a carnivorous race" (Adams 1991, 124).

The Social Movement for Vegetarianism

In the middle of the nineteenth century, in Germany, the Netherlands, England and the U.S., the vegetarian cause began to coalesce as a social movement. The first secular vegetarian society in England was formed in 1847 at Ramsgate, at which time the term *vegetarian* replaced the more common *Pythagorean* as the official word for someone who abstained from flesh foods. In 1850, William Metcalfe founded a similar organization in New York, The American Vegetarian.

Support for vegetarianism in the mid-nineteenth century was fueled, in part, by the findings of evolutionary science, which had begun to demonstrate the similarities between human and nonhuman animals. With the publication of Charles Darwin's (1809–1882) *Descent of Man* in 1871, the privileged position of humans was further eroded.

The humane movement developed from the belief that if human beings were, in fact, superior it behooved them to act civilized by controlling their "animal passions" and practicing benevolence to animals. Although most members of the humane movement were not vegetarian, some of the most vocal activists were, including Bernard Shaw (1856–1950), the philanthropist Lewis Gompertz, Anna Kingsford and the author and social reformer Henry S. Salt (1851–1939).

Salt's writings had a wide-ranging impact, including on Mohandas Gandhi (1869–1948). Gandhi was inspired by the connections Salt made between animal rights and social justice, to move beyond his previous traditional Hindu vegetarianism to see vegetarianism as a movement for the moral and spiritual progress of the human race.

Gandhi's conversion to ethical vegetarianism illustrates the cross-fertilization of ideas between East and West that characterizes much of the modern vegetarian movement. Gandhi went on to influence millions of Hindus to adopt vegetarianism. Eastern thought, in turn, has had a profound influence on vegetarianism in the West. The influence of Hinduism and Buddhism on theosophy was an important factor in theosophy's endorsement of vegetarianism. The influx of Eastern ideas that began in the 1960s also had a large influence on the adoption of vegetarianism. The Krishna cult, in particular, had a profound impact in the west through their dispensing of free vegetarian food.

The Modern Vegetarian Movement

Vegetarianism was largely eclipsed by the two world wars. A number of factors contributed to its increased acceptance in the postwar years. Beginning in the 1920s, there had been a growing appreciation for the benefits of vegetables and fruits due to the discovery of vitamins. Additional studies in the 1950s, including research on the Seventh Day Adventists, confirmed the health benefits of a vegetarian diet. In the 1970s, many people also became concerned over the purity of food, and in particular meat. Concerns focused on the effects of pesticides, chemicals, and bacterial contamination, all of which are found in greater concentrations in meat. People became additionally worried about the purity of meat as a result of the outbreak of B.S.E (mad cow disease) and foot-and-mouth disease in England and Europe. The publicity surrounding these outbreaks served to educate people about the contents of the food fed to farm animals, including sludge, carcasses, and the excrement of other animals, thereby providing people with additional incentive to adopt a vegetarian diet.

A number of health studies in the 1980s and 1990s also helped to fuel interest in vegetarianism, including the China Health Project directed by the Cornell professor of nutrition, Colin Campbell. Campbell's cross-cultural research involving over 10,000 people in the U.S. and China concluded that human beings are not anatomically designed to eat meat, and that there is an inverse correlation between the amount of animal products that one eats and the benefits that accrue to one's health. The physician Dean Ornish's research, first published in 1983 in *Stress, Diet and Your Heart*, also demonstrated that arterial sclerosis could be reversed through a vegetarian diet.

The growth of the animal advocacy movement in the U.S. and England in the 1970s also helped to advance the vegetarian cause. In previous centuries, vegetarians tended to focus on the cruelty inherent in the slaughter of innocent beings. The modern animal advocacy movement, in addition, has called attention to the conditions in which animals live throughout their lives, promoting vegetarianism as a means of protesting this treatment. Significant influences on the development of vegetarianism in the animal advocacy movement include Peter Singer's utilitarian arguments for the equal consideration of the interests of both humans and nonhumans, Tom Regan's case for the "inherent worth" of animals, and the writings of Carol Adams as well as the literature of Feminists for Animal Rights, which underline the commonalities in meat dominance and male dominance.

Veganism also developed increasing support in the 1980s and 1990s. Rejection of dairy products had begun in the nineteenth century, but it was not until 1944 that the first Vegan Society was formed in Leicester, England.

Vegetarianism and the Environment

Beginning in the 1970s ecological arguments also became an important motive for many people to adopt a vegetarian diet. In *Diet for a Small Planet*, published in 1971, Frances Moore Lappe criticized the inefficiency of a meat-based diet, arguing that only a small proportion of the nutrients that are fed to nonhuman animals return to humans as nutrients. Moore contended that in 1968 the amount of edible protein that was wasted by America's animal based diet was equivalent to the world protein shortage. *Diet for a Small Planet* provided a major impetus for people to either cut back on or eliminate meat from their diets.

In the following two decades, numerous articles and books advanced similar environmental critiques of a meat-based diet, including Jeremy Rifkin's *Beyond Beef*, Howard Lyman's *Mad Cowboy*, and John Robbins's *Diet for a New America* and *The Food Revolution*. These authors highlighted the link between animal agriculture and a host of environmental problems: soil and water depletion, desertification, air and water pollution, global warming, the waste of valuable grain resources, and the destruction of the tropical rain forests. Current estimates are that 90 percent of all agricultural land, more than one half the total land area of the U.S., is devoted to the production of animal products. Cattle now occupy 70 percent of rangeland in the American west and are a major contributor to both agricultural runoff and desertification. Beef production is also a major factor in the destruction of half the tropical rain forest of southern Mexico and Central America.

Animal agriculture has also been blamed as a major contributor to global warming. Greenhouse gases are produced from grain fertilizers and from the methane released from animals. American waterways are equally threatened. According to the Environmental Protection Agency, animal waste poses a greater threat to American waterways than all other industrial sources combined. In a 1999 report by the Union of Concerned Scientists, meat-eating is cited, along with driving automobiles, as one of the two most damaging lifestyle factors contributing to environmental destruction.

Not all environmentalists believe that meat-eating and animal agriculture are inherently harmful to the environment. Advocates for mixed farming and biodynamic farming argue that some use of animals on small-scale farms is necessary, due to the usefulness of their manure for fertilizing the soil. A number of environmentalists also support meat-eating as long as the meat is "organic" and the animals are raised "humanely."

While studies show that the number of people adopting vegetarianism has been slowly increasing throughout most of the Western world, vegetarianism has not followed a steadily uphill course. Meat-eating has actually increased throughout the world. Consumption of chicken has also sharply risen, in part because of concerns over the purity of beef. In the West, the rise in meat consumption has been attributed to the proliferation of fast food restaurants, and in the East and developing world to the desire to imitate Western society's affluent lifestyle, symbolized by meat. Studies vary around the world as to the number of people who are currently vegetarian, ranging from a low of 0.2 percent in Poland to a high of 4.4 percent in the Netherlands. In the U.S. estimates range from a low of 0.3 percent to a high of 7 percent of the population. The higher numbers generally represent people who claim to be vegetarian but who sometimes eat meat, including fish. Most studies suggest that women have been, cross-culturally and throughout history, about 70 percent of vegetarians.

In his book *Meat: A Natural Symbol* Nicke Fiddes suggests that meat has functioned throughout history as a means of asserting human dominance over the natural world. By eating nonhuman animals, humans show their superiority over the "lower" animals. Both religious vegetarians as well as those motivated by health have at times demonstrated the reverse side of this phenomenon. Rather than dominating the external environment, some vegetarians (and perhaps mostly men) have sought to tame the "beast within" as a means of attaining a physical or spiritual purity.

The modern vegetarian movement is part of a long continuous history. Although compassion for nonhuman animals and environmental concerns are parts of this history, they have moved to the fore in recent years. The modern vegetarian movement deviates from the past, however, in focusing less on self-denial and ritual purity and more on the idea of embracing vegetarianism as a positive ethical choice.

Marti Kheel

Further Reading

Adams, C. J. (1991). *The sexual politics of meat: A feminist-vegetarian critical theory*. New York: Continuum.

Akers, K. (1993). *A vegetarian sourcebook: The nutrition, ecology, and ethics of a natural food diet*. Denver: Vegetarian Press.

Barkas, J. (1975). *The vegetable passion: A history of the vegetarian state of mind*. New York: Charles Scribner's Sons.

Bentham, J. (1988). *Introduction to the principles of morals and legislation*. Buffalo, NY: Prometheus Books. (Original work published 1780)

Berry, R. (1998). *Food for the gods: Vegetarianism and the world's religions: Essays, conversations, recipes*. New York: Pythagorean.

Dombrowski, D. (1984). *The philosophy of vegetarianism*. Amherst: University of Massachusetts Press.

Fiddes, N. (1991). *Meat: A natural symbol*. New York: Routledge.

Fox, M. A. (1999). *Deep vegetarianism*. Philadelphia: Temple University Press.

Gandhi, M. (1999). Diet and morality. In K. Walters & L. Portmess (Eds.), *Ethical vegetarianism: From Pythagoras to Peter Singer* (pp. 139–144). New York: State University of New York Press.

Gregerson, J. (1994). *Vegetarianism: A history.* Fremont, CA: Jain Pub. Co.

Leneman, L. (1997). The awakened instinct: Vegetarianism and the women's suffrage movement in Britain. *Women's History Review, 6*(2), 271–286.

Marcus, E. (1998). *Vegan: The new ethics of eating.* Ithaca, NY: McBooks.

Maurer, D. (2002). *Vegetarianism: Movement or moment?* Philadelphia: Temple University Press.

Meyer-Renschlausen, E., & Wirz, A. (1999). Dietetics, health reform and social order: Vegetarianism as a moral physiology: The example of Maximilian Bircher-Benner. *Medical History, 43,* 323–341.

Ornish, D. (1983). *Stress, diet and your heart.* New York: Henry Holt & Co.

Paley, W. (1999). The dubious right to eat flesh. In K. Walters & L. Portmess (Eds.), *Ethical vegetarianism: From Pythagoras to Peter Singer* (pp. 65–67). New York: State University of New York Press.

Pythagoras (1999). The kinship of all life. In K. Walters & L. Portmess (Eds.), *Ethical vegetarianism: From Pythagoras to Peter Singer* (pp. 113–125). New York: State University of New York Press.

Rifkin, J. (1992). *Beyond beef: The rise and fall of the cattle culture.* New York: Dutton.

Robbins, J. (1987). *Diet for a new America.* Walpole, NH: Stillpoint.

Robbins, J. (2001). *The food revolution: How your diet can help save your life.* Berkeley, CA.: Conari Press.

Rosen, S. (1997). *Diet for transcendence: Vegetarianism and the world religions.* Badger, CA.: Torchlight.

Shelley, P. B. (1999). A vindication of natural diet. In K. Walters & L. Portmess (Eds.), *Ethical vegetarianism: From Pythagoras to Peter Singer* (pp. 69–74). New York: State University of New York Press.

Spencer, C. (1995). *The heretic's feast: A history of vegetarianism.* Hanover, NH: University Press of New England.

Venezuela

(2001 est. pop. 24 million)

Venezuela is the northernmost country in continental South America. It can be divided into four main geographical regions. The most important region is the Venezuelan highlands, an extension of the Andes Mountains that runs east-west in a gentle arc from western Venezuela along the Caribbean coast. The Venezuelan highlands have always been home to the vast majority of Venezuela's population. In the northwestern corner of the country lie the Maracaibo lowlands, which include Lake Maracaibo, the largest lake in Latin America. South of the highlands lie the vast Orinoco llanos, or plains. The fourth region is the Guiana highlands, a sparsely populated region that constitutes almost half of Venezuela's national territory.

Pre-Columbian Venezuela was much less densely populated than other parts of the Caribbean basin. The densest populations lived in the cool climate of the Venezuelan highlands. These highland groups, including the Timoto-Cuica and Caquetío, had developed settled agriculture using techniques including irrigation and terracing and supplemented their diets through hunting, fishing, and trading. Groups in the lowlands, related to the Carib and Arawak groups of the Caribbean, depended heavily on fishing from the lakes and rivers. Archeological evidence suggests that many pre-Columbian Indian groups developed along strips of land running from the Caribbean coast up to the highlands so that they could consume products from the different ecological zones. Even where such formal groups did not exist, most groups supplemented their diets by exchanging food and goods with groups from other regions.

The Spanish conquest in the sixteenth century produced a new environmental order, although the environmental transformation of Venezuela was slower than that in other parts of Latin America. The demographic collapse of Venezuela's native populations was the fastest and most catastrophic environmental transformation. The main cause of this complex phenomenon was the introduction of Old World epidemic diseases such as smallpox, measles, and influenza. Numbers for Venezuela are difficult to find, but in nearby regions each pandemic outbreak could carry away as much as half the indigenous population. Warfare, Spanish slaving raids, and rapidly declining birth rates also contributed to the demographic collapse. Records from late sixteenth-century Caracas suggest that the indigenous population there had declined between 50 and 75 percent. Some groups in the lowlands and along the coasts disappeared entirely. The Spanish also quickly stripped Venezuela of the few natural resources that interested them. The earliest explorers had discovered rich beds of pearls in eastern Venezuela, a region that came to be known as the Pearl Coast. Harvesting began in 1519, and by 1537 the pearl beds had been completely fished out. With a low indigenous population and few natural resources of interest to the Spanish, the colony languished until the early eighteenth century.

The Cacao Boom

The pace of environmental change began to accelerate in the late seventeenth century. Venezuela entered a period of economic growth based on agricultural exports that lasted until the 1920s. Venezuela's first agricultural boom was based on cacao, a New World crop that was the basic ingredient for chocolate. Demand for chocolate, both in Latin America and in Europe, grew rapidly in the 1700s, and cacao became a highly profitable crop. From the early 1700s to the early 1800s, Venezuela was the world's largest producer of cacao. The cacao boom stimulated population growth. Between 1772 and 1812 the population of Caracas alone almost doubled from 24,000 to 42,000. The boom also changed Venezuela's demographic makeup, attracting the voluntary immigration of Spaniards from Europe and the forced migration of slaves from Africa. By the late eighteenth century, Venezuela's population was roughly 20 percent European, 10 percent Indian, 20 percent African, and 50 percent mixed.

The increasing dynamism of the coast produced environmental changes in other parts of the country. To feed the growing urban and agricultural populations of the highlands, ranchers introduced cattle to the llanos, where large herds—with no predators and no competition—soon ran wild. Meat from these cattle was directed to domestic consumption, and the hides were exported. Venezuela's cacao industry was destroyed during the long, violent war of independence from Spain (1811–1821). After independence, growers began cultivating coffee in the former cacao lands and opened new coffee frontiers in the Andean states of Merida, Táchira, and Trujillo. Between 1830 and 1930, Venezuela's coffee production increased tenfold, making it the world's second-largest exporter of coffee after Brazil. This growth was not, however, environmentally sustainable. In many coffee zones, poor agricultural techniques led to soil erosion, changes in rainfall, and soil exhaustion. By the 1920s coffee yields in many Venezuelan plantations were half of yields in neighboring Colombia, where coffee planters had made a more concerted effort to create a sustainable coffee agriculture. Venezuela's coffee industry quickly fell into decline during the 1920s, when petroleum surpassed cash crops as Venezuela's major export.

The Oil Boom

The discovery of petroleum in the Maracaibo basin during the 1910s inaugurated the most recent phase of Venezuela's environmental history. Between 1928 and 1970 Venezuela was the world's leading exporter of oil and continues to be a major exporter today. The petroleum industry has transformed the Maracaibo basin's landscapes, most significantly in the pollution of Lake Maracaibo from leaks in oil wells and underwater pipelines. On a national level, the growth of the petroleum industry coupled with the collapse of the agricultural export sector caused rapid urbanization. Whereas in 1941 only 33 percent of Venezuela's population lived in cities, by 1999, 87 percent did. During the prosperous decades from the 1930s to the 1970s, the Venezuelan state created several national parks and enacted pioneering environmental policies. In the early 1980s, however, oil prices collapsed, and the government entered a long period of economic and political crisis, during which it has been unable or unwilling to enforce these environmental policies. National and municipal social services have not been able to keep up with the rapid population growth and urbanization. Venezuela's major metropolitan centers all suffer from critical environmental problems of air pollution, water shortages, and inadequate waste disposal. The landslides that destroyed several shantytowns around Caracas in December 1999, leaving several thousand people dead or missing, are an apt symbol of Venezuela's urban environmental crisis. During the 1980s Venezuelan professionals and grassroots activists established more than forty environmental nongovernmental organizations. These organizations are often small and ideologically divided, making it difficult for them to act in concert to effect change.

Stuart McCook

Further Reading

Christen, C., Herculano, S., Hochstetler, K., Prell, R., Price, M., & Roberts, J. T. (1998, summer). Latin American environmentalism: Comparative views. *Studies in Comparative International Development, 33*, 58–87.

Cook, N. D. (1993). *Born to die: Disease and the New World conquest, 1492–1650.* Cambridge, UK: Cambridge University Press.

Haggerty, R. A. (Ed.). (1990). *Area handbook for Venezuela* (4th ed.). Washington, DC: U.S. Government Printing Office.

Helms, M. W. (1984). The Indians of the Caribbean and Circum-Caribbean at the end of the fifteenth century. In L. Bethell (Ed.), *Cambridge history of Latin America* (Vol. 1, pp. 37–57). Cambridge, UK: Cambridge University Press.

Lombardi, J. V. (1982). *Venezuela: The search for order: The dream of progress.* New York: Oxford University Press.

Sánchez-Albornóz, N. (1974). *The population of Latin America: A history.* Berkeley & Los Angeles: University of California Press.

Sauer, C. O. (1966). *The early Spanish main.* Berkeley & Los Angeles: University of California Press.

Yarrington, D. (1997). *A coffee frontier: Land, society, and politics in Duaca, Venezuela, 1830–1936.* Pittsburgh, PA: University of Pittsburgh Press.

Volga River

At 3,700 kilometers in length, the Volga is the longest river in Europe. The Volga and its basin are located in western Russia. The Volga has been Russia's most significant waterway throughout history. As such, the river has been referred to as "the Soul of Russia," "the Mother Volga," and "Russia's Main Street."

The Volga River originates northwest of Moscow at an elevation of only 225 meters above sea level in the Valdai Hills, which are situated between the cities of Moscow and Novgorod. This low elevation is sometimes cited as the reason why the river lacks the capacity to "flush" itself clean; a history of excessive diversions and extreme contamination from a variety of sources is the more probable reason why the river has problems with pollution. From its source the Volga flows northeast of Moscow to the Rybinsk Reservoir. Through the Rybinsk Reservoir and a set of canals one can travel from the Volga River all the way to the Baltic Sea by water. Indeed, most of the Volga is navigable. Yearly statistics concerning river-borne freight in Russia typically cite the Volga as carrying at least half of all such freight.

From Yaroslavl' the Volga River begins to flow southward, eventually constituting a large delta of almost three hundred channels and emptying into the Caspian Sea. On its course southward it passes through or near numerous cities of significance, such as Nizh-niy Novgorod, Kazan, Samara, Saratov, Volgograd, and Astrakhan. Among its many tributaries are the Oka, Belaya, Vyatka, and Kama Rivers.

Throughout the twentieth century the Volga was manipulated and contaminated. Most notable among early diversions of the river was the Great Volga project, which was promoted under the Soviet leader Joseph Stalin. Because the country's leadership, beginning with the Russian Communist leader Vladimir Lenin, was fond of large-scale water projects, the Volga and its tributaries were dammed under the Great Volga project, and thirty-four hydroelectric stations were constructed. The reservoirs that were created along the Volga are immense and are sometimes referred to as "inland seas." During storms the ocean-sized waves produced on these reservoirs jeopardize the fragile soils of the area's shorelines. The dams also reduce spawning grounds of fish by obstructing their natural runs. The consequence has been a dwindling fish industry.

Urban, agricultural, and industrial effluents pollute the river and its reservoirs. From many of the cities along the Volga's course, polluted wastewaters are discharged from inadequate sanitation facilities. In the middle Volga region in the vicinity of Samara, the Volga-Ural oil fields and former state farms also contribute to pollution. In the lower Volga region dioxin pollution from the use of herbicides and insecticides and the production of chemicals has been high for decades. Contamination by this carcinogen has been demonstrated to be harmful to humans, threatening especially their reproductive, endocrine, and immune systems. It is also a problem for the fauna of the region.

In the region's agricultural sectors runoff of nitrates from fertilizers into the reservoirs of the river causes problems with algae in the summer. Because of the chemical contamination from agricultural and industrial sectors, much of the wildlife in the area has been eradicated. As a source of irrigation for crops, contaminated reservoir water returns to affect the foods grown in the wider region. An additional source of contamination is the petrochemical industries in the vicinity of Astrakhan. Runoff of industrial by-products in this region is severe, and there are frequent leaks from pipelines and refineries.

Although there have been efforts to control pollution of the river, its overexploitation, and increasing rates of water consumption, such as the effort made by the 1989 Public Committee to Save the Volga, environmental concerns are a low priority in Russia today. Even national reserves and wetlands that the international Ramsar Convention designated significant are in a precarious situation.

Kyle Evered

Further Reading

Mordukhai-Boltovskoi, F. D. (1979). *The river Volga and its life*. The Hague, Netherlands: W. Junk.

Pryde, P. R. (1991). *Environmental management in the Soviet Union*. Cambridge, UK: Cambridge University Press.

von Humboldt, Alexander

(1769–1859)

German geographer

Alexander von Humboldt used modern scientific techniques to observe and analyze the environment. His fame arose from his self-financed exploration of South America, Mexico, and Cuba in 1799–1804, accompanied by the botanist Aimé Bonpland (1773–1858). Humboldt negotiated Napoleon's European wars as he collaborated with French and German specialists to analyze thousands of observations and specimens. Although Prussian by birth, Humboldt moved to the scientific and political capital of Europe, Paris, to write the more than thirty volumes of topical works known collectively as *Voyage du Humboldt et Bonpland*. Nineteenth-century founders of evolution and ecology Charles Darwin, Alfred Russel Wallace, Louis Agassiz, and Henry Walter Bates acknowledged the importance of the *Voyage* to their work. Humboldt's significance for environmental history arises from his collections, measurements, collaboration, interpretations, and publications. By publishing his generalizations about the distribution of plant species and environmental conditions, Humboldt laid the foundation for the study of ecology and biogeography. In combination with Humboldt's sympathy for the peoples he encountered on his travels, these accomplishments inspire environmental historians to explain how people and the environment influence each other through time.

Humboldt's expedition to South America traversed several countries, including a few weeks in Philadelphia and Washington, D.C. He assisted President Jefferson in understanding the Spanish territories won by Napoleon and recently acquired as the Louisiana Purchase. Before his return to Europe, Humboldt created interest in his expedition by sending entertaining letters to European and American newspapers. His attention to native cultures and colonialism expanded on popular works by men such as François-René de Chateaubriand. Humboldt and Bonpland tapped the knowledge of missionaries and isolated scientists, including the famous botanist Don José Celestino Mutis in Bogotá, Colombia. Humboldt and his collaborator, Karl Sigismund Kunth, honored Mutis by featuring his portrait as the frontispiece to *Plantes equinoxiales* (Paris and Tübingen, 1805–1817). Humboldt and Bonpland paid great attention to taking specimens and observations and sent duplicate collections to Europe by different routes whenever possible. The thousands of pressed plants, beetles, bird skins, minerals, and pages of observations formed the raw material for the multi-decade publication of *Voyage.*

Humboldt's early training as a mining engineer enabled him to use instruments to make careful, repeated measurements of magnetism, temperature, barometric pressure, and location. In his South American wanderings over 115° of longitude and 64° of latitude, Humboldt's measurements showed that the intensity of magnetism increased with latitude, an insight which Carl F. Gauss (1777–1855) later used to develop his theory of terrestrial magnetism. Humboldt measured the temperature of the ocean on all his voyages; his data characterized the cold current along Peru and Chile that carries an abundance of marine life, a feature eventually named after him as the Humboldt Current. Humboldt used his surveying instruments to identify the longitude and latitude of river mouths and mountain passes. On his journey to Peru, he paired geographic and barometric readings, using a formula devised by Pierre-Simon Laplace (1749–1827) to translate the barometric readings into elevations and thereby create a topographic map of his route over the Andes. In his famous ascent and study of Mount Chimborazo in Ecuador, Humboldt drew the distribution of plants on the slopes of the volcano, initiating the discipline of biogeography with his novel depiction.

Humboldt financed his travels and publications by spending the fortune he received from family estates in Poland, but his books also drew on the talents of those supported by Napoleon's patronage. The emperor supported scientists who investigated basic phenomena and the larger world and artists who created printmaking techniques that reproduced beautiful scientific images. Paris savants such as Georges Cuvier wrote up the comparative anatomy and zoology of Humboldt's animal specimens, though the German

Karl Sigismund Kunth wrote most of the volumes on botany. French artists transformed Humboldt's skins and ink sketches into hundreds of beautiful colored prints of birds, plants, and views. Publishing his findings ensured that Humboldt's knowledge would become a foundation for subsequent nineteenth-century scientists.

Betsy Mendelsohn

Further Reading

Botting, D. (1973). *Humboldt and the cosmos.* New York: Harper & Row.

Fiedler, H. & Leitner, U. (2000). *Alexander von Humboldts Schriften: Bibliographie der selbständig erschienenen Werke.* Berlin, Germany: Akademie Verlag.

Kellner, L. (1963). *Alexander von Humboldt.* New York: Oxford University Press.

Wallace, A. R.
(1823–1913)
English biogeographer

Alfred Russel Wallace was joint discoverer with Charles Darwin of the theory of evolution by natural selection, and an innovative scientific thinker, field zoologist, and biogeographer. His extensive fieldwork among the rich habitats of the Amazon and the Malay Archipelago prompted him in the direction of increasingly bold scientific theory. His writings on the evolution and distribution of animals and plants in space and time and on the complex relationship between human beings and their environment retain much of their validity. Wallace was born 8 January 1823 near Usk, Monmouthshire. Wallace's formal education ended when he was fourteen. Apprenticed to his brother, a surveyor, he began a long process of self-education. At Leicester, he met Henry Walter Bates (1825–1892), who enthused him about beetles. They sailed to South America together in 1848, as self-financed professional collectors, although they soon split up, with Wallace concentrating on the Rio Negro and its tributaries. During this expedition, to the Amazon, which lasted from May 1848 to July 1852, he collected widely, identified many new species, and explored the upper reaches of the river Vaupes. Wallace undertook a second expedition, to the Malay Archipelago, between April 1854 and February 1862. In the course of this he wrote two significant papers, "On the Law which has regulated the introduction of New Species," from Sarawak, Borneo, and "On the Tendency of Varieties to Depart Indefinitely from the Orig-

inal Type," from Ternate, which prompted a joint publication, together with extracts from Darwin's writing, at the Linnean Society's meeting of 1 July 1858 (and nudged Darwin into writing *The Origin of Species*). Wallace, while traveling from Bali to Lombok, deduced by observation that there was a major dividing line between the Asian and Australian biological regions, now known as the Wallace Line.

Wallace specialized in birds, butterflies, and fishes, recorded vocabularies and customs of the local peoples, and forged a lifelong friendship with the botanist Richard Spruce (1817–1893). Wallace lost much of his collections and journals in a shipboard fire on the voyage home from the Amazon expedition. Undeterred, he prepared for a second expedition, with some initial support from the Royal Geographical Society. Arriving in Singapore, he traveled extensively throughout the Malay Archipelago, with several long and hazardous voyages. He made important visits to Sarawak (Borneo), where he obtained orangutan specimens, the Moluccas, the Aru Islands, and Papua New Guinea, searching in particular for birds of paradise. The impact of his Ternate paper effectively transformed him from working naturalist to scientific theorist.

On his return to England, Wallace wrote extensively. He became a fellow of the Geographical, Linnean, and Zoological Societies, president of the Entomological Society, and was on friendly terms with Darwin, Joseph Hooker (1817–1911), Charles Lyell (1797–1875), and T. H. Huxley (1825–1895). Never wholly at ease in London scientific circles, he preferred the peace of domestic life after his marriage to Anne Mitten, who shared his deep love of plants. His books on biogeography were hugely influential, in particular his two books *The Geographical Distribution of Animals* (1876) and *Island Life* (1880), in which his lucid synthesis of contemporary research is grounded and illuminated by first-hand knowledge. In spite of his works' influence, Wallace was regarded as something of a maverick, partly because of his interest in spiritualism. He developed a distinctly un-Darwinian view of man's consciousness, as having come about by a process additional to natural selection, though in other respects he was a partisan Darwinist. He never obtained a regular salaried post, and was especially disappointed not to be named superintendent of Epping Forest, for which he had ambitious plans. In 1881, he was granted a civil pension, largely through Darwin's efforts. He lectured in the United States in 1886 and 1887, at the invitation of the Lowell Institute, and was greatly struck by his visit to Yosemite, and the giant sequoias, which increased his awareness of environmental issues and the need for preservation. Wallace was a prolific writer on scientific and social issues, with a clear engaging style that conveys his enthusiasm for intellectual enquiry, and for all aspects of the natural world.

Peter Raby

Further Reading

Brooks, J. L. (1984). *Just before the origin: Alfred Russel Wallace's theory of evolution*. New York: Columbia University Press.

Camerini, J. R. (Ed.). (2002). *The Alfred Russel Wallace reader: A selection of writings from the field*. Baltimore & London: Johns Hopkins University Press.

Knapp, S. (1999). *Footsteps in the forest: Alfred Russel Wallace in the Amazon*. London: Natural History Museum

McKinney, H. L. (1972). *Wallace and natural selection*. New Haven, CT: Yale University Press.

Raby, P. (2001). *Alfred Russel Wallace: A life*. London and Princeton, NJ: Chatto and Windus, Princeton University Press.

Smith, C. H. (Ed.). (1991). *Alfred Russel Wallace: An anthology of his shorter writings*. Oxford: Oxford University Press.

Wallace, A. R. (1869). *The Malay archipelago: The land of the orang-utan and the bird of paradise: A narrative of travel with studies of man and nature*, 2 vols. London: Macmillan and Co.

Wallace, A. R. (1876). *The geographical distribution of animals; with a study of the relations of living and extinct faunas as elucidating the past changes of the earth's surface*, 2 vols. London: Macmillan and Co.

Wallace, A. R. (1880). *Island life: or, the phenomenon and causes of insular faunas and floras, including a revision and attempted solution of the problem of geological climates*. London: Macmillan and Co.

War

War is as ancient as human settlement on the land and the invention of iron and bronze tools for farming and fighting. For example, four thousand years ago and more in the Near East, in the Fertile Crescent (the area from the southeastern coast of the Mediterranean Sea around the Syrian Desert north of the Arabian Peninsula to the Persian Gulf) of the Tigris and Euphrates River valleys, an elaborate system of irrigation canals watered farmers' fields. These canals were vulnerable to destruction by warring armies, contributing to long-term ecological degradation from siltation and waterlogging.

Environmental change caused by war appeared in the northern Mediterranean Sea basin twenty-five hundred years ago. The Mediterranean ecosystem is naturally fragile, featuring long, hot summers and short, wet winters; the topography is mostly mountainous, with soils that are light and easily eroded after natural vegetation is removed. A slowly rising population used wood for forging or building chariots and for making battering rams, siege machines and fortifications, and tools for farming. In a perennially warring region, the rulers of the city-states that emerged in Greece and adjacent lands raised armies and navies and consumed both human and natural resources to confront their enemies. Defensive fortifications and siege warfare were well developed when Babylonian king Nebuchadnezzar's army besieged the fortified city of Lachish in 588 BCE, placing great piles of wood from stripped forests against the wooden ramparts and burning them until the fortifications collapsed.

In military campaigns as early as the Persian invasion of Greece in 512 BCE, armies burned their enemies' forests and pillaged their farmlands. These attacks on civilian populations and lands were the grim precursors of modern "total war." Rural people fled to safety in the forest ahead of advancing military columns; if they stayed for any time, their new fields and pastures damaged fragile woodlands.

On coastlands downstream from forests, ports developed at the mouths of rivers; there shipbuilders

In Flanders Fields

Major John McCrae was a Canadian physician who fought at the Western Front in 1914, before being reassigned to a hospital in France. He died of pneumonia while on active duty in 1918. His "In Flanders Fields" is probably the most often recited poem from the war. He wrote it in May 1915, shortly after the Battle of Ypres. It was published in his collection of poetry, *In Flanders Fields and Other Poems*, in 1919. He described the scene before him, where poppies—whose seeds lie dormant for years—bloomed in fields and meadows torn up in the fighting. Thus nature survives the violence of humans, a symbol of hope and regeneration, but at the same time a piercing reminder of war, bloodshed, and loss. The poem, helped make the red field poppy the symbol of remembrance with paper poppies worn by millions every year on Armistice Day (11 November) in Europe and on Memorial Day in the United States.

In Flanders fields the poppies blow
Between the crosses, row on row
That mark our place; and in the sky
The larks, still bravely singing, fly
Scarce heard amid the guns below.

We are the Dead. Short days ago
We lived, felt dawn, saw sunset glow,
Loved and were loved, and now we lie
In Flanders fields.

Take up our quarrel with the foe:
To you from failing hands we throw
The torch; be yours to hold it high.
If ye break faith with us who die
We shall not sleep, though poppies grow
In Flanders fields.

---

built ships of all sizes for peaceable trade and the great triremes (ancient galleys) for naval warfare; woodsmen gradually cleared forested watersheds upstream to meet the shipyards' needs. As local timber supplies ran low, strategic needs demanded control of more-distant stands of timber. In the protracted Peloponnesian War (431–404 BCE), which ended the golden age of Athens, great naval battles between Sparta and its allies on one hand and the Athenian Empire on the other destroyed hundreds of triremes; the prime trees of whole forests were lost as the ships burned and sank. This was a bitter irony because one of Athens's purposes in the long Sicilian Campaign was to capture forests for shipbuilding.

The Roman Empire produced the greatest environmental transformations that were yet experienced in Mediterranean and European landscapes. In coastal zones timber harvests for shipbuilding produced defo-restation and soil loss. In North Africa, Roman armies damaged croplands and water systems in the conquest of Carthage. Also, as the Roman general Julius Caesar's forces moved northward in the conquest of Gaul and then Germany and Britain, they built a system of roads so superbly engineered that many are still in use today. On the moving northern frontiers of the empire, a string of military fortifications established garrisons of troops with ancillary communities to provide food and forest products for them. These engineering works opened wide areas of forest to settled agriculture.

A long series of invasions of Italy from the north ultimately crippled Rome's empire. Urban centers declined, and rural medieval Europe slowly emerged in its aftermath. Warfare was endemic (native), interlacing with civilian life on the land. In the feudal era warriors' weapons were no more powerful than in earlier times, so the environmental impacts of organized violence revolved around fortifications and siege warfare. The lords of the land defended their headquarters by building gradually more massive, intricately designed forts surrounded by earthen ramparts with wooden palisades (fences of stakes for defense). Sieges of fortresses and fortified towns could last for years, devouring both woods and croplands. In the twilight zone between mass violence and peaceful times, brigandage (plundering hardly distinguishable from regular soldiering) festered. Peasant populations were terrorized by raids on food and livestock. Lands deserted when rural people became refugees reverted to natural woodlands and wetlands. These wars took western Europe to the beginning of the industrial, nation-state era, with its unprecedented acceleration of the scale of warfare and the scope of its environmental impacts.

But European societies were by no means the only ones whose mass conflicts produced environmental change in the long centuries before modern times. In the varied landscapes and climates of Asia, China stands out, with its great river basins draining wide mountain systems, its dense lowland populations, and its long north-south distances. Cycles of stability followed by civil war revolved there for more than twenty centuries as imperial dynasties struggled to establish and maintain control over regional warlords. Within China's heartland the complex irrigation systems of the Yangtze and Yellow Rivers were repeated targets of armies disrupting their enemies' food supplies. Refugees from flood waters, like refugees from war throughout history, caused additional environmental disruptions where they wandered and settled. Also, on China's northwest frontier, facing perennial threats from nomadic warriors of the central Asian grasslands, emperors built the Great Wall and protected forest zones, to guard against invading cavalry.

The Indian subcontinent has an equally long history of urban civilizations. Beginning with the Maurya Empire nearly twenty-five hundred years ago, Indian kingdoms developed the capacity to mount extended wars for control of river basins and hill forest hinterlands. Royal armies led by elephant corps slowly devoured the land on long campaigns. In the upper Ganges River basin from 997 CE onward, Muslim conquest states from farther northwest—the Delhi sultanate and then the great Mughal Empire—mounted sustained campaigns that had widespread environmental impacts. Cavalry swept the countryside, and the royal elephant corps required massive amounts of fodder. The Mughal imperial army, in its late seventeenth-

century campaigns in south India, was a mobile city of nearly 1 million fighters, camp followers, and suppliers.

Throughout the premodern world many conflicts were frontier wars, either fought as wars between two states or fought as wars of conquest. Often protracted and intermittent, these wars were precursors of modern guerrilla warfare and counterinsurgency, although they did not produce the devastation of today's counterinsurgency weapons. Many were fought in hill areas, usually forested and on slopes with easily eroded soils. They were characterized by seasonal skirmishes, fortified outposts, and capture of loot, including movable natural resources. In one of many instances, the Nepal Himalayas, the armies of the rising Gurkha state conquered peripheral hill areas of western Nepal and Kumaon in the eighteenth century. They destroyed crop terraces and irrigation systems, thus producing soil erosion that permanently reduced the productivity of the land. In other settings where depopulation occurred and human pressures receded, food crops gave way to increased populations of domestic livestock, including cattle, sheep, and goats, because less labor was needed to maintain livestock than to till soil. More dramatically, farmland often reverted to secondary woodland, where wildlife flourished and local biodiversity (biological diversity as indicated by numbers of species of animals and plants) increased in the newly verdant habitat where few hunters roamed. However, these changes were usually temporary because victorious regimes soon settled a new generation of farmers to renew the agricultural landscape.

Global Empires in the Modern Era

Except for the impacts of regional empires such as Rome and China, the ecological impacts of wars were largely local and short-lived until Europe's power began to extend globally in the sixteenth century. The emerging era of the imperial nation-state and large-scale capital and industry accelerated the technological impacts associated with global trade and transport. The rise of bureaucratic administration meant increasingly efficient taxation power, the capacity to channel social and economic resources toward systematic violence against enemies. Funding for military research and development inexorably increased in the wars between European states and in accelerating arms races, and the wars between these states ultimately engulfed every continent. Early ecological damage outside Europe reflected these states' navies' needs for construction timber and naval stores. By the 1700s European navies began cutting the hardwood and white pine stands of northeastern North America, the coastal hardwoods of Brazil, and later the teak forests of monsoon Asia to find substitutes for the depleted English oak and Scandinavian conifers. These environmental costs of naval warfare were confined to the land; the seas themselves suffered little pollution or biological reduction from naval wars until the great wars of the twentieth century.

The most fundamental ecological impacts of Europe's global conquests occurred in the Americas, where Europeans brought with them epidemic diseases that were a holocaust for Native Americans. Up to 90 percent of the Native American population died by the late sixteenth century. This depopulation led to widespread abandonment of cultivated lands and reversion to secondary forest, often for long periods. In Latin America even in the 1500s the impacts of conquest registered both on lowland coastal zones and riverine forests, the highlands of Mexico and the Andes, where sheep and goats came to rule degraded pasture lands and the wide, natural grasslands where cattle soon prevailed.

In North American woodland ecosystems the impact of endemic frontier warfare was somewhat different. There Europeans were able to follow up their conquests by settling in and clearing temperate forests far more readily than they could anchor themselves in tropical rain forest zones. In contrast to Latin America, where populations did not recover to their pre–1492 levels until around 1800, the native populations of North America were fully replaced by northern European immigrants in much shorter order.

Wars of the Industrial Era

The great escalation of modern warfare and its impacts began in Europe in the 1790s, when revolutionary France and its ruler, Napoleon, expanded both the intensity of warfare and its continent-wide reach. The Napoleonic wars also disrupted intercontinental transport of supplies, in one case resulting in a major long-term change in cropping patterns. The British naval blockade after 1805 cut off supplies of cane sugar to French ports from the Caribbean. In response new techniques of extracting sugar from beets led to an explosion of sugar beet farming in the heavy soils and cool climate of northern Europe. Meanwhile the former

slaves of Haiti turned their work from half-deserted cane plantations in the fertile lowlands to subsistence cropping in the erosive hill woodlands, and Haiti became one of the most degraded landscapes in the Americas. In this way Europe's revolutionary wars had unintended ecological consequences across the oceans.

From the mid-nineteenth century onward western European and U.S. industry produced a leap in destructive capacity through revolutionary innovations in mass production. By the end of the 1800s highly accurate breech-loading rifles and machine guns transformed the battlefield, and more powerful explosives began to ravage both urban and rural targets. Moreover, railroads and steamships gave industrialized nations far greater mobility and international reach. In addition to their civilian uses, trains and ships moved troops and materiel rapidly, inexpensively, and far, making possible the conquest of the rest of the world.

The U.S. Civil War demonstrated the ecological impacts of the new industrial warfare. When it began in 1861, no one expected the war to grind on for over four years, but its glacial momentum toward exhaustion of the South produced widespread destruction of croplands and fodder resources by Northern armies, extending to deliberate scorched earth campaigns in its final year. These strategies were nothing new in the history of warfare, but their scale and intensity were unprecedented. Ultimately the human resources, economic wealth, and industrial power of the North prevailed. Northern armies could be supplied and supported more consistently by the Northern railroad network connecting military movements back to factories and farms. Also, the Northern navy's blockade of Southern ports and rivers interdicted the South's raw cotton exports to Europe. The increasingly global impact of war was evident in immediately intensified cotton production on other continents, especially the rich black soils of central India, where small farmers switched from food crops to cotton by 1862 and tilled even some previously forested land until the war ended in 1865.

In Europe in the same decade Germany harnessed the Industrial Revolution to accelerated military mobilization. Rapid victories over the Austro-Hungarian Empire and then France resulted from skillful movement of German armies over the new railway networks, while more powerful artillery damaged woodlands and cities. However, in terms of ecological violence, these mid-nineteenth-century European wars were merely overtures to the two world wars that followed, when the environmental impacts of warfare became truly global.

World War I

On both sides of World War I (the "Great War"), improved long-distance food transport enabled mass armies to be sustained year around. Conversely, on a scale greater than ever before, armies deprived both enemy units and civilians of food, fiber, and fodder by ravaging land and destroying stored crops.

The war also brought the first large-scale use of chemical warfare. Germany's chemical industry, which had recently emerged as the world's leader, forged close cooperation with its military, enabling the German army to use massive amounts of mustard gas on Allied troops. By the war's end chemical war produced 1.3 million casualties, including ninety thousand deaths, and temporarily poisoned lands around the battlefields.

Europe's forests came under unprecedented pressures during the war. Seemingly endless bombardments in battle zones shattered forests that had been carefully managed for centuries. In addition—and this was new in history—for hundreds of miles behind the lines, emergency fellings of timber were carried out in France and elsewhere around Europe. Only the great forest zone of Russia escaped heavy exploitation because imperial Russia's railway system was still rudimentary. The British, Canadians, and U.S. armies organized large timber imports into Europe from both North America and India's monsoon forests. However, this war began only the beginnings of tree cutting from tropical rain forests because logging and transport facilities were still in their infancy in the wet tropics. Perhaps equally important for the longer run, government forestry agencies in many countries took greater control over forest resources during the war. The postwar recovery period brought reforestation programs in both Europe and North America in which single-species tree plantations replaced the greater variety of species in the former natural forests.

World War II

Further industrialization between the two world wars enabled militarized states from 1939 to 1945 to mobilize far greater resources from around the world than a quarter-century before and to inflict new levels of destruction. The U.S. Army Air Corps, using a new generation of bombers, destroyed the Moehne and

Eder dams in the German Ruhr Valley, destroying or crippling over 125 factories and 46 bridges and inundating 3,000 hectares of cropland. Also, using incendiary bombs produced by the rapidly maturing U.S. chemical industry, the same planes almost totally destroyed the German cities of Hamburg and Dresden from the air.

In combat zones the forests of Europe were once again battered by fighting. Behind the lines of combat, timber was cut at the most urgent speed that limited human power could achieve, and wide forest regions of Norway and Poland were looted of their timber wealth. This time, even more than in the previous war, the battle zones of Europe, North Africa, and the Middle East could call upon timber resources from other continents. Timber-harvesting machinery and transport networks, from forest roads to harbor facilities to oceanic ships, were more highly developed than in the previous war, although strikingly, the vast forest resources of Asian Russia were still largely inaccessible. British Columbia was now a leading source of military timber for Great Britain, while Washington and Oregon provided massive amounts of spruce for the Allied air forces. Innovations in airplane design, combined with recently acquired knowledge of the tropical forests of the Americas, led to harvesting even balsa, one of the lightest of tropical woods. The postwar impact of these timber harvests was largely the result of the roads that penetrated previously inaccessible forests, encouraging new frontier settlements after the fighting stopped. Once again wartime and subsequent peacetime together produced long-term changes on the land; neither can be understood without the other.

The impact of the war on fragile islands in the Pacific had no previous parallel in that ocean's web of life. Small islands have limited varieties of plant and animal species, and many have thin or fragile soils; they are exceptionally vulnerable to the impacts of human conflict. On both steep volcanic islands and coral atolls throughout the Pacific, the fighting produced fundamental ecological degradation of forests, watersheds, coastal swamplands, and coral reefs.

In this war, as in others, the spread of epidemic diseases accelerated longer trends in human and animal populations. Diseases of both humans and livestock had spread into the Pacific with traumatic impacts ever since the 1770s, but the Pacific war accelerated the process in some instances. Allied disease-control teams succeeded in containing the spread of malaria from the islands where it was already widespread, but the cattle tick reached New Caledonia, infecting livestock and damaging agricultural systems there. Malaria itself caused nearly ten times as many casualties as battles for the U.S. forces until 1943. However, a new chemical, DDT, largely controlled the disease among the troops before the war's end. No one at the time foresaw the massive environmental damage that DDT would produce in the following peacetime.

For the marine resources of the Pacific the war had paradoxical effects. Commercial fisheries and whaling fleets were largely destroyed, docked, or transformed into military uses until 1945, leaving fish stocks and marine mammal populations to recover somewhat, although submarine warfare killed some whales, and any increase in their numbers proved to be temporary. Overall, this war initiated major environmental damage to the planet's oceans.

In the home islands of Japan the war had tragic ecological as well as human impacts. The Japanese war machine had attempted to command the mineral and forest resources of southeastern Asia, to compensate for its limited resource base at home, but that effort was brief and limited by the Allied counterattacks. However, the domestic damage in Japan was appalling. For Japan's forest resources the wartime loss of import sources (especially the northwestern coast of North America) meant intensive cutting of domestic forests for charcoal, firewood, and construction, even ancient stands that had been preserved for centuries. In many locations the direct result was loss of soil and damage to water regimes (regular patterns of occurrence or action). On Japan's farms food production expanded urgently, especially on marginal lands, and even songbirds were virtually wiped out for emergency food.

The U.S. Army Air Corps played a decisive role here, too. U.S. incendiary bombing almost totally destroyed Japan's urban areas, which were built of wood. Postwar rebuilding of the ravaged cities of Europe and Asia required continuing large-scale harvesting of forests from boreal (northern), temperate, and tropical forests.

The ultimate environmental disaster, the impact of nuclear bombs, was also Japan's fate. The cities of Hiroshima and Nagasaki were rapidly rebuilt after 1945, in part because the local flora made a surprisingly rapid recovery from radioactive pollution, but the human costs of the two bombs are still being counted.

By August 1945 the United States was triumphant, having suffered relatively little long-term damage to its domestic resources and ecosystems or to its additional resource areas in Latin America. Its military

industry had grown exponentially, and military-industrial coordination had reached high levels. Hence, that war sowed the seeds of later disasters, which began to be evident as the Cold War deepened after 1948.

The Late Twentieth Century

The global arms race after 1945 accelerated production of every tool of destruction. One of the smallest weapons, multiplied almost countless times, has been land mines. Some 100 million unexploded antipersonnel mines remain around the planet now, littering rural Vietnam, Afghanistan, and many other war-torn countries and grievously retarding the restoration of postwar farms, pastures, forests, and water regimes.

Equally widespread by the time the Cold War ended in 1990 were the long-term pollution effects of military industry, which left many locations severely poisoned. Many weapons-production sites and testing grounds in the United States required massively expensive cleanups. Large areas of Soviet and eastern European land and air had become virtual wastelands, and even the Arctic Ocean north of Russia was severely polluted, in part from nuclear radiation.

Chemical warfare produced a new range of destruction in the Vietnam War (1961–1975) as the U.S. Air Force applied Agent Orange and other defoliants to the forests of Indochina. In addition to 12.7 million metric tons of bombs and shells, U.S. planes dropped 49,800 metric tons of herbicides, permanently destroying or seriously damaging 1.5 million hectares of upland forest and mangrove marshes.

In the post–1945 years nuclear technology, designed for both bombs and power plants, became the most ominous environmental threat in history, although its greatest impact resulted from the peacetime armament race rather than from actual war. In the United States nuclear facilities in Washington State, Colorado, and elsewhere became radioactive sewers, and entire Pacific islands and their coastal reefs became unfit for life as a result of U.S. and French nuclear weapons testing. Soviet sites of both weapons manufacturing and power plants were even more highly radioactive. The meltdown at the Chernobyl nuclear power plant in 1986 poisoned wide agricultural, forest, and urban areas for centuries to come.

Finally, twentieth-century warfare has made a major contribution even to warming of the global atmosphere. Military establishments consume great amounts of fossil fuels, contributing directly to global warming. The Persian Gulf War of 1991 was the most notorious case of atmospheric pollution in wartime, as the plumes of burning oil wells darkened skies for months far downwind. It now seems that the fires caused less regional and global air pollution than was feared in their immediate aftermath, although they dropped heavy pollution on nearby desert, farmland, and the gulf's waters.

War and Resource Conservation

As war has concentrated power in the hands of the military and the state, it has also enhanced the power of governments to regulate the use of natural resources. In the twentieth century warfare has resulted in rapid strengthening of regimes for resource management that have shaped postwar years. Under the United Nations the Forestry Division of the Food and Agricultural Organization created a global network of professional foresters in the late 1940s. Within member countries in Europe and North America and colonial countries, governments' forestry services extended their authority to manage forest reserves, limiting private owners' ability to sell or cut timber for short-term financial gain. However, close relations between forest departments and timber corporations have often minimized this distinction. In the United States and Canada, as well as countries newly independent after 1945 such as India, Malaysia, Indonesia, and the Philippines, the enhanced power of governments over timber resources often led to more efficient clear-cutting of forests.

On the other hand, wildlife conservation also received new emphasis after both world wars. In World War I the trauma and disillusionment that people experienced at the devastation of entire landscapes, including their wildlife, led to links between the postwar peace movement and the international wildlife conservation movement, plus the first efforts to survey and protect endangered species. The wildlife conservation movement was abandoned during World War II, and wild flora and fauna suffered grievously in and near war zones. Warplanes used wildlife reserves such as flamingo marshes in the Caribbean for target practice or for dumping unused bombs.

TTX>However, war sometimes reduces pressure on wildlife populations. In the war in Nicaragua in the late 1980s, Contra troops forced rural subsistence hunters to leave Caribbean lowland forests for several years. By 1990 wildlife in the rain forest flourished, but this was only a temporary reprieve from human pressures, just as whenever humans have been forced off land by war. Equally ironic, military reservations such as the severely polluted Rocky Mountain Arsenal Wildlife Refuge in Colorado often act as de facto wildlife reserves, in peacetime as well as war.

In sum, the ecological consequences of war are complex and even paradoxical. They are often difficult to separate from the impacts of human population growth and industrial expansion in peacetime. However, in many ways war's environmental impacts have been distinctive and widespread, and they have been accelerating ominously over the past century.

Richard P. Tucker

Further Reading

Albion, R. G. (1926). *Forests and sea power: The timber problem of the Royal Navy, 1652–1862*. Cambridge, MA: Harvard University Press.

Austin, J. E., & Bruch, C. E. (Eds.). (2000). *The environmental consequences of war*. Cambridge, UK: Cambridge University Press.

Bamford, P. W. (1956). *Forests and French sea power, 1660–1789*. Toronto, Canada: University of Toronto Press.

Bennett, J. (2001). War, emergency and the environment: Fiji, 1939–1946. *Environment and History, 7*(3), 255–287.

Best, G. (1982). *War and society in revolutionary Europe, 1770–1870*. London: Fontana.

Bond, B. (1984). *War and society in Europe, 1870–1970*. London: Fontana.

Creveld, M. V. (1989). *Technology and war: From 2000 B.C. to the present*. New York: Free Press.

Crosby, A. W. (1972). *The Columbian exchange: Biological and cultural consequences of 1492*. Westport, CT: Greenwood Press.

Crosby, A. W. (1986). *Ecological imperialism: The biological expansion of Europe, 900–1900*. Cambridge, UK: Cambridge University Press.

Danielssohn, B., & Danielssohn, T. M. (1986). *Poisoned reign: French nuclear colonialism in the Pacific*. Harmondsworth, UK: Penguin.

Elvin, M., & Liu, T.-J. (Eds.). (1998). *Sediments of time: Environment and society in Chinese history*. Cambridge, UK: Cambridge University Press.

Firth, S. (1987). *Nuclear playground*. Honolulu: University of Hawaii Press.

Gleick, P. W. (1994). Water, war, and peace in the Middle East. *Environment, 36*(3), 6–42.

Hale, J. R. (1985). *War and society in Renaissance Europe, 1450–1620*. London: Fontana.

Hastings, T. H. (2000). *Ecology of war and peace: Counting costs of conflict*. Lanham, MD: University Press of America.

Headrick, D. R. (1981). *The tools of empire: Technology and European imperialism in the nineteenth century.* Oxford, UK: Oxford University Press.

Homer-Dixon, T. F. (1998). *Ecoviolence: Links among environment, population and security.* Lanham, MD: Rowman and Littlefield.

Homer-Dixon, T. F. (1999). *Environment, scarcity and violence.* Princeton, NJ: Princeton University Press.

Hughes, J. D. (1994). *Pan's travail: Environmental problems of the ancient Greeks and Romans.* Baltimore: Johns Hopkins University Press.

Kiple, K. F. (1993). *The Cambridge world history of human disease.* Cambridge, UK: Cambridge University Press.

Lanier-Graham, S. (1993). *The ecology of war: Environmental impacts of weaponry and warfare.* New York: Walker and Company.

McNeill, J. R. (1992). *Mountains of the Mediterranean world: An environmental history.* Cambridge, UK: Cambridge University Press.

McNeill, J. R. (2000). *Something new under the sun: An environmental history of the twentieth-century world.* New York: W. W. Norton.

McNeill, W. H. (1976). *Plagues and peoples.* Garden City, NY: Anchor Books.

McNeill, W. H. (1982). *The pursuit of power: Technology, armed force, and society since A.D. 1000.* Chicago: University of Chicago Press.

Meiggs, R. (1982). *Trees and timber in the ancient Mediterranean world.* Oxford, UK: Clarendon Press.

Melville, E. (1994). *A plague of sheep.* Cambridge, UK: Cambridge University Press.

Miller, S. W. (2000). *Fruitless trees: Portuguese conservation and Brazil's colonial timber.* Stanford, CA: Stanford University Press.

Mintz, S. (1985). *Sweetness and power: The place of sugar in modern history.* New York: Viking.

Nietschmann, B. (1990, November). Conservation by conflict in Nicaragua. *Natural History, 99*(11), 42–48.

Pounds, N. J. G. (1973). *An historical geography of Europe, 450 B.C.–A.D. 1330.* Cambridge, UK: Cambridge University Press.

Richards, J. F., & McAlpin, M. B. (1983). Cotton cultivating and land clearing in the Bombay Deccan and Karnatak: 1818–1920. In R. P. Tucker & J. F. Richards (Eds.), *Global deforestation and the nineteenth-century world economy* (pp. 68–94). Durham, NC: Duke University Press.

Russell, E. (2001). *War and nature: Fighting humans and insects with chemicals from World War I to Silent Spring.* Cambridge, UK: Cambridge University Press.

Sauer, C. (1966). *The early Spanish main.* Berkeley and Los Angeles: University of California Press.

Strachan, H. (1983). *European armies and the conduct of war.* London: George Allen and Unwin.

Thirgood, J. V. (1981). *Man and the Mediterranean forest: A history of resource depletion.* London: Academic Press.

Thomas, W. L. (1956). *Man's role in changing the face of the Earth.* Chicago: University of Chicago Press.

Tucker, R. P. (1987). The British empire and India's forest resources: The timberlands of Assam and Kumaon, 1914–1950. In J. F. Richards & R. P. Tucker (Eds.), *World deforestation in the twentieth century* (pp. 91–111). Durham, NC: Duke University Press.

Tucker, R. P. (2000). *Insatiable appetite: The United States and the ecological degradation of the tropical world.* Berkeley and Los Angeles: University of California Press.

Turner II, B. L., Clark, W. C., Kates, R. W., Richards, J. F., Mathews, J. T., Meyer, W. B. (Eds.). (1990). *The Earth as transformed by human action.* Cambridge, UK: Cambridge University Press.

Vayda, A. P. (1974). Warfare in ecological perspective. *Annual Review of Ecology and Systematics, 5,* 183–193.

Wawro, G. (2000). *Warfare and society in Europe, 1792–1914.* New York: Routledge.

Westing, A. (1976). *Ecological consequences of the second Indochina war.* Stockholm, Sweden: Almqvist and Wiksell International.

Westing, A. (1980). *Warfare in a fragile world: Military impact on the human environment.* London: Taylor & Francis.

Westing, A. (1984). *Environmental warfare: A technical, legal and policy appraisal.* London: Taylor & Francis.

Westing, A. (Ed.). (1984). *Herbicides in war: The long-term ecological and human consequences.* Philadelphia: Taylor & Francis.

Westing, A. (Ed.). (1990). *Environmental hazards of war: Releasing dangerous forces in an industrialized world.* London: Sage Publications.

Williams, M. (1989). *Americans and their forests.* Cambridge, UK: Cambridge University Press.

Waste Management

Over the years and around the world, solid waste—garbage, trash, or rubbish—has been abundant, cumbersome, and often polluting. But many factors besides waste itself combine to produce a waste problem, including perception and the conditions under which

---

Dig a trench through a landfill and you will see layers of phone books like geographical strata or layers of cake. . . . During a recent landfill dig in Phoenix, I found newspapers dating from 1952 that looked so fresh you might read one over breakfast

Source: Rathje, William. "Garbage archaeologist." *The Economist*, September 8, 1990.

---

people live. The greatest refuse-management problems exist in cities.

Waste Practices before the Industrial Revolution

Humans began abandoning the nomadic life around 10,000 BCE. Tribes that followed game left their wastes behind. In towns and cities such habits could not be tolerated by the citizenry, but methods of dealing effectively with refuse took time. In ancient Troy, food and human wastes were sometimes dropped on the floors of houses or dumped into the streets. When the stench became unbearable, people covered the droppings with a fresh supply of dirt or clay. In the streets, pigs, dogs, birds, and rodents ate the organic material. The debris accumulation in Troy amounted to 4.7 feet per century, and as much as 13 feet per century in other cultures.

While the state of sanitation was appalling in many parts of the ancient world, there were some signs of progress. In Mohenjo Daro, founded in the Indus Valley about 2500 BCE, central planning led to the construction of built-in home rubbish chutes and to the institution of scavenger services. In Heracleopolis, founded in Egypt about 2100 BCE, wastes were collected in areas of the privileged, but dumped primarily in the Nile River. About the same time, the homes of the Sea Kings in Crete had bathrooms connected to trunk sewers, and by 1500 BCE the island had land set aside for disposal of garbage.

Religion sometimes was important in enforcing sanitary practices. About 1600 BCE, Moses wrote a sanitary law code under which Jews were expected to bury their waste far from living quarters. The Talmud required that the streets of Jerusalem be washed daily despite the scarcity of water.

In the classical period, waste plagued even the high culture of Athens. About 500 BCE, Greeks organized the first municipal dumps in the Western world, and the Council of Athens began enforcing an ordinance requiring scavengers to dispose of wastes no less than one mile from the city walls. Athens also issued the first known edict against throwing garbage into the streets, and established compost pits.

Ancient Mayans in the New World also placed their organic waste in dumps and used broken pottery and stones as fill. Records from second-century BCE China reveal "sanitary police" who were charged with removing animal and human carcasses and "traffic police" responsible for street sweeping.

Because of its size and dense population, Rome faced sanitation problems unheard of elsewhere. While garbage collection and disposal were well organized by the standards of the day, they did not meet the city's needs. General collection was restricted to state-sponsored events, and property owners were responsible for cleaning abutting streets—although the laws were not always enforced. Wealthy Romans used slaves to dispose of their wastes, and some independent scavengers gathered garbage and excreta for a fee and sold the material as fertilizer. When Rome's power waned, the quality of the city's environment deteriorated.

As western Europe deurbanized in the Middle Ages—due in great degree to widespread plagues—

A recycling bin in a subway station in Seoul, South Korea, in August 2002. COURTESY KAREN CHRISTENSEN.

Waste Management in Early American Cities

We arrived in Cincinnati in February, 1828, and I speak of the town as it was then; several small churches have been built since, whose towers agreeably relieve its uninteresting mass of buildings. At that time I think Main street, which is the principal avenue, (and runs through the whole town, answering to the High street of our old cities), was the only one entirely paved. The *troittoir* is of brick, tolerably well laid, but it is inundated by every shower, as Cincinnati has no drains whatever. What makes this omission the more remarkable is, that the situation of the place is calculated both to facilitate their construction and render them necessary. Cincinnati is built on the side of a hill that begins to rise at the river's edge, and were it furnished with drains of the simplest arrangement, the heavy showers of the climate would keep them constantly clean; as it is, these showers wash the higher streets, only to deposit their filth in the first level spot; and this happens to be in the street second in importance to Main street, running at right angles to it, and containing most of the large warehouses of the town. This deposit is a dreadful nuisance, and must be productive of miasma during the hot weather.

Source: Trollope, Fanny. (1984). *Domestic Manners of the Americans.* London: Alan Sutton Publishing, pp. 27–28. (Originally published 1832)

---

people were spared the massive waste problems experienced by densely populated cities. Despite the crudity of medieval dwellings and living conditions, the eventual rise of new cities was accompanied by greater attention to health practices. Cities began paving and cleaning streets at the end of the twelfth century.

The migration of rural peoples to urban places also meant the migration of hogs, geese, ducks, and horses into the cities. In 1131 a law was passed prohibiting swine from running loose in Paris after young King Philip was killed in a riding accident caused by an unattended pig. But animals continued to roam the streets as scavengers.

In the great Islamic cities and in China, however, public areas were better maintained than in Europe during the Middle Ages and Renaissance.

The Waste Problem in the Industrial Age

With the onset of the Industrial Revolution in the 1760s, urban sanitation took a turn for the worse first in England then on the European continent. The inability to house the growing population migrating to the industrial centers led to serious overcrowding and health problems. As late as 1843, a major section of Manchester had only one toilet for every 212 people.

English cities, however, were the first to establish city services to confront the problems. (Some research suggests that Vienna established a refuse collection system that was one of the earliest on record in the eighteenth century.) While it is easy to exaggerate the

range and quality of services provided, the largest industrial cities in England and elsewhere had rudimentary public works and public health agencies by the early nineteenth century.

The rise of public health science was crucial. Cholera epidemics ravaged England in the early nineteenth century, and in the late 1820s many people accepted chronic dysentery and other endemic diseases as normal. The 1842 Poor Law Commission's *Report on the Sanitary Condition of the Labouring Population of Great Britain*, authored by Edwin Chadwick, came to the conclusion that communicable disease was related to filthy environmental conditions. The filth—or miasmatic—theory of disease was the most significant force for promoting environmental sanitation until the twentieth century, when the germ theory identified bacteria as the culprit in spreading communicable diseases.

While Europe was in the throes of its Industrial Revolution, the United States was just emerging as a nation. Many of the European lessons about sanitation, therefore, were not applied immediately. Early America was highly decentralized, and the smaller towns and cities did not face the enormous waste problems of London or Paris. Yet habits of neglect affected these communities too. Casting rubbish and garbage into the streets was done casually and regularly, despite the fact that crude sanitary regulations were common by the late seventeenth century in major towns. In 1634 Boston officials prohibited residents from throwing fish or garbage near the common landing. In 1657 the burghers of New Amsterdam passed laws against casting waste into streets.

By and large, sanitation in preindustrial America was determined by local circumstances. Some city leaders placed a high priority on city cleanliness, applying the principles of environmental sanitation. Others simply ignored the problem. Individuals or private scavengers usually collected refuse. Boards of health were slow in developing, understaffed, and limited in power. It was not until 1866 that New York City became the first American city to establish a systematic public health code.

The solid waste problem became a serious issue in American cities during the Industrial Revolution. Crowded cities produced mounds of garbage. Coal mines left hills of slag. Pigs or turkeys still roamed the streets and alleys in some towns looking for scraps; horses dumped tons of manure into thoroughfares; and rivers, lakes and the oceans became sinks for tons of urban discards.

Boston authorities estimated that in 1890 scavenging teams collected approximately 350,000 loads of garbage, ashes, rubbish, and street sweepings. In Chicago 225 street teams gathered approximately 2,000 cubic yards of refuse daily. In Manhattan in 1900, scavengers collected an average of 612 tons of garbage daily. Because of seasonal variations in available fruits and vegetables, that amount increased to 1,100 tons daily in July and August. One hundred years later, the United States produces more than 250 million tons of municipal solid waste each year, and possibly as much as 380 million tons per year. This represents more than 4 pounds per person per day.

The Worldwide Waste Stream

Unfortunately, the United States is a leader in many categories associated with municipal solid waste generation, although the waste problem is not restricted to the United States. While the composition of solid waste varies considerably throughout Europe, organic material and paper dominate the waste stream. These two categories account for between 50 and 80 percent of residential waste materials. Glass, plastics, and metals make up as little as 10 percent to as much as 25 percent. In eastern Europe, organic materials are more plentiful than glass, plastics, and metals. Overall figures suggest substantially less use of packaging material in Europe as a whole, for example, than in the United States.

Affluence is a strong dictator of waste volume and variety. For example, in higher-income economies in Israel, Saudi Arabia, and the United Arab Emirates, abandoned cars, furniture, and packaging are openly discarded. In Asia, paper and plastics waste are generally greatest in Tokyo and Singapore, while very low in Beijing and Shanghai (due in part to recovery and recycling). On the Indian subcontinent organic and inert matter dominates waste disposal, and per capita per day disposal rarely exceeds 0.8 kilograms (less than 2 pounds). The same is true for African cities, where waste is high in organic material and also rarely exceeds 0.8 kilograms. Waste in Latin America generally is high in organic material, but can average 1 kilogram per day (2.2 pounds).

While the discards of nineteenth-century America were largely food wastes, wood and coal ash, rubbish, and horse manure, the current waste stream includes a complex mix of hard-to-replace as well as recyclable materials, and a variety of toxic substances to a much greater extent than anywhere else in the world. Of all current discards, paper, plastics, and aluminum have increased the most. Paper makes up about 38 percent of the U.S. waste stream; plastics, 11 percent; metals and glass, 19 percent; and yard waste, 12 percent.

Waste Management: Public and Private

The way solid waste is managed—or mismanaged—is crucial to the success of collection and disposal practices. Beginning in the late nineteenth century, a major concern of city government in the United States was to determine responsibility for delivering needed services such as refuse collection and disposal. For many years, the question was whether public or private service was better. Between the 1890s and the 1960s, publicly managed systems dominated. Today, the United States has a mixed system of service providers in the solid waste field, with the trend toward increased privatization. Whatever the system, local governments in North America in general retain primary responsibility for managing or overseeing solid waste management. In Canada the approach favors more decentralization than in the United States.

The recent interest in "integrated waste management" systems, that is, systems that will use some or all disposal options, requires cooperation between public and private parties. In the United States, the Environmental Protection Agency's promotion of integrated waste management also suggests a significant role for the federal government in setting a national agenda for solid waste, as well as having an expanded regulatory function.

Since the 1960s, the U.S. federal government has played a greater role in addressing the waste problem, underscoring its significance as an environmental issue with national repercussions. The 1965 Solid Waste Disposal Act was the first major federal law to recognize solid waste as a national problem. Since that time new laws have been added, shifting attention among issues of recycling, resource recovery, conversion of waste to energy, hazardous wastes, and more traditional concerns over municipal solid wastes.

While the United States seeks to implement an integrated solid waste management system, western Europe leads the world in such an endeavor. Governments in all Western European countries are required to design their systems around integrated models with waste prevention at the core. While the public sector has been at the center of these programs for years, private companies increasingly carry out waste management services. Even in Eastern Europe where state-run programs have been the norm, private companies are making headway. In many countries, legislation to improve solid waste management at the highest levels is insufficient, and private sector initiatives increasingly compete with governments to carry out of waste services.

Collection Practices

Collection of solid wastes has been made difficult throughout the world by the growing volumes and kinds of materials discarded, the larger populations to be served, and the greater distances that sanitation workers are required to cover. There is no "best" method of collection. Before 1900, some American cities chose to collect unseparated discards, and others experimented with source separation. Historically, collections were most frequent in the business districts, less frequent in outlying areas or poorer neighborhoods. As more affluent suburbs grew, cities diverted collection teams from inner-city routes to upper- and middle-class neighborhoods.

After World War II, technical advances helped to ease the problems of collection especially in the United States and Europe with the introduction of compaction vehicles and transfer stations (used as central drop-off points for collected refuse). But over the years collection remained heavily dependent on hand labor in many parts of the world. No matter the method, collection is difficult because it is costly and does not serve every citizen equally well, especially the poor. Surveys

estimate that from 70 to 90 percent of the cost of solid waste service in the United States goes for collection. Equally high or higher collection ratios can be found in other areas such as Africa.

Collection of wastes is an imposing task throughout the world. In some cities, such as Kathmandu, Nepal, there is no formal waste collection service of any kind. In Mexico City, the national government controls collection and disposal arrangements, and does not allow private contractors to operate. Throughout Latin America collection coverage is reasonably good in the large cities such as Buenos Aires, Sao Paolo, Rio de Janeiro, Caracas, Santiago, and Havana, although it is uncertain whether squatter settlements receive adequate collection service. Privatizing collection operations, which became more popular in the United States in the 1960s, also has caught on in several large cities in Latin America.

Conditions in Europe vary greatly. In western Europe and Scandinavia collection is frequent and highly mechanized; in eastern Europe, where much of the housing is multifamily apartments, quality of service is uneven. Like Europe, cities in the industrialized countries of Asia—Australia, New Zealand, Hong Kong, Japan, and Singapore—have waste collection that is mechanized and capital-intensive. In developing countries much of collection is done by hand labor, with the exception of some large cities that maintain motorized collection fleets. In the poorest countries, collection rates may not exceed 50 percent and may not extend to the poor.

Privatization also is gaining a foothold in some countries. Most interestingly in East Asia and the Pacific, women often manage garbage in the household, pay for collection service, separate recyclables, and sell items to private waste collectors. In South and West Asia, for example, labor unrest and civil disturbances have affected municipal service periodically. In much of Africa the municipality, through a combination of motorized vehicles, animal-drawn carts, and human-drawn wheelbarrows and pushcarts, carries out collection. As in many developing regions, transfer stations are uncommon and collection reliability is often low.

Disposal Options: Landfills and Incinerators

Modern sanitary landfills evolved from those originating in Great Britain in the 1920s, and American attempts in the 1930s in New York City, San Francisco, and especially Fresno, California. The sanitary landfill is composed of systematically dug trenches, where layers of solid waste alternate with layers of dirt. The trenches are then covered with a layer of dirt so that odors could not escape and rodents and other vermin could not enter. Newer landfills utilize plastic liners to retard leaching, and monitoring devices to detect methane emissions and various other pollutants.

Through the 1950s and 1960s engineers and waste managers believed that the sanitary landfill was the most economical and safest form of disposal. By the 1970s, experts began to doubt that landfills could serve the future needs of cities, not only because of the paucity of land but also because of citizen resistance and increasingly rigid environmental standards. The NIMBY syndrome—Not in My Back Yard—spread across the country as some neighborhoods refused to act as dumping grounds for the whole community. In some cases, the placing of dumps in minority neighborhoods was and is challenged as a form of environmental racism. Many times sanitary landfills did not live up to their name, becoming a haven for insects and rodents, threatening groundwater, producing methane gas linked to ozone depletion, and containing various hazardous materials.

By recent estimates, 55–70 percent of the waste generated in North America ends up in landfills. However, the total number of sites in the United States particularly declined substantially through the late 1980s and 1990s, from approximately 8,000 in 1988 to 2,300 in 1999. By 2008, the Environmental Protection Agency (EPA) predicts that the number of landfills will fall to about 1,200. The major reason for the decline, in addition to siting problems, is Subtitle D of the Resource Conservation and Recovery Act (1976), which set and enforced rigorous national standards for municipal solid waste (MSW) landfills in the 1990s. In essence, newer, larger, but fewer landfills could meet the new standards, while smaller and older ones simply stopped operating.

The lack of sites in the United States, especially in the East and parts of the Midwest, forced several states to export their garbage. New York is the top exporter with 5.6 million tons per year, followed by New Jersey (1.8 million tons), Missouri (1.79 million tons), and Maryland (1.55 million tons). The major importer of waste is Pennsylvania with 9.76 million tons per year followed at some distance by Virginia (3.89 million tons) and Michigan (3.12 million tons).

There is a clear split between northern and southern/eastern Europe in the use of landfills. In some northern European countries landfill practices parallel current U.S. experience with approximately half of the waste finding its way to landfills. In Greece, Spain, Hungary, and Poland, virtually all collected waste goes into the ground. Many of the landfills in Europe are of the small, uncontrolled municipal type, but efforts are being made to shift toward larger regional types. Unlike in the U.S., NIMBYism is unlikely to influence the siting of landfills.

Landfilling has been the cheapest and most typical form of disposal in East Asia and the Pacific. But in countries such as Australia, Japan, and Singapore, costs have risen sharply in recent years. In developing countries open dumping rather than sanitary landfilling has dominated disposal practices. The same is true in South and West Asia and in much of Africa. Egypt and South Africa tried to upgrade landfills, but this objective has yet to achieve success. Waste pickers—sometimes operating under municipal authority or on their own—work the open dumps to find materials to utilize or sell. Ocean dumping is still common in these regions as well, although the practice is banned or restricted in most places.

The use of landfills—many of them private—in Latin America and the Caribbean is on the rise, especially in large cities. However, these sites more closely resemble controlled dumps than sanitary landfills. In Mexico, for example, there are nearly 100 controlled disposal sites, but only about 10 percent (mostly in the north) can be considered sanitary landfills. Waste pickers also are common in Latin America, and while attempts have been made to prevent them from entering the dumps, such efforts normally fail.

Of the available alternatives, incineration has had the strongest following. The first systematic incineration of refuse at the municipal level was tested in Nottingham, England, in 1874. Two years later in Manchester, Alfred Fryer built an improved "destructor" and subsequently the British led in the development of the technology for several decades. The British were the first to attempt to convert the heat from burning waste into steam to produce electricity. The first American "cremators" were built in 1885.

Two types of combustion facilities were developed in the late nineteenth and early twentieth centuries. The first is a mass burn unit used to reduce the total volume of waste; the second is the waste-to-energy facility, pioneered by the British, meant to produce steam to generate electricity or to be sold directly to customers as a heating source. Waste-to-energy became popular in the United States in the 1970s in the wake of the energy crisis, but did not gain widespread support, nor did incineration in general.

Despite the fact that incineration drastically reduces the volume of waste, the cost of the technology and chronic problems with air pollution made it a weak competitor in contests with the sanitary landfill. In the 1990s, however, incineration rebounded, especially built on the hope of an improved competitive edge because of rising landfill fees and the promise of cleaner energy production. In 1996, 110 combustors with energy recovery were in operation in the United States with a capacity to burn up to 100,000 tons of MSW per day. The number is much lower in Canada. Overall, waste-to-energy incineration handles approximately 10 to 15 percent of the solid waste stream in North America.

Incineration also has a checkered history internationally. In Africa any kind of burning and waste-to-energy—except medical waste incineration—are little used because of high costs. The same is true in Latin America. In Asia, only cities in the most industrialized countries use modern incinerator technology. Japan leads the way, with Tokyo having 13 incinerators. The increasing lack of landfill space and the dense population has put Japan on the forefront of incineration use and development. In developing countries, many problems have arisen with imported incinerators. Some units do not operate at high enough temperatures to destroy the high moisture content in the waste, fail to destroy pathogens, and contribute substantial air pollution.

Europe's commitment to incineration since the early successes in England has been mixed. Northern European countries, particularly Sweden, rely heavily on mass-burn incineration in association with energy generation. In western Europe anywhere from 35 to 80 percent of residential waste is incinerated. The lack of landfill space and energy needs have been powerful forces in promoting the burning of waste, but not without controversy. Emissions of acid gases, heavy metals, dioxin, and mercury have caused serious concern, and have led the European Union to enforce stringent emissions standards for incinerators. Older incinerators that do not generate energy are being phased out.

European countries have been active in producing by-products from incineration residue, using fly ash, for example, in a variety of road products. Europeans also have led the way in developing refuse-derived fuels. The experiences in eastern Europe have been less successful, especially because of the older incineration facilities in use and the inability to upgrade or replace them.

Recycling and Recovery

Only in the last several years has recycling emerged as an alternative disposal strategy to landfilling and incineration, particularly in the United States. Once regarded as a grassroots method of source reduction and a protest against overconsumption in a "throw-away society," recycling arose in the 1980s as a disposal method in its own right. In 1988 about 1,000 communities in the United States had curbside collection service; in 2000 the number exceeded 7,000. The province of Ontario initiated its first curbside program in 1983, and by 1987 at least 41 communities had such programs in Canada. The EPA estimated that recycling and composting diverted 57 million tons of material away from landfills and incinerators in the United States in 1996 (up from 34 million tons in 1990), with the most typical recyclables being aluminum cans, batteries, paper and paperboard, and yard trimmings.

A major goal of many communities and the nation in general is to increase the recycling rate, which stood at 10 percent in the late 1980s. The EPA's 1988 draft report on solid waste called for a national recycling goal of 25 percent by 1992. In the late 1990s, the EPA raised the goal to at least 35 percent of MSW by 2005, and called for reducing the generation of solid waste to 4.3 pounds per capita per day. The actual rate of recycling in the late 1990s was about 20 to 25 percent in North America.

The U.S. experience with recycling, while vastly changed from years past, falls short of recycling and recovery efforts in other parts of the industrialized world. Germany and Denmark, in particular, have aggressive recycling policies. Denmark, for example, recycles about 65 percent of its waste. One of the most unique aspects of recovery of materials in western Europe is the pervasive idea of "producer responsibility" for proper disposal of packaging and other products. In some western European countries packaging reduction goals have been set at 75 percent by 2002. Recycling and recovery in southern and eastern Europe and in other parts of the world is more uneven. Throughout Latin America and the Caribbean materials recovery is extensive with recycling programs in all large cities and most moderate-sized communities. In smaller towns and rural areas, where much of the waste is organic, composting is the only form of recovery in use. However, centralized composting has not been successful in Latin America as a rule. By contrast, backyard composting is more widespread in Australia, Japan, and New Zealand. In Asia a large portion of household organic waste is fed to animals. The large composting plants that were so prevalent throughout developing countries in Asia—including those pioneered in India—are out of use and not working at full capacity.

In East Asia and the Pacific, formal and informal source separation and recycling programs are practiced. The highest degree of waste reduction takes place in the thriving urban areas of Australia, New Zealand, Japan, Korea, and Hong Kong. There also are waste recovery programs and recycling efforts sponsored by cities and national ministries in the People's Republic of China and Vietnam.

Informal waste picking is widespread throughout the world, particularly in developing countries. In several locations, such as in South and West Asia and Africa, there are informal networks of pickers, buyers, traders, and recyclers in place of formal public systems or private companies. Materials recovery takes on a different form in the developing world as opposed to highly industrialized regions. For the former, materials recovery becomes a necessity in areas of poorly paid or unemployed people and in areas where resources are scarce. In industrialized areas, materials recovery is an attempt to lessen the wastefulness of growing economies and reduce environmental costs.

The waste problem is a part of life—ancient and modern. Strides have been made throughout the world to confront the complex problems of waste generation, collection, disposal, and materials recovery. Finding a way to manage solid waste in order to preserve resources and minimize pollution is a constant challenge.

Martin V. Melosi

Further Reading

American Public Works Association. (1970). *Municipal refuse disposal.* Chicago: Public Administration Service.

American Public Works Association. (1975). *Solid waste collection practice.* Chicago: American Public Works Association.

Armstrong, E. L., Robinson, M. C., & Hoy, S. M. (1976). *History of public works in the United States.* Chicago: American Public Works Association.

Bonomo, L., & Higginson, A. E. (Eds.). (1988). *International overview on solid waste management.* London: Academic Press.

Carra, J. S., & Cossu, R. (Eds.). (1990). *International perspectives on municipal solid wastes and sanitary landfilling.* London: Academic Press.

Gandy, M. (1993). *Recycling and waste.* Aldershot, England: Ashgate Publishing.

Grover, V. I., Guha, B. K., Hogland, W., & McRae, S. G. (Eds.). (2000). *Solid waste management.* Rotterdam, Netherlands: A. A. Balkema.

Gunnerson, C. G. (June, 1973). Debris accumulation in ancient and modern cities. *Journal of the Environmental Engineering Division, ASCE, 99,* 229–43.

Kemper, P., & Quigley, J. M. (1976). *The economics of refuse collection.* Cambridge, MA: Ballinger.

Kharbanda, O., & Stillworthy, E. A. (1990). *Waste management.* New York: Auburn House.

Kirov, N. Y. (Ed.). (1972). *Solid waste treatment and disposal.* Ann Arbor, MI: Ann Arbor Science Publishers.

Melosi, M. V. (1981). *Garbage in the cities.* College Station: Texas A & M University Press.

Melosi, M. V. (2000). *The sanitary city.* Baltimore: Johns Hopkins University Press.

Melosi, M. V. (2001). *Effluent America.* Pittsburgh: University of Pittsburgh Press.

Neil, H. A., & Schubel, J. R. (1987). *Solid waste management and the environment.* Englewood Cliffs, NJ: Greenwood.

Pollock, E. (December, 1985). Wide world of refuse. *Waste Age, 16,* 89–90.

Rathje, W., & Murphy, C. (1992). *Rubbish!* New York: Harper Perennial.

Rose, P. (1988). Solid waste. In N. Ball (Ed.), *Building Canada* (pp. 245–61). Toronto, Canada: University of Toronto Press.

Savas, E. S. (1977). *The organization and efficiency of solid waste collection.* Lexington, MA: D. C. Heath and Co.

Small, W. E. (1970). *Third pollution.* New York: Praeger Publishing.

Strasser, S. (1999). *Waste and want.* New York: Metropolitan Books.

Tillman, D. A., Rossi, A. J., & Vick, K. M. (1989). *Incineration of municipal and hazardous solid wastes.* San Diego, CA: Academic Press.

United Nations Environment Programme, Division of Technology, Industry, and Economics. (2002). *Newsletter and technical publications: Municipal solid waste management.* Retrieved December 5, 2002, from http://www.unep.or.jp/ietc/ESTdir/Pub/MSW/RO

United States Environmental Protection Agency, Office of Solid Waste. (2002). *Basic facts: Municipal solid waste.* Retrieved December 5, 2002, from http://www.epa.gov/epaoswer/non-hw/muncpl/facts/htm

Zero Waste. (2002). Waste & recycling: Data, maps & graphs. Retrieved December 5, 2002, from http://www.zerowasteamerica.org/Statistics.htm

Water

Humankind's ancient, massive, and growing intervention in natural hydrological processes, including capturing and rerouting flows of water and altering water quality, has resulted in improved human health and longevity, and created opportunities for humans to live in places, numbers, and comfort that otherwise wouldn't be possible. Between 1700 and 1900, human withdrawals of freshwater from aquifers, rivers, and lakes increased five times, from 110 cubic kilometers to 580 cubic kilometers. Over the next hundred years, withdrawals increased another nine times to 5,190 cubic kilometers, which is more than 10 percent of the Earth's available flows. Although the same water can be used repeatedly, different uses require different levels of quality, quantity, and flow characteristics. Today societies are grappling with how to manage water resources to achieve multiple goals. Environment-related goals include protection of endangered species, provision of recreational and wilderness experiences, and allowing natural systems to provide services that humans would otherwise have to provide themselves.

The Physical and Biological Context

The ongoing exchange of seawater and freshwater is called the hydrologic cycle, and is powered by the sun's energy causing evaporation. As evaporated water cools in the upper atmosphere, it condenses and falls as rain or snow. Although most evaporation and precipitation occur over oceans, clouds are also carried inland by winds, bringing the water that fills rivers, recharges groundwater aquifers, and rejuvenates the Earth's terrestrial biomass. The cycle continues as the water eventually evaporates again.

Key physical aspects of water enable it to play its central role. Substances can dissolve or be suspended in water. This enables flowing water to transport them from one place to another. Rivers carry nutrients from mountains to valleys to soils in flood plains. Poisons and pathogens also reside in water, making it a common source of disease to humans and other species.

Evaporating water leaves minerals behind. Unless replenished with a new inflow, the minerals left behind become more concentrated, rendering the remaining water less fit for use. Water can impart energy both in terms of its elevation (falling water drives hydropower turbines), and in terms of heated water molecules (the evaporation process transfers energy from liquid water to the atmosphere). But the energy in water also propels floods, one of Earth's most devastating natural disasters. Since the hydrogen side of a water molecule is more positively charged and the oxygen side more negatively charged, liquid water molecules tend to align their positive and negative poles and pull together. This property facilitates water flow from roots to leaves of plants, and enables water to serve as a solvent. Finally, water freezes from the top down, allowing fish and other species to survive the winter in unfrozen depths, which has enabled more long-lived and complex organisms and food webs to emerge.

Water's origins on Earth remain a mystery. It may have been released from within the floating rocky debris that first formed the Earth, or it may have arrived little by little in the form of icy meteors striking the dry young planet. Today, twice as much of the Earth is covered by water as is covered by land. Ninety-seven percent of all of Earth's water is found in oceans, and 2 percent is located in polar and mountain ice. Of the remainder, 95 percent is located in underground aquifers, and the rest can be found in lakes, inland seas, surface soils, the atmosphere itself, living biomass, and stream channels. The ironic phrase "as predictable as weather" summarizes the variable nature of water's stocks and flows: wet and dry periods, droughts, and floods all are common occurrences, though their exact timing and magnitude cannot be predicted.

Freshwater ecosystems contain a large proportion of the world's biodiversity compared to their size. While comprising just 1 percent of the Earth's surface, they serve as home to 40 percent of the world's fish species, while 12 percent of animal species reside in fresh water. As of 2000, 34 percent of fish species, primarily located in freshwater habitats, were threatened with extinction.

Wetlands—regions where the prevalence of water results in saturated soils and that support life adapted to saturated soil conditions—are among the world's most biologically productive. They also provide such beneficial services to humans as filtering water, slowing and capturing flood flows, and serving as fish and wildlife habitat. Biological processes in wetlands are mimicked in today's wastewater treatment facilities,

A cistern at Acoma Pueblo in New Mexico in 1992. This and two other cisterns were the only sources of water for the community, located on a mesa several hundred feet above the valley floor. COURTESY DAVID LEVINSON.

which concentrate and accelerate the natural processes that break down and remove solids and pathogens from fresh water.

Irrigation

Irrigation remains the leading human use of water, accounting for 70 percent of all freshwater consumption. Forty percent of all crops produced today have been irrigated. Irrigated agriculture may have originated with the Sumerians of Mesopotamia around 4000 BCE. By 3200 BCE, Egyptians were digging irrigation canals off of the Nile River. As of 700 BCE, *qanats*—deep tunnels that deliver water from an underground aquifer to a farming region—were well established in Persia. The Sabeans living in Marib (modern-day Yemen) built a large agricultural diversion dam in roughly 500 BCE. In North America, by 200 BCE the Hohokam tribes located in current-day Arizona had established extensive irrigation canals drawing from the Gila and Salt Rivers. By 1900, roughly 40 million hectares were irrigated worldwide. This quantity grew sevenfold in the twentieth century to 270 million hectares. Irrigation particularly accelerated after 1950 with the introduction of "Green Revolution" high-yielding seed varieties that required extensive and well-regulated inputs of water.

The environmental impacts of irrigation canals include reducing the amount of water available for instream ecological processes and for riparian (at or near the riverbank) wetlands, and altering riparian zones in the places where diversion works exist. Further environmental impacts occur along canal routes where dry terrestrial ecosystems are transformed into flowing water systems, terrestrial habitats are fragmented, and migratory paths of terrestrial animals are blocked. Although irrigation canals do support wildlife, the flow regime of canals is keyed toward agricultural production, not a region's natural hydrological processes, creating adaptation challenges for local water-dependent species. While irrigated agriculture may increase overall biotic productivity, especially in dry regions, it may also reduce a region's biodiversity as farmers devote fields to a few or a single food-crop species (called monocropping).

In regions where salts naturally occur in the soil column, intensive irrigation can lead to soil salinization. As irrigation water rises to the surface and evaporates or transpires, salts concentrate, ultimately rendering the root zone infertile. Soil salinization is blamed for the destruction of numerous early agriculture-dependent civilizations of Mesopotamia and possibly South America. Today, 20 percent of irrigated acreage worldwide has elevated quantities of salts.

Hydropower

Waterwheels are among humanity's earliest machines, being utilized by the early Greek, Egyptian, and Chinese civilizations. The earliest waterwheels were used to grind grain and to lift water out of a river into another channel. Over the centuries, other applications emerged, with over 500,000 waterwheels existing in Europe by 1800. Hydropower consisted of transforming the movement of water directly into the movement of machinery until 1882 when the world's first hydroelectric plant was built on Wisconsin's Fox River. The growing demand for electricity spurred by the industrial era helped launch an era of large dam building worldwide. As of 1900, roughly 700 dams higher than 15 meters had been commissioned, with 220 located in England. By the end of the century, nearly 50,000 had been commissioned, though not all provided hydropower. China was the leading builder: at the time of its 1949 revolution, it had 8 large dams; by 2002, the number was roughly 22,000. There are an estimated 800,000 dams of all sizes worldwide. Reservoir volume is estimated at 10,000 cubic kilometers, or 5 times the volume of the world's rivers, covering 400,000 square kilometers, roughly the size of California.

Large hydropower dams that create reservoirs dramatically alter the ecology of river systems. Above the dam, flowing water regimes become standing water regimes and riparian habitat is flooded. Shorelines of reservoirs often are barren since plant and animal life

Water and the Growth of Cities

I have left to last the dynamic component of the city, without which it could not have continued to increase in size and scope and productivity; this is the first efficient means of mass transport, the waterway. That the first growth of cities should have taken place in river valleys is no accident; and the rise of the city is contemporaneous with improvements in navigation, from the floating bundle of rushes or logs to the boat powered by oars and sails.

Source: Mumford, Lewis. (1961). *The City in History: Its Origins, Its Transformations, and Its Prospects.* New York: Harcourt, Brace & World.

are not adapted to ever-shifting reservoir elevations determined by hydropower, agricultural, urban, downstream environmental, and recreational needs. Dams block sediment flows, causing siltation above the dam, alteration or loss of habitat for bottom-dwelling species, and a reduction in the deposition of nutrients in the floodplain. Dams also block passageways for migratory fish. By retaining flood flows in reservoirs, dams de-link the main channels of rivers from nearby wetlands, reducing the contribution each makes to ecological processes occurring in the other. Water temperature increases behind dams due to prolonged exposure of standing water to sunlight, which can degrade downstream fish spawning habitat when the warmer water is released.

There have been profound indirect environmental effects of hydropower and large dams. Hydropower provided a large proportion of the energy that fueled the Industrial Revolution. In the early 1900s, 40 percent of all U.S. electricity was generated by hydropower. By 2000, hydropower provided roughly 10 percent of U.S. electricity and 15 percent of the world's electricity. Large dam/reservoir systems enabled vast regions to transition from undeveloped wetland ecosystems to agricultural ecosystems. By 1980 California had lost 91 percent of its original wetlands largely as a result of the transformation of its great central valley from wetlands to agriculture. This substantially reduced available habitat and population sizes of numerous bird, terrestrial, and aquatic species.

Transportation

Rivers have served as commercial highways since ancient times. Civilizations have built dams and canals both to stabilize the elevation of waterways and to extend their reach. Rivers, including the Mississippi and the Rhine, have been dredged and straightened to permit the passage of longer barges with deeper drafts. Obstructions such as submerged boulders, branches, and tree trunks have also been removed from river channels. Environmental impacts include disturbing biotic activity in the benthic (river bed) zone due to dredging; curtailing annual flood events; accelerating the velocity and intensity of floods; and reducing shade and protection provided by submerged and partially submerged objects. Over the twentieth century, the number of rivers altered to improve transportation increased from roughly 9,000 to 500,000.

Canals also have played crucial roles in extending the range of human habitation and increasing the intensity of economic activity on frontiers. Canals enable building materials and machinery to be transported to frontiers while also enabling crops and natural resources to be shipped cheaply and quickly back to urban centers. China's 2,500-year-old Grand Canal extends over 1,600 kilometers enabling extensive agriculture and other industry to occur far from natural rivers. Completed in 1825, North America's 580-kilometer Erie Canal helped link New York Harbor to the Great Lakes, facilitating the rapid westward expansion and industrial growth of the United States.

Flood Control

Floods arise naturally due to heavy rainfall and/or rapid snowmelt, and on rare occasions result from catastrophic dam failure. Some 10,000 floods occur each year worldwide. Modern history's worst recorded flood occurred in 1887 along China's Huang-Ho (Yellow) River. A million people died as the waters engulfed eleven large towns and hundreds of villages. As recently as 1993, flooding on the Mississippi River resulted in 48 deaths and physical damages estimated at $15–$20 billion.

Environmental impacts of flooding include transfer of sediments and nutrients from uplands to the floodplain; creation of temporary aquatic links between rivers and nearby lakes and wetlands enabling the relocation of aquatic species; and re-routing of rivers into alternate or new channels. Floods help make soils fertile and aid forest growth. Levees (embankments that confine a flood), while protecting the immediate area from flooding, often serve to accelerate floodwaters, increasing their potential for devastation downstream. Levees also alter flood-dependent ecological processes where they are located. Restoration of upstream wetlands and forests, which serves to slow down floodwaters, became a part of flood-management planning in the 1990s.

Water for Cities

The ancient Romans took immense pride in their aboveground aqueducts, which by 300 BCE were delivering more than 1.5 million liters of water per day to Roman citizens. Roman cities also included extensive systems of pipes that delivered water from the aqueducts to houses and baths, as well as separate systems that carried sewage wastes away from homes. Today, roughly 95 percent of all urban dwellers have access to a fresh water supply, and 86 percent have access to sanitation facilities.

Throughout human history, societies have utilized rivers to carry wastes away, increasing the risk of contamination downstream. Water quality impacts can be divided between biological contaminants and chemical contaminants, the importance of the latter growing since the dawn of the industrial era. Though some ancient societies, such as the Chinese, adopted practices that separated human wastes from waters intended for human consumption, until the mid-nineteenth century, links between history's many plagues and the human relationship with water were only vaguely understood. Water-related diseases such as typhoid, cholera, and malaria took their toll worldwide. As recently as 1885, a cholera epidemic killed over 80,000 people in Chicago. Advances in epidemiology (the study of diseases in large populations) also occurred during this period. In 1854, Dr. John Snow linked London's cholera outbreaks to a public well that drew water from the Thames River just downstream from the city's raw sewage outfalls. His discovery launched

investigations in England and elsewhere into alternative designs for wastewater treatment facilities.

In the twentieth century, as growing cities in Europe and eastern North America increasingly released concentrated biological and industrial wastes into waterways, severe environmental degradation resulted. Biological impacts included a reduction in the quantity of dissolved oxygen in the rivers as living microbial matter multiplied and consumed biological wastes. Oxygen depletion led to die-offs of fish populations.

Pollution generated by industrial and agricultural activities often cannot be broken down by natural processes. Trace elements (including heavy metals), pesticides, petroleum, and petroleum by-products may leach from mining or farming operations or be flushed away from metal-plating, chemical, refining, and other facilities. They can be damaging or fatal to fish and other aquatic species. Some elements, including mercury and arsenic, bio-accumulate along food chains, reaching concentrations dangerous to humans and birds who eat fish caught in polluted waters.

Water for the Environment

A galvanizing event in U.S. public demand for river clean-up occurred in 1969 when Ohio's Cuyahoga River, saturated with petroleum wastes, ignited. Since the 1970s, industrialized nations have taken significant steps to reduce the loading of industrial pollution into rivers and lakes, including in the United States' passage of the Clean Water Act of 1972. The environmental health of European and North American waterways has improved, symbolized by the capture of an Atlantic salmon in a Rhine River tributary in 1990, twenty-two years after the previous catch occurred. Developing-world waterways remain under environmental pressure from untreated industrial and urban effluents, both of which continue to grow in quantity.

Another environmental risk to rivers involves industrial accidents that cause massive pulses of pollutants to enter a waterway. In 1986 a fire at a chemical plant near Basel, Switzerland, sent a plume of poisons down the Rhine River, killing nearly all plant and animal life for 180 kilometers. In January of 2000, the holding pond of a mine-metal recovery facility based in Baia Mare, Hungary, breached its dam during a heavy storm, releasing lethal cyanide and other metals into the Tiza River, a tributary of the Danube. Near the site of the breach, plankton and mollusk species were wiped out. Over a thousand tons of fish were destroyed in Hungarian rivers, with additional impacts in downstream nations.

Few water-management regulations focus exclusively on environmental benefits. The free-flowing characteristics of some U.S. rivers have been protected through the Wild and Scenic Rivers Act of 1968. The U.S. Endangered Species Act of 1973 can require far-reaching restrictions on the quality, quantity, and timing of flows that serve as habitat for endangered and threatened species. Since the 1990s, legislation has emerged to fight the growing costs imposed by such invasive species as the zebra mussel, a native of Eastern Europe, which now clogs North American freshwater intake pipes. Tort law (allowing lawsuits when damage has been done) and application of the Public Trust Doctrine have also served to protect environmental uses of water in the United States.

Internationally, *The Convention on Wetlands of International Importance Especially as Waterfowl Habitat*, or "Ramsar Convention," of 1971, maintains a list of Wetlands of International Importance that by 2001 included over 1,070 sites covering 81 million hectares. A growing number of national park systems worldwide also provide protection to aquatic ecosystems located within their boundaries.

Of the many uses of water described in this selection, some are complementary to each other and to environmental protection while others are not. Sorting out water rights—what they are, who has them, and how they are transferred—will be a prime challenge for years to come for citizens and water managers alike.

Brent M. Haddad

See also Aral Sea; Dams, Reservoirs, and Artificial Lakes; Droughts; Floods

Further Reading

Cech, T. V. (2003). *Principles of water resources: History, development, management, and policy*. New York: John Wiley & Sons.

Dahl, T. E. (1990). *Wetlands losses in the United States 1780's to 1980's*. Washington, DC: U.S. Department of the Interior, Fish and Wildlife Service. Retrieved July 16, 1997, from http://www.npwrc.usgs.gov/resource/othrdata/wetloss/wetloss.htm

McCully, P. (1996). *Silenced rivers: The ecology and politics of large dams*. London: Zed Books.

McNeill, J. R. (2000). *Something new under the sun: An environmental history of the 20th century*. New York: W. W. Norton.

United Nations Environment Programme (2000). *Report of the International Task Force for Assessing the Baia Mare Accident*.

World Commission of Dams (2000). *Dams and development*. London: Earthscan Publications Ltd.

Wolf, A. T., Natharius, J. A., Danielson, J. J., Ward, B. S., & Pender, J. K. (1999). International river basins of the world. *International Journal of Water Resources Development 15*(4), 387–427.

World Conservation Union (IUCN) (1996). *1996 IUCN Red List of Threatened Animals*. Gland, Switzerland: IUCN.

World Resources Institute (1998). *World Resources 1998–1999*. Washington, DC: World Resources Institute.

Water Energy

Mechanical (kinetic) energy of flowing or falling water was traditionally converted to rotary motion by a variety of waterwheels, and, starting in the early nineteenth century, by water turbines that have been used since the 1880s to turn generators. Unlike the combustion of fossil fuels, this form of electricity generation does not produce directly any air pollution, but its other environmental impacts have become a matter of considerable controversy.

It is not known by how many generations or centuries do the origins of waterwheels predate the first reference to their existence by Antipater of Thessalonica, who wrote during the first century BCE about their use in grain milling. A millennium later such simple devices were common in parts of Europe: In 1086 the Domesday Book listed 5,624 mills in southern and eastern England, one for every 350 people. The usual arrangement was to channel flowing water through a sloping wooden trough onto wooden paddles, often fitted to a sturdy shaft that was directly attached to a millstone above. Vertical waterwheels, first mentioned by Vitruvius in 27 BCE, were much more efficient. All of them turned the millstones by right-angle gears but they were propelled in three distinct ways.

Wheels and Turbines

Undershot wheels were driven by kinetic energy of moving water. As doubling the speed boosts the capacity eightfold, they were preferably located on swift-flowing streams. The best designs could eventually convert 35–45 percent of water's kinetic energy into useful rotary motion. Breast wheels were powered by a combination of flowing and falling water and operated with heads between 2 to 5 meters. Overshot wheels were driven primarily by the weight of descending water and hence could be located on streams with placid water flows. With heads over 3 meters their conversion efficiencies were commonly in excess of 60 percent with peaks of up to 85 percent. Wheels, as well as shafts and gears, were almost completely wooden until the beginning of the eighteenth century; hubs and shafts were the first iron parts and the first all-iron wheel was built early in the nineteenth century.

Besides the wheels fixed in streams there were also floating wheels on barges and tidal mills and common uses of waterwheels eventually expanded far beyond grain milling to power machines ranging from wood saws and oil presses to furnace bellows and forge hammers, and to mechanize manufacturing processes ranging from wire pulling to tile glazing. Even as their uses widened, capacities of waterwheels remained limited, averaging less than 4 kilowatts in Europe of the early 1700s. Post-1750 innovations led to a rapid increase of individual capacities as arrays of waterwheels, sometimes rating in excess of 1 megawatt, became the leading prime movers of expanded mass manufacturing in Europe and North America. In 1832 Benoit Fourneyron's invention of the reaction turbine ushered in the era of much more powerful water-driven machines. James B. Francis designed an inward-flow turbine in 1847, A. Pelton patented his jet-driven turbine in 1889, and V. Kaplan introduced his axial flow turbines in 1920.

Hydroelectricity

The first water turbines were used merely to replace waterwheels as the prime movers in many industries but by the late 1880s the machine began to be coupled with generators to produce electricity. The first American hydroelectric plant was built in 1882 in Wisconsin. More than a century later, water turns turbines that supply almost 20 percent of the world's electricity. In dozens of tropical countries, water power is the dominant means of electricity production.

Most of the world's hydro energy remains to be tapped. Worldwide total of economically feasible hydro generation is over 8 petawatthours (PWh, that is 1015 watthours) or roughly three times the currently exploited total. Europe has the highest share of exploited capacity (more than 45 percent), Africa the lowest (below 4 percent). The greatest boom in construction of large dams took place during the 1960s and 1970s, with about 5,000 new structures built per decade.

Advantages and Drawbacks

The air pollution advantage of hydropower is the most obvious one: If coal-fired power plants were to generate electricity that is currently produced worldwide by running water, the global emissions of CO_2 and SO_2 would be, respectively, 15 percent and 35 percent higher. Hydrogeneration also has low operating costs and its spinning reserve (zero load synchronized to the system) in particular is an excellent way to cover peak loads created by sudden increases in demand. Moreover, many reservoirs built primarily for hydrogeneration have multiple uses—serving as sources of irrigation and drinking water, as protection against flooding, and as resources for aquaculture and recreation. But during the closing years of the twentieth century, large dams came to be widely seen as economically dubious, socially disruptive, and environmentally harmful.

Displacement of a large number of usually poor people has been the most contentious matter. Construction of large dams dislocated at least 40 million people during the twentieth century (some estimates go as high as 80 million), and during the early 1990s, when the work began on 300 new large dams every year, the annual total reached 4 million people. China and India, the two countries that have built nearly 60 percent of the world's large dams, had to relocate most people: more than 10 million in China and at least 16 million in India. Large hydro projects also have a multitude of undesirable environmental impacts, and recent studies of these previously ignored changes have helped to weaken the case for hydrogeneration as a clean source of renewable energy and a highly acceptable substitute for fossil fuels.

Perhaps the most surprising finding is that large reservoirs in warm climates are significant sources of greenhouse gases emitted by decaying vegetation. Water storage behind large dams has increased the average age of river runoff and lowered the temperature of downstream flows. Several of the world's largest rivers have reservoir-induced ageing of runoff exceeding six months or even one year (Colorado, Rio Grande del Norte, Nile, Volta). Many tropical reservoirs create excellent breeding sites for malaria mosquitoes and for the schistosomiasis-carrying snails, and most dams present insurmountable obstacles to the movement of migratory fish. Multiple dams have caused river channel fragmentation that now affects more than three quarters of the world's largest streams.

Other environmental impacts caused by large dams now include massive reduction of aquatic biodiversity both upstream and downstream, increased evaporative losses from large reservoirs in arid climates, invasion of tropical reservoirs by aquatic weeds, reduced dissolved oxygen and H_2S toxicity in reservoir waters, and excessive silting. The last problem is particularly noticeable in tropical and monsoonal climates. China's Huang River, flowing through the world's most erodible area, and India's Himalayan rivers carry enormous silt loads. Silt deposition in reservoirs has effects far downstream as it cuts the global sediment flow in rivers by more than 25 percent, and reduces the amount of material, organic matter, and nutrients available for alluvial plains and coastal wetlands downstream, and hence increases coastal erosion.

The ultimate life span of large dams remains unknown. Many have already served well past their designed economic life of fifty years but silting and structural degradation will shorten the useful life of many others. As a significant share of the Western public sentiment has turned against new hydro projects, some governments took action. Sweden has banned further hydrostations on most of its rivers and Norway has postponed all construction plans. Since 1998, the decommissioning rate for large U.S. dams has overtaken the construction rate. Major hydro projects of the twenty-first century thus will be built only in Asia, Latin America, and Africa.

Vaclav Smil

Further Reading

Devine, R. S. (1995). The trouble with dams. *The Atlantic Monthly, 276*(2), 64–74.

Gutman, P. S. (1994). Involuntary resettlement in hydropower projects. *Annual Review of Energy and the Environment, 19*, 189–210.

International Hydropower Association. (2000). *Hydropower and the world's energy future*. Sutton: IHA.

Leyland, B. (1990). Large dams: Implications of immortality. *International Water Power & Dam Construction, 42*(2), 34–37.

Moxon, S. (2000). Fighting for recognition. *International Water Power & Dam Construction 52*(6), 44–45.

Reynolds, J. (1970). *Windmills and watermills*. London: Hugh Evelyn.

Shiklomanov, I. A. (1999). *World water resources and water use*. St. Petersburg: State Hydrological Institute.

Smil, V. (1994). *Energy in world history*. Boulder, CO: Westview.

Smil, V. (2003). *Energy at the crossroads*. Cambridge, MA: The MIT Press.

World Commission on Dams. (2000). *Dams and Development*. London: Earthscan Publisher.

Water Pollution

Large-scale pollution of the hydrosphere (the aqueous envelope of the Earth including bodies of water and vapor in the atmosphere), including contamination of major rivers, lakes, seas, oceans, and groundwater, is largely a product of four forces: natural resource exploitation, industrialization, urbanization, and agriculture, primarily dating from the nineteenth century. Pollution of local drinking water sources from human and other wastes, however, has probably existed since humans first created cities, and waterborne disease has historically been responsible for countless urban epidemics. Records of contamination of the Thames River in England—for instance, by wastes from tanneries, slaughterhouses, and textile mills, as well as by human sewage—date back to the fourteenth century. However, in these cases the waters involved were finite and the pollution more temporary. During the last two centuries pollution has occurred on a scale not previously experienced.

Nineteenth-Century Industrial and Municipal Water Pollution

Water pollution, like that of air and land, was initially most severe in those nations that industrialized and urbanized first, such as Great Britain, Germany, and the United States, but these nations were also often the first to attempt extensive control and reduction strategies. During the nineteenth century, wherever industrialization and urbanization developed, water pollution was a major consequence. Many industries were large water users, but they also required a "sink" in which to dispose of their wastes. The preferred site for a sink was usually the river on which the industries were located. The major industrializing nations in the nineteenth century—Great Britain, Germany, the United States, and Japan—all experienced severe river pollution from industrial activities and natural resource development, such as mining of coal, lead, and copper. Rivers such as the Thames and the Calder in Great Britain, the Rhine in Germany, the Blackstone and Connecticut in the United States, and the Watarase in Japan became contaminated by industrial wastes that destroyed fish, shellfish, and vegetation, altered stream ecology, and rendered the water unusable for drinking and other purposes. In addition, the pollution undoubtedly had damaging but unrecorded health effects. Fishers and farmers were often the primary economic losers from such pollution.

Growing urbanization and the use of waterways as a disposal place for sewage carrying human wastes produced another destructive influence on water quality. Many of the waterways receiving raw sewage were also the source of drinking water supplies for downstream or neighboring cities. Thus municipal building of sewage systems to improve local sanitary conditions (such as advocated by Edwin Chadwick in Great Britain) and to collect storm water resulted in threats to the health of inhabitants of downstream cities. Nineteenth-century cities in Europe and the United States frequently suffered from epidemics of waterborne diseases such as cholera and typhoid because of a failure to separate water supply and sewage disposal. In contrast, Tokyo, one of the largest cities in the world in the nineteenth century, separated water supply and sewage disposal and provided higher sanitary conditions for its inhabitants than did most U.S. and European cities. Sanitarians and authorities in these latter cities, however, rationalized the use of streams for sewage disposal by advancing the hypothesis that running water purifies itself. Although urbanites had dumped human wastes into neighboring waterways for centuries, the volume of wastes greatly increased in the last decades of the nineteenth century as hundreds of cities constructed sewage systems. The 1861 British Sewage Commission, for instance, reported that nearly one hundred rivers were in "an absolutely poisonous condition" because of sewage discharges. In the United States in 1904, the effluent from about 27 million urbanites, most of the sewered population, was discharged untreated into waterways, often with a devastating effect on drinking water quality and stream ecology. The situation was similar in other urbanizing and industrializing nations.

During the nineteenth century cities that experienced epidemics of waterborne infectious diseases such as cholera and typhoid that were related to sewage pollution included Chicago and Pittsburgh in the United States; Hamburg and Posen in Germany; Paris; Stockholm, Sweden; St. Petersburg, Russia; and Montreal, Canada. Cities—such as Boston and New York and Turin (Italy)—that shifted their sources of water supply from local sources or abutting rivers and instead drew water from protected upcountry watersheds sharply reduced the risk of epidemics of waterborne disease. Although some antipollution legislation was passed during the late nineteenth century, such as Great Britain's river pollution statutes (1876), Italy's Sanitary Law (1888), and the Massachusetts Act to Protect the Purity of Inland Water (1886), they had only a limited effect on reducing pollution.

Improving Drinking Water Quality through Science

Part of the difficulty in controlling waterborne disease was a failure to understand its epidemiology. For much of the nineteenth century physicians and sanitarians were divided between those who believed in the theory of contagionism—epidemics are caused by contagion (contamination by touch)—and those who believed in the theory of anticontagionism—contamination caused by miasmas (vaporous exhalations believed to cause disease), where decaying organic matter polluted the air. Those who believed in contagionism advocated the use of quarantines to control epidemics, whereas anticontagionists advocated sanitary approaches such as cleaning privies and streets. The latter efforts actually produced some healthful effects by improving urban sanitation, but cholera and typhoid epidemics still continued in numerous cities in spite of a cleaner environment.

In the 1880s and 1890s, however, the work of French scientist Louis Pasteur and the development of the germ theory resulted in improved understanding of the methods of transmission of infectious diseases. The research of German scientist Robert Koch, who maintained that germ theory rather than contagionism or anticontagionism best explained how epidemics of cholera and typhoid were transmitted, proved most critical for comprehending waterborne diseases. In the early 1890s in the United States, biologist William T. Sedgwick, basing his research on the work of Koch, directed an interdisciplinary group of investigators at the Massachusetts Board of Health in clarifying the relationship of typhoid fever to sewage. Most sanitary engineers and physicians in the western European nations and the United States accepted these findings during the next decade. In the United States, for in-

This stream in Iowa lacks conservation buffers, which would help protect against erosion and contamination, and would support wildlife. COURTESY LYNN BETTS, USDA NATURAL RESOURCES CONSERVATION SERVICE.

stance, by 1905 thirty-six states had enacted legislation protecting drinking water, with enforcement by state boards of health. In 1912 concern over pollution and health led the U.S. Congress to create the Public Health Service (PHS) and to provide it with the function of investigating "the diseases of man and conditions influencing the propagation and spread thereof, including sanitation and sewage and the pollution, either directly or indirectly, of the navigable streams and lakes of the United States" (Mullan 1989, 58). In 1914 the PHS established the first water-quality standards for interstate commerce, based upon bacterial methods of water analysis, and these were copied by many states. However, few stringent laws limiting water pollution were actually enacted, and municipal pollution of waterways continued largely unabated through the 1920s except in cases of severe nuisance. Western Euro-

pean nations had a pattern similar to that of the United States, with little statutory protection for water bodies from municipal and industrial pollution.

But while the discharge of raw sewage into streams continued largely unabated, drinking water quality greatly improved in the United States and western European nations such as Great Britain and Germany. The technologies of water filtration and chlorination, rather than regulation, were responsible for reducing the incidence of waterborne disease. German cities such as Altona and Bremen pioneered in the application of water filtration techniques, and at the turn of the century London, Liverpool, and Birmingham in Great Britain and Berlin, Hamburg, and Bresslau in Germany all used sand filters for water protection. U.S. cities eventually followed this lead as American sanitary engineers teamed with biologists and chemists to perfect the techniques of slow sand and mechanical filtration. The use of chlorination (1908) to disinfect water was also developed in the United States and advanced rapidly among U.S. cities. By approximately 1940 most urbanites in the United States and western Europe were drinking potable (suitable for drinking) water that was either filtered or came from protected sources, and a steep decline in morbidity and mortality from typhoid fever as well as other waterborne diseases had occurred.

Although advances were also made in sewage treatment methods, such as the trickling filter and activated sludge, implementation proceeded at a much slower rate. Sewage treatment was not viewed as necessary to protect drinking water quality but rather as a means to prevent nuisances; it primarily benefited downstream cities but was paid for by the upstream cities. As a result, many waterways in Europe and the United States, as well as other areas of the world where urbanization had advanced, became badly polluted with sewage.

Old and New Sources of Industrial Pollution

Although fishers, farmers, operators of water filtration plants, and people requiring clean water in manufacturing processes objected to pollution from industrial wastes, such pollution received only limited attention from state authorities and sanitarians. The political power of industry and the belief in industrial nations such as Germany, Japan, and the United States that rivers in industrial areas are intended to serve as sewers prevented the passage of strong legislation. In some cases litigation led to damages being paid to those who sued, but seldom were conditions improved.

The two world wars greatly exacerbated the pollution of water bodies because of the wartime emphasis on production and the resultant weakening of environmental controls. The destructive nature of war itself, of course, greatly injured many aspects of the environment. During World War I industries such as metals, chemicals, food processing, petroleum refining, and coal mining and processing greatly expanded without attention to pollution controls. Sharp declines in the water quality of many waterways resulted. In the period between the wars, the growth in the number of motor vehicles led to major increases in petroleum use, with increased waterway contamination from petroleum spills and the dumping of waste oil. In reaction to the oil contamination of waterways and beaches, the U.S. Congress in 1924 passed the Oil Pollution Control

Act, the first national environmental regulatory legislation passed in the United States. The opposition of the petroleum industry, however, limited the act to offshore spills and did not include onshore refineries. During the 1930s, in spite of the worldwide depression, some advances were made in the United States and western European nations in improving drinking water quality and in sewage treatment through state programs, but the coming of World War II brought a halt to environmental improvements.

Like World War I, World War II had a devastating effect on waterways and for many of the same reasons—industrial production greatly increased, environmental controls were not enforced, and war's devastation drastically harmed environmental quality. For instance, the sinking of ships substantially increased oil pollution in oceans. During the war, industries in the combatant nations, especially the United States and Germany, produced a range of new chemical substances as part of their war efforts. Some were new products, such as rayon, artificial rubber, and synthetic detergents. Effluents from chemical manufacturers, in addition to discharges of the chemicals themselves, not only increased water pollution but also produced long-lasting environmental damage. Most significant were the pesticides and herbicides based on the chlorinated hydrocarbons (DDT, chlordane, endrin, etc.), which had long-lasting effects on plant and animal ecology in and out of water bodies. Indiscriminate spraying of these chemicals sharply harmed bird and insect life in many areas. Through bioaccumulation, these chemicals moved higher and higher up the food chain with devastating effects on birds and fish. Agricultural runoff containing toxic pesticides and herbicides became major sources of river and estuary contamination. Runoff containing artificial fertilizers led to increased nitrogen and phosphorous loads with consequent eutrophication (the process by which a body of water becomes enriched in dissolved nutrients) and hypoxic (deficient in oxygen) conditions. In addition, the development of the nuclear industry resulted in nuclear power plant wastes and other radioactive materials becoming a source of water pollution, as did polychlorinated biphenyls (PCBs), widely used in electrical transformers.

Water Quality Improvements through Regulation

During the postwar period, although a number of pollution-control measures were submitted to legislative bodies, war recovery and an increase in production were the prime national goals of the former combatants. In the United States, for example, although some progress was made in controlling municipal pollution because of increases in sewage treatment (in 1948, 1956, and 1961 Congress approved versions of the Water Pollution Control Act, providing limited subsidies for research and sewage treatment), industrial pollution from both old and new industries continued. The same was true in other industrialized nations. Many industrial rivers, such as the Monongahela and the Cuyahoga in the United States and the Emscher and the Rhine in Germany, remained open sewers. However, during the 1960s and 1970s the development of a heightened environmental consciousness in the United States, Canada, western Europe, and Japan resulted in much stronger pollution-control legislation and major improvements in water quality.

The United States provides a good example of the manner in which water-quality standards were strengthened, shifting from the state level to the national level as a means to secure improved control of pollution. Driving these changes was a heightened concern with environmental quality and its relationship to human health. The most significant change in regard to water pollution came in 1972, when Congress enacted the Federal Water Pollution Control Act Amendments, moving control over environmental pollution from the states to the federal government. This act, which was passed over President Richard M. Nixon's veto, aimed at the far-reaching goal of complete elimination of pollutant discharges into the nation's waters by the mid-1980s. The act called for industrial implementation of the "best practicable" water-pollution control technology by mid-1977 and the "best available" technology by mid-1983. Municipalities had to implement secondary treatment (biological treatment that goes beyond primary treatment, which removes suspended matter only) or better by mid-1977 and "best practicable" treatment by mid-1983. In order to pay for these technology improvements, the construction grants program provided massive federal subsidies to pay for the costs of construction of publicly owned wastewater treatment plants. This spending enabled the Clean Water Act, enacted in 1972, to produce major reductions in waterborne pollution from urban and industrial sources. Following the Clean Water Act, in 1974 Congress approved the Safe Drinking Water Act, which authorized the Environmental Protection Agency to set national health-based drinking water standards.

Although most western European nations also adopted drinking water regulations designed to protect the public health, they varied in terms of the degree of state enforcement. Today water quality concerns in the United States and western Europe focus largely on issues of nonpoint source pollution from pesticides and herbicides from agricultural areas, on industrial residues such as PCBs and heavy metals in sediments, on contamination from mining sources such as mine acid, on groundwater pollution by toxic chemicals such as trichloroethylene, on the parasites *Cryptosporidium* and *Giardia*, and on raw sewage inputs into waterways during wet weather. The latter problems are common in urban areas that have older combined sewer systems or overloaded sanitary sewers.

Water Quality Problems in the Former Soviet Union

Whatever the problems of the United States and western Europe in regard to water pollution, they were far less than those of Russia, East Germany, Poland, and Romania. These central and eastern European nations, all of which had lagged behind the nations of western Europe before World War II in regard to environmental and sanitary measures, experienced increases in urbanization and forced industrialization after World War II. Most of these nations lacked even the minimal environmental controls present in western Europe. Many of the rivers, lakes, and bays in Russia and the rest of the Soviet Union were subjected to extensive municipal and industrial pollution as the Soviet Union focused on natural resource development and industrial production. Because of the discharge of raw sewage, Russian rivers still carry waterborne diseases that have long ago disappeared from the United States and western Europe. In addition, industries dumped large amounts of heavy metals, phenols, and toxic chemicals into waterways, destroying stream ecology and damaging water quality. Massive agricultural runoff has contributed to eutrophication of rivers such as the Volga and Dnepr. The Black Sea and the Caspian Sea have lost many of their indigenous fish species due to pollution, and Lake Baikal, the world's oldest, deepest, and most voluminous lake, suffered for decades from pollution from pulp and paper plants on its shores. Recently a cooperative environmental policy among several nations has reduced the flow of effluents into this critical body of water.

Water Problems in the Developing World

The regions of the world where water pollution is growing most rapidly today are those where rapid urbanization, industrialization, and intensive agricultural development are occurring. That is, most at risk are the newly developing nations in Asia (the world's largest water user) and Africa as well as some parts of South America. In many of these regions of the world, freshwater supplies are inadequate because of growing populations and economies. Those supplies that do exist are frequently polluted. Cities in these regions have often suffered for centuries from inadequate and polluted water supplies and poor sanitation, although there were some improvements under colonialism. In cities such as Kampala (Uganda), Hong Kong, Manila, and Calcutta, for instance, colonial administrators often installed European-type sanitation and water supply systems, but these systems seldom provided full services for native populations. Population growth soon overwhelmed these systems, with reversion to more rudimentary methods. Studies today report that over 2 billion people worldwide suffer from waterborne and water-based diseases such as diarrhea and schistosomiasis. In some African nations, such as Mali, Zaire, and Niger, cholera outbreaks have occurred. Thirty-five percent of the population of sub-Saharan Africa does not have access to potable water, and it is estimated that 10–12 percent of the region's morbidity and mortality is related to water-based diseases.

In many cases large cities in the developing world—megacities such as Tianjin (China), Jakarta (Indonesia), Calcutta, and Bombay—lack the clean water resources acquired by most Western cities before World War II through the use of filtration and chlorination. Many draw upon shrinking groundwater supplies, frequently polluted with nitrates, mercury, and even arsenic. The situation, however, varies from country to country, with rural populations usually worse off than urban. Only 60 percent of the population in Indonesia has access to safe drinking water, as compared to over 90 percent in Korea and the Philippines. In southeastern Asia only approximately half of its 1 billion people have access to safe drinking water.

Most developing nations lack adequate sewage treatment facilities. In India during the 1990s only about 10 percent of the urban population had their sewage treated, with raw sewage and garbage often discharged into rivers from which the water supply was drawn. In China substantial sections of the Huike, Chang (Yangtze), and Huang (Yellow) Rivers as well as other rivers were heavily polluted by human and industrial wastes and not potable. Many large cities in Asia, such as Manila, Karachi, and Calcutta, lack sewage facilities for large fractions of their population. In Africa, with the fastest-growing urban population of any of the continents, large and growing cities such as Accra (Ghana), Addis Ababa (Ethiopia), and Dar es Salaam (Tanzania) suffer from similar deficiencies in regard to potable water. In Zaire only 50 percent of the urban population has access to safe drinking water, with much smaller percentages in the rural areas. South American cities, such as La Paz (Bolivia) and Santiago (Chile), which have experienced rapid growth of squatter settlements, also have serious water supply problems.

Nations with the highest disease rates caused by the water supply are also among the world's poorest, reducing the resources that can be spent for environmental improvement. Groups such as the United Nations Environmental Programme (UNEP), Organization for Economic Cooperation and Development (OECD), and the World Health Organization have attempted to improve water supply and sanitary conditions in these nations with some success, although surging urban populations continually strain resources. And, even though water supply has been improved in some locations, sanitation and waste removal continue to lag behind, providing a repetition of the experience in the United States and western Europe.

Oceans

Although the oceans historically have been largely free of pollution, this situation has begun to change in the last several decades. There are numerous signs of ocean degradation. These include the reduction and disappearance of supplies of fish and shellfish, the dying of sea grass beds, and increased sedimentation. Some fish, whale, and dolphin meat, designated for human consumption, contains dangerous levels of toxins such as PCBs and heavy metals. Although it is not clear whether anthropogenic (human-caused) pollution is the cause, coral reefs are dying in many coastal areas. Seas such as the Baltic, the Black, and the Mediterranean, as well as the Gulf of Mexico, have increased pollution from nutrient loads from agricultural fertilizer runoff and deposits of heavy metals such as mercury. The Gulf of Mexico contains a large oxygen-depleted area or "dead zone" formed by excessive nitrogen inputs from agricultural areas. Many thousands of square kilometers of seas around China are no longer suitable for marine life because of nonpoint source runoff containing excess nitrogen and phosphates from chemical fertilizers as well as because of supertanker oil leaks. One of the commonest human-made elements found in the oceans today is plastic, which can be extremely damaging to seabirds, turtles, and mammals such as seals. Large oil spills have devastating effects on sea animals and birds as well as on coastal beaches. And sedimentation from agricultural development and settlement in low-lying coastal areas has badly polluted coastal waters. Even the formerly most untainted areas, such as the Arctic and Antarctic seas, are beginning to show signs of human pollution.

The history of water pollution reveals several patterns relating to human uses of water bodies. The basis of any discussion of water and its pollution is that humans cannot survive on Earth without clean water. Today people are putting increased pressure on this precious resource. Historically humans have used waterways for two main purposes—as sources of water for a variety of social purposes and as a sink or disposal place for human, manufacturing, and agricultural wastes and for other types of debris. Frequently these two purposes have clashed as wastes of various sorts have polluted water sources of clean water.

As history has shown, however, human society has followed definite patterns in regard to the generation of water pollution and its remediation. That is, although there were many isolated incidents of human-caused water pollution before the nineteenth century, their scale was relatively small and damages temporary. Urbanism and industrialization in western European nations and the United States altered this pattern. As cities grew, increasingly they constructed sewage systems to remove human wastes to neighboring waterways. Industries also discharged directly into both waterways and sewer systems. The result was the increasing contamination of rivers, lakes, and bays, reducing their ability to assimilate wastes and damaging their ecology. Most serious, however, was sewage contamination of waterways from which cities drew their water supply, with resulting epidemics of waterborne diseases such as cholera and typhoid.

By the twentieth century, however, technologies such as water filtration and chlorination had controlled waterborne diseases. Pollution, however, continued, with waterways becoming increasingly degraded. In 1950, for instance, American cities still discharged half of their raw sewage untreated into waterways. Most European nations had similar patterns. New chemical constituents further damaged water quality. During the last quarter of the century, however, stricter regulation and control of wastewater discharges were imposed as a result of the environmental movements in wealthier nations such as the United States, Great Britain, Germany, France, and Japan. Consequently, water quality in many formerly polluted water bodies improved. In contrast, the nations of central and eastern Europe continued to pollute their water bodies. In addition, the developing world experienced the greatest increases in water contamination and degradation, producing severe health effects among its population. The poverty of many of these nations helps explain their failure to develop means to reduce their pollution. Finally, ocean pollution grew in scale and in previously pristine locations. Thus, as the world enters the twenty-first century, it continues to face severe problems of water pollution that threaten the health both of populations and of the environment.

Joel A. Tarr

Further Reading

Anderson, D., & Grove, R. (Eds.). (1987). *Conservation in Africa: Peoples, policies and practice*. New York: Cambridge.

Bernhardt, C., & Massard-Guillbaud, G. (Eds.). (2002). *The modern demon: Pollution in urban and industrial European societies*. Clermont-Ferrand, France: Presses Universitaires Blaise-Pascal.

Bernhardt, C. (Ed.). (2000). *Environmental problems in European cities in the 19th and 20th century*. New York: Waxmann Verlag.

Breeze, L. E. (1993). *The British experience with river pollution, 1865–1876*. New York: Peter Lang.

Brimblecombe, P., & Pfister, C. (Eds.). (1990). *The silent countdown: Essays in European environmental history*. Berlin: Springer-Verlag.

Burger, J. (1997). *Oil spills*. New Brunswick, NJ: Rutgers University Press.

Carter, F. W., & Turnock, D. (Eds.). (1993). *Environmental problems in eastern Europe*. London: Routledge.

Chioc, M. (2002). *The Rhine: An eco-biography 1815–2000*. Seattle: University of Washington Press.

De Walle, F. B., Nikolopoulou-Tamvakli, M., & Hinen, W. J. (Eds.). (1993). *Environmental condition of the Mediterranean Sea*. Dordrecht, Netherlands: Kluwer Academic.

Evans, R. J. (1987). *Death in Hamburg: Society and politics in the cholera years 1830–1910*. New York: Oxford University Press.

Feshbach, M. (1995). *Ecological disaster: Cleaning up the hidden legacy of the Soviet regime*. New York: Twentieth Century Fund Press.

Ghose, N. C., & Sharma, C. B. (1989). *Pollution of Ganga River: Ecology of mid-Ganga Basin*. New Delhi, India: Ashish Publishing House.

Gleicik, P. (Ed.). (1993). *Water in crisis*. New York: Oxford University Press.

Gorman, M. (1993). *Environmental hazards: Marine pollution*. Santa Barbara, CA: ABC-Clio Press.

Goubert, J. (1989). *The conquest of water: The advent of health in the industrial age*. Princeton, NJ: Princeton University Press.

Grove, R. H. (1998). *Ecology, climate and empire: Studies in colonial environmental history*. London: White Horse Press.

Hamlin, C. (1997). *A science of impurity: Water analysis in nineteenth-century Britain*. Berkeley and Los Angeles: University of California Press.

Hanley, S. (1997). *Everyday things in premodern Japan: The hidden legacy of material culture*. Berkeley and Los Angeles: University of California Press.

Kobori, I., & Glantz, M. H. (Eds.). (1998). *Central Eurasian water crisis*. Tokyo: U.N. University Press.

Luckin, B. (1986). *Pollution and control: A social history of the Thames in the nineteenth century*. Boston: Adam Hilger.

McMichael, T. (2001). *Human frontiers, environments and disease: Past patterns, uncertain futures*. New York: Cambridge University Press.

Melosi, M. V. (2000). *The sanitary city: Urban infrastructure in America from colonial times to the present*. Baltimore: Johns Hopkins University Press.

Micklin, P., & Williams, W. D. (Eds.). (1995). *The Aral Sea basin*. Berlin: Springer-Verlag.

Mishima, A. (1992). *Bitter sea: The human cost of minamata disease*. Tokyo: Josei.

Mullan, F. (1989). *Plagues and politics: The story of the United States Public Health Service*. New York: Basic Books.

Outwater, A. (1996). *Water: A natural history*. New York: Basic Books.

Pointing, C. (1991). *A green history of the world*. New York: Penguin Books.

Rogers, P., & Lydon, P. (Eds.). (1994). *Water in the Arab world*. Cambridge, MA: Harvard University Press.

Said, R. (1993). *The river Nile: Geology, hydrology and utilization*. Oxford, UK: Pergamon Press.

Smil, V. (1993). *China's environmental crisis: An inquiry in the limits of national development*. Armonk, NY: M. E. Sharpe.

Tarr, J. A. (1996). *The search for the ultimate sink: Urban pollution in historical perspective*. Akron, OH: University of Akron Press.

Turner, B. L., II, Clark, W. C., Kates, R. W., Richard, J. F., Mathews, J. T., & Meyer, W. B. (Eds.). (1990). *The Earth as transformed by human action: Global and regional changes in the biosphere over the past 300 years*. New York: Cambridge University Press.

Ui, J. (1992). *Industrial pollution in Japan*. Tokyo: U.N. University Press.

Weather Events, Extreme

Weather consists of the temperature, humidity, precipitation, air pressure, and wind in a region at a particular time. Climate is the composite of weather conditions over a long period, usually taken as thirty years. Extreme weather events involve enormous forces of nature; for example, the energy released per day in a hurricane is the equivalent of 500,000 atomic bombs of the size that were dropped on Nagasaki. Extreme weather is nevertheless part of the rhythm of nature: Drought-provoked wildfires and ice storms, for example, are not disasters for nature (although they may be for humans); on the contrary, they rejuvenate the forest.

Extreme Weather Events That Became Disasters

On 5 January 1998 freezing rain started falling on northeastern North America. This occurs about a dozen times each winter, so residents treated it as a minor inconvenience, as did power companies and governments. It left a clear, thick coating of ice on every tree and shrub, which recast them into marvelous crystalline figures. Even meteorologists did not expect the intensity, persistence, and scope of the freezing rain: wave after wave kept falling on a huge territory for five days. The ice loading brought trees, power lines, and even transmission towers crashing to the ground. More people were directly affected by this extreme weather event than any other in North America: 4.7 million were deprived of electricity in Canada and 1.5 million in the United States. For most, that meant they were deprived of heat, light, often water, and other essential services—some for three weeks—in a dark, frigid winter climate. It was the most costly disaster in Canadian history. The 19 January issue of *Time* magazine described it as a "grim fairyland . . . in a glittering

Tikopia After the Hurricane of 1952

Tikopia is a small island in the Solomon Islands in the South Pacific. The following is the first impression of British anthropologist Raymond Firth, upon arriving on the island in early 1952.

When the expedition arrived at Tikopia on March 13, 1952, it was quite obvious that the island had suffered terribly. The Tikopia young men aboard were greatly disturbed at its ravaged appearance. They said "The land has been destroyed." The deep green of the vegetation was interspersed by odd large patches of brown and red, indicating bare soil showing through in a most unusual way. Leafless trees along the strand indicated the destruction wrought by the wind. The crests of the island looked ragged. Many trees had disappeared altogether and coconut palms, formerly abundant on the hill slopes, stood, sparsely, with a few gaunt fronds at curious angles. When we later walked round the island we saw that the beaches of Faea were strewn with wreckage which had not yet been fully cleared away since the people had only just finished dealing with the debris in their orchards. Some houses had been broken down and even the solid walls of coral stones of a church had been torn apart. Practically all the canoes were intact, though rumours in the Solomons had said that they were all destroyed. But sand lay thick all through the villages of Faea, covering the bases of the trees. No coconuts or bananas were to be seen; many large breadfruit trees were in ruins. Some of the low-lying areas were still flooded. Food shortage had already set in, and it was quite apparent to both Tikopia and Europeans that difficult times were ahead. The major question was, how difficult?

Source: Firth, Raymond. *Social Change in Tikopia*. (1959). New York: Macmillan, pp. 47–48.

state of emergency" (Purvis 1998, 12). Since problems only began with the collapse of the electric system upon which people had become dependent, this was not a natural disaster but rather an extreme weather event that precipitated a technological disaster. Centralized, electrically based heating and lighting had increased vulnerability to freezing rain. The ice storm paradoxically resulted from warming: Unusually warm, moisture-laden winds blowing across the continent from the El Niño Southern Oscillation (a warm-surface-water effect) in the Pacific Ocean collided with the usual stagnant cold air mass in the valleys of the St. Lawrence River and Lake Champlain. The ocean and the atmosphere interacted on one side of the continent to produce extreme weather on the other.

Unlike the ice storm, most extreme weather events are ugly, even though some have temporary appeal. On the morning of 8 September 1900, the residents of Galveston, Texas, went to the beach to watch the pounding breaker waves. By early afternoon the storm had become a hurricane, and it was too late to evacuate the barrier reef, which became completely flooded by more than three meters of water. Between six and eight thousand of its thirty-eight thousand residents drowned, a record that persists as the worst loss of life in an American natural disaster. The hurricane was so

strong that it was still a storm after it had crossed the Atlantic Ocean, Europe, and entered Siberia. The disaster was not entirely natural, because it resulted from the decision to construct a city on a hurricane-prone barrier reef and from decisions not to build adequate defenses because they were judged too expensive. After the disaster the residents reconstructed the reef, bringing in an enormous amount of fill to raise the city by 3.4 meters and constructing a huge concrete seawall around it. This was a major engineering accomplishment of the early twentieth century and succeeded in protecting Galveston against subsequent hurricanes. However, it was enormously expensive, and the very reason for living on a barrier reef—the spectacular beach—had to be sacrificed. No other barrier reef has been defended in this way.

Extreme weather is usually thought to be of short duration, but that is not always the case. The year 1816 was known as the one without a summer. In northeastern United States there was snowfall in June and crop-destroying frosts in June, July, and August. Food shortages occurred in Germany, France, the Netherlands, and Switzerland. Grain prices tripled leading to food riots. Ireland suffered a horrible famine and subsequent disease that killed 65,000 people. Scientists only recently found the cause of this extreme weather and human misery on the opposite side of the planet a year earlier. On 13 April 1815, Mt. Tambora in Indonesia erupted in a cataclysmic volcanic explosion that ejected 160 cubic kilometers of ash into the upper atmosphere, where it was dispersed by the jet stream around the planet, blocking out sunlight. The ash did not descend for a year. In this case, then, what occurred on the surface of the Earth and beneath it (the eruption) affected the atmosphere and weather globally.

Drought is another form of long-lasting extreme weather. It is a slow-onset event that results in famines and many fatalities. In 1991 and 2000, for example, 42 percent of disaster-related deaths were attributable to drought.

Earthquakes can unleash extreme weather, as when an earthquake, tsunami ocean waves, and high winds that spread devastating fires struck Lisbon, Portugal, in 1755. The city took centuries to be constructed but was destroyed in hours.

Bangladesh is the world's most densely populated country and one of the poorest. About 80 percent of Bangladesh is a flat plain barely above sea level. It is crisscrossed by rivers and has one of the rainiest climates in the world. Floods during the monsoon season are common, and if they coincide with a tropical storm that raises tides to extreme heights, then wind-driven waves push violently inland along backed-up rivers. This conjuncture of social dynamics and those of nature renders its population particularly vulnerable to extreme weather. In one twenty-eight-year period during the twentieth century, Bangladesh suffered seven major floods that killed 22,000 (1963), 17,000 (1965), 30,000 (1965), 10,000 (1965), 300,000 (1970), 10,000 (1985), and 131,000 (1991).

Although tornadoes hit many countries, they are most frequent and strongest in the United States. Southwestern Oklahoma has the greatest number, but because of its small population it has a much lower casualty potential than Chicago, which has half as many tornadoes. In the United States the worst killer tornadoes were in 1884 (800 deaths), 1925 (792 deaths), and 1936 (658 deaths).

Preventing Extreme Weather Events from Becoming Disastrous

The heaviest rainfall ever recorded in a 24-hour period was caused by a cyclone that poured 1.58 meters of water on a mountain slope of Réunion Island in 1958. It was not a populated area so this was not a disaster. The disastrousness of extreme weather for humans depends not only the power of the weather event, but also on the size of the human population, the value of its constructions, its willingness to acknowledge risk, and capacity to defend itself.

Death tolls remain highest in densely populated, poor countries: Hurricane Mitch killed 10,000 people in 1998 in Central America, and cyclones in India killed 10,000 in 1998 and 50,000 in 1999. The geologist Edward Tenner remarked in his 1996 book *Why Things Bite Back: Technology and the Revenge of Unintended Consequences* that while the wealthy nation of Japan lost an average of 63 people in forty-three disasters, the much poorer nation of Peru lost an average of 2,900 in thirty-one. The Netherlands is a low-lying country like Bangladesh, but differs in that it is prosperous and has protected itself with an expensive array of dikes and sea gates. In wealthy, modern societies lives are being saved from extreme weather by costly defenses. These usually involve attempts at mitigation, evacuation, and other forms of emergency preparedness. In the last quarter of the twentieth century, no set of tornadoes (they come in sets) in the United States has killed more than a hundred people. It has been estimated that every dollar spent on mitigation saves seven spent on damage recovery costs. Property damage is nevertheless escalating. Tenner remarks, "Since 1900, deaths from tropical cyclones in the United States have declined from six thousand per year to only a few dozen; yet property damage has soared to over $1.5 billion in recent decades because of the amount of new construction in hurricane-prone areas" (Tenner 1996, 74). Hurricane Andrew of 1992 in Florida killed only 43 people but resulted in property damage of $25 billion and bankrupted six insurance companies.

One reason for the increase in property damage involves people's reactions to defenses and disaster. As Doppler radar systems give more accurate evacuation information for storms and as people have come to feel entitled to government compensation after a disaster, no matter where their homes happen to have been located, people have come to believe they can live safely in harm's way. Disaster researchers call the result "disaster by design," a phenomenon that leads to repeat disasters and unnatural disasters. Decisions about the location and type of development determine the damage from extreme weather. More than 25 percent of the damage from Hurricane Andrew could have been avoided if Florida's building codes had been enforced. What is called a natural disaster is actually a hybrid of the forces of nature and the characteristics of society. Many defenses depend on prediction, which is particularly difficult because extreme weather events in any locality are rare and forecasts are often based on inadequate data. The hundred-year flood or ice storm is a probabilistic abstraction that does not inform planners whether they should be ready in a century or tomorrow. The United Nations declared the 1990s the decade of natural disaster reduction, but disasters and their costs have instead increased.

In many cases good fortune rather than the defenses of modern society has protected it from extreme weather. Tenner notes that Florida was fortunate that Hurricane Andrew didn't strike Miami directly; if it had, its cost could have tripled. South Carolina was spared when Hurricane Hugo came ashore in a park rather than in the nearby city of Charleston.

The Causes of Extreme Weather

Our planet is speeding through space at variable distances from its huge source of energy, the sun. Its present equilibrium is maintained because the energy it receives equals the energy it irradiates into space. Earth is spinning on its axis, dragging the oceans and the atmosphere as it rotates. The amount of solar energy that is received by any one region on Earth changes as Earth rotates. The energy emitted from the sun varies according to solar activity. The warming of certain parts of the atmosphere more than others sets in motion currents of hot air rising and cool air falling. Water currents are set up in the ocean for similar reasons and because of the wind. In the hot areas of the planet a great deal of evaporation occurs over the oceans, and these masses of hot, humid air travel long distances before cooling and releasing their moisture in one form of precipitation or another. Floods in one region and droughts in another are the consequence. The motion of the air masses results in cyclones (called hurricanes over the Atlantic, typhoons over the Pacific) and tornadoes. The El Niño Southern Oscillation also produces extreme weather over a wide area in some years, as in 1982–1983, when it caused droughts in Australia, flooding along the western coast of South America, and record summer temperatures in western Europe.

Only a relatively thin crust of the surface of the Earth is solid, and this is divided into plates that float on a molten core and grind against one another. The hot, molten material from the interior explodes periodically in the form of a volcano, which can produce extreme weather. When earthquakes or volcanoes occur in the ocean, the sudden release of enormous energy displaces a huge quantity of water, resulting in a gigan-

tic wave referred to as a tsunami. Societies exist in this vortex of autonomous dynamics and flux of energy transformations that we call nature. The effects of any of these depend on the geophysical and built structures lying in their path.

Fortunately extreme weather is rare in most regions in the time span of a human life. There seem to be self-regulating mechanisms in nature that keep climate in a steady state and usually make change gradual over the periods of time that are pertinent to humans. Most of nature's fluctuations, such as the seasons, day and night, and so forth, are regular. The tides, for example, are based on such astronomical regularity that they can be calculated two years in advance.

The present steady state could however be tipped into one with characteristics that may not be as supportive of human society. Human activities may inadvertently produce a positive-feedback loop that disrupts nature's balance. Climatologists do not have definitive evidence that human-induced global climate change will result in more frequent and intense extreme weather, but they argue the hypothesis is plausible. The fact that nature itself produces extreme weather has been used imprudently as an excuse to avoid rectifying human activity that could unleash more of it.

Raymond Murphy

See also Droughts; Earthquakes; Floods

Further Reading

Abley, M. (1998). *The ice storm.* Toronto, Canada: McClelland and Stewart.

Larson, E. (2000). *Isaac's storm.* New York: Vintage.

Mileti, D. (1999). *Disasters by design.* Washington, DC: Joseph Henry Press.

Murphy, R. (2001). Nature's temporalities and the manufacture of vulnerability. *Time and Society, 102/3),* 329–348.

Platt, R. (1999). *Disasters and democracy: The politics of extreme natural events.* Washington, DC: Island Press.

Purvis, A. (1998, January 19). Grim Fairytale. *Time* (Canadian edition), *151*(2), 12–15.

Quarantelli, E. L. (1998). *What is disaster?* New York: Routledge.

Tenner, E. (1996). *Why things bite back: Technology and the revenge of unintended consequences.* New York: Alfred A. Knopf.

Worster, D. (1994). *Nature's economy* (2nd ed.). Cambridge, UK: Cambridge University Press.

Zebrowski, E., Jr. (1997). *Perils of a restless planet: Scientific perspectives on natural disasters.* Cambridge, UK: Cambridge University Press.

Weeds

In the Western world weeds have been defined and redefined according to the cultural ideas and outlooks of peoples who have tried to compete with them for open places, over many millennia.

The word itself has no intrinsic meaning. Its origins are obscure. Etymological evidence suggests that the ninth-century Old English noun *wēod* and the verb *wēodian*, which refer to fern-like plants growing on waste places and the clearing of them for agricultural purposes, are the most likely source. The botanical evidence points to the proto-German *weyt* (c. 1150) or the later Belgian *weedt* (c. 1576) and Dutch *weet*, each of which refers to the dye-plant woad, once widespread in Europe, North Africa, and Asia.

In modern times, Ralph Waldo Emerson thought weeds were plants whose virtues had not yet been discovered. The American agriculturist L. H. Bailey held that Nature knows no plants as weeds. Sir Edward Salisbury, sometime director of the Botanical Gardens at Kew, England, characterized a weed as a plant growing where we do not want it. To Oliver Rackham, the historian of the British countryside, weeds were specialized plants, intimately linked to farming. The French naturalist Jean Rostand believed that in naming a plant a weed "man gives proof of his personal arrogance."

Glacial Retreat, Neolithic Agriculture, and Early Civilizations

Weeds have been competing with us for something like ten thousand years. Paleobotanists believe that the plants we now call weeds had long inhabited the interglacial and post-glacial landscapes. But the great cultural changes of the early Neolithic period, around 10,000 years ago, fundamentally altered the people-Nature relationship. Agriculture, rippling outwards from the Fertile Crescent in the Near East, replaced hunting and gathering just at the time when the rapidly retreating European glaciers of the last Ice Age uncovered new lands for settlement.

Young, rich post-glacial soils favored plant species that already had many of the characteristics of weeds: rapid colonization of bare ground, fast breeding, wide dispersal, domination of an environment, and a tolerance of close human settlement. As well, northern swidden agriculture, beginning between 7,000 and 5,000 years ago, involved repeated cycles of clearing and planting followed by long fallow periods, which imitated the ecology of glacial retreat. Thus Neolithic agriculture, with its monocultures and open places, gave the late-glacial survivors a new lease on life. Other plants, introduced from the Near Eastern homelands of agriculture, became closely associated with farming.

Egyptian, Sumerian, and Assyrian civilizations had no collective term for weeds. All plants were equally valued. The classical Greeks, however, had a word. Theophrastus, in one of his treatises on plants used the term *botáne* as noxious herb, thus weed. Roman writers such as Pliny, Virgil, and Columella used weeding concepts, but the modern term has no apparent direct Latin counterpart. "Runcinate," a word now used to describe the lobed or toothed leaf-edge of some plants, is derived from Latin *runcina*, a weeding hook, and *Runcina* the rural goddess of weeding.

Conceptual Transitions

Relative "certainties" about which plants are weeds and which are not is comparatively modern. Tollund Man, a bog-preserved corpse from the Danish Iron Age, ate goosefoot in his measure of porridge. Roman introductions into northern Europe, like ground elder, remained garden plants until quite recently. The land of Virgil's *Georgics* (30 BCE), which needed no farming is, however, a far cry from our weeds and the hard labor they demand.

In the Judeo-Christian tradition, the transition from Arcadia to "a battle with weeds . . . a hard life of seat and toil" came with the Old Testament Fall (Genesis 1: 4). Thenceforth, the Other had always to be contended with: "And on the hill that shall be digged with the mattock, there shall not come thither the fear of briars and thorns" (Isaiah 7:25).

The New Testament parable of the sower carries a similar message, couched in the language of grim competition. "And [some] seed fell among thorns; and the thorns sprang up; and choked them" (Matthew 13: 7). The same imagery is explicit in the "Parable of the Weeds Explained" (Matthew 13:33): "The one who sowed the good seed is the Son of Man. . . . The weeds are the sons of the evil one and the enemy who sows them is the devil."

Weeds and the Balance of Nature

Such well known weeds as the sorrels, docks, fat-hens and thistles would in the original primeval world each have its proper place in the primitive plant-association to which it might belong, and would be present in no extraordinary numbers. It was the changes brought about by cultivation in its various forms, fires, and close grazing of domestic animals which upset the balance of nature. . . . Thus, through the many centuries of cultivation in Europe, aided by ever expanding intercourse with other lands, the great army of now almost cosmopolitan weeds has been gathered together—the very pick of the vegetable world in temperate climes for thriving under the artificial conditions imposed by man. It is the old story that when one interferes with nature she exacts remorselessly her tribute.

Source: Cockayne, Leonard. (1919). *New Zealand Plants and Their Story*.

Medieval and Early Modern Notions

The Middle Ages saw a degree of ambivalence towards weedy plants. For Medieval herbalists, each plant had its "virtues" and "signatures." The virtues of the bramble were that it could heal sore ears or ease menstruation. The red juice of St. John's wort signified its power to heal wounds. But other scholars, like the early thirteenth-century prelate Alexander of Neckham, believed that after the Fall the Earth was governed by moral rather than biological causes. The Fall reminded mankind of the world as it once was. Poisonous plants were a constant reminder of humanity's pride and deceit.

The English playwright-poet William Shakespeare used weeds as a malevolent metaphor in several of his plays. Dark forces emanated from Elsinore as Hamlet pondered on his father's death.

Fie on't! O fie! tis an unweeded garden,
That grows to seed; things rank and gross in
nature
Possess it merely. That it should come to this!
(Hamlet, I:ii)

Antony FitzHerbert's *Boke of Husbandry* (1523) reflected Elizabethan attitudes to weeds. The month of May heralded the "tyme to wede thy corn." The sixteenth century farmer had to deal with "divers manner of wedes." Nettles and dodder "doe moche harme." Thistles, docks and kedlokes (charlock), darnolde (darnel) and gouldes (corn marigold) were bad enough. Dog fennel (stinking mayweed) "is the worst weed that is except terre" (hairy vetch).

Post-Reformation "Improvement"

Protestant reinterpretations of the biblical basis for the human condition developed the notion that the Earth had deteriorated after the Fall. While thorns and thistles grew up where once there were fruits and flowers, and mankind had to accept the consequences, there was also the injunction, in Psalm 8:3: "Thou has given him dominion over the works of thy hands; thou hast put all things under his feet."

The herbalist William Cole in his *Art of Simples* (1656) thought that weeds and poisonous plants had a definite purpose. It required "the industry of men to weed them out. . . . Had he nothing to struggle with, the fire of his spirit would be half extinguished." The English jurist Sir Matthew Hale, in *The Primitive Organization of Mankind* (1667) advanced the notion of "improvement" a step further. He believed, from his reading of Genesis, that "Man was invested with the power, authority, right, dominion, trust and care . . . to preserve the Species of divers Vegetables, to improve them and others, to correct the redundancies of unprofitable Vegetables [weeds], to preserve the face of the Earth in beauty, usefulness and fruitfulness."

By the seventeenth century agricultural improvers like Walter Blith, in *The English Improver Improved* (1649), drew a harder line between crops and weeds. The latter had become "an obscenity, the vegetable equivalent of vermin." Gorse, ferns, bracken, and broom were "such filth." But for some the line remained fuzzy. Seventeenth-century London gardeners grew foxglove, willow herb, and poppies, the bane of wheat growers, as decorative plants. Others, wrote the herbalist William Gerard, were wont to "feast themselves [aesthetically] even with varieties of those things the vulgar call weeds."

Eighteenth-Century Enlightenment

Throughout the eighteenth century many naturalists, philosophers, and agricultural writers continued to diverge from the hard-line improvers. The gardener William Hanbury thought heather "very elegant" and "looked kindly" on meadow sweet and thistles. The agricultural writer William Marshall considered blackberry flowers "beautiful beyond expression." The herbalist William Turner worried that "precious herbs" were dismissed as "weeds or grass" by the ignorant. "Botanists," Samuel Pegge wrote in his *Curialia Miscellanea* (1796), "allow nothing to be weeds." There is even a tradition that the great Swedish naturalist Carolus Linnaeus fell on his knees at the sight of English gorse "the enemy of every improver . . . and gave thanks for so beautiful a plant."

The German poet-philosopher Johann Wolfgang von Goethe, in *An Attempt to Evolve a General Comparative Theory* wrote that he could understand the farmer who attributed the existence of weeds to "the curse of an enraged benevolent spirit, or the malice of a sinister one." But he placed himself among those who saw weeds as "children of universal Nature, cherished as much by her as the wheat [the farmer] carefully cultivates and values so highly."

The North American New World

Across the Atlantic a similar ambivalence prevailed. European weeds arrived with the pilgrims or even earlier, with European fisher-folk. Weeds came in their foodstuffs and that of their livestock, in their straw bedding, their chests of clothing, and in their bags and packets of seeds. Weeds came, too, from the bilges of their ships, in unwanted ballast thrown ashore to make room for cargoes for Europe. Worn out ships, left to rot on the shores of coves and bays, contributed foreign seeds from the crevices of their timbers. Weeds followed the colonists inland, on their shoes and the feet of their animals, in wool, hair, and fur, spilling off wagons and carts and sprouting up wherever a coarse sack or bag was cast aside. Plantain became, for indigenous peoples, symbolic of the white man's footstep.

The pilgrims and their successors encountered indigenous plants that did not conform with, or yield to, a "perfect system of economy." For the Philadelphia physician Benjamin Rush, the cultivation of a new land rendered it healthy by "draining swamps, destroying [indigenous] weeds, burning brush and exhaling the unwholesome or superfluous moisture of the air."

The clergyman-physician Jared Eliot, ever the theologian-improver, in *Essays upon Field Husbandry in New England and Other Papers, 1748–62*, regarded the work of draining swamps, clearing out brambles, thickets

and poisonous weeds, replacing them with pasture and crops, as "a Resemblance to Creation." But the botanist John Bartram, with the better eye for natural processes, begged to differ. Clearing out swamp "weeds" prevented the deposition of flood debris and contributed to soil erosion.

In the New World, however, as in the Old, the improvers took the moral high ground. The transformation from savage to civilized was "the planting of a garden, not the fall from one; any change in the New England environment was divinely ordained and wholly positive." That, unfortunately, included the introduction of Old World weeds like barberry, which carried wheat blast disease. Divinely ordained or not, the eighteenth-century governments of Connecticut, Massachusetts, and Rhode Island attempted to control it by introducing the first-ever noxious weeds laws.

The late-eighteenth-century American agricultural writer John Lorain stood apart, however, from this form of debate. Lorain anticipated the nineteenth- and early-twentieth-century ecological sciences. He indicated, in *Nature and Reason Harmonized in the Practice of Husbandry* (1825), that he recognized the interdependence of plant species, including weeds, and their role in maintaining soil fertility, "notwithstanding [that] slovenly farmers complain more loudly of the injury done by them." Lorain was ahead of his time in believing that neither weeds nor biblical curses were the causes of soil impoverishment.

Nineteenth- and Twentieth-Century Science

The English botanist Sir Joseph Hooker, the evolutionist Charles Darwin, and the American diplomat-geographer George Perkins Marsh profoundly influenced much of the nineteenth-century scientific and popular discourse about weeds and weediness as a global phenomenon. Both Hooker and Darwin witnessed the spread of European and North American flora into the Pacific, the Americas, and British colonies. Both commented on the often-rampant, weedy habit some hitherto innocuous plants assumed in new locations and sought explanations. Marsh stood the existing Man-Nature paradigm on its head. (*Man* is used here in the same sense Marsh used the term.) The evidence he collected during long foreign sojourns pointed to Man as the modifier of Nature, the antithesis of the world of the natural theologians, in which God displayed himself in his natural works. Marsh found weeds that were equally at home in Upper Egypt wheat fields, Bosphorus gardens, or New England cultivations. Man transplanted them. Nature merely propagated them.

Darwin's work on natural selection led him to the view that Old World plants had a competitive edge over their New World counterparts, derived from the "longer period they have been engaged in strife, and consequent vigor they have acquired." Linking Darwin's "struggle for existence" with philosopher Herbert Spencer's earlier "survival of the fittest" theories, Hooker developed and disseminated a Displacement-Replacement model to explain the ascendant and often weedy nature of exotic plants in such widely separated places as Madeira, St. Helena, Mauritius, Argentina, India, Oceania, Polynesia, and Australasia.

Although Hooker, Director of the Royal Botanical Gardens at Kew, was very influential, his model was not universally accepted. In the South Pacific islands of New Zealand, a small group of naturalists was uniquely placed to observe and record, for the first time, the introduction of exotic plants and their effects on the indigenous biota, from initial European contact in the late eighteenth century. Some of them subscribed to Hooker's model. Two of them, L. Cockayne and G. T. Thomson, began to question it and in the early 1900s arrived at a quite different explanation for weediness, based on ecological principles.

Both noticed, like Marsh, that human agency, particularly aspects of agriculture and horticulture, determined whether many exotic plants, including weeds, survived or not. Both came to understand that as long as New World farmers perpetuated the practices that mimic post-glacial European landscapes, European weeds thrived. The same principle applied to any exotic plant: re-create preferred habitats and in the absence of other checks such as predation, they thrive; allow farmland or a garden to revert to its native plant cover and in the end the exotic plant may well lose the struggle for existence.

Weed Control

Today, the application of ecological principles to agricultural practice is one use of science and technology in weed control. Others, including biological control using plant predators, usually viral or bacterial plant pathogens and insects, and the use of herbicidal sprays, are of relatively recent origin. For most of the past ten millennia only primitive, labor-intensive means of control were available.

Hand weeding, using simple technologies like the mattock, weed hook and hand hoe, prevailed from classical and biblical times well into the nineteenth century. In some situations, cattle, both small and large, were used to reduce perennial weeds by grazing fallow ground. In others, domesticated free-ranging fowl helped to control barnyard, vineyard, and garden weeds, both annual and perennial. Some weed seeds could be separated from cereals by winnowing or using sieves and corn screens. Efficient seed cleaning machinery, capable of eliminating most weed seeds, was not developed until the late nineteenth century.

Annual weeds could be removed from crops while they were growing, at some risk to the crop. The use of fallow periods—resting the land between crops—helped to control perennial weeds, particularly if stock was used to graze the fallow. Alternatively, it was repeatedly plowed, cross-plowed, and harrowed. During the eighteenth century, systematic crop rotation over several years was found to reduce weeds, particularly if fodder crops with heavy foliage, like turnips, were used to smother weeds.

During the nineteenth century many legislatures in North America and parts of the British colonies introduced legislation in a futile effort to force landholders to control what came to be called noxious weeds, on their properties and roadsides. "Californian" or "Canadian" thistle, originally from Europe, was a typical target. Once established in a pasture, its underground rhizome defeated limited farming technology and the weed laws. Legislation continues, however, to be used as a coercive tool, requiring land users to attempt to control nuisance weeds.

Looking Ahead

In the twenty-first century, the discourse about weeds, at least in the Western world, centers principally on economics and biodiversity. The means available to control them continue to be limited. Often, as with herbicide effects on humans, they are controversial. Genetic engineering has provided herbicide resistant crops but is also controversial. Debate continues about the effectiveness of international border controls and biosecurity systems.

Jean Rostand accused humanity of arrogance in naming a plant a weed. To control them remains difficult. To eliminate them has so far proved impossible. Perhaps it is a symptom of our arrogance as a species that we aspire to do either.

Neil Clayton

Further Reading

Cockayne, L. (1928). *The vegetation of New Zealand*. Leipzig, Germany: W. Engelmann.

Crosby, A. (1986). *Ecological imperialism: The biological expansion of Europe, 900–1900*. Cambridge, UK: Cambridge University Press.

Glacken, C. J. (1990). *Traces on the Rhodian shore—nature and culture in western thought from ancient times to the end of the eighteenth century*. Berkeley: University of California.

Grove, R. H. (1996). *Green imperialism: Colonial expansion, tropical island Edens and the origins of environmentalism, 1600–1860*. Cambridge, UK: Cambridge University Press.

Holzner, W., & Numata, M. (Eds.). (1982). *Biology and ecology of weeds*. The Hague, Netherlands: Junk.

Hooker, J. (1864). Note on the replacement of species in the colonies and elsewhere. *Natural History Review, 12*, 123–127.

Jones, P. (1991). *Just weeds—history, myths and uses*. New York: Prentice Hall.

King, L. J. (1966). *Weeds of the world: Biology and control*. London: Hill.

Knobloch, F. (1996). *The culture of wilderness: Agriculture as colonization in the American West*. Chapel Hill, NC: University of North Carolina Press.

Marsh, G. P. (1965) *Man and nature, or physical geography as modified by human action*. Cambridge, MA: Harvard University Press.

Pollan, M. (1991). *Second nature: A gardener's education*. New York: Dell.

Price, A. G. (1963). *The western invasion of the Pacific and its continents: A study of moving frontiers and changing landscapes, 1513–1958*. Oxford, UK: Clarendon Press.

Rackham, O. (1986). *The history of the countryside—The full fascinating story of Britain's landscape*. London: Dent.

Salisbury, E. (1961). *Weeds and aliens*. London: Collins.

Shewell-Cooper, W. E. (1962). *Plants and fruit of the Bible*. London: Darton, Longman and Todd.

Thomas, K. (1983). *Man and the natural world: Changing attitudes in England 1500–1800*. London: Allen Lane.

Williams, R. (1973). *The country and the city*. New York: Oxford University Press.

Worster, D. (Ed.). (1994) *The ends of the earth: Perspectives on modern environmental history*. Cambridge, UK: Cambridge University Press.

Zohary, M. (1982). *Plants of the Bible*. New York: Cambridge University Press.

Wetlands

The term *wetlands* refers to a broad collection of water-based ecosystems. It includes salt marshes and cypress swamps, mangrove thickets and bogs; all wetlands are places where water floods or saturates the soil most of the time so that only plants specially adapted to wet, anaerobic conditions can thrive. Found in estuaries at the mouths of rivers, in protected embayments of the sea, along rivers, and in other topographic low spots where water tends to collect, wetlands vary widely in size and character owing to differences in climate, vegetation, soils, and hydrological conditions. In northern latitudes, bogs with highly acidic soils often support unusual plant life, including insectivorous pitcher plants and shrubby heath vegetation, which forms peat and, in some places, a distinctive floating mat of decaying plant life. Marshes, which form in interior plains or in coastal zones, are broad expanses of water-tolerant sedges, rushes, or grasses. Usually associated with the flood plains of rivers, swamps are vegetated with trees and shrubs that can endure standing water. In tropical latitudes, dense stands of mangroves with their characteristic prop roots form coastal wetlands flooded daily by tides.

Though they differ, all wetlands are places where water and land intermingle, providing invaluable services to people. By retarding runoff and allowing water to seep back into the ground, many wetlands play a critical role in recharging the aquifers that people rely on for agricultural and domestic water supplies. With their sponge-like soils, wetlands absorb and store water, providing natural flood control along many rivers. It is estimated that an acre of wetland can store up to 1.6 million gallons of floodwater. Coastal wetlands also buffer the shoreline from storms and floods. Many wetlands preserve water quality by filtering out excess nutrients and pollutants; an acre of wetland can filter up to an estimated 7.3 million gallons of polluted runoff per year. Finally, wetlands provide critical habitat, offering nursery grounds for shrimp and fish, and food and shelter for wildlife and migratory waterfowl. More than one-third of all endangered species in the United States depend on wetlands during some phase of their life. Quietly and freely, wetlands have long offered their services to society, but it is only recently, in the wake of centuries of drainage and destruction, that scientists and citizens have come to recognize these valuable contributions.

Early Attitudes Toward Wetlands

For much of history, wetlands were regarded as wastelands. Standing water and thick muck often made wetlands buggy and difficult to travel through. Many believed that miasma, or moist air emanating from swamps, caused malaria and other debilitating diseases. (Scientists came to realize that mosquitoes carried the malarial parasites only in the late nineteenth century.) Worse still, wetlands were impossible to farm. All these traits made wetlands seem frightening and useless. The epic eighth-century Anglo-Saxon poem *Beowulf* offers early evidence of such fearful attitudes; its hero fought two terrifying monsters that dwelled in the "moors" (an English variety of marsh). Wetlands were regarded as places to avoid or, increasingly, as places to transform.

As early as the days of the Roman Empire, engineers experimented with draining wetlands. In England, Romans oversaw the construction of raised banks that kept the sea from the marshes on the Medway estuary in Kent and of Car Dyke, a catchment that encircled the western edge of the Fens (a marshy region in southeastern England).

Through the Middle Ages, attempts at drainage continued in Europe. In Holland, the Dutch excluded tides from the extensive marshes of the Low Country with dikes. When the dikes alone proved inadequate for keeping the sea-level wetlands dry, they pioneered the use of windmill-powered pumps in the fifteenth and sixteenth centuries to flush excess water out. Eventually steam pumps and later diesel and electric pumps would make it possible to drain increasingly larger wetland areas of northern Europe for agriculture.

Wetlands in Columbia County, New York, in 2003. Despite the name, land does not have to be wet to be a wetland. COURTESY MARCY ROSS.

Despite the prevalent negative associations that encouraged wetland drainage, some people made their livelihoods in those shunned landscapes. On the moors of England, commoners cut peat for fuel, grazed livestock, fished for eels, and hunted waterfowl until enclosure acts consolidated landholdings and permitted extensive drainage in the eighteenth and nineteenth centuries. In North America, many indigenous tribes used moist soil at the edges of swamps to grow corn, and hunted and fished in wetland areas.

When European settlers traveled to the New World, they carried Old World attitudes (and malaria) with them, regarding wetlands with a mixture of favor and disdain. Coastal and riverside marshes with their rich grasses provided essential fodder for their livestock, which in turn provided manure for upland farms. Yet forested interior swamps seemed mysterious and wicked. In the earliest conflicts between Native Americans and Puritan settlers, natives hid in swamps, reinforcing the settlers' perceptions of the wetlands as dangerous places. Meanwhile in England, the 1678 book *The Pilgrim's Progress* depicted swamps as miry, sinful places, where lost souls could get stuck. Nearly a thousand years after *Beowulf*, wetlands were still regarded as a useless and dangerous.

Wetland Drainage and Development in America

In North America, fearful attitudes were gradually overcome when the draw of wetland resources attracted colonists' attention. In the South, valuable wood from cypress swamp forests was cut and sold for barrels and shingles. In cutover areas, planters began to experiment with rice cultivation in tidewater wetlands. Eventually, slaves cleared swamp forests and built levees around the rice fields along most rivers on the southeast coast.

As settlers pressed westward, they encountered enormous freshwater marshes in the Midwest and impenetrable swamps in the lower Mississippi valley. In 1849 and 1850, the U.S. Congress passed the Swamp Land Acts, which granted more than 24 million hectares of so-called swamplands to the states, to be sold into private ownership to promote drainage and farming. As settlers tried to ditch and drain the water from wetlands, they encountered difficulties. When one landowner built a ditch to shunt water off his swampland property, the water simply flooded neighbors' farms. After decades of haphazard, piecemeal attempts, engineers and farmers realized that successful drainage would require planning and cooperation among landowners. Between 1870 and 1900, twelve states adopted laws to establish drainage districts that taxed landowners within their jurisdiction to pay for ditches and levees to transform wetlands into farmlands.

During the same period, technological innovations, such as development of steam-operated dredges, made the building of levees and the drainage of wetlands along large rivers more feasible. In the poorly drained areas of the Midwest, the mass production of drainage tiles and ditch diggers made drainage of large areas possible. The U-shaped clay tiles could be buried in long lines to create underground conduits that carried water away from fields like gutters. In the sixteen years between 1906 and 1922, nearly 3.6 million hectares of swampland were drained in just seven Midwestern states. By 1955, 41.2 million hectares had been organized into drainage districts, converting more wetlands to farmlands than to any other purpose. In a short period, extensive inland marshes were entirely replaced with corn crops.

After World War II, brisk demand for housing raised another threat, as roadways and suburban developments began to encroach on formerly avoided wetlands. Between 1954 and 1959, the spread of the New York City urban area alone swallowed up 12.5 percent of Long Island's wetlands. All in all, between the mid 1950s and the mid 1970s, 4.4 million wetland hectares were converted to shopping centers, airports, suburbs, farms, and other uses. Pesticides sprayed for insect control made wetlands more habitable for people, but they killed off fish and birds and devastated whole ecosystems.

For centuries, the conviction that swamps and marshes were worthless and troublesome went hand in hand with people's actions and government policies: citizens drained swamps, and government land grants and subsidies encouraged even more drainage. In 1982, the U.S. Fish and Wildlife Service reported that the United States had lost 54 percent of its wetlands.

New Attitudes toward U.S. Wetlands

With the striking transformation of these landscapes came a new attitude toward wetlands. By the mid-nineteenth century, influential Romantic thinkers and artists had begun to recognize that the unique beauty of America lay in its disappearing natural features, wetlands included. As early as 1862, Henry David Tho-reau had recognized wild swamps as "sacred places" (Vileisis 1997, 96). In the 1870s and 1880s, painter Martin Johnson Heade captured the quiet beauty of many marshes with brush and canvas. In the first decade of the twentieth century, novelist Gene Stratton Porter lamented the demise of the Limberlost Swamp in northwestern Indiana in her best-selling novels.

As consequences of drainage became evident, others too began to reevaluate wetlands. Sport hunters directed crucial attention to swamps and marshes after they noticed that waterfowl populations—dependent on wetlands for nesting and breeding—were declining. To cope with the decline, in the first decades of the twentieth century Congress passed a series of laws that regulated hunting and created wildlife refuges, but it failed to authorize sufficient funding. When continuing loss of wetland habitat was exacerbated by the great drought of the 1930s, the continental waterfowl population dropped to an all-time low. Not until the New Deal, when the Bureau of Biological Survey head Jay Norwood "Ding" Darling spearheaded efforts to garner funding through the Duck Stamp program, did the federal government begin to purchase and protect significant wetlands as national wildlife refuges.

By the 1950s, scientists had begun to realize that the value of wetlands went far beyond waterfowl habitat. Coastal wetlands provided a rich source of nutrients for ocean-dwelling organisms and offered critical nursery grounds for young fish and marine invertebrates. As such, their destruction could have severe consequences for ocean fisheries. For example, one study near Palm Beach, Florida found a direct correlation between drastic declines in fish populations and the widespread filling of mangrove wetlands for vacation home development. Reflecting a broadening awareness of the values of marshes and swamps, ecologists coined the word "wetland" in the 1950s. When citizens recognized the consequences of extensive drainage and development of wetlands in their own communities, they began to organize to restore and protect these landscapes. In 1947, the unique marshes of south Florida were protected as Everglades National Park. In 1963, Massachusetts passed the nation's first wetland protection law, which required developers to obtain a permit from the state before they could fill and build in a wetland. Many other states passed similar legislation to maintain open space, fish and wildlife habitat, water quality, and flood absorption capacity. Citizen concern for environmental quality also spread to Congress, which enacted the federal Clean Water Act and other laws that benefited wetlands in the 1970s.

Contemporary U.S. Wetland Conflicts and Politics

Though their reputation has markedly improved, wetlands have recently landed at the center of a new conflict. From an ecological perspective, wetlands offer innumerable public services (water quality, flood control, habitat), but from a legal and social perspective, wetlands are seen primarily as private property.

The Clean Water Act requires developers to obtain Section 404 permits from the Army Corps of Engineers before they fill in wetlands. Agencies charged with protecting the public value of fish, wildlife, and water quality then make recommendations, which may lead to project modifications that minimize wetland destruction. Since its enactment, bitter conflict about enforcement of the Clean Water Act has grown. Those who oppose the regulations dislike the delays inherent in the permit process and argue that private landowners have the right to do what they want with their land. They claim wetland regulations that limit how landowners can use their land are tantamount to the unconstitutional taking of property by the government.

However, those who favor stronger wetland protection contend that the Corps only rarely denies permit requests. A report by the General Accounting Office in 1988 backed this claim, revealing that the Corps far more frequently provided than blocked permits for activities that destroyed wetlands. Moreover, wetland advocates deny that Clean Water Act regulations "take" property. They argue that the rules are intended to protect the public from the harm that results from wetland loss, such as poor water quality and flooding. For example, the regulations that may prevent a housing development in a wetland on a bay also protect fishermen whose livelihoods depend on healthy wetland nursery grounds and nearby communities that depend on wetlands to absorb floodwater.

Despite ongoing conflicts, changes in agricultural policies and economic circumstances have recently slowed the rate of wetland destruction in the United States from 200,000 hectares per year in 1985 to an estimated 23,400 hectares per year in 2002. However, with development pressures mounting and so many public services at stake, how we protect our diminishing wetlands promises to be the source of continuing debate.

World Wetlands in Crisis

Despite growing attention to conservation, wetlands worldwide continue to be threatened by pollution, drainage for agriculture, and overextraction of fresh water. Some wetlands are endangered by dams that would block their source of water, while thousands of hectares of mangrove swamps are threatened by the expanding shrimp aquaculture industry. Few national governments have been able to regulate development and industry adequately to protect or provide conservation, restoration, and mitigation measures for nearby wetlands. It is now estimated that more than 50 percent of the world's wetlands have been destroyed, with some countries having already lost up to 80 percent of their wetlands.

The degradation and loss of wetlands puts countless communities at risk. Worldwide, polluted water is estimated to affect the health of 120 million people, and freshwater shortages are predicted to worsen in at least 60 countries by 2050. Moreover, with climate change, some predict that flood-related disasters will become more frequent. As the world's population grows, threats to wetlands will undoubtedly increase even as these scarce ecosystems become ever more valuable to society.

Ann Vileisis

Further Reading

Blake, N. M. (1980). *Land into water—water into land: A history of water management in Florida.* Tallahassee: University Presses of Florida.

Kelly, R. (1989). *Battling the inland sea: American political culture, public policy, and the Sacramento Valley, 1850–1986.* Berkeley: University of California Press.

Miller, D. C. (1989). *Dark eden: The swamp in nineteenth century American culture.* Cambridge, UK: Cambridge University Press.

Mitsch, W., & Gosselink, J. (1993) *Wetlands* (2nd ed.). New York: Van Nostrand Reinhold Co.

Preston, W. C. (1981). *Vanishing landscapes: Land and life in the Tulare Lake basin.* Berkeley: University of California Press.

Prince, H. C. (1997). *Wetlands of the American Midwest: A historical geography of changing attitudes.* University of Chicago Geography Research Papers, No 241.

Purseglove, J. (1988). *Taming the flood: A history and natural history of rivers and wetlands.* Oxford,UK: Oxford University Press.

Siry, J. V. (1984). *Marshes of the ocean shore: Development of an ecological ethic.* College Station: Texas A&M Press.

Tiner, R. W., Jr. (1984). *Wetlands of the U.S.: Current status and recent trends.* Washington, DC: U.S. Department of the Interior, Fish and Wildlife Service.

United States Environmental Protection Agency. (2002). *Wetlands.* Retrieved May 30, 2002, from: http://www.epa.gov/owow/wetlands/

Vileisis, A. (1997). *Discovering the unknown landscape: A history of America's wetlands.* Washington, DC: Island Press.

Whale

Whales are a group of marine mammals that includes seventy-eight species in the order Cetacea, which traces its evolutionary path back 40 to 50 million years to forebears that lived on land. Biologists classify whales in two general groups: toothed whales and baleen whales. The former range from sperm whales to the smaller dolphins and porpoises, and the latter, named for the large fibrous plates that they use to strain food from the ocean, range from minkes to the blue whale, the largest organism ever. Cetaceans are distributed over all of the world's seas and a few of the rivers.

It is, perhaps, ironic that the largest whales eat the smallest food. The Antarctic baleen whales, which have adult weights of from 10 to 100 tons, subsist largely on krill, a crustacean only a few centimeters long, with the occasional small fish thrown in. The smaller toothed whales generally feed on larger sea creatures, from midsized fish to giant squid and other mammals. The baleen whales tend to migrate from the equator toward the poles, where they spend the summer feasting on the rich aquatic resources and building up a layer of fat, whereas the toothed whales have a more general distribution.

Just as whales can be classified in two groups, so, too, can whalers. For untold years, people around the world have used small boats to catch whales close to shore, dragging them onto land for processing; for at least one thousand years, since the Basque whalers first began hunting right whales in the Bay of Biscay, others have pursued whales on the high seas. Those who operate shore stations have to choose their locations carefully and take what comes by, but the pelagic whalers can be much more effective and selective as they seek out specific species. Pelagic whalers need to be more effective because they have to take elaborate equipment with them to process their catch, a very capital-intensive process.

A Source of Meat and Oil

Whales have supplied two main products for people: meat and oil, although a host of other products has evolved from the whaling industry, such as ambergris (a waxy substance used in perfumery), scrimshaw, bone meal, and liver oil. Whale meat has long been a source of food for people and their animals, and in the last forty years it has been the main product of the whaling industry. Whale oil was a very desirable commodity from the middle of the nineteenth century until the 1960s. Oil from the head cases of sperm whales has been used as a high-quality industrial lubricant. Oil from the blubber and flesh of baleen and sperm whales served into the twentieth century as a fuel until the rise of the petroleum industry made it uneconomical. Then, in the 1920s, scientists invented a way to refine baleen whale oil into margarine. This refining technique was one of several breakthroughs that revived the whaling industry. It was perhaps the most important because it created a new market for the whalers, but without new technology in hunting and processing of whales, whaling would have continued its decline. The whalers of previous centuries had been so efficient that the only major pocket of whales left was in the Antarctic seas, where hundreds of thousands of huge blue and fin whales lived. Given their size and speed, these species could not be caught by men in small boats throwing harpoons. Instead, catching and killing them required an exploding harpoon mounted on a small steam-powered ship that could travel at at least fifteen knots. Flensing (stripping blubber) and processing such huge animals presented new challenges that were solved by the invention of the floating factory: a huge vessel with a stern slipway for dragging the behemoths on board and an array of equipment for rendering them into oil.

Conservation Efforts Begin

In the 1930s the industry boomed, leading to a series of efforts to conserve whale stocks and culminating in creation of the International Whaling Commission (IWC) in 1946. Whaling on the high seas proved to be difficult to regulate, and despite efforts by conservationists the catch of whales grew until, in the 1963–1964 season, whalers took more than sixty-six thousand whales. The industry declined after that because

Supplies and Equipment for the Sixteenth-Century English Whaler
The following is essentially a shopping list for a whaling ship in 1575:

A proportion for the setting forth of a ship of 200 tons, for the killing of the whale.

There must be 55 men who departing for Wardhouse in the month of April, must be furnished with 4 quintals and a half of bread for every man.

250 hogsheads to put the bread in.

150 hogsheads of cider.

6 quintals of oil.

8 quintals of bacon.

6 hogsheads of beef.

10 quarters of salt.

150 pound of candles.

8 quarters of beans and peas.

Saltfish and herring, a quantity convenient.

4 tuns of wines.

Half a quarter of mustard seed, and a quern.

A grindstone.

800 empty shaken hogsheads.

350 bundles of hoops.

800 pair of heads for the hogsheads.

10 estachas for harpoon irons.

3 pieces of baibens for the javelins small.

2 tackles to turn the whales.

A hawser of 27 fathoms long to turn the whales.

15 great javelins.

18 small javelins.

50 harpoon irons.

6 machicos to cut the whale withall.

2 dozen of machetos to mince the whale.

2 great hooks to turn the whale.

Continues

Continued

3 pair of canhooks.

6 hooks for staves.

3 dozen of staves for the harpoon irons.

6 pulleys to turn the whale with.

10 great baskets.

10 lamps of iron to carry light.

5 kettles of 150 lbs the piece, and 6 ladles.

1000 of nails for the pinnaces.

500 of nails for the houses, and the wharf.

18 axes and hatchets to cleave wood.

12 pieces of lines, and 6 dozen of hooks.

2 beetles of rosemary.

4 dozen of oars for the pinnaces.

6 lanterns.

Item, gunpowder and matches for arquebuses as shall be needful. Item, there must be carried from hence 5 pinnaces, five men to strike with harpoon irons, two cutters of whale, 5 coopers, and a purser or two.

Source: Hakluyt, Richard. (1972). *Voyages and Discoveries: The Principal Navigations, Voyages, Traffiques and Discoveries of the English Nation.* New York: Penguin Books, pp. 159–161.

blue, fin, and humpback whales had all been driven to the edge of extinction, with the Sei and Bryde's whales following shortly thereafter. Most striking was the decline of the blue whale, from perhaps 200,000 before whaling began to about 3,000 today. Likewise, there may have been as many as 125,000 humpback whales before widespread commercial hunting, but there are only about 20,000 left in 2002. Today, only the minke whale exists in numbers that might make commercial whaling feasible, but those numbers are a matter of some debate. In 1982 the IWC voted to ban all commercial whaling, but Japanese whalers in particular continue to catch minkes in the name of scientific research, a highly controversial practice because the meat ends up on the market in Japan.

Until the 1970s most people saw whales as commodities to be exploited rapidly or slowly, depending both on how many were left and the demand for their products. Since then, though, whales have become a symbol of environmentalism, species with special qualities that deserve protection under most circumstances. This change in attitude was in part also a product of technology as people in 1967 heard for the first time recordings of humpback whale songs and soon became exposed to many television shows about whales, all of which suggested that whales are more than just really large slabs of meat or tubs of margarine. The clearest sign of this new attitude toward whales has been seen in the rise of whale-watching, which draws millions of participants each year.

But even as environmentalists have celebrated the growth of whale-watching, they have been struggling to reconcile the whales' new status as icons with the continued desire to hunt whales among some Native

An Inuit grave in Alaska marked by a whale shoulder blade.
COURTESY JOHN AND KAREN HOLLINGSWORTH/U. S. FISH AND WILDLIFE SERVICE.

peoples in North America. The Inuit in Alaska won a bruising battle with the IWC, environmentalists, and the U.S. government in the 1970s and 1980s to allow continued harvesting of bowhead whales, and in the 1990s the Makah tribe of Washington won a similar fight to take one gray whale per year. Environmentalists frequently argue that whales are sentient beings and that even one killed is too many, but the native peoples contend that whaling is an integral part of their culture. Because Japanese and Norwegians often make similar claims, the victories of the Makah and Inuit have compromised the argument of the United States government that Japan and Norway should cease whaling. This problem was quite clear at the 2002 IWC meeting in Shimonoseki, Japan, when the Japanese delegates made a strong case that aboriginal whaling in the United States should face similar levels of scrutiny to Japanese whaling.

Kurk Dorsey

See also International Whaling Commission

Further Reading

Connor, R. C., & Peterson, D. M. (1994). *The lives of whales and dolphins.* New York: Henry Holt.

Ellis, R. (1991). *Men and whales.* New York: Knopf.

Evans, P. G. H. (1987). *The natural history of whales and dolphins.* New York: Facts on File.

Scheffer, V. (1969). *The year of the whale.* New York: Scribners.

Starbuck, A. (1989). *History of the American whale fishery.* Secaucus, NJ: Castle Books.

Tønnessen, J. N., & Johnsen, A. O. (1982). *The history of modern whaling.* Berkeley & Los Angeles: University of California Press.

White, Gilbert

(1720–1793)
British naturalist

British naturalist Gilbert White was the author of the classic *The Natural History of Selborne* (1789). Born in Selborne, Hampshire, fifty miles southwest of London, White at age nineteen entered Oriel College, Oxford. After completing his degree in 1743, he became a Fellow at Oriel, beginning an occasionally troubled but lifelong professional association. In 1747, White began a career in the Church of England, the other affiliation that would define his working life. Although White traveled widely in southern Britain, his main interest remained his eastern corner of Hampshire, where he lived most of his last five decades.

White's early writings show a predilection for natural observation. He began keeping the *Garden Kalendar* in 1751, which was succeeded by his *Naturalist's Journal* in 1767. His masterwork, *The Natural History of Selborne*, began as a series of letters to noted fellow naturalists Thomas Pennant (1726–1798) and Daines Barrington (1727–1800). In its original form, the *Natural History* was paired with the *Antiquities of Selborne*, observations about the local human inhabitants and culture. However, it was in the minute examination and description of nature that White excelled. He was the first to identify the British harvest mouse and the noctule bat, and to observe that earthworms are hermaphroditic. He was especially interested in birds, differentiating three species of "willow wren" and observing how swifts copulate in flight. Species interaction also fascinated White, as when he detailed the symbiotic relationship of cows, insects, and fish at the edge of local ponds: "During this great proportion of the day, they [the cows] drop much dung, in which insects nestle; and so supply food for the fish, which would be poorly subsisted but from this contingency" (White 1997, 27).

White's *Natural History* influenced generations of naturalists. Charles Darwin (1809–1882) read it while in school and recalled, "From reading White's 'Selborne,' I took much pleasure in watching the habits of birds, and even made notes on the subject. In my simplicity I remember wondering why every gentleman did not become an ornithologist" (Darwin 1958, 7). Darwin also cited White in four chapters of *The Descent of Man* (1871). For W. H. Hudson (1841–1922), best known for the novel *Green Mansions* (1904) but also an accomplished naturalist, reading *Selborne* sparked "an overmastering urge to see with his own eyes the England that it depicted" (Allen 1994, 206).

Because White so successfully conveyed passion through his precise descriptions, he found avid readership among Romantic poets William Wordsworth (1770–1850) and Samuel Taylor Coleridge (1772–1834), and painter John Constable (1776–1837). More recent writers have continued to admire White's prose. Virginia Woolf saw the *Natural History* as "one of those ambiguous books that seem to tell a plain story . . . and yet by some apparently unconscious device of the author's has left a door open, through which we hear distant sounds" (in Mabey 1999, 6). However, it was probably American poet James Russell Lowell (1819–1891) who best described the book's enduring appeal (Lowell 1871, 5): "Open the book where you will," he wrote, "it takes you out of doors."

Michael R. Hutcheson

Further Reading

Allen, D. E. (1994). *The naturalist in Britain: A social history.* Princeton, NJ: Princeton University Press.

Barber, L. (1980). *The heyday of natural history 1820–1870.* Garden City, NY: Doubleday.

Darwin, C. (1958). *The autobiography of Charles Darwin and selected letters.* New York: Dover.

Lowell, J. R. (1871) *My garden acquaintance.* Boston: Houghton Mifflin.

Mabey, R. (1999). *Gilbert White: A biography of the naturalist and author of* The natural history of Selborne. London: Pimlico.

White, G. (1997). *The natural history of Selborne.* New York and London: Penguin Books.

White, Laura Lyon

(1839–1916)
U.S. conservationist

In the early twentieth century the U.S. conservation movement was directed from Washington by President Theodore Roosevelt and the U.S. Forest Service chief Gifford Pinchot. But it would not have been successful without the support of a broad-based national constituency concerned about the efficient use of natural resources. In the forefront of this constituency were members of women's clubs throughout the country. And foremost among women's club leaders who saw conservation as a crucial issue was Laura Lyon White, a San Francisco socialite. She led the long battle to stop the logging of ancient sequoia trees in the Calaveras area of the Sierra Nevada Mountains of California, and she was actively engaged in the forestry and irrigation issues that would come to be the core of the conservation movement, the forerunner of today's environmental movement.

White, the wife of banker Lovell White, who was an associate of financier William Ralston, held important positions in both the state and national Federation of Women's Clubs. The national group backed state and federal efforts to save Niagara Falls in New York, an island in the Florida Everglades, Mount Rainier in Washington, the White Mountains in New Hampshire, the southern Appalachian Mountains, the Chippewa forest reserve in Minnesota, and the big trees of Calaveras County, California. White was one of only two women in attendance at the 1908 Governors Conference on the Conservation of Natural Resources hosted by Teddy Roosevelt in Washington. Not long after, she was a delegate to the Women's National Rivers and Harbors Congress (of which she was state president). In 1914 she was even rumored as a possible candidate for lieutenant governor of California on the Republican ticket.

Born in Indiana, Laura Lyon attended Oberlin College, where she wrote a sketch, "Children's Rights," which was later adapted into a children's play. After college she settled in Des Moines and was active in the successful campaign to make that city the capital of Iowa. Following her marriage to White, the couple immigrated via Panama to California, where for five years they operated a general merchandising store in the gold country. There Lovell White met Ralston, who offered him a job with the Bank of California in San Francisco. In the city both Laura and Lovell White wrote articles for Bret Harte's literary magazine, the *Overland Monthly*. Laura White was an ardent supporter of women's suffrage and fought in both the 1896 and 1911 elections for the right of women to vote. After the unsuccessful first campaign she founded the California Club, one of the first civics clubs for women, and worked to improve conditions for working women and to expand educational and recreational opportunities for children. She also led the City Beautiful movement by founding branches of the Outdoor Art Club in San Francisco and Mill Valley.

From 1900 until her death, Laura White campaigned, with the support of her club associations, to preserve the Calaveras big trees in a public park, personally carrying petitions signed by hundreds of thousands of women to several presidents in Washington. She also corresponded with a succession of California governors, but the purchase of land for a park was not made until 1926, and Calaveras did not become a state park until 1931. Laura White and her army of women conservationists were given credit for the victory.

William Yaryan

Further Reading

Barker, P. (1994). The domestication of politics: Women and American political society, 1780–1920. In V. Ruiz & E. C. DuBois (Eds.), *Unequal sisters: A multicultural reader in U.S. women's history* (pp. 66–91). New York: Routledge.

Blair, K. J. (1989). *The clubwoman as feminist: True womanhood redefined, 1868–1914.* Boston: G. K. Hall.

Davis, R. (1967). *California women: A guide to their politics, 1885–1911.* San Francisco: California Scene.

Engbeck, J. H., Jr. (1973). *The enduring giants: The giant sequoias, their place in evolution and in the Sierra Nevada forest community; history of the Calaveras big trees; the story of Calaveras Big Trees State Park.* Berkeley and Los Angeles: University of California, University Extension.

Hoy, S. M. (1980). Municipal housekeeping: The role of women in improving urban sanitation practices, 1880–1917. In M. V. Melosi (Ed.), *Pollution and reform in American cities, 1870–1930* (pp. 173–198). Austin: University of Texas Press.

Kaufman, P. W. (1996). *National parks and the woman's voice: A history.* Albuquerque: New Mexico University Press.

Matthews, G. (1992). *The rise of public woman: Woman's power and woman's place in the United States, 1630–1970.* New York: Oxford University Press.

Riley, G. (1999). *Women and nature: Saving the "wild" West.* Lincoln: University of Nebraska Press.

Smith, M. L. (1987). *Pacific visions: California scientists and the environment, 1850–1915.* New Haven, CT: Yale University Press.

Starr, K. (1973). *Americans and the California dream, 1850–1915.* New York: Oxford University Press.

Yaryan, W., Verardo, J., & Verardo, D. (2000). *The Sempervirens story.* Los Altos, CA: Sempervirens Fund.

White, Lynn, Jr.

(1907–1987)
Historian of medieval technology

Lynn White Jr.'s major contribution to environmental history was a lecture that he gave in 1966 to the American Association for the Advancement of Science, entitled "The Historical Roots of the Ecologic Crisis." This lecture was published as an article in the journal *Science* and became one of the most influential articles on the environment published in the twentieth century. It not only influenced biologists and environmental activists but also invited response from theologians and historians, many of whom were eager to prove him wrong. White's central argument was that the attitudes that allow the exploitation of nature originated out of Judeo-Christian beliefs that became predominant in the Middle Ages. "Christianity has a lot to answer for" in the ecological disaster that followed the Industrial Revolution, he said, because Latin (Western) Christianity facilitated the rise of environmentally destructive technology and science.

Those who appropriate White to argue for the abandonment of Christianity have failed to read on and see that he was instead suggesting that there are other strands in Christianity, represented by Eastern Orthodoxy and by St. Francis of Assisi, that have a less human-oriented view of nature. White was a lifelong Presbyterian, son of a Presbyterian minister, and earned a master's degree at Union Theological Seminary in New York before he did further graduate work in history at Harvard. He was not really suggesting that Christians become Zen Buddhists or secularists. Instead, he was on the leading edge of a significant group of ecotheologians and environmental ethicists who began writing in the 1970s and of a great expansion of religiously based environmental organizations in the 1990s.

The influence of White's article must have surprised and amused him. It does not represent the kind of carefully documented research that he did in his major work on the history of technology. The *Science* article reads more like a witty, lighthearted attempt to

> The victory of Christianity over paganism was the greatest psychic revolution in the history of our culture. By destroying pagan animism, Christianity made it possible to exploit nature in a mood of indifference to the feelings of natural objects.
>
> Lynn I. White Jr., *Science*, March 10, 1967.

show a group of scientists, "See, the obscure work of a medievalist can have some relevance for the modern world." White took a similar approach when he gave his Presidential Address to the American Historical Association in 1973, referring to the newly formed Office of Technology Assessment of the U.S. government. He said that it could improve its cost-benefit assessments of nuclear weapons and transportation systems by paying attention to the history of technological innovations in the Middle Ages.

White was born in San Francisco and died in Los Angeles. Before becoming a professor of history at the University of California in Los Angeles, he was president of Mills College in Oakland, California, from 1943 to 1958. Earlier in his career he had taught at Princeton and Stanford.

Patricia Townsend

Further Reading

Barbour, I. G. (Ed.). (1973). *Western man and environmental ethics: Attitudes toward nature and technology*. Reading, MA: Addison-Wesley.

Barrett, G. W., & Mabry, K. E. (2002). Twentieth-century classic books and benchmark publications in biology. *BioScience, 52*(3), 282–286.

Glick, T. (1999). White, Lynn, Jr. *Encyclopedia of historians and historical writing* (pp. 1295–1296). Chicago: Fitzroy Dearborn.

Nelson, M. P. (2001). Lynn White, Jr. 1907–1987. In Joy A. Palmer (Ed.), *Fifty key thinkers on the environment* (pp. 200–205). London: Routledge.

White, L., Jr. (1967). The historical roots of our ecologic crisis. *Science, 155*(3767), 1203–1207.

White, L., Jr. (1973). Technology assessment from the stance of a medieval historian. Retrieved July 6, 2002, from http://www.theaha.org/info/AHA_History/lwhite.htm

Whitney, E. (1993). Lynn White, ecotheology, and history. *Environmental Ethics, 15*(2), 151–169.

White-Tailed Deer

White-tailed deer evolved in North America 4 million years ago. East of the Rocky Mountains, deer adapted to a wide variety of habitats, including grasslands, oak forests, and the brushy edge areas near savannas and swamps. White-tailed deer were especially important to Native Americans of the Southeast, who relied on deer much like Great Plains Native Americans relied on buffalo. Venison provided sustenance, and deerskins furnished leather for clothing and moccasins.

To kill deer in quantity, Native Americans used fire to drive them into confined areas, where they could be quickly killed. The natives also set seasonal ground fires in forested regions to create new vegetation and the edge habitats that deer favored. Deer had an exalted place in Native American cosmology and ritual. Young men rarely ate the first deer they killed for fear that other deer might never allow themselves to be killed. That belief system and the practice of killing deer primarily for food and necessities helped preserve the herds. Perhaps 40 million white-tailed deer inhabited North America in 1492.

Those numbers diminished sharply as European colonists sought deerskins for the Atlantic market. In European tanneries, American deerskins became gloves, bookbindings, harnesses, and buckskin breeches favored by English aristocrats as casual attire. In exchange for the skins, colonial traders offered Native Americans guns, cloth, knives, metal utensils, and rum. As Native Americans became dependent on European trade goods during the eighteenth century, they hunted primarily for the European market. By the 1750s over half a million deerskins were shipped from southern ports each year. Colonial governments tried to protect diminishing deer herds by establishing closed seasons on commercial hunting, but enforcement was lax, and deer numbers declined 35 to 50 percent by 1800. During the nineteenth century, market hunting by midwestern settlers and improved railway transport made venison and deerskins important commodities in eastern cities. By 1870 venison sold for less than beef and pork in urban hotels and eateries. That market took a heavy toll. In 1890 government agencies estimated that only 300,000 white-tailed deer remained in America. They were all but extinct in several states.

The Lacy Act, a federal law passed in 1900 to prohibit interstate shipment of any animals not taken in accord with state regulations, curtailed market hunting and set white-tailed deer on the path to a dramatic recovery. Sportsmen and wilderness advocates lobbied for the restocking of deer on public lands. Until the 1930s, wildlife managers also promoted systematic killing of wolves, coyotes, mountain lions, and other predators of deer. An abundance of abandoned farmland in the South and Northeast provided deer with new and favorable habitat.

As a result, white-tailed deer numbers have risen dramatically since the 1940s to a current estimated population of 25 million. In the East deer routinely encounter food shortages, disease, and other problems of overpopulation. Expanding human populations have also infringed on the natural habitat of deer. Many suburbanites now regard white-tailed deer as nuisance animals that devour shrubbery, carry deadly ticks, and create hazards for motorists. Despite lenient hunting regulations, culling of large herds, and sterilization of wild deer, the trend shows no sign of abatement.

Timothy Silver

Further Reading

Halls, L. K. (Ed.). (1984). *White-tailed deer: Ecology and management.* Harrisburg, PA: Stackpole Books.

Krech, S., III. (1999). *The ecological Indian: Myth and history.* New York: W. W. Norton.

Nelson, R. (1997). *Heart and blood: Living with deer in America.* New York: Random House.

Silver, T. (1990). *A new face on the countryside: Indians, colonists, and slaves in South Atlantic forests, 1500–1800.* New York: Cambridge University Press.

Wild Turkey

The wild turkey (*Meleagris gallopavo*) is a bird species unique to North America. Scientists recognize six subspecies of wild turkey, which is a member of the pheasant (*Phasianini*) family. The eastern wild turkey is found over most of eastern and central United States from southern Maine to northern Florida, westward through southern New England, New York, and southern Ontario to southeastern South Dakota. Eastern wild turkeys range southward through the eastern portions of Nebraska, Kansas, Oklahoma, and Texas. The Florida wild turkey is found in central and southern Florida. The Rio Grande wild turkey is found in central and western Texas, western Oklahoma, and southwestern Kansas. The Merriam's wild turkey is found in northeastern Mexico, Arizona, New Mexico, Colorado, and the western tip of Oklahoma. The Gould's wild turkey is found in north-central Mexico, southeastern Arizona, and southwestern New Mexico. The Mexican wild turkey is native to central Mexico. A separate species, the ocellated turkey (*Meleagris ocellata*), is native to the Yucatan Peninsula of Mexico and adjacent portions of Guatemala and Belize. The eastern, Rio Grande, and Merriam's subspecies have been widely introduced into many areas of North America, some of which are outside of the original range occupied by the subspecies.

Throughout human occupation of North America the wild turkey has held cultural significance. From prehistoric to modern times Native Americans used wild turkeys for food and for ceremonial purposes. It is believed that the Anasazi people in Colorado, Utah, and New Mexico domesticated turkeys and that Aztecs in Mexico domesticated Mexican wild turkeys prior to the arrival of the Spanish in the 1500s. Domesticated turkeys were taken to Europe by Spaniards by 1520. Later English colonists returned "domestic" turkeys to North America.

When Europeans began settling North America, they found the wild turkey in abundance in many areas, particularly the eastern United States. The value of the wild turkey to U.S. colonial settlement is exemplified by the symbolism of the turkey at Thanksgiving. Benjamin Franklin (1706–1790), one of the founding fathers of the United States, wanted the wild turkey adopted as the national symbol. However, Franklin was outvoted, and the national symbol became the bald eagle.

Throughout settlement of the United States the wild turkey was an important source of food. Wild turkeys were hunted first as subsistence food and later commercially to feed an ever-urbanizing United States. Slowly the combination of unrestricted hunting and loss of habitat led to the demise of the wild turkey. Wild turkeys were completely eliminated in many areas and were reduced to small numbers in other areas. By the early twentieth century wild turkeys no longer were found in eighteen of the thirty-nine states where they originally had occurred.

A male Eastern Wild Turkey in Louisiana. COURTESY GARY M. STOLZ/
U.S. FISH AND WILDLIFE SERVICE.

In the 1930s the U.S. forester Aldo Leopold (1887–1948) emerged as a philosophical and scientific leader in a new field that became known as "wildlife management." In 1937 the U.S. Congress passed the Federal Aid in Fish and Wildlife Restoration Act, which established an excise tax on certain guns and ammunition used for hunting. The taxes collected by the U.S. government were then apportioned back to individual states to fund wildlife restoration and research. Thus an era of modern wildlife conservation began. Because of their scarcity, wild turkeys became one of the subjects of restoration and scientific research.

From the 1950s to 1999 wild turkeys were restored to the entire historical range and beyond. During the winter of 2001–2002, 5,500 wild turkeys were captured in eleven states and released into new habitats in eight states and one Canadian province. Legal hunting harvests of wild turkeys now exceed 700,000 annually.

Roger D. Applegate

Further Reading

Dickson, J. G. (1992). *The wild turkey—biology and management*. Harrisburg, PA: Stackpole Books.

Hewitt, O. H. (1967). *The wild turkey and its management*. Washington, DC: Wildlife Society.

Kallman, H. (1987). *Restoring America's wildlife 1937–1987*. Washington, DC: U.S. Fish and Wildlife Service.

Pedersen, J. L. (2002). A successful Making Tracks trapping season. *Turkey Call, 29*(4), 20–21.

Porter, W. F., & Fleming, K. K. (2001). *Proceedings of the eighth National Wild Turkey Symposium*. Edgefield, SC: National Wild Turkey Federation.

Schorger, A. W. (1966). *The wild turkey—its history and domestication*. Stillwater: Oklahoma State University Press.

Taylor, C. I., Quigley, H. B., & Gonzalez, M. J. (n.d.). *Ocellated turkey (Meleagris ocellata)* (Wildlife Bulletin No. 6). Edgefield, SC: National Wild Turkey Federation.

Williams, L. E., Jr. (1991). *Wild turkey country*. Minocqua, WI: Northword Press.

Wilderness

People have had and continue to have differing ideas of wilderness. The etymology of the word defies easy characterization, and definition is complicated by the interweaving of the word with the semantic history of other terms. For example, *wild nature* connotes a habitat without human-introduced plants and animals, as distinct from a habitat that contains species introduced by humans. One of the closest antecedents of "wilderness" is the Anglo-Saxon *wilddéoren*, meaning the place or habitat of wild deer. The *Oxford English Dictionary* provides a comprehensive history of English usage of "wilderness" dating from approximately 1200 CE. Linguistic convention defines "wilderness" as natural landscapes, free of human modification, and devoid of settlement; they are landscapes in which humans are only visitors.

Wilderness Themes

As with all ideas, the notion of wilderness is understood in a variety of ways, with differing emphases. The following contemporary interpretations of wilderness are noteworthy.

Wilderness and the Conservation of Biodiversity

This theme is articulated especially by conservation biologists. The scientific consensus is that extinctions are increasing in frequency on all scales (local to global) and for all types (genetic to ecosystemic). As the human population grows, the habitats that are home to myriad other species are subject to development and fragmentation. In order to conserve biodiversity, there must exist wild lands that are not subject to development. Proposed solutions for the biodiversity crisis range from the short-term and regional (for example, the outright purchase of critical habitat for endangered species), to the long-term and continental, such as the

Y2Y (Yellowstone to Yukon) Re-Wilding and the Wild Lands Project. These projects aim to designate and restore core habitats capable of sustaining the predisturbance suite of species and natural processes. Whether on a regional or a continental scale, the biodiversity view of wilderness entails a core commitment to the protection and management of wilderness as habitat for indigenous plant and animal species.

Wilderness and the Human Condition

This theme is reflected in such ancient textual sources as the Mesopotamian *Epic of Gilgamesh* and the Hebrew Scripture, in the works of the nineteenth-century Romantic poets and Henry David Thoreau, in the twentieth-century writings of Aldo Leopold, and in disciplines such as environmental history and ecological psychology. Whether the writings are secular or sacred, a central question is the place of humans in the natural scheme. In one interpretation of Judeo-Christian texts, while Adam and Eve were expelled from the Garden of Eden, humans have nevertheless been placed in the role of stewards of creation. Certain naturalistic accounts argue that wild places and creatures are essential to the psychological well-being of humans. A variation on this theme is that wilderness is a necessary condition for human self-understanding, for what we have become as cultural beings can only be gauged against the wildness of nature. Ecologists argue that human ecology cannot be separated from biological ecology; therefore, if we perturb wild nature, we risk perturbing ourselves in ways that are hard to predict. Ethicists such as Charles Taylor argue that the natural world makes moral claims on humans because of its intrinsic value and because its destruction diminishes the human estate. In combination, such notions challenge anthropocentrism, which views nature as raw material for economic exploitation.

Bioregionalism and Reinhabitation

Sometimes termed "the practice of the wild," bioregionalism attempts to reestablish humans as dwellers within the wild, and thus demurs from the conventional definition of wilderness. The basic premise is that cultures that are connected to natural processes and places are qualitatively richer and probably more sustainable than the dominant cultural forms of industrial-consumerism, which disconnect people from place. Differences exist across bioregional narratives, reflecting the commitment to the importance of place. Characteristically, bioregionalists engage in the work of ecological restoration. Freeman House, an articulate reinhabitant and member of the Mattole River Watershed Group, writes, "Patterns of mutuality flow out of the wild center to empower a community engaged in envisioning a sustainable future" (House 1999, 211).

Ethical Themes

Ethical considerations of the wilderness idea are diverse, yet typically converge on questions involving humankind's place within and relation to the naturally evolved world. As distinct from scientific assessments, ethical considerations are invariably qualitative, such as Thoreau's arguments that wildness is a necessary condition for the preservation of the world, and John Muir's notions that going into the mountains is going home, as well as contemporary iterations such as evolutionary arguments, posthistoric primitivism, and deep ecology. Evolutionists such as Edward O. Wilson argue that the natural history of humankind forces recognition of the continuing importance of wild places. Posthistoric primitivism, associated with the work of Paul Shepard and others, combines evolutionary biology with anthropological, paleontological, psychological, and other human sciences to argue that humans remain social primates who are deformed by cultural systems. By "coming home to the Pleistocene," we can reintegrate ourselves with the evolved wildness that surrounds us and also exists within human nature. Deep ecology, associated with the work of Arne Naess, George Sessions, and others, argues that the intrinsic value of native species obligates the preservation and restoration of wild habitats, and that such obligations are fully consonant with an ecological understanding of human nature.

Issues and Controversies

Countervailing discourses to either the received or to contemporary ideas of wilderness exist, including the following.

The Social Critique

The received idea of wilderness has been attacked as harboring classist, sexist, and racist dogma. That is, the wilderness idea reflects the interests of white, Euro-American males. According to this argument, the idea served first to legitimate colonization, since wild lands were presumed to be devoid of humans and therefore open for the taking, and later to displace indigenous people from lands that became national parks, forests,

1333

and designated wilderness areas. Further, critics charge, the wilderness idea serves the interests of an economically privileged and politically powerful leisure class that converts wild nature into a recreational playground, engaging in activities (skiing, hunting, fishing, snowmobiling) that ultimately degrade nature.

Third World Criticism

Third World critics argue that the received idea of wilderness, and its variation as habitat for the conservation of biodiversity, harbors remnants of colonialism and imperialism. Indian intellectuals offer several criticisms. Madhav Gadgil and Ramachandra Guha confront wilderness preservationists with arguments that the First World, having exploited its own ecologies, now wants the Third World to become the refuge of biodiversity. Vandana Shiva challenges the policies and philosophies of Third World elites who advocate technological modernization and industrialization as the keys to economic and social progress, and the creation of nature reserves for the preservation and conservation of indigenous species. She argues that those policies displace subsistence farmers from their native landscapes, with disastrous social and ecological consequences.

Revisionist Arguments

These include arguments that the so-called New World first encountered by European explorers, and later the colonists, was not pristine wilderness, but a landscape shaped for thousands of years by humans. Environmental historians argue variations on this theme. For example, William Cronon states that colonial New England was not a savage, howling wilderness but a domesticated landscape. Shepard Krech III argues that indigenous people transformed the American landscape from coast to coast through fire. Amazonia itself has come under scrutiny, with persuasive arguments being advanced for significant human modification of the tropical rain forest over millennia. Dissenters from revisionism, such as E. O. Wilson, concede that humans have found niches in virtually all terrestrial environments. "But to claim that the surviving wildernesses are less than the name implies, and have in some sense become part of the human domain, is false" (Wilson 2002, 145).

Ecological Restoration

Ecological restoration of degraded landscapes, especially in the public lands of the American West, raises a variety of wilderness issues. A restored landscape, critics charge, is an artifice. Critics believe that ecological restoration has been co-opted by land management agencies. Guided by the idea of sustainable development, ecosystem health rather than a return to the predisturbance state, becomes the goal of restoration. Thus ecological restoration becomes a legitimating rationale for remaking nature according to criteria of sustainability rather than criteria that move degraded landscape off trajectories of decline onto trajectories of recovery. Critics argue that only those landscapes allowed to heal themselves qualify as wilderness.

In contrast, advocates of ecological restoration argue that rather than imposing artificial schemes, restoration actually mimics natural processes, reestablishes indigenous flora and fauna, and deflects damaged ecosystems onto trajectories of recovery. "Strong restoration" is a term used to describe this kind of activity, implying that the restoration of predisturbance composition, structure, and function of wild lands is the goal, that invasive means are to be limited, that natural processes are to be mimicked, and that ultimately humans should be causally uncoupled from the restored wilderness ecosystem.

The Idea of Wilderness and Environmental History

Environmental history and associated disciplines, such as historical ecology, landscape history, and cultural geography, all address the human influence on and place within natural systems. Different ideas of wilderness influence environmental historians in a variety of ways, including how they select and interpret relevant materials. At least three different ideas of wilderness can be discerned in environmental history. One is the theory of inevitable decline; that is, the interpretation of human impacts on the wild earth as leading toward (often inadvertent) ruination. Revolutionary changes, such as were occasioned by the agricultural and industrial revolutions, are subject to reinterpretation according to that theory. Variations on this theme range across spatial and temporal scales, whether it is the extinction of megafauna being caused by Paleolithic hunters, the collapse of the ancient Egyptian civilization (beginning with deforestation and culminating in desertification), or the present-day impact of the chemical industry on people of color. The second idea of wilderness discernible in environmental history is revisionism, discussed earlier. The third idea of wilderness in environmental history is framed by ecological science. Environmental histories of forest and fishery management, agriculture, and water resource development are being written using interpretive principles rooted in the ecosystem concept.

The Twenty-First Century

Ongoing reinterpretations of the wilderness idea promise a more scientifically robust, historically articulated, and ethically leavened wilderness idea. Given the complexity of the idea of wilderness, no foundational discourse that resolves all questions can be anticipated. However, several salient themes are apparent in the early years of the twenty-first century.

One is the recognition that pristine natural systems (free of human control) are an endangered, indeed, almost nonexistent, species. Simon Levin argues that human domination of natural systems offers a fragile dominion at best. A variety of responses to environmental dysfunctions, such as adaptive management and ecosystem management, have been articulated, emphasizing the ongoing importance of conserving and restoring the biodiversity without which any notion of wilderness is an empty concept. The work of conserving and restoring biodiversity envisions replacing degraded ecosystems and landscapes on evolutionary trajectories from which humans are causally disconnected and natural subsidy (as distinct from inputs of cultural resources, such as chemicals) is optimized.

A second theme is the deconstruction of exceptionalism, that is, the notion that the human species has escaped natural selection. The cultural schemes that mediate human behavior are now clearly understood as subject to natural selection. It is now recognized that cultures are only viable if they are sustainable; that is, a viable culture can only be achieved through adaptive engagement with nature. The future of human society is arguably dependent upon restoring and sustaining ecosystem health, and therefore the conservation of biodiversity, including wild ecosystems.

A third theme is woven from stands of evolutionary biology and natural history. The human and chimpanzee genomes are more than 99 percent the same, yet the little bit of difference makes all the difference. Humankind has become a symbol-using species, time-binders who accrete and interpret experience through language. Many wilderness discourses are thus appropriately seen as contemporary versions of perennial philosophical and religious questions concerning the meaning of life. We now know that, whatever the pretense, humankind remains profoundly dependent upon the naturally evolved world. The redefinition of humanity that follows from historical ecology, human ecology, and evolutionary biology indicates that regardless of culturally evolved features of life, such as the domestication of animals and the creation of built environments, the continuing practice of the wild—living in ways that harmonize with the naturally evolved world—is fundamental.

While the natural, social, and human sciences articulate diverse wilderness themes, there is also convergence on a common center. Humankind remains embedded within and profoundly dependent upon the wild Earth. Pulitzer Prize–winning poet Gary Snyder writes that "a culture that alienates itself from the very ground of its own being—from the wilderness outside . . . and from that other wilderness, the wilderness within—is doomed to a very destructive behavior, ultimately perhaps self-destructive behavior" (Snyder 1974, 106). Given the ever-increasing pressures humanity places upon the wild Earth, conserving and restoring biodiversity has become even more crucial to humanity's long-term prospects. In context, then, the twenty-first-century idea of wilderness might be understood as a part of the process of cultural adaptation to environmental exigencies. Which is to say that the forces of natural selection still operate on humankind, and that Thoreau's intuition that in wildness is the preservation of the world has been borne out in fact.

Max Oelschlaeger

Further Reading

Bickerton, D. (1990). *Language and species*. Chicago and London: University of Chicago Press.

Bratton, S. P. (1993). *Christianity, wilderness, and wildlife: The original desert solitaire*. Scranton, PA: University of Scranton Press.

Callicott, J. B., & Nelson, M. P. (Eds.). (1998). *The great new wilderness debate*. Athens & London: University of Georgia Press.

Cavalli-Sforza, L. L. (2000). *Genes, peoples, and language* (M. Seielstad, Trans.). New York: North Point Press.

Cronon, W. (1983). *Changes in the land: Indians, colonists, and the ecology of New England*. New York: Hill & Wang.

Diamond, J. (1992). *The third chimpanzee: The evolution and future of the human animal*. New York: HarperCollins.

Ehrlich, P. (2000). *Human natures: Genes, cultures, and the human prospect*. Washington, DC: Island Press.

Eisenberg, E. (1998). *The ecology of Eden*. New York: Alfred A. Knopf.

Fisher, A. (2002). *Radical ecopsychology: Psychology in the service of life*. Albany: State University of New York Press.

Foreman, D., & Wouk, H. (1992). *The big outside: A descriptive inventory of the big wilderness areas of the United States*. New York: Harmony Books.

Gadgil, M., & Guha, R. (1993). *This fissured land: An ecological history of India*. Berkeley and Los Angeles: University of California Press.

Grumbine, R. E. (1992). *Ghost bears: Exploring the biodiversity crisis*. Washington, DC: Island Press.

House, F. (1999). *Totem salmon: Life lessons from another species*. Boston: Beacon Press.

Krech, S., III. (1999). *The ecological Indian: Myth and history*. New York: W. W. Norton.

Lentz, D. L. (Ed.). (2000). *Imperfect balance: Landscape transformations in the precolumbian Americas*. New York: Columbia University Press.

Leopold, A. (1970). *A Sand County almanac: With essays on conservation from Round River*. San Francisco: Sierra Club Books.

Levin, S. (1991). *Fragile dominion: Complexity and the commons*. Reading, MA: Perseus Books.

Merchant, C. (1989). *Ecological revolutions: Nature, gender and science in New England*. Chapel Hill: University of North Carolina Press.

Nash, R. (1982). *Wilderness and the American mind* (3rd ed.). New Haven & London: Yale University Press.

Oelschlaeger, M. (1991). *The idea of wilderness: From prehistory to the age of ecology*. New Haven & London: Yale University Press.

Oelschlaeger, M. (Ed.). (1992). *The wilderness condition: Essays on environment and civilization*. San Francisco: Sierra Club Books.

Rudzitis, G. (1996). *Wilderness and the changing American West*. New York: Wiley & Sons.

Sessions, G. (Ed.). (1995). *Deep ecology for the 21st Century: Readings on the philosophy and practice of the new environmentalism*. Boston: Shambhala.

Shepard, P. (1998). *Coming home to the Pleistocene*. Washington, DC: Island Press.

Shiva, V. (1989). *Staying alive: Women, ecology, and development*. London: Zed Books.

Snyder, G. (1974). *Turtle Island*. New York: New Directions Publishing.

Snyder, G. (1990). *The practice of the wild*. San Francisco: North Point Press.

Soulé, M. E. (Ed.). (1986). *Conservation biology: The science of scarcity and diversity*. Sunderland, MA: Sinauer Associates.

Wilson, E. O. (1992). *The diversity of life*. Cambridge, MA: The Belknap Press of Harvard University Press.

Wilson, E. O. (2002). *The future of life*. New York: Alfred A. Knopf.

Wright, W. (1992). *Wild knowledge: Science, language, and social life in a fragile environment*. Minneapolis: University of Minnesota Press.

Wilderness Society

The Wilderness Society is a conservation group that works through public education, scientific analysis, and advocacy to protect U.S. wilderness areas and pass them on to future generations. Focusing on the 623 million acres of public land in the country, the Wilderness Society protects clean air and water, wildlife, beauty, and opportunities for recreation.

During the 1930s a growing number of wilderness enthusiasts were becoming disillusioned with road-building projects of the National Park Service, particularly the highways through Shenandoah National Park of Virginia and Great Smoky Mountains National Park of Tennessee and North Carolina. In 1935 the Wilderness Society was formed by a group of men who, according to its mission statement, wanted to "save from invasion" the "minor fraction of outdoor America which yet remains free from mechanical sights and sounds and smells" (Wilderness Society n.d.). Founding members included Robert Sterling Yard (1861–1945), publicist of the National Park Service; Benton MacKaye (1879–1975), the "father of the Appalachian Trail"; Robert Marshall (1901–1939), chief of recreation and lands for the U.S. Forest Service; and Aldo Leopold (1887–1948), wildlife ecologist at the University of Wisconsin.

In 1936 Marshall spoke on behalf of the Wilderness Society in favor of establishing Olympic National Park in the state of Washington. Within a year, the organization had grown to 576 members. It was supported by donations—mainly from Marshall, in the early years—and membership dues.

The Wilderness Act, signed by President Lyndon B. Johnson in 1964, was instrumental to the Wilderness Society in its quest to save America's vanishing wild lands. The act enabled Congress to set aside portions of national forests, national parks, and national wildlife refuges as units to be kept free from the influence of humans—without roads, structures, or vehicles. The

Wilderness Society has helped pass legislation that has increased the acreage protected in the National Wilderness Preservation System. In 1980 the Alaska National Interest Land Conservation Act protected 56 million acres; and in 1994 the California Desert Protection Act saved 8 million acres of fragile desert lands.

The Wilderness Society continues to take action on controversial issues, such as the Roadless Area Conservation Rule, which was adopted by the federal government in 2001 but remains unimplemented. This rule protects 58.5 million acres of national forests and national grasslands from road construction, commercial logging, new oil and gas leases, and mineral development. The Wilderness Society supports the protection of roadless areas (representing less than 2 percent of America's landscape), which provide refuge for vanishing wildlife and fish species and sources of clean drinking water for millions of Americans. Boise Cascade, a major logging corporation, has been vocal in its opposition to the roadless rule and continues to seek timber industry rights in old-growth forests. Another opponent of the Wilderness Society's efforts is the Society of American Foresters, which maintains that roadless areas are not in the best interest of forest management.

In other recent campaigns, the Wilderness Society has fought a proposed U.S. Air Force bombing range in the Owyhee Canyonlands, located in Idaho, Oregon, and Nevada; has asked Congress to protect Baca Ranch in New Mexico, an important elk habitat; and has been working on a long-term management plan for wilderness and parks in the Sierra Nevada Range.

The Wilderness Society headquarters is in Washington, D.C., and there are eight regional offices across the country. The society has 200,000 members and publishes the annual *Wilderness* magazine.

Robin O'Sullivan

Further Reading

Glover, J. M. (1986). *A wilderness original: The life of Bob Marshall.* Seattle, WA: The Mountaineers.

Leopold, A. (1987). *A Sand County almanac.* New York: Oxford University Press.

Rennicke, J. (1998, June 1). The geography of hope. *Backpacker*, 38–40.

Roberts, A. (1995). The Endangered Species Act: A commitment worth keeping. *Animal Guardian, 8*(3), 5–8, 15. Retrieved January 7, 2003, from http://www.awionline.org/wildlife/ag-esa.htm

Rupp, D. (1998, August). Playing in the zones. *Sports Afield*, 76–80.

The Wilderness Society. (n.d.). *The Wilderness Society's Roots.* Retrieved May 13, 2002, from http:// http://www.wilderness.org/abouttws/history.htm

Wind Energy

Only a small portion of incoming solar radiation (less than 2 percent) powers the atmospheric motion. The combination of diurnal and seasonal changes of insolation (exposure to sun's rays) and of differential heating of surfaces (vegetated vs. barren, land vs. water) mean that wind frequencies and velocities range from prolonged spells of calm to episodes of violent cyclonic (rainstorms, tornadoes, hurricanes) flows. Sail ships, used by the earliest civilizations of the Old World, were undoubtedly the first converters of wind energy into useful motion. And before the end of the twentieth century, one of the world's oldest energy sources has become one of the most promising modern providers of renewable energy as wind-generated electricity has been the fastest growing segment of modern renewable energetics.

The first written record of windmills comes a millennium after the first mention of waterwheels: al-Masudi's report of 947 CE notes the use of simple vertical-shaft windmills in Seistan (in today's eastern Iran) to raise water for irrigating gardens. The first European record comes only from the closing decades of the twelfth century. Subsequent development of windmills was uneven in both time and space.

Windmills and Their Uses

The earliest vertical designs were used basically unchanged for many centuries in the Near East, as were the horizontal European machines. These mills pivoted on a massive central post that was supported usually by four diagonal quarterbars and the whole enginehouse had to be turned to face the wind. Post mills were unstable in high winds, vulnerable to storm damage, and their low height limited their efficiency. Still, unlike in China and India where wind power made historically little difference, post mills became a major source of rotary motion in Atlantic Europe.

As with watermills, grain milling and water pumping (the Dutch drainage mills being the most prominent examples of this application) were the most common applications of wind power. Other common uses included grinding and crushing, papermaking, sawing, and metalworking. Post mills were gradually replaced by tower mills and smock mills. Only the top cap of these machines had to be turned into the wind, and after 1745 the English introduction of the fantail made it possible to turn the sails automatically. The fantail catches the wind bearing away from the sails and it turns the cog ring at the top of the tower until the sails are returned square on to the wind. More than a century before this innovation the Dutch millers introduced the first relatively efficient blade designs that provided more lift while reducing drag. But true airfoils, aerodynamically contoured blades with thick leading edges, were introduced in England only by the end of the nineteenth century.

America's westward expansion on the windy Great Plains created demand for smaller machines to pump water for steam locomotives, households, and cattle. These windmills were made of a large number of fairly narrow blades or slats that were fastened to solid or sectional wheels and they were usually equipped either with the centrifugal or the side-vane governor and with independent rudders.

Windmills reached the peak of their importance during the latter half of the nineteenth century: in 1900 about 30,000 machines with a total capacity of some 100 megawatts worked in countries around the North Sea, and the U.S. sales of smaller brands of American windmills amounted to millions of units during the second half of the nineteenth century.

Wind Electricity

Many machines that continued operating in the twentieth century were connected to generators to produce electricity for immediate household use and for storage in lead-acid batteries. Gradual extension of electricity networks ended this brief era of wind-generated electricity and little research and even less field testing on converting wind into useful energy was done until the early 1970s, when the Organization of Petroleum Exporting Countries suddenly quintupled the price of crude oil, reigniting the interest in renewable energies.

Modern Wind-Driven Electricity Generation

The first modern boom in wind energy was launched by the U.S. tax credits during the early 1980s. By 1985 the country's wind turbines had installed capacity of just over 1 gigawatt and the world's largest wind facility (637 megawatts) was at Altamont Pass in California. Low load factors, poor turbine designs, and the expiration of tax credits in 1985 ended this first wind wave. Better turbine designs, with blades optimized for low speeds, and larger turbine sizes have led the expansion that began around 1990. The average size of new machines rose from mere 40–50 kilowatts in the early 1980s to over 200 kilowatts a decade later. Today's commercial market is dominated by turbines rated at 500–750 kilowatts. The first machines with power of more than 1 megawatt have entered service, and 4–5 megawatt turbines, with rotor diameters of 110–112 meters, are in design stage. Germany, Denmark, and Spain have been the leaders of this expansion. New laws that guarantee higher fixed price for wind-generated electricity have been essential, and the Danish government has been particularly active in promoting wind power: The country now has the highest per capita installed capacity and it dominates the world export market in efficient wind turbines. Germany is the world leader in absolute terms, with more than 9,000 machines and about 6.1 gigawatts of installed capacity at the end of 2000.

United States' wind-generating capacity rose from 1 gigawatt in 1985 to 2.5 gigawatts by the end of 2000, with half of it in California. Spain, India, the Netherlands, Italy, and the U.K. are next in line. Global capacity of wind turbines reached 1 gigawatt in 1985, 10 gigawatts in 1998 (equal to nuclear plants in 1968), and 17.3 gigawatts in 2000. As a result wind-driven electricity generation is seen as the most promising of all new renewable conversions, far ahead of other solar-based techniques both in terms of operational reliability and unit cost. Some experts argue that at the best windy sites, even unsubsidized wind electricity is already competitive with fossil-fueled generation, or even cheaper than coal or gas-fired production, and hence we should go for a more aggressive maximization of wind's potential. Some plans foresee 10 percent of the world's electricity supply generated by wind by the year 2020. That is not a modest goal considering that in the year 2000 wind generated less than 0.5 percent of the world's electricity.

Available resource is no obstacle to even the boldest dreams. Only about 2 percent of all solar energy received by the Earth is needed to drive the atmospheric motion, and if a mere 1 percent of this flux could be converted to electricity, the global capacity would be some 35 terawatts, or more than 10 times the 2000 total installed in all fossil, nuclear, and hydro stations. A much more restrictive estimate that considers only wind speeds above 5 meters per second up to 10 meters above ground puts the global wind power potential at about 6 terawatts, or about 350 times larger than the total installed in 2000. The main problems associated with tapping this potential result from the fact that wind is unevenly distributed in both space and time.

Many windy sites are far away from centers of electricity consumption, and many densely populated areas with high electricity demand experience long seasonal periods of calm or low wind speeds and hence are utterly unsuitable, or only marginally suited, for harnessing wind's energy. Virtually the entire southeastern United States, northern Italy, and Sichuan, China's most populous province, are in the latter category. Wind's intermittence means that it cannot be used for base-load generation. Its fluctuations are only imperfectly predictable, and peak wind flows only rarely coincide with the time of the highest demand. Inevitably, these realities complicate efficient commercial utilization. The visual aspect of siting large turbines and building connection and transmission lines is another concern. Offshore siting of wind turbines should help to minimize or eliminate these impacts.

Vaclav Smil

Further Reading

Braun, G. W., & Smith, D. R. (1992). Commercial wind power: Recent experience in the United States. *Annual Review of Energy and the Environment, 17,* 97–121.

Danish Wind Industry Association. (2002). Read about wind energy. Retrieved December 3, 2002, from http://www.windpower.dk/core.htm

McGowan, J. G., & Connors, S. R. (2000). Windpower: A turn of the century review. *Annual Review of Energy and the Environment, 25,* 147–197.

Pasqualetti, M. J., Gipe, P., & Righter, R. W. (2002). *Wind power in view: Energy landscapes in a crowded world.* San Diego, CA: Academic Press.

Reynolds, J. (1970). *Windmills and watermills.* London: Hugh Evelyn.

Smil, V. (1994). *Energy in world history.* Boulder, CO: Westview.

Smil, V. (2003). *Energy at the crossroads.* Cambridge, MA: The MIT Press.

Sørensen, B. (1995). History of, and recent progress in, wind-energy utilization. *Annual Review of Energy and the Environment, 20,* 387–424.

Stockhuyzen, F. (1963). *The Dutch windmill.* New York: Universe Books.

Wolff, A. R. (1900). *The windmill as prime mover.* New York: John Wiley.

Wise-Use Movement

The term *wise use* originally appeared in the biography of the U.S. forester Gifford Pinchot, *Breaking New Ground*, in 1947. Pinchot (1865–1946), who was the first chief of the U.S. Forest Service in 1905, used the term synonymously with *conservation*. At the turn of the twentieth century *conservation* referred to using, rather than preserving, natural resources. Pinchot's view was in contrast to that of the U.S. naturalist John Muir (1838–1914), who believed in protecting wild areas and their resources from development forever.

Today, those who believe in the wise use of natural resources are remnants of a social movement that has its roots in the Sagebrush Rebellions of the late 1800s, when public land issues and concerns about natural resources were only beginning to be identified, and similar debate over resource extraction and grazing in the late 1940s. Between 1978 and 1981, activists in the West opposed the federal government's land-use policies under federal acts such as the 1976 Federal Land Policy and Management Act and the 1964 Wilderness Act. Although loosely organized, opponents of the two acts argued that the government was "locking up" public lands that were originally designed for recreational use and resource extraction. They sought to use constitutional language to have forest reserves and other land in the public domain transferred from federal control to the states. This became a legal issue based on the idea of states' rights and state sovereignty—giving states the power to control the land for their own citizens. But the Sagebrush rebels were unsuccessful in their efforts, and the "rebellion" appeared to end.

Contemporary Wise-Use Movement

The ideas that formed the philosophical and legal basis for the Sagebrush Rebellions began to resurface in the late 1980s, and a social movement began to rebuild itself. Although many of the Sagebrush rebels were no longer politically active, they were replaced or supported by advocates who believed in the same ideas.

The wise-use movement, as it has come to be called, was motivated by the political ideals of President Ronald Reagan, whose values were grounded in western culture. He and members of his administration, including Secretary of the Interior James Watt, were sympathetic to the appeals of angry timber workers as logging operations diminished, to snowmobilers and four-wheel-drive club members who were barred from using trails on public lands, and to ranchers caught up in the contentious debate over grazing livestock on public lands. They were joined in their opposition by individuals who owned property located within the boundaries of national parks—called "inholders"—who had begun organizing in the mid-1970s.

That opposition began to coalesce around 1988 near the end of the Reagan administration. In August 1988 nearly three hundred people gathered in Reno, Nevada, at a national conference sponsored by the Center for the Defense of Free Enterprise. The center brought together representatives from various extractive resource industries, trade group and government officials, and public interest membership organizations that dealt with environmental or resource issues. The participants produced the Wise Use Agenda—a list of twenty-five goals that would become the basis for the movement. The conference also brought together allied groups that were unaware that they shared many common perspectives about the environment.

The Wise Use Agenda was printed and distributed nationally, and a copy was transmitted to President George H. W. Bush as a blueprint of recommendations for his new administration's resource policies. The agenda included broad policy goals that promoted the use of the environment for social and economic well-being; the identification and wise use of technologies that work in productive harmony with nature; public awareness; the discouraging of extremist attitudes toward resource use and protection; and sensitivity toward natural and human values. Specifically, movement leaders sought to have control and management of public lands turned over to state or county officials rather than being retained by the federal government. They believed that local citizens know more about the "wise use" of land and resources than does a distant Washington bureaucracy. This is especially true in the West, where wise-use advocates believed the "public" has the right to use "public lands" as it sees fit.

The Wise-Use Controversy

After the agenda was issued environmental organizations began to criticize the wise-use movement and its leaders. They argued that the umbrella organizations that served as the connections among wise-use advocates were actually front groups funded by extractive industries, thinly disguised as grassroots organizations, or connected to Eastern religious sects. The wise-use movement's leaders, such as Alan Gottlieb and Ron Arnold of the Center for the Defense of Free Enterprise, were both charismatic and controversial as they traveled around the United States seeking support for the movement's goals. Criticism was also directed at individual organizations such as the Blue Ribbon Coalition and the Alliance for America, whose names, environmental groups believed, were not indicative of their true purpose of resource development. Others tried to connect wise-use advocates to militia organizations. Bill Clinton's presidential election in 1992 virtually ended their hope for legislative success as the new president embarked upon a more moderate environmental agenda than those of his predecessors. What little momentum wise-use leaders had under Reagan and Bush has never returned.

Movement Strategies

The wise-use movement may have become so controversial because of the success it once had in mobilizing its membership. Those who supported the Wise Use Agenda were well connected through the Internet and through the organizations to which they belonged. They could be quickly informed about pending legislation that affected their interests and kept abreast of key issues through facsimile machines and direct mail campaigns. The Wise Use Agenda had also expanded to include groups previously working outside the movement, such as fish processors, shrimpers along the Gulf Coast, motorcycle clubs (including the radical Sahara Club), and those opposed to gun control or supportive of private property rights. Although the wise-use groups could never point to any major legislative successes, some note that they were, at least for a short time, effective in gaining a seat at the policy table as part of the natural resources debate. They achieved legitimacy in some sectors of government, although at best, they may be said to have stalled, rather than rolled back, environmental legislation. Groups such as People for the West, for instance, played a key role in influencing the development of the comprehensive planning document, Yellowstone Vision for the Future in 1990–1991 and developed a persuasive message on public lands use that brought support from western ranchers, mining interests, and recreationists. But the group, which changed its name to "People for the USA," folded in 2001 when it ran out of funds. Other groups closed their doors as the momentum of the early 1990s began to wane.

A number of changes occurred during the administrations of Bill Clinton and George W. Bush. Several watchdog organizations were established or expanded to monitor wise-use groups and their activities, such as the Clearinghouse on Environmental Advocacy and Research (CLEAR) and Political Research Associates. Wise-use advocates began to characterize their membership as richly diverse, although the groups were still more active in the West than in other regions of the country, especially when the interests of rural residents collided with urban and suburban values. The concept of wise use is now often referred to as "environmental backlash" to encompass a broader spectrum of issues and advocates. Under President George W. Bush those advocates have found support in the administration's appointments to the Department of Interior, the Department of Agriculture, and other key natural resource agencies and commissions.

From the perspective of grassroots activism, the wise-use movement has certainly not kept pace with Americans' enduring values of environmental protection and wilderness preservation, and one Sierra Club article noted that few "foot soldiers" are left. It remains a movement that shadows the ups and downs of partisan politics, gaining momentum during times of conservative political power and subsiding periodically, as it did after the Sagebrush Rebellions and the Clinton administration.

Jacqueline Vaughn

Further Reading

Arnold, R., & Gottlieb, A. (1994). *Trashing the economy: How runaway environmentalism is wrecking America* (2nd ed.). Bellevue, WA: Free Enterprise Press.

Brick, P. D., & McGreggor Cawley, R. (Eds.). (1996). *A wolf in the garden: The lands rights movement and the new environmental debate.* Lanham, MD: Rowman and Littlefield.

Echeverria, J., & Booth Ely, R. B. (Eds.). (1995). *Let the people judge: Wise use and the private property rights movement.* Washington, DC: Island Press.

Gottlieb, A. (Ed.). (1989). *The wise use agenda: A task force report sponsored by the wise use movement.* Bellevue, WA: Free Enterprise Press.

Helvarg. D. (1994). *The war against the Greens: The "wise use" movement, the new right, and anti-environmental violence.* San Francisco: Sierra Club Books.

Switzer, J. V. (1997). *Green backlash: The history and politics of environmental opposition in the U.S.* Boulder, CO: Lynne Rienner.

Women and Conservation

Women who are active in conserving natural resources live on every continent. At the turn of the twentieth century, during the conservation movement of the Progressive Era, the goals of members of women's clubs in the United States were to protect forests and watersheds and to guarantee the preservation of the country's unique landscapes. By mid-twentieth century women in the United States advocated the creation and monitoring of public lands as a means to support conservation. Women in other developed countries supported efforts to create sustainable agricultural and forestry practices. By the end of the century women in developing countries were joining in such indigenous efforts as the greenbelt movement in Kenya to plant trees to reverse the desertification of their land.

In the United States the General Federation of Women's Clubs (GFWC) organized its Forestry Division in 1902 and for a time reported to the male-dominated American Forestry Association and Conservation Congress about women's work in conserving forests and protecting watersheds. The GFWC supported the Minnesota Federation of Women's Clubs in saving the state's Chippewa Forest Reserve, the California Federation in establishing Big Basin State Park to protect a grove of redwoods, and the passage of the federal Weeks Bill in 1911 to establish national forests in the East. The Louisiana Federation led in the development of the Waterways Committee that spawned water conservation projects in thirty-nine states with goals of protecting pure drinking water and clean waterfronts.

Inspired by the California Federation, members of the GFWC—by then numbering 800,000 women—broke with the American Forestry Association over the issue of the preservation of Hetch Hetchy Valley in Yosemite National Park. The women joined naturalist John Muir in unsuccessfully opposing a plan to create a reservoir for the city of San Francisco in that valley. GFWC members responded to the loss by putting their efforts behind what they called "the conservation of natural scenery" and the development of national parks. Under the direction of GFWC president Mary

Belle King Sherman, they lobbied Congress to pass the bill that established the National Park Service in 1916.

Preservation of Species

American women of the early twentieth century also led in the preservation of bird and plant species. Women of the Audubon societies faced an issue with women's fashionable hats. The use of bird feathers as decoration, in particular the "aigrette" feathers from snowy egrets and great white herons, threatened those birds with extinction. Mabel Osgood Wright, president of the Connecticut Audubon Society and editor of *Bird Lore*, organized the secretaries of the initial nineteen state Audubon societies, who were all women but one, to campaign against the practice and to support protective legislation.

In the 1930s and 1940s Rosalie Edge broke with the National Audubon Society to form the Emergency Conservation Committee (ECC) to publish pamphlets condemning actions that threatened conservation. She believed that the National Audubon Society's alliance with hunters made the Society oppose a federal bag limit on migratory birds and accept the practice of baiting ducks. The ECC's efforts stopped park rangers from controlling the white pelican population in Yellowstone National Park, protected a grove of sugar pines in Yosemite National Park, and rescued old-growth forests by helping to develop a constituency to create Olympic National Park.

The women-run Garden Club of America, organized nationally in 1913, supported the work of state and local garden clubs to protect native plants and birds. Minerva Hamilton Hoyt, conservation chair of the California Garden Club, protected desert plants by her drive to establish Joshua Tree National Monument in 1936. In the 1940s the Garden Club of America organized its eight thousand members to oppose mining in Organ Pipe Cactus National Monument in Arizona and the lumbering of virgin timber in Olympic National Park. Later they joined the successful protest against building Echo Park Dam in Dinosaur National Monument in Utah and Colorado.

By midcentury one of the ways by which U.S. women preserved species and landscapes was to seek federal and state protection of public lands in addition to monitoring existing public lands. Marjory Stoneman Douglas became a spokesperson for the importance of the Florida Everglades as a habitat for vanishing species. Bettie Willard and Estella Leopold helped establish Florissant fossil beds in Colorado to save a deposit of fossils that are 38 million years old. Among women who organized to protect the shorelines of the Great Lakes by working to establish state and national parks were Genevieve Gillette in Michigan and Dorothy Buell, president of the Save the Dunes Council in Indiana. Biologist Liane Russell organized the Tennessee Citizens for Wilderness Planning to keep dams out of wild rivers in Tennessee. Members of the Ohio League of Women Voters, shocked by the fires that erupted from the oil and debris in the Cuyahoga River, put their membership behind establishing a national park in the Cuyahoga Valley. Hundreds of women worked to protect the Alaskan wilderness by lobbying for the Alaska Lands Bill passed in 1980. They included the long-time environmentalist Margaret E. Murie and the Alaskan Celia Hunter, the first woman president of the Wilderness Society.

Developing Countries

By the late twentieth century the conservation ethic was also well established in developing countries. Women's concerns stemmed from their need to provide food, fuel, and water for their families and communities in a sustainable way. In Kenya, Wangari Maathai founded the greenbelt movement in 1977 to transform women from "tree killers" into "tree planters" (Vollers 1988, 11). Within ten years more than five hundred communities had developed tree nurseries, and twenty-five thousand households had established wood lots. Women in Ghana in Africa conserved wood by developing a device for smoking fish that uses one-tenth as much wood as before, and women of the Chipko ("hug a tree") movement in the Himalayan region of India filed a successful suit to shut down limestone mines that were denuding hillsides.

In 2001 the World Wildlife Fund (WWF) instituted its Women and Conservation Initiative to offer grants, training, and technical assistance to women in conservation in addition to giving annual awards for accomplishments. For the first awards, WWF selected Meidi Kasmidi from Sulawesi, Indonesia, who worked to establish Bunaken Marine Park and introduce concepts of marine conservation to fishers outside the park, and Mauricia Gonzalez Garcia from Chiapas, Mexico, whose organization, Linea Biosfera, has trained a network of advocates in agro-ecology, human rights, and health in ten Central American communities.

Polly Welts Kaufman

See also Chipko; Douglas, Marjorie Stone; Wright, Mabel Osgood

Further Reading

Englehardt, N. (2001) *World Wildlife Fund acknowledges women's contribution to conservation*. Retrieved June 20, 2001, from http://www.worldwildlife.org

Kaufman, P. W. (1996). *National parks and the woman's voice: A history*. Albuquerque: University of New Mexico Press.

Maathai, W. (1988). *The green belt movement: Sharing the approach and the experience*. Nairobi, Kenya: Environment Liaison Centre International.

Merchant, C. (1996). *Earthcare: Women and the environment*. New York: Routledge.

Norwood, V. (1993). *Made from this Earth: American women and nature*. Chapel Hill: University of North Carolina Press.

Shiva, V. (1988). *Staying alive: Women, ecology, and development*. London: Zed Books.

Vollers, M. (1988). Healing the ravaged land. *International Wildlife, 18*(1), 4–9.

Wood

Ancient writers observed that forests always recede as civilizations grow. The Roman poet Ovid wrote, for example, that during the "Golden Age," before civilization began, "even the pine tree stood on its own hills" but that when the Iron Age began, "the mountain oak, the pine were felled" (Ovid 1976, 1.94–1.95). This change occurred because wood has been the principal fuel and building material for almost every society for over five thousand years, from the Copper Age until the middle of the nineteenth century. Without access to vast supplies of wood, the great civilizations of Sumer, Assyria, Egypt, China, Knossos (in ancient Crete), ancient Greece and Rome, western Europe, and the Western Hemisphere after European settlement would have never emerged. Wood, in fact, is the unsung hero of the technological revolution that has brought civilization from a stone-and-bone culture to the present age.

Wood before Civilization

As important as wood has been in the development of civilization, it played an even more important role in human evolution. Wood provided some of the first humans, *Homo erectus*, with fuel for fire. The discovery of how to make fire from wood allowed *Homo erectus*, from which *Homo sapiens* evolved, to migrate from the ubiquitous warmth of their original equatorial habitat in Africa to lands throughout the Old World, where heat from fire made these colder climates habitable. Fire released *Homo erectus* from restraints of climate, allowing the species to create its own indoors. Increasing the range of habitat gave the genus better odds for survival. Light from wood fires permitted *Homo erectus* to continue working after nightfall. Hence, the discovery liberated humanity from the confines of night. Wood fires also diversified the diet of *Homo erectus*. Armed with torches, *Homo erectus* hunted at night with more effective fire-hardened wooden spears. Nor did these ancestors have to live by the vagaries of game because vegetable matter like tubers, when cooked over fire, became eatable as well. Hence, fire gave humanity an enhanced degree of stability. Fire also provided humans with greater security because they could sleep at night knowing that its flames warded off predators and lessened the danger of stepping on venomous snakes or tripping over rocks by improving vision at night. The availability of wood fuel changed not only the social evolution of the human genus but also its physical development. Cooking-softened food led to smaller molars. Although many animals like the chimpanzee and otter have used tools to aid in their pursuit of food, no other animal except for those in the genus from *Homo erectus* to *Homo sapiens* has ever built fires.

The Uses of Wood

Wood, as humanity's principal fuel for fire, has allowed the human species to reshape the Earth for its use. With heat from wood fires, humanity has settled throughout the globe, making even very cold regions habitable. Grains became edible when cooked over wood fires. Agriculture could then spread, resulting in settlements that grew from isolated rural houses to great cities. In charcoal-fueled kilns where temperatures rose above 900° C, potters could change earth into durable ceramics to store and ship goods. Metallurgists stoked charcoal fires to extract metal from stone. They revolutionized tools and weaponry to such a degree that historians categorize the various ages of civilization according to the dominant metal in use at the time.

Transportation—and, by extension, trade—the accumulation of wealth, exploration, and colonization would have been unthinkable without wood. From the Bronze Age until the two ironclad ships clashed by Hampton Roads, Virginia, in 1862, almost every ship, whether involved in commerce or war, was built with timber. Carts, chariots, and wagons were also built primarily of wood. Early steamboats and railroad locomotives in the United States ran on wood fuel. Wooden ships tied up to wooden piers and wharves. Wooden carts, chariots, and wagons crossed wooden bridges and, in the United States during the nineteenth century, traveled on wooden roads. Railroad ties, of course, were wooden.

Wood was also used for the beams that propped up mine shafts and supported almost every type of building. Waterwheels and windmills—the major means of mechanical power before steam was harnessed—were usually built of wood. The peasant could not farm without wooden tool handles or wood plows; the soldier could not throw his spear or shoot his arrows without their wooden shafts; he could not hold his gun without its wooden stock. What would archers have done lacking wood for bows; the brewer and vintner, lacking wood for their barrels and casks; or the woolen industry, lacking wood for its looms?

Recognizing the Importance of Wood

Great thinkers in times past recognized their society's debt to wood as its principal building block. The Greek philosopher Plato, according to Diogenes Laertius, wrote that all technology was derived from mining and forestry. Lucretius, one of the foremost Roman philosophers, argued that wood made mining, and as a result, civilization, possible. Great fires, according to Lucretius, "devoured the high forests and thoroughly heated the earth," melting metal from ore. When people came to observe the burned-down forest and saw the solidified metal lying on the ground, "the thought came to them," Lucretius continued, "that these pieces could be made liquid again by fire and cast into the form and shape of anything, and then by hammering, could be drawn into the form of blades as sharp and thin as one pleased so they might equip themselves with tools. . . ." Tools, in turn, Lucretius concluded, made forestry and carpentry possible, enabling humans "to cut forests, hew timber, smooth, and even fashion it with auger, chisel and gouge" (Lucretius 1997, 5.1255–1268). In this way, Lucretius surmised, civilization emerged.

Pliny, the great Roman natural historian, concurred with Lucretius's judgment that wood was "indispensable for carrying on life" (Pliny 1938–1963, 12.5). The Roman statesman Cicero explained the importance of

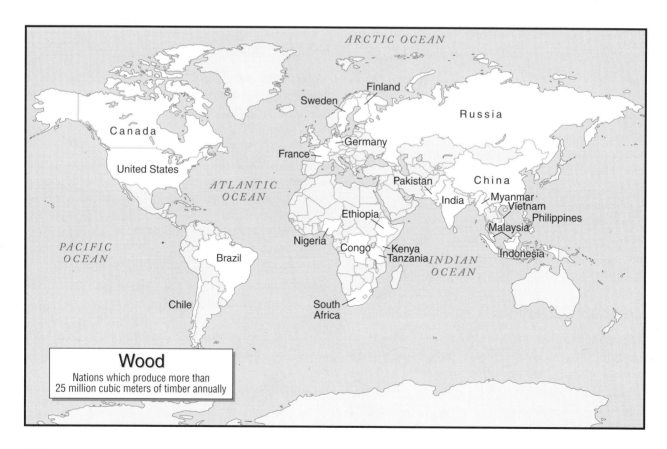

wood to Roman civilization when he wrote, "We cut up trees to cook our food . . . for building . . . to keep out heat and cold . . . and also to build ships, which sail in all directions to bring us all the needs of life" (Cicero 1997, 2.150–151).

Respected commentators of life in later times also talked about the importance of wood for their societies. Arab philosopher Ibn Khaldun, writing in the fourteenth century CE, discussed the crucial role wood played in the medieval Muslim world. "God made all created things useful for humanity," Khaldun wrote in his major work, the *Muqaddimah*, "so as to supply all their necessities and needs. Trees belong among these things. They have innumerable uses for everyone. Wood gives people fuel to make fires," which, in Khaldun's estimation, they "need to survive. Bedouins use wood for tent poles and pegs, for came litters for their women, and for the lances, bows, and arrows they use for weapons," while "sedentary people use wood for the roofs of their houses, for the locks for their doors, and the chairs on which they sit." Therefore, the carpenter "is necessary to civilization" (Ibn Khaldun 1958, 2.363–364).

The government of the Venetian Republic, once the world's major maritime power, acknowledged its debt to wood for the development and hegemony of the Venetian state. As a nation whose wealth was based on sea power, Venice regarded its forests as "the very sinews of the Republic" (Perlin 1991, 152).

The English of the sixteenth and seventeenth centuries also recognized the crucial role of wood in their lives. Gabriel Plattes, who wrote on technological matters in the seventeenth century, observed that all "tools and instruments" used in Europe at that time "are made of wood and iron." But of the two materials, Plattes deemed wood as more crucial because without wood fuel, "no iron," the principal metal of that time, "can be provided" (Plattes 1639, 9). Likewise, the English of that age realized their dependence on wood for trade and navigation that gave the nation preeminence both commercially and economically. As one naval official declared, "As the Navy hath no being without ships, so no ships without timber" (Perlin 1991, 30).

Leading officials of the new American nation quickly realized the importance of forests to the development of the country. Alexander Hamilton, in his *Report on Manufactures*, informed the American people of their good fortune to have both iron "in great abundance" and cheap and plentiful supplies of charcoal, "the chief instrument in manufacturing it" (Hamilton 1961–1987, 10.314). Tench Coxe, a close friend of Thomas Jefferson and James Madison as well as an economic writer in his own right, made a similar observation in the 1790s that the new nation's great forests would provide the young country with an "immense and unequalled" store of "wooden raw materials and fuel for invaluable and numerous manufactures" (Coxe 1794, 450–451). James Hall's seminal work on pioneer society in the Ohio River valley showed how those settling in lands west of the Allegheny Mountains relied almost entirely on indigenous timber for all their needs. Not only did these pioneers use wood for building houses, bridges, and fencing and for fuel, but also they substituted, according to Hall, wooden pins for iron nails, curbed wells with hollow logs, had their doors "swinging on wooden hinges" as well as fastened with a wooden latch." Because pioneers so often used wood in place of "stone, iron and even leather," the American frontier, according to Hall, could indeed be called "a wooden country" (Hall 1836, 101).

Wood and Language

Language through the ages also demonstrates the important role that wood played in the lives of human ancestors. The Sumerians, who established the first written language more than four thousand years ago, used the cuneiform sign "gis" as the root for building words relating to wood. These words included *plan, model,* and *archetype. Architectron,* which in classical Greece came to mean "chief builder" and is the word from which *architect* comes, originally meant "leading wood worker." The Romans used the expression "carrying a load of timber to the forest" to signify a redundant act, similar to the English expression "carrying coals to Newcastle"—which came into being when coal replaced wood as England's principal fuel and Newcastle was the regional center where most of England's coal was found. For the ancient Greeks and Romans the words meaning "wood"—*hulae* and *materia*—came to mean "primary matter." The merging of these two meanings suggests that people living in classical times regarded wood as the basic material from which everything else was derived. The word *legno,* "wood" in Italian, could also be used for "ship" in the days when timber was used for shipbuilding. Trees were so important to life in ancient Ireland that the old names of the letters in the Irish alphabet were names of trees, beginning with *alim* (elm), *beith* (birch), *coll* (hazel), *dair* (oak), and so on.

John Evelyn, a leading figure in seventeenth-century England, summed up the significance of wood to past societies with the observation that "all arts and artisans"—technology—"must fail and cease if there were no timber and wood. . . ." Evelyn did not resort to hyperbole when he stated that the England of his day would be better off "without gold than without timber" (Evelyn 1786, 2.216).

By the beginning of the nineteenth century wood started to lose its crucial role in the evolution of civilization. Beginning in England in the late eighteenth century, the transition from charcoal to coal in iron smelting allowed Western society to begin freeing itself from the fetters of wood. No longer dependent on scarce wood for fuel, iron production in Great Britain mushroomed, and Great Britain soon became the leading industrial power of the nineteenth-century world. Other European nations soon followed England's lead. The availability of iron to build all sorts of machinery and the availability of seemingly unlimited coal to power them ushered in a new era qualitatively separating those people living since the middle of the nineteenth century from the rest of history. This new age of unprecedented growth is called the "Industrial Revolution."

The naval clash in 1862 between the first two iron-clad warships off the eastern American coast put an end to an era—dating back to ancient Egypt—of society's reliance on wooden ships for commerce and war. Hence, with wooden ships made obsolete by that one clash, wood lost its geopolitical importance. Ironically, the force that relegated wood to just another commodity—the rise in importance of fossil fuels and iron—increased qualitatively society's demand for wood and its ability to meet this demand. The Industrial Revolution greatly enlarged the consumer base for paper products ranging from books and newspapers to toilet paper. It also greatly increased population and its wealth, resulting in increased house construction and therefore stimulating a growing need for lumber products. Machinery made from iron and powered by fossil fuels has provided these wood products in ever-greater amounts by revolutionizing access to the forest, transport of wood to points of manufacture, and delivery of finished products to consumers.

John Perlin

Further Reading

Cicero. (1997). *The Nature of the gods* (H. Rackham, Trans.). New York: Garland.
Coxe, T. (1794). *A view of the United States of America*. Philadelphia: William Hall.
Drushka, K., & Konttinen, H. (1997). *Tracks in the forest*. Helsinki, Finland: Harbour Publishing Company.
Evelyn, J. (1786). *Silva*. York, UK: A. Ward for J. Dodsey.
Hall, J. (1836). *Statistics of the West at the close of the year 1836*. Cincinnati, OH: J. A. James.
Hamilton, A. (1961–1987). *Papers* (H. Syrett, Ed.). New York: Columbia University Press.
Khaldun, I. (1958). *Muqaddimah* [An introduction to history]. New York: Pantheon.
Lucretius. (1997). *On the nature of the universe* (R. Melville, Trans.). New York: Oxford University Press.
Nef, J. (1923). *The rise of the British coal industry*. London: Cass.
Ovid. (1976). *Metamorphoses* (G. Sandys, Trans.). New York: Garland.
Perlin, J. (1991). *A forest journey: The role of wood in the development of civilization*. Cambridge, MA: Harvard University Press.
Plattes, G. (1639). *A discovery of infinite treasure hidden since the world's beginning*. Amsterdam: Theatrum Orbis Terrarum.
Pliny the Elder. (1938–1963). *Natural history* (H. Rackham, Trans.). Cambridge, MA: Harvard University Press.
Tucker, R. P., & Richards, J. F. (Eds.). (1983). *Global deforestation and the nineteenth-century world economy*. Durham, NC: Duke University Press.

World Bank

The World Bank is a group of multilateral lending organizations that forms the major source of financial assistance to more than one hundred developing countries. The World Bank was established at an international conference held in Bretton Woods, New Hampshire, in 1944, with the goal of supporting recovery of nations affected by World War II. Within a few years the goal had broadened to one of financing economic development of poor countries. The International Monetary Fund (IMF), established at the same time, works to stabilize currency exchange throughout the world.

The main organizations that make up the World Bank, based in Washington, D.C., are the International Bank for Reconstruction and Development (IBRD), and the International Development Association (IDA). The IDA makes loans on favorable terms to the poorest countries, allowing long repayment and low interest. The IDA was founded in 1960 and is supported by funds from donor countries, whereas the IBRD charges market interest rates and is expected to pay its own way.

Together the IBRD and IDA made new loans totaling over $17 billion in 2001. That amount understates the true influence of the World Bank because the willingness of the World Bank to make loans to a project reassures individuals and private banks that invest additional money. Another member of the World Bank group, the Multilateral Investment Guarantee Agency (MIGA), insures multinational corporations against political risks when they invest in developing countries. Through MIGA the bank attempts to exert some leverage to protect the environment, for example, by putting pressure on a mine in Indonesia that dumps its wastes into the river.

The first environmental advisor at the World Bank was appointed in 1971 but had relatively little influence over projects supported by the bank. It was only in 1989 that all projects were required to undergo an environmental assessment and that substantial time was devoted to environmental concerns. The pressure to improve the bank's environmental record came from environmental organizations that publicized the damage to tropical forests and indigenous people caused by large projects such as Polonoroeste in Brazil, which opened roads into Amazonia. Another project that was subjected to criticism was the huge Sardar Sarovar dam in the Narmada Valley of India. As a result, its World Bank funding was withdrawn in 1993 while it was still under construction.

Ironically, just as the environmental assessment of World Bank projects was becoming well accepted, less bank money was going to specific projects and more to structural adjustment loans (loans given only if the government of the recipient country is willing to undertake reforms of its economy along free market principles). These loans went into countries' general budgets and were not subject to environmental assessment. The stringent conditions of structural adjustment affected the environment in many ways, such as encouraging indebted countries to export their natural capital of forests and minerals. Environmental economists, anthropologists, and ecologists on the bank staff, notably Herman Daly, Michael Cernea, and Robert Goodland, attempted to "green" their colleague economists, but the basic purpose of the bank, to promote economic growth, seemed to many environmentalists to be at odds with the long-term survival of life on the planet.

Popular resistance to the effects of economic globalization led to protests against global financial institutions, including the Jubilee 2000 movement that proposed forgiving the debts of the most heavily indebted nations. Although the World Bank has been at the environmental cutting edge among the various agencies that provide development funding, because it is the biggest and most visible, it has also been at the center of protest.

Patricia K. Townsend

Further Reading

Cobb, J. B. (1999). *The earthist challenge to economism: A theological critique of the World Bank.* New York: St. Martin's.

George, S., & Sabelli, F. (1994). *Faith and credit: The World Bank's secular empire.* Boulder, CO: Westview.

Goodland, R. (2000). *Social and environmental assessment to promote sustainability: An informal view from the World Bank* (Environment Department paper No. 74). Retrieved June 28, 2002, from http://www.wds.worldbank.org

Rich, B. (1994). *Mortgaging the earth: The World Bank, environmental impoverishment, and the crisis of development.* Boston: Beacon Press.

Wade, R. (1997). Greening the bank: The struggle over the environment, 1970–1995. In D. Kapur (Ed.). *The World Bank: Its first half-century: Vol. 2. Perspectives* (pp. 611–734). Washington, DC: Brookings Institution.

World Wildlife Fund

Founded as a charity in 1961 in Switzerland by scientists and conservationists who were alarmed at the rate at which wild animal species were disappearing, especially in Africa, the World Wildlife Fund (WWF) has become one of the world's largest independent organizations dedicated to the conservation of nature. The mission of the World Wildlife Fund (WWF) is to build a future in which humans live in greater harmony with nature. In particular, the WWF works to promote activities that help to conserve the world's biological diversity, ensure that the use of renewable natural resources is sustainable, and reduce waste and pollution.

The WWF now operates in around a hundred countries, and its panda logo is one of the most widely known logos in the world. Since 1961, the WWF's work has broadened from the conservation of specific animals and plants threatened with extinction to general environmental protection.

The WWF claims to have around 5 million supporters spread across all continents. It has over twenty-eight national organizations. Since its inception the WWF has invested in more than 13,000 projects in 157 countries. All these play a part in the campaign to stop the accelerating degradation of Earth's natural environment.

In partnership with the International Union for the Conservation of Nature (IUCN) and the United Nations Environment Programme (UNEP), the WWF produced *The World Conservation Strategy* in 1980, one of the first major statements of how social development and environmental protection might harmonize. Since then, some fifty countries have formulated and initiated their own national conservation strategies, based on its recommendations. By the mid-1980s, the WWF felt that it needed to change its name from World Wildlife Fund to the World Wide Fund for Nature in order to reflect its broadened range of concerns; now it is known simply as WWF. The United States and Canada, however, retained the old name.

The WWF has tended to take a less critical view of business and government than many environmental organizations. This stance, the WWF would argue, enables it to maintain a dialogue with business and political leaders. The WWF has tried to build links with religious organizations as well.

The WWF played a significant role in building an international consensus to protect whales and has fought hard against the destruction of elephant populations by ivory poachers. It has also played a major part in the promotion of so-called debt-for-nature swaps, under which a portion of a country's foreign debt is converted into funds for conservation.

In 1991, the WWF, IUCN, and UNEP joined forces again to publish *Caring for the Earth: A Strategy for Sustainable Living*. It lists 132 actions people at all social and political levels can take to enhance their environment while simultaneously increasing the quality of their life. In the later 1990s, the WWF began to focus its activities on three key areas: forests, freshwater ecosystems, and oceans and coasts. The organization seems set to play a major role in future conservation efforts.

Sandy Irvine

Further Reading

WWF. (2002). *WWF Global Network.* Retrieved May 29, 2002, from http://www.panda.org

Wright, Mabel Osgood
(1859–1934)
Nature writer and conservationist

Mabel Osgood Wright was not only one of the most popular woman nature writers of the Progressive Era, but also one of its most influential woman conservationists. The author of more than twenty-five works of fiction and nonfiction, Wright founded the Connecticut Audubon Society, served as associate editor of *Bird-Lore* magazine (now *Audubon*), helped to organize one of the first privately owned bird sanctuaries in the United States, and educated thousands of children in the art and science of nature study.

Born in New York City to Samuel Osgood (1812–1880), a Unitarian minister, and Ellen Haswell Murdock, Wright was raised in the family's Greenwich Village home and educated at Miss Lucy Green's school for girls at 1 Fifth Avenue. Her father, the influential pastor of the Church of the Messiah, introduced Wright to William Cullen Bryant, Oliver Wendell Holmes, and other prominent literary figures, and he also encouraged her interest in nature, which she developed during regular visits to the family's summer home in Fairfield, Connecticut. After her 1884 marriage to James Osborne Wright (1852–1920), a rare book dealer, Wright began living much of the year in Fairfield, where she watched the small, coastal New England town gradually become a suburb of New York City.

Wright's nature writing included natural history essays, field guides, children's books, and garden books. Her first major publication, *The Friendship of Nature* (1894), collected her essays on the birds and flowers surrounding her Fairfield home. It was hailed by readers and critics alike as a sensitive and accurate portrayal of the Connecticut landscape. Equal acclaim was accorded to Wright's two field guides: *Birdcraft* (1895), which became the leading guide to bird identification until the publication of Roger Tory Peterson's *Field Guide to the Birds* (1934), and *Flowers and Ferns in Their Haunts* (1901), a companion guide to plant life. Her writing for children included works of nature fiction, such as *Tommy-Anne and the Three Hearts* (1896), and introductions to bird and animal life, such as *Citizen Bird* (1897), written with the naturalist Elliott Coues. Of Wright's fictional works for adults, the most popular were her semiautobiographical books—written under the pseudonym "Barbara"—which contained various nature observations and gardening tips. The best of these is *The Garden of a Commuter's Wife* (1901).

A Selection from Mabel Osgood Wright's *The Friendship of Nature*

A morning in winter; can there be morning in the dead season? There is no dead season. Men say that it is summer, or autumn, or winter, but Nature has set no fixed bounds to her actions, and does not perish when she casts off her apparel, but, gathering her forces to herself, prepares for new effort. Nature knows but two changes, putting forth and withdrawing, and between these there is a constant transition. We call the first of them birth, the last, death, and choose to surround them with mystery. Nature, left to herself, has gentle gradations, blending all from the first breath to the last, as she mingles the prismatic colours, with no gap to measure where youth ends or age begins. We fasten attributes to things, and hold them there by mere persistency. There is no really dead season; there are no snows so deep but somewhere in the firs the crossbill holds his sign of the sacred legend, no ice so thick but under it the warm current stirs, no age so dreary that love may not quicken it until eternal spring.

Source: Wright, M. O. (1999). *The friendship of nature: A New England chronicle of birds and flowers* (D. J. Philippon, Ed.). Baltimore: Johns Hopkins University Press. (Original work published 1894)

As a conservationist, Wright sought to protect endangered songbirds, educate children about suburban nature, and encourage other women to do the same. In 1898 she founded the Audubon Society of the State of Connecticut (now the Connecticut Audubon Society) and served as its first president until 1925. She also served on the board of directors of the National Association of Audubon Societies (now the National Audubon Society) from its organization in 1905 until 1928; worked as associate editor of *Bird-Lore* from 1899 to 1911; and in 1914 helped create Fairfield's Birdcraft Sanctuary, a wildlife refuge that is still an active facility of the Connecticut Audubon Society. Wright died at home and was buried with her husband at Oaklawn Cemetery in Fairfield. She had no children.

Daniel J. Philippon

Further Reading

Barrow, M. V. (1998). *A passion for birds: American ornithology after Audubon*. Princeton, NJ: Princeton University Press.

Doughty, R. W. (1975). *Feather fashions and bird preservation: A study in nature protection*. Berkeley: University of California Press.

Gibbons, F., & Strom, D. (1998). *Neighbors to the bird: A history of birdwatching in America*. New York: W. W. Norton.

Norwood, V. (1993). *Made from this earth: American women and nature*. Chapel Hill: University of North Carolina Press.

Wright, M. O. (1999). *The friendship of nature: A New England chronicle of birds and flowers* (D. J. Philippon, Ed.). Baltimore: Johns Hopkins University Press. (Original work published 1894)

Y

Yam

The yam, *Dioscorea batatas*, is a member of the Dioscoreaceae family of tropical and subtropical herbs and shrubs with starchy rhizomes, which has been cultivated for food since prehistoric times. Yam plants have climbing stems, leaves, flowers, and fleshy tubers that can grow up to 2.1 meters in length and weigh up to 54 kilograms. The yam tuber, the edible part of the plant, has a dark brown or black scaly skin that resembles the bark of a tree and off-white, golden, red, or purple flesh, depending on the variety. Yams thrive in the warm, frost-free, tropical climates of South America, Africa, and the Caribbean and are rarely found in American markets. Only one species, *Dioscorea rotundata*, is grown around the world. Yams are often identified by their Spanish names, *boniato* and *ñame*, and by their Japanese name, *daisho*. Although more than six hundred species of yams exist, only six are edible.

Civilizations have long cultivated the yam. More than fifty thousand years ago, the yam was domesticated simultaneously in different places, including parts of Africa, South America, and tropical Asia, where it became a staple of subsistence agriculture. West African artifacts depict the yam on pottery. In east Africa during the first centuries of the common era, Bantu peoples practiced forest agriculture based on the yam. The word *yam*, in fact, derives from the African verbs *njam*, *nyami*, or *djambi*, which all mean "to eat." Today the yam still holds tremendous economic and symbolic importance in African culture. Western Africa (Cameroon, Nigeria, Benin, Togo, Ghana, and Ivory Coast), for example, produces 90 percent of the world's yams, and 95 percent of all yams are grown in sub-Saharan Africa. In parts of Nigeria and Ghana, villagers celebrate the annual yam festival of Iri-ji ("new yam eating") to thank their ancestral gods for a new harvest. The yam is also a powerful marriage symbol in parts of African culture.

The yam is commonly mistaken for the sweet potato, a member of the morning glory family that originated in Peru and Ecuador in prehistoric times. The yam and sweet potato, however, are not even distantly related. The existence of the yam was mistakenly recorded in North America in 1676 by African slaves, who called the American sweet potato by its African names. Indeed, the African presence in the American South made the sweet potato—which reminded blacks of the African yam—a crucial food in southern cuisine. Yams, however, contain more natural sugar than sweet potatoes, have higher moisture contents, take much longer to mature, and can be stored much longer—up to six months.

Besides culinary, economic, and cultural value, the yam has many medicinal uses. Since 1850, species in the *Dioscorea* genus, including some edible yams, have been used to treat abdominal pain, rheumatoid arthritis, and muscular rheumatism. In 1942 American Russell Macherane extracted diosgenin, a female hormone precursor, from one yam species and converted it into progesterone, facilitating the development of the birth control pill. The yam has many experimental medical uses as well.

Jessica Teisch

Further Reading

Degras, L. (1993). *The yam: A tropical root crop*. London: Macmillan.

Marking Out the Yam Field

The yam is a major crop for many farming people in Africa, such as the Tiv described below, who each year carefully mark out their fields.

In the Kparev lineages, the compound head first of all himself erects one large yam heap on which he will then erect an *akombo*, or magical emblem. This mound, with the *akombo* set either on it or just in front of it, is the centre point of the top (*ityough*) side of the field of the senior woman of the compound, usually the mother or wife of the compound head. He then takes 58 (more or less) paces in a straight line to the bottom (*ityo*) of the field and marks the spot.

Most Tiv say that yam mounds should be one pace (32–33 inches) apart, and that there should be 58 mounds in a row (*iba*); hence the compound head should take 58 steps. There is some variation in the number of mounds said to compose a row; though the most common number is 58, the range is from 50 to 80. There is, of course, even greater variation in the number of heaps actually found in rows.

Source: Bohannan, Paul. (1954). *Tiv Farm and Settlement*. London: Her Majesty's Stationery Office, p. 16.

Dounias, E. (2001, March). The management of wild yam tubers by the Baka pygmies in southern Cameroon. *African Study Monographs, Suppl. 26*, 135–156.

Gebremeskel, T. (1987). *Yam in Africa*. Ibadan, Nigeria: Socioeconomic Unit, International Institute of Tropical Agriculture.

Headland, T. N. (1987). The wild yam question: How well could independent hunter-gatherers live in a tropical rain forest ecosystem? *Human Ecology, 15* [4]463–491.

Onwueme, I. C. (1978). *The tropical tuber crops: Yam, cassava, sweet potato, and cocoyams*. New York: Wiley.

Yellow Sea

The Yellow Sea is a semi-enclosed sea bounded by China to the north and west, North and South Korea to the east, and the East China Sea to the south. It covers approximately 39 million hectares. The Yellow Sea is relatively shallow, with an average depth of 45 meters. The western coastal waters along China are marked by the two large delta systems of the Huang (Yellow) and Chang (Yangtze) Rivers, separated by the Shang-dung Peninsula. Along the coast of North and South Korea, the Yellow Sea has long stretches of tidal flats punctuated by numerous rocky islands and small river mouths. The seabed is mostly flat, featureless, and covered by large layers of sand and mud sediments from the Huang and Chang Rivers, which together deposit over 1.3 billion metric tons of sediment each year into the Yellow Sea.

The Yellow Sea has a rich variety of marine life, and more than one hundred species of commercially exploited fish live in its waters. Although fishing vessels have operated in the Yellow Sea for hundreds of years, large-scale commercial fishing increased significantly during the last decades of the twentieth century. By the mid-1980s almost 5 million metric tons of fish were taken each year from the Yellow Sea by boats operating out of China, North and South Korea, and Japan. The Yellow Sea also has large suspected offshore reserves of oil and gas, and all of its bordering countries have invested heavily in efforts to develop and exploit these reserves. In recent years parts of the Chinese and South Korean coastline have also grown into important centers for recreational tourism.

During the past two decades parts of the Yellow Sea have become heavily contaminated with a variety of pollutants. Although pollution levels in midocean are still relatively low, the coastal waters have experienced significant increases in heavy metals and chemical contamination as wastewater discharges from developing industrial centers in China and South Korea have risen sharply. The rapid expansion of urban areas in the region has also led to much higher quantities of untreated domestic sewage being funneled into the river systems that flow into the Yellow Sea. And rising levels of oil pollution, stemming from offshore drilling, increased marine transportation, and a series of accidents involving oil tankers, have begun to create problems for the area's fishing industry.

Efforts to encourage regional cooperation in addressing these problems have been hampered by political and economic disputes among the Yellow Sea's bordering countries. All of the Yellow Sea falls within the territorial claims of China, North Korea, and South Korea. However, in some cases these claims overlap, with disputes over contested areas of potential oil and gas reserves being the most contentious. Although the bordering countries have signed several bilateral agreements, efforts to develop a more cohesive, regional approach toward exploitation and preservation of Yellow Sea's natural resources have had only limited success.

James H. Lide

Further Reading

Cannon, T., & Jenkins, A. (Eds.). (1990). *The geography of contemporary China: The impact of Deng Xioping's decade.* New York: Routledge.

Chao, S. (1994). *Geography of China: Environment, resources, population, and development.* New York: John Wiley.

Edmonds, R. L. (1994). *Patterns of China's lost harmony: A survey of the country's environmental degradation and protection.* New York: Routledge.

Geping, Q., & Jinchang, L. (1994). *Population and the environment in China.* Boulder, CO: Lynne Rienner.

Leeming, F. (1993). *The changing geography of China.* Cambridge, MA: Blackwell.

Park, C., Kim, D., & Lee, S. (Eds.). (1990). *The regime of the Yellow Sea: Issues and policy options for cooperation in the changing environment.* Seoul, South Korea: Institute for East and West Studies, Yonsei University.

Z

Zebra Mussel

The most notorious "stowaway" to enter North America in a cargo ship's ballast water is the zebra mussel. More than any other species, this thumbnail-sized, black-and-white-striped freshwater mollusk has brought the growing economic and ecological problems stemming from invasive nonindigenous (exotic) species to American public and governmental attention, precipitating passage of the Nonindigenous Aquatic Species Nuisance Prevention and Control Act (1990). The mussel was largely confined to the Black, Aral, and Caspian Seas until canal construction and growing commerce in timber between Russia and western Europe facilitated expansion of its range as far as London by 1824. On the city's outskirts in 1912, 81 metric tons of the mussels were removed from a .4-kilometer stretch of unfiltered water main, which mussel encrustations had reduced from 1 meter to less than .3 meter in diameter. The first observers remarked on the mussel's ability to survive for weeks out of water, clinging to logs in the damp holds of timber ships. Elsewhere in Britain, a mollusk described by the first British observers as "tenacious and exceedingly prolific" completely plastered the walls of docks where timber was bonded and was transferred inland by barges to "pave and line" most British rivers and canals by the early 1840s.

The mussel's North American history replicated its European history. In 1988 specimens were detected in western Lake Erie and Lake St. Clair. (Because it was already so abundant, however, the mussel probably arrived in the larval stage in mid-decade, although the "culprit" ship was never traced.) Larvae were trans-

ported beyond these lakes by being carried in bait buckets and bilge water and by clinging to weeds entangled in boat propellers and boat trailers. By 1990 it was present throughout the Great Lakes, spreading to the Hudson, Mohawk, Ohio, and Mississippi River drainages at an expansion rate generally considered to be the fastest on record for an invasive exotic. Possessing filaments with a remarkable ability to attach themselves to solid surfaces, the mollusk can reach a density of 627,000 per square meter, a density unprecedented among native freshwater invertebrates such as clams. This filter feeder also removes plankton from the aquatic food web, thus altering basic energy flows and clarifying water. It has crowded out—and, in some cases, virtually wiped out—native bivalves. Moreover, the water intake systems of power plants designed to withstand earthquakes, fires, and floods are disabled by its "biofouling" impact. Attempted methods of control, including physical removal, high-pressure hosing with hot water, ultraviolet radiation, and chlorine dousing, have proved largely ineffectual.

In the mussel's defense, some biologists have stressed its water-purifying role, which has assisted in the reappearance of native plants in Lake Erie, and accumulations of its fecal matter have indirectly encouraged the revival of native fishes by providing a rich food source for the invertebrates they feed on.

Although the mussel is presently found from Quebec to Louisiana, European lessons may be worth heeding. In Europe the mussel has been mostly confined to lakes, rivers, and other waterways directly connected to infested waters. Expansion beyond has been slow. Because this pattern has been replicated in North America and because the belief that it takes only two specimens to create a viable population has been undermined (the "Noah fallacy"), biologists now debate whether birds' feet or boats' bottoms will be the most powerful mechanism of further dispersal. If studies indicate the predominance of natural mechanisms of dispersal, then the controversial regulation of boating and boat movements may be seen as redundant.

Peter Coates

Further Reading

D'Itri, F. M. (Ed.). (1997). *Zebra mussels and aquatic nuisance species*. Chelsea, MI: Ann Arbor Press.

Johnson, L. E., & Carlton, J. T. (1996, September). Post-establishment spread in large-scale invasions: Dispersal mechanisms of the zebra mussel *Dreissena polymorpha. Ecology, 77* (6), 1686–1690.

Johnson, L. E., & Padilla, D. K. (1996). Geographic spread of exotic species: Ecological lessons and opportunities from the invasion of the zebra mussel *Dreissena polymorpha. Biological Conservation, 78*, 23–33.

Nalepa, T. F., & Schloesser, D. W. (Eds.). (1993). *Zebra mussels: Biology, impacts, and control*. Boca Raton, FL: Lewis.

O'Neill, C. R., & Pohl, S. E. (Eds.). (1996). *Zebra mussel: Impacts and control*. Ithaca, NY: Cornell University Cooperative.

Zoos

Although their collections, designs, and operations have changed over time, zoos have been found wherever humans have displayed captive animals in permanent exhibits for the purposes of entertainment and enlightenment. Throughout their history these institutions have sparked both enormous popularity and heated controversy. To some observers zoos perform valuable work in natural-history education, wildlife conservation, and scientific research; to others zoos represent the worst kind of "speciesism"—an arrogant assertion of human dominion over the natural world. Whatever one's opinion, though, it is clear that zoos reveal much about the complicated history of the human relationship with the nonhuman environment.

From Ancient Menageries to Zoological Gardens

In some respects zoos are as old as human civilizations. In ancient societies from Mesopotamia to Egypt to China, ruling elites collected and displayed wild animals as symbols of their power and prestige, their domination of both humans and nature. Similar menageries later appeared in Greco-Roman cities, in the courts of medieval Europe, and in the imperial centers of the Aztecs in Mexico and the Moguls in India. In most cases these collections were not open to the public but rather served to entertain a select audience of nobles or to impress visiting dignitaries.

By the eighteenth century, though, a different organizing model had begun to take hold. The Enlightenment fostered an obsession with reason, order, and scientific inquiry. At the same time the rise of substantial middle classes in many Western nations created greater demands for public cultural institutions. Finally, the Industrial Revolution separated many urbanites from the natural landscape and prompted calls to establish outposts of "nature" within the modern city. These trends all came together in the "zoological garden" (soon nicknamed the "zoo"), a neatly organized, pleasantly landscaped collection of exotic animals, managed by scientific "experts" and dedicated to popular instruction and rational amusement. By the early nineteenth century public zoological gardens had opened in London (1828), Amsterdam (1838), and Berlin (1844); within a generation, the concept had crossed the Atlantic to the United States, with Philadelphia (1874) and Cincinnati (1875) leading the way. Yet, despite their founders' claims of enlightened management and zoological expertise, these modern gardens often remained places of pure entertainment for their visitors, who were more concerned with feeding the animals than with learning their Latin names. In this way modern zoos were little different from the menageries of centuries past.

Moreover, just as ancient menageries had depended on military and political power to obtain their specimens, modern zoos relied upon the imperial reach of Western powers to secure their exotic creatures. Capitalizing on the "new imperialism" that spread across Asia and Africa during the late nineteenth and early twentieth centuries, animal dealers established international trade networks in order to capture, transport, buy, and sell the charismatic creatures that zoos most desired—big cats and pachyderms, giraffes and camels, apes and monkeys. Strangely enough, imperial authorities also founded zoological gardens in many colonial cities, presenting native fauna as if they were exotic attractions (which, of course, they were back in the West). Whether in

Egypt or England, though, zoo animals were presented out of their natural environmental context, packaged for popular consumption in a pastoral urban park.

From Zoological Parks to Conservation Centers

One of the most prominent animal dealers, Carl Hagenbeck (1844–1913) of Germany, helped to usher in a revolution in zoo design in the early twentieth century. At his Tierpark (1907) in Stellingen, Germany, Hagenbeck developed striking panoramas, outdoor exhibits that used hidden moats and artificial rockwork to simulate the animals' native landscapes. Yet, Hagenbeck's designs succeeded less because they provided a more "natural" environment for the animals and more because they provided a spectacular stage upon which zoogoers could view the inhabitants. Similarly, although the U.S. movement to establish more expansive "zoological parks"—most notably in Washington (1891) and the Bronx, New York (1899)—began as a conservationist project to preserve endangered native species, public demand soon turned these facilities into more traditional collections of more popular animals. Through the middle of the twentieth century, then, zoos continued to emphasize entertainment over education.

The global connections that bound together zoological parks and natural environments became evident once again in the decades after World War II. As independence movements swept across Africa and Asia, Western zoo leaders worried that precious wildlife habitat would be sacrificed to economic development under the new postcolonial governments. Yet, these conservationist concerns tended to focus primarily on preserving a steady supply of those charismatic species that zoo audiences had come to expect. To be sure, over the next several decades many zoos worked to save these endangered creatures both by promoting field research in the wild and by inaugurating captive-reproduction programs. Multinational agreements, such as the Convention on International Trade in Endangered Species of Wild Fauna and Flora (CITES) and the International Species Information System (ISIS), both instituted in 1973, allowed zoo officials from across the globe to monitor and coordinate their captive-breeding efforts. Again, however, popular Western attitudes often dictated which animals received the lion's (or tiger's or panda's) share of attention and funding.

The "New Zoo"?

By the dawn of the twenty-first century many zoos around the world had become big business. In the United States alone, zoos spent well over $1 billion during the 1990s on increasingly sophisticated exhibits, most notably so-called landscape immersion displays that seem to place both visitors and animals within realistic replicas of the animals' native habitats. Yet, such increased expenses have often led to increased commercialization, as zoos turn to merchandising and corporate sponsorship to balance their budgets. Competition from for-profit rivals, such as Sea World and Disney's Animal Kingdom, has made these financial challenges even greater, creating potential conflicts between environmental ideals and economic imperatives.

Still, many zoo professionals would argue that the twenty-first-century zoo is truly a "new zoo"—a conservation center far removed from the menageries and zoological gardens of the past. In some respects, such as veterinary expertise and educational programs, this assertion does ring true. Yet, the zoogoing experience itself remains much the same as it has been for centuries. The World Zoo Organization claims that its 550 member zoos attract a collective annual attendance of 600 million visitors. For most of those millions, the zoo is less a place to learn about the environment than a place to satisfy their curiosity about the animal world, to enjoy the thrill of staring across the species barrier and having a "wild" creature stare back.

Jeffrey Hyson

Further Reading

Bell, C. E. (Ed.). (2001). *Encyclopedia of the world's zoos.* Chicago: Fitzroy Dearborn.

Croke, V. (1997). *The modern ark: The story of zoos, past, present, and future.* New York: Scribner.

Hancocks, D. (2001). *A different nature: The paradoxical world of zoos and their uncertain future.* Berkeley and Los Angeles: University of California Press.

Hanson, E. (2002). *Animal attractions: Nature on display at American zoos.* Princeton, NJ: Princeton University Press.

Hoage, R. J., & Deiss, W. A. (Eds.). (1996). *New worlds, new animals: From menagerie to zoological park in the nineteenth century.* Baltimore: Johns Hopkins University Press.

Hyson, J. (2000). Jungles of Eden: The design of American zoos. In M. Conan (Ed.), *Environmentalism in landscape architecture*. Washington, DC: Dumbarton Oaks.

Kisling, V. N., Jr. (Ed.). (2001). *Zoo and aquarium history: Ancient animal collections to zoological gardens*. Boca Raton, FL: CRC Press.

Koebner, L. (1994). *Zoo book: The evolution of wildlife conservation centers*. New York: Forge.

Mullan, B., & Marvin, G. (1999). *Zoo culture* (2nd ed.). Urbana: University of Illinois Press.

Norton, B. G., Hutchins, M., Stevens, E. F., & Maple, T. L. (Eds.). (1995). *Ethics on the ark: Zoos, animal welfare, and wildlife conservation*. Washington, DC: Smithsonian Institution Press.

Rothfels, N. (2002). *Savages and beasts: The birth of the modern zoo*. Baltimore: Johns Hopkins University Press.

Index